Swami Vivekananda's Vedāntic Cosmopolitanism

Swami Vivekananda's Vedāntic Cosmopolitanism

SWAMI MEDHANANDA

OXFORD
UNIVERSITY PRESS

OXFORD
UNIVERSITY PRESS

Oxford University Press is a department of the University of Oxford. It furthers the University's objective of excellence in research, scholarship, and education by publishing worldwide. Oxford is a registered trade mark of Oxford University Press in the UK and certain other countries.

Published in the United States of America by Oxford University Press
198 Madison Avenue, New York, NY 10016, United States of America.

Library of Congress Cataloging-in-Publication Data
Names: Medhananda, Swami, author.
Title: Swami Vivekananda's vedāntic cosmopolitanism / Swami Medhananda.
Description: New York, NY, United States of America : Oxford University Press, 2022. |
Includes bibliographical references and index.
Identifiers: LCCN 2021037343 (print) | LCCN 2021037344 (ebook) |
ISBN 9780197624463 (hardback) | ISBN 9780197624470 | ISBN 9780197624494 |
ISBN 9780197624487 (epub)
Subjects: LCSH: Vivekananda, Swami, 1863–1902.
Classification: LCC BL1280.292.V58 M43 2022 (print) |
LCC BL1280.292.V58 (ebook) | DDC 294.5/55092—dc23
LC record available at https://lccn.loc.gov/2021037343
LC ebook record available at https://lccn.loc.gov/2021037344

DOI: 10.1093/oso/9780197624463.001.0001

আমার motto এই যে, যেখানে যাহা কিছু উত্তম পাই, তাহাই শিক্ষা করিব।
—স্বামী বিবেকানন্দ
(১৮৯০-এ স্বামী অখন্ডানন্দকে লেখা চিঠি)

My motto is to learn whatever is great wherever I may find it.
—Swami Vivekananda
(1890 Letter to Svāmī Akhaṇḍānanda)

Contents

Acknowledgments xi
Abbreviations of Texts xiii
A Note on Sanskrit and Bengali Transliteration xv

Introduction: Swami Vivekananda as an Immersive Cosmopolitan Philosopher 1

I. *INTEGRAL ADVAITA*

1. The Making of an Integral Advaitin: Vivekananda's Intellectual and Spiritual Tutelage under Sri Ramakrishna 17
   1. 1878 to 1884: From Brāhmo Theism to Advaita Vedānta 19
   2. 1884 to 1886: From Acosmic Advaita to Integral Advaita 25
   3. Ramakrishna's Scriptural Support for Integral Advaita 35
   4. Ramakrishna's Legacy: From Narendranāth Datta to Swami Vivekananda 38
2. "The Deification of the World": The Metaphysics and Ethics of Oneness in Vivekananda's Integral Advaita 43
   1. Vivekananda's Two-Pronged Hermeneutic Method 48
   2. The Impersonal-Personal God 50
   3. The World as a Real Manifestation of God 58
   4. The Divinity of the Soul 68
   5. Practical Vedānta: The Ethics of Oneness 73
   6. The Four Yogas as Direct Paths to Liberation 78
   7. Harmonizing the Vedāntic Schools of Dvaita, Viśiṣṭādvaita, and Advaita 85
3. Grounding Religious Cosmopolitanism: Three Phases in the Evolution of Vivekananda's Doctrine of the Harmony of Religions 91
   1. Doctrinal Truth and Salvific Efficacy: Two Ways of Conceptualizing the Threefold Typology 94
   2. The Early Phase (September 1893 to March 1894): Salvific and Doctrinal Pluralism and the Ideal of a "Universal Religion" 97
   3. The Middle Phase (September 1894 to May 1895): A Vedāntic Universal Religion Based on the Three Stages of Dvaita, Viśiṣṭādvaita, and Advaita 101

4. The Final Phase (Late 1895 to 1901): A Vedāntic Universal Religion Based on the Four Yogas 106
5. Vivekananda on the Definition of Religion, Degrees of Salvific Efficacy, and the Problem of Conflicting Religious Truth-Claims 124
6. The Problem of Non-Substantialist Buddhism: Addressing Ninian Smart's Objection 129
7. The Contemporary Relevance of Vivekananda's Vedāntic Universal Religion 135

II. *THE EXPERIENTIAL BASIS OF RELIGION*

4. "The Science of Religion": Vivekananda's Critique of Scientism and His Defense of the Scientific Credentials of Religion 141
1. Vivekananda's Appeal to Spiritual Experience as a Response to the Global Crisis of Religious Belief 142
2. Vivekananda's Critique of Scientism 146
3. Vivekananda's Defense of a Wide Empiricism 153

5. Perceiving God: A Vivekanandan Argument for the Epistemic Value of Supersensuous Perception 162
1. Perception and Testimony in Traditional Indian *Pramāṇa* Epistemology 163
2. Reconstructing and Refining Vivekananda's Argument 170
3. Premises 1 and 2: Perceiving Ultimate Reality 174
4. Premise 3: Perception as Epistemic Justification 178
5. Premise 6: Perceptual Testimony as Epistemic Justification 187
6. Premises 4 and 7: Absence of Rebutting and Undercutting Defeaters 193

6. Addressing Philosophical Challenges to Supersensuous Perception 197
1. The Crosscheckability Objection to Premise 2 199
2. The Speckled Hen Objection to Premise 3 203
3. The Gullibility Objection to Premise 6 206
4. Objections to Premises 4 and 7: The Conflicting Claims Objection and Kumārila's Criticisms of Yogic Perception and Testimony 209
5. Anantanand Rambachan's Criticisms of Vivekananda's Views on Spiritual Experience 217

III. *FAITH AND REASON*

7. From Agnosticism to "Metagnosticism": Vivekananda's Kantian-Vedāntic Critique of Theological Reason 235
1. The Indian Background: Nyāya, Śaṅkara, and Ramakrishna 236
2. Can We Have Faith in an Unknowable God? Kant, Hamilton, Spencer, and Mill 242
3. Vivekananda's Cosmopolitan Views on the Powers and Limits of Reason 249

4. Vivekananda on Arguments for God's Existence 255
5. Vivekananda's Rational Response to the Problem of Evil 259

8. The Will to Realize: Vivekananda's Doxastic Involuntarism and His Three-Rung Ladder of Religious Faith 264
1. Evidentialism versus the Will to Believe: Clifford, Huxley, and James 265
2. Vivekananda's Vedāntic Intervention in Late Nineteenth-Century Debates about Faith 272
3. Stage 1: Faith as Sub-Doxastic Intellectual Assent 276
4. Stage 2: Faith as Belief 280
5. Stage 3: Faith as Self-Authenticating Realization 283
6. Vivekananda's Relevance to Contemporary Debates about Faith 286

IV. *CONSCIOUSNESS*

9. Panentheistic Cosmopsychism: Vivekananda's Sāṃkhya-Vedāntic Solution to the Hard Problem of Consciousness 299
1. Contemporary Analytic Responses to the Hard Problem of Consciousness 302
2. Late Nineteenth-Century Western Views on Consciousness 305
3. Ramakrishna's Mystically Grounded Panentheistic Cosmopsychism 311
4. Vivekananda's Provisional Sāṃkhyan Mind-Consciousness Dualism 313
5. Vivekananda's Sāṃkhya-Vedāntic Metaphysics of Panentheistic Cosmopsychism 324

10. Vivekananda's Justification of Panentheistic Cosmopsychism: Involution, Mystical Experience, and Grounding by Self-Limitation 332
1. Reconstructing Vivekananda's Argument for Panentheistic Cosmopsychism 333
2. Refining and Developing Vivekananda's Argument 340
3. Grounding by Self-Limitation and the Individuation Problem 345
4. Addressing Objections to Vivekananda's Panentheistic Cosmopsychism 356
5. Which Advaita? Bringing Vivekananda into Dialogue with Miri Albahari 363

Epilogue: From "Neo-Vedānta" to Cosmopolitan Vedānta 372

Bibliography 377
Index 399

Acknowledgments

I am grateful to Revered Swami Muktidananda for providing me with an intellectually and spiritually congenial atmosphere to conduct research at the Ramakrishna Institute of Moral and Spiritual Education. In the course of researching and writing this book, I benefited from conversations with the following scholars: Ermine Algaier, Rupa Bandyopadhyay, Arindam Chakrabarti, Amit Churvedi, Nilanjan Das, Matthew Dasti, Jonardon Ganeri, Jonathan Gold, Malcolm Keating, James Madaio, Joseph Milillo, Arpita Mitra, Todd Leroy Perreira, Stephen Phillips, Sister Gayatri Prana, Anantanand Rambachan, Prabal Kumar Sen, Itay Shani, Linda Simon, and Anand Vaidya. For insightful feedback on one or more chapters of the book, I am grateful to Jonardon Ganeri, Itay Shani, Anand Vaidya, Norris Frederick, Matt Seidel, Joseph Milillo, Swami Mahayogananda, Swami Chidekananda, and four anonymous peer reviewers for Oxford University Press. I also had helpful discussions with the following monks of the Ramakrishna Order: Revered Swamis Shivavratananda, Atmavidananda, Bhajanananda, Nityasthananda, Atmarupananda, Atmapriyananda, Balabhadrananda, Muktidananda, Sarvapriyananda, Divyasukhananda, Chandrakantananda, Chidvikashananda, Mahayogananda, Vedanishthananda, Harinamananda, Sukalyanananda, Paramahamsananda, Vedarthananda, Tadvratananda, Pravrajika Vrajaprana, and Brahmacharis Subrata and Nachiketa.

Joseph Milillo, Apala Das, Swami Mahamedhananda, and Brahmachari Nachiketa kindly sent me articles and book chapters that I had trouble finding in local libraries. Swami Atmarupananda provided me with more accurate and precise dates and titles of some of Vivekananda's lectures and writings than the dates and titles found in the *Complete Works*. Swami Divyavibhananda, Head Librarian at the Ramakrishna Mission Institute of Culture, and Swami Bhavantakananda, Head Librarian at RKMVERI, kindly allowed me to use their libraries to my heart's content. I would also like to thank Hannah Doyle and Lucy Randall at Oxford University Press for their support and guidance throughout the process.

Finally, I owe a special debt of gratitude to Most Revered Swami Smarananananda, President of the Ramakrishna Math and Mission, and Revered Swami Suvirananda, General Secretary of the Ramakrishna Math and Mission, for their kind encouragement and unfailing support of my work. It should be noted that this book was not vetted in any way by the Ramakrishna Order. All views expressed in this book are mine alone.

Abbreviations of Texts

Texts Relating to Swami Vivekananda

[Throughout this book, whenever I cite a passage from any of the works listed below, I use parenthetical citations in the body of the text. In case of multi-volume works like *The Complete Works of Swami Vivekananda* (CW), I cite the abbreviated title, followed by the volume number and page number. Whenever I cite a passage from an originally Bengali text written or spoken by Vivekananda, I first cite the Bengali original and then the English translation.]

CW Vivekananda, Swami. [1957–1997] 2006–2007. *The Complete Works of Swami Vivekananda: Mayavati Memorial Edition*. 9 vols. Calcutta: Advaita Ashrama.

BCW Vivekānanda, Svāmī. [1964] 2009. *Svāmī Vivekānander Vāṇī o Racanā*, fourth edition. 10 vols. Kolkātā: Udbodhan.

LSV Anonymous. 1989. *The Life of Swami Vivekananda by His Eastern and Western Disciples*, sixth edition. 2 vols. Kolkata: Advaita Ashrama.

Texts Relating to Sri Ramakrishna

[Whenever I cite a passage from Svāmī Sāradānanda's *Śrīśrīrāmakṛṣṇalīlāprasaṅga*, I first cite the volume number, fascicle number, and page number of the Bengali text (*LP*) and then cite the page number of Swami Chetanananda's single-volume English translation (*DP*).]

K Gupta, Mahendranāth. [1902–1932] 2010. *Śrīśrīrāmakṛṣṇakathāmṛta: Śrīma-kathita*. 1 vol. Kolkātā: Udbodhan.

G Gupta, Mahendranath. [1942] 1992. *The Gospel of Sri Ramakrishna*, translated by Swami Nikhilananda. New York: Ramakrishna-Vedanta Center.

LP Sāradānanda, Svāmī. [1909–1919] 2009. *Śrīśrīrāmakṛṣṇalīlāprasaṅga*. 2 vols. Kolkātā: Udbodhan. Volume 1 contains three separately paginated fascicles, and Volume 2 contains two separately paginated fascicles.

DP Saradananda, Swami. 2003. *Sri Ramakrishna and His Divine Play*, translated by Swami Chetanananda. St. Louis: Vedanta Society of St. Louis.

Sanskrit Commentaries of Śaṅkarācārya

[Unless otherwise noted, translations of Sanskrit passages from Śaṅkarācārya's commentaries are my own.]

BSBh Śaṅkarācārya. 2007. *Brahmasūtram: Śāṅkarabhāṣyopetam*. Delhi: Motilal Banarsidass.

BhGBh Śaṅkarācārya. 2012. *Śrīmadbhagavadgītā Śāṅkarabhāṣya Hindī-anuvādasahita*. Gorakhpur: Gita Press.

BṛUpBh Śaṅkarācārya. 2013. *Bṛhadāraṇyaka Upaniṣad*. Gorakhpur: Gita Press.

ĪUpBh Śaṅkarācārya. 2011. *Īśādi Nau Upaniṣad: Śāṅkarabhāṣyārtha*. Gorakhpur: Gita Press.

Works by Immanuel Kant

[As is standard in Kant scholarship, I cite the *Critique of Pure Reason* using the A/B edition pagination, and I cite all other works by volume and page of the Akademie Ausgabe (Ak.): Immanuel Kant, *Gesammelte Schriften* (Berlin: Königlich-Preussischen Akademie der Wissenschaften zu Berlin [now de Gruyter], 1902–).]

CPR Kant, Immanuel. 1998. *Critique of Pure Reason*, translated by Paul Guyer and Allen Wood. Cambridge: Cambridge University Press.

CPrR Kant, Immanuel. 1996. *Critique of Practical Reason*. In Immanuel Kant, *Practical Philosophy*, translated by Mary J. Gregor, 133–271. Cambridge: Cambridge University Press.

LM Kant, Immanuel. 1997. *Lectures on Metaphysics*, translated by Karl Ameriks and Steve Naragon. Cambridge: Cambridge University Press.

OPA Kant, Immanuel. 1992. *The Only Possible Argument in Support of a Demonstration of the Existence of God*. In Immanuel Kant, *Theoretical Philosophy: 1755–1770*, translated by David Walford, 107–202. Cambridge: Cambridge University Press.

RB Kant, Immanuel. 1996. *Religion within the Boundaries of Mere Reason*, translated by George di Giovanni, in Immanuel Kant, *Religion and Rational Theology*, 39–216. Cambridge: Cambridge University Press.

A Note on Sanskrit and Bengali Transliteration

Throughout the book, I transliterate Sanskrit words using the standard International Alphabet of Sanskrit Transliteration (IAST) scheme. The original editors of the nine-volume *Complete Works of Swami Vivekananda* used an outdated and inconsistent method of transliterating Sanskrit terms. For instance, in Vivekananda's lecture "Māyā and Illusion" (*CW* 2:88–104), the original editors rendered the first instance of "Māyā" as "Mâyâ" but all subsequent instances as "Maya" without any diacritics. For the sake of accuracy and clarity, I have consistently transliterated all Sanskrit terms in cited passages from the *Complete Works* using the IAST scheme.

There is no standard transliteration scheme for Bengali, so I have adopted the scheme that I think will be most helpful to my expected readers. Whenever possible, I transliterate Sanskritic Bengali words in such a way that the Sanskrit root words are easily identifiable by those who have some knowledge of Sanskrit but little or no knowledge of Bengali. For instance, I render the Bengali word "*bijñān*" as "*vijñāna*," and I render "*bidyā*" as "*vidyā*."

Throughout the book, I generally transliterate the names of Bengali figures using the appropriate diacritical marks, *except* in the case of very well-known Bengali figures, the English spelling of whose names are already familiar, including "Swami Vivekananda," "Sri Ramakrishna," "Keshab Chandra Sen," and "Debendranath Tagore." Moreover, I cite the names of Indian authors in exactly the way the authors themselves wrote their names. For instance, I refer to "Swami Tapasyananda" instead of "Svāmī Tapasyānanda," since Swami Tapasyananda printed his name in his English-language books without diacritics. However, I always use diacritics when citing the names of authors of texts in an Indian language such as Bengali or Sanskrit. For instance, I refer to "Dineścandra Bhaṭṭācārya Śāstrī" and "Svāmī Gambhīrānanda" as authors of Bengali books.

Introduction

Swami Vivekananda as an Immersive Cosmopolitan Philosopher

Truth is my God, the universe my country.

—Swami Vivekananda (1895; *CW* 5:92)

Swami Vivekananda (1863–1902), the Bengali spiritual figure who played a pivotal role in reviving Hinduism in India and introducing Vedānta and Hinduism to the West, is also one of modern India's most important philosophers. Unfortunately, his philosophy has too often been interpreted through reductive hermeneutic lenses that fail to capture the sophistication and originality of his thinking. Typically, scholars have argued either that he simply gave a modern ethical twist to the eighth-century Śaṅkarācārya's philosophy of Advaita Vedānta[1] or that he championed a "Neo-Vedāntic" philosophy shaped more by Western outlooks and expectations than by indigenous Indian traditions.[2] Rejecting both of these prevailing interpretive approaches, this book offers a new interpretation of Vivekananda's philosophy that highlights its originality, contemporary relevance, and cross-cultural significance. Vivekananda, I argue, is best seen as a cosmopolitan Vedāntin who developed distinctive new philosophical positions through creative dialectical engagement with thinkers in both Indian and Western philosophical traditions.

The young Vivekananda's upbringing and education in Calcutta, then the cultural and intellectual hub of British-ruled India, were thoroughly cosmopolitan. His father, Viśvanāth Datta, was a successful lawyer proficient in Bengali, English, Sanskrit, Persian, Arabic, Urdu, and Hindi. Endowed with a broad religious outlook, Viśvanāth was fond of reciting passages from the Bible and the *Dewan-i-Hafiz*, and he sometimes asked his son Narendranāth—Vivekananda's pre-monastic name—to read aloud from these books as well (Gambhīrānanda

[1] For references, see note 2 of chapter 2.

[2] See, for instance, Hacker (1995: 227–350), Halbfass ([1995] 2007: 169–82), Fort (2007: 489–504), Baumfield (1991).

Swami Vivekananda's Vedāntic Cosmopolitanism. Swami Medhananda, Oxford University Press. © Oxford University Press 2022. DOI: 10.1093/oso/9780197624463.003.0001

1984, vol. 1: 16). Meanwhile, Vivekananda's mother, Bhuvaneśvarī Devī, was a traditional pious Hindu woman who performed daily worship of Śiva and regularly studied the *Rāmāyaṇa* and *Mahābhārata* (*LSV* 1:8).

From 1881 to 1884, Narendranāth studied at the General Assembly's Institution (now known as Scottish Church College) in Calcutta, where he took numerous courses in Western philosophy from mostly European professors, including Reverend William Hastie. As a college student, he studied such thinkers as Descartes, Hume, Spinoza, Kant, Fichte, Hegel, Schopenhauer, Auguste Comte, Charles Darwin, John Stuart Mill, and Herbert Spencer.[3]

As we will see in the course of this book, Vivekananda's early study of Western thought had an enormous impact on his thinking. As he himself later admitted in his lecture on "Soul, God and Religion" (1895), when he was "a boy," he got swept up in the "surging tide of agnosticism and materialism" and became skeptical of the very existence of God: "[I]t seemed for a time as if I must give up all hope of religion" (*CW* 1:317–18). However, in late 1881 or early 1882, his life took a decisive turn when he met the mystic Sri Ramakrishna (1836–1886), who would become his guru. In an 1896 lecture, Vivekananda described his first life-changing encounter with Ramakrishna: "For the first time I found a man who dared to say that he saw God, that religion was a reality to be felt, to be sensed in an infinitely more intense way than we can sense the world" (*CW* 4:179). As I will discuss in detail in the first chapter, Ramakrishna trained and guided Narendra both spiritually and intellectually from 1882 to 1886, and shortly after Ramakrishna's passing in August 1886, Narendra became a *sannyāsin*, eventually assuming the name "Swami Vivekananda." After traveling throughout India as a wandering monk from 1888 to March 1893, Vivekananda took two extended trips to the West, giving lectures and classes on Hinduism and Vedānta in America and England from 1893 to 1896 and again from 1899 to 1901.

In a letter dated June 22, 1895, Vivekananda told Mary Hale, "I intend to write a book this summer on the Vedānta philosophy" (*CW* 8:341). Unfortunately, he never ended up writing that planned book on Vedānta, likely because he did not live long and spent so much of his time and energy lecturing and traveling. Nonetheless, those interested in Vivekananda's thought will find philosophical ideas and arguments scattered throughout the nine-volume *Complete Works of Swami Vivekananda*, which contains an eclectic mix of his prose writings, transcribed lectures, often sketchy notes jotted down by students in his classes, letters originally written mostly in English and Bengali, recorded dialogues between Vivekananda and some of his disciples like Saratcandra Cakravarti in English

[3] For detailed information on Vivekananda's studies at Scottish Church College, see Dhar (1975: 51–61).

and Bengali, and poems and devotional hymns (*stotras*) originally written in English, Bengali, and Sanskrit.

Reconstructing Vivekananda's philosophical views is a formidable task, not only because of the eclectic nature of the available texts but also because of the way that the *Complete Works* has been organized and edited. The early editors of the *Complete Works* made numerous silent changes to Vivekananda's lectures and writings, sometimes modifying his language and, at times, combining or grouping his lectures and classes in ways that are counterintuitive or confusing. To mention just one example, Vivekananda's June 1896 lecture on "The Necessity of Religion" (*CW* 2:57–69), a wide-ranging sociological and philosophical discussion of the historical origins of religion and its essence, appears in the second volume of the *Complete Works* as the first of a series of lectures on *Jñāna-Yoga*, even though the lecture has nothing to do with the path of knowledge as taught in Advaita Vedānta.

Two other textual difficulties are worth mentioning. First, the English translations of Vivekananda's Bengali writings and dialogues in the *Complete Works* are often rather loose and sometimes inaccurate. Hence, throughout this book, whenever I refer to a passage from one of his Bengali works, I will also cite the original Bengali from *Vāṇī o Racanā*, the Bengali edition of Vivekananda's collected works, and I will modify the English translations of Bengali passages as provided in the *Complete Works* whenever I deem appropriate.

Second, as the *Complete Works* is not chronologically ordered, it is difficult to determine whether and how Vivekananda's views on certain philosophical issues evolved in the course of his thinking. Fortunately, two intrepid researchers, Terrance Hohner and Carolyn Kenny (2014), have compiled an enormously helpful, day-by-day chronology of Vivekananda's lectures and classes in the West from 1893 to 1901. In compiling this chronology, Hohner and Kenny consulted numerous texts in addition to the *Complete Works*, especially Marie Louise Burke's *Swami Vivekananda in the West: New Discoveries*, an invaluable six-volume biographical and historical work on Vivekananda's time in the West based on careful original research (Burke 1992–1999). At various points in my book, I have consulted both Hohner and Kenny's chronology as well as Burke's six-volume work.

At the methodological level, one of the primary aims of this book is to reconstruct Vivekananda's philosophical views on a variety of topics while keeping in mind the various textual issues just discussed. However, I will also make a sustained case that his philosophical positions and arguments are not merely of historical interest. Past scholars have tended to paint Vivekananda either as a modern-day exponent of Śaṅkara or as a colonial subject whose views were largely a reaction to Western hegemony and the British occupation of India. Instead, I join a growing chorus of recent scholars in advocating a more nuanced "cosmopolitan" approach to his thought.[4] In an important recent book, Nalini Bhushan and Jay L. Garfield argue that colonial philosophers such as Vivekananda, K. C. Bhattacharyya, and Sri Aurobindo exhibited a "cosmopolitan consciousness"—an intensely creative and agential philosophical intelligence that thrived on engaging a global intellectual community (Bhushan and Garfield 2017: 20–38). My book explores how Vivekananda exemplified this cosmopolitan consciousness both in his subtle development of ideas in Indian philosophical traditions and in his searching critico-constructive engagement with a host of modern Western thinkers.

However, since there are many varieties of cosmopolitanism (Scheffler 1999), an important question arises: what kind of cosmopolitan was Vivekananda? In confronting this question, I have found Jonardon Ganeri's recent article (Ganeri 2017) on the "immersive cosmopolitanism" of K. C. Bhattacharyya (1875–1949), a younger contemporary of Vivekananda, especially helpful. Ganeri focuses on Bhattacharyya's famous talk "Svaraj in Ideas" (1928), which diagnosed some of the main forms of intellectual "slavery" exhibited by colonial Indian philosophers and outlined a vision for achieving *svarāj*—that is, "self-determination" or "freedom"—in the sphere of thought (Bhattacharyya [1928] 2011). Bhattacharyya's "immersive cosmopolitanism," Ganeri argues, is embodied particularly in three key features of his vision for an intellectual *svarāj*.

First, Bhattacharyya stresses the need for reverential immersion in one's own indigenous tradition, calling on his Indian philosophical peers to "resolutely think in our own concepts" ([1928] 2011: 110). He contrasts this conception of an immersive cosmopolitanism with a radically unrooted cosmopolitanism that is equally critical of *all* traditions, including one's own. For Bhattacharyya, this kind of unrooted cosmopolitanism amounts to a mere "patchwork of ideas of different cultures" ([1928] 2011: 106), collapsing into a radical subjectivism that arbitrarily privileges "the accidental likes and dislikes of the person judging" ([1928] 2011: 108). While some of Bhattacharyya's critics have argued that his emphasis on "reverence" for the Indian tradition amounts to another form of intellectual slavery, Ganeri justly claims that Bhattacharyya actually views reverential immersion as an act of freedom. As Ganeri puts it, "it is not that one simply finds oneself with roots in the ancient tradition, but rather one must actively plant oneself somewhere there. The activity of imagining with humility an ancient idea is a way of taking root in the tradition, and this is not passivity but spontaneity" (2017: 725). For Bhattacharyya, then, reverential immersion—far from being a passive and uncritical acquiescence—is a critical and dynamic

[4] See, for instance, Madaio (2017), Barua (2020), Ganeri (2017: 718–36), Bhushan and Garfield (2017), Hatcher (2004: 201–203), Maharaj (2020b: 185–186), Medhananda (2020: 3–6).

excavation of one's own tradition that involves revising or rethinking aspects of that tradition when necessary.

Second, Bhattacharyya claims that the uncritical acceptance of Western ideas, which was prevalent during his time, amounts to a form of intellectual bondage. According to him, foreign ideas should be approached with "critical reserve and not docile acceptance . . . docile acceptance without criticism would mean slavery" ([1928] 2011: 110). Third, he contrasts the slavish acceptance of Western ideas with his preferred method of thought: "vital assimilation," a dialectical engagement with Western views that combines receptive openness with critical scrutiny ([1928] 2011: 104). The truly free cosmopolitan thinker, Bhattacharyya affirms, should be equally ready to accept (though perhaps with some revision) or criticize any foreign ideas, depending on their intrinsic value. Finding such an attitude rare among his fellow Indian thinkers, he laments the fact that "[t]here is nothing like a judgment on western systems from the standpoint of Indian philosophy" ([1928] 2011: 105).

Vivekananda, I would argue, both explicitly theorized as well as practiced the kind of immersive philosophical cosmopolitanism that Bhattacharyya would champion decades later. In 1895 letters to his disciple Alasinga Perumal, Vivekananda affirmed that "truth is my God, the universe my country" (*CW* 5:92), and that "I belong as much to India as to the world, no humbug about that" (*CW* 5:95). Similarly, in an 1897 letter to Mary Hale, he gave voice to his self-consciously cosmopolitan identity: "What am I? Asiatic, European, or American? I feel a curious medley of personalities in me" (*CW* 8:395). In all of these statements, he declared himself to be a cosmopolitan in its etymological meaning of "citizen of the world/universe." Vivekananda often specifically emphasized the cosmopolitan imperative to seek knowledge from the people and cultures of other countries. As he put it in a March 1890 letter to Svāmī Akhaṇḍānanda, "My motto is to learn whatever is great wherever I may find it" (*BCW* 6:250 / *CW* 6:234).

In fact, in his lecture "The Work Before Us" delivered in Madras on February 9, 1897, he went so far as to claim that India's *lack* of a cosmopolitan openness to other cultures was one of the main reasons for its protracted "slavery" at the hands of Muslim and British rulers:

> To become broad, to go out, to amalgamate, to universalise, is the end of our aims. . . . With all my love for India, and with all my patriotism and veneration for the ancients, I cannot but think that we have to learn many things from other nations. We must be always ready to sit at the feet of all, for, mark you, every one can teach us great lessons. . . . We cannot do without the world outside India; it was our foolishness that we thought we could, and we have paid the penalty by about a thousand years of slavery. That we did not go out to

> compare things with other nations, did not mark the workings that have been all around us, has been the one great cause of this degradation of the Indian mind. We have paid the penalty; let us do it no more. (*CW* 3:270–71)

Vivekananda's immersive cosmopolitanism, like K. C. Bhattacharyya's, combined a "veneration" for ancient Indian traditions with the imperative to "universalise" one's outlook, to "amalgamate" the ideas of different global cultures, and to "learn many things from other nations." Anticipating Bhattacharyya's canny linkage of political and intellectual forms of slavery, Vivekananda traced India's long-term political subjugation to its intellectual and cultural parochialism, its arrogant refusal to "go out to compare things with other nations."[5]

On numerous occasions, Vivekananda likened the parochial attitude of many of his fellow Indians to the mindset of "frogs in a well" (*kūpa-maṇḍukas*) who think that their well is the whole world. As he put it in a letter to Svāmī Rāmakṛṣṇānanda dated March 19, 1894, "Nowhere in the world have I come across such 'frogs in the well' as we are. Let anything new come from some foreign country, and America will be the first to accept it. But we?—oh, there are none like us in the world, we men of Aryan blood!!!" (*BCW* 6:324 / *CW* 6:256). Likewise, in an 1895 letter to Rāmakṛṣṇānanda, Vivekananda specifically remarked that a cosmopolitan outlook is the precondition for intellectual originality and creativity: "Had I the money I would send each one of you to travel all over the world. No great idea can have a place in the heart unless one steps out of his little corner" (*BCW* 7:169 / *CW* 6:331).

However, just as K. C. Bhattacharyya would later warn against the "docile acceptance" of foreign ideas, Vivekananda, in his 1899 Bengali essay "*Vartamān Bhārat*" ("Modern India"), scathingly referred to the "mere echoing of others" (*parānuvāda*) as a "slavish weakness" that had become fashionable among his fellow Indians (*BCW* 6:194 / *CW* 4:477). In the same essay, he also indicated his cosmopolitan alternative to such blind imitation: "O India, this is your terrible danger! The intoxication of imitating the West has grown so strong that what is good or what is bad is no longer decided by reason, judgment, scripture, or discrimination (*buddhi vicār śāstra vivek*)" (*BCW* 6:193 / *CW* 4:477). For Vivekananda, cosmopolitan engagement with foreign ideas and values involves not servile acceptance but active assimilation through critical discernment.

At the same time, his reference to "scripture" signals his recognition of the importance of his own nation's ideals and values. In his "Reply to the Address at Ramnad" delivered on January 25, 1897, Vivekananda called on Indians to cultivate a cosmopolitan receptivity to foreign ideas while remaining rooted in their own great Indian tradition:

[5] He made a similar point at *CW* 5:220.

> Stand on your own feet, and assimilate what you can; learn from every nation, take what is of use to you. But remember that as Hindus everything else must be subordinated to our own national ideals. Each man has a mission in life, which is the result of all his infinite past Karma. Each of you was born with a splendid heritage, which is the whole of the infinite past life of your glorious nation. (*CW* 3:152)

Vivekananda's exhortation anticipated K. C. Bhattacharyya's ideal of "vital assimilation," which involves engaging with other traditions autonomously and critically while holding on to one's "national ideals." Vivekananda's cosmopolitan ideal can also be seen as a kind of "rooted cosmopolitanism," which—according to the contemporary philosopher Kwame Anthony Appiah (1997: 618)—balances an openness and receptivity to other cultures with a "patriotic" love for one's own country, with its "own cultural particularities."

In the course of this book, I will examine how Vivekananda put this immersive cosmopolitan method into practice by actively reinterpreting and broadening his own inherited Vedāntic tradition and by critically engaging a variety of Western thinkers. Along the way, I will myself employ a cosmopolitan methodology to demonstrate the contemporary relevance of his views. As a cosmopolitan philosopher, I aim not so much to compare Vivekananda's positions with those of recent Western philosophers as to show how he directly contributes to contemporary philosophical debates by developing innovative approaches to long-standing problems.[6] While there are a large—and ever growing—number of book-length historical and biographical studies of Vivekananda,[7] books focusing on his philosophical thought are much rarer.[8] This is the first book-length philosophical study of Vivekananda that examines his cosmopolitan engagement with global thinkers as well as the contemporary value of his ideas and arguments.[9]

The book has four parts, each of which focuses on one important dimension of Vivekananda's cosmopolitan Vedāntic thought. Part I ("Integral Advaita"), comprising chapters 1 to 3, examines how he systematically reinterprets the fundamental tenets of traditional Advaita Vedānta in light of his guru Ramakrishna and the ancient Vedāntic scriptures. Part II ("The Experiential

[6] For some discussions of the difference between comparative philosophy and cosmopolitan/global/cross-cultural philosophy, see Ganeri (2016), Mills (2009), and Maharaj (2018: 4–5).

[7] For instance, see Sil (1997), Beckerlegge (2006), J. Sharma (2013), Sen (2013), Green (2016), and Paranjape (2020). In Medhananda (2020), I argue against interpretations of Vivekananda as a Hindu supremacist, especially Jyotirmaya Sharma's *A Restatement of Religion* (2013).

[8] Two of the most academically serious book-length studies of Vivekananda's philosophy in English are Rambachan (1994a) and Devdas (1968). I critically engage both of these books at relevant points in my study.

[9] In this book, I do not discuss Vivekananda's extensive critical engagement with Arthur Schopenhauer's philosophy, since I have already discussed this topic in detail in Maharaj (2017a).

Basis of Religion"), comprising chapters 4 to 6, analyzes Vivekananda's efforts to reconceive religion as an experientially grounded science and then reconstructs and further develops his sophisticated argument for the epistemic value of supersensuous perception. Part III ("Faith and Reason"), comprising chapters 7 and 8, examines his cosmopolitan views on the powers and limits of reason and the dynamics of religious faith. Finally, Part IV ("Consciousness"), comprising chapters 9 and 10, reconstructs his doctrine of panentheistic cosmopsychism, situating it within his late nineteenth-century historical milieu and demonstrating its importance for contemporary philosophical debates about the hard problem of consciousness.

I will now walk through the book's arguments chapter by chapter. Chapter 1 elucidates Ramakrishna's crucial role in shaping the young Vivekananda's intellectual and spiritual development. Prior to meeting Ramakrishna, Vivekananda was committed to the rational theism of the Brāhmo Samāj. However, as a result of Ramakrishna's close guidance between 1882 and 1886, Vivekananda's worldview evolved dramatically. While he initially leaned toward the world-negating and quietistic outlook of traditional Advaita Vedānta, he eventually came to embrace what I call "Integral Advaita," the nonsectarian and life-affirming Advaita philosophy championed by Ramakrishna himself.

With this background in place, chapter 2 provides a detailed reconstruction of the main tenets of Vivekananda's philosophy of Integral Advaita, as expounded in lectures and writings in the 1890s. Militating against the dominant view that his philosophy follows Śaṅkara's Advaita Vedānta in all or most of its essentials, I contend that Vivekananda, under the influence of Ramakrishna, reconceived Advaita Vedānta as a nonsectarian, world-affirming, and ethically oriented philosophy. According to my reconstruction, Vivekananda, in contrast to Śaṅkara, held that (1) the impersonal Brahman and the personal Śakti are equally real aspects of one and the same Infinite Divine Reality; (2) the universe is a real manifestation of Śakti; (3) since we are all living manifestations of God, we should make Vedānta practical by loving and serving human beings in a spirit of worship; and (4) each of the four Yogas (i.e., basic forms of spiritual practice)—Bhakti-Yoga, Jñāna-Yoga, Karma-Yoga, and Rāja-Yoga—is a direct and independent path to salvation. Vivekananda also criticized the "text-torturing" of traditional scriptural commentators like Śaṅkara and Rāmānuja, anchoring his own Integral Advaita philosophy in a subtle reinterpretation of the Upaniṣads, the *Bhagavad-Gītā*, and the *Brahmasūtra*.

Chapter 3 examines Vivekananda's views on the harmony of religions. Most scholars claim that in spite of his pluralist-sounding statements that the different world religions are equally valid paths to the same goal, he was actually more of an inclusivist, since he affirmed the superiority and uniqueness of Advaita Vedānta and Hinduism vis-à-vis other religions. I argue that these scholars overlook the fact that his views on the harmony of religions *evolved* from 1893 to 1901 in three phases. In the first phase from September 1893 to March 1894, Vivekananda defended the equal salvific efficacy of the major world religions but claimed that a "universal religion" that would harmonize all the world religions was an "ideal" that did not yet exist. In the second phase from September 1894 to May 1895, he claimed that the universal religion *already exists* in the form of Vedānta, which he expounded in terms of the "three stages" of Dvaita, Viśiṣṭādvaita, and Advaita. However, by late 1895, he decisively abandoned his earlier attempt to ground the harmony of religions in the three stages of Vedānta. Instead, in the third and final phase of his thinking from December 1895 to 1901, he consistently conceived the Vedāntic universal religion in terms of his Integral Advaitic paradigm of four Yogas. According to his final position, every religion corresponds to at least one of the four Yogas, each of which is a direct and independent path to salvation. On this basis, he defended not only a full-blown religious pluralism but also the more radical cosmopolitan ideal of learning from—and even practicing—religions other than our own. On the basis of my diachronic examination of Vivekananda's views, I argue that the vast majority of scholars have seriously misrepresented his mature Vedāntic doctrine of the harmony of religions by taking it to be based on the three stages of Vedānta rather than on the four Yogas.

Chapter 4 examines Vivekananda's doctrine of the "science of religion," which involved both a defense of the scientific credentials of religion and a Vedāntic critique of the scientism that was becoming prevalent during his time. Situating him in his late nineteenth-century historical context, I argue that his sustained attempt to reground religion in spiritual experience was a cosmopolitan response to the global crisis of religious belief. Vivekananda's science of religion had both a negative and a positive dimension. Negatively, he criticized various forms of scientism, the tendency to overvalue the natural sciences and to deny the existence of realities that cannot be investigated through these sciences. As we will see, his prescient critique of scientism anticipated numerous contemporary arguments in the philosophy of science. Positively, Vivekananda defended what I call a "wide empiricism," the view that while experience is the primary source of knowledge, the category of experience encompasses both the sensory and the supersensuous. While sensory experience is the basis of the natural sciences, supersensuous experience is the basis of the science of religion.

Central to Vivekananda's science of religion, then, is the controversial assumption that supersensuous experience is a genuine source of knowledge. He defended this assumption by presenting a sophisticated argument for the epistemic value of supersensuous perception (hereafter AEV), which I reconstruct and further develop in chapter 5. To my knowledge, no scholar has even acknowledged, let alone grappled with, this strain of Vivekananda's work. One of the key premises of his AEV is an epistemic principle of perceptual justification that he adapted from traditional Indian *pramāṇa* epistemology—namely, *svataḥ-prāmāṇyatā*, the doctrine of the "intrinsic validity" of cognitions defended by Bhāṭṭa Mīmāṃsakas and Vedāntins. According to Vivekananda, it is a mark of rational behavior to take our perceptual experience of *F* as evidence that we really do perceive *F* in the absence of reasons for doubt. For instance, I am justified in taking my perception of a wall as evidence that there really is a wall in front of me, so long as I have no good reason to doubt the veridicality of my perception of the wall. It is equally rational, he claims, to trust the testimony of others regarding their perceptual experiences in the absence of reasons for doubt. On the basis of these epistemic principles, he argues that we are justified in believing the testimony of mystics who claim to have directly perceived supersensuous realities. In the course of the chapter, I refine and develop Vivekananda's AEV into a seven-premise argument (AEV$_s$) by drawing upon Vivekananda's own ideas as well as contemporary analytic philosophy.

Chapter 6 addresses some of the most important objections to different premises of AEV$_s$ as well as Anantanand Rambachan's influential criticisms of Vivekananda's views on supersensuous perception. I respond to these objections and criticisms by engaging recent work in philosophy of religion and epistemology and by building on Vivekananda's arguments.

Chapter 7 examines Vivekananda's views on the powers and limits of theological reason, which he developed through a subtle cosmopolitan engagement with two groups of thinkers: Immanuel Kant, William Hamilton, Herbert Spencer, and John Stuart Mill on the one hand and Śaṅkara and Ramakrishna on the other. Siding with Ramakrishna against Śaṅkara, Vivekananda held that spiritual experience is the only authoritative means of knowing Brahman. Moreover, while he followed Vedānta and the Kantian tradition in arguing that reason can neither prove nor disprove the existence of supersensuous entities like God or the soul, he also criticized Kantian thinkers from a Vedāntic standpoint, arguing that they were not justified in ruling out the possibility of supersensuous knowledge. I contend, however, that Vivekananda, in spite of his rational agnosticism, defended the (limited) rational force of the argument from religious experience, an argument based on AEV that infers God's existence from the testimony of mystics who claim to have perceived God. He also followed Mill and Ramakrishna in granting some degree of rational force to the argument from design for God's existence, though he maintained that this was weaker than the argument from religious experience. Finally, I show how Vivekananda employed rational arguments—drawn especially from Śaṅkara and Ramakrishna—to refute the argument from evil against God's existence, advanced by Mill and many others.

Building on these claims, chapter 8 reconstructs Vivekananda's nuanced cosmopolitan account of the dynamics of religious faith. I argue that he made a unique intervention in late nineteenth-century debates about faith and reason by steering a middle course between the stringent evidentialism of W. K. Clifford and T. H. Huxley and the anti-evidentialist fideism of William James. Vivekananda justifies religious faith on the basis of what I call an "expanded evidentialism," arguing that supersensuous perception and mystical testimony are valid sources of evidence that support the rationality of religious belief. Having identified his intervention, I then argue that Vivekananda's various remarks about faith hint at a dynamic conception of religious faith, according to which one's faith evolves in the following three stages: (1) faith as sub-doxastic intellectual assent, (2) faith as belief, and (3) faith as self-authenticating realization. According to Vivekananda, the vast majority of sincere spiritual aspirants occupy the first stage of faith, since they do not yet *believe* that God exists, but they "assent" intellectually to God's existence; these aspirants strive to attain the second stage of belief in God by purifying their minds through ethical and spiritual practices. In the context of the second stage of faith-as-belief, I argue that Vivekananda subscribed to what contemporary epistemologists call "doxastic involuntarism," the view that beliefs are not subject to direct voluntary control. For Vivekananda, the belief that God exists arises spontaneously in those who have attained a sufficiently high level of mental purity. Nonetheless, he maintains that the journey of faith culminates not in belief but in the direct supersensuous perception of God, which removes all doubts. I conclude the chapter by bringing Vivekananda into critical dialogue with William Alston, who was one of the first Western philosophers to distinguish doxastic and non-doxastic forms of religious faith.

The final chapters of this book concern what contemporary philosopher David Chalmers has called the "hard problem of consciousness"—the problem of explaining how conscious experience arises. Chapters 9 and 10 provide an in-depth reconstruction of Vivekananda's Sāṃkhya-Vedāntic solution to the hard problem of consciousness and demonstrate its relevance to contemporary philosophical debates. In chapter 9, I first outline Ramakrishna's mystically grounded views on consciousness and the views of five of Vivekananda's prominent Western contemporaries. I then examine Vivekananda's own approach to the hard problem of consciousness and his critique of modern materialist theories of consciousness. Combining elements from Sāṃkhya, Advaita Vedānta, and the teachings of Ramakrishna, Vivekananda defends a metaphysics of panentheistic cosmopsychism, according to which the sole reality is Divine Consciousness, which manifests as everything in the universe.

Chapter 10 reconstructs Vivekananda's philosophical justification of panentheistic cosmopsychism and his account of how the single Divine Consciousness individuates into the varied conscious perspectives of humans and animals. I suggest that he provides two complementary arguments in favor of panentheistic cosmopsychism: (1) an "involution argument" for panpsychism, which is based on the Sāṃkhyan *satkāryavāda*, the doctrine that an effect pre-exists in its material cause; and (2) an argument for panentheistic cosmopsychism, which is based on two sub-arguments—namely, the argument from design and the argument for the epistemic value of supersensuous perception (i.e., AEV, discussed in chapter 5). Vivekananda, we will see, defends the premises of both these arguments through a cosmopolitan engagement with Indian and Western thought. I then explain what I call his account of "grounding by self-limitation," which lies at the core of his panentheistic cosmopsychism. Following Ramakrishna, Vivekananda holds that the single, impersonal-personal Divine Consciousness manifests as everything in the universe by playfully limiting, or veiling, Herself through the individuating principle of *māyā*. I conclude the chapter by bringing Vivekananda into dialogue with the contemporary philosopher of mind Miri Albahari, who has recently defended a "perennial idealist" theory of consciousness derived from the world-denying metaphysics of classical Advaita Vedānta. Since Vivekananda's panentheistic cosmopsychism holds that the world is a real manifestation of Divine Consciousness, I argue that it has considerable advantages over Albahari's perennial idealist theory, which ultimately denies the reality of both the world and the grounding relation.

Before we conclude the introduction, it is worth addressing an important hermeneutic issue. Many scholars have distinguished between "insider" or "emic" work on Ramakrishna and Vivekananda and "outsider" or "etic" work.[10] Not surprisingly, self-styled "outsider" scholars have tended to denigrate "insider" literature as uncritical and hagiographic, while "insiders"—that is, monks and devotees of the Ramakrishna-Vivekananda tradition—have often faulted "outsider" scholarship for its "cultural monovision" (Tyagananda and Vrajaprana 2010: 241), its scrutiny of Ramakrishna and Vivekananda through the distortive lenses of contemporary Western conceptual categories and cultural assumptions. While there is some truth in these criticisms from both sides, I believe the insider-outsider dichotomy is largely unhelpful and misleading, both because some scholarship on the Ramakrishna-Vivekananda tradition cannot be so easily pigeonholed as *either* "insider" or "outsider," and because the insider-outsider dichotomy wrongly implies that the two approaches are mutually exclusive. As a scholar-monk of the Ramakrishna Order who was educated at major American and European universities, I see myself as straddling the border between "insider" and "outsider." Indeed, for me, the hermeneutic ideal is

[10] See, for instance, Beckerlegge (2013: 445), De Michelis (2004: 119, 182), Rigopoulos (2019: 450n1, 451n2), and Olson (2011).

to combine the virtues of both "insider" and "outsider" approaches. Accordingly, I have attempted throughout this book to combine a critical and scholarly approach with a sensitivity to the specific historico-cultural *Weltanschauung* within which Vivekananda developed and expressed his philosophical ideas. To what extent I have succeeded I leave to readers to judge.

PART I
INTEGRAL ADVAITA

1

The Making of an Integral Advaitin

Vivekananda's Intellectual and Spiritual Tutelage under Sri Ramakrishna

Now I happened to get an old man [Ramakrishna] to teach me, and he was very peculiar. He did not go much for intellectual scholarship, scarcely studied books; but when he was a boy he was seized with the tremendous idea of getting truth direct. . . . Now, all the ideas that I preach are only an attempt to echo his ideas.

—Swami Vivekananda, "My Life and Mission" (1900; *CW* 2:149)

In order to gain a thorough understanding of a philosopher's mature thought, it is often helpful to determine how the philosopher arrived at his or her mature view. In the case of Swami Vivekananda (1863–1902), two of the most important early influences were undoubtedly the Brāhmo Samāj, a Hindu reform organization popular during his time, and the Hindu mystic Sri Ramakrishna (1836–1886), who would become Vivekananda's guru. However, I believe scholars have tended to underestimate the extent of Ramakrishna's influence on Vivekananda and have not paid sufficient attention to the precise ways that Ramakrishna shaped his young disciple's thinking. Elizabeth De Michelis (2004: 49), for instance, argues that the charismatic Brāhmo leader Keshab Chandra Sen (1838–1884), rather than Ramakrishna, was "the most influential role model for Vivekananda" and that "Vivekananda's debt to the Brahmo Saṃaj cannot be overstated."[1] Numerous scholars have claimed, in a similar vein, that Vivekananda's Vedāntic philosophy bears little resemblance to the teachings of Ramakrishna.[2]

In the course of this book, I will challenge this scholarly orthodoxy by arguing that Vivekananda's formative training under Ramakrishna played a pivotal role in shaping his mature spiritual and philosophical outlook. This chapter makes the case that while the teenager Narendranāth Datta—who would go on to become Vivekananda—was initially drawn toward the ideology of the Brāhmo

[1] Kopf (1979: 205–6) defends a similar view.
[2] See, for instance, Devdas (1968: 12–39), Neevel (1976), Matchett (1981), and J. Sharma (2013).

Swami Vivekananda's Vedāntic Cosmopolitanism. Swami Medhananda, Oxford University Press. © Oxford University Press 2022. DOI: 10.1093/oso/9780197624463.003.0002

Samāj, Ramakrishna gave an entirely new orientation to Narendra's intellectual and spiritual life in the course of their meetings between 1882 and 1886. To be sure, as I will note in relevant places in subsequent chapters of this book, Vivekananda did continue to accept some ideas of the Brāhmo Samāj, but he developed and reworked these ideas in the light of what he had learned from Ramakrishna.

Prior to meeting Ramakrishna, Narendra was committed to the rational monotheism of the Brāhmo Samāj. However, as a result of Ramakrishna's close intellectual and spiritual guidance between 1882 and 1886, Narendra's philosophico-spiritual worldview evolved dramatically in two main phases, which I discuss in sections 1 and 2 of this chapter respectively. In the first phase from 1882 to early 1884, Ramakrishna taught Narendra traditional Advaita Vedānta, which holds that the sole reality is the impersonal nondual Brahman and that the world, the personal God, and individual souls are all ultimately as unreal as a dream. Under his guru's guidance, Narendra studied Advaitic texts like the *Aṣṭāvakra-Saṃhitā* and, even more importantly, had several transformative Advaitic spiritual experiences, which led him to move away from Brāhmo theism and to embrace Advaita Vedānta instead. However, in the second phase from 1884 to 1886, Ramakrishna gradually led Narendra to reject the world-negating and quietistic outlook of traditional Advaita Vedānta in favor of a more expansive and ethically oriented Advaitic philosophy, according to which the static nondual Brahman is inseparable from the dynamic personal Śakti, which actually manifests as everything in this world.

Section 3 further illuminates this second phase by discussing some of the key scriptures to which Ramakrishna frequently appealed in support of the harmonizing and world-affirming Advaitic philosophy he encouraged Narendra to accept, including the *Bhagavad-Gītā* and the *Bhāgavata-Purāṇa*. Section 4 briefly discusses Vivekananda's intensive study of a vast range of philosophical texts and scriptures during the period after Ramakrishna's passing in 1886 and prior to his first trip to the West in 1893. During this formative period, his study of the Vedāntic scriptures and his critical examination of Śaṅkara's commentaries on these scriptures were crucially informed by his early training under Ramakrishna. Overall, this chapter provides the necessary background for the subsequent nine chapters of this book, which reconstruct and analyze Vivekananda's mature philosophical views and arguments, contained primarily in lectures, writings, and recorded dialogues from 1893 to 1901.

Since I will be referring to Vivekananda's reported spiritual experiences at various points in this chapter and in later chapters, a brief note is in order regarding how we should approach them. I wish to emphasize that I am not presupposing the veridicality of the young Vivekananda's putative spiritual experiences. Whether or not his spiritual experiences were veridical, he certainly *took* them to be veridical and explicitly acknowledged their transformative impact on his intellectual and spiritual development. Accordingly, throughout this book, I will rely only on his own first-hand reports of his spiritual experiences, since what is important for the purposes of this philosophical study is his own understanding of their nature and significance. That said, I will also show, in chapter 5, that Vivekananda himself presented a sophisticated philosophical argument in support of the epistemic value of mystical experience, which—if sound—would make it reasonable for us to believe that the reported experiences of mystics like himself are veridical.

1. 1878 to 1884: From Brāhmo Theism to Advaita Vedānta

As a teenager in the late 1870s, Narendranāth felt drawn toward the Brāhmo Samāj, visiting Brāhmo leaders and attending many Brāhmo programs.[3] All Brāhmos upheld the monotheistic doctrine that God is personal (*saguṇa*) but formless (*nirākāra*). Hence, they rejected all forms of image worship, and they denied the possibility of God incarnating as a human being. Debendranath Tagore (1817–1905), an early leader of the Brāhmo Samāj, claimed that the Upaniṣads affirmed such a rational monotheism. At the same time, Debendranath subordinated all religious scriptures—including the Upaniṣads—to the direct spiritual realization of God:

> I came to see that the pure heart, filled with the light of intuitive knowledge (*ātmapratyayasiddhajñānojjvalita viśuddha hṛdaya*),—this was its basis [i.e., the basis of Brahmoism]. Brahma reigned in the pure heart alone. . . . We could accept those texts only of the Upanishads which accorded with that heart. (Tagore 1916: 161; quoted in Halbfass 1988: 223)

Tellingly, Debendranath also rejected Śaṅkara's Advaita Vedānta, which he felt effaced the distinction between the worshipper and the object of worship:

[3] For the biographical information in this section, I rely primarily on *LP* 2.ii.33–187, Gambhīrānanda (1984), Nikhilananda (1953), Chetanananda (1997: 19–73), *LSV* 1 and *LSV* 2, Dhar (1975), M. Datta (1912), and B. Datta (1954). I do not rely on Narasingha Sil's polemical book-length "reassessment" of Vivekananda (Sil 1997), which sets out to remove the "hagiographical halo" (1997: 23) surrounding Vivekananda, since the book is seriously flawed from a scholarly standpoint. Sil has a tendency to shroud his baseless speculations in the guise of biographical facts—claiming, for instance, that Vivekananda only joined the Sādhāran Brāhmo Samāj "because of his musical expertise" (1997: 34) and insinuating, without any evidence, a "homoerotic" relationship between him and Ramakrishna (1997: 42–43).

> Our relation with god is that of worshipper and worshipped—this is the very essence of Brâhmaism. When we found the opposite conclusion to this arrived at in Shankaracharya's *Śârirak mimâmsâ* of the *Vedanta Darśana* we could no longer place any confidence in it; nor could we accept it as a support of our religion. (Tagore 1916: 160–61; quoted in Rambachan 1994a: 21)

Keshab Chandra Sen (1838–1884) was a prominent and charismatic member of Debendranath's Brāhmo Samāj, but in 1866, he broke away from the organization due to ideological differences. After this schism, Debendranath renamed his organization the "Ādi Brāhmo Samāj," and Keshab became the leader of the Brāhmo Samāj of India, which continued to uphold rational monotheism and went even further than Debendranath in privileging spiritual realization over religious scriptures and dogmas (Rambachan 1994a: 24–31). However, unlike Debendranath, Keshab strongly emphasized social reform initiatives—including widow remarriage, social equality, and intercaste marriage—and championed the harmony of the world's religions (Stevens 2018). In 1875, Keshab became closely acquainted with Ramakrishna, even writing about Ramakrishna's spiritual greatness in newspapers and encouraging his own followers to visit him. In 1878, Śivanāth Śāstrī and Vijayakṛṣṇa Gosvāmī broke from Keshab's Brāhmo sect due to ideological differences and formed the Sādhāran Brāhmo Samāj. While there were many reasons for this schism, two of them are especially worth mentioning in this context. First, Śivanāth and Vijayakṛṣṇa were suspicious of Keshab's increasing tendency to claim that his decisions were "motivated by *ādeśa* (divine command)" and the consequent "attitude of hero worship that was growing around him" (Rambachan 1994a: 28; see also Sastri 1911: 268). Second, Keshab had consented to the marriage of his fifteen-year-old daughter with the Maharaja of Cooch Behar, directly flouting the official Brāhmo stance against the marriage of girls under the age of eighteen (Stevens 2018: 154–200). The Sādhāran Brāhmo Samāj, like Keshab's organization, upheld rational monotheism and strongly emphasized social reform. However, while Keshab lauded the British colonial rule of India as divinely ordained, the Sādhāran Brāhmo Samāj took steps to challenge British imperialism, helping to paving the way for the Indian National Congress (Stevens 2018: 185–86).

In 1879, Keshab founded the "Nava Vidhān" (New Dispensation), a new Brāhmo sect emphasizing the underlying unity of all religions. It is significant, however, that Keshab had already established a close association with Ramakrishna several years earlier in March 1875 (*LP* 2.ii.9 / *DP* 725). While there is a great deal of controversy regarding the extent to which Ramakrishna influenced Keshab's Nava Vidhān,[4] it is clear that Keshab viewed Ramakrishna as

[4] For a thorough discussion of this controversy, see Basu (1977: 188–244).

the living embodiment of the ideals of the Nava Vidhān. As Svāmī Sāradānanda recalls, "When Keshab came to see the Master [Ramakrishna] at Dakshineswar, many of us saw him take the dust of the Master's feet while loudly repeating, 'Victory to the Nava Vidhān! Victory to the Nava Vidhān!'" (*LP* 2.ii.10 / *DP* 726).

Narendra met and spoke to Debendranath Tagore and Keshab on several occasions, but he felt especially drawn toward the Sādhāran Brāhmo Samāj, which he formally joined in 1878 or 1879 (Gambhīrānanda 1984, vol. 1: 55; Dhar 1975, vol. 1: 85).[5] In the March 1882 entry of the *Kathāmṛta*, Gupta recorded that Narendra "frequents the Sādhāran Brāhmo Samāj" (*K* 22 / *G* 84). The extent of Narendra's association with Keshab remains a matter of dispute. According to Narendra's brother Mahendranāth Datta, Narendra had joined Keshab's "Band of Hope," a youth group advocating temperance (M. Datta 1943: 12).[6] In 1883, Narendra also acted in Trailokyanāth Sānyāl's play *Nava Vṛndāvan*, which was inspired by Keshab's Nava Vidhān and very likely by Ramakrishna as well, and both Ramakrishna and Keshab were present during one of Narendra's performances (Cetanānanda 1969; M. Datta 1943: 13).

However, as far as I am aware, there is no reliable evidence that Narendra joined Keshab's Nava Vidhān or was closely associated with Keshab in any way.[7] Kopf (1979: 205) claims that Vivekananda joined "Keshub's Brahmo Samaj in 1880," citing as evidence a page from Christopher Isherwood's biography, *Ramakrishna and His Disciples* (Isherwood 1965: 192). However, on the page cited by Kopf, Isherwood only states that "Naren joined the Brahmo Samaj," not specifying there or anywhere else in the book that it was Keshab's Nava Vidhān in particular and not mentioning any date. More recent scholars (De Michelis 2004: 99; Stevens 2018: 211) have repeated Kopf's mistake, claiming that Narendra had joined Keshab's Nava Vidhān in 1880, but only citing as evidence Kopf's erroneous citation of Isherwood.

Moreover, there is strong evidence that Narendra was actually turned off by aspects of Keshab's personality and, hence, chose not to associate with him. In an 1894 letter to the Harvard professor John Henry Wright, Vivekananda himself remarked, "I *never* identified myself anyway with Mr. [Pratap Chandra] Mazoomdar's party chief [i.e., Keshab]" (*CW* 7:468). In the postscript to the same letter, Vivekananda added this clarification: "I had connection with Pundit Shiva Nath Shastri's party [i.e., the Sādhāran Brāhmo Samāj]—but only on

[5] Vivekananda himself mentioned that he had been a member of the Sādhāran Brāhmo Samāj (*K* 1134 / *G* 981; *CW* 7:468).

[6] For details on Keshab's "Band of Hope," see Sastri (1911: 243–44).

[7] Priya Nath Mallik, a member of the Nava Vidhān, wrote: "At the very first he [Vivekananda] made acquaintance of the Sadharan Brahmo Samaj, then, after he came to know me, he began to have leanings towards Navavidhan" (Banerji 1942: 277). However, as Stevens (2018: 268n61) notes, "Mallik may have had a vested interest in magnifying Keshab's influence," so Mallik cannot be taken as a trustworthy source.

points of social reform. Mazoomdar and Chandra Sen—I always considered as not sincere, and I have no reason to change my opinion even now" (*CW* 7:468). Vivekananda's brother Bhupendranath Datta likewise noted that Narendra "became a member of the Sadharan Brahmo Samaj" perhaps because "the mysticism of Keshabchandra seemed too much irrational to him" (Datta 1954: 154).[8] Such textual evidence calls into question attempts by scholars like De Michelis (2004) to prove that Keshab was a formative influence on Vivekananda. It is also important to note that by the time Narendra had met Keshab, Keshab had already come under the influence of Ramakrishna—a fact that complicates any attempt to make a clear-cut distinction between Keshab's influence on Vivekananda and Ramakrishna's influence on Vivekananda.

What we can say with confidence, then, is that between roughly 1878 and 1882, Narendra was an active member of the Sādhāran Brāhmo Samāj and a staunch advocate of its ideology of rational monotheism and social reform. He also met both Debendranath Tagore and Keshab on several occasions, though he had an especially close association with Śivanāth Śāstrī, one of the leaders of the Sādhāran Brāhmo Samāj.

According to Narendra's younger brother Bhupendranath Datta, Narendra would often tell his classmate Haromohan Mitra, "But for Ramakrishna I would have been a Brahmo missionary" (Datta 1954: 154). This statement makes clear that it was Narendra's momentous encounter with Ramakrishna that changed the course of his life by turning him away from Brāhmoism. Narendra likely first met Ramakrishna in November 1881 at the age of eighteen, when he had just begun studying Western philosophy at Scottish Church College (Dhar 1975, vol. 1: 80). Narendra visited Ramakrishna regularly in Dakshineswar and Calcutta from early 1882 to 1886, the year his beloved guru passed away. I would distinguish two key phases in the evolution of Narendra's thinking during this period. In the first phase, Narendra moved away from Brāhmo theism and embraced Advaita Vedānta, which maintains that the sole reality is the impersonal and formless Brahman. In the second phase, Narendra's Advaitic outlook itself evolved and broadened, as he felt compelled to accept the reality not only of the impersonal Brahman but also of the personal God—whom he also referred to as "Śakti" or "Kālī"—and as he began to look upon the world as a real manifestation of Śakti. We will discuss the first phase in this section and the second phase in the next section.

Ramakrishna singled out Narendra as a person of the highest spiritual caliber, an "*īśvarakoṭi*"—that is, a spiritually perfect, divinely commissioned soul who takes birth not because of his own past *karma* but in order to help others attain

[8] Likewise, Vivekananda's other brother Mahendranāth Datta (1912: 9) noted that while Narendra occasionally visited Keshab, he joined the Sādhāran Brāhmo Samāj soon after it was formed.

salvation (*LSV* 2:853–54; *K* 357 / *G* 364). Ramakrishna specifically remarked that Narendra "belonged to the realm of the formless Absolute" (*nirākārer ghar*), which is why he chose to teach Advaita Vedānta to Naren, even though he taught *bhakti* (the path of devotion) to almost everyone else (*K* 357 / *G* 364).

In late 1881 or early 1882, Narendra went to visit Ramakrishna in Dakshineswar for the second time. When Narendra was sitting alone with Ramakrishna in his room, the latter went into an ecstatic mood and touched Narendra on the chest. Vivekananda later described what ensued in vivid detail:

> One day in the temple-garden at Dakshineswar, Ṭhākur [Ramakrishna] touched me, and first of all I began to see that the houses—rooms, doors, windows, verandahs—the trees, the sun, the moon—all were, as it were, dissolving and ultimately merging in the *ākāśa* [ether]. Gradually again, the *ākāśa* also vanished, and what happened next I do not recollect. But I do remember that I became frightened and cried out to Ṭhākur, "Ah, what are you doing to me? Don't you know I have parents at home?" When Ṭhākur heard this, he gave a loud laugh and then touched me again with his hand and said, "All right, let it stop for now." After that, I gradually returned to my normal state and once again saw the houses, doors, windows, verandahs, and other things just as they were before. (*BCW* 9:87 / *CW* 5:392; translation modified)[9]

This was Narendra's first glimpse of the heady Advaitic state of *nirvikalpa samādhi*, during which his mind merged into nondual Brahman and the world of differentiation began to vanish. After he returned to a normal state of consciousness, Narendra was left feeling bewildered by the experience and was amazed by Ramakrishna's ability to "destroy the strong structure of my mind at will" (*LP* 2.ii.51–52 / *DP* 772). However, in spite of this overwhelming Advaitic experience, Narendra was not yet ready to accept the teachings of Advaita Vedānta. Indeed, in the March 1882 entry of the *Kathāmṛta*, Mahendranāth Gupta introduces Narendra as a nineteen-year-old college student "who frequents the Sādhāran Brāhmo Samāj" (*K* 22 / *G* 84)—which suggests that he was still committed to Brāhmo theism at the time.

During Narendra's subsequent visits to Ramakrishna, his guru would encourage Narendra to read aloud from the Advaitic treatise *Aṣṭāvakra-Saṃhitā*, which affirms the sole reality of Pure Consciousness. There are several verses in the first chapter of this text that must have impressed Narendra deeply. First, the sage Aṣṭāvakra's declaration in verse 6 that "you are already eternally liberated" (*mukta evāsi sarvadā*) emerged as a prominent theme in Vivekananda's lectures

[9] Another very similar version of Vivekananda's account of this *samādhi* experience is found in *LP* 2.ii.51 / *DP* 771.

and writings in the 1890s (Nityaswarupananda 2008: 7). As we will see in section 6 of the next chapter, Vivekananda repeatedly taught that the aim of spiritual practice is not to *attain* liberative knowledge but to remove the layers of ignorance and impurity that veil our already pure and liberated Self. Second, the idea conveyed in the first line of verse 11—"The person who considers himself liberated is liberated indeed, and the person who considers himself bound remains bound" (Nityaswarupananda 2008: 10)—became a keynote of the later teachings of Vivekananda, who constantly exhorted people to think of themselves not as sinners but as "spirits free, blest and eternal" (*CW* 1:11).

However, Ramakrishna knew that Narendra would be less persuaded by intellectual teaching than by direct spiritual experience. Vivekananda himself recounted the decisive spiritual experience that finally compelled him to accept Advaita Vedānta. As a Brāhmo theist, Narendra initially followed Debendranath Tagore in dismissing Advaita Vedānta as a "blasphemous" atheistic philosophy that taught the "absurd" and sinful doctrine that we are "identical with the Creator" (Chetanananda 1997: 27). One day,[10] while Narendra was ridiculing the Advaitic idea that "[t]his jug is God, this cup is God, and we too are God," Ramakrishna touched Narendra, who immediately went into an ecstatic spiritual state that lasted for several days. Vivekananda later described this spiritual experience as follows:

> That day my mind underwent a complete revolution (*bhāvāntara*) at the marvelous touch of the Master. I was stupefied to find that there was really nothing in the universe but God (*īśvara bhinna viśvabrahmāṇḍe anya kichuī ār nāi*)! . . . [E]verything I saw was God. I sat down to take my meal, but found that everything—the food, the plate, the person who served, and even myself—was nothing but God. . . . [F]rom then on I kept having the same experience, no matter what I was doing—eating, sitting, lying down, or going to college. . . . When that first intoxication lessened a bit, the world began to appear to me as a dream (*jakhan pūrvokta ācchanna bhābṭā ekṭu komiyā jāito, takhan jagaṭṭāke svapna boliyā mone hoyto*). . . . This state of things continued for some days. When I became normal again, I realized that I must have had a glimpse of the knowledge of Advaita (*advaitavijñāner ābhās*). Then it struck me that the words of the scriptures were not false. Thenceforth I could not deny the conclusions of the Advaita philosophy. (*LP* 2.ii.81–82 / *DP* 802; translation modified)

[10] The precise date of this incident is unknown, but it definitely occurred sometime between 1882 and January 1884, since Vivekananda mentions that he was attending "college" at the time, and he passed his BA examination at Scottish Church College in January 1884 (a fact noted in Paranjape 2015: xlvi).

According to Vivekananda, this decisive experience precipitated his philosophico-spiritual conversion from Brāhmo theism to the philosophy of Advaita Vedānta. His nuanced diachronic description of the phenomenology of his Advaitic experience is revealing. Initially, he seems to have had a panentheistic experience of everything in the world as a real manifestation of God. However, after this state "lessened a bit," he began to look upon the world as unreal and dreamlike. In other words, this single prolonged spiritual experience enabled him to inhabit firsthand two distinct nondual standpoints: first, an integral, all-encompassing nondual standpoint akin to Tantra and Śaiva Nondualism; and subsequently, a more traditional, world-denying nondual standpoint.

2. 1884 to 1886: From Acosmic Advaita to Integral Advaita

With this transformative nondual experience, Narendra entered into the second phase of his spiritual tutelage under Ramakrishna. Although Narendra now accepted Advaita Vedānta, he was not yet able to assimilate fully what he had experienced, nor was he able to reconcile the two different nondual states he had experienced in succession. Indeed, as we will see, Narendra, for some time after this spiritual experience, seemed to prefer a quietistic, world-denying Advaita worldview; he was less intent on seeing the world as God than on forgetting the world altogether and immersing himself in the nondual state of *nirvikalpa samādhi*. He was also skeptical of Ramakrishna's visions of God. He would bluntly tell Ramakrishna, "The forms of God that you see are a fiction of your mind" (*K* 826 / *G* 772).[11] However, as I will show in this section, Ramakrishna gradually led Narendra to accept a more integral, world-affirming Advaitic outlook through a combination of philosophical instruction and personal spiritual guidance.

A keynote of Ramakrishna's teachings, as I have discussed in detail in the first chapter of my book *Infinite Paths to Infinite Reality: Sri Ramakrishna and Cross-Cultural Philosophy of Religion* (Maharaj 2018), is his distinction between two fundamental stages of spiritual realization, which he called "*jñāna*" and "*vijñāna*" respectively. For instance, on September 14, 1884, Ramakrishna, addressing Narendra and other devotees, contrasted the spiritual outlooks of the *jñānī* and the *vijñānī*:

[11] Similarly, on March 25, 1887, Narendra told Mahendranāth Gupta, "I used to dismiss his [Ramakrishna's] words. . . . I told him that his visions of God were all hallucinations of his mind" (*K* 1133 / *G* 981).

> The *jñānī* says, "This world is a 'framework of illusion' (*dhokār ṭāti*)." But he who is beyond both knowledge and ignorance describes it as a "mansion of mirth" (*majār kuṭi*). He sees that it is God Himself (*īśvara*) who has become the universe, all living beings, and the twenty-four cosmic principles. . . . He alone who, after reaching the *nitya* [Eternal Reality], can dwell in the *līlā* [God's cosmic play], and again climb from the *līlā* to the *nitya*, has ripe knowledge and devotion (*pākā jñāna, pākā bhakti*). Sages like Nārada cherished love of God after attaining the Knowledge of Brahman. This is called *vijñāna*.
>
> Mere dry knowledge (*śudhu śuṣka jñāna*) is like an ordinary rocket: it bursts into a few sparks and then dies out. But the Knowledge of sages like Nārada and Śukadeva is like a good rocket: for a while it showers balls of different colors, and then it stops; again it throws out new balls, and again it stops; and thus it goes on. Those sages had *prema* [supreme love] for God. *Prema* is the rope by which one can reach Saccidānanda. (*K* 534 / *G* 523, translation modified)

The *jñānī*, according to Ramakrishna, is the traditional Advaitin who has attained the spiritual realization that the impersonal nondual Brahman alone is real and the universe is unreal. The *vijñānī*, however, first attains knowledge of Brahman and then achieves the even greater, and more comprehensive, realization that Brahman "has become the universe and its living beings." For Ramakrishna, then, both the *jñānī* and the *vijñānī* are Advaitins, since they both maintain that Brahman is the sole reality. However, while the *jñānī* has the *acosmic* realization of nondual Brahman in *nirvikalpa samādhi*, the *vijñānī* returns from the state of *nirvikalpa samādhi* to attain the richer, world-inclusive nondual realization that the same Brahman realized in *nirvikalpa samādhi* has also manifested as everything in the universe. Hence, unlike the *jñānī*, the *vijñānī* combines knowledge and devotion by worshipping everything and everyone as real manifestations of God. I call Ramakrishna's philosophy "Vijñāna Vedānta" or "Integral Advaita," because it harmonizes various religious paths and approaches to God on the experiential basis of the nondual state of *vijñāna* (Maharaj 2018: 13–50).

Ramakrishna's telling reference to "mere dry knowledge" indicates his preference for *vijñāna* over mere *jñāna*. On other occasions, he contrasted the spiritual selfishness of *jñānī*s with the spiritual compassion of *vijñānī*s. He likened *jñānī*s, who seek only their own salvation, to "a hollow piece of drift-wood" that "sinks if even a bird sits on it" (*K* 482 / *G* 479). By contrast, *vijñānī*s like Nārada, who strive to help others achieve spiritual enlightenment, "are like a huge log that not only can float across to the other shore but can carry many animals and other creatures as well" (*K* 482 / *G* 479). Ramakrishna would often describe himself as a *vijñānī*: "I do not have the nature of a *jñānī*. . . . The Divine Mother has kept me in the state of a *bhakta*, a *vijñānī*" (*K* 391 / *G* 393). Moreover, as we will see,

Ramakrishna repeatedly encouraged Narendra to be a spiritually compassionate *vijñānī* rather than a mere *jñānī*.

Ramakrishna's key distinction between the spiritual experiences of *jñāna* and *vijñāna*, I would suggest, helped the young Narendra make sense of his own earlier multifaceted Advaitic experience, discussed at the end of the previous section. It is significant that Vivekananda himself later claimed, in the passage already quoted, that this momentous spiritual experience gave him a glimpse of "*advaita-vijñāna*." It seems likely that he had in mind here Ramakrishna's concept of *vijñāna*. Vivekananda, we should recall, described his initial Advaitic experience as the realization that "there was really nothing in the universe but God," which corresponds quite closely to the Ramakrishnan *vijñānī*'s realization that God "has become the universe, all living beings, and the twenty-four cosmic principles." Narendra's subsequent Advaitic state, when he began to see the world "as a dream," corresponds to the traditional Advaitic *jñānī*'s experience of the world as a "framework of illusion."

On another occasion in 1884, Ramakrishna was explaining to Narendra and other devotees that one of the main religious practices of Vaiṣṇavas is "showing compassion to all beings" (*sarva jīve dayā*) (*LP* 2.ii.131 / *DP* 852). Suddenly, just after uttering this phrase, Ramakrishna reportedly went into a deep state of *samādhi*. After a while, he came down to a semi-ecstatic state and said: "How foolish to speak of compassion! Human beings are as insignificant as worms crawling on the earth—and they are to show compassion to others? That's absurd. It must not be compassion, but service to all. Serve them, knowing that they are all manifestations of God (*śivajñāne jīver sevā*)" (*LP* 2.i.131 / *DP* 852). Crucially, Ramakrishna's ethics of service is based on the panentheistic outlook of the *vijñānī*: since God manifests in the form of human beings, one actually serves God by serving others. Ramakrishna's teaching affected the young Narendra so deeply that he took his friends aside afterward and explained its far-reaching significance to them:

> What Ṭhākur [Ramakrishna] said today in his ecstatic mood is clear: One can bring Vedānta from the forest to the home and practice it in daily life. Let people continue with whatever they are doing; there's no harm in this. People must first fully believe and be convinced that God has manifested Himself before them as the world and its creatures. . . . If people consider everyone to be God, how can they consider themselves to be superior to others and harbor attachment, hatred, arrogance—or even compassion (*dayā*)—toward them? Their minds will become pure as they serve all beings as God (*śivajñāne jīver sevā*), and soon they will experience themselves as parts of the blissful God. They will realize that their true nature is pure, illumined, and free. (*LP* 2.ii.131 / *DP* 852; translation modified)

As I will discuss in section 5 of the next chapter, this remark contains in a nutshell the ethically oriented "Practical Vedānta" Vivekananda would go on to preach throughout the world a decade later. The key to making Vedānta practical and efficacious in everyday life, Narendra realized, is to recognize that "God has manifested Himself" as "the world and its creatures." In other words, Narendra learned from Ramakrishna that the ethico-spiritual practice of serving "all beings as God" finds its justification not in the world-denying metaphysics of traditional Advaita Vedānta but in the world-inclusive metaphysics of Ramakrishna's Vijñāna Vedānta.

On February 25, 1884, Narendra's father died and his family was suddenly plunged into dire poverty. Sometime later in 1884 or in 1885, Narendra, in desperation, begged Ramakrishna to pray to the Divine Mother for the material welfare of his family. Ramakrishna responded: "My boy, I can't make such demands. But why don't you go and ask the Mother yourself? All your sufferings are due to your disregard of Her" (*LSV* 1:127). Vivekananda later recounted what transpired that night:

> About 9 o'clock the Master commanded me to go to the temple. As I went, I was filled with a divine intoxication. My feet were unsteady. My heart was leaping in anticipation of the joy of beholding the living Goddess and hearing Her words. . . . Reaching the temple, as I cast my eyes upon the image, I actually found that the Divine Mother was living and conscious, the Perennial Fountain of Divine Love and Beauty. I was caught in a surging wave of devotion and love. In an ecstasy of joy I prostrated myself again and again before the Mother and prayed, "Mother, give me discrimination! Give me renunciation! Give unto me knowledge and devotion! Grant that I may have an uninterrupted vision of Thee!" A serene peace reigned in my soul. The world was forgotten. Only the Divine Mother shone within my heart. (*LSV* 1:128)

Swept up in ecstatic love of Kālī, Narendra could only pray to Her for spiritual virtues and entirely forgot about his family's material difficulties. At the suggestion of Ramakrishna, Narendra went twice more to the Kālī Temple, but each time he entered the temple, he became so full of devotional fervor that he was unable to pray for the alleviation of his family's poverty.

A day after this incident, Ramakrishna joyfully recounted to his devotee Vaikuṇṭhanāth Sānyāl what had transpired with Narendra the day before and then told him with "unfeigned delight": "He [Naren] would not accept the Divine Mother before, but did so yesterday. . . . Isn't it wonderful that Narendra has accepted Mother?" (*LSV* 1:129). Years later, on May 29, 1899, Vivekananda, in a private conversation with his disciple Sister Nivedita, seemed to refer to this transformative incident when he explained to her how Ramakrishna finally led him to accept the reality and supremacy of Śakti. Nivedita recounts this conversation in a letter:

S. [Swami Vivekananda] How I used to hate Kali and all Her ways. *That* was my 6 years' fight, because I would not accept Kali.
N. [Nivedita] But now you have accepted Her specially, have you not, Swami?
S. I *had* to—Ramakrishna Paramahamsa dedicated me to Her. And you know I believe that She guides me in every little thing I do—and just does what She likes with me. Yet I fought so long.—I loved the man you see, and that held me. I thought him the purest man I had ever seen, and I knew that he loved me as my own father and mother had not power to do. . . . His greatness had not dawned on me then. That was afterwards, when I had given in. At that time I thought him simply a brain-sick baby, always seeing visions and things. I hated it—and then *I* had to accept Her too!
N. Won't you tell me what made you do that Swami? What broke all your opposition down?
S. No that will die with me. I had great misfortunes at that time you know. My father died, and so on. And She saw Her opportunity to make a slave of me. They were her very words.—"To make a slave of you." And R.P. [Ramakrishna Paramahamsa] made me over to Her-----Curious, He only lived 2 years after doing that. . . . Yes, I think there's no doubt that Kali worked up the body of Ramakrishna for Her Own Ends. You see Margot I cannot *but* believe that there is, somewhere, a Great Power that thinks of itself as Feminine and called Kali, and the Mother!--------And I believe in Brahman, too—that there is nothing but Brahman ever—but you see it's always like that. It's the multitude of cells in the body that make up the person—the *many* brain-centres that produce the one consciousness.
N. Yes—always Unity *in Complexity.*
S. Just so! And why should it be different with Brahman? It is Brahman—the One—and yet it is the gods too! (Basu 1982: vol. 1, 157)[12]

Several clues in this passage suggest that he had in mind his ecstatic experiences of the Divine Mother in the Kālī Temple in 1884 or 1885. Vivekananda himself, as we have seen, remarked that it was precisely this incident in the Kālī Temple that led him to accept the reality and greatness of Śakti, the Divine Mother. The fact that he mentioned that his father had just died also makes it likely that he had this particular incident in mind. Vivekananda specifically notes that during this incident, he heard Kālī say that She had made "a slave" of him. Indeed, from that point on, he would often tell his intimate friends and disciples, especially toward

[12] For a slightly different version of the same passage, see *CW* 8:263.

the end of his life, that he felt himself to be a mere instrument of the Divine Mother.[13] Moreover, after this spiritual experience of Śakti, Narendra began to have spiritual visions of various forms of the personal God. This is clear from the fact that on August 9, 1885, Ramakrishna remarked that "even Naren is seeing forms of God (*īśvarīya rūpa*) nowadays" (*K* 897 / *G* 834).

Tellingly, in the 1899 dialogue just quoted, Vivekananda remarked that his decisive spiritual experience of the Divine Mother in 1884 or 1885 made him realize that the one Divine Reality is at once "Brahman" and a "great Power . . . called Kali and Mother." As is clear from this dialogue between Ramakrishna and Narendra on March 11, 1885, it was Ramakrishna who helped Narendra to arrive at this spiritual insight into the inseparability of the impersonal Brahman from the personal dynamic Śakti:

NARENDRA (TO SRI RAMAKRISHNA): "Why, I have meditated on Kālī for three or four days, but nothing has come of it."

SRI RAMAKRISHNA: "All in good time, my child. Kālī is none other than Brahman. That which is Brahman is also Kālī. Kālī is the Primal Śakti. When the Divine Reality is inactive (*niṣkriya*), I call It 'Brahman,' and when It creates, preserves, and destroys, I call It 'Śakti' or 'Kālī.' What you call 'Brahman' I call 'Kālī.' Brahman and Kālī are inseparable (*abheda*). They are like fire and its power to burn: if one thinks of fire one must think of its power to burn. If one accepts Kālī one must also accept Brahman; again, if one accepts Brahman one must also accept Kālī." (*K* 779–80 / *G* 734; translation modified)

Significantly, Ramakrishna also repeatedly emphasized to Narendra and others that it is the *vijñānī*, rather than the mere *jñānī*, who realizes the inseparability of Brahman and Śakti. As he put it, "The *vijñānī* sees that the Reality which is impersonal (*nirguṇa*) is also personal (*saguṇa*). . . . The *vijñānī* sees that the Reality which is Brahman is also *Bhagavān*; That which is beyond the three *guṇa*s is also *Bhagavān* endowed with the six divine attributes" (*K* 51 / *G* 104). According to Ramakrishna, the *jñānī*, after realizing the impersonal nondual Brahman in the state of *nirvikalpa samādhi*, considers both Śakti and the world to be illusory. By contrast, the *vijñānī*, after attaining the knowledge of the "inactive" nondual Brahman in *nirvikalpa samādhi*, remains in the world as a *bhakta* and realizes that Śakti, far from being unreal, is the same ultimate reality in its dynamic aspect as the omnipotent and loving Lord who creates, preserves, and destroys the universe. From a philosophical standpoint, then, it is the *vijñānī* who realizes that the personal God of *bhakta*s and the impersonal Absolute of *jñānī*s are equally real. Moreover, since Śakti is the real personal/dynamic aspect of the

[13] See, for instance, *BCW* 9:122 / *CW* 7:206–7.

impersonal-personal Infinite Reality, the *vijñanī* looks upon the world as a real manifestation of Śakti.

In an important conversation on March 11, 1885, Ramakrishna further explained to Narendra how Vijñāna Vedānta harmonizes the apparently conflicting Vedāntic philosophies of Śaṅkara and Rāmānuja:

SRI RAMAKRISHNA: "In Vedānta, there is Śaṅkara's Advaitic interpretation, and there is also Rāmānuja's Viśiṣṭādvaitic interpretation."

NARENDRA: "What is Viśiṣṭādvaita?"

SRI RAMAKRISHNA: "Viśiṣṭādvaita is Rāmānuja's doctrine. According to this view, Brahman is qualified by the universe and its living beings. These three—Brahman, the insentient world, and living beings—together constitute One Reality. (*jīva-jagat-viśiṣṭa brahma. sab joḍiye ekṭi.*). Take the instance of a bel-fruit. A man wanted to know the weight of the fruit. He separated the shell, the flesh, and the seeds. But can a man get the weight of the whole fruit by weighing only the flesh? He must weigh flesh, shell, and seeds together. At first it appears that the real thing in the fruit is the flesh, and not its seeds or shell. Then by reasoning you find that the shell, seeds, and flesh all belong to the fruit; the shell and seeds belong to the same thing that the flesh belongs to. Likewise, in spiritual discrimination one must first reason, following the method of 'Not this, not this': God is not the universe; God is not the living beings; Brahman alone is real, and all else is unreal. Then one realizes, as with the bel-fruit, that the Reality from which we derive the notion of Brahman is the very Reality from which come living beings and the universe. The *nitya* and the *līlā* are the two aspects of one and the same Reality. (*tārpar anubhab hoy, jār śā̆s tārī kholā, bici. jā theke brahma bolcho tāi theke jīvajagat. jā̆rī nitya tā̆rī līlā.*). Therefore, Rāmānuja held that Brahman is qualified by the universe and the living beings. This is called Viśiṣṭādvaita."

(*To M.* [Mahendranāth Gupta]) "I do see God directly. What shall I reason about? I clearly see that She Herself has become everything; that She Herself has become the universe and all living beings. . . ." (*K* 778–79 / *G* 733–34; translation modified)

For Ramakrishna, Śaṅkara's Advaita Vedānta corresponds to the "*jñāna*" stage of spiritual experience, the realization—in the state of *nirvikalpa samādhi*—that the impersonal nondual Brahman alone is real and that Śakti and the world are "unreal." Rāmānuja's Viśiṣṭādvaita philosophy, he claims, corresponds to the subsequent "*vijñāna*" stage of spiritual experience, the realization that "Brahman, the world, and living beings together constitute One Reality" (*sab joḍiye ekṭi*). While the *jñānī* subscribes to a world-denying Advaitic philosophy, the *vijñānī* holds the Integral Advaitic view that the "One Reality" encompasses not only the impersonal Brahman but also the dynamic Śakti, which manifests as all the sentient and insentient entities in the world. At the end of the passage, Ramakrishna made clear that he himself was currently enjoying the Integral Advaitic state of *vijñāna*: "I clearly see that She Herself has become everything."

The fact that Ramakrishna, both here and elsewhere, appealed to Rāmānuja's philosophy to explain his own Integral Advaitic philosophy of *vijñāna* led Mahendranāth Gupta, the author of the *Kathāmṛta*, to infer that he was a Viśiṣṭādvaitin. Gupta remarks: "Ṭhākur [Ramakrishna] does not say that this universe is unreal like a dream. He says, 'If we say so, then the weight of the bel-fruit will fall short.' His view is not the doctrine of *māyā* [of Śaṅkara's Advaita Vedānta] but the doctrine of Viśiṣṭādvaita" (*K* 698).[14] However, Gupta overlooks the crucial fact that Ramakrishna does not fully subscribe to *either* Śaṅkara's Advaita Vedānta *or* Rāmānuja's Viśiṣṭādvaita Vedānta, since he rejects the doctrinal exclusivism of both philosophies. Śaṅkara holds that the ultimate reality is *exclusively* impersonal (*nirguṇa*) and, therefore, not personal (*saguṇa*);[15] Rāmājuna, by contrast, holds that the ultimate reality is *exclusively* personal and, therefore, not impersonal.[16] Ramakrishna departs from both Śaṅkara and Rāmānuja in holding that the ultimate reality is *both* the impersonal Brahman *and* the personal Śakti. At the same time, he harmonizes the views of Śaṅkara and Rāmānuja at the level of spiritual experience.[17] Although he does not accept wholesale the doctrines of either Śaṅkara or Rāmānuja, Ramakrishna accepts the spiritual core of both philosophies by arguing that Śaṅkara's Advaita Vedānta corresponds to the spiritual stage of *jñāna* while Rāmānuja's Viśiṣṭādvaita corresponds to the post-*brahmajñāna* stage of *vijñāna*. From Ramakrishna's perspective, Rāmānuja's Viśiṣṭādvaita resembles, but is not identical to, his own Vijñāna Vedānta, since Rāmānuja does not even accept the reality of *nirguṇa* Brahman and, therefore, would not accept Ramakrishna's claim that the *vijñānī* views everything in the world as God *after* having attained the knowledge of *nirguṇa* Brahman in *nirvikalpa samādhi*.

Likewise, Ramakrishna taught the harmony of all religious doctrines to Narendra and others from the spiritual standpoint of *vijñāna*. For instance, on September 29, 1884, Ramakrishna told Narendra: "There are various paths to

[14] Nikhilananda omits this passage from his translation of the *Kathāmṛta*.

[15] As Ramakrishna was no doubt aware, "*nirguṇa*" literally means "without attributes," not "impersonal." Nonetheless, "attributes" include all the omni-attributes of the personal God, such as omniscience, omnipotence, and omnibenevolence. Hence, Śaṅkara holds that Brahman is ultimately only "impersonal" in the sense of being devoid of all the omni-attributes of the personal God. Śaṅkara makes this point explicitly in his commentary on *Brahmasūtra* 2.1.14, which I discuss in section 2 of chapter 2.

[16] For more details on Śaṅkara's and Rāmānuja's views of ultimate reality, see Maharaj (2018: 53–63).

[17] See Maharaj (2018: 23–26) for a fuller account of Ramakrishna's method of harmonizing conflicting philosophical sects.

reach God. Each view is a path. It is like reaching the Kālī Temple by different roads. . . . Many views, many paths—and I have seen them all" (*K* 594 / *G* 571–72). As I have argued in detail elsewhere (Maharaj 2018: 85–116), Ramakrishna championed the pluralist doctrine that various religious faiths and spiritual philosophies are different paths to the common goal of God-realization. He derived this religious pluralism from his *vijñāna*-based ontology of the impersonal-personal Infinite Divine Reality. As he put it, "God is infinite, and the paths to God are infinite" (*K* 511 / *G* 506). Since God is infinite—both personal and impersonal, with and without form, immanent and transcendent—there must be correspondingly infinite ways of approaching and ultimately realizing God. For Ramakrishna, the infinite impersonal-personal God is conceived and worshipped in different ways by people of varying temperaments, preferences, and worldviews. Hence, a sincere practitioner of any religion can realize God in the particular form he or she prefers. Non-theistic spiritual practitioners, such as Advaitins and Buddhists, can realize the impersonal aspect of the Infinite Reality. He added, however, that *bhakta*s who believe in the personal God—whether Hindu, Christian, or Muslim—can realize the same Infinite Reality as "eternally endowed with form and personality" (*nitya sākāra*) (*K* 152 / *G* 191). Hence, both theistic and non-theistic spiritual practitioners can realize God through sincere spiritual practice, even though they will end up realizing different aspects or forms of one and the same Infinite Reality. I will argue in chapter 3 that most scholars have not sufficiently appreciated the extent to which Vivekananda's later views on the harmony of all religions were shaped by Ramakrishna's *vijñāna*-based religious pluralism.

On March 11, 1886, Ramakrishna encouraged Narendra to be a many-sided *vijñānī bhakta* rather than a "dry," one-sided *jñānī*:

SRI RAMAKRISHNA (*to Narendra*): "Brahman is without taint. . . . Brahman and *māyā*. The *jñānī* rejects *māyā*. . . . The *bhakta*, however, does not ignore *māyā*. He worships *Mahāmāyā*. Taking refuge in Her, he says: 'O Mother, please stand aside from my path. Only if You step out of my way shall I have the Knowledge of Brahman.' The *jñānī*s explain away all three states—waking, dream, and deep sleep. But the *bhakta*s accept them all. As long as there is the ego, everything else exists. So long as the 'I' exists, the *bhakta* sees that it is God who has become *māyā*, the universe, the living beings, and the twenty-four cosmic principles."

Narendra and the other devotees sat silently listening.

SRI RAMAKRISHNA: "But the doctrine of *māyā* is dry." (*To Narendra*) "Repeat what I said."

NARENDRA: "*Māyā* is dry."

Ramakrishna affectionately stroked Narendra's face and hands and said: "Your face and hands show that you are a *bhakta*. But the *jñānī* has different features;

> they are dry. Even after attaining *jñāna*, the *jñānī* can live in the world, retaining *vidyāmāyā* [the *māyā* of knowledge], that is to say, *bhakti*, compassion, renunciation, and such virtues. This serves him two purposes: first, the teaching of men (*lokaśīkṣā*), and second, the enjoyment of divine bliss. If a *jñānī* remains silent, merged in *samādhi*, then men's hearts will not be illumined. . . . And further, a *jñānī* lives as a devotee, in the company of *bhakta*s, in order to enjoy and drink deep of the Bliss of God. . . . Remaining in the *līlā* after reaching the *nitya* is like coming back to this shore of a river after going to the other side. Such a return to the plane of *līlā* is for the teaching of humanity and for enjoyment—joyful participation in the divine sport in the world." (*K* 1020 / *G* 939–40; translation modified)

Ramakrishna contrasts the philosophical standpoint of the Advaitic *jñānī*, who dismisses *māyā*—including Śakti and the world—as unreal, with the outlook of the *bhakta*, who "sees that it is God who has become *māyā*, the universe, the living beings, and the twenty-four cosmic principles." Clearly, he refers here not to an ordinary *bhakta* but to a *vijñānī bhakta* who, after having attained the knowledge of nondual Brahman (the *nitya*) in *nirvikalpa samādhi*, comes down from the state of *samādhi* and sees everything in the world as the sportive play (*līlā*) of Śakti. Moreover, here and elsewhere, he reminds Narendra that a *jñānī* who always remains in the state of *nirvikalpa samādhi* cannot help others and is, therefore, ethically inferior to the spiritually compassionate *vijñānī* who chooses to come back from *samādhi* for the purpose of teaching and helping others. Tellingly, Ramakrishna explicitly instructs Narendra to reject the *jñānī*'s "dry" Advaitic doctrine of illusory *māyā* and tells him that his features indicate that he is actually a *vijñānī bhakta* at heart. On another occasion, Ramakrishna made a similar remark after examining Narendra's face: "Could one who is a dry *jñānī* have such eyes? *Jñāna* and feminine *bhakti* are blended in you" (*LP* 2.ii.105 / *DP* 826).

In spite of Ramakrishna's repeated exhortations to Narendra to be a *vijñānī*, Narendra was still eager to forget the world and immerse himself in the blissful Advaitic state of *nirvikalpa samādhi*. One day, shortly before Ramakrishna passed away in August 1886, Narendra asked Ramakrishna for the experience of *nirvikalpa samādhi*. Ramakrishna then rebuked him:

> Shame on you! You are asking for such an insignificant thing. I thought you would be like a great banyan tree, and that thousands of people would rest in your shade. But now I see that you are seeking your own liberation. There is a state higher than that. It is you who sing, "O Lord, Thou art all that exists." (Chetanananda 1997: 36)[18]

[18] Nicholson (2020) rightly cites this passage as strong evidence for the influence of Ramakrishna on Vivekananda's Vedāntic ethics.

Ramakrishna reminds Narendra that he is not an ordinary soul but an *īśvarakoṭi* for whom the exalted state of *nirvikalpa samādhi* is an "insignificant thing." Significantly, Ramakrishna tells him that the state higher than *nirvikalpa samādhi* is the realization that God is "all that exists"—which is, of course, none other than the state of *vijñāna*. In other words, he tells Narendra not to be a self-centered *jñānī* but a compassionate *vijñānī*. Instead of seeking his own liberation as *jñānī*s do, Narendra should work for the benefit of humanity by seeing God in everyone and serving them in a spirit of worship.

Years later, in 1898, Vivekananda, in conversation with Sister Nivedita, confirmed Ramakrishna's insight into his innately devotional nature. According to Nivedita, "He [Vivekananda] said one day that Ramakrishna, while seeming to be all Bhakti, was really within all Jñāna; but he himself, apparently all Jñāna, was full of Bhakti, and that thereby he was apt to be as weak as any woman" (*CW* 9:355). In fact, while Vivekananda possessed both *bhakti* and *jñāna*, there is strong evidence that in the last few years of his life, the devotional side of his nature became paramount. In a letter to Sister Christine dated October 25, 1898, Vivekananda wrote: "Never mind, 'Mother' knows what is best for us. She will show the way. I am now in Bhakti. As I am growing old, Bhakti is taking the place of Jñāna" (*CW* 9:107). Similarly, in a letter dated April 12, 1900, he echoed Ramakrishna's oft-repeated teaching that we are all "instruments" of the Divine Mother: "I am Mother's child. She works, She plays. Why should I plan? What should I plan? Things came and went, just as She liked, without my planning. We are Her automata. She is the wirepuller" (*CW* 8:517). A few months later, in a letter to Mary Hale dated June 17, 1900, he remarked that "Kali worship is my special *fad*. . ." (*CW* 8:522).

This section has made the case that Ramakrishna carefully groomed the young Vivekananda to be a many-sided and compassionate *vijñānī*, an Integral Advaitin who upholds the inseparability of the impersonal nondual Brahman from the dynamic personal Śakti and who looks upon everything in the world as a playful manifestation of Śakti. In chapters 2 and 3, I will argue that Vivekananda's formative training under Ramakrishna played a decisive role in his later philosophical exposition of Advaita Vedānta in lectures and writings from 1893 to 1901.

3. *Ramakrishna's Scriptural Support for Integral Advaita*

Ramakrishna impressed on the minds of Narendra and his other visitors that the Integral Advaitic outlook of the *vijñānī*, far from being something newfangled or idiosyncratic, finds support in numerous traditional Vedāntic scriptures. For instance, on October 29, 1885, he explained that the "superior devotee" (*uttam bhakta*)—another name for the *vijñānī*—"sees that God alone has become everything," and he then immediately added, "Read the *Gītā*, the *Bhāgavata*, and the Vedānta, and you will understand all this" (*K* 985 / *G* 910).[19] Although Ramakrishna did not mention any specific verses from the *Gītā* in this context, he may have had in mind 7.19, in which Kṛṣṇa declares: "Very rare is the great soul who knows that Vāsudeva is all that is (*vāsudevaḥ sarvam*)." On November 28, 1883, Ramakrishna quoted *Gītā* 18.66 and encouraged his visitors to take refuge in God:

> The Lord says in the *Gītā*: "O Arjuna, take refuge in Me. I shall deliver you from all sins." Take refuge at His feet: He will give you right understanding. He will take entire responsibility for you. . . . Can we ever know God unless He lets us know Him? Therefore I say, take refuge in God. Let Him do whatever He likes. He is self-willed. What power is there in a man? (*K* 316 / *G* 329)

On May 8, 1887, less than a year after Ramakrishna's passing, Narendra quoted verses 18.61–62 and 18.66 of the *Gītā* and then said to his brother disciple Prasanna:

> Did you notice what Krishna said? "Mounted on a machine" (*yantrārūḍhāṇi*). The Lord, by His *māyā*, causes all beings to revolve as if mounted on a machine. To seek to know God? You are but a worm among worms—and you to know God? . . . Don't you remember Ramakrishna's words? God is the hill of sugar and you are but an ant. One grain is enough to fill your stomach, and you think of bringing home the entire hill! . . . God is the Ocean of Mercy. Take refuge in Him. He will show compassion. (*K* 1154–55 / *G* 997–98)

It is significant that Narendra appealed not only to Ramakrishna's teaching about the ant and the sugar hill but also to one of his guru's favorite verses from the *Gītā* to support the view that it is not possible to attain liberation without God's grace. As we will see in section 6 of the next chapter, Vivekananda, in his later lectures and writings, followed Ramakrishna rather than Śaṅkara in claiming that the *Gītā* teaches that Bhakti-Yoga and Jñāna-Yoga are equally direct and effective paths to liberation (*CW* 1:93).

Vivekananda likewise pursued his guru's hint that the *vijñānī*'s standpoint can be found in the *Bhāgavata-Purāṇa*. In *Bhakti-Yoga* (1896), Vivekananda quotes *Bhāgavata* 1.7.10 in support of the view that the *vijñānī* remains as a *bhakta* "even

[19] In numerous other places, Ramakrishna also remarks that the standpoint of *vijñāna* can be found in the *Adhyātma-Rāmāyaṇa*, a book that—he claims—is "filled with ideas of *jñāna* and *bhakti*" and that holds that "God alone has become the universe and its living beings" (*K* 901 / *G* 836–37).

after liberation": "These are they who have been spoken of in the *Bhāgavata-Purāṇa* thus: 'O king, such are the glorious qualities of the Lord that the sages whose only pleasure is in the Self, and from whom all fetters have fallen off, even they love the Omnipresent with the love that is for love's sake' " (*CW* 3:40). Shortly thereafter, he cites *Bhāgavata* 10.32.2, claiming that the "blessed Gopis" had attained the heights of both *jñāna* and *bhakti*: "So long as they had lost sense of their own personal identity and individuality, they were all Krishnas, and when they began again to think of Him as the One to be worshipped, then they were Gopis again" (*CW* 3:41).

In an important recent article, James Madaio has made a convincing case that Vivekananda's understanding of Advaita Vedānta was shaped not only by Śaṅkara's Advaita Vedānta but also by a host of post-Śaṅkaran Advaitic texts that Vivekananda had read and to which he referred at various points in his lectures and writings (Madaio 2017).[20] Madaio notes, for instance, that Vivekananda's emphasis on *nirvikalpa samādhi* and meditation may be traced to a number of medieval Advaitic texts with which he was familiar, including *Jīvanmuktiviveka*, *Pañcadaśī*, *Yogavāsiṣṭha*, *Vivekacūḍāmaṇi*, and *Aparokṣānubhūti* (2017: 5–6).[21] I would only add that it was Ramakrishna who introduced Narendra to many of these medieval Advaitic texts and even suggested to him how they should be interpreted. As I already mentioned in section 1, Ramakrishna asked Narendra to read aloud from *Aṣṭāvakra-Saṃhitā*. Ramakrishna also owned a copy of Bipin Bihārī Ghoṣāl's *Mukti o tāhār Sādhan* (*Liberation and Spiritual Practice*; 1881), an eclectic Bengali compilation of passages from various Indian philosophical texts, including Advaita Vedāntic texts like *Pañcadaśī*, *Yogavāsiṣṭha*, *Vivekacūḍāmaṇi*, *Aṣṭāvakra-Saṃhitā*, *Avadhūta-Gītā*, *Vedāntasāra*, and *Ātmabodha* (Ghoṣāl [1881] 1987). Moreover, Ramakrishna's guru Totāpurī, a wandering Advaita Vedāntin monk who was influenced by the yoga-oriented strain of post-Śaṅkara Advaita, taught Ramakrishna an Advaitic doctrine emphasizing the need for constant meditation on the Ātman and the importance of *nirvikalpa samādhi* for the attainment of *brahmajñāna*.[22] Ramakrishna, in turn, taught Narendra an Advaitic philosophy that was indirectly shaped by the yogic strain of post-Śaṅkara Advaita Vedānta.

[20] Nicholson (2020) makes a similar argument.

[21] For discussion of some of these texts in relation to Vivekananda, see section 1 of chapter 5.

[22] See, for instance, Ramakrishna's references to Totāpurī's Advaitic teachings at *K* 991 / *G* 915 and Sāradānanda's detailed account of Ramakrishna's training under Totāpurī at *LP* 1.ii.159–71 / *DP* 303–15.

4. *Ramakrishna's Legacy: From Narendranāth Datta to Swami Vivekananda*

In this chapter, I have begun to make the case that the single most formative influence on Vivekananda's mature philosophical thought was his guru Ramakrishna. The extent of Ramakrishna's impact on Vivekananda is evidenced by the period after Ramakrishna's passing in August 1886 and prior to Vivekananda's first departure for the West in 1893. Immediately after his guru's passing, Narendra gathered together a core group of his brother disciples who chose to renounce the world in the name of Ramakrishna, who represented for them the ideal embodiment of renunciation, purity, and holiness. In January 1887, Narendra and his brother disciples took the formal vows of *sannyāsa*, at which point he assumed the name "Swami Vivekananda."

From 1888 to early 1893, Vivekananda traveled throughout India as a wandering monk before leaving for America in March 1893. In 1890, in a place called Kakrighat near Almora in the Himalayas, he had a transformative spiritual experience, which revealed to him—as he put it to Svāmī Akhaṇḍānanda—"the oneness of the macrocosm with the microcosm" (*LSV* 1:250). He wrote in a notebook what he had learned from the spiritual experience:

> The microcosm and the macrocosm are built on the same plan. Just as the individual soul is encased in the living body, so is the universal Soul in the Living Prakṛti [Nature]—the objective universe. Śivā [i.e., Kālī] is embracing Śiva: this is not a fancy. . . . This dual aspect of the Universal Soul is eternal. So what we perceive or feel is this combination of the Eternally Formed and the Eternally Formless. (*LSV* 1:250)[23]

It is significant that during this spiritual experience, he seems to have directly perceived the Integral Advaitic truths about God taught to him by Ramakrishna several years earlier—that the impersonal Brahman and personal Śakti are inseparable and that God is both with and without form.

During his wandering years, Vivekananda also studied a variety of scriptures and philosophical texts. In his 1889 Bengali translation of *The Imitation of Christ*, he cited the *Gītā*, the Vedas, Kaṭha Upaniṣad, *Adhyātma-Rāmāyaṇa*, *Vivekacūḍāmaṇi*, *Mahābhārata*, and *Manusmṛti* (*CW* 9:292–99). In several 1889 letters to the Advaita Vedānta pundit Pramadadās Mitra, Vivekananda raised a number of searching questions regarding the philosophical and social views expressed in texts like the Vedas, Upaniṣads, *Bhagavad-Gītā*, *Brahmasūtra*, Śaṅkara's Sanskrit commentaries on these Vedāntic scriptures, *Mahābhārata*,

[23] Unfortunately, the original Bengali statement is lost (Gambhīrānanda 1984, vol. 1: 230–31).

Pañcadaśī, *Avadhūta-Gītā*, the Buddhist Mahāyāna text *Prajñāpāramitāsūtra*, Gautama's *Nyāyasūtra*, and *Bhāgavata-Purāṇa* (*CW* 6:209–14).

While a full-scale examination of Vivekananda's critical engagement with these texts is beyond the scope of this chapter, I will indicate very briefly three of the ways that his reception of these scriptural and philosophical texts—as reflected in his 1889 letters to Pramadadās Mitra—was mediated by the influence of Ramakrishna. First, in these letters, the young Vivekananda persistently questioned Śaṅkara's casteism and attempted to refute Śaṅkara's arguments that *śūdras* should not be allowed to study the Vedas (*CW* 6:208–9). Tellingly, he mentions, in this context, that he learned from his "guru" Ramakrishna that it "means grave harm if one bent on going beyond *guṇa* and *karma* cherishes in mind any caste distinctions" (*CW* 6:210).

Second, in the same letter, he suggests that the Brahman of Vedānta is the same as the Śūnyatā of the Buddhists:

> In the Tantra, Ācārya [Śaṅkara] has been called a crypto-Buddhist; views expressed in the Buddhist text *Prajñāpāramitā* perfectly tally with the Vedāntic views propounded by the Ācārya. The author of *Pañcadaśī* also says that what we call Brahman is the same truth as the Śūnya of the Buddhist. (*BCW* 6:230 / *CW* 6:211; translation modified)

It was likely Ramakrishna who first suggested to Vivekananda such a Vedāntic interpretation of Buddhist Śūnyatā. On April 9, 1886, Ramakrishna explained to Narendra that the Buddha's realization of *nirvāṇa* is the same as the Advaitic realization of Pure Consciousness:

> SRI RAMAKRISHNA: "Why should Buddha be called an atheist? He simply could not express the Reality in words. Do you know what 'Buddha' means? By meditating on one's own *bodha svarūpa* [one's true nature as Pure Consciousness], one *becomes* that *bodha svarūpa*."
> NARENDRA: "Yes, sir." (*K* 1028 / *G* 947–48; translation modified)

Third, as early as 1889, we find the young Vivekananda distinguishing between the original meaning of Vedāntic scriptures and the sometimes distortive interpretations of these scriptures advanced by the *ācārya*s of various schools (*sampradāya*s) like Advaita Vedānta. For instance, in a letter to Mitra dated August 17, 1889, Vivekananda raised a query about Caitanya's non-Advaitic interpretation of the *Brahmasūtra*:

> Caitanyadev is said to have told Sārvabhauma at Puri, "I understand the *Vyāsasūtra* [i.e., *Brahmasūtra*], they are dualistic; but the commentator

> makes them Advaitic, which I don't understand." Is this true? Tradition says, Caitanyadev had a dispute with Prakāśānanda Sarasvatī on the point, and Caitanyadev won. (*BCW* 6:230 / *CW* 6:211; translation modified)

Indeed, as we will see in section 2 of the next chapter, in many of his later lectures and classes, Vivekananda faulted traditional commentators for "text-torturing" (*CW* 3:328) and called for an "independent" interpretation of the Vedāntic scriptures in the nonsectarian spirit of Ramakrishna (*CW* 3:233).

Between 1893 and 1896, Vivekananda gave lectures and classes on Hinduism and Vedānta in America and England, returning to India in January 1897. In January 1899, he established the Ramakrishna Mission, a monastic organization based on the twin ideals of striving for one's own liberation and serving humanity—embodied in the organization's Sanskrit motto, "*ātmano mokṣārthaṃ jagaddhitāya ca*," coined by Vivekananda himself. He took a second trip to America and Europe from spring 1899 to December 1900 and then returned to India, living mostly in Belur Math, the main monastery of the Ramakrishna Mission, where he passed away on the fourth of July 1902 at the age of thirty-nine.

In the next two chapters, I will argue that the core doctrines of the Integral Advaitic philosophy expounded by Vivekananda in his lectures and writings from 1893 to 1901 were shaped primarily by his extended discipleship under Ramakrishna. In chapters 4 through 10, I will explore how he developed sophisticated new philosophical views on the epistemology of spiritual experience, the dynamics of faith and reason, and the hard problem of consciousness through a subtle cosmopolitan engagement with indigenous Indian traditions and figures like Mīmāṃsā, Nyāya, Ramakrishna, and Śaṅkara as well as a variety of Western thinkers, including Immanuel Kant, William Hamilton, Herbert Spencer, and T. H. Huxley.

Taken as a whole, this book militates against the view of scholars like De Michelis (2004) and Baier (2019), who claim that Vivekananda's thought was shaped less by Ramakrishna than by Keshab Chandra Sen and Western occult traditions like Theosophy, Spiritualism, and New Thought. I have already noted in section 1 of this chapter that the extent of the young Narendra's association with Keshab has been exaggerated by these scholars, due in part to their dependence on unreliable sources. That said, as I will note at relevant points in later chapters, I do agree with these scholars that certain major themes in Vivekananda's thought—including the framework of "four Yogas," the harmony of religions, and the attempt to harmonize science and religion—were anticipated in Keshab's lectures. Nonetheless, I will argue that Vivekananda developed these themes in new and distinctive ways in the light of the Integral Advaitic philosophy he had learned from Ramakrishna.

De Michelis and Baier claim that Vivekananda was "influenced" by numerous Western occult ideas like faith-healing (De Michelis 2004: 159–60), the New Thought doctrine of "positive thinking" (De Michelis 2004: 116), and the Theosophical conception of religion as a science (Baier 2019: 244–48). However, their claims about "influence" fail to capture the subtle dynamics of Vivekananda's cosmopolitan engagement with modern Western spiritual practices. During his visits to America and England, Vivekananda quite naturally became acquainted with many of the Western occult and Spiritualist thought-currents that were popular at the time—as is evident from his numerous (often sardonic) references to seances (*CW* 4:32), "faith-healers" (*CW* 1:171), hypnotism (*CW* 1:172), and "Theosophy," which he branded as an "Indian grafting of American Spiritualism" (*CW* 4:317). His stance toward such Western occult ideas was characteristically nuanced and dialectical: while some of them have a grain of truth, they also have dangerous elements which may lead to "ultimate ruin" (*CW* 1:172).

For instance, in *Rāja-Yoga*, he frames his discussion of the Yogic practice of *pratyāhāra*—which he defines as "checking the outgoing powers of the mind" (*CW* 1:174)—by noting that modern Western "faith-healers" and "hypnotists" employ a form of *pratyāhāra* without knowing it:

> Where they [faith-healers] succeed in making a person throw off suffering by denying it, they really use a part of Pratyāhāra, as they make the mind of the person strong enough to ignore the senses. The hypnotists in a similar manner, by their suggestion, excite in the patient a sort of morbid Pratyāhāra for the time being. (*CW* 1:172)

However, in cosmopolitan fashion, Vivekananda then goes on to *criticize* the practices of faith-healing and hypnotism from the standpoint of traditional Indian Yoga:

> Now the control of the centres which is established in a hypnotic patient or the patient of faith-healing, by the operator, for a time, is reprehensible, because it leads to ultimate ruin. It is not really controlling the brain centres by the power of one's own will, but is, as it were, stunning the patient's mind for a time by sudden blows which another's will delivers to it. . . . Every attempt at control which is not voluntary, not with the controller's own mind, is not only disastrous, but it defeats the end. The goal of each soul is freedom, mastery—freedom from the slavery of matter and thought, mastery of external and internal nature. (*CW* 1:172)

According to Vivekananda, faith-healing and hypnotism, instead of inculcating self-control, involve the control and manipulation of one person's mind by another, thereby weakening the person's will and turning her mind into "a shapeless, powerless mass" (*CW* 1:172). Vivekananda then contrasts these degenerate and dangerous Western forms of *pratyāhāra* with the authentic Yogic practice of *pratyāhāra*, which results in the development of true "character" and freedom from the "thraldom of the senses" (*CW* 1:174).

Claiming that Vivekananda was straightforwardly "influenced" by Western practices of faith-healing and hypnotism hardly captures his nuanced and critical stance toward these occult practices. In fact, in response to articles claiming that he and other Hindus were passing off Theosophical ideas as their own, he wrote:

> The articles in question are libels on the Hindus and their religion. We Hindus . . . have no need nor desire to import religion from the West. Sufficient has been the degradation of importing almost everything else. The importation in the case of religion should be mostly on the side of the West, we are sure, and our work has been all along in that line. (*CW* 4:318)

Here, Vivekananda cannily anticipated contemporary scholars like De Michelis and Baier who claim that he borrowed Western occult ideas. Vivekananda's aim, rather, was to identify the limited value of modern Western occult practices, as well as their dangers and weaknesses, and to educate Westerners about the more morally and spiritually beneficial practices taught in ancient Indian spiritual traditions.

Bearing in mind Vivekananda's training under Ramakrishna and his critico-constructive engagement with Western thought-currents, I will reconstruct in the next two chapters the central tenets of Vivekananda's life-affirming and ethically oriented philosophy of Integral Advaita, which he expounded in lectures and writings from 1893 to 1901.

2

"The Deification of the World"

The Metaphysics and Ethics of Oneness in Vivekananda's Integral Advaita

I never read of any more beautiful conception of God than the following: "He is the Great Poet, the Ancient Poet; the whole universe is His poem, coming in verses and rhymes and rhythms, written in infinite bliss." When we have given up desires, then alone shall we be able to read and enjoy this universe of God. Then everything will become deified.

—Swami Vivekananda, "God in Everything" (1896; *CW* 2:149)

After his formative training under Ramakrishna and his travels through India as a wandering monk, Vivekananda made two visits to the West from 1893 to 1896 and from 1899 to 1900, delivering lectures to rapt audiences on Hinduism, Vedānta, and the harmony of all religions (*CW* 8:301). While it is clear from his lectures and writings that he championed the philosophy of Advaita Vedānta, scholars have debated two key interpretive questions concerning his Advaitic worldview. First, to what extent, if at all, does Vivekananda's Advaita philosophy differ from the traditional Advaita Vedānta of the eighth-century Śaṅkarācārya and his followers? Second, what is the relationship between Vivekananda's Advaita Vedānta and the philosophical worldview of his guru Ramakrishna?[1] We can group scholars into three main camps, depending on how they have answered these two questions.

According to the majority of scholars, Vivekananda accepts wholesale the *metaphysical* tenets of Śaṅkara's Advaita Vedānta, but he differs from Śaṅkara in emphasizing the social and ethical implications of Advaita philosophy.[2] Swami Satprakashananda's interpretation of Vivekananda is typical:

[1] For a helpful survey of different scholarly approaches to this controversial issue, see Beckerlegge (2000: 27–51).

[2] See, for instance, Devdas (1968), Bhaṭṭācārya Śāstrī (1990), Dhīreśānanda (1962), Gambhīrānanda (1988), Medhācaitanya (1988), Chaudhuri (1995), Mahadevan (1965), Srivastava (1965: 43), Banhatti (1989: 96–108), Dutta (1982), and Satprakashananda (1978). Bhushan and Garfield have recently argued that Vivekananda provides a realist reinterpretation of the Advaitic

Swami Vivekananda's Vedāntic Cosmopolitanism. Swami Medhananda, Oxford University Press. © Oxford University Press 2022. DOI: 10.1093/oso/9780197624463.003.0003

> It is Śaṅkara's Advaita philosophy that he [Vivekananda] accepted and expounded in modern terms. . . . So far as the basic ideas of Advaita Vedānta are concerned he does not differ from Śaṅkara, but there are some differences in his way of presentation and the emphasis laid by him on its practical aspects. (Satprakashananda 1978: 70)

Proponents of this line of approach argue that Vivekananda accepted Śaṅkara's basic metaphysical framework, according to which the impersonal and attributeless (*nirguṇa*) Brahman alone exists from the ultimate (*pāramārthika*) standpoint, while individual souls (*jīvas*), the universe (*jagat*), and the personal God (*saguṇa* Brahman or *īśvara*) are real from the empirical (*vyāvahārika*) standpoint but ultimately non-existent.[3]

We can further divide proponents of this Śaṅkaran approach to Vivekananda's philosophy into two subgroups, depending on how they understand the relation between Vivekananda and Ramakrishna. Some scholars discern a *continuity* between the philosophical views of Vivekananda and Ramakrishna, claiming that both of them espoused Śaṅkara's Advaita Vedānta in all its essentials (Bhaṭṭācārya Śāstrī 1990; Dhīreśānanda 1962; Mahadevan 1965: 45–73). Other scholars argue that there is a radical *discontinuity* between Vivekananda's world-denying Śaṅkaran philosophy and Ramakrishna's world-affirming monistic philosophy, which comes closer to Tantra than to Śāṅkara Advaita (Devdas 1968: 12–39; Neevel 1976; Matchett 1981).

A second group of scholars has adopted a more critical stance toward Vivekananda, contending that there are fundamental tensions and inconsistencies in his thought, which may stem in part from his conflicting allegiances to Śaṅkara and Ramakrishna.[4] For instance, Thomas J. Green claims that there is a tension between Vivekananda's traditional Advaitic commitment to the ultimate unreality of the world and his repeated emphasis on serving God in the form of human beings, which presupposes that the divine is "really present in the individuated universe" (2016: 34). In a similar vein, Amiya P. Sen claims that Vivekananda was unable to reconcile satisfactorily "what appear to be polar

doctrine of *māyā*, but they leave open the possibility that this interpretation is consistent with Śaṅkara's philosophy (2017: 217–23).

[3] For a good overview of Śaṅkara's Advaitic metaphysics, see Chatterjee and Datta (2008: 365–412). Some scholars (De Smet 1987; Malkovsky 1997) have interpreted Śaṅkara's philosophy in a more realist manner. It would take me too far afield to defend adequately my non-realist interpretation of Śaṅkara, but at various points in this chapter, I try to show that numerous passages from his commentaries are strongly non-realist in their import.

[4] Halbfass (1988: 228–46), Rambachan (1994a), Sen (2013: 101), J. Sharma (2013: 119), Green (2016: 34), Baier (2019: 255).

opposites, a radical, this-worldly approach to human existence and an extremely abstract philosophical viewpoint in which life and its several problems were insubstantial and transitory" (2013: 101). According to such scholars, Vivekananda was not a systematic or consistent thinker, so we should not be surprised to find tensions and contradictions in his philosophy.

Meanwhile, a third group of scholars argues that Vivekananda consistently championed a nonsectarian and life-affirming Advaitic philosophy that differs from Śaṅkara's Advaita Vedānta in key respects.[5] Many of these scholars—including Swami Tapasyananda (1990: ix–xxxiii), Satischandra Chatterjee (1995), and R. K. Dasgupta (1999)—further trace Vivekananda's nonsectarian Advaita philosophy to Ramakrishna's harmonizing, *vijñāna*-based philosophical worldview. According to these scholars, Vivekananda followed Ramakrishna, rather than Śaṅkara, in holding that (1) the impersonal Brahman and the personal Śakti are equally real aspects of one and the same Infinite Divine Reality; (2) the universe is a real manifestation of Śakti; and (3) all four Yogas—Bhakti-Yoga, Jñāna-Yoga, Karma-Yoga, and Rāja-Yoga—are direct and independent means to salvation.

How are we to adjudicate these long-standing debates about the nature and coherence of Vivekananda's philosophy of Advaita Vedānta? Too often, scholars have tended one-sidedly to emphasize those passages from his corpus that support their own favored interpretation while overlooking or downplaying the numerous other passages that seem to support one of the other two interpretive approaches. What I will attempt in chapters 2 and 3 is a more comprehensive reconstruction of Vivekananda's Advaitic philosophy that takes into account all, or at least most, of the major strands of his Vedāntic thought. Building on chapter 1, I will defend the third interpretive approach in a new way by arguing that Vivekananda, primarily under the influence of Ramakrishna, reconceptualized Advaita Vedānta as a nonsectarian and life-affirming philosophy that differs substantially from Śaṅkara's philosophy. At the same time, I will try to show that there is some truth to the first and second approaches as well.

As I explained in the previous chapter, Ramakrishna encouraged the young Narendra to reject the quietistic, world-denying Advaitic outlook of the *jñānī* in favor of the world-affirming and ethically oriented Advaitic outlook of the *vijñānī*, who sees that everything and everyone in the world, far from being unreal, are so many manifestations of God. In this and the next chapter, I will make

[5] Majumdār (1988), Dhyānānanda (1988), Tapasyananda (1990: ix–xxxiii; 1995), Śraddhānanda (1994: 103–41), S. C. Chatterjee (1995), R. K. Dasgupta (1999), Long (2008), Bhajanananda (2010), MacPhail (2013), Maharaj (2019; 2020a), Nicholson (2020), and Paranjape (2020: 89–113). Panday (2012) is hard to categorize, because he vacillates between claiming that Vivekananda follows Śaṅkara and claiming that Vivekananda departs from Śaṅkara in fundamental respects.

the case that the philosophy of Advaita Vedānta that Vivekananda preached throughout the world in the 1890s was not the traditional Advaita Vedānta of Śaṅkara and his followers but the world-affirming, *vijñāna*-based Advaita philosophy taught to him by Ramakrishna. Throughout this book, I will refer to Vivekananda's world-affirming, ethically oriented Advaita Vedānta as "Integral Advaita." Although he never referred to his own philosophy as "Integral Advaita," I believe this designation aptly captures the expansive and harmonizing nature of his Advaitic philosophical worldview.[6] Vivekananda's philosophy of Integral Advaita, I argue, upholds an all-inclusive Divine Oneness that encompasses not only the impersonal Brahman but also the dynamic Śakti as well as the entire universe of sentient and insentient entities. As Ramakrishna taught Vivekananda in 1885, "These three—Brahman, the insentient world, and living beings—together constitute One Reality (*sab joḍiye ekṭi*)" (*K* 778 / *G* 733).

This chapter has seven sections. Section 1 sets the stage for my reconstruction of Vivekananda's Integral Advaita by outlining his hermeneutic method. Those defending a Śaṅkaran interpretation of Vivekananda's philosophy, I suggest, are correct that Vivekananda frequently appeals to traditional Advaitic doctrines, including impersonality, *māyā*, *vivartavāda*, and the ontological distinction between *pāramārthika* and *vyāvahārika* levels of reality. However, I will argue that he subtly reconceptualizes these traditional Advaitic doctrines in the light of Ramakrishna. Once we recognize his distinctive hermeneutic method, we will be able to resolve many, but not all, of the apparent contradictions in his thought.

In sections 2 through 7 as well as in the next chapter, I provide a detailed reconstruction of the main tenets of Vivekananda's Integral Advaita.[7] In my reconstruction of each philosophical tenet, I not only draw upon his lectures, writings, and recorded conversations but also trace his views to Ramakrishna's teachings, anticipate potential objections to my interpretations, and examine how Vivekananda supports his philosophical views through novel interpretations of the Upaniṣads, the *Bhagavad-Gītā*, and the *Brahmasūtra*.

Section 2 reconstructs Vivekananda's views on ultimate reality. Following Ramakrishna, he claims that God is "personal-impersonal" (*CW* 3:336)—both

[6] I borrow the term "integral" from Sri Aurobindo, who frequently used it to characterize his own philosophico-spiritual worldview. Significantly, Aurobindo acknowledged the formative influence of both Ramakrishna and Vivekananda on his Integral Vedāntic thought (Maharaj 2018: 120–24).

[7] Unlike some scholars, I will argue that Vivekananda's exposition of Vedānta—with the major exception of his views on the harmony of religions—remained largely consistent from 1894 to 1901 and that there are no substantial philosophical differences in how he taught Vedānta in India and in the West. There are certainly differences in *emphasis* at different times and places, but I will argue that he consistently espoused all the key tenets of Integral Advaita reconstructed in this chapter. However, in chapter 3, I argue that his views on the harmony of religions *did* evolve substantially from 1893 to 1901.

the impersonal nondual Brahman realized in *nirvikalpa samādhi* as well as the dynamic personal Śakti who creates, preserves, and destroys the universe. While Śāṅkara Advaitins ontologically privilege the impersonal Brahman over the personal God, Vivekananda reinterprets impersonality from the expansive standpoint of Ramakrishna, arguing that "impersonality includes all personalities" (*CW* 2: 319).

Section 3 examines Vivekananda's views on the nature and ontological status of the world. He contends that the world is a real manifestation of God, reinterpreting the traditional Advaitic doctrines of *māyā* and *vivarta* in a non-illusionistic manner. Tellingly, he departs from Śaṅkara in defending a realist interpretation of key passages from Chāndogya Upaniṣad and Īśā Upaniṣad. Section 4 discusses Vivekananda's doctrine of the innate divinity of the soul, which strives to harmonize apparently conflicting Vedāntic conceptions of the *jīva*'s relation to Brahman. Section 5 shows how Vivekananda, under the influence of Ramakrishna, derives an ethics of social service—what he calls "Practical Vedānta"—from his panentheistic metaphysics of Integral Advaita. Section 6 discusses his pluralistic doctrine that all four Yogas are direct and independent paths to *mokṣa* and examines how he grounds this doctrine in his Integral Advaitic metaphysics.

Finally, section 7 critically probes Vivekananda's doctrine that the Vedāntic schools of Dvaita, Viśiṣṭādvaita, and Advaita correspond to three necessary "stages" of spiritual development. Building on an insight of Sister Nivedita, I argue that Vivekananda's "three stages" doctrine stands in tension with the other tenets of his Integral Advaita reconstructed in sections 2 through 6. In particular, his insistence on the *necessity* of all three stages entails that all worshippers of the personal God (*bhakta*s)—who occupy the stage of either Dvaita or Viśiṣṭādvaita—must eventually go on to attain the highest Advaitic realization in order to achieve spiritual fulfillment. This necessity claim, I suggest, contradicts his Integral Advaitic position that *bhakti* and *jñāna* are on an equal salvific footing and that the personal God and the impersonal Brahman are different but equally real aspects of the same Infinite Divine Reality. Hence, in partial agreement with the second group of scholars, I argue that there *is* a genuine tension between Vivekananda's Integral Advaitic philosophy and his hierarchical doctrine of the "three stages" of Vedānta—a tension that he could have avoided if he had conceived Dvaita and Viśiṣṭādvaita not as "lower" stages on the way to Advaita but simply as different, but equally true, ways of conceiving and experiencing the impersonal-personal Infinite Reality. Chapter 3 will then examine in detail how, beginning in late 1895, he presented a sophisticated doctrine of the harmony of all religions on the basis of the tenets of Integral Advaita discussed in this chapter.

1. Vivekananda's Two-Pronged Hermeneutic Method

As I will argue in the course of this chapter, Vivekananda expounded and justified the main tenets of his philosophy of Integral Advaita on the basis of a two-pronged hermeneutic method: first, a radical refashioning of traditional Advaita Vedāntic concepts; and second, a novel interpretation of key passages from the Upaniṣads, *Bhagavad-Gītā*, and *Brahmasūtra*. I believe one of the main reasons that so many scholars have interpreted Vivekananda as a follower of Śaṅkara is that he repeatedly appealed to a whole host of traditional Advaitic concepts, including *māyā*, *vivartavāda*, impersonality, and the distinction between "relative" and "absolute" standpoints. However, if we carefully analyze how he *interprets* these traditional Advaitic concepts, we will find that he deviates significantly from Śaṅkara and his followers. In other words, while Vivekananda undoubtedly aligned himself with the tradition of Advaita Vedānta, he should be seen as one of the most radical innovators within this tradition, often reconceptualizing traditional Advaitic doctrines beyond recognition.

It is worth asking *why* he employs such a complicated—and, frankly, sometimes confusing—hermeneutic method of explicitly subscribing to traditional Advaitic doctrines which he, nonetheless, reinterprets (often tacitly) from the standpoint of Ramakrishna's world-affirming Vijñāna Vedānta. After all, he could have simply rejected traditional Advaita Vedānta and called his own Advaitic philosophy by a different name so as to differentiate it clearly from Śaṅkara's philosophy. Indeed, this is precisely what Sri Aurobindo did in the decades following Vivekananda's death. In *The Life Divine* (1940), Aurobindo explicitly criticized the "Illusionism" and "Mayavada" of traditional Advaita Vedānta (2005: 455–98), contrasting it with his own "integral," world-affirming Advaitic philosophy, which he traced to the "real Adwaita" of the *Bhagavad-Gītā* and the Upaniṣads (1997: 448). Accordingly, Aurobindo characterized the world not as an illusory *māyā* but as *līlā*, the real playful manifestation of the Lord. Nalini Bhushan and Jay Garfield have aptly contrasted the differing hermeneutic styles of Aurobindo and Vivekananda: "While Aurobindo is most directly associated with the *līlāvāda* interpretation and an explicit critique of *māyāvāda*, we will see that Vivekananda, while using the rhetoric of *māyāvāda*, is already adopting a perspective that leads in the *līlāvāda*, or this-worldly direction" (2017: 217–18).

If Vivekananda championed the world-affirming and ethically oriented Advaitic philosophy taught to him by Ramakrishna, why did he choose to expound his philosophy using so many of the concepts and doctrines of the traditional, world-denying Advaita Vedānta of Śaṅkara and his followers? Although a full answer to this question is beyond the scope of this study, I believe part of the reason is that Vivekananda was torn between conflicting impulses. On the one hand, he was reluctant to start a new Vedāntic sect in the name of Ramakrishna. As he put it in an 1897 conversation with his brother disciple Swami Yogananda, "I haven't been born to found one more sect (*sampradāya*) in a world already teeming with sects" (*BCW* 9:35 / *CW* 6:478). Hence, he preferred to align himself with the tradition of Advaita Vedānta while, at the same time, advancing innovative interpretations of its key philosophical doctrines.

On the other hand, Vivekananda was fully aware that the nonsectarian Vedānta he espoused had a number of novel features that distinguished it from Śaṅkara's Advaita Vedānta. In a remarkable 1894 letter to his disciple "Kidi" (Singaravelu Mudaliar), he declared, paradoxically, that he had started a "non-sectarian sect": "For a religion to be effective, enthusiasm is necessary. At the same time we must try to avoid the danger of multiplying creeds. We avoid that by being a non-sectarian sect, having all the advantages of a sect and the broadness of a universal religion" (*CW* 4:356). Instead of creating a new sect per se, Vivekananda chose to align himself with the existing tradition of Advaita Vedānta while at the same time reconceptualizing it as a nonsectarian "universal religion."

The second key aspect of Vivekananda's hermeneutic method was his conscious effort to reinterpret the Upaniṣads, *Bhagavad-Gītā*, and *Brahmasūtra* from the nonsectarian standpoint of his Integral Advaitic philosophy. In his lectures in India and the West, he often accused traditional commentators like Śaṅkara and Rāmānuja of text-torturing:

> Coming to our commentators again, we find another difficulty. The Advaitic commentator, whenever an Advaitic text comes, preserves it just as it is; but the same commentator, as soon as a dualistic text presents itself, tortures it if he can, and brings the most queer meaning out of it. . . . In the same way, if not in a still worse fashion, the texts are handled by the dualistic commentator. Every dualistic text is preserved, and every text that speaks of non-dualistic philosophy is tortured in any fashion he likes. (*CW* 3:233)

In other words, Vivekananda faulted traditional commentators for lapsing into eisegesis—that is, imposing their own philosophical assumptions and doctrines onto the text instead of trying to understand the text on its own terms. On one occasion, he likewise remarked that "all the great commentators . . . were at times 'conscious liars' in order to make the texts suit their philosophy" (*CW* 7:36).

Breaking with traditional commentators, Vivekananda called for a new hermeneutic approach that strives to harmonize the various apparently conflicting passages of the scriptures without resorting to text-torturing (Maharaj 2020a).

Significantly, he claimed that he learned this non-eisegetic hermeneutic approach to the scriptures from Ramakrishna:

> It was given to me to live with a man [Ramakrishna] who was as ardent a dualist, as ardent an Advaitist, as ardent a *bhakta*, as a *jñānī*. And living with this man first put it into my head to understand the Upaniṣads and the texts of the scriptures from an independent and better basis than by blindly following the commentators; and in my opinion and in my researches, I came to the conclusion that these texts are not at all contradictory. So we need have no fear of text-torturing at all! The texts are beautiful, ay, they are most wonderful; and they are not contradictory, but wonderfully harmonious, one idea leading up to the other. (*CW* 3:233)

For Vivekananda, Ramakrishna's life and teachings exemplified a perfect philosophical synthesis of Advaita, Viśiṣṭādvaita, and Dvaita and an ideal practical synthesis of the yogas of *jñāna*, *bhakti*, *karma*, and *dhyāna*. Inspired by the ideals of Ramakrishna, Vivekananda advocated a non-eisegetic hermeneutic approach to the *prasthānatraya*—the Upaniṣads, the *Bhagavad-Gītā*, and the *Brahmasūtra*—that refrains from one-sidedly privileging certain teachings of the scriptures while downplaying or distorting other teachings.

As we will see in the course of this chapter, Vivekananda articulated many of the main tenets of his philosophy of Integral Advaita not only by reconceptualizing the doctrines of traditional Advaita Vedānta but also by providing new interpretations of passages from the *prasthānatraya* that often deviated quite drastically from Śaṅkara's interpretations.

2. The Impersonal-Personal God

As we saw in the previous chapter, the young Narendra, under the guidance of Ramakrishna, gradually came to accept the reality of Śakti, the Divine Mother. In a conversation with his guru in March 1885, Narendra specifically learned from him that "Brahman and Kālī are inseparable" (*K* 780 / *G* 734). In the same conversation, Ramakrishna clarified the inseparability of the impersonal nondual Brahman from the personal Śakti as follows: "When the Divine Reality is inactive (*niṣkriya*), I call It 'Brahman,' and when It creates, preserves, and destroys, I call It 'Śakti' or 'Kālī' " (*K* 779–80 / *G* 734).

In his lectures and writings from the 1890s, Vivekananda often echoed Ramakrishna's teachings on the inseparability of Brahman and Śakti. For instance, in his lecture "The Women of India" (1894), he observes:

> [T]he central conception of Hindu philosophy is of the Absolute; that is the background of the universe. This Absolute Being, of whom we can predicate nothing, has Its powers spoken of as She—that is, the real personal God in India is She. This Śakti of the Brahman is always in the feminine gender. (*CW* 9:195)

Following Ramakrishna, Vivekananda holds that while the impersonal nondual Brahman is utterly transcendent and ineffable, Śakti is the same Absolute in its dynamic aspect as the "real personal God" who creates, preserves, and destroys the universe. Notice his emphasis on the *reality* of the personal God, which—as we will soon see—is more consistent with Ramakrishna's Vijñāna Vedānta than with Śaṅkara's Advaita Vedānta.

In his Calcutta lecture "The Vedānta in All its Phases" (1897), he clarifies his Integral Advaitic conception of the "personal-impersonal" God as follows:

> The next point, which all the sects in India believe in, is God. Of course their ideas of God will be different. The dualists believe in a Personal God, and a personal only. I want you to understand this word ["]personal["] a little more. This word ["]personal["] does not mean that God has a body, sits on a throne somewhere, and rules this world, but means Saguṇa, with qualities. There are many descriptions of the Personal God. This Personal God as the Ruler, the Creator, the Preserver, and the Destroyer of this universe is believed in by all the sects. The Advaitists believe something more. They believe in a still higher phase of this Personal God, which is personal-impersonal. (*CW* 3:335–36)

Who are these "Advaitists" who believe in a "personal-impersonal" God? I believe Vivekananda has in mind not Śaṅkara and his followers but *bhakti*-oriented Advaitins like the author of the medieval text *Adhyātma-Rāmāyaṇa*, which Ramakrishna often singled out as a book that harmonizes Advaita Vedānta with intense devotionalism (*K* 901 / *G* 836–37).[8]

Since Vivekananda had read Śaṅkara's commentaries carefully, he was certainly aware of Śaṅkara's understanding of the personal God. In his commentary on *Brahmasūtra* 2.1.14, Śaṅkara explains the ontological status of *īśvara*, the personal God, as follows:

> Thus *īśvara*'s rulership, omniscience, and omnipotence are dependent on the limiting adjuncts conjured up by ignorance; but from the ultimate standpoint,

[8] Both Tapasyananda (1988: vi–vii) and Matchett (1981: 176–77) have helpfully traced some of Ramakrishna's teachings about God and *bhakti* to specific verses of the *Adhyātma-Rāmāyaṇa*. Another *bhakti*-oriented Advaitic text is Madhusūdana Sarasvatī's *Bhaktirasāyanam*, but I have found no evidence that Vivekananda read this text.

> such terms as "the ruler," "the ruled," "omniscience," etc. cannot be used with regard to the Ātman in its true nature after the removal of all limiting adjuncts through knowledge.[9]

For Śaṅkara and his followers, the impersonal, attributeless (*nirguṇa*) Brahman and the personal God (*saguṇa* Brahman or *īśvara*) are not equally real. Rather, from the ultimate standpoint, only the impersonal nondual Brahman is real, while the personal God is empirically real but ultimately unreal, since it is the same *nirguṇa* Brahman with the unreal "limiting adjuncts" (*upādhi*s) of "lordship" (*īśvaratva*), "omnipotence," and so on.[10] In contrast to Vivekananda, then, Śaṅkara holds that the "higher phase" of the personal God is not the "personal-impersonal" God but the impersonal Brahman alone, which *excludes* personality.

Unlike Śaṅkara, Vivekananda does not claim that the personal God is ultimately unreal. Following Ramakrishna, Vivekananda maintains that the personal God, far from being sublated upon attaining knowledge of the impersonal Brahman, is *included* in the "personal-impersonal" Infinite Reality. Accordingly, in his lecture "The Sages of India" (1897), he declares that "our religion preaches an Impersonal Personal God" (*CW* 3:249). In an 1896 letter to his disciple E. T. Sturdy, Vivekananda sketched a diagram illustrating the inseparability of Brahman and Śakti, which he planned to include in a book on Vedānta that he ended up never writing:

Brahman	=	The Absolute
|		
Mahat or Īśvara	=	Primal Creative Energy (*CW* 5:102)

[9] *tad evam avidyātmakopādhiparicchedāpekṣam eva īśvarasya īśvaratvaṃ sarvajñatvaṃ sarvaśaktitvaṃ ca na paramārthato vidyayā apāstasarvopādhisvarūpe ātmani īśitrīśitavya-sarvajñatvādivyavahāra upapadyate* (*BSBh* 2.1.14, p. 201).

[10] There is a complexity here. As Hacker (1995: 85–96) notes, Śaṅkara frequently uses the term "*īśvara*" as a synonym for *nirguṇa* Brahman, and in only a few instances—such as in his commentary on *Brahmasūtra* 2.1.14—uses "*īśvara*" in the narrower sense of the personal God. However, I think it would be a serious mistake to infer from this terminological haziness that Śaṅkara granted equal ontological status to both the personal God and *nirguṇa* Brahman. In fact, in all the places where Śaṅkara employs "*īśvara*" as a synonym for *nirguṇa* Brahman, he conceives *īśvara* not as the personal God but as *nirguṇa* Brahman itself. And in those few places where he defines "*īśvara*" in the narrow sense of the personal God, as in his commentary on *Brahmasūtra* 2.1.14, he clearly holds that the personal God is non-existent from the ultimate standpoint. Hence, I disagree with scholars like De Smet (1972) and Malkovsky (1997) who claim that Śaṅkara conceived the highest Brahman as "personal." Mitra (2020) argues that Śaṅkara, like Ramakrishna, ascribes equal ontological status to *nirguṇa* Brahman and the personal *īśvara*, but Mitra overlooks the key passage from Śaṅkara's commentary on *Brahmasūtra* 2.1.14 just discussed, where he clearly states that the personal *īśvara* is ultimately non-existent.

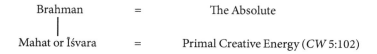

For Vivekananda, Brahman is the impersonal (*nirguṇa*) nondual Absolute, and the vertical line indicates that it is inseparable from Mahat/Īśvara, the "Primal Creative Energy," which he also refers to as "Śakti." The provenance of Vivekananda's expansive conception of ultimate reality, I would suggest, is not Śaṅkara's Advaita Vedānta but the *bhakti*-oriented, world-affirming Advaita philosophy of his guru Ramakrishna.

However, there are also numerous passages where Vivekananda seems to suggest that the impersonal is higher than the personal. For instance, in his notes for a planned book on Vedānta, he claims that the "Absolute or Brahman, the Sat-Chit-Ananda, is Impersonal and the real Infinite" (*CW* 5:433). How are we to reconcile this impersonal conception of ultimate reality with his acceptance, in numerous places, of a "personal-impersonal" God? The key to answering this question is to recognize that he subtly reconceptualizes the traditional Advaitic doctrine of impersonality (*nirguṇatva*) to include, rather than exclude, personality. Take, for instance, this passage from his second "Practical Vedanta" lecture (1896):

> The Impersonal God is a living God, a principle. The difference between personal and impersonal is this, that the personal is only a man, and the impersonal idea is that He is the angel, the man, the animal, and yet something more which we cannot see, because impersonality includes all personalities, is the sum total of everything in the universe, and infinitely more besides. (*CW* 2:319)

For Śaṅkara and his followers, impersonality *excludes* all personality: Brahman is ultimately only impersonal (*nirguṇa*), and the personal God is that same impersonal Brahman with the false superimposition of *īśvaratva*. For Vivekananda, by contrast, "impersonality *includes* all personalities" (emphasis added). Vivekananda reiterates this point just a few pages later: "It is all yours, for the Impersonal includes the Personal. So God is Personal and Impersonal at the same time" (*CW* 2:323). Notice here that he explicitly equates his doctrine that impersonality "includes" all personalities with the doctrine of the impersonal-personal God, which he espouses in various other places.

In fact, there are numerous places where he closely echoes Ramakrishna's language. For instance, in his lecture "Worshipper and Worshipped" (1900), Vivekananda remarks: "Naturally the universal Absolute must have two aspects; the one representing the infinite reality of all things; the other, a personal aspect, the Soul of our souls, Lord of all lords" (*CW* 6:51). Similarly, in his lecture on "The Divine Mother" (1895), he explains, in a Ramakrishnan vein, that the Divine Mother has both "conditioned" and "unconditioned" natures:

> Every manifestation of power in the universe is "Mother." She is life, She is intelligence, She is Love. She is in the universe yet separate from it. She is a person

> and can be seen and known (as Ramakrishna saw and knew Her).... Divine Mother can have form (Rūpa) and name (Nāma) or name without form; and as we worship Her in these various aspects we can rise to pure Being, having neither form nor name.... The sea calm is the Absolute; the same sea in waves is Divine Mother. She is time, space, and causation. God is Mother and has two natures, the conditioned and the unconditioned. As the former, She is God, nature, and soul (man). As the latter, She is unknown and unknowable. (*CW* 7:26–27)

Vivekananda follows Ramakrishna in affirming the ontological reality of the Divine Mother. As the "unconditioned" *nirguṇa* Brahman, She is "unknown and unknowable," in the sense that nondual Brahman can never be an object of knowledge but one can nonetheless realize one's identity with Brahman in *nirvikalpa samādhi*. As the "conditioned" *saguṇa* Brahman or Śakti, She manifests as "God, nature, and soul." Ramakrishna would often illustrate the idea that "Brahman and Śakti are inseparable" by using the analogy of still and agitated water: "The water is the same, whether it remains calm or takes the form of waves and bubbles" (*K* 254 / *G* 277). Echoing Ramakrishna's language almost verbatim, Vivekananda declares, "The sea calm is the Absolute; the same sea in waves is Divine Mother." It is clear from this Ramakrishnan analogy of the sea that Vivekananda does not take the Divine Mother's "conditioned" status to imply her unreality. Interestingly, Śaṅkara, in his commentary on Bṛhadāraṇyaka Upaniṣad 5.1.1, explicitly rejects the Bhedābhedavādin Bhartṛprapañca's view that both Brahman and its manifestations have ontological reality—a view that Bhartṛprapañca illustrates by likening Brahman to an ocean and Brahman's manifestations to the waves of the ocean. For Śaṅkara, the problem with Bhartṛprapañca's analogy is precisely that the waves are as real as the ocean water, which would mean that "the entire dual universe, corresponding to the waves etc. on the water, is ultimately real (*paramārthasatyam*)" (*BṛUpBh* 5.1.1, p. 1164). Tellingly, Vivekananda sides with Bhartṛprapañca and Ramakrishna *against* Śaṅkara by appealing to the analogy of the ocean and its waves to illustrate the ontological reality of both Brahman and its manifestation as the personal God and the universe.

However, one might object at this point that there are places where Vivekananda seems to suggest that the impersonal Brahman alone is ultimately real, while the personal God is only empirically or relatively real.[11] As we have seen, Śaṅkara and his followers distinguish between *pāramārthika* (absolute) and *vyāvahārika* (empirical or relative) standpoints and maintain that *īśvara* is only real from the *vyāvahārika* standpoint—that is, so long as we remain ignorant of our true nature as the impersonal nondual Brahman. Although Vivekananda

[11] Both Bhaṭṭācārya Śāstrī (1990: 97–98) and Devdas (1968: 51–64) argue along these lines.

almost never uses the Sanskrit terms "*vyāvahārika*" and "*pāramārthika*," he does often use the English terms "relative" and "absolute," frequently referring to the "relative" status of both the personal God and the universe as opposed to the "absolute" status of the impersonal Brahman.[12] If we take the term "relative" to be synonymous with "*vyāvahārika*," then it does seem as if Vivekananda is committed to the Śaṅkaran view that the world and the personal God are ultimately unreal.[13]

We can begin to address this serious objection by examining an important passage from the "Philosophy of Īśvara" section of *Bhakti-Yoga* (1896), where Vivekananda explains the precise sense in which he takes *īśvara* to be "relative":

> Who is Īśvara? *Janmādyasya yataḥ*—"From whom is the birth, continuation, and dissolution of the universe," [*Brahmasūtra* 1.1.2]—He is Īśvara—"the Eternal, the Pure, the Ever-Free, the Almighty, the All-Knowing, the All-Merciful, the Teacher of all teachers" [perhaps adapted from *Yogasūtra* 1.25–26]; and above all, *sa īśvaraḥ anirvacanīya-premasvarūpaḥ*—"He the Lord is, of His own nature, inexpressible Love" [adapted from *Nārada-Bhaktisūtra* 51]. These certainly are the definitions of a Personal God. Are there then two Gods—the "Not this, not this" [Bṛhadāraṇyaka Upaniṣad 3.9.26], the Sat-cit-ānanda, the Existence-Knowledge-Bliss of the philosopher, and this God of Love of the Bhakta? No, it is the same Sat-cit-ānanda who is also the God of Love, the impersonal and personal in one. It has always to be understood that the Personal God worshipped by the Bhakta is not separate or different from the Brahman. All is Brahman, the One without a second; only the Brahman, as unity or absolute, is too much of an abstraction to be loved and worshipped; so the Bhakta chooses the relative aspect of Brahman, that is, Īśvara, the Supreme Ruler. (*CW* 3:37)

In the final sentence, Vivekananda claims that the impersonal Brahman alone is "absolute," while *īśvara* is the "relative aspect of Brahman." Crucially, however, he follows Ramakrishna in holding that "it is the same Sat-cit-ānanda who is also the God of Love, the impersonal and personal in one." Śaṅkara conceives the relative (*vyāvahārika*) status of the personal God in ontological terms as a merely provisional reality that is sublated by the liberative knowledge of the impersonal nondual Absolute. Vivekananda, by contrast, conceives the "relative" status of the personal God in *relational* terms: the nondual Saccidānanda, when seen in relation to individual souls (*jīva*s) and the universe (*jagat*), is the personal God (*īśvara*). From the relative standpoint, Saccidānanda manifests as the personal

12 See, for instance, *CW* 2:132–33, *CW* 5:276, and *CW* 3:37.

13 Bhaṭṭācārya Śāstrī assumes that Vivekananda's English terms "relative" and "absolute" do correspond to the traditional Advaitic terms "*vyāvahārika*" and "*pāramārthika*" (1990: 97–98).

God who creates, preserves, and destroys the universe and with whom we can enter into a loving relationship through prayer and worship. Lest we assume that Vivekananda follows Śaṅkara in granting only provisional reality to the personal God, he notes that "Creation is eternal, and so also is Īśvara" (*CW* 3:37). Just a few pages later, he explicitly states that the relative status of *īśvara* does not entail its unreality: "to say that Iśvara is unreal, because He is anthropomorphic, is sheer nonsense" (*CW* 3:42).

Interestingly, Vivekananda then goes on to compare Madhva's, Rāmānuja's, and Śaṅkara's respective interpretations of *Brahmasūtra* 4.4.17–18, which concern the fate of those who worship the personal God (*CW* 3:37–42). After discussing Madhva's and Rāmānuja's interpretations, Vivekananda explains how "the Advaita system maintains all the hopes and aspirations of the dualist intact, and at the same time propounds its own solution of the problem in consonance with the high destiny of divine humanity" (*CW* 3:40). Tellingly, instead of quoting Śaṅkara directly, Vivekananda explains *sūtras* 17 and 18 from the standpoint of his own Integral Advaita philosophy: "Those who aspire to retain their individual mind even after liberation and to remain distinct will have ample opportunity of realising their aspirations and enjoying the blessing of the qualified Brahman" (*CW* 3:40). In corroboration of this claim, he cites passages about ecstatic *bhakti* from the *Bhāgavata-Purāṇa*, and he notes that while some liberated souls attain the nondual state "which the Śrutis declare as 'Not this, not this,'" there are others "who cannot, *or will not* reach this state" (*CW* 3:40; emphasis added). As the italicized words indicate, Vivekananda's "Advaita system" explicitly accommodates those liberated *bhaktas* who choose to remain in an eternal loving relationship with the personal God in a transcendental realm.[14] By contrast, Śaṅkara holds that worshippers of the personal God attain *brahmaloka* but cannot remain there eternally. Instead, Śaṅkara upholds the doctrine of liberation by stages (*krama-mukti*),[15] according to which *bhaktas* in *brahmaloka* must eventually attain the nondual state of liberation upon the dissolution of the universe.

It is highly significant that when Vivekananda finally goes on to quote Śaṅkara's commentary on *sūtra* 17 in the next paragraph of "The Philosophy of Īśvara," he conspicuously refrains from mentioning—let alone endorsing—the doctrine of *krama-mukti*, which frames Śaṅkara's interpretation of the *sūtra*. Instead, Vivekananda quotes Śaṅkara's "conclusion" that "the wills of the liberated are dependent on the will of the Supreme Ruler," thereby making it seem as if Śaṅkara himself accommodates the possibility of an eternal loving relationship with the personal God (*CW* 3:41–42). Vivekananda's comparative discussion of

[14] For more detailed discussion of this point, see section 7 of this chapter.

[15] See, for instance, Śaṅkara's commentary on *Brahmasūtra* 4.3.10.

Brahmasūtra 4.4.17–18, then, is a good example of his subtle, albeit confusing, hermeneutic strategy of explicitly endorsing Śaṅkara's interpretation while implicitly deviating from it. By omitting the framework of *krama-mukti* from Śaṅkara's interpretation of 4.4.17, Vivekananda quietly turns Śaṅkara into an Integral Advaitin who upholds the equal status and value of the nondualist's goal of identity with the impersonal Absolute and the *bhakta*'s goal of eternal loving communion with the personal God.

It is significant that in a letter to his disciple Alasinga Perumal dated August 20, 1893, Vivekananda explicitly distanced himself from the traditional Advaitic doctrine of *pāramārthika* and *vyāvahārika* levels of reality:

> No religion on earth preaches the dignity of humanity in such a lofty strain as Hinduism, and no religion on earth treads upon the necks of the poor and the low in such a fashion as Hinduism. The Lord has shown me that religion is not in fault, but it is the Pharisees and Sadducees in Hinduism, hypocrites, who invent all sorts of engines of tyranny in the shape of doctrines of Pāramārthika and Vyāvahārika. (*CW* 5:15)

He suggests here that the traditional Advaitic two-tier ontology, by dismissing the *vyāvahārika* or empirical realm as ultimately unreal, had the pernicious consequence of justifying social oppression and tyranny. As I will discuss in more detail in section 5 of this chapter, Vivekananda specifically criticized Śaṅkara for his "narrowness of heart," since he excluded the lower castes from the study of Vedānta and failed to develop an ethics of service and universal love on the basis of Advaita philosophy. Hence, I believe there is strong evidence that Vivekananda rejected the traditional Advaitic equation of the *vyāvahārika* realm with the realm of ignorance.[16]

Indeed, in his third "Practical Vedanta" lecture, he argues that the philosophy of Advaita, as he conceives it, actually provides ontological justification for the *reality* of the personal God:

> What is the outcome of this philosophy? It is that the idea of Personal God is not sufficient. We have to get to something higher, to the Impersonal idea. It is the only logical step that we can take. Not that the personal idea would be destroyed by that, not that we supply proof that the Personal God does not exist, but we must go to the Impersonal for the explanation of the personal, for the Impersonal is a much higher generalization than the personal. The Impersonal only can be Infinite, the personal is limited. Thus we preserve the personal and

[16] Bhajanananda (1994: 571) is one of the few scholars to have recognized Vivekananda's realist reconceptualization of the traditional Advaitic two-tier ontology.

> do not destroy it. Often the doubt comes to us that if we arrive at the idea of the Impersonal God, the personal will be destroyed, if we arrive at the idea of the Impersonal man, the personal will be lost. But the Vedāntic idea is not the destruction of the individual, but its real preservation. (*CW* 2:333)

According to Vivekananda, the idea of the impersonal Brahman is "higher" than that of the personal God, not in the sense that the former is real while the latter is unreal but in that the former *grounds* the latter. Inspired by Ramakrishna, he aims to establish the reality of the personal God by showing that it is actually the dynamic aspect of the absolute Brahman itself. Vivekananda's insistence that impersonality *preserves* the personal God signals his implicit break with traditional Advaita Vedāntins like Śaṅkara, who maintain that impersonality entails the ultimate sublation of the personal God.

3. *The World as a Real Manifestation of God*

As we saw in section 2 of the previous chapter, Ramakrishna's philosophico-spiritual worldview is based on a key distinction between two stages of spiritual realization: *jñāna* and *vijñāna*. According to Ramakrishna, the *jñānī* practices "*neti, neti*" *sādhana*, rejecting everything in the world as unreal, until he attains *brahmajñāna*, the knowledge of the impersonal nondual Brahman. The *vijñānī*, however, goes one step further than the *jñānī*: after the attainment of *brahmajñāna*, the *vijñānī* realizes that "the Reality which is impersonal (*nirguṇa*) is also personal (*saguṇa*)" and that the world, far from being an illusion, is a "mansion of mirth," a real manifestation of God (*K* 534 / *G* 523). As Ramakrishna puts it, the *vijñānī* sees that "it is Brahman that has become the universe and its living beings" (*K* 51 / *G* 104).

Although Vivekananda does not use the term "*vijñāna*" frequently, there are several places where he does seem to use the term in Ramakrishna's sense. In his "Discourses on Jñāna-Yoga" (1896), he defines "*Vijñāna*" as "real knowing," a feeling of "the Eternal Unity," and he goes on to characterize it as the realization that "all is one" and "all is love" (*CW* 8:23).[17] Even more importantly, he appeals to the philosophico-spiritual *standpoint* of *vijñāna* throughout his lectures and writings. At various places, he echoes very closely Ramakrishna's teachings on the spiritual stages of *jñāna* and *vijñāna*, as for instance in this passage from his lecture "Realisation" (1896):

[17] Somewhat similarly, in his lecture on "Sāṃkhya and Vedānta," he remarks: "That knowledge itself is Vijñāna, neither intuition, nor reason nor instinct. The nearest expression for it is all-knowingness" (*CW* 2:459).

> [W]e have to go through the negation, and then the positive side will begin. We have to give up ignorance and all that is false, and then truth will begin to reveal itself to us. When we have grasped the truth, things which we gave up at first will take new shape and form, will appear to us in a new light, and become deified. They will have become sublimated, and then we shall understand them in their true light. But to understand them, we have first to get a glimpse of truth; we must give them up at first, and then we get them back again, deified. We have to give up all our miseries and sorrows, all our little joys. (*CW* 2:167)

The spiritual realization Vivekananda describes here, I would suggest, is not the Advaitic *jñānī*'s realization that Brahman alone is real and everything else is unreal, but the Ramakrishnan *vijñānī*'s realization that everything in the world is God Himself in various forms.[18] Moreover, Vivekananda emphasizes that the way to achieve this "positive" realization is through "negation"—that is, the renunciation of all worldly pleasures and attachments. In one of his 1896 lectures on "Practical Vedānta," he describes the transformed outlook of the God-realized soul in very similar terms: "The whole vision is changed, and instead of an eternal prison this world has become a playground; instead of a land of competition it is a land of bliss, where there is perpetual spring, flowers bloom and butterflies flit about" (*CW* 2:324). Since the impersonal Brahman and dynamic Śakti are inseparable aspects of the same Infinite Reality, the world, far from being unreal, is a real manifestation of Śakti. Vivekananda's world-affirming Integral Advaita philosophy, as we will see, bears much greater affinities with Ramakrishna's *vijñāna*-based doctrine of an all-inclusive oneness than with Śaṅkara's Advaita Vedānta. For Vivekananda, Advaita is not the One *excluding* the many but a panentheistic oneness—the "One, *manifesting* Himself as many," as he puts it in his first "Practical Vedānta" lecture (*CW* 2:304; emphasis added).

Vivekananda elaborates his Integral Advaitic conception of the world through a subtle reinterpretation of the traditional Advaitic doctrines of *māyā* and *vivarta*. He also justifies his world-inclusive Advaita by appealing to passages from various Upaniṣads that indicate that everything in the world is a real manifestation of God. In his lecture "Māyā and Illusion" (1896), he notes that the word "*māyā*" is generally "used, though incorrectly, to denote illusion, or delusion, or some such thing" (*CW* 2:88). He clearly has in mind the traditional Advaitic conception of *māyā* as a principle of illusion. Although Śaṅkara does not use the word "*māyā*" all that frequently, when he does use the word, he tends to use it in the sense of magic, deception, and sometimes—though rarely—illusion.[19] For

[18] S. C. Chatterjee cites this key passage and rightly traces it to Ramakrishna's standpoint of *vijñāna* (1995: 265–66).

[19] See the helpful discussion of this issue in Hacker (1995: 78–81).

instance, Śaṅkara claims that "the whole creation is merely *māyā*," and it is clear from the context that he means that the world is an illusory appearance (*BSBh* 3.2.4, pp. 346–47). Post-Śaṅkara Advaitins, who tended to place much greater emphasis on *māyā* than Śaṅkara himself did, frequently used the term as a synonym for "illusion"—which led some philosophical schools to label Advaita Vedānta "*māyāvāda*."[20]

Vivekananda boldly rejects the prevailing illusionistic interpretation of *māyā* in favor of a novel phenomenological interpretation:

> Thus we find that Māyā is not a theory for the explanation of the world; it is simply a statement of facts as they exist, that the very basis of our being is contradiction, that everywhere we have to move through this tremendous contradiction, that wherever there is good, there must also be evil, and wherever there is evil, there must be some good, wherever there is life, death must follow as its shadow, and everyone who smiles will have to weep, and vice versa. Nor can this state of things be remedied. (*CW* 2:97)

Rejecting the view that *māyā* is an ontological theory of the unreality of the world, Vivekananda reinterprets it phenomenologically as a "statement of facts as they exist." From a phenomenological standpoint, *māyā* denotes the inherently contradictory nature of life—that good and evil, life and death, joy and sorrow are mutually entailing opposites. For Vivekananda, then, the world as perceived by ignorant people is *māyā* in the sense that nothing in the world can give us lasting fulfillment.

However, he also repeatedly states that this very world of *māyā* becomes transformed—"deified"—for those who have realized God. For instance, in his second "Practical Vedānta" lecture, he explains his world-inclusive Advaita philosophy through a reinterpretation of passages from the Chāndogya Upaniṣad:

> And this is the real, practical side of Vedānta. It does not destroy the world, but it explains it; it does not destroy the person, but explains him; it does not destroy the individuality, but explains it by showing the real individuality. It does not show that this world is vain and does not exist, but it says, "Understand what this world is, so that it may not hurt you." The voice did not say to Upakosala that the fire which he was worshipping, or the sun, or the moon, or the lightning, or anything else, was all wrong, but it showed him that the same spirit which was inside the sun, and moon, and lightning, and the fire, and the earth, was in him, so that everything became transformed, as it were, in the eyes of Upakosala. The fire which was merely a material fire before, in which

[20] See, for instance, *Pañcadaśī* 9.88.

> to make oblations, assumed a new aspect and became the Lord. The earth became transformed, life became transformed, the sun, the moon, the stars, the lightning, everything became transformed and deified. Their real nature was known. The theme of the Vedānta is to see the Lord in everything, to see things in their real nature, not as they appear to be. (*CW* 2:312)

According to Vivekananda, Vedānta does not teach that the world "does not exist"; rather, it teaches us to "see the Lord in everything." He finds support for this world-inclusive Advaita Vedānta in Chāndogya Upaniṣad 4.11.1 to 4.13.1, where the *brahmacārin* Upakosala is taught to meditate on the sun, moon, fire, food, and so on as God. What appear to the ignorant to be merely material phenomena are actually manifestations of God Himself. According to Śaṅkara, this passage from Chāndogya Upaniṣad enjoins meditations that lead to inferior results such as dwelling in the world of fires, whereas *ātmavidyā* (knowledge of the nondual Ātman) alone constitutes the highest liberative knowledge.[21] In contrast to Śaṅkara, Vivekananda claims that Upakosala's knowledge that the same God who dwells in the sun, moon, and fire also dwells in him *is* the highest Advaitic knowledge.

Likewise, several pages later in the same lecture, Vivekananda interprets "*sarvaṃ khalvidaṃ brahma*" ("All this is, indeed, Brahman")—the famous statement from Chāndogya Upaniṣad 3.14.1—in a world-affirming manner:

> This is the line of thought in the passage I have read to you; the earth is a symbol of the Lord, the sky is the Lord, the place we fill is the Lord, everything is Brahman. And this is to be seen, realised, not simply talked or thought about. We can see as its logical consequence that when the soul has realised that everything is full of the Lord, of Brahman, it will not care whether it goes to heaven, or hell, or anywhere else; whether it be born again on this earth or in heaven. These things have ceased to have any meaning to that soul, because every place is the same, every place is the temple of the Lord, every place has become holy and the presence of the Lord is all that it sees in heaven, or hell, or anywhere else. Neither good nor bad, neither life nor death—only the one infinite Brahman exists. (*CW* 2:318)

According to Śaṅkara's interpretation of "*sarvaṃ khalvidaṃ brahma*," the word "*sarvam*" is brought into apposition with "*brahma*" in order to "dissolve the universe" (*prapañcapravilāpanārtham*).[22] All is Brahman, Śaṅkara claims, in the sense that the *substratum* of everything is Brahman, while this entire universe of

21 See Śaṅkara's commentary on Chāndogya Upaniṣad 4.14.2.
22 This statement occurs in Śaṅkara's commentary on the *Brahmasūtra* (*BSBh* 1.3.1, pp. 94–95).

names and forms is unreal.[23] For Vivekananda, by contrast, "*sarvaṃ khalvidaṃ brahma*" contains the quintessence of a world-affirming Advaita philosophy: everything in this universe is a real manifestation of the "one infinite Brahman." Echoing Ramakrishna, he describes the highest Advaitic realization not as the state of *nirvikalpa samādhi* in which the world is not perceived but as the world-embracing realization that "everything is full of the Lord." He also elaborates in this passage one radical consequence of this view: instead of championing the traditional goal of liberation (*mukti*) from this transmigratory cycle, he claims that the fully enlightened soul does not "care" whether it is born again on earth or finds itself in heaven or hell, since it sees nothing but God everywhere. As we will see in section 5 of this chapter, Vivekananda draws an important ethical consequence from his integral reconception of the spiritual ideal: it is far nobler to serve others in a spirit of worship than to seek one's own salvation alone.

In his tellingly titled lecture "God in Everything" (1896), Vivekananda reinterprets the Īśā Upaniṣad in a similarly world-affirming (or, perhaps better, world-*transforming*) manner that contrasts sharply with Śaṅkara's world-denying interpretation. For the sake of brevity, I will only compare here Vivekananda's and Śaṅkara's respective interpretations of the first verse of the Īśā Upaniṣad, which runs as follows:

> *īśā vāsyam idaṃ sarvaṃ yatkiñca jagatyāṃ jagat*
> *tena tyaktena bhuñjīthā mā gṛdhaḥ kasya svid dhanam.*

According to Śaṅkara, the meaning of the first line is that "all this that is unreal (*anṛtam*), whether moving or not moving, is to be covered (*ācchādaniyam*) by one's own Supreme Ātman" (*ĪUpBh* 1, p. 4). By glossing "*idaṃ sarvam*" as "*anṛtam idaṃ sarvam*," Śaṅkara boldly claims that the first line supports the Advaitic doctrine of the unreality of the world, even though the verse itself does not suggest the world's unreality in any way. Śaṅkara's interpretive acrobatics are equally on display in his commentary on the phrase, "*tena tyaktena bhuñjīthāḥ*," in the second line of the first verse. The word "*bhuñjīthāḥ*," the *ātmanepadī* form of the second person, singular, optative tense (*vidhi liṅg*) of √*bhuj*, means "enjoy" or "eat" according to Pāṇinī's grammar.[24] While Śaṅkara generally follows Pāṇinī, he notably departs from Pāṇinī here in glossing "*bhuñjīthāḥ*" as "*pālayethāḥ*" ("protect"), since this meaning accords better with his Advaitic reading. Taking the Ātman to be the implied direct object of "*bhuñjīthāḥ*," Śaṅkara claims that "*tena tyaktena bhuñjīthāḥ*" means that through the renunciation of all works and

[23] S. C. Chatterjee succinctly explains the difference between Ramakrishnan and Śaṅkaran interpretations of "*sarvaṃ khalvidaṃ brahma*" ([1963] 1985: 112–13). I also discuss this issue in Maharaj (2018: 38–41).

[24] For a more detailed discussion of this issue, see Maharaj (2020c: 319–20).

sense-pleasures, the renunciate should "protect" the Ātman by practicing "steadfast devotion to knowledge of the Ātman" (*ĪUpBh* 1, p. 5).

Vivekananda's interpretation of the first verse of the Īśā Upaniṣad differs radically from Śaṅkara's:

> Here I can only lay before you what the Vedānta seeks to teach, and that is the deification of the world. The Vedānta does not in reality denounce the world. The ideal of renunciation nowhere attains such a height as in the teachings of the Vedānta. But, at the same time, dry suicidal advice is not intended; it really means deification of the world—giving up the world as we think of it, as we know it, as it appears to us—and to know what it really is. Deify it; it is God alone. We read at the commencement of one of the oldest of the Upaniṣads, "Whatever exists in this universe is to be covered with the Lord." (*CW* 2:146)

While Śaṅkara takes the first line of the first verse to imply the unreality of the world, Vivekananda claims that it teaches the "deification of the world." For Śaṅkara, the word "*vāsyam*" ("to be covered") means that the Advaitin *sannyāsin* should reject the unreal world and focus on the nondual Ātman alone. Vivekananda, by contrast, interprets "*vāsyam*" to mean that we should "cover" the world "with the Lord" in the sense of seeing everything in the world as a real manifestation of the Lord.

Vivekananda's interpretation of the second line of the first verse of the Īśā Upaniṣad also contrasts sharply with Śaṅkara's:

> We have to cover everything with the Lord Himself, not by a false sort of optimism, not by blinding our eyes to the evil, but by really seeing God in everything. Thus we have to give up the world, and when the world is given up, what remains? God. What is meant? You can have your wife; it does not mean that you are to abandon her, but that you are to see God in the wife. Give up your children; what does that mean? To turn them out of doors, as some human brutes do in every country? Certainly not. That is diabolism; it is not religion. But see God in your children. So, in everything. In life and in death, in happiness and in misery, the Lord is equally present. The whole world is full of the Lord. Open your eyes and see Him. This is what Vedānta teaches. . . . When we have given up desires, then alone shall we be able to read and enjoy this universe of God. Then everything will become deified. Nooks and corners, byways and shady places, which we thought dark and unholy, will be all deified. (*CW* 2:146–49)

Śaṅkara, as we have seen, interprets "*tena tyaktena bhuñjīthāḥ*" as an injunction for Advaitin monks to "protect" the Ātman by physically renouncing all possessions and works. In contrast to Śaṅkara, Vivekananda takes "*bhuñjīthāḥ*" at face value, interpreting it as "enjoy": "When we have given up desires, then alone shall we be able to read and enjoy this universe of God." According to Ramakrishna, while the *jñānī* dismisses the world as a "framework of illusion," the *vijñānī* embraces the world as a blissful manifestation of God (*K* 479 / *G* 478). For Vivekananda, the first verse of the Īśā Upaniṣad supports the standpoint of the Ramakrishnan *vijñānī* rather than that of the Śaṅkaran *jñānī*: we can only truly enjoy the world when we see God in everything. Notably, Vivekananda also departs from Śaṅkara in interpreting "*tyaktena*" as the *inner* renunciation of selfish "desires," thereby expanding the scope of the first verse to include householders as well as monks. According to Vivekananda, the verse does not instruct us to renounce our spouse and children but to renounce our selfish attachment to them by seeing God in them.[25]

At this point, one might object that while Vivekananda does sometimes seem to hold that the world is a real manifestation of God, he is not entirely consistent on this point, since there are several passages where he explicitly uses the word "*māyā*" in the sense of illusion. For instance, in his lecture "One Existence Appearing as Many" (1896), he directly equates "Māyā" with "illusion": "I am that One Existence. This is the last conclusion. There are neither three nor two in the universe; it is all One. That One, under the illusion of Māyā, is seen as many, just as a rope is seen as a snake" (*CW* 3:21). It might seem as if Vivekananda contradicts himself here, since—as we have seen—he rejects the illusionistic interpretation of *māyā* at other places.

However, I would argue that this contradiction is only apparent. The context of the statement just quoted makes clear that what he means is that the world *as perceived by the ignorant*—that is, the world of material objects existing independently of God—is illusory.[26] Accordingly, he remarks earlier in the same paragraph:

> We have seen how in the whole of this universe there is but One Existence; and that One Existence when seen through the senses is called the world, the world of matter. When It is seen through the mind, It is called the world of thoughts and ideas; and when It is seen as it is, then It is the One Infinite Being. . . . There is but one Being which the ignorant call the world. (*CW* 2:20–21)

[25] Other Upaniṣadic passages Vivekananda marshals in support of his world-affirming Integral Advaita include Kaṭha Upaniṣad 2.2.8 and 2.2.10 (*CW* 2: 182–83) and Śvetāśvatara Upaniṣad 4.3 (*CW* 2: 211).

[26] Bhushan and Garfield (2017: 222) interpret Vivekananda in a similar manner: "But that illusory status does not entail the nonexistence of a material world, only the falsification of its nature."

Vivekananda articulates here a world-inclusive Advaita philosophy, according to which the sole reality is the "One Infinite Being," which *manifests* as the world. Those who have not yet realized this Infinite Being see the world not as God but as a realm of independently existing material objects or mental ideas. It is in this context that he goes on to state that the "One, under the illusion of Māyā, is seen as many." I take him to mean, then, that the world as perceived by the ignorant is illusory, since they fail to recognize that the world is actually the "One Existence" manifesting in various forms.

He clarifies the ontological status of *māyā* in his lecture "The Real and the Apparent Man" (1896):

> There is, therefore, but one Ātman, one Self, eternally pure, eternally perfect, unchangeable, unchanged; it has never changed; and all these various changes in the universe are but appearances in that one Self. Upon it name and form have painted all these dreams; it is the form that makes the wave different from the sea. Suppose the wave subsides, will the form remain? No, it will vanish. The existence of the wave was entirely dependent upon the existence of the sea, but the existence of the sea was not at all dependent upon the existence of the wave. The form remains so long as the wave remains, but as soon as the wave leaves it, it vanishes, it cannot remain. This name and form is the outcome of what is called Māyā. It is this Māyā that is making individuals, making one appear different from another. Yet it has no existence. Māyā cannot be said to exist. Form cannot be said to exist, because it depends upon the existence of another thing. It cannot be said as not to exist, seeing that it makes all this difference. According to the Advaita philosophy, then, this Māyā or ignorance—or name and form, or, as it has been called in Europe, "time, space, and causality"—is out of this one Infinite Existence showing us the manifoldness of the universe; in substance, this universe is one. (*CW* 2:275)

Here, Vivekananda equates *māyā* with "ignorance," "name and form," and the network of "time, space, and causality." For Śaṅkara, *māyā* "cannot be described either as real or as unreal" (*tattvānyatvābhyām anirvacanīya*); *māyā* is not real, since it is sublated upon the attainment of the knowledge of Brahman, and it is not unreal, since the appearance of this universe cannot be denied (*BSBh* 2.1.14, p. 201).[27] In a subtle move, Vivekananda follows traditional Advaitins in characterizing *māyā* as neither existent nor non-existent, but he departs from traditional Advaitins in his precise understanding of the non-existence pole of *māyā*. According to Vivekananda, *māyā*—understood as name and form—does not exist in the sense that it has no *independent existence*: "Form cannot be said to exist, because it depends upon the existence of another thing." Accordingly, he

[27] See also Sadānanda's similar definition of *māyā* in para. 34 of the *Vedāntasāra* (Sadānanda 1931: 22).

likens *māyā* to the wave of an ocean: while the wave was emphatically real while it lasted, "[t]he existence of the wave was entirely dependent upon the existence of the sea. . . . " He makes precisely the same point in his "Hints on Practical Spirituality" (1899): "The reality of everything is the same infinite. This is not idealism; it is not that the world does not exist. It has a relative existence, and fulfils all its requirements. But it has no independent existence. It exists because of the Absolute Reality beyond time, space, and causation" (*CW* 2:32–33). For Vivekananda, then, the world of names and forms does exist, but depends for its existence on Brahman.

Likewise, in his "God in Everything" lecture, he equates *māyā* with "dream" just after declaring that Vedānta teaches "the deification of the world":

> The whole world is full of the Lord. . . . Give up the world which you have conjectured, because your conjecture was based upon a very partial experience, upon very poor reasoning, and upon your own weakness. Give it up; the world we have been thinking of so long, the world to which we have been clinging so long, is a false world of our own creation. Give that up; open your eyes and see that as such it never existed; it was a dream, Māyā. What existed was the Lord Himself. It is He who is in the child, in the wife, and in the husband; it is He who is in the good and in the bad; He is in the sin and in the sinner; He is in life and in death. (*CW* 2:146–47)

The context makes clear that the apparent world of independently existing entities is "a dream, Māyā," but that the world, when seen aright, is "the Lord Himself," who actually manifests in the form of child, wife, husband, and so on. More generally, I would suggest that in all those passages where Vivekananda aligns *māyā* with "dream" or "illusion," the context of these statements indicates that the very world which is illusory when seen as a Godless realm of independently existing material objects is *real* when seen as a playful manifestation of God.

He further clarifies his understanding of *māyā* in his lecture "Māyā and Freedom" (1896), which crescendoes in an eloquent passage describing the transformed outlook of one who has realized God:

> Then, and then alone, will all difficulties vanish, then will all the perplexities of heart be smoothed away, all crookedness made straight, then will vanish the delusion of manifoldness and nature; and Māyā, instead of being a horrible, hopeless dream, as it is now, will become beautiful, and this earth, instead of being a prison-house, will become our playground, and even dangers and difficulties, even all sufferings, will become deified and show us their real nature, will show us that behind everything, as the substance of everything, He is standing, and that He is the one real Self. (*CW* 2:129)

Vivekananda describes, in effect, the integral outlook of the Ramakrishnan *vijñānī* who sees everything in the world as a manifestation of God. Moreover, he notes that the very *māyā* which is a "dream" and "prison-house" in the eyes of the ignorant becomes a joyous "playground" for the realized soul who sees everything as God. From this standpoint of *vijñāna*, I believe we can reconcile all of his various statements about *māyā*. When Vivekananda refers to *māyā* as a "statement of facts," he is making the *phenomenological* claim that the world is full of contradictions and can never provide us with lasting fulfillment. When he refers to *māyā* as a "dream" or "illusion," he is making the *ontological* claim that the world as perceived by the ignorant—that is, as a Godless realm of independently existing entities—is illusory but that the very same world of *māyā*, when seen as a manifestation of God, is emphatically real and blissful.

One potential problem for my interpretation is that Vivekananda, in several places, explicitly endorses the doctrine of *vivarta*. Certain theistic traditions of Vedānta, including Viśiṣṭādvaita, accept *pariṇāmavāda*, the doctrine that Brahman actually transforms into the world. Traditional Advaita Vedāntins, by contrast, accept *vivartavāda*, the doctrine that the world is merely an "illusory appearance" (*vivarta*) of Brahman. Hence, for traditional Advaitins, Brahman only *appears* to transform into the world but, in reality, remains unchanged.[28] The Advaitin Sadānanda, in the *Vedāntasāra*, succinctly explains the difference between *pariṇāmavāda* and *vivartavāda*: "*Vikāra* is the actual modification of a thing altering into another substance; while *vivarta* is only an apparent modification" (Sadānanda 1931: 84; para. 138). According to Śaṅkara Advaitins, then, this world of plurality appears to us because of our ignorance; the moment we attain the knowledge of nondual Brahman, this world will vanish. As Śaṅkara puts it, this entire world of names and forms is "conjured up by ignorance" (*avidyākalpita*), and Brahman "in its ultimate nature remains unchanged and beyond all empirical dealings."[29]

Let us now examine carefully a passage from Vivekananda's lecture "Vedānta and Privilege," where he explicitly endorses *vivartavāda*:

> God has not changed at all, and has not become the universe at all. We see God as the universe, because we have to look through time, space, and causation. It is time, space, and causation that make this differentiation apparently, but not really. This is a very bold theory indeed. Now this theory ought to be explained a little more clearly. It does not mean idealism in the sense in which it is generally understood. It does not say that this universe does not exist; it exists, but at the same time it is not what we take it for. . . . What becomes of this phenomenal

[28] For a detailed discussion of Advaitic *vivartavāda*, see Hacker (1953).

[29] *pāramārthikena ca rūpeṇa sarvavyavahārātītam apariṇatam avatiṣṭhate* (*BSBh* 2.1.27, p. 213).

> world? This world is admitted as an apparent world, bound by time, space, and causation, and it comes to what is called the Vivarta-vāda in Sanskrit, evolution of nature, and manifestation of the Absolute. The Absolute does not change, or re-evolve. (*CW* 1:420)

I would argue that Vivekananda reconceptualizes *vivartavāda* so as to steer a middle course between *pariṇāmavāda* and the illusionistic *vivartavāda* of Śāṅkara Advaita. He clearly sides with traditional Advaitins in rejecting *pariṇāmavāda*: "God has not changed at all. . . . " At the same time, he rejects the traditional Advaitic view that the "universe does not exist" from the ultimate standpoint. In Vivekananda's hands, *vivartavāda* means that the world, far from being an illusory appearance of the Absolute, is a real "manifestation of the Absolute." His understanding of *vivartavāda* presupposes his realist conception of *māyā*, discussed earlier in this section. For Vivekananda, *māyā*, understood as the network of time-space-causality, is real but depends for its existence on the Absolute. Hence, the Absolute, through *māyā*, actually manifests as everything in the universe.[30] For Śaṅkara and his followers, the world of names and forms is a product of ignorance, so it is sublated the moment we attain the knowledge of Brahman. For Vivekananda, by contrast, the world *remains* even after we attain the knowledge of Brahman, but it becomes "deified": "Māyā," as he puts it, becomes transformed into "our playground," since we see everything as a real manifestation of God (*CW* 2:129).

4. *The Divinity of the Soul*

A keynote of Vivekananda's teachings is his emphasis on our innate divinity and perfection. From the standpoint of his Integral Advaita, since there is nothing but God, and God actually manifests as individual souls, every soul must be inherently divine. For instance, in his "Paper on Hinduism" (1893), he addressed his audience at the Parliament of the World's Religions in Chicago with this startling message:

> "Children of immortal bliss"—what a sweet, what a hopeful name! Allow me to call you, brethren, by that sweet name—heirs of immortal bliss—yea, the Hindu refuses to call you sinners. Ye are the Children of God, the sharers of immortal bliss, holy and perfect beings. Ye divinities on earth—sinners! It is a sin

[30] Vivekananda endorses *vivartavāda* in numerous other passages, including *CW* 1:362–63 and *CW* 1:418–19. I believe these passages can be interpreted along the same realist lines as suggested here.

> to call a man so; it is a standing libel on human nature. Come up, O lions, and shake off the delusion that you are sheep; you are souls immortal, spirits free, blest and eternal. . . . (*CW* 1:11)

Fully aware that the American Christians in his audience were used to being told that they were "sinners," Vivekananda declared, from a Vedāntic perspective, that they are actually "Children of immortal bliss," his translation of the phrase "*amṛtasya putrāḥ*" from Śvetāsvatara Upaniṣad 2.5. He echoed his guru Ramakrishna, who frequently contrasted the Christian emphasis on sin with the Vedāntic doctrine of the divinity of all human beings. On one occasion, for instance, Ramakrishna told his visitors:

> Once someone gave me a book of the Christians. I asked him to read it to me. It talked about nothing but sin. [To Keshab Chandra Sen] Sin is the only thing one hears of at your Brāhmo Samāj, too. The wretch who constantly says, "I am bound, I am bound" only succeeds in being bound. He who says day and night, "I am a sinner, I am a sinner," verily becomes a sinner.
>
> One should have such burning faith in God that one can say: "What? I have repeated the name of God, and can sin still cling to me? How can I be a sinner any more? How can I be in bondage any more?" (*K* 88 / *G* 138)

Notice that Ramakrishna finds a doctrinal emphasis on sin not only in Christianity but also in the Brāhmo Samāj, the modern Hindu reform movement to which Vivekananda himself had once belonged. A crucial aspect of the young Vivekananda's spiritual evolution, discussed in the previous chapter, consisted in his moving away from the Christian-Brāhmo doctrine of our inherent sinfulness to the positive Ramakrishnan/Vedāntic doctrine of our inherent divinity. To that end, Ramakrishna instructed him to read the *Aṣṭāvakra Saṃhitā*, which affirms, in the sixth verse: "You are already eternally liberated" (*mukta evāsi sarvadā*).

In his later lectures, Vivekananda attempted to reconcile various conflicting Vedāntic conceptions of the soul's relation to God by emphasizing what all these conceptions share—namely, the doctrine of the innate divinity and perfection of the soul. In his lecture "The Work Before Us" (1897), delivered in Madras, he articulates very clearly his nonsectarian position on this issue:

> For if there is one common doctrine that runs through all our apparently fighting and contradictory sects, it is that all glory, power, and purity are within the soul already; only according to Rāmānuja, the soul contracts and expands at times, and according to Śaṅkara, it comes under a delusion. Never mind these differences. All admit the truth that the power is there—potential or manifest it is there—and the sooner you believe that, the better for you. (*CW* 3:284)

For Rāmānuja, the soul is "contracted" (*saṅkucita*) in a state of ignorance but gradually expands through spiritual practice and God's grace. For Śaṅkara, by contrast, the soul is always identical with nondual Brahman in its essence but fails to realize its divine nature due to ignorance (what Vivekananda here calls "delusion"). Vivekananda conspicuously refrains from taking sides in this long-standing debate between Advaitins and Viśiṣṭādvaitins. Instead, he points out that for all their differences, all Vedāntic sects fundamentally agree that "all glory, power, and purity are within the soul already." From Vivekananda's nonsectarian perspective, these sects differ only on the relatively minor issue of whether we are *already* fully divine (Śaṅkara's position) or whether we are only *potentially* divine (Rāmānuja's position).

In his commentary on Patañjali's *Yogasūtra* 2.25 in his book *Rāja-Yoga*, Vivekananda sums up his view of the soul in the succinct statement: "Each soul is potentially divine" (*CW* 1:257). While it might seem as if he sides here with Rāmānuja against Śaṅkara in holding that the soul is only potentially divine, I believe that in this context, he uses the term "potentially divine" in a broader sense so as to accommodate a variety of different views on the soul's relation to God. Hence, even Śaṅkara would accept the "potential" divinity of the soul in this broader sense, since we cannot realize our identity with nondual Brahman until we purify ourselves through spiritual practice and eradicate our spiritual ignorance.

In his lecture "The Common Bases of Hinduism" (1897), Vivekananda once again emphasizes the common ground of all Vedāntic sects but this time strives to accommodate Dvaita Vedānta as well:

> There may be differences as to the relation between the soul and God. According to one sect the soul may be eternally different from God, according to another it may be a spark of that infinite fire, yet again according to others it may be one with that Infinite. It does not matter what our interpretation is, so long as we hold on to the one basic belief that the soul is infinite, that this soul was never created, and therefore will never die, that it had to pass and evolve into various bodies, till it attained perfection in the human one—in that we are all agreed. . . . [W]e all hold in India that the soul is by its nature pure and perfect, infinite in power and blessed. (*CW* 3:375)

In the second sentence of this passage, Vivekananda mentions, respectively, the Dvaitic, Viśiṣṭādvaitic, and Advaitic views of the soul's relation to God. And once again, he refrains from taking sides in these sectarian disputes, foregrounding instead what he takes to be the fundamental doctrine shared by all these Vedāntic sects: namely, that "the soul is infinite" and that every soul will eventually attain "perfection." However, Madhva's Dvaita Vedānta poses a serious problem for Vivekananda, since Dvaita Vedāntins do not accept universal salvation and deny that the soul is "infinite." According to Madhva, all *jīvas* are *pratibimbas* ("reflections") of God in the sense that they are entirely dependent on God and resemble God only in certain respects (B. N. K. Sharma 1962: 307). Hence, for Madhva, God alone is infinite in the fullest sense, while *jīvas* remain eternally different from Him, though they share some of God's essential features to a much lesser degree. Madhva also upholds *svarūpa-tāratamya*, the hierarchical doctrine that *jīvas* have varying degrees of intrinsic knowledge, power, and bliss in bondage as well as in liberation.[31] According to Madhva, *jīvas* fall into one of three categories: *mukti-yogyas* (those who are capable of attaining liberation), *nitya-saṃsārīs* (the eternally transmigrating), and *tamo-yogyas* (those condemned to eternal damnation). When one of these *mukti-yogyas* attains salvation through spiritual practice, it dwells eternally in Vaikuṇṭhaloka after leaving the physical body and enjoys loving communion with Viṣṇu. From the Dvaita standpoint, not all souls are destined to attain salvation, and the *tamo-yogyas* are definitely not by nature "pure and perfect" but are, in fact, inherently evil and, therefore, doomed to eternal damnation. Hence, I believe Dvaita Vedāntins would not subscribe fully to Vivekananda's view that "the soul is by its nature pure and perfect, infinite in power and blessed," though they *would* accept that all *jīvas*—even the *tamo-yogyas*—have some degree of God's essential features: namely, Truth (*satyam*), Consciousness (*jñānam*), and Bliss (*ānandam*).

In fact, Vivekananda seems to have been aware of the Dvaita doctrine of *svarūpa-tāratamya*, as is clear from the following remark in his London lecture "The Absolute and Manifestation" (1896): "Some dualists are so narrow as to insist that only the few that have been predestined to the favour of God can be saved; the rest may try ever so hard, but they cannot be accepted" (*CW* 2:142). Although he does not explicitly mention Madhva's Dvaita Vedānta here, he almost certainly has in mind followers of Madhva, who subscribe to the doctrine that some, but not all, souls are predestined for salvation.[32] On the other hand, in the passage quoted in the previous paragraph, he seems to imply that all Dvaitins believe that every soul will eventually be saved. Indeed, in his lecture on "The Ātman" (1896), he is even more explicit in claiming that dualists accept universal salvation: "Another peculiar doctrine of the dualists is, that every soul must eventually come to salvation" (*CW* 2:242). How are we to reconcile his apparently conflicting statements about the Dvaita stance on the question of universal salvation? One possibility is that when Vivekananda claimed that "dualists" accept universal salvation, he may have been thinking of non-Mādhva sects of dualism.

31 For a good discussion of the Mādhva doctrine of *svarūpa-tāratamya*, see Buchta (2014).

32 In light of the fact that he made this statement in a lecture delivered in London, it is possible that he was also thinking of certain Christian "dualists" like Calvinists, who also subscribe to the doctrine of divine predestination.

Another possibility is that in his attempt to establish common ground among the Vedāntic sects, he consciously suppressed the Dvaita doctrine of *svarūpa-tāratamya*, which he found to be troublingly "narrow."

Interestingly, in a little-known conversation with his disciple Svāmī Śuddhānanda—which is recorded in Svāmī Abjajānanda's Bengali work, *Svāmijīr Padaprānte*, and not in the *Complete Works*—Vivekananda appealed to *Brahmasūtra* 1.1.19—"*asminnasya ca tadyogaṃ śāsti*" ("The scriptures teach the union [*yogam*] of the *jīva* and Brahman")—as scriptural support for his nonsectarian view of the divinity of the soul:

> Who has told you that the *sūtras* [*Brahmasūtra*] support the Advaita philosophy alone? Śaṅkarācārya was an Advaitin, so he tried to interpret the *sūtras* in terms of Advaita philosophy. But you should try to understand the literal meaning (*akṣarārtha*) of the *sūtras* themselves, the true intention (*abhiprāy*) of Vyāsa [the author of the *Brahmasūtra*]. Take, for example, the *sūtra*, "*asminnasya* [*ca*] *tadyogaṃ śāsti*" [1.1.19]. I think that if we interpret this *sūtra* correctly, we will find that Bhagavān Vedavyāsa indicated both Advaita and Viśiṣṭādvaita through it (*ete advaita o viśiṣṭādvaita ubhay vādī bhagavān vedavyāsa kaṛtrk sūcita hoyeche*). (Abjajānanda 1983: 15; my translation)[33]

Vivekananda tells Svāmī Śuddhānanda not to rely only on Śaṅkara's sectarian Advaitic interpretation of *Brahmasūtra* 1.1.19. Instead, he encourages his disciple to adopt a broadminded and unbiased approach to the *Brahmasūtra*, striving to understand the meaning of the *sūtras* themselves, independently of traditional commentaries.[34] According to Vivekananda, 1.1.19 equally supports both Advaitic and Viśiṣṭādvaitic conceptions of the soul's relationship to Brahman. More specifically, he suggests that the author of the *Brahmasūtra* deliberately employed the capacious and open-ended language of "*yogam*" ("union") in 1.1.19 in order both to harmonize a variety of apparently conflicting scriptural passages concerning the *jīva*'s relation to Brahman and to accommodate numerous sectarian interpretations of these passages. From Vivekananda's perspective, the "union" (*yogam*) of the soul with Brahman encompasses not only the absolute Advaitic identity with Brahman but also the Viśiṣṭādvaitic unity of part (*aṃśa*) and Whole (*aṃśī*).

[33] For a somewhat inaccurate English translation of the passage, see Abjajananda (2003: 25).

[34] I discuss Vivekananda's nonsectarian approach to the *Brahmasūtra* in detail in Maharaj (2020a).

5. *Practical Vedānta: The Ethics of Oneness*

Although Vivekananda often praised Śaṅkara for his extraordinary intellect, he also faulted him repeatedly for his "narrowness of heart" (*CW* 6:392). As early as 1889, Vivekananda questioned Śaṅkara's attempt to justify barring low-caste *śūdra*s from the study of the Upaniṣads (*CW* 6:208–9). In a February 1890 letter to Svāmī Akhaṇḍānanda, he wrote: "Śaṅkara had not the slightest bit of Buddha's wonderful heart, dry intellect merely!" (*BCW* 6:248 / *CW* 6:227). In an 1898 conversation with Saratcandra Cakravarti, Vivekananda referred to Śaṅkara's "specious arguments" for the view that "non-Brahmin castes will not attain to a supreme knowledge of Brahman" (*BCW* 9:71 / *CW* 7:117). Vivekananda's criticisms of Śaṅkara's casteism may have been inspired, in part, by Ramakrishna, who frequently recited a legendary story about Śaṅkara found in the *Śaṅkaradigvijaya*:

> Śaṅkarācārya was a *brahmajñānī*, to be sure. But at the beginning he too had the feeling of differentiation. He didn't have absolute faith that everything in the world is Brahman. One day as he was coming out of the Ganges after his bath, he saw an untouchable, a butcher, carrying a load of meat. Inadvertently the butcher touched his body. Śaṅkara shouted angrily, "Hey there! How dare you touch me?" "Revered sir," said the butcher, "I have not touched you, nor have you touched me. The Pure Self cannot be the body nor the five elements nor the twenty-four cosmic principles." Then Śaṅkara came to his senses. (*K* 217 / *G* 248)

From Ramakrishna's perspective, anyone who has truly attained the Advaitic realization that "everything in the world is Brahman" should not make caste distinctions or consider some people to be inferior to others. In Ramakrishna's telling of the incident, Śaṅkara only fully internalized this truth after his encounter with the wise untouchable. Although Vivekananda never explicitly referred to this legendary incident involving Śaṅkara and the untouchable, he found in Śaṅkara's scriptural commentaries the very casteism for which the untouchable in the incident reproached him.[35]

However, Vivekananda's criticism of Śaṅkara went well beyond the issue of casteism. In a scathing letter to the pundit Pramadadās Mitra dated May 20, 1897, Vivekananda reproached Śaṅkara and other traditional commentators for their lack of social concern in general:

[35] I discuss in detail Vivekananda's views on caste in Medhananda (2020: 14–21).

> The Upaniṣads and the *Gītā* are the true scriptures; Rāma, Kṛṣṇa, Buddha, Caitanya, Nānak, Kabīr, and so on are the true Avatāras, for their hearts were as infinite as the sky—and above all, Ramakrishna. Rāmānuja, Śaṅkara etc., seem to have been mere Pundits with much narrowness of heart (*saṅkīrṇa-hṛday*). Where is that love, that weeping heart at the sorrow of others?—Dry pedantry of the Pundit—and the feeling of only oneself getting to salvation hurry-scurry! (*BCW* 7:266 / *CW* 6:394; translation modified)

Here, Vivekananda criticizes Śaṅkara and other traditional *ācārya*s not specifically for their casteism but for their spiritual selfishness, which led them to neglect the suffering of others. Tellingly, he contrasts the "narrowness of heart" of *ācārya*s like Śaṅkara and Rāmānuja with the spiritual compassion of broad-hearted *avatāra*s like Buddha, Caitanya, and especially Ramakrishna.

From a philosophical standpoint, Vivekananda traced Śaṅkara's narrowness of heart to his ontological denigration of the world. In a passage from an 1893 letter already quoted in section 2 of this chapter, Vivekananda scathingly remarked that it is the "hypocrites," who have invented "all sorts of engines of tyranny in the shape of doctrines of Pāramārthika and Vyāvahārika," who are responsible for social oppression and exploitation (*CW* 5:15). Although he did not explicitly refer in this passage to Śaṅkara or traditional Advaitins, his reference to the distinctively Advaitic doctrine of "Pāramārthika and Vyāvahārika" levels of reality suggests that he had traditional Advaitins in mind. For Vivekananda, the lack of social concern of traditional Advaitins like Śaṅkara—recall his criticism of Śaṅkara's "narrowness of heart"—stems from their ontological doctrine that the world is empirically real but ultimately unreal. By relegating the world to merely *vyāvahārika* status, traditional Advaitins ended up devaluing the world, thereby justifying selfishness and morally reprehensible social practices that contradict the true Advaitic doctrine of the divinity and oneness of all human beings. Hence, for Vivekananda, an ethics of compassion and social service must be grounded not in the world-denying metaphysics of traditional Advaita but in the world-affirming Integral Advaita taught in the original Vedāntic scriptures and by Ramakrishna.

For Vivekananda, it was Ramakrishna who pushed Advaita Vedānta to its logical conclusion by showing how the metaphysical doctrine of the oneness of all beings entails social concern. Vivekananda, as we discussed in the previous chapter, arrived at this insight as early as 1884, when Ramakrishna taught him the spiritually grounded ethics of "*śivajñāne jīver sevā*"—the practice of serving others in a spirit of worship, "knowing that they are all manifestations of God" (*LP* 2.i.131 / *DP* 852). Ramakrishna explicitly grounded this ethics of social service in his life-affirming philosophy of Vijñāna Vedānta, according to which everything is a real manifestation of God.

In a series of four lectures on "Practical Vedānta" delivered in November 1896, Vivekananda followed Ramakrishna in deriving an ethics of social service from the Integral Advaitic metaphysics explained in sections 2 through 4 of this chapter. As he put it, "My idea is to show that the highest ideal of morality and unselfishness goes hand in hand with the highest metaphysical conception . . . " (*CW* 2:355). This "highest metaphysical conception," I would argue, is not Śaṅkara's Advaita Vedānta but the more expansive philosophy of Integral Advaita. Accordingly, in a passage from his second "Practical Vedanta" lecture already quoted earlier, he observed that "impersonality includes all personalities, is the sum total of everything in the universe, and infinitely more besides" (*CW* 2:319). In other words, the impersonal-personal Infinite Reality is not only transcendent but also immanent in the world, manifesting in endless forms.

Vivekananda elaborated the ethical implications of this panentheistic metaphysics as follows:

> But what is more practical than worshipping here, worshipping you? I see you, feel you, and I know you are God. The Mohammedan says, there is no God but Allah. The Vedānta says, there is nothing that is not God. . . . The living God is within you, and yet you are building churches and temples and believing all sorts of imaginary nonsense. The only God to worship is the human soul in the human body. Of course all animals are temples too, but man is the highest, the Taj Mahal of temples. If I cannot worship in that, no other temple will be of any advantage. (*CW* 2:320–21)

For Vivekananda, the panentheistic metaphysics of Vedānta has a crucial practical implication: since we are all living manifestations of God, we should make Vedānta practical by loving and serving human beings in a spirit of worship. Moreover, it is clear from his private utterances that this "practical Vedānta" was not merely an intellectual theory but a deeply rooted spiritual conviction. In a letter to Mary Hale dated July 9, 1897, he wrote: "[M]ay I be born again and again, and suffer thousands of miseries so that I may worship the only God that exists, the only God I believe in, the sum total of all souls—and above all, my God the wicked, my God the miserable, my God the poor of all races, of all species, is the special object of my worship" (*CW* 5:137).

In opposition to my interpretation, scholars such as Bhaṭṭācārya Śāstrī and Svāmī Gambhīrānanda admit that Vivekananda's practical emphasis on serving human beings as manifestations of God is not found in Śaṅkara's work, but they claim that Vivekananda's practical Vedānta is nonetheless compatible with Śaṅkara's Advaitic metaphysics. Since Śaṅkara accepts the empirical (*vyāvahārika*) reality of the world, individual souls, and the personal God, these scholars argue that the practice of serving others in a spirit of worship can be easily accommodated within the traditional Advaitic framework as a potent means of purifying the mind, thereby making one fit to practice the more advanced *sādhana* of Jñāna-Yoga, which alone leads to *mokṣa* (Bhaṭṭācārya Śāstrī 1990: 140–62; Gambhīrānanda 1988). According to these scholars, then, Vivekananda accepted the traditional Advaitic doctrine that the world is ultimately unreal, but he prescribed an ethics of *sevā* at the *vyāvahārika* level for inferior spiritual aspirants who still think that the world and the personal God are real.[36] In support of their interpretation, they both quote this passage from one of Vivekananda's transcribed talks: "The highest Advaitism cannot be brought down to practical life. Advaitism made practical works from the plane of Viśiṣṭādvaitism. . . . In Advaitism 'I' loses itself in God" (*CW* 6:122).

However, I think there is strong evidence that Vivekananda did not articulate his ethics of serving God in human beings within a traditional Advaitic metaphysical framework. First of all, as I have just shown, the metaphysical foundation of his ethics of social service—as elaborated in his four "Practical Vedānta" lectures—is not Śaṅkara's Advaita Vedānta but the philosophy of Integral Advaita, which holds that God is both personal and impersonal and that the world is a real manifestation of God. Second, the context of the statement quoted by Bhaṭṭācārya and Gambhīrānanda suggests that what Vivekananda refers to as the "highest Advaitism" is the spiritual experience of *nirvikalpa samādhi* in which one's individuality is merged in nondual Brahman. For one who is immersed in the state of *nirvikalpa samādhi*, neither one's individuality nor the world is perceived, so there is no question of serving anyone. As Vivekananda put it in a 1900 dialogue with Chakravarti, "The knowledge of Brahman is the ultimate goal—the highest destiny of man. But man cannot remain absorbed in Brahman all the time. When he comes out of it, he must have something to engage himself. At that time he should do such work as will contribute to the real well-being of people. Therefore do I urge you to serve Jīvas, knowing that we are all one (*abheda-buddhite jīvasevārūp karma karo*)" (*BCW* 9:116 / *CW* 7:197–99; translation modified). For Vivekananda, while the "highest Advaitism" of *nirvikalpa samādhi* precludes any possibility of ethical action, so long as one is *not* in *nirvikalpa samādhi*, one should make Advaita practical by serving *jīvas* "in a spirit of oneness."

Moreover, his statement that "Advaitism made practical works from the plane of Viśiṣṭādvaitism" is perfectly consonant with my view that his "Practical Vedānta" is grounded in the panentheistic metaphysics of his *vijñāna*-based Integral Advaita. As I discussed in section 2 of the previous chapter, Ramakrishna himself would often liken the *vijñānī*'s Integral Advaitic worldview to Viśiṣṭādvaita, since in both philosophies, God actually manifests as the

[36] Baier (2019: 243) also supports this interpretation of Vivekananda's Practical Vedānta.

universe.[37] However, as I pointed out there, it would be a mistake to think that Ramakrishna simply *equates* Vijñāna Vedānta with Rāmānuja's Viśiṣṭādvaita. Rāmānuja accepts the personal God but denies the reality of the impersonal Brahman, while the *vijñānī* accepts the reality of *both* the impersonal Brahman and the personal God, since he sees that the very Brahman realized in the state of *nirvikalpa samādhi* has become everything in the universe. With Ramakrishna's teachings on *vijñāna* in the background, I would suggest that when Vivekananda claims that Practical Vedānta "works from the plane of Viśiṣṭādvaitism," he means that the ethics of serving God in human beings operates on the spiritual plane of *vijñāna*. After returning from *nirvikalpa samādhi*, the *vijñānī* sees that all beings are various manifestations of God, and hence, serving these beings becomes the highest form of worship.

It is also worth addressing briefly Paul Hacker's influential argument that Vivekananda's doctrine of practical Vedānta was likely inspired not by any indigenous Indian ideas but by the pseudo-Vedāntic ethical doctrine of the German indologist Paul Deussen (1845–1919), who had extended conversations with Vivekananda in London in September 1896. Hacker hypothesizes that Deussen suggested to Vivekananda a pseudo-Vedāntic ethics rooted in Arthur Schopenhauer's ethical interpretation of the Upaniṣadic teaching "*tat tvam asi*" (Hacker 1995: 239–41, 273–318). It is no coincidence, Hacker claims, that just weeks after his meeting with Deussen, Vivekananda delivered his lectures on "Practical Vedānta" in which he presented a Vedāntically grounded ethics for the first time.

Since I have refuted Hacker's argument in detail elsewhere (Maharaj 2018: 45–50; Maharaj 2020b),[38] I will only point out here that Hacker is definitely mistaken in assuming that Vivekananda championed an ethics of serving God in human beings only after he had met Deussen in 1896. As I noted in the previous chapter, Ramakrishna explicitly taught the young Vivekananda the *vijñāna*-based ethical doctrine of *śivajñāne jīver sevā* as early as 1884. Moreover, in several 1894 letters, Vivekananda emphasized the importance of *śivajñāne jīver sevā*. In one such letter, for instance, he exhorted his brother disciples of Ramakrishna: "If you want any good to come, just throw your ceremonials overboard and worship the Living God, the Man-God (*nara-nārāyaṇa*)—every being that wears a human form—God in His universal as well as individual aspect (*virāṭ o svarāṭ*). The universal aspect of God means this world, and worshipping it means serving it (*tār sevā*) . . . " (*BCW* 7:52–53 / *CW* 6:264; translation modified). Crucially, Vivekananda justified *sevā* as a spiritual practice by appealing to Ramakrishna's

[37] See, for instance, *K* 778 / *G* 733.

[38] For further criticisms of Hacker's argument, see Beckerlegge (2006: 218–19), Green (2016: 130–31), Killingley (1998: 145–59), Paranjape (2020: 89–113), and Nicholson (2020).

panentheistic metaphysics of Vijñāna Vedānta. Since God has actually become all human beings, the best way to worship God is to serve them—particularly, "the poor, the miserable, the weak" (*CW* 5:51). As Gwilym Beckerlegge points out, these 1894 letters are conclusive evidence that, *contra* Hacker and his followers, Vivekananda explicitly articulated a Vedāntic ethics of *sevā* well before he met Deussen (2006: 201–2). Hence, I believe the available evidence strongly indicates that the main inspiration for Vivekananda's Vedāntic ethics of social service was neither Śaṅkara nor Deussen but his own guru Ramakrishna.[39]

6. *The Four Yogas as Direct Paths to Liberation*

According to Vivekananda, each of the four main kinds of spiritual practice—Karma-Yoga (the Yoga of selfless work), Bhakti-Yoga (the Yoga of devotion), Rāja-Yoga (the Yoga of meditation), and Jñāna-Yoga (the Yoga of knowledge)—is a direct and independent path to salvation. In a class on "Karma-Yoga" given on January 3, 1896, he declared:

> Each one of our Yogas is fitted to make man perfect even without the help of the others, because they have all the same goal in view. The Yogas of work, of wisdom, and of devotion are all capable of serving as direct and independent means for the attainment of Mokṣa. "Fools alone say that work and philosophy are different, not the learned." The learned know that, though apparently different from each other, they at last lead to the same goal of human perfection. (*CW* 1:93)

Vivekananda unambiguously states here that each Yoga is a "direct and independent" path to *mokṣa* and, accordingly, that all the Yogas have equal salvific efficacy. Vivekananda, in support of this view, quotes the first line of *Bhagavad-Gītā* 5.4 (*sāṃkhyayogau pṛthag bālāḥ pravadanti na paṇḍitāḥ*), which he takes at face value to mean that Karma-Yoga and Jñāna-Yoga lead directly to the same goal of salvation. He thereby deviates from Śaṅkara and his followers, who adopt the traditional Advaitic view that Jñāna-Yoga alone is a direct path to *mokṣa*. Śaṅkara, in his commentary on *Gītā* 18.55, defines Bhakti-Yoga as the "worship of God through one's own actions" (*svakarmaṇā bhagavataḥ abhyarcana*), taking

[39] Of course, it is still *possible* that Vivekananda's conversations with Deussen gave him further impetus to develop a Vedāntic ethics. However, there is no evidence that the ethical implications of Vedānta were even a topic of their conversations, and Vivekananda nowhere refers to the possibility of a Vedāntic ethics in any of his numerous statements about Schopenhauer and Deussen (cf. Maharaj 2017a). Hence, *contra* Hacker, I believe the available evidence establishes only that it is *possible*, but not *probable*, that Vivekananda was influenced by Schopenhauer and Deussen with respect to his Vedāntic ethics.

it to be synonymous with Karma-Yoga. Śaṅkara then goes on to claim that the "fruit" of the successful practice of Bhakti-Yoga-cum-Karma-Yoga is the attainment of "fitness" for the practice of Jñāna-Yoga (*jñānaniṣṭhāyogyatā*), which alone leads directly to *mokṣa* (*BhGBh* 18.55, p. 454). Hence, in stark contrast to Vivekananda, Śaṅkara maintains that Bhakti-Yoga and Karma-Yoga can only lead *indirectly* to *mokṣa* by purifying the mind, thereby making one fit to practice Jñāna-Yoga.[40]

The passage quoted earlier from Vivekananda's "Karma-Yoga" class only states that three of the Yogas are direct paths to *mokṣa* but leaves out Rāja-Yoga. At other places, however, he mentions all four Yogas as direct paths, such as in his well-known summing-up of his Integral Advaita philosophy in *Rāja-Yoga*:

> Each soul is potentially divine. The goal is to manifest this Divinity within, by controlling nature, external and internal. Do this either by work, or worship, or psychic control, or philosophy—by one or more or all of these—and be free. This is the whole of religion. Doctrines, or dogmas, or rituals, or books, or temples, or forms, are but secondary details. (*CW* 1:257)

He mentions here that each of the four Yogas—including Rāja-Yoga, the Yoga of "psychic control"—leads to the same goal of the manifestation of the "Divinity within."[41] Moreover, the crucial qualifying phrase, "by one or more or all of these," indicates that while each Yoga is sufficient on its own for salvation, one can also combine the Yogas, since they are complementary rather than mutually exclusive.

Indeed, in numerous other lectures and writings, he goes much further by claiming that we should all strive to attain the ideal of a perfect combination of all four Yogas. For instance, he expresses this ideal in his lecture "The Ideal of a Universal Religion" (1896):

> Would to God that all men were so constituted that in their minds *all* these elements of philosophy, mysticism, emotion, and of work were equally present in full! That is the ideal, my ideal of a perfect man. Everyone who has only one or two of these elements of character, I consider "one-sided"; and this world is almost full of such "one-sided" men, with knowledge of that one road only in which they move; and anything else is dangerous and horrible to them. To

[40] See also Śaṅkara's commentary on *Gītā* 5.26, where he states that Karma-Yoga "leads to liberation through the stages of mental purification, attainment of Knowledge, and renunciation of all actions" (*sattvaśuddhijñānaprāptisarvakarmasannyāsakrameṇa mokṣāya*) (*BhGBh* 5.26, p. 164).

[41] Other passages where Vivekananda claims that all four Yogas are direct paths to salvation include *CW* 1:55 and *CW* 7:111–12.

become harmoniously balanced in all these four directions is *my* ideal of religion. (*CW* 2:388)

Vivekananda elaborates here the Integral Advaitic rationale for a correspondingly integral approach to personality development. Combining the four Yogas, he suggests, not only fosters the development of a balanced and many-sided personality but also makes for a more peaceful and loving global community by enhancing our ability to empathize with others. In section 4 of the next chapter, I will discuss in detail how Vivekananda, on the basis of this ideal of combining the four Yogas, championed the radical cosmopolitan imperative to learn from, and even to practice, religions other than our own.

Crucially, his thesis that all four Yogas are direct paths to salvation is grounded in his Integral Advaitic ontology of the impersonal-personal Infinite Reality discussed in section 2 of this chapter. On the basis of this expansive ontology, he is able to maintain that different Yogas are direct paths to the realization of different aspects or forms of one and the same Infinite Reality.[42] The Bhakti-Yogī, for instance, can realize the personal aspect of the Infinite Reality, while the Jñāna-Yogī can realize the impersonal aspect of the same Divine Reality. As we saw in chapter 1, it was Ramakrishna who helped Vivekananda to arrive at this insight.[43] As Ramakrishna put it, "The *vijñānī* sees that the Reality which is *nirguṇa* is also *saguṇa*. . . . The *jñānī*'s path leads to Truth, as does the path that combines *jñāna* and *bhakti*. The *bhakta*'s path, too, leads to Truth. Jñāna-Yoga is true, and Bhakti-Yoga is true. God can be realized through all paths" (*K* 51 / *G* 103–4).

In his class on "The Naturalness of Bhakti-Yoga," held on February 3, 1896, Vivekananda clarifies precisely how Bhakti-Yoga is a direct and independent path to salvation. The goal of Bhakti-Yoga is the attainment of "Parā-Bhakti," an exalted state of "supreme devotion" toward God in which no worldly "bondages" remain to fetter the soul (*CW* 3:72). As he puts it, "A ship, all of a sudden, comes near a magnetic rock, and its iron bolts and bars are all attracted and drawn out, and the planks get loosened and freely float on the water. Divine grace thus loosens the binding bolts and bars of the soul, and it becomes free" (*CW* 3:72–73). It is significant that he borrows this metaphor of a ship from Ramakrishna, who invoked it in the specific context of the *vijñānī*: "The eight fetters have fallen from the *vijñānī*. . . . Once a ship sailed into the ocean. Suddenly its iron joints,

42 Long (2020) makes a similar argument, partly on the basis of my earlier work.

43 As De Michelis (2004: 86–87), Baier (2019: 249), and Stevens (2018: 129) have noted, Brāhmos like Akshay Kumar Dutt and Keshab Chandra Sen had already emphasized the complementarity of the four Yogas well before Vivekananda and may, indeed, have influenced him. However, I believe Vivekananda's specific doctrine that each of the four Yogas is a direct path to realizing the impersonal-personal Divine Reality was shaped by Ramakrishna rather than by Dutt or Keshab, who neither taught such a doctrine nor would have accepted it in light of their monotheistic commitments.

nails, and screws fell out. The ship was passing a magnetic hill, and so all its iron was loosened" (*K* 480 / *G* 476). For Vivekananda, Bhakti-Yoga, when practiced sincerely, is sufficient on its own to lead to perfect mental purity and, by God's "grace," to a state of perfect freedom from all bondages. Tellingly, he quotes verses 6–7 from chapter 12 of the *Gītā* in support of the view that Bhakti-Yoga is a direct path to salvation: "Those who, having offered up all their work unto Me, with entire reliance on Me, meditate on Me and worship Me without any attachment to anything else—them, I soon lift up from the ocean of ever-recurring births and deaths, as their mind is wholly attached to Me" (*CW* 3:77). Śaṅkara, we should recall, interprets such verses in the *Gītā* to mean that Bhakti-Yoga leads *indirectly* to salvation by making one fit to practice Jñāna-Yoga, which is the only direct path to salvation. Vivekananda, in contrast to Śaṅkara, takes these *Gītā* verses at face value to mean that the *bhakta*, by God's grace, can attain *mokṣa* directly, without having to practice Jñāna-Yoga at all. He then goes on to quote verses 5.13.21–22 of the *Viṣṇu-Purāṇa*, which show how the "blessed Gopis" attained *mukti* through *bhakti* alone:

> Here is a passage showing how, in the case of one of the blessed Gopis, the soul-binding chains of both merit and demerit were broken. "The intense pleasure in meditating on God took away the binding effects of her good deeds. Then her intense misery of soul in not attaining unto Him washed off all her sinful propensities; and then she became free." (*CW* 3:78)

Vivekananda, then, clearly sides with Ramakrishna against Śaṅkara in holding that Bhakti-Yoga, through a combination of mental purification and God's grace, leads ultimately to the supreme love of God, which is sufficient, by itself, to destroy all bondages and to lead to freedom from rebirth.

In his book *Bhakti-Yoga* (1896), he explicitly states that through the practice of Bhakti-Yoga, one can attain both the supreme love for God *and* the knowledge of nondual Brahman. As he puts it, "with perfect love true knowledge is bound to come even unsought" (*CW* 3:34). Here again, Vivekananda follows Ramakrishna, who frequently taught that God, "if it pleases Him," can give "His devotee both the Love of God and the Knowledge of Brahman" (*K* 471 / *G* 468). In "The Philosophy of Īśvara" section of *Bhakti-Yoga* (*CW* 3:37–42), Vivekananda elaborates the Integral Advaitic basis for his view that Bhakti-Yoga leads both to supreme devotion and to Advaitic knowledge. Echoing Ramakrishna's favorite teaching that "Brahman and Śakti are inseparable," Vivekananda claims that "it is the same Sat-cit-ānanda who is also the God of Love, the impersonal and personal in one" (*CW* 3:37). Hence, the nondual Brahman of Advaitins and the personal God of *bhakta*s are different aspects of one and the same impersonal-personal Infinite Reality. From this Integral Advaitic standpoint, he goes on to explain that perfected *bhakta*s like Prahlāda and the *gopī*s can choose either to merge their individuality in nondual Brahman or to remain in loving communion with the personal God:

> Those who attain to that state where there is neither creation, nor created, nor creator, where there is neither knower, nor knowable, nor knowledge, where there is neither *I*, nor *thou*, nor *he*, where there is neither subject, nor object, nor relation, "there, who is seen by whom?"—such persons have gone beyond everything to "where words cannot go nor mind," gone to that which the Śrutis declare as "Not this, not this"; but for those who cannot, or will not[,] reach this state, there will inevitably remain the triune vision of the one undifferentiated Brahman as nature, soul, and the interpenetrating sustainer of both—Īśvara. (*CW* 3:40)

As I already noted in section 2, Vivekananda claims here that *bhakta*s, through the practice of Bhakti-Yoga, may attain the Advaitic state in which there is no subject-object duality whatsoever, but they may also choose to retain their individuality in order to enjoy the love of the personal God. This, I take it, is the thrust of the key phrase "for those who cannot, or *will not*[,] reach" the Advaitic state. For Vivekananda, while some *bhakta*s may not be *able* to reach the Advaitic state, other *bhakta*s *choose* not to attain this nondual state, preferring instead to remain in loving communion with the personal God.

In his class on Bhakti-Yoga held on February 16, 1896, he appealed to Ramakrishna's metaphor of sugar[44] to convey the attitude of those perfected *bhakta*s who prefer the love of God to Advaitic knowledge:

> "Who cares to become sugar?" says the Bhakta, "I want to taste sugar." Who will then desire to become free and one with God? "I may know that I am He; yet will I take myself away from Him and become different, so that I may enjoy the Beloved." That is what the Bhakta says. Love for love's sake is his highest enjoyment. (*CW* 3:99)

It is clear, then, that for Vivekananda, Bhakti-Yoga is capable, on its own, of leading *both* to supreme love of the personal God as well as to Advaitic knowledge of the impersonal Brahman. Nonetheless, he notes that most *bhakta*s prefer the bliss of loving communion with God to Advaitic realization.

Anantanand Rambachan has argued that Vivekananda fails to provide a clear and rigorous account of the precise mechanism by which each of the four Yogas

[44] See, for instance, *K* 481 / *G* 478.

leads directly to *mokṣa*. According to Rambachan, Vivekananda unjustifiably assumes that through the practice of any of the four Yogas, "*avidyā* [ignorance], by some means or other, spontaneously falls away in the automatic manifestation of *brahmajñāna*" (1994a: 72). The best way to address Rambachan's criticism of Vivekananda is to examine carefully passages where Vivekananda clarifies the common mechanism at the heart of all the Yogas. For instance, in his essay "Four Paths of Yoga," he writes:

> Our main problem is to be free. It is evident then that until we realise ourselves as the Absolute, we cannot attain to deliverance. Yet there are various ways of attaining to this realisation. These methods have the generic name of Yoga (to join, to join ourselves to our reality). These Yogas, though divided into various groups, can principally be classed into four; and as each is only a method leading indirectly to the realisation of the Absolute, they are suited to different temperaments. Now it must be remembered that it is not that the assumed man becomes the real man or Absolute. There is no becoming with the Absolute. It is ever free, ever perfect; but the ignorance that has covered Its nature for a time is to be removed. Therefore the whole scope of all systems of Yoga (and each religion represents one) is to clear up this ignorance and allow the Ātman to restore its own nature. (*CW* 8:152)

Superficially, it may seem as if Vivekananda contradicts himself by stating that each of the four Yogas leads "indirectly" to the realization of the Ātman. How are we to reconcile this statement with his repeated assertions that each of the Yogas is a "direct and independent" path to *mokṣa*? The key to understanding his position is his thesis that the Absolute, which is our true nature, is "ever free, ever perfect." Since we are *already* the Ātman, the purpose of all the Yogas is simply to remove our *ignorance* of our true divine nature by "purifying the mind" (*CW* 8:152). For Vivekananda, our impurities cause us to identify mistakenly with the body-mind complex. Therefore, when we become pure through the practice of *any* of the Yogas, our true nature as the Ātman spontaneously manifests itself, and this manifestation of the Ātman is tantamount to *mokṣa*.

For traditional Advaitins like Śaṅkara, Jñāna-Yoga alone is a direct path to *mokṣa*, since only *śruti*—specifically, the Upaniṣadic teaching of our identity with the nondual Ātman—is able to generate the knowledge of Brahman.[45] In contrast to Śaṅkara, Vivekananda maintains that we are *already* knowers of Brahman, so the knowledge of Brahman need not be generated. For instance, in a passage from *Karma-Yoga*, he explains how Karma-Yoga leads directly to

[45] Rambachan makes this point repeatedly. See, for instance, Rambachan (1994a: 71).

salvation: "We may all hope that some day or other, as we struggle through the paths of life, there will come a time when we shall become perfectly unselfish; and the moment we attain to that, all our powers will be concentrated, and the knowledge which is ours will be manifest" (*CW* 1: 35). For Vivekananda, the aim of all Yogas is not the *attainment* of the knowledge of Brahman but the *manifestation* of "the knowledge which is ours." In an 1898 conversation with Saratcandra Cakravarti, he made the same point even more emphatically: "work has no power of directly manifesting the Ātman, it is only effective in removing some veils that cover knowledge. Then the Ātman manifests by Its own effulgence" (*BCW* 9:102 / *CW* 7:178).[46] Vivekananda's view, in short, is that all four Yogas are direct and independent paths to *mokṣa*, since they are all equally effective means of purifying the mind, thereby removing the "veils" that cover our ever-present knowledge of our true nature as the Ātman.

Rambachan's criticism of Vivekananda, I would suggest, stems from his Śaṅkaran assumption that the knowledge of Brahman must be *generated*. According to Rambachan, Śaṅkara justifies the direct salvific efficacy of Jñāna-Yoga by providing a clear explanation of how *śruti* alone generates the knowledge of Brahman.[47] He claims that Vivekananda, by contrast, does not explain clearly how the other three Yogas can generate the knowledge of Brahman. However, Rambachan overlooks the fact that, according to Vivekananda, the knowledge of Brahman is already "ours," so it need not be generated. Vivekananda's position on this issue can be seen as a development of Ramakrishna's succinct teaching that "Pure Mind, Pure Intelligence, and Pure Ātman, are one and the same" (*śuddhaman, śuddhabuddhi, ār śuddha ātmā—ekī jinis*) (*K* 536 / *G* 524), which suggests that the achievement of absolute mental purity is a sufficient precondition for—in effect, tantamount to—the manifestation of the Ātman. Vivekananda may also have been thinking of verses 3.38–39 of the *Bhagavad-Gītā*, which state that our "knowledge" (*jñānam*) of the Ātman is "covered" by desire (*kāma*), just as fire is covered by smoke and a mirror by dust. For Ramakrishna and Vivekananda, when our minds become pure through spiritual practice, our innate knowledge of our true nature as the Pure Ātman manifests spontaneously. For Śaṅkara, by contrast, the mental purification acquired through disciplines such as Karma-Yoga and Bhakti-Yoga only makes us fit to practice Jñāna-Yoga, which alone *generates* the knowledge of the Ātman that we did not previously have.

[46] *karmer nijer sākṣāt ātmaprakāśer śakti nei; katakguli āvaraṇke dūr kore dei mātra. tārpar ātmā āpon prabhāy āpni udbhāsita hoy.*

[47] In his book *Accomplishing the Accomplished*, Rambachan (1991) discusses in detail Śaṅkara's understanding of how the Upaniṣads generate the knowledge of Brahman.

7. Harmonizing the Vedāntic Schools of Dvaita, Viśiṣṭādvaita, and Advaita

One of the recurring themes in Vivekananda's lectures and writings from December 1894 onward was his attempt to harmonize three of the main schools of Vedānta: namely, Dvaita, Viśiṣṭādvaita, and Advaita. In light of his philosophy of Integral Advaita reconstructed in the previous sections of this chapter, we might expect him to have harmonized the three schools roughly as follows. In his 1896 lecture on "Ramakrishna," he explicitly credited his guru with teaching him the "central secret that the truth may be one and yet many at the same time, that we may have different visions of the same truth from different standpoints" (*CW* 4:181). Accordingly, as we saw in section 2, he follows Ramakrishna in holding that *bhakta*s who worship the personal God and traditional Advaitins who contemplate the impersonal Absolute are actually viewing the same Infinite Divine Reality from different, but equally true, standpoints. Since Vivekananda also holds that all four Yogas are direct and independent paths to salvation, he maintains that *bhakta*s directly attain the same goal of God-realization as Advaitins do, even if the salvific goal for most *bhakta*s is not to become one with God but to dwell eternally in loving communion with Him. In light of his Integral Advaitic philosophy, then, he could simply have held the non-hierarchical view that the *bhakti* schools of Dvaita and Viśiṣṭādvaita—both of which conceive God as personal—are on a salvific par with Advaita, since all three Vedāntic philosophies lead to salvific realization of the same ultimate reality viewed from different standpoints.

Indeed, Ramakrishna unambiguously held this non-hierarchical position. He would often refer to Hanumān as the paradigmatic example of a *vijñānī* who revels in adopting various spiritual attitudes toward God:

> Hanumān, after realizing God in both His personal and His impersonal aspects, cherished toward God the attitude of a servant, a devotee. He said to Rāma: "O Rāma, sometimes I think that You are the whole and I am a part of You. Sometimes I think that You are the Master and I am Your servant. And sometimes, Rāma, when I contemplate the Absolute, I see that I am You and You are I." (*K* 483 / *G* 480)

Hanumān's three attitudes toward Rāma—the relationship of part to whole, the relationship of servant to master, and the relation of absolute identity—correspond to the Vedāntic schools of Viśiṣṭādvaita, Dvaita, and Advaita respectively. Significantly, there is no hint here of any kind of hierarchical privileging of the Advaitic realization. Instead, Ramakrishna views the three different standpoints as equally true spiritual attitudes (or *bhāva*s). Indeed, on the basis of his own spiritual experience of *vijñāna*, he declared that the ability to enjoy and commune with God in all three ways is the summit of spiritual realization: "I have come to the final realization that God is the Whole and I am a part of Him, that God is the Master and I am His servant. Furthermore, I think every now and then that He is I and I am He" (*K* 594 / *G* 638). Accordingly, Ramakrishna points out that the highest goal for many *bhakta*s is not Advaitic realization but eternal loving communion with God as "eternally endowed with form and personality" (*nitya sākāra*) (*K* 152 / *G* 191). He would often appeal to the metaphor of sugar to convey the *bhakta*'s attitude: "I don't want to *be* sugar; I love to *eat* sugar" (*K* 481 / *G* 478). Indeed, on May 23, 1885, in the young Vivekananda's presence, Ramakrishna explicitly stated that for many *bhakta*s, the salvific goal is not Advaitic *nirvāṇa*—the total dissolution of one's individuality in nondual Brahman—but eternal loving communion with the personal God: "It can't be said that *bhakta*s need *nirvāṇa*. According to some schools there is an eternal Kṛṣṇa and there are also His eternal devotees. Kṛṣṇa is Spirit embodied, and His Abode also is Spirit embodied (*cinmay śyām, cinmay dhām*)" (*K* 834 / *G* 779). Hence, from Ramakrishna's standpoint of *vijñāna*, Dvaita and Viśiṣṭādvaita—both of which conceive salvation as eternal communion with the personal God—are on a salvific par with Advaita Vedānta.

Puzzlingly, however, Vivekananda seems to deviate from his guru and his own Integral Advaitic philosophy by adopting the hierarchical view that Dvaita and Viśiṣṭādvaita are true but "lower" stages on the way to the highest truth of Advaita Vedānta. In numerous lectures delivered in both the West and India from late 1894 onward, he championed this hierarchical doctrine of the "three stages" of Vedānta.[48] For instance, in his lecture "The Ātman" delivered in New York on February 2, 1896, he provides a mostly accurate[49] summary of the schools of Dvaita, Viśiṣṭādvaita, and Advaita and then summarizes his hierarchical doctrine as follows:

> These are the salient points of the three steps which Indian religious thought has taken in regard to God. We have seen that it began with the personal, the extra-cosmic God. It went from the external to the internal cosmic body, God immanent in the universe, and ended in identifying the soul itself with that God and making one Soul, a unit of all these various manifestations in the

[48] See, for instance, "The Ātman" (*CW* 2:238–53), "Practical Vedānta: Part IV" (*CW* 2:341–58), "Soul, Nature and God" (*CW* 2:423–31), and "The Highest Ideal of Jñāna-Yoga" (*CW* 1:393–404).

[49] As far as I can tell, his only mistake—or, at least, overgeneralization—in this lecture is his claim that "[a]nother peculiar doctrine of the dualists is, that every soul must eventually come to salvation" (*CW* 2:242). As discussed in section 4, Madhva's school of Dvaita Vedānta does not accept universal salvation.

universe. This is the last word of the Vedas. It begins with dualism, goes through a qualified monism, and ends in perfect monism. . . .

Now, as society exists at the present time, *all these three stages are necessary*. The one does not deny the other, one is simply the fulfilment of the other. The Advaitin or the qualified Advaitin does not say that dualism is wrong; it is a right view, but a *lower* one. It is on the way to truth. (*CW* 2:253; emphasis added)

Two features of Vivekananda's position—indicated by the italicized words in the passage—are worth highlighting. First, his view is overtly hierarchical, since he holds that Dvaita and Viśiṣṭādvaita are true but "lower" stages "on the way to" the highest truth of Advaita. Second, he insists, both here and in numerous other places, that all three stages are "necessary."[50] It is also important to note that he conceives the three stages of Vedānta both as philosophical stages and as stages of spiritual experience. From a philosophical standpoint, he holds that Dvaita and Viśiṣṭādvaita are lower stages in a philosophical dialectic culminating in the most logical, rationally satisfying, and comprehensive doctrine of Advaita Vedānta (*CW* 2:430–31). From the standpoint of spiritual experience, he claims, as he puts it in a letter dated May 6, 1895, that Dvaita, Viśiṣṭādvaita, and Advaita are "the three stages of spiritual growth in man," and he then immediately adds: "Each one is necessary" (*CW* 5:81). Moreover, as I will discuss in detail in section 3 of the next chapter, for a brief period from mid-1894 to mid-1895, he attempted to establish the harmony of the world's religions on the basis of the three stages of Vedānta.

The problem lies in the fact that Vivekananda insists that all three stages of spiritual experience are "necessary," since this necessity claim seems to entail that all *bhakta*s must ultimately transcend the experience of the personal God and attain the highest Advaitic realization in order to attain salvation. This necessity claim, which is built into his doctrine of the "three stages" of Vedānta, contradicts not only Ramakrishna's non-hierarchical teachings on *bhakti* and *jñāna* but also two key tenets of Vivekananda's own Integral Advaita. As we have seen in section 2, Vivekananda follows Ramakrishna in holding the non-hierarchical view that personal and impersonal conceptions of the ultimate reality are equally true, since they describe the same Infinite Reality from different standpoints. Moreover, as discussed in section 6, on the basis of this non-hierarchical ontology of the impersonal-personal Infinite Reality, Vivekananda maintains that Bhakti-Yoga is a direct and independent path to salvation. Through the practice of Bhakti-Yoga, *bhaktas* can either attain the Advaitic realization of nondual

50 For other passages where he makes this necessity claim, see *CW* 1:323 ("The different stages of growth are absolutely necessary to the attainment of purity and perfection"), *CW* 1:404 ("every individual will have to take" the "three steps"), and *CW* 2:347 ("all these various steps through which humanity has to pass").

Brahman or choose to remain in eternal loving communion with the personal God.

However, Vivekananda's doctrine that Dvaita, Viśiṣṭādvaita, and Advaita are *necessary* stages of "spiritual growth" seems to contradict these tenets of his Integral Advaita. After all, according to the doctrine of "three stages," the *bhakta*'s realization of the personal God is insufficient for salvation, since it is a "lower" stage on the way to the highest goal of Advaitic realization. He makes this point explicitly in his account of the three Vedāntic stages in his fourth lecture on "Practical Vedānta" (1896). After noting that "[s]ome dualists conceive of the goal as the highest heaven, where souls will live with God forever," Vivekananda immediately goes on to add: "Of course we know that the Advaita holds that this cannot be the goal or the ideal: bodilessness must be the ideal" (*CW* 2:349–50). He makes clear here that his hierarchical subordination of Dvaita and Viśiṣṭādvaita to Advaita entails that the *bhakta*'s goal of attaining eternal loving communion with the personal God is salvifically inferior to the highest Advaitic ideal of "bodilessness"—that is, the total dissolution of one's individuality in the impersonal nondual Brahman.

Interestingly, in this same lecture, he insists that his privileging of Advaita over Dvaita and Viśiṣṭādvaita is not meant to be "patronising": "Dualism and all systems that had preceded it are accepted by the Advaita not in a patronising way, but with the conviction that they are true manifestations of the same truth, and that they all lead to the same conclusions as the Advaita has reached" (*CW* 2:347). His insistence notwithstanding, it is difficult to see how his gesture of relegating Dvaita and Viśiṣṭādvaita to "lower" stages or "lower" truths in a hierarchy culminating in Advaita is *not* patronizing, since he thereby denies the self-understanding of the many *bhakta*s who take the ultimate salvific goal to be eternal communion with the personal God.

Sister Nivedita (born Margaret Noble), one of Vivekananda's own disciples and one of the most astute interpreters of his work, was perhaps the first to have detected this conceptual tension between his hierarchical doctrine of three stages and his more egalitarian Integral Advaitic philosophy. In her insightful 1907 introduction to his *Complete Works*, she wrote:

> It must never be forgotten that it was the Swami Vivekananda who . . . also added to Hinduism the doctrine that Dvaita, Viśiṣṭādvaita, and Advaita are but three phases or stages in a single development, of which the last-named constitutes the goal. This is part and parcel of the *still greater and more simple doctrine* that the many and the One are the same Reality, perceived by the mind at different times and in different attitudes; or as Ramakrishna expressed the same thing, "God is both with form and without form. And He is that which includes both form and formlessness." (*CW* 1:xv; emphasis added)

Immediately after noting that Vivekananda's doctrine of the three stages of Vedānta is one of his most original contributions to Hindu thought, she provides a very subtle, almost veiled, *critique* of this very doctrine in the next sentence. His hierarchical "three stages" doctrine, she claims, stands in tension with the "still greater and more simple doctrine"—also endorsed by him—that the many and the one are the "same Reality" seen from different standpoints.[51] Nivedita also reminds us that his guru Ramakrishna endorsed the latter non-hierarchical doctrine that the personal God and the impersonal nondual Brahman are both equally true aspects of the same Infinite Reality—a doctrine that entails, as we have seen, that the *bhakta*'s goal of eternal loving communion with the personal God is in no way salvifically inferior to the Advaitin's goal of absolute identity with the impersonal Brahman. Unfortunately, Nivedita does not clarify precisely why she thinks that this non-hierarchical doctrine is "greater" and "more simple" than the "three stages" doctrine. Nonetheless, our critical examination of the "three stages" doctrine in this section can help us read between the lines of her philosophically rich and nuanced suggestion. The non-hierarchical doctrine—endorsed by both Ramakrishna and Vivekananda—is "greater" than Vivekananda's own "three stages" doctrine, I would suggest, since the former doctrine avoids the patronizing gesture of relegating theistic spiritual experiences to "lower" stages in a hierarchy culminating in Advaitic realization. Moreover, this non-hierarchical doctrine is "more simple" than the "three stages" doctrine, since the former doctrine is able, *by itself*, to harmonize the schools of Dvaita, Viśiṣṭādvaita, and Advaita in an egalitarian manner. Since the personal God of Dvaitins and Viśiṣṭādvaitins and the impersonal Brahman of Advaitins are one and the same Divine Reality seen from equally true standpoints, Dvaita and Viśiṣṭādvaita enjoy an equal footing with Advaita. From this standpoint, the hierarchical doctrine of "three stages" proves to be an unnecessary complexity. At the same time, however, Nivedita tries to mitigate the tension between Vivekananda's two doctrines by suggesting that the "three stages" doctrine is "part and parcel" of the broader non-hierarchical doctrine. It must be said, however, that she does not explain precisely how the former doctrine can be plausibly subsumed under the latter doctrine, and I have not been able to find any evidence that Vivekananda himself reconciled the two doctrines in such a manner.

In accordance with Nivedita's suggestion that Vivekananda's non-hierarchical Ramakrishnan doctrine is "greater" and "more simple" than his own "three stages" doctrine, I suggest that he would have been more philosophically consistent and less "patronising"—to use his own word—had he harmonized the

[51] For instance, Nivedita records that Vivekananda once told someone in Paris that "what Ramakrishna Paramahamsa and I" have taught is that "the Many and the One are the same Reality, perceived by the same mind at different times and in different attitudes" (Nivedita 1910: 31–32).

three Vedāntic schools from *within* his Integral Advaitic framework, which places *bhakti* and *jñāna* on an equal footing. As it stands, however, I believe there is a tension between his egalitarian Integral Advaitic framework and his "three stages" doctrine, which places the devotional schools of Dvaita and Viśiṣṭādvaita on a lower salvific footing than Advaita.

In the next chapter, I will argue in detail that between mid-1894 and mid-1895, Vivekananda attempted to harmonize the world religions on the basis of the three stages of Vedānta, but by late 1895, he abandoned this attempt in favor of a broader and more egalitarian doctrine based on the equal salvific efficacy of each of the four Yogas. In the context of the harmony of religions, then, it seems that he had come to realize fairly quickly that the hierarchical "three stages" doctrine was neither helpful nor necessary. Likewise, in the context of his exposition of Vedānta, it is possible that if he had lived longer, he might have recognized eventually—as Nivedita had—that his Integral Advaitic framework is perfectly sufficient on its own to harmonize the schools of Dvaita, Viśiṣṭādvaita, and Advaita in an elegant and non-hierarchical manner. Accordingly, he might very well have dropped the "three stages" doctrine from his Vedāntic philosophy altogether. Alternatively, had he lived longer, he might have *retained* his "three stages" doctrine but dropped his thesis that all three stages are "necessary," since it is this *necessity* claim in particular, as I have argued, that comes into direct conflict with key tenets of his Integral Advaitic philosophy.

These speculative possibilities aside, I have suggested in this section, by building on Nivedita's critical insight, that there is an internal tension between Vivekananda's Integral Advaitic philosophy reconstructed in sections 2 through 6 of this chapter and his own hierarchical doctrine of the three necessary stages of Vedānta.

3

Grounding Religious Cosmopolitanism

Three Phases in the Evolution of Vivekananda's Doctrine of the Harmony of Religions

In his famous "Paper on Hinduism" delivered at the World's Parliament of Religions in Chicago on September 19, 1893, Vivekananda declared that "the whole world of religions is only a travelling, a coming up, of different men and women, through various conditions and circumstances, to the same goal" (*CW* 1:18). Indeed, the doctrine that religions are different paths to the same goal—which, as we saw in chapter 1, was taught to him by Ramakrishna—was to become a keynote of his lectures in the West, during his visits from 1893 to 1896 and again from 1900 to 1901.

Although it is uncontroversial that Vivekananda championed the harmony of all religious paths, there has been a great deal of scholarly controversy concerning precisely *how* he harmonized the world religions. In 1983, the Christian theologian Alan Race introduced a threefold typology of exclusivism, inclusivism, and pluralism that has been extremely influential in shaping recent discussions of religious diversity in philosophy and theology (Race 1983). Scholars of Vivekananda have debated where in this typology to place his views on religious diversity. We can divide these scholars into four main groups.

Many scholars argue that although Vivekananda may *seem* to have championed the pluralist doctrine that all religions have equal truth and salvific efficacy, he actually subscribed to a "hierarchical inclusivism," according to which different religions occupy different stages leading to the highest truth of Advaita Vedānta.[1] As Stephen Gregg contends, Vivekananda was "no simplistic pluralist, as portrayed in hagiographical texts, nor narrow exclusivist, as portrayed by some modern Hindu nationalists, but a thoughtful, complex inclusivist" (2019: 1) who upheld "the superiority of a monistic, *Advaita Vedanta* interpretation of reality" (2019: 120).

[1] See Hacker (1977 [1971]: 565–79), Neufeldt (1987, 1993), Halbfass (1991: 51–86), Barua (2014: 77–94), Raghuramaraju (2015: 185–205), Rigopoulous (2019: 438–60), Gregg (2019), Baier (2019: esp. 254–55).

Swami Vivekananda's Vedāntic Cosmopolitanism. Swami Medhananda, Oxford University Press. © Oxford University Press 2022. DOI: 10.1093/oso/9780197624463.003.0004

By contrast, some scholars claim that Vivekananda held a consistently pluralist stance that did not privilege either Hinduism or Advaita Vedānta over other religions (Elkman 2007; Bhajanananda 2008; Mitra 2018). Meanwhile, still other scholars argue that Vivekananda's position on the world religions combines elements of both pluralism and inclusivism, with some claiming that he *vacillates* between religious pluralism and Advaitic inclusivism[2] and others contending that his views fall somewhere *between* pluralism and inclusivism.[3]

It is worth noting that scholars in all three of these camps, in spite of their differences, adopt a *synchronic* approach to Vivekananda, since they assume that his views on religious diversity did not evolve significantly from 1893 to 1901. By contrast, Thomas J. Green (2016: 150) and Gwilym Beckerlegge (2006: 220–21) adopt a *diachronic* approach, arguing that he advocated a pluralist stance between 1893 and 1894 but later shifted to a more inclusivist Advaitic position beginning in 1895.

This chapter proposes to make a fresh intervention in these ongoing debates by defending a new interpretation of Vivekananda's views on religious diversity. The first step in adjudicating these debates is to note that different interpreters of Vivekananda have employed the terms "inclusivism" and "pluralism" in a variety of ways, and often without sufficient conceptual precision or consistency. Section 1, building on the recent work of Robert McKim and Paul Griffiths, argues that it is especially important to distinguish questions about the salvific efficacy of religions from questions about their doctrinal truth. Accordingly, I first provide one set of definitions of exclusivism, inclusivism, and pluralism in terms of salvific efficacy and then provide another set of definitions in terms of doctrinal truth.

With this conceptual background in place, the remaining six sections of the chapter provide an in-depth examination of Vivekananda's views on the harmony of religions. Militating against the synchronic approach of the vast majority of scholars, I side with Green and Beckerlegge in adopting a diachronic approach, arguing that his views evolved significantly from 1893 to 1901. However, while Green and Beckerlegge distinguish only two phases in Vivekananda's thinking, I distinguish three key phases in the evolution of his views.

In section 2, I discuss the first phase from September 1893 to March 1894, during which he defended the equal salvific efficacy of the major world religions but had not yet developed fully and explicitly the philosophical underpinnings of religious pluralism. Indeed, during this early phase, he claimed that a

2 Aleaz (1993: esp. 214), Schmidt-Leukel (2017: 55–58), Paranjape (2020: 102).

3 See, for instance, Long (2017: 249–61). According to Long, Vivekananda's views occupy "a position on the boundary between inclusivism and pluralism" (2017: 256). I discuss Long's interpretation in note 15.

"universal religion" that would harmonize all the world religions was an "ideal" that did not yet exist. In section 3, I examine the second phase in Vivekananda's thinking from September 1894 to May 1895. During this period, he claimed that the universal religion *already exists* in the form of Vedānta, which he expounded in terms of the "three stages" of Dvaita, Viśiṣṭādvaita, and Advaita. He vacillated, however, between the Advaitic inclusivist view that non-Advaitic religions were lower stages on the way to Advaita and the more pluralist view that all the major world religions contained, at least in germ, all three stages of Vedānta. While Green and Beckerlegge take this to be Vivekananda's final view on the harmony of religions, I argue that this was merely a transient phase in his thinking.

As we will see in section 4, Vivekananda, by late 1895, decisively abandoned his earlier attempt to ground the harmony of religions in the three stages of Vedānta. Instead, in his work from December 1895 to 1901, he consistently conceived the Vedāntic universal religion in terms of the paradigm of four Yogas, a crucial aspect of his Integral Advaita already discussed in section 6 of the previous chapter. According to his final position, every religion corresponds to at least one of the four Yogas, each of which is a direct and independent path to salvation. On this basis, he defended not only a full-blown religious pluralism but also the radical cosmopolitan ideal of enriching our spiritual lives by learning from, and even practicing, religions other than our own. On the basis of my diachronic examination of Vivekananda's views in sections 2 through 4, I argue that the vast majority of scholars have seriously misrepresented Vivekananda's mature Vedāntic doctrine of the harmony of religions by taking it to be based on the three stages of Vedānta rather than on the four Yogas.

Section 5 examines some of the nuances of his final religious pluralist position, including his understanding of what counts as a "religion" in the first place, his view that some religions (like Haṭha-Yoga) have less salvific efficacy than others, and his response to the problem of conflicting religious truth-claims. Section 6 addresses Ninian Smart's important objection to Vivekananda's "Neo-Advaitic" harmonization of the world religions. According to Smart, the Theravāda and Mahāyāna schools of Buddhism pose a serious problem for Vivekananda since they deny the existence of any eternal underlying reality. By examining Vivekananda's various statements on Buddhism, I argue—contrary to Smart—that he explicitly accommodated the non-substantialist schools of Buddhism within the Vedāntic universal religion. Finally, section 7 demonstrates the contemporary relevance of Vivekananda's views on religious harmony by bringing him into dialogue with John Hick and Perry Schmidt-Leukel, two prominent Christian advocates of religious pluralism.

1. *Doctrinal Truth and Salvific Efficacy: Two Ways of Conceptualizing the Threefold Typology*

Before embarking on our diachronic examination of Vivekananda's views on religious diversity, we should define as precisely as possible the range of possible positions on this issue. As Robert McKim (2012) and Paul Griffiths (2001) have shown, it is crucial to distinguish questions about the *truth* of religions from questions about their *salvific efficacy*. Questions about truth concern the extent to which religions provide an accurate account of reality. Questions about salvific efficacy concern the extent to which religions are effective in leading to salvation (however salvation and effectiveness are understood).

McKim rightly notes that positions on truth and salvific efficacy are logically independent:

> Truth and salvation are very different matters. No particular position on the one entails or requires the corresponding position (or the most closely related position) on the other. For example, someone can consistently believe that members of some or all other traditions will, or can, achieve salvation, even in cases in which the distinctive beliefs associated with the relevant tradition, or traditions, are believed to be largely or even entirely mistaken. (2012: 8)

Hence, it is perfectly possible for a pluralist about salvation to be an inclusivist or even exclusivist about truth. In scholarship on Vivekananda, I believe there has been a great deal of confusion and misunderstanding concerning his views on religious diversity, in part because scholars have not been sufficiently careful about specifying whether they are defining pluralism and inclusivism in terms of truth, salvific efficacy, or both.

I define the three basic positions on the question of salvation as follows:

> *Exclusivism about Salvation* (ES): Only one religion has a high degree of salvific efficacy, and no other religion has any salvific efficacy at all.
>
> *Inclusivism about Salvation* (IS): Multiple religions have salvific efficacy, but one of them has greater salvific efficacy than all the others.
>
> *Pluralism about Salvation* (PS): Multiple religions have an equally high degree of salvific efficacy.

There are two points worth noting about the definitions of IS and PS. First, the word "multiple" means "more than one," not "all." A pluralist about salvation need not hold that *all* religions have an equally high degree of salvific efficacy.

Indeed, some proponents of salvific pluralism have argued that it is implausible to make the sweeping claim that all religions, across the board, have an equally high degree of salvific efficacy.[4] Hence, the view that some religious paths are less salvifically efficacious than others is perfectly compatible with PS, which holds only that *more than one* religion has maximal salvific efficacy. Second, in the definition of IS, the phrase "greater salvific efficacy" is deliberately vague so as to accommodate a variety of possible inclusivist views. For instance, one form of IS may hold that only one religion delivers the *highest* form of salvation, while some other religions deliver *lesser* forms of salvation. Another form of IS may hold that only one religion delivers salvation most *quickly* or *directly*, while some other religions deliver the same form of salvation, only more *slowly* or *indirectly*. Yet another form of IS may hold that only one religion delivers salvation most *easily*, while some other religions deliver the same form of salvation, only with greater *difficulties* or *impediments*.

Conceptualizing the threefold typology in terms of doctrinal religious truth is considerably more complicated for a number of reasons, one being that it is surprisingly difficult to provide plausible and coherent definitions of exclusivism and pluralism about truth. To see why this is the case, let us start provisionally with fairly intuitive and straightforward definitions of the three positions on truth (with the subscript "p" standing for "provisional"):

> *Exclusivism about Truth*$_p$ (ET$_p$): The doctrines of only one religion are true, while the doctrines of other religions are false.

> *Inclusivism about Truth*$_p$ (IT$_p$): The doctrines of only one religion *R* have the most truth, but the doctrines of other religions have some truth as well, though not as much truth as *R*.

> *Pluralism about Truth*$_p$ (PT$_p$): The doctrines of all religions are equally true.

The most obvious problem with ET$_p$ is that multiple religions *share* certain doctrines (McKim 2012: 14–34). For instance, Judaism, Christianity, and Islam all accept a monotheistic God. Therefore, a Christian who subscribes to ET$_p$ would be committed to the self-contradictory claim that the doctrine of a monotheistic God is true and not true at the same time. Meanwhile, the most obvious problem with PT$_p$ is that different religions often make conflicting truth-claims. For instance, Christians believe that Christ died on the cross, while Muslims deny this. Therefore, a Christian who subscribes to PT$_p$ would be committed to the self-contradictory claim that Christ died on the cross and did not die on the

[4] See, for instance, Hick (1988: 453; 1991: 83; 1995: 79–81) and Schmidt-Leukel (2005: 20).

cross. As McKim rightly notes, in order for pluralism about truth to be a coherent position, it most likely has to be restricted to a particular area of inquiry (2012: 103–5).

Indeed, as I will suggest in the remainder of this chapter, this is precisely Vivekananda's line of approach. He finds a unity in multiple religions with respect to their fundamental claims about ultimate reality. At the same time, he acknowledges that religions often differ with respect to relatively minor claims about issues like rebirth, historical events, and so on. For the purposes of this chapter, then, it will be useful to reformulate the definitions of exclusivism, inclusivism, and pluralism about truth with respect to fundamental claims about ultimate reality (with the subscript "f" standing for "fundamental"), and in a way that avoids the obvious problems with the provisional definitions of doctrinal exclusivism (ET_P) and doctrinal pluralism (ET_P) given earlier:

Exclusivism about Truth$_f$ (ET_f): The doctrines about ultimate reality in one religion are true, while contradictory claims in other religions are false.

Inclusivism about Truth$_f$ (IT_f): The doctrines about ultimate reality in only one religion *R* have the most truth, but the doctrines about ultimate reality in other religions have some truth as well, though not as much truth as *R*.

Pluralism about Truth$_f$ (PT_f): The doctrines about ultimate reality in multiple religions are equally true.

Several points should be noted here. It is perfectly possible for someone to subscribe to PT_f while being an inclusivist or exclusivist with respect to religious doctrines that do not concern ultimate reality. With respect to ET_f, to avoid the problem of self-contradiction entailed by ET_P discussed in the previous paragraph, ET_f has the added clause about "contradictory claims." Hence, for instance, a Christian who subscribes to ET_f allows that any doctrines in other religions that are also found in Christianity—such as the doctrine of a monotheistic God—are true.

It is also important to distinguish two kinds of inclusivism about truth (IT_f). In particular, I follow Griffiths (2001: 60–64) and McKim (2012: 48–49) in distinguishing "closed" and "open" forms of inclusivism about truth, with the latter emphasizing the value, if not the necessity, of learning from religions other than one's own. With respect to doctrines concerning ultimate reality, the closed and open forms of inclusivism can be defined as follows:

Closed Inclusivism about Truth$_f$ (CIT_f): The doctrines about ultimate reality in only one religion *R* have the most truth, but the doctrines about ultimate reality in other religions have some truth as well, though not as much truth as *R*. All the true doctrines in religions other than *R* are already known to, and explicitly taught by, *R* in some form. Therefore, nothing new can be learned by studying and coming to know what it is that any religion other than *R* teaches.[5]

Open Inclusivism about Truth$_f$ (OIT$_f$): The doctrines about ultimate reality in only one religion *R* have the most truth, but the doctrines about ultimate reality in other religions have some truth as well, though not as much truth as *R*. Religions other than *R* have some true doctrines about ultimate reality that are not already known to, and not explicitly taught by, *R* in some form. Therefore, it is beneficial for practitioners of all religions—including *R*—to learn from religions other than their own.

Finally, it should be noted that while a doctrinally inclusivist position can be either open or closed, doctrinal pluralism (PT$_f$) is *necessarily* open (OPT$_f$). The openness of PT$_f$ follows from the fact that PT$_f$, by definition, holds that religions other than our own teach different but equally true doctrines about the ultimate reality. Therefore, if we accept PT$_f$, we must accept OPT$_f$: we can gain a more complete understanding of the ultimate reality by learning from religions other than our own.

Now that we are equipped with precise definitions of the threefold typology with respect to both salvific efficacy and doctrinal truth, we can proceed to examine Vivekananda's subtly evolving views on religious diversity from 1893 to 1901.

2. *The Early Phase (September 1893 to March 1894): Salvific and Doctrinal Pluralism and the Ideal of a "Universal Religion"*

In his early lectures from September 1893 to March 1894, one of Vivekananda's primary aims was to educate Americans about the Hindu religion, removing misconceptions about it and highlighting the religious tolerance and acceptance of Hindus. In his six addresses at the World's Parliament of Religions in Chicago, delivered between September 11 and 27, 1893, he made the case that Hinduism accepts other religions because it contains the rudiments of a pluralistic "universal religion" that does not yet exist (*CW* 1:19). In this section, I will focus on his especially detailed "Paper on Hinduism" delivered at the Parliament on September 19, but I will also refer to other lectures up to March 1894, wherever relevant.

[5] Some of the language in this formulation is borrowed from Griffiths's definition of closed inclusivism in Griffiths (2001: 59).

In the "Paper on Hinduism," he identifies what he takes to be the pluralistic elements within Hinduism:

> To the Hindu, then, the whole world of religions is only a travelling, a coming up, of different men and women, through various conditions and circumstances, to the same goal. Every religion is only evolving a God out of the material man, and the same God is the inspirer of all of them. Why, then, are there so many contradictions? They are only apparent, says the Hindu. The contradictions come from the same truth adapting itself to the varying circumstances of different natures.
>
> It is the same light coming through glasses of different colours. And these little variations are necessary for purposes of adaptation. But in the heart of everything the same truth reigns. The Lord has declared to the Hindu in His incarnation as Krishna, "*I am in every religion as the thread through a string of pearls. . . .* " And what has been the result? I challenge the world to find, throughout the whole system of Sanskrit philosophy, any such expression as that the Hindu alone will be saved and not others. (*CW* 1:18)

According to Vivekananda, the "same truth"—namely, God—reigns in every religion. In support of this view, he quotes the second line of verse 7.7 of the *Bhagavad-Gītā* (*mayi sarvam idaṃ protaṃ sūtre maṇigaṇā iva*), which could be literally translated as follows: "On Me is all this here strung like pearls on a thread." While this line does not explicitly concern religious pluralism, Vivekananda gives it a pluralistic twist by adding "religion" to it: God is "in every religion." One could argue that he willfully distorts the meaning of this verse, but on a more charitable reading, he could be seen as drawing out the implications of this ancient verse for a modern, globally conscious audience.

In the same passage, he also explicitly raises the problem of conflicting religious truth-claims: "The contradictions come from the same truth adapting itself to the varying circumstances of different natures." If the same God is the central theme of all religions, why do different religions seem to hold so many conflicting views about God?[6] These doctrinal contradictions, he claims, are "only apparent," and he clarifies this idea by appealing to a metaphor: "It is the same light coming through glasses of different colours." Likening each religion to a differently colored lens, he claims that the "same light" of God, therefore, *appears* to be different when it passes through lenses of different colors. Notice the pluralistic thrust of this metaphor of lenses. Just as it would not make sense to say that red light is somehow truer than, or superior to, green or blue light, it does

[6] For detailed discussion of Vivekananda's response to the problem of conflicting religious truth-claims, see section 5 of this chapter.

not make sense to claim that one religion is superior to other religions in its conception of God. Moreover, there is no suggestion that the "light" of God shines more fully in one religion than in all the others. Hence, I think he is best understood as championing PT_f, the non-hierarchical view that the doctrines about ultimate reality in multiple religions are equally true, since they conceive and describe the same God in different ways.

Significantly, he also derives salvific pluralism (PS) explicitly from PT_f: since different religions have the same God at their center, they are equally effective paths to the same goal of God-realization. As he puts it, "the whole world of religions is only a travelling, a coming up, of different men and women, through various conditions and circumstances, to the same goal." There is no suggestion here or elsewhere that there is a single royal road to salvation that is superior to all the rest. By means of this metaphor of paths, he means to convey PS: multiple religions have an equally high degree of salvific efficacy. Accordingly, in his first Parliament address on September 11, he conveyed this metaphor of paths to the same goal by appealing to verse 7 of the *Śivamahimnastotram*: "*As the different streams having their sources in different places all mingle their water in the sea, so, O Lord, the different paths which men take through different tendencies, various though they appear, crooked or straight, all lead to Thee*" (*CW* 1:4; emphasis in original).[7] Here again, he foregrounds the pluralistic thrust of the metaphor of various religious paths by rendering, with reasonable accuracy, the original Sanskrit phrase "*rucīnāṃ vaicitryāt*" as "through different tendencies." Since different religious paths suit "different tendencies," there is no single religious path that is superior to all the others. Hence, he clearly upholds salvific pluralism (PS). At the same time, however, he notes that these "paths" are "crooked or straight" (*ṛjukuṭila*), which implies that not *all* religious paths are on a salvific par. Just as a straight path will take us to the goal faster than a crooked path, some religions can take us to the goal of salvation more quickly, or more effectively, than others can. In section 5, I will discuss some of the religious paths—including Haṭha-Yoga and corrupted forms of *vāmācāra*, the "left-handed" form of Tantra—that Vivekananda took to be salvifically inferior to the major world religions.

Toward the end of his "Paper on Hinduism," his argument takes an interesting turn, when he introduces the ideal of a "universal religion":

> The Hindu may have failed to carry out all his plans, but if there is ever to be a universal religion, it must be one which will have no location in place or time; which will be infinite like the God it will preach, and whose sun will shine upon the followers of Krishna and of Christ, on saints and sinners alike; which will not be Brahminic or Buddhistic, Christian or Mohammedan, but the sum total

[7] *rucīnāṃ vaicitryād ṛjukuṭilanānāpathajuṣāṃ nṛṇām eko gamyas tvam asi payasām arṇavam iva.*

> of all these, and still have infinite space for development; which in its catholicity will embrace in its infinite arms, and find a place for every human being, from the lowest grovelling savage not far removed from the brute, to the highest man towering by the virtues of his head and heart almost above humanity, making society stand in awe of him and doubt his human nature. It will be a religion which will have no place for persecution or intolerance in its polity, which will recognise divinity in every man and woman, and whose whole scope, whose whole force, will be created in aiding humanity to realise its own true, divine nature. (*CW* 1:19)

Vivekananda suggests that the pluralistic elements within Hinduism hint at an ideal "universal religion," a broad, second-order religion that would provide the philosophical rationale for the salvific efficacy and doctrinal truth of all first-order religions, including Hinduism, Christianity, Buddhism, and so on. Some scholars, including Wilhelm Halbfass (1991: 51), have claimed that Vivekananda straightforwardly equates this "universal" metareligion with Hinduism. However, it is clear from this passage that Vivekananda makes a distinction between Hinduism, understood as one first-order religion among others, and a second-order "universal religion" that is the "sum total of all" first-order religions, including Hinduism. It is also significant that he couches this entire paragraph in the future tense: the universal religion "*will* be infinite like the God it *will* preach," and so on. As we will see in the two subsequent sections, this is one of the key respects in which his thinking evolved after 1894, since he would soon go on to argue that the universal religion already exists in the form of Vedānta.

In his final address at the Parliament delivered on September 27, 1893, he went even further by defending a religious cosmopolitanism:

> The Christian is not to become a Hindu or a Buddhist, nor a Hindu or a Buddhist to become a Christian. But each must assimilate the spirit of the others and yet preserve his individuality and grow according to his own law of growth. (*CW* 1:24)

The strong language of "must" here is significant. Every religious practitioner "must assimilate the spirit" of other religions while remaining rooted in her own home tradition. Similarly, in his later lecture on the "Harmony of Religions" delivered in Michigan on March 22, 1894, he expressed the complementarity of all religions by using the metaphor of a symphony:

> Why take a single instrument from the great religious orchestras of the earth? Let the grand symphony go on. . . . All the religions are good since the essentials are the same. Each man should have the perfect exercise of his individuality but

> these individualities form a perfect whole. *This marvellous condition is already in existence.* Each creed has had something to add to the wonderful structure. (*CW* 2:483; emphasis added)

Since all religions center on the same Infinite God and since they all have different strengths and suit varying temperaments, each religion—which he likens to a musical instrument—contributes something valuable and unique to the "grand symphony" of religious life across the globe. Hence, Vivekananda clearly champions OPT_f, the view that we can gain a more complete understanding of the ultimate divine reality by learning from religions other than our own. Moreover, the italicized sentence at the end of this passage signals a subtle, but important, shift in his thinking about the "universal religion," which he had introduced in his earlier "Paper on Hinduism" as an ideal that had yet to be realized. By March 1894, we find him claiming that the "wonderful structure," the "perfect whole" that would provide the rationale for the complementarity of all religions, "is already in existence." Although he did not refer specifically to a "universal religion" anywhere in this lecture, I think it is plausible to assume that he had in mind this second-order "universal religion" that he had explicitly mentioned in his "Paper on Hinduism." Indeed, as we will see in subsequent sections, in his lectures from mid-1894 to 1900, he was even more explicit and emphatic in declaring that the "universal" or "eternal" religion already existed in the form of Vedānta.

In sum, between September 1893 and March 1894, Vivekananda already championed both salvific pluralism (PS) and open doctrinal pluralism (OPT_f), but he had not yet elaborated fully the tenets of the second-order "universal religion" that would provide the philosophical rationale for the harmony of all religions and for the cosmopolitan imperative to learn from religions other than our own.

3. *The Middle Phase (September 1894 to May 1895): A Vedāntic Universal Religion Based on the Three Stages of Dvaita, Viśiṣṭādvaita, and Advaita*

Vivekananda's lectures from September 1893 to mid-1894 focused on Hinduism and the need for religious tolerance. However, as Marie Louise Burke has meticulously documented, his lectures and writings after September 1894 began to focus less on Hinduism in general and more on Vedānta (Burke 1994, vol. 2: 330–93). His first recorded statement on Vedānta is contained in his lengthy "Reply to the Madras Address" (*CW* 4:331–53), which he wrote in September 1894. This document, I will argue, marked the beginning of the second phase in his thinking about the harmony of religions, which lasted until May 1895.

In the "Reply to the Madras Address," he claimed, for the first time, that the philosophical basis of the "Hindu religion" is the "three Prasthānas . . . in their different explanations as Dvaita, Viśiṣṭādvaita, or Advaita" (*CW* 4:335). These three *prasthānas* ("pillars"), he pointed out, are the foundational scriptures of Vedānta—namely, the Upaniṣads, the *Bhagavad-Gītā*, and the *Brahmasūtra* (*CW* 4:335)—which were interpreted in various ways by Śaṅkara, Rāmānuja, Madhva, and others. He went on to argue that Vedānta provides the philosophical basis for the harmony of all the world's religions:

> As absolute, Brahman alone is true; as relative truth, all the different sects, standing upon different manifestations of the same Brahman, either in India or elsewhere, are true. Only some are higher than others. Suppose a man starts straight towards the sun. At every step of his journey he will see newer and newer visions of the sun—the size, the view, and light will every moment be new, until he reaches the real sun. He saw the sun at first like a big ball, and then it began to increase in size. . . . Still is it not true that our traveller always saw the sun, and nothing but the sun? Similarly, all these various sects are true—some nearer, some farther off from the real sun which is our *ekam eva advitīyam*—"One without a second."
>
> And as the Vedas are the only scriptures which teach this real absolute God, of which all other ideas of God are but minimised and limited visions; as the *sarvalokahitaiṣiṇī* Śruti [the Vedic scripture that wishes for the good of all beings everywhere] takes the devotee gently by the hand, and leads him from one stage to another, through all the stages that are necessary for him to travel to reach the Absolute; and as all other religions represent one or other of these stages in an unprogressive and crystallized form, all the other religions of the world are included in the nameless, limitless, eternal Vedic religion. (*CW* 4:343)

In contrast to his earlier religious pluralism (OPT_f and PS), Vivekananda now champions an Advaita Vedāntic inclusivism. The Vedas alone, by which he means the Upaniṣads as interpreted from an Advaitic standpoint, teach the "real absolute God"—that is, the nondual Brahman—while the ideas of God found in other religious scriptures "are but minimised and limited visions." Hence, with respect to the truth of religious doctrines about ultimate reality, he was clearly an inclusivist (IT_f). Since the different world religions represent different "stages" on the way toward the "Absolute," they are all "included" in the "eternal Vedic religion." Strikingly, he now equates the "universal religion"—which he had earlier projected as an unrealized ideal in his "Paper on Hinduism" (*CW* 1:19)—with Vedānta, which encompasses all the world's religious and spiritual traditions as various stages, some of which "are higher than others." It is not entirely clear in this passage whether his Advaitic inclusivism about ultimate reality (IT_f) entails a corresponding inclusivism about salvation (IS). Nonetheless, his claim that the various stages are "necessary . . . to reach the Absolute" suggests salvific inclusivism (IS), since it seems to imply that the realization of the more "limited" forms of God taught in other religions is not sufficient for salvation. It is also worth noting that in this "Reply to the Madras Address," he does not explicitly state that Dvaita and Viśiṣṭādvaita are lower stages leading to the highest stage of Advaita, though he does seem to imply as much.

In his lecture on "The Religions of India" delivered in New York on December 30, 1894, he more explicitly grounded the harmony of all religions in his doctrine of "three stages":

> We believe in a God, the Father of the universe, infinite and omnipotent. But if our soul at last becomes perfect, it also must become infinite. But there is no room for two infinite unconditional beings, and hence we believe in a Personal God, and we ourselves are He. These are the three stages which every religion has taken. First we see God in the far beyond, then we come nearer to Him and give Him omnipresence so that we live in Him; and at last we recognise that we are He. The idea of an Objective God is not untrue—in fact, every idea of God, and hence every religion, is true, as each is but a different stage in the journey, the aim of which is the perfect conception of the Vedas. (*CW* 1:331)

Although he had already introduced the notion of various "stages" on the way toward the Absolute in his earlier "Reply to the Madras Address," he now claims that there are specifically "three stages" in the development of our understanding of God: (1) feeling that God is far away from us, (2) feeling that God is omnipresent, and (3) feeling that we *are* God. Moreover, in his "Reply to the Madras Address," he claimed that each religion corresponded to one particular stage on the way to the Absolute, thereby seeming to imply salvific inclusivism (IS). In this passage, by contrast, he claims that there are "three stages which *every* religion has taken." Hence, he now seems to champion salvific pluralism (PS), since a practitioner of any religion can reach the Advaitic summit through the practice of her own religion. Nonetheless, he embeds his salvific pluralism in a Vedic doctrinal inclusivism (IT_f), according to which the doctrines about ultimate reality in non-Vedic religions are less perfect and less complete than the "perfect conception" of God in the Vedas.

In his lecture on "Soul, God and Religion" delivered in Connecticut on March 8, 1895, he claimed that all religions have "the same foundation principles" (*CW* 1:318), which he proceeded to explain in terms of the "three different stages of ideas with regard to the soul and God" (*CW* 1:318):

> In the New Testament it is taught, "Our Father who art in heaven"—God living in the heavens separated from men. We are living on earth and He is living in heaven. Further on we find the teaching that He is a God immanent in nature; He is not only God in heaven, but on earth too. He is the God in us. In the Hindu philosophy we find a stage of the same proximity of God to us. But we do not stop there. There is the non-dualistic stage, in which man realises that the God he has been worshipping is not only the Father in heaven, and on earth, but that "I and my Father are one." . . . The gulf between God and man is thus bridged. Thus we find how, by knowing God, we find the kingdom of heaven within us. . . . But I and my Father are one: I find the reality in my soul. These ideas are expressed in some religions, and in others only hinted. In some they were expatriated. Christ's teachings are now very little understood in this country. If you will excuse me, I will say that they have never been very well understood. (*CW* 1:323)

He clarifies here in what sense religions other than Hinduism have expressed the three stages in our understanding of God. Although he finds all three stages in Christ's teachings in the New Testament, he claims that modern Christians have tended to misinterpret his teachings. While the three stages are explicitly stated in some religions, they are only "hinted" at in other religions. When he remarks that the three stages were "expatriated" in some religions, I think it is plausible to assume that he is making the historical claim that some religions—he likely has in mind Christianity and Islam—have downplayed or even suppressed Advaitic spiritual experience, even though Advaitic ideas are present, explicitly or implicitly, in many religions. Vivekananda might have been thinking, for instance, of the persecution and execution of the Sufi mystic Manṣur al-Ḥallāj, who famously declared, "I am the Absolute" (*ana al-Ḥaqq*) (quoted in Glassé and Smith 2001: 166).

Hence, he clearly champions salvific pluralism (PS), since he claims that a sincere practitioner of any religion can attain the highest nondual spiritual experience. With respect to religious doctrine, his position seems to lie somewhere *between* doctrinal pluralism (PT_f) and doctrinal inclusivism (IT_f). He comes close to doctrinal pluralism when he claims that some religions other than Hinduism have "expressed" the three stages. Arguably, however, he seems to imply, in a doctrinally inclusivist manner, that the most accurate and perspicuous account of the three stages is found in the Vedāntic scriptures alone, while other religious scriptures have also sometimes expressed these three stages, but in a less perspicuous manner.

A bit later in the same lecture, Vivekananda reaffirms salvific pluralism (PS) in the context of what he calls "the one universal religion":

> It is not what you read, nor what dogmas you believe that is of importance, but what you realise. . . . The end of all religions is the realising of God in the soul. That is the one universal religion. If there is one universal truth in all religions, I place it here—in realising God. Ideals and methods may differ, but that is the central point. (*CW* 1:324)

Here, he derives salvific pluralism from the "one universal religion," which holds that the aim of all religions is the realization of God. It is clear from the broader context of this lecture that what he means by God-realization is the nondual experience of God as our own Self, which can be attained through any religion by first passing through the two lower stages in which there remains some degree of separation between us and God. As he puts it, "The different stages of growth are absolutely necessary to the attainment of purity and perfection. The varying systems of religion are at bottom founded on the same ideas" (*CW* 1:323–24). It is also significant that in the first sentence of this passage, he downplays the importance of religious doctrine, emphatically subordinating it to God-realization. Hence, for Vivekananda, the fact that a particular religion does not teach the three stages in a clear way—or at all—does not substantially diminish its salvific efficacy, since a practitioner of any religion can attain the highest nondual realization if she is sincere.

In a letter to his disciple Alasinga Perumal dated May 6, 1895, Vivekananda made one final attempt to explain the harmony of religions on the basis of the three stages of Vedānta:

> Now I will tell you my discovery. All of religion is contained in the Vedānta, that is, in the three stages of the Vedānta philosophy, the Dvaita, Viśiṣṭādvaita and Advaita; one comes after the other. These are the three stages of spiritual growth in man. Each one is necessary. This is the essential of religion: the Vedānta, applied to the various ethnic customs and creeds of India, is Hinduism. The first stage, i.e. Dvaita, applied to the ideas of the ethnic groups of Europe, is Christianity; as applied to the Semitic groups, Mohammedanism. The Advaita, as applied in its Yoga-perception form, is Buddhism etc. Now by religion is meant the Vedānta; the applications must vary according to the different needs, surroundings, and other circumstances of different nations. (*CW* 5:81–82)

In this letter, he hearkens back to his position in the "Reply to the Madras Address." Conceiving Vedānta as a universal religion based on the "three stages" of "Dvaita, Viśiṣṭādvaita and Advaita," he goes on to claim that Hinduism alone encompasses all three stages, while non-Hindu religions correspond to only one of the three stages: Christianity and Islam are at the Dvaita stage, while Buddhism corresponds to the Advaita stage. In light of his earlier lectures "Soul,

God and Religion" and "The Religions of India," it seems likely that he continues to assume in this letter that all the major world religions contain all three stages, though he does not say so explicitly. Presumably, then, his position in this letter is that the predominant emphasis of devotional religions like Christianity and Islam is on dualism but that sincere practitioners of these devotional religions may eventually attain the higher stages of qualified nondualism and nondualism as well. Nonetheless, this letter does seem to imply, at best, a very narrow form of salvific pluralism: while he is willing to place Buddhism on an equal salvific footing with Advaita Vedānta, he places all devotional religions on a lower salvific footing, since they correspond to inferior spiritual stages on the way to the highest Advaitic stage of realization. Moreover, since he makes the very strong claim that all three stages are "necessary" for our "spiritual growth," all practitioners of devotional religions *must* eventually go on to attain Advaitic realization in order to achieve the highest salvation.

It is also significant that in this letter, he distinguishes the second-order universal religion of "Vedānta" from the first-order "ethnic" religion of Hinduism. Hence, he seems to subscribe to doctrinal inclusivism at both the first- and second-order levels (IT_f). He is a second-order *Vedāntic* doctrinal inclusivist, since he claims that all the various first-order religions—including Hinduism—are "contained" in Vedānta. However, he also seems to be a first-order *Hindu* doctrinal inclusivist, since he holds that Hinduism is the only first-order religion that encompasses all three stages, whereas every non-Hindu religion corresponds only to *one* of the three stages.

To sum up, in writings and lectures between September 1894 and May 1895, Vivekananda taught the harmony of all religions on the basis of a doctrinally inclusivist Advaita Vedāntic "universal religion," according to which the aim of all religions is the salvific realization of God, which is reached through the three necessary stages of Dvaita, Viśiṣṭādvaita, and Advaita. Moreover, while he granted the highest salvific efficacy to both Buddhism and Advaita Vedānta, he placed all devotional religions on a lower salvific footing, since they correspond to lower stages in a salvific hierarchy culminating in the highest Advaitic realization.

4. *The Final Phase (Late 1895 to 1901): A Vedāntic Universal Religion Based on the Four Yogas*

As far as I am aware, the passage from Vivekananda's May 6, 1895 letter quoted in the previous section was his final attempt to harmonize the world religions on the basis of the "three stages" of Vedānta. To be sure, he did continue to teach the three stages of Vedānta in subsequent years, in both India and the

West—for instance, in his 1896 lecture on "The Vedānta Philosophy" at Harvard University (*CW* 1:357–65) and his 1897 lecture on "The Vedānta in All Its Phases" in Calcutta (*CW* 1:322–54). Crucially, however, after May 1895, he never again appealed to the three stages of Vedānta *in the specific context of the harmony of religions*. Instead, in his lectures and writings from late 1895 to 1901, Vivekananda taught the harmony of all religions on the basis of a Vedāntic universal religion grounded in the four Yogas.[8] Building on section 6 of the previous chapter, this section reconstructs in detail his final view on the harmony of religions based on the four Yogas and explores why he ended up preferring this view to his earlier position based on the "three stages" of Vedānta, which he had fleetingly endorsed from mid-1894 to mid-1895.

In numerous lectures and writings from late 1895 to 1901, while Vivekananda continued to hold that Vedānta is the universal basis of all religions, he consistently theorized Vedānta not in terms of the three stages of Dvaita, Viśiṣṭādvaita, and Advaita but in terms of the four Yogas.[9] During an interview in London held on October 23, 1895, he declared: "I propound a philosophy which can serve as a basis to every possible religious system in the world . . . " (*CW* 5:187). Similarly, in a February 1897 interview held in Madras, Vivekananda asserted that "Vedānta is the rationale of all religions" (*CW* 5:212). Moreover, while he projected the "universal religion" as an ideal rather than an actuality in his 1893 "Paper on Hinduism," in his lecture "The Sages of India," delivered on February 11, 1897, he explicitly declared that "Vedānta . . . is already the existing universal religion in the world, because it teaches principles and not persons" (*CW* 3:250).

Toward the end of his lecture on "The Methods and Purpose of Religion" delivered in London on May 14, 1896, he provided one of his clearest and most succinct accounts of the Vedāntic philosophical basis of all religions:

[8] As Rambachan (1994a: 29) has noted, Keshab Chandra Sen's doctrine of a universal religion may have influenced Vivekananda. Keshab conceived his New Dispensation not as "an isolated creed, but the science which binds and explains and harmonizes all religions" (quoted in Rambachan 1994a: 29). For discussion of Keshab's universal religion, see Stevens (2018: 154–200) and A. Sharma (1998: 33–41). While both Ramakrishna and Keshab may have played a role in inspiring Vivekananda to formulate a second-order "universal religion," I believe that Vivekananda was the first to theorize a universal religion in terms of the Vedāntic framework of four Yogas, though he himself noted that the main inspiration for this idea was Ramakrishna (*CW* 4:178–82).

[9] In chronological order, his lectures and writings relating to the harmony of religions from late 1895 to 1901, all of which appeal to the four Yogas, are as follows: "Abou Ben Adhem's Ideal" (December 7, 1895; *CW* 9:482–83); "The Ideal of a Universal Religion: How It Must Embrace Different Types of Minds and Methods" (January 12, 1896; *CW* 2:375–96); "Four Paths of Yoga" (essay written during his first visit to America [exact date unknown]; *CW* 8:152–55); "The Doctrine of the Swami" (January 19, 1896; *CW* 9:484); "The Ideal of a Universal Religion" (January 31, 1896; *CW* 9:484–87); "Ramkrishna Paramahamsa" (fall 1896; *CW* 4:160–87 [title in *CW*: "My Master"]); "The Ideal of a Universal Religion" (March 4, 1896; *CW* 9:487–88); "Philosophy of Freedom" (March 21, 1896; *CW* 9:489–91); "Ideal of a Universal Religion" (March 26, 1896; *CW* 9:493–96); "The Methods and Purpose of Religion" (May 14, 1896; *CW* 6:3–17); "The Way to the Realisation of a Universal Religion" (January 28, 1900; *CW* 2:359–74); "Hinduism and Sri Ramakrishna" (1901; *BCW* 6:3 / *CW* 6:181–82).

> The plan of Vedānta, therefore, is: first, to lay down the principles, map out for us the goal, and then to teach us the method by which to arrive at the goal, to understand and realise religion.
>
> Again, these methods must be various. Seeing that we are so various in our natures, the same method can scarcely be applied to any two of us in the same manner. We have idiosyncrasies in our minds, each one of us; so the method ought to be varied. Some, you will find, are very emotional in their nature; some very philosophical, rational; others cling to all sorts of ritualistic forms—want things which are concrete. . . . If there were only one method to arrive at truth, it would be death for everyone else who is not similarly constituted. Therefore the methods should be various. Vedānta understands that and wants to lay before the world different methods through which we can work. . . . Take any path you like; follow any prophet you like; but have only that method which suits your own nature, so that you will be sure to progress. (*CW* 6:15–17)

In his exposition of the Vedāntic universal religion throughout this lecture, the "three stages" of Vedānta are conspicuously absent. Instead, in the first sentence of this passage, he specifies that the Vedāntic universal religion has three fundamental components: (1) the "principles" underlying all religions, (2) the "goal" of all religions, and (3) the various "methods" by which we can all reach this goal. Earlier in the lecture, he explains that the "grand principle" of Vedānta is "that there is that One in whom this whole universe of matter and mind finds its unity," known as "God, or Brahman, or Allah, or Jehovah, or any other name" (*CW* 6:11). The fundamental principle of Vedānta, in other words, is that the same Infinite God is conceived differently by different people, and called by various names, depending on their temperament, spiritual capacity, and individual circumstances. We should recall that this principle is identical to the foundational tenet of Vivekananda's Integral Advaita philosophy, discussed in section 2 of the previous chapter. The "goal" mapped out by Vedānta is the salvific realization of the impersonal-personal Infinite God in whatever aspect or form one prefers (*CW* 6:13–14). Finally, Vedānta teaches that there are various "methods" for attaining this common goal of God-realization. Crucially, he does not privilege any one method over all the others. Instead, he claims that any given religious practitioner will make the most rapid spiritual progress by adopting the method that best suits his or her particular "nature"—be it "emotional," "philosophical," "ritualistic," or otherwise.

Although he did not explicitly explain these various methods in terms of the four Yogas in this particular lecture, he did so in numerous other lectures and writings from 1896 to 1900. Take, for instance, this passage from his lecture on "The Ideal of Karma-Yoga" delivered in New York on January 10, 1896:

> The grandest idea in the religion of Vedānta is that we may reach the same goal by different paths; and these paths I have generalized into four, namely those of work, love, psychology, and knowledge. But you must at the same time remember that these divisions are not very marked and quite exclusive of each other. Each blends into the other. But according to the type which prevails, we name the divisions. It is not that you can find men who have no other faculty than that of work, nor that you can find men who are no more than devoted worshippers only, nor that there are men who have no more than mere knowledge. These divisions are made in accordance with the type or the tendency that prevails in a man. We have found that, in the end, all these four paths converge and become one. All religions and all methods of work and worship lead us to one and the same goal. (*CW* 1:108)

According to Vivekananda, we can reach the same goal of God-realization through "different paths," which he generalizes into the four Yogas: Karma-Yoga ("work"), Bhakti-Yoga ("love"), Rāja-Yoga ("psychology"), and Jñāna-Yoga ("knowledge"). Two points are worth noting. First of all, he is careful to emphasize that his division of paths into the four Yogas is not meant to be restrictive or exhaustive. Indeed, in a statement entitled "Four Paths of Yoga," which he wrote at some point during his first visit to America, he explicitly notes that there may be religious paths that do not fall neatly into any one of the four Yogas. As he puts it, the "Yogas, though divided into various groups, can *principally* be classed into four . . . " (*CW* 8:152; emphasis added). His view seems to be, then, that most, but not necessarily all, of the various religious paths can be grouped into one of the four Yogas. Second, he notes that the four Yogas should not be understood as airtight compartments. Each Yoga, as he puts it, "blends into the other," since each Yoga contains elements of the other three Yogas to varying degrees. Moreover, the frequently overlapping nature of the Yogas reflects the fact that no human being exclusively embodies only one personality type. Nonetheless, he claims that most human beings exhibit a prevailing "type" or "tendency," which corresponds to one of the four Yogas, while also having other tendencies to a lesser extent.

In his lecture "Ramkrishna Paramahamsa,"[10] delivered in Wimbledon, England in the fall of 1896, he provided a very clear and detailed exposition of a Vedāntic universal religion based on the four Yogas. As we will see, it is hardly

[10] The text entitled "My Master" (*CW* 4:154–87) in the *Complete Works* actually combines two of Vivekananda's lectures: "Sri Ramakrishna: His Life and Teachings" (delivered in New York on February 23, 1896) and "Ramkrishna Paramahamsa" (delivered in Wimbledon, England, in the fall of 1896). His Wimbledon lecture was first published in 1897, in two parts, in the journal *Brahmavadin*. On this basis, we can determine that his Wimbledon lecture, to which I refer here, comprises *CW* 4:160–87.

a coincidence that we find this exposition in the context of a lecture on his guru Ramakrishna. After briefly describing Ramakrishna's practice of various Hindu traditions as well as his practice of Islam and Christianity, Vivekananda observes: "Thus from actual experience, he came to know that the goal of every religion is the same, that each is trying to teach the same thing, the difference being largely in method and still more in language" (*CW* 4:174). He is alluding here, of course, to Ramakrishna's teachings on the harmony of religions, which I discussed briefly in section 2 of chapter 1.

On the basis of his varied spiritual experiences of God culminating in the unique state of *vijñāna*, Ramakrishna taught that the Infinite God is both impersonal (*nirguṇa*) and personal (*saguṇa*), both with form (*sākāra*) and without form (*nirākāra*). From this expansive standpoint of *vijñāna*, he taught the harmony of all religious paths: "God is infinite, and the paths to God are infinite" (*K* 511 / *G* 506). Since God is infinite, there must be correspondingly infinite ways of approaching and ultimately realizing God.[11] According to Ramakrishna, the same Infinite God is conceived and described by different people in different ways, depending on their particular temperament and cultural background.

Ramakrishna was fond of appealing to two parables to illustrate this truth: that of the chameleon and the blind men and the elephant. According to the chameleon parable, there is a chameleon on a tree which changes colors throughout the day, but different people who see the chameleon at various times think that the chameleon is only one particular color—say, green, or red, or colorless—and then quarrel among themselves about the color of the chameleon (*K* 101 / *G* 149–50). Ramakrishna draws the following lesson from this parable:

> In like manner, one who constantly thinks of God can know God's real nature; he alone knows that God reveals Himself to seekers in various forms and aspects. God is personal (*saguṇa*) as well as impersonal (*nirguṇa*). Only the man who lives under the tree knows that the chameleon can appear in various colors, and he knows, further, that the animal at times has no color at all. It is the others who suffer from the agony of futile argument. (*K* 101 / *G* 149–50)

The various people seeing the chameleon as only one color represent the various religions, each of which conceives God from a true but partial standpoint. The man sitting under the tree, who tells these people that they are all correct and that they need not quarrel with one another, represents the *vijñānī*—such as Ramakrishna himself—who has realized various forms and aspects of God and hence affirms on the basis of his own spiritual experience that all religions describe the same God in different ways.

[11] I discuss Ramakrishna's views on religious pluralism in detail in Maharaj (2018: 85–152).

Ramakrishna's parable of the blind men and the elephant has a similar structure and message (*K* 151 / *G* 191). Just as each of the five blind men touches a different part of the elephant and takes that part to represent the elephant as a whole, religious practitioners often make the mistake of assuming that the particular aspect of God they value or experience represents the whole of God. Moreover, just as the person with sight can see the elephant as a whole, the *vijñānī* sees that all religions—represented by the blind men—make contact with a real aspect of God, though none of them captures the whole of God, who is infinite and illimitable.

Vivekananda often appealed to the chameleon parable and the parable of the blind men and the elephant to illustrate the harmony of religions.[12] However, here in the "Ramkrishna Paramahamsa" lecture, instead of mentioning these parables, he provides a highly original interpretation of Ramakrishna's teachings on the harmony of religions:

> The second idea that I learnt from my Master, and which is perhaps the most vital, is the wonderful truth that the religions of the world are not contradictory or antagonistic. They are but various phases of one eternal religion. That one eternal religion is applied to different planes of existence, is applied to the opinions of various minds and various races. There never was my religion or yours, my national religion or your national religion; there never existed many religions, there is only the one. One infinite religion existed all through eternity and will ever exist, and this religion is expressing itself in various countries in various ways. Therefore we must respect all religions and we must try to accept them all as far as we can. Religions manifest themselves not only according to race and geographical position, but according to individual powers. In one man religion is manifesting itself as intense activity, as work. In another it is manifesting itself as intense devotion, in yet another, as mysticism, in others as philosophy, and so forth. It is wrong when we say to others, "Your methods are not right."
>
> To learn this central secret that the truth may be one and yet many at the same time, that we may have different visions of the same truth from different standpoints, is exactly what must be done. Then, instead of antagonism to anyone, we shall have infinite sympathy with all. Knowing that as long as there are different natures born in this world, the same religious truth will require different adaptations, we shall understand that we are bound to have forbearance with each other. (*CW* 4:180–81)

[12] See, for instance, *CW* 6:120 and *CW* 7:416–17.

Strikingly, while Ramakrishna himself rarely, if ever, appealed to an "eternal religion" when teaching the harmony of religions, Vivekananda claims that he learned from his guru that there is only "one eternal religion," which expresses and manifests itself in the form of the various religious traditions of the world. As Vivekananda puts it in the final sentence of the same lecture, "He [Ramakrishna] left every religion undisturbed because he had realised that in reality they are all part and parcel of the one eternal religion" (*CW* 4:187). The "central secret" of this eternal religion taught to him by Ramakrishna is that different religions have "different visions" of the same Infinite God "from different standpoints." In effect, then, Vivekananda identifies the eternal religion with the expansive viewpoint of the *vijñānī*, who has realized various forms and aspects of the same God—the one represented, in Ramakrishna's two parables, by the person sitting under the tree who sees the chameleon in various colors and by the sighted person who sees the elephant as a whole. Hence, for Vivekananda, the eternal religion is a second-order religion, or a metareligion, that explains and justifies the salvific efficacy of all the various first-order religions.

In this lecture, he does not explicitly equate the "eternal religion" with Vedānta. Nonetheless, it is evident from this passage that the Vedāntic universal religion he expounds in numerous other lectures from 1896 to 1901—grounded, as we have seen, in the principle of an Infinite God and the doctrine of four Yogas—is identical to the second-order "eternal religion" taught to him by Ramakrishna. Accordingly, he claims, in this passage from his "Ramkrishna Paramahamsa" lecture, that the eternal religion encompasses all the methods taught by the various first-order religions, which he groups into the four Yogas: "work," "devotion," "mysticism," and "philosophy."

A bit earlier in the same lecture, Vivekananda explains precisely how the framework of four Yogas serves as the basis of the harmony of religions: "He [Ramakrishna] had the same sympathy for all sects; he had found the harmony between them. A man may be intellectual, or devotional, or mystic, or active; *the various religions represent one or the other of these types*" (*CW* 4:178; emphasis added). The final clause is crucial to understanding Vivekananda's final view on the harmony of religions: each religion corresponds to one of the four Yogas.[13] He presupposes here his fundamental thesis—discussed in section 6 of the previous chapter—that each of the four Yogas is a "direct and independent" path to salvation, since each Yoga is equally capable of removing the mental impurities that prevent us from realizing and manifesting our own innate divinity (*CW* 1:93). Salvific pluralism (PS) follows directly from this thesis: since each Yoga has

[13] He similarly claims, in his undated written piece "Four Paths of Yoga," that "each religion represents one" of the "systems of Yoga" (*CW* 8:152).

equal salvific efficacy, and each religion corresponds to one of the Yogas, all of the major world religions have equal salvific efficacy.

Indeed, a few pages later in the same lecture, Vivekananda explicitly champions salvific pluralism and contrasts it with a "patronising" inclusivism:

> "As different rivers, taking their start from different mountains, running crooked or straight, all come and mingle their waters in the ocean, so the different sects, with their different points of view, at last all come unto Thee." This is not a theory, it has to be recognised, but not in that patronising way which we see with some people: "Oh yes, there are some very good things in it. These are what we call the ethnical religions. These ethnical religions have some good in them." Some even have the most wonderfully liberal idea that other religions are all little bits of a prehistoric evolution, but "ours is the fulfilment of things." One man says, because his is the oldest religion, it is the best: another makes the same claim, because his is the latest.
>
> We have to recognise that each one of them has the same saving power as the other. What you have heard about their difference, whether in the temple or in the church, is a mass of superstition. The same God answers all. . . . (*CW* 4:182)

After quoting the seventh verse of *Śivamahimnastotram*, he points out that the doctrine that various religions are different paths leading to the same goal can be interpreted either inclusivistically or pluralistically. He then goes on to champion the salvific pluralist view (PS) that each world religion "has the same saving power as the other." Tellingly, he contrasts his own salvific pluralist position with the "patronising" inclusivist view (IS) that one's own religion is the highest one, while other religions are "all little bits of a prehistoric evolution"—that is, lower stages leading eventually to the one highest religion, which alone affords salvation. Vivekananda may have had in mind, in part, Śaṅkara's Advaitic inclusivist view that Jñāna-Yoga alone leads directly to *mokṣa*, while the other three Yogas lead indirectly to *mokṣa* by purifying and concentrating the mind, thereby making one fit to practice the highest path of Jñāna-Yoga.

However, I believe his description of a "patronising" inclusivist position also serves as an *implicit autocritique* of his own earlier attempt to harmonize the world religions on the basis of the three stages of Vedānta. As we should recall from the previous section, between mid-1894 and mid-1895, he sometimes held the salvific inclusivist view that theistic religions like Christianity and Islam occupied the lowest stage in the Vedāntic hierarchy of Dvaita, Viśiṣṭādvaita, and Advaita. It is possible that one of the reasons he soon went on to abandon this inclusivist position in favor of his final pluralist view is that he recognized that his "three stages" view patronizingly relegated non-Advaitic religions to a salvifically inferior position vis-à-vis Advaita Vedānta. It is also significant that Vivekananda's explicit critique of salvific inclusivism occurred in a lecture on Ramakrishna, since it may very well have been his renewed reflection on Ramakrishna's pluralist teachings that led him to recognize that his own earlier inclusivist position was not in line with his guru's religious pluralism, which was not based on any kind of hierarchy of lower and higher stages.

Similarly, in his lecture "The Ideal of a Universal Religion: How It Must Embrace Different Types of Minds and Methods," delivered in New York on January 12, 1896, he harmonized the world religions by appealing to a universal religion based not on the three stages of Vedānta but on the four Yogas (*CW* 2:387–88). In this lecture, he provided another clue as to why he moved away from his earlier inclusivist position:

> That plan alone is practical, which does not destroy the individuality of any man in religion and at the same time shows him a point of union with all others. But so far, all the plans of religious harmony that have been tried, while proposing to take in all the various views of religion, have, in practice, tried to bind them all down to a few doctrines, and so have produced more new sects, fighting, struggling, and pushing against each other. (*CW* 2:384)

He notes here that previous efforts to harmonize the world religions have failed because they were based on rigid and narrow doctrinal frameworks that failed to honor the "individuality" and self-understanding of the various religions. He may have been thinking here, in part, of his own previous attempt to harmonize the world religions on the basis of the doctrine of the three stages of Dvaita, Viśiṣṭādvaita, and Advaita. By 1896, he seems to have recognized the danger of "binding" all religions down to this single controversial doctrine, which not all—or even most—religions would accept.

By replacing the framework of three stages with that of the four Yogas, Vivekananda not only broadened the Vedāntic universal religion from a doctrinal standpoint but also avoided his earlier "patronising" relegation of theistic religions to inferior stages in an Advaitic hierarchy. Accordingly, beginning in late 1895, he consistently upheld both doctrinal pluralism and salvific pluralism. The doctrines in numerous religions are equally true, since they conceive and describe the same ultimate reality from different, but equally accurate, standpoints (PT_f). Moreover, numerous religions have the "same saving power," since they correspond to one or more of the four Yogas, each of which is a direct and independent path to salvation (PS).

Significantly, the various analogies he employed to illustrate the harmony of religions in lectures from late 1895 to 1901 have a pluralistic, non-hierarchical thrust. In "The Ideal of a Universal Religion" (1896), he employed two analogies to convey doctrinal pluralism and salvific pluralism respectively. The first analogy is as follows:

> We must learn that truth may be expressed in a hundred thousand ways, and that each of these ways is true as far as it goes. We must learn that the same thing can be viewed from a hundred different standpoints, and yet be the same thing. . . . Suppose we all go with vessels in our hands to fetch water from a lake. One has a cup, another a jar, another a bucket, and so forth, and we all fill our vessels. The water in each case naturally takes the form of the vessel carried by each of us. . . . So it is in the case of religion; our minds are like these vessels, and each one of us is trying to arrive at the realisation of God. God is like that water filling these different vessels, and in each vessel the vision of God comes in the form of the vessel. Yet He is One. He is God in every case. (*CW* 2:383)

From Vivekananda's perspective, various religions provide apparently conflicting conceptions of God because the same God is conceived in a variety of ways by people of varying natures. Hence, different religious conceptions of God are actually complementary, since they all describe the same ultimate reality from "different standpoints." Just as it would not make sense to say that a jar holds water better than a cup does, it is wrong to claim that one religion's conception of God is truer than that found in other religions. Hence, by means of this analogy of water and differently shaped vessels, Vivekananda expresses a pluralist stance toward various religious conceptions of ultimate reality (PT_f).

A bit later in the same lecture, he invokes a striking analogy in order to convey *salvific* pluralism (PS):

> If it be true that God is the centre of all religions, and that each of us is moving towards Him along one of these radii, then it is certain that all of us *must* reach that centre. And at the centre, where all the radii meet, all our differences will cease; but until we reach there, differences there must be. All these radii converge to the same centre. One, according to his nature, travels along one of these lines, and another, along another; and if we all push onward along our own lines, we shall surely come to the centre, because, "All roads lead to Rome." (*CW* 2:384–85)

By likening the various religions to different "radii" converging toward the same "centre" of God-realization, he affirms a robust salvific pluralism, since the circumferential endpoints of all the radii are equidistant from the center, which implies that the various religions have equal salvific efficacy. Each radius, representing one particular religion, is different from all the other radii, since different religions are suited to different natures. Nonetheless, since every religion corresponds to one of the four Yogas, each of which has equal salvific efficacy, all *religions* also have the same salvific efficacy.

In his lecture "The Way to the Realisation of a Universal Religion," delivered at the Universalist Church in Pasadena, California, on January 28, 1900, he came up with an analogy tailored to the venue to convey doctrinal pluralism (PT_f):

> Take four photographs of this church from different corners: how different they would look, and yet they would all represent this church. In the same way, we are all looking at truth from different standpoints, which vary according to our birth, education, surroundings, and so on. (*CW* 2:366)

The pluralist thrust of this analogy is clear: just as all four photographs of the church from different corners are equally accurate, all religions provide equally accurate accounts of the ultimate reality. People in different religious traditions describe the same ultimate reality from "different standpoints," depending on their individual temperament and circumstances.

Shortly thereafter, Vivekananda goes on to convey salvific pluralism (PS) by appealing to a different analogy:

> The greater the number of sects, the more chance of people getting religion. In the hotel, where there are all sorts of food, everyone has a chance to get his appetite satisfied. So I want sects to multiply in every country, that more people may have a chance to be spiritual. (*CW* 2:368)

Just as different kinds of food appeal to people with varying preferences, different religious sects appeal to people with varying temperaments and preferences. The pluralistic thrust of this analogy is clear from the fact that every person, no matter what kind of food he eats, gets "his appetite satisfied." Just as it would be foolish to claim that one type of food is objectively better at satisfying a person's appetite than other types of food, it is foolish to claim that one particular religion has greater salvific efficacy than all other religions.

It is, of course, perfectly possible to accept salvific pluralism and still maintain that there is little or no need to learn from religions other than one's own. After all, if my own religion is as salvifically efficacious as any other, why should I even bother to learn about other religious paths? For Vivekananda, however, the Vedāntic universal religion based on the four Yogas provides a philosophical rationale for deepening salvific pluralism into a full-blown religious cosmopolitanism—the endeavor to learn from, and assimilate the spirit of, other religions.

As we saw in section 2, he had already advocated a form of religious cosmopolitanism as early as September 1893, when he called on every religious practitioner to "assimilate the spirit" of other religions (*CW* 1:24). However, in that early phase in his thinking, he had not yet specified precisely what the "spirit" of different religions consists in, and he had not yet explicitly and fully worked out the philosophical basis for such a religious cosmopolitanism. I would argue that it was only after he had developed a Vedāntic universal religion based on the four Yogas in late 1895 that he was able to provide a strong philosophical justification for a radical religious cosmopolitanism.

I will now briefly reconstruct the four main facets of Vivekananda's mature doctrine of religious cosmopolitanism, presented in lectures from late 1895 to 1901. First, since different religions provide different, but complementary, accounts of one and the same Infinite Divine Reality, every religious practitioner can enrich and broaden her understanding of God by learning about other religions. From Vivekananda's standpoint, we can all think of God in the way we prefer, but we should never *limit* God to what we can understand of Him. In an important statement made in 1897 or 1898, he notes that he learned this insight from his guru: "If there is anything which Sri Ramakrishna has urged us to give up as carefully as lust and wealth, it is the limiting of the infinitude of God by circumscribing it within narrow bounds" (*CW* 7:412). Vivekananda was thinking, of course, of Ramakrishna's oft-repeated teaching that "there is no limit to God" (*tā̐r iti nai*) (*K* 997 / *G* 920). According to Vivekananda, the greatest help in remaining alive to God's infinitude and illimitability is to acquaint ourselves with various religious views of ultimate reality, ranging from the loving personal God of theistic traditions to the Śūnyatā of Mahāyāna Buddhism and the impersonal nondual Brahman of Advaita Vedānta (OPT_f).

Second, in his lecture "The Way to the Realisation of a Universal Religion" (1900), he claims that every religion has a unique "soul," which he defines as a "particular excellence" (*CW* 2:370). He then goes on to specify that the soul of Islam is universal brotherhood, the soul of Hinduism is God-realization, and the soul of Christianity is purification of mind through social service (*CW* 2:371–72). Since the souls of all religions are "supplementary" rather than "contradictory," we should strive to enrich our own spiritual life by assimilating the unique soul of every religion (*CW* 2:365).

The highly original third and fourth facets of Vivekananda's religious cosmopolitanism are grounded directly in the paradigm of four Yogas. In section 6 of the previous chapter, I mentioned briefly his view that although each of the four Yogas is a direct and independent path to salvation, it is better to *combine* all four Yogas to the best of our ability. In his summer 1896 class "Lessons on Bhakti-Yoga" held in London, he elaborates the cosmopolitan implications of this view:

> We want to become harmonious beings, with the psychical, spiritual, intellectual, and working (active) sides of our nature equally developed. Nations and individuals typify one of these sides or types and cannot understand more than

> that one. They get so built up into one ideal that they cannot see any other. The ideal is really that we should become many-sided. . . . We must be as broad as the skies, as deep as the ocean; we must have the zeal of the fanatic, the depth of the mystic, and the width of the agnostic. . . . We must become many-sided, indeed we must become protean in character, so as not only to tolerate, but to do what is much more difficult, to sympathise, to enter into another's path, and feel *with him* in his aspirations and seeking after God. (*CW* 6:137–38)

For Vivekananda, even though any one of the Yogas can take us to salvation, we can accelerate our spiritual progress and develop a "many-sided" personality by combining the four Yogas. Moreover, since each religion corresponds to one of the four Yogas, and the ideal is to combine all four Yogas to the fullest extent, the greatest help in realizing this ideal is to learn from—and, indeed, even *practice*—religions other than our own. Hence, Vivekananda's doctrine of the four Yogas serves as the basis for a radicalized version of what contemporary theologians call "multiple religious belonging" (Oostveen 2018; Drew 2011). While remaining firmly rooted in our own religious tradition, we should strive not only to incorporate the spiritual practices of other religions into our own practice but also to remain open to all the new religions that are yet to come.

He makes this point forcefully at the end of "The Way to the Realisation of a Universal Religion" (1900):

> Our watchword, then, will be acceptance, and not exclusion. . . . I accept all religions that were in the past, and worship with them all; I worship God with every one of them, in whatever form they worship Him. I shall go to the mosque of the Mohammedan; I shall enter the Christian's church and kneel before the crucifix; I shall enter the Buddhistic temple, where I shall take refuge in Buddha and in his Law. I shall go into the forest and sit down in meditation with the Hindu, who is trying to see the Light which enlightens the heart of every one.
>
> Not only shall I do all these, but I shall keep my heart open for all that may come in the future. . . . We stand in the present, but open ourselves to the infinite future. We take in all that has been in the past, enjoy the light of the present, and open every window of the heart for all that will come in the future. (*CW* 2:373–74)

According to Vivekananda, the perfect embodiment of this religious cosmopolitan ideal was Ramakrishna, who had practiced multiple religions and fully harmonized all four Yogas. As he puts it, "Such a unique personality, such a synthesis of the utmost of Jñāna, Yoga, Bhakti and Karma, has never before appeared among mankind" (*CW* 7:412).

To understand the fourth facet of Vivekananda's religious cosmopolitanism, we should recall his assertion that his grouping of religious methods into four Yogas is a "generalisation" and that there are, in fact, "thousands and thousands of varieties of minds and inclinations" (*CW* 2:387). Indeed, in numerous lectures, he goes even further. He claims that every single human being has a unique nature, and he derives from this premise the radical cosmopolitan ideal that every person should have his or her own individualized religion. Take, for instance, this passage from his lecture on "The Methods and Purpose of Religion" (1896):

> Seeing that we are so various in our natures, the same method can scarcely be applied to any two of us in the same manner. We have idiosyncrasies in our minds, each one of us; so the method ought to be varied. . . . It is a most glorious dispensation of the Lord that there are so many religions in the world; and would to God that these would increase every day, until every man had a religion unto himself! (*CW* 6:15)

Since every person has a unique nature, the cosmopolitan ideal is for each person to have a religion that is tailor-made, as it were, for her own individual nature. In an undated lecture on "Religion and Science," he makes this point very succinctly: "No man is born to any religion; he has a religion in his own soul" (*CW* 6:82). In "The Ideal of a Universal Religion" (1896), he similarly claims: "No sooner does a religion start than it breaks into pieces. The process is for the religion to go on dividing until each man has his own religion, until each man has thought out his own thoughts and carved out for himself his own religion" (*CW* 9:488).[14] The historical fact that virtually every religion has eventually split into different sects and schools, he claims, constitutes strong evidence that different people, even *within* a particular religion, have different natures. The logical—and, indeed, desirable—endpoint of such a process is that each person will have "carved out" a religious framework that is uniquely suited to his or her particular nature and temperament. Moreover, we will be in a better position to carve out our own individualized religion by learning about the spiritual practices taught in other religions.

Before concluding this section, it is important to address some philosophical complexities in Vivekananda's mature understanding of the Vedāntic universal religion and its relation to the various world religions, including Hinduism. Significantly, he is careful to distinguish the Vedāntic universal religion from Hinduism. Take, for instance, this passage from his lecture "The Methods and Purpose of Religion" (1896):

[14] For similar statements, see *CW* 2:364 and *CW* 6:17.

> Vedānta . . . preaches the one principle and admits various methods. It has nothing to say against anyone—whether you are a Christian, or a Buddhist, or a Jew, or a Hindu. . . . It only preaches the principle which is the background of every religion. . . . (*CW* 6:17)

It is clear from such passages that he conceives "Vedānta" as a second-order universal religion that propounds the equal truth and salvific efficacy of various first-order religions, *including* Hinduism. Indeed, in his 1897 lectures in India, one of his primary aims was to harmonize the various conflicting Hindu sects by explaining to all Hindus the underlying Vedāntic universal religion that united all these sects. He put this point as follows in his lecture "The Future of India," delivered in Madras on February 14, 1897:

> All of us have to be taught that we Hindus—dualists, qualified monists, or monists, Śaivas, Vaiṣṇavas, or Pāśupatas—to whatever denomination we may belong, have certain common ideas behind us, and that the time has come when for the well-being of ourselves, for the well-being of our race, we must give up all our little quarrels and differences. (*CW* 3:287–88)

Hence, his position is that the second-order Vedāntic universal religion, based on the four Yogas, establishes the equal salvific efficacy and doctrinal truth of the various first-order world religions, including all the numerous sects of Hinduism.

At the same time, however, Vedānta itself is, of course, a philosophy found *within* Hinduism—in particular, as Vivekananda often emphasized, in the Upaniṣads, the *Bhagavad-Gītā*, and the *Brahmasūtra* (*CW* 3:395–96). He makes this clear in his 1901 essay "Hinduism and Sri Ramakrishna," originally written in Bengali:

> The Veda is the only exponent of the universal religion (*sārvajanīn dharma*). Although the supersensuous vision of truths is to be met with in some measure in our Purāṇas and Itihāsas and in the religious scriptures of other races, still the fourfold scripture known among the Aryan race as the Veda being the first, the most complete, and the most undistorted collection of spiritual truths, deserves to occupy the highest place among all scriptures, command the respect of all nations of the earth, and furnish the justification (*pramāṇabhūmi*) of all their respective scriptures. . . . It is the Jñāna-kāṇḍa [the knowledge portion of the Veda, i.e., the Upaniṣads] or the Vedānta only that has for all time commanded recognition for leading men across Māyā and bestowing salvation on them through the practice of Yoga, Bhakti, Jñāna, or Niṣkāma Karma [selfless work]; and as its validity and authority remain unaffected by any limitations of time,

> place or persons, it is the only exponent of the universal and eternal religion for all humanity (*sārvalaukik, sārvabhauma o sārvakālik dharmer ekmātra upadeṣṭā*). (*BCW* 6:3 / *CW* 6:181–82; translation modified)

According to Vivekananda, the Vedāntic scriptures occupy the "highest place" among the world's religious scriptures, since they alone teach the "universal religion" based on the four Yogas. In such passages, he clearly subscribes to Hindu inclusivism with respect to doctrinal truth (IT_f): Hinduism is more "complete" and comprehensive than other world religions, since it alone teaches the Vedāntic universal religion, which harmonizes all the various religions. Hence, Vivekananda's views on Hinduism's status vis-à-vis other religions are complex. On the one hand, when he conceives Hinduism as a category denoting the various Hindu sects (like Śāktism, Gauḍīya Vaiṣṇavism, Advaita Vedānta, Dvaita Vedānta, and so on), he holds the pluralist view that all the world religions—including all the various sects within Hinduism—have equally true doctrines regarding ultimate reality (PT_f). On the other hand, when he emphasizes that the Vedāntic universal religion is found within Hinduism alone, he holds the inclusivist position that Hinduism provides a more comprehensive and complete account of ultimate reality than any other religion does (IT_f). At the same time, he clearly and consistently champions the *salvific* pluralist position that all the major world religions have equal and maximal salvific efficacy (PS), and he in no way privileges Hinduism over other religions in this regard.[15]

Vivekananda's appeal to a second-order "universal religion" raises another important issue that has been discussed by recent philosophers and theologians—most fully and persuasively, I believe, by Robert McKim. McKim rightly argues that there is necessarily an "inclusivist dimension to pluralism," since the very acceptance of pluralism about the doctrinal truth of different first-order religions (PT_f) entails a *second-order inclusivism* about truth (IT_f):

> According to pluralism about truth, one can look to the other relevant religious traditions to supplement the account of reality offered by any single tradition, thereby arriving at an account of reality that is more complete than that proposed by any particular tradition. . . . Someone who embraces the full pluralist

[15] Long has argued that Vivekananda's views occupy "a position on the boundary between inclusivism and pluralism," since passages like the one above suggest a "Vedāntic inclusivism," while Vivekananda elsewhere champions the pluralist view that different religions are so many paths to the same goal (2017: 256). However, Long's definitions of inclusivism and pluralism are somewhat imprecise. He defines inclusivism in terms of doctrinal truth: it is "the view that one's own religion possesses a final, definitive truth available only imperfectly in other traditions . . . " (2017: 250). Confusingly, however, Long defines pluralism in terms of both doctrinal truth and salvific efficacy: pluralism, he claims, "sees the world's religions as more or less equal in terms of their ability to express and embody truth *and* salvation" (2017: 250; emphasis added).

> account will be an inclusivist with respect to the particular accounts of the various traditions that are being accommodated in that account. The truths of any particular tradition, however significant they may be, are incomplete and hence second-class in comparison with the more comprehensive picture offered by pluralism and are incorporated within the comprehensive pluralist analysis. . . . Actually, someone who asserts PT2 [pluralism about truth] wears two hats. She is a member of a religious tradition, and she believes that tradition to do very well in terms of truth and believes other traditions to do equally well. But she also subscribes to a deeper truth, a metalevel truth that other members of her own tradition, not to mention members of other traditions, may not be aware of. As a pluralist, therefore, she feels she understands the situation of others better than they themselves understand it. (2012: 105–6)

McKim's cogent reasoning here can be applied easily enough to Vivekananda's approach to religious diversity. According to Vivekananda's first-order PT_f, many first-order religions—including all the various Hindu sects, Christianity, Islam, and so on—have equally true doctrines about ultimate reality. However, he justifies PT_f by appealing to a second-order Vedāntic "universal religion"—what McKim calls a "metalevel truth"—which is *inclusivist* with respect to the truth of all first-order religions. We need only recall the first principle of Vivekananda's "universal religion," according to which different religious accounts of the ultimate reality are equally correct, because they are different but complementary ways of viewing the same Infinite God. This first principle, therefore, is inclusivist, since it provides an account of ultimate reality that is *more comprehensive* than the partial accounts of ultimate reality found in any given first-order religion. Likewise, according to Vivekananda, while different first-order religions typically correspond to only one of the four Yogas, the Vedāntic universal religion encompasses *all four* Yogas. Bearing in mind this distinction between first- and second-order levels, we can say that Vivekananda establishes the equal salvific efficacy (PS) and doctrinal truth (PT_f) of numerous *first-order* religions on the basis of a *second-order* Vedāntic doctrinal inclusivism (IT_f). That Vivekananda himself was aware of the second-order inclusivist dimension of his first-order religious pluralist position is clear from numerous passages in his lectures, such as his explicitly inclusivistic statement in his 1896 lecture on "Ramkrishna Paramahamsa" that all religions are "part and parcel of the eternal religion" (*CW* 4:187).[16]

From late 1895 onward, then, Vivekananda envisioned an ideal future in which all religious practitioners would "wear two hats" (to use McKim's apt phrase): they would belong to a particular first-order religion of their choice while

[16] Similarly, in his 1897 "Reply to the Madras Address," he claims that "all the other religions of the world are included in the nameless, limitless, eternal Vedic religion" (*CW* 4:343).

also accepting the second-order Vedāntic universal religion. They would also be religious cosmopolitans who strive to broaden their understanding of the ultimate reality and enrich and deepen their spiritual practice by learning from, and practicing, religions other than their own. Vivekananda's strong emphasis on religious cosmopolitanism reflects the fact that the second-order Vedāntic inclusivism he endorses is an open, rather than closed, one (OIT_f). Since the account of ultimate reality in any given first-order religion is necessarily incomplete and partial, we all stand to learn a great deal from other religions. Let us return, for a moment, to Vivekananda's analogy of viewing the same church from four different corners. Just as someone viewing the church from the front can learn more about the church by walking around the church and viewing it from different standpoints, each of us can gain greater insight into the Infinite Divine Reality by learning how other religions conceive the ultimate reality. Moreover, by learning about, and engaging in, the spiritual practices taught in other religions, we come closer to discovering what Vivekananda calls the unique religion of our "own soul" (*CW* 6:82), since we can "custom-design," as it were, the particular combination of spiritual practices that is uniquely suited to our individual nature and temperament.

In this section, then, I have made the case that beginning in late 1895, Vivekananda harmonized the world religions on the basis of a Vedāntic universal religion, which has three basic tenets: (1) All religions have at their center the same impersonal-personal Infinite Divine Reality, (2) The salvific goal of all religions is the realization of this Infinite Divine Reality in some form or aspect, and (3) There are numerous equally effective methods for attaining this goal, which can be generalized into the four Yogas, and each religion typically corresponds to one of these Yogas. Crucially, from late 1895 until his death, he consistently conceived this universal religion in terms of the four Yogas rather than in terms of the three stages of Dvaita, Viśiṣṭādvaita, and Advaita. Moreover, his Vedāntic universal religion is best understood as a second-order open inclusivist framework (OIT_f) that provides the philosophical basis for first-order salvific and doctrinal pluralism (PS and PT_f) as well as a radical religious cosmopolitanism. Indeed, with McKim's reasoning in the background, we can see that second-order doctrinal inclusivism is not a "bug," but a feature, of *any* coherent pluralist theory concerning the doctrinal truth of multiple religions—be it Vivekananda's, Ramakrishna's, John Hick's,[17] or otherwise. The pluralist thesis that various religious conceptions of ultimate reality are equally true and complementary (PT_f) *logically necessitates* a more comprehensive second-order framework that encompasses all first-order religious accounts of ultimate reality as partial truths (OIT_f).

[17] For a detailed critical discussion of Hick's theory of religious pluralism vis-à-vis Ramakrishna's, see Maharaj (2018: 117–52).

5. *Vivekananda on the Definition of Religion, Degrees of Salvific Efficacy, and the Problem of Conflicting Religious Truth-Claims*

Some important questions regarding Vivekananda's final view on the harmony of religions remain to be answered. First, how does he define "religion" in the first place? Second, does he hold that *all* religions have equal salvific efficacy or that some religions have greater salvific efficacy than others? Third, how does he address the problem of conflicting religious truth-claims? In this section, I will briefly discuss his answers to these three questions in turn.

In his lecture "The Necessity of Religion," delivered in London on June 7, 1896, he argues that it is necessary to define religion very broadly so as to accommodate as many paths to salvation as possible—those that already exist and those that are yet to come. Accordingly, he claims that every religion posits an "Ideal Unit Abstraction" that cannot be perceived through the senses:

> Thus, this one fact stands out from all these different religions, that there is an Ideal Unit Abstraction, which is put before us, either in the form of a Person or an Impersonal Being, or a Law, or a Presence, or an Essence. We are always struggling to raise ourselves up to that ideal. (*CW* 2:62)

Significantly, he is careful *not* to claim that all religions posit some kind of God or ultimate reality, since such a narrow definition of religion would exclude atheistic and agnostic religions, including Jainism, non-substantialist schools of Buddhism, and ethical humanism. Instead, he claims that all religions posit an "Ideal Unit Abstraction" (hereafter IUA), which he defines very broadly. For Vivekananda, the IUA takes a wide variety of forms in different religions, including the Personal God of theistic religions, the "Impersonal Being" of Advaita Vedānta and certain schools of Buddhism, the "Moral Law" of "Buddhists as represented by the Southern sect" and of some "modern" thinkers (Vivekananda may have had in mind Kantians), the "Ideal Unity," and the "Ideal Human Being" of ethical humanists (*CW* 2:60–62). All religions, he claims, share the belief in an ideal state, reality, or condition that is "not in the senses," however that ideal is understood (*CW* 2:62). For instance, with respect to modern ethical humanism, which was gaining currency during his time,[18] he observes: "None of us have yet seen an 'Ideal Human Being,' and yet we are told to believe in it" (*CW* 2:62).

[18] Vivekananda had read the work of Auguste Comte, who defended an atheistic "Religion of Humanity." For a good discussion of nineteenth-century humanism, see Davies (1997: 7–40).

In the same lecture, Vivekananda goes on to argue that every religion must not only posit an IUA but also prescribe ethical disciplines through the practice of which one can realize the ideal of one's religion. All ethical practices, he claims, have the aim of "self-abnegation," the complete elimination of selfishness and egoism:

> Ethics always says, "Not I, but thou." Its motto is, "Not self, but non-self." . . . You have to put *yourself* last, and others before you. The senses say, "Myself first." Ethics says, "I must hold myself last." Thus, all codes of ethics are based upon this renunciation. . . . Perfect self-annihilation is the ideal of ethics. (*CW* 2:62–63)

According to Vivekananda, then, a religion must fulfil two criteria: (1) it must posit an ideal beyond the senses, and (2) it must prescribe ethical practices that lead to the realization of this ideal. For Vivekananda, any agnostic or atheistic doctrine that meets these two criteria counts as a religion. On the other hand, self-styled "religions" that do not meet the second ethical criterion are *not*, in fact, religions proper. For instance, he was often scathing about the "horrible practices" of "the present corrupted form of *vāmācāra* of the Tantras"—that is, the "left-handed" path of Tantra based on sexual practices (*BCW* 9:127 / *CW* 7:215).[19] Hence, I believe he would not consider the modern corrupted form of Tāntrika *vāmācāra* to be a true religion. Likewise, contemporary self-styled "religions" like ISIS and Aum Shinrikyo—which encourage their followers to engage in violence and other unethical acts—would not count as true religions in Vivekananda's sense, since they fail to meet the ethical criterion of his definition. By defining religion in terms of these two broad criteria, Vivekananda accommodates atheistic and agnostic religions like Jainism, Buddhism, and ethical humanism while *excluding* self-styled "religions" that prescribe unethical practices.

Regarding Vivekananda's salvific pluralism, it is important to note that while he held that more than one religion has maximal salvific efficacy, he nonetheless believed that some religions have greater salvific efficacy than others. For instance, he clearly believed that Rāja-Yoga has greater salvific efficacy than Haṭha-Yoga, the aim of which is "to make the physical body very strong" (*CW* 1:138). In his book *Rāja-Yoga* (1896), he claims that the "practices" of Haṭha-Yoga "are very difficult, and cannot be learned in a day, and, after all, do not lead to much spiritual growth" (*CW* 1:138). Likewise, he remarks in numerous places that some religious practices, though valid, are nonetheless "lower" than others.

[19] However, he goes on to add that he "did not denounce . . . the real *vāmācāra*," which suggests that he would grant some salvific efficacy to the original form of *vāmācāra* (*BCW* 9:127 / *CW* 7:215).

For instance, in "The Ideal of a Universal Religion," he refers to the practice of "fetishism" as a lower stage of spiritual progress on the way to the goal of God-realization (*CW* 2:383).

The fact that Vivekananda considered some religions to have greater salvific efficacy than others does not make him any less of a salvific pluralist. In section 1, I defined salvific pluralism (PS) as the view that *multiple*, but not *all*, religions have equal and maximal salvific efficacy. Indeed, numerous contemporary pluralists—including John Hick (1989: 233–51) and Perry Schmidt-Leukel (2005: 20)—have followed Vivekananda in holding that some, but not all, religions have an equally high degree of salvific efficacy. Hick, for instance, defends the delimited pluralist hypothesis that the "great world faiths" have equal salvific efficacy (1989: 240). Like Hick, Vivekananda, in "The Way to the Realisation of a Universal Religion" (1900), speaks of the equal salvific efficacy of the "great religions of the world," under which he includes Christianity, Judaism, Islam, Hinduism, Buddhism, and Zoroastrianism (*CW* 2:361–62). In an undated essay on "The Fundamentals of Religion," he provides a list of the "great religions of the world today," which includes all the religions just mentioned as well as Taoism and Confucianism (*CW* 4:374–75). Vivekananda's position, then, is that at least all the great world religions have the highest degree of salvific efficacy, and that some religious paths—like Haṭha-Yoga and fetishism—have less salvific efficacy than the great world religions.[20]

Finally, it is important to understand Vivekananda's basic approach to the problem of conflicting religious truth-claims. The key to his approach is his emphatic subordination of religious doctrine to spiritual practice. In a famous passage from *Rāja-Yoga* (1896) already quoted in section 6 of the previous chapter, he claims that the essence of all religions is to "manifest" our innate divinity through the practice of one or more of the four Yogas—"by work, or worship, or psychic control, or philosophy"—and he then adds: "Doctrines, or dogmas, or rituals, or books, or temples, or forms, are but secondary details" (*CW* 1:257). By privileging spiritual practice and reducing religious doctrines to non-essential "secondary details," he prises apart a given religion's salvific efficacy from its doctrinal truth. Hence, from Vivekananda's perspective, even if a particular religion teaches mostly false doctrines, it can still have salvific efficacy so long as it prescribes ethical and spiritual practices that aim to eliminate egoism.

It is from this fundamental perspective that he addresses the problem of apparently conflicting religious truth-claims. In "The Way to the Realisation of a Universal Religion" (1900), he explicitly raises this problem:

[20] One complication here is that since Haṭha-Yoga is itself a tradition within Hinduism, Vivekananda, strictly speaking, would hold that some traditions within Hinduism have the greatest degree of salvific efficacy, while other Hindu traditions, like Haṭha-Yoga, do not.

> Then arises the question: How can all these varieties be true? If one thing is true, its negation is false. How can contradictory opinions be true at the same time? This is the question which I intend to answer. But I will first ask you: Are all the religions of the world really contradictory? (*CW* 2:365)

Vivekananda clearly recognizes the contradictions involved in making the sweeping statement that "all religions are true." If what is meant by this statement is that all the doctrines of every religion are true, then the statement violates the law of non-contradiction. For instance, if the doctrine of reincarnation is true, then Hinduism, Buddhism, and Jainism are correct on this issue, while religions that deny reincarnation must be wrong on this issue. Likewise, if it is true that Christ died on the cross, then Christianity is correct on this issue, while Islam—which denies that Christ died on the cross—is wrong.

In "The Ideal of a Universal Religion" (1896), he claims that there are "three parts" in every major religion: philosophy, mythology, and ritual (*CW* 2:377–78). Philosophy encompasses a religion's basic doctrines, mythology encompasses historical claims about "the lives of men, or of supernatural beings," and ritual encompasses "forms and ceremonies" and so on (*CW* 2:377). He goes on to argue that religions *do* often conflict in their philosophical doctrines, their historical truth-claims, and their ritualistic practices (*CW* 2:377–79). Hence, to refer back to the examples mentioned in the previous paragraph, Vivekananda would agree that not all religions can be correct on the metaphysical question of whether there is reincarnation or on the historical question of whether Christ died on the cross, since different religions provide conflicting answers to these questions. However, as we have seen, he insists that the doctrines and rituals taught in different religions are merely "secondary details," by which he means that they are not essential for salvation. Therefore, even if orthodox Christianity is wrong, say, in denying reincarnation, this doctrinal error in Christianity does not substantially detract from its salvific efficacy.

At the same time, as we have already seen in the previous section, Vivekananda argues that there are three key respects in which the various religions actually *complement*, rather than conflict, with one another. First, the "internal soul" of every religion—such as universal brotherhood in Islam and spiritual realization in Hinduism—complements one another, so it is not only possible, but desirable, to incorporate the spirit of other religions into one's own religious practice (*CW* 2:365). Second, even though different religions prescribe different ethical and spiritual practices, most of these practices correspond to one or more of the four Yogas, each of which leads to salvation. Moreover, Vivekananda champions the cosmopolitan ideal of combining the four Yogas to the best of our ability, since each of them develops different, but equally important, aspects of the human personality (*CW* 6:137–38). Hence, the ethical and spiritual practices taught in different religions are actually complementary, and all religious practitioners can enrich their spiritual lives by incorporating some of the disciplines taught in other religions into their own spiritual practice (*CW* 2:373–74). Third, various conceptions of ultimate reality taught in different religions—such as Allah, Viṣṇu, Christ, God the Father, Śiva, Kālī, the impersonal Brahman, and so on—are not conflicting but complementary, since they correspond to different aspects or forms of one and the same Infinite Divine Reality (*CW* 2:366, *CW* 6:11).

But what about religions that deny the existence of *any* kind of ultimate reality? As I discussed earlier in this section, Vivekananda defines religion very broadly so as to include even atheistic and agnostic doctrines like ethical humanism and Southern Buddhism (i.e., what is now known as Theravāda). In a class lecture on Karma-Yoga delivered in New York on January 10, 1896, he also accepts both theistic and atheistic forms of Karma-Yoga:

> Here are the two ways of giving up all attachment. The one is for those who do not believe in God, or in any outside help. They are left to their own devices; they have simply to work with their own will, with the powers of their mind and discrimination, saying, "I must be non-attached." For those who believe in God there is another way, which is much less difficult. They give up the fruits of work unto the Lord; they work and are never attached to the results. (*CW* 1:102)

Since his Vedāntic universal religion accepts Karma-Yoga as one of the four Yogas leading to salvation, he clearly accepts the salvific efficacy of atheistic Karma-Yoga. According to Vivekananda, we can attain the ideal of perfect "selflessness" through the performance of unattached action even without believing in God (*CW* 1:111). At the same time, since his Vedāntic universal religion posits the realization of God as the common goal of all religions, he would claim that the atheistic Karma-Yogī's goal of "selflessness" is actually tantamount to God-realization, even though the atheistic Karma-Yogī would obviously not accept this characterization of the goal. Hence, there is a second-order *inclusivist* dimension to Vivekananda's stance toward religions that deny the existence of an ultimate divine reality. He accommodates atheistic and agnostic religions within his Vedāntic universal religion by holding that practitioners of these religions are, as it were, anonymous Vedāntins who will ultimately attain the goal of God-realization *even though* they neither believe in God nor accept God-realization as their goal. From Vivekananda's perspective, then, this second-order Vedāntic inclusivism (IT_f) is necessary to establish a common ontological basis for all religions and to uphold the salvific efficacy even of atheistic and agnostic religions.

6. *The Problem of Non-Substantialist Buddhism: Addressing Ninian Smart's Objection*

As I already noted in this chapter's introduction, by far the most common objection to Vivekananda's doctrine of the harmony of religions is that he was less a religious pluralist than an Advaitic inclusivist, since he considered non-Advaitic paths to be inferior stages on the way to the goal of Advaitic realization. This entire chapter can be seen as a rebuttal to this objection. As I have argued, these scholars have failed to recognize the *evolution* in Vivekananda's thinking about the harmony of religions. My diachronic examination has shown that it was only for a brief period—roughly, from mid-1894 to mid-1895—that he harmonized the world religions on the basis of the three stages of Vedānta. The vast majority of scholars have overlooked the fact that Vivekananda, beginning in late 1895, reconceived the Vedāntic universal religion as a pluralistic framework based on the four Yogas.

In this concluding section, I will address an important objection that applies even to Vivekananda's final view on the harmony of religions. Ninian Smart argues that Buddhism poses a serious problem for Vivekananda's position. Taking Vivekananda to be a paradigmatic "Neo-Advaitin," Smart claims: "the ultimate reality is presented in a substantialist way in Neo-Advaita: this does not seem to square with Theravādin *nirvāṇa* or with Mahāyāna *śūnyatā* (though the latter sometimes functions a bit like a ghost-substance)" (2009: 268). Smart rightly notes that a Vedāntic model of religious pluralism like Vivekananda's presupposes a "substantialist" conception of the ultimate reality as a positive entity or reality, whether that positive reality is conceived as a personal God (by theists) or as the impersonal Brahman (by Advaita Vedāntins).[21] According to Smart, however, since both the Theravāda school of Buddhism and at least certain strains of Mahāyāna Buddhism *reject* a substantialist understanding of the ultimate reality, these Buddhistic schools cannot easily be accommodated within Vivekananda's Vedāntic model of religious pluralism.

It is worth noting that Smart completely ignores Vivekananda's own fairly nuanced views on the Buddha's teachings and on the doctrines of later schools of Buddhism. In fact, Vivekananda explicitly acknowledged the non-substantialist strains of Buddhism and explained how they can be accommodated within his Vedāntic universal religion. His understanding of the Buddha's teachings seems to have evolved from 1893 to 1901. In his lectures from 1893 and 1896, he consistently claimed that the Buddha was "a perfect agnostic" with respect to the

[21] In his use of the term "substantialist," Smart does not mean to imply that the ultimate reality is conceived as a substance. I take it that Smart uses the term "substantialist" in a very broad sense to denote any conception of the ultimate reality as a positive entity or reality.

existence of "a Personal God or a personal soul" (*CW* 2:352).[22] By contrast, in his lectures from 1897 to 1901, he claimed that the Buddha outright denied the existence of God and the soul. For instance, in his lecture on "Buddhistic India" delivered in Pasadena on February 2, 1900, he remarked:

> You know he [Buddha] denied that there was any soul in man—that is, in the Hindu sense of the word. Now, we Hindus all believe that there is something permanent in man, which is unchangeable and which is living through all eternity. And that in man we call Ātman, which is without beginning and without end. And [we believe] that there is something permanent in nature [and that we call Brahman, which is also without beginning and without end]. He denied both of these. He said there is no proof of anything permanent. It is all a mere mass of change; a mass of thought in a continuous change is what you call a mind. . . . The torch is leading the procession. The circle is a delusion. (*CW* 3:529)[23]

After 1896, then, Vivekananda seems to have moved away from his earlier agnostic interpretation of the Buddha's teachings, holding instead that the Buddha was an atheist and a non-substantialist who denied the existence of God and the soul. It is not clear to me what led Vivekananda to modify his interpretation of the Buddha's doctrine.

Vivekananda also often discussed the doctrines of the "Mahāyāna" (or "Northern") school of Buddhism and the "Southern school" of Buddhism (which, a few years after Vivekananda's passing in 1902, came to be known as "Theravāda" Buddhism).[24] From 1889 to 1902, he consistently held the view that the majority of Mahāyāna Buddhists subscribed to a substantialist doctrine that is essentially the same as Advaita Vedānta, while the Southern Buddhists subscribed to the non-substantialist doctrine that there is no eternal underlying reality at all—neither God nor a soul. As he put it in a class at Ridgley Manor in New York on August 4, 1895, "The great majority of the adherents of Northern Buddhism believe in Mukti and are really Vedāntists. Only the Ceylonese [i.e., Southern Buddhists] accept Nirvāṇa as annihilation" (*CW* 7:94). Likewise, in several lectures, he claims that the "Southern school of Buddhists" holds

[22] For other references to Buddha's agnosticism in his lectures up to 1896, see *CW* 1:18, *CW* 2:484, and *CW* 4:135–37.

[23] The transcript of this lecture is incomplete in places. Phrases in square brackets were inserted by the editor of *CW*. For other references to Buddha as an atheist and non-substantialist, see *CW* 3:529 ("Buddhistic India," February 2, 1900) and *CW* 8:98–99 ("Buddha's Message to the World," March 18, 1900).

[24] For a detailed historical account of how the "Southern" school of Buddhism first came to be known as "Theravāda" in 1907, see Perreira (2012).

that "nothing unchanging exists" (*CW* 1:329)—in other words, that there is no eternal reality beneath this ever-changing phenomenal world.[25]

According to Vivekananda, Mahāyāna Buddhism, in stark contrast to the Southern school, posits an eternal nondual Reality at the basis of this phenomenal flux. Accordingly, in a Bengali letter dated August 17, 1889, Vivekananda observed that the "views expressed in *Prajñāpāramitā*, the Buddhist Mahāyāna book, perfectly tally with the Vedāntic views propounded by Ācārya [Śaṅkara]" (*CW* 6:211). Although he did not refer to any particular verses from the *Prajñāpāramitāsūtra*, he may have been thinking, in part, of the numerous verses which characterize reality or "Suchness" (*tathatā*) as "nondual" (*advaya*).[26] In a much later letter dated February 9, 1902, he similarly claimed that "the Mahāyāna school of Buddhism is even Advaitistic," and he goes on to add: "Why does Amara Singha, a Buddhist, give as one of the names of Buddha—Advayavādī? . . . I hold the Mahāyāna to be the older of the two schools of Buddhism" (*CW* 5:172). In support of his claim that Mahāyāna Buddhism is actually "Advaitistic," he refers to the Mahāyāna Buddhist Amarasiṃha's famous Sanskrit thesaurus *Amarakośa*, which notes, at 1.1.27, that one of the names for the Buddha is *advayavādī* (Amarasiṃha 1968: 9). Vivekananda also claims here that the Mahāyāna school is older than the Southern school of Buddhism.

Obviously, scholarship on Buddhism has advanced considerably since Vivekananda's time. It is interesting to note, however, that even now there is still no consensus among scholars regarding the nature of the Buddha's teachings as recorded in the *Tipiṭaka*, with some defending a substantialist/Vedāntic interpretation,[27] others defending an agnostic interpretation,[28] and still others favoring non-substantialist interpretations of various sorts.[29] Moreover, the vast majority of recent scholars have followed Vivekananda in adopting a non-substantialist interpretation of the "Southern" (i.e., "Theravāda") school of Buddhism (Harvey 2013: 57–62; Ñāṇamoli and Bodhi 1995: 27–29). With respect to Mahāyāna Buddhism, scholars continue to debate how its doctrines should be interpreted. Numerous scholars from the early twentieth century up to the present have defended the Advaitic interpretation of Mahāyāna Buddhism favored by Vivekananda. For instance, T. R. V. Murti argues that Nāgārjuna's *śūnyatā* denotes a positive ineffable Reality that can neither be said to exist nor not to exist (1955: 329–31). In support of his interpretation, Murti quotes a striking passage

[25] See also *CW* 5:279.

[26] See especially chapter 16 ("Suchness") of *Prajñāpāramitā*, translated into English by Conze (1975: 193–99).

[27] Rhys Davids (1934), Coomaraswamy (1964: 199–221), Bhattacharya (1973), Grimm (1958), Jennings (1948), Reigle and Reigle (2015), Conze (1962: 129–34), Albahari (2002: 5–20), Reigle (2015: ix–xviii), Schmidt-Leukel (2007), Drew (2011: 57–61).

[28] Keith (1923: 62–63), Frauwallner (1953: 217–34), Batchelor (1997: 14–20).

[29] Collins (1982: 135–38), Hayes (1994), Harvey (2013: 57–62).

from the Mahāyāna text *Ratnakūṭasūtra*: " 'that ātman is' is one end; 'that ātman is not' is another; but the middle between the ātma and nairātmya views is the Inexpressible. . . . It is the reflective review of things" (quoted in Murti 1955: 27–28). More recently, David Reigle has argued that major Mahāyāna thinkers such as Nāgārjuna, Vasubandhu, and Candrakīrti "thought that the Buddha's *anātman* teaching was directed against a permanent personal *ātman*" rather than against the Upaniṣadic Ātman (2015: ix).[30] Reigle further suggests that the "Buddha Nature" (*Buddha-dhātu*) mentioned in the Mahāyāna *Tathāgatagarbhasūtra* bears a strong resemblance to the Vedāntic Ātman (2015: xvi–xvii). On the other hand, scholars like Jonathan C. Gold and Richard King have defended non-substantialist interpretations of major Mahāyāna thinkers like Vasubandhu and Nāgārjuna.[31] Since the Mahāyāna tradition of Buddhism is vast and internally variegated, most recent scholars have rightly eschewed monolithic interpretations of Mahāyāna Buddhism in favor of more specific interpretations of particular Mahāyāna texts and thinkers. Vivekananda acknowledged some of this internal diversity within the Mahāyāna tradition when he remarked, in one of his more nuanced statements, that the "great majority" of Mahāyāna Buddhists "are really Vedāntists" (*CW* 7:94), thereby implying that at least some Mahāyāna thinkers were non-substantialists.

As for Vivekananda's claim that Mahāyāna Buddhism historically preceded Southern Buddhism,[32] the reigning orthodoxy among twentieth-century scholars was, to the contrary, that the Southern (Theravāda) school predates the Mahāyāna school, since the former was taken to be a subgroup of one of the schools emerging from the *sthavira* side of the early split between the Sthavira and Mahāsaṅgika factions of Buddhism.[33] More recently, however, numerous scholars have begun to question this standard historical narrative, arguing that it is simplistic and inaccurate in a number of respects.[34] While it is uncontroversial that the Theravāda school has always *claimed* to be the older of the two schools, it is far from clear to what extent its self-representation is an accurate one. Moreover, in a new book, Joseph Walser lends considerable support to

[30] Other contemporary scholars defending Advaitic interpretations of Mahāyāna Buddhism include Loy (1988: 194–97) and Davis (2010).

[31] Gold (2015: 59–93), R. King (1989: 385–405), and Siderits (2011).

[32] In light of Perreira's groundbreaking new research (Perreira 2012: 498–526), it seems that Vivekananda may have arrived at this view in part due to the influence of some of the Japanese Buddhist delegates at the 1893 World's Parliament of Religions in Chicago. During the Parliament, Noguchi Zenshirō distributed copies of a 17-page pamphlet entitled *Outlines of the Mahâyâna as Taught by Buddha* written by Shintō Kuroda, which stated that the "precepts and doctrines of 'Mahâyâna' and 'Hînayâna' were both taught by one Buddha . . . " (Perreira 2012: 517).

[33] Bareau (2013 [1955]: 275–326), Warder (2004: 277–400), Nakamura (1980: 90–234, esp. 117), and Lamotte (1988: 520).

[34] See especially Perreira (2012: 1–4).

Vivekananda's position by arguing that key Mahāyāna doctrines like *śūnyatā* ("emptiness") and *vijñaptimātra* ("mind-only") can be traced to early texts that preceded the advent of the Mahāyāna school itself, including the *Tipiṭaka*, the *Saddharmasmṛtyupasthānasūtra*, and the Maitrāyaṇīya Upaniṣad (Walser 2018).

Let us now return to Smart's objection that Vivekananda's substantialist Vedāntic framework is unable to accommodate the non-substantialist Buddhist traditions of Theravāda and Mahāyana. Vivekananda, as I have just shown, held that while most Mahāyāna Buddhists accepted the existence of a nondual ultimate reality, the Buddha himself, as well as Southern (i.e., Theravāda) Buddhists and a minority of Mahāyāna Buddhists, subscribed to the *non*-substantialist view that there is no unchanging reality—neither God nor an eternal soul—behind this phenomenal flux. Nonetheless, he explicitly accommodated *both* the substantialist and non-substantialist strains of Buddhism within his Vedāntic universal religion. For instance, during a question-and-answer session at Harvard University in March 1896, he remarked:

> The Vedānta has no quarrel with Buddhism. The idea of the Vedānta is to harmonise all. With the Northern Buddhists we have no quarrel at all. But the Burmese and Siamese and all the Southern Buddhists say that there is a phenomenal world, and ask what right we have to create a noumenal world behind this. (*CW* 5:279)

With sections 4 and 5 of this chapter in the background, it is easy to see how Vivekananda accommodated what he took to be the mainstream nondual strain of Mahāyāna Buddhism. For Vivekananda, the *śūnyatā* of mainstream Mahāyāna Buddhism is nothing but a negative characterization of the nondual Brahman of Advaita Vedānta. Moreover, although he does not discuss Mahāyāna spiritual practice anywhere in his work, he would presumably have taken it to be a form of Jñāna-Yoga. Hence, I believe Vivekananda would hold that mainstream Mahāyāna doctrines about the ultimate reality are as true as the doctrines of other world religions (PT_f). And since he takes Jñāna-Yoga to be a direct and independent path to salvation, he would also grant maximal salvific efficacy to mainstream Mahāyāna Buddhism (PS).

How did Vivekananda accommodate the non-substantialist strains of Buddhism—including the Buddha's own teachings (as interpreted by Vivekananda in his lectures after 1896) as well as Southern/Theravāda Buddhism? In "The Necessity of Religion" (1896), he explicitly addressed this question:

> Some exceptions may be taken in the case of the Buddhists as represented by the Southern sect. It may be asked—if the Buddhists do not believe in any God

> or soul, how can their religion be derived from the supersensuous state of existence? The answer to this is that even the Buddhists find an eternal moral law, and that moral law was not reasoned out in our sense of the word. But Buddha found it, discovered it, in a supersensuous state. (*CW* 2:60–61)

From Vivekananda's perspective, even though both the Buddha himself and Southern Buddhists denied the reality of God and the soul, they nonetheless accepted an "eternal moral law"—presumably Vivekananda's English rendering of the Pāli term *dhamma*—which can only be realized by transcending the ordinary mind and senses. Moreover, he frequently praised the Buddha for his unselfishness and compassion, claiming that he attained *nirvāṇa* through the "distinterested performance of action"—in other words, through the practice of an atheistic form of Karma-Yoga (*CW* 4:137). At the same time, Vivekananda was forthright in rejecting the non-substantialist Buddhist interpretation of *nirvāṇa* as "annihilation" (*CW* 7:94), as is clear from this response to a question posed to him in Madras in February 1897:

> *Q.* —What is the notion of Mukti, according to the Advaita philosophy, or in other words, is it a conscious state? Is there any difference between the Mukti of the Advaitism and the Buddhistic Nirvāṇa?
>
> *A.* —There is a consciousness in Mukti, which we call superconsciousness. It differs from your present consciousness. It is illogical to say that there is no consciousness in Mukti. The consciousness is of three sorts—the dull, mediocre, and intense—as is the case of light. When vibration is intense, the brilliancy is so very powerful as to dazzle the sight itself and in effect is as ineffectual as the dullest of lights. The Buddhistic Nirvāṇa must have the same degree of consciousness *whatever the Buddhists may say.* Our definition of Mukti is affirmative in its nature, while the Buddhistic Nirvāṇa has a negative definition. (*CW* 5:206; emphasis added)

Critics like Smart would likely pounce on the italicized phrase in this passage, which clearly indicates that Vivekananda denied the self-understanding of non-substantialist Buddhists. Vivekananda claims here that the non-substantialist interpretation of *nirvāṇa* advocated by Southern Buddhists is mistaken, since he takes *nirvāṇa* to be a negative term for the ineffable reality of pure nondual Consciousness. However, Smart and most other scholars have overlooked Vivekananda's crucial distinction between a religion's salvific efficacy and its doctrinal truth—a distinction, as we have seen, emphasized only recently by philosophers like McKim. Although Vivekananda thinks the non-substantialist interpretation of *nirvāṇa* is indeed mistaken, he nowhere suggests that this doctrinal error detracts from the salvific efficacy of non-substantialist Buddhism as a religious path. Moreover, we should remind ourselves of his emphatic insistence that the heart of religion consists not in religious "doctrines" or "dogmas"—which he considers to be mere "secondary details"—but in spiritual practice (*CW* 1:257). Hence, there is no reason to think that he granted any less salvific efficacy to non-substantialist Buddhism than he did to Mahāyāna Buddhism and the other major world religions.

In sum, I think Vivekananda would hold that while non-substantialist Buddhism is mistaken in denying the existence of an ultimate reality, it is nonetheless as salvifically efficacious as any of the other major world religions (PS), *in spite* of its erroneous views about ultimate reality. And at a second-order level, Vivekananda accommodates non-substantialist Buddhism within his Vedāntic universal religion by reconceiving the goal of *nirvāṇa* as the salvific realization of the nondual Ātman. Hence, I think Vivekananda would be happy to concede to Smart that he rejects the non-substantialist Buddhist understanding of *nirvāṇa*, but Vivekananda would argue that this second-order Vedāntic inclusivism is a very small price to pay for placing non-substantialist Buddhism on a salvific par with all the other major world religions. Indeed, without some such second-order philosophical framework, religious pluralism would devolve into what Alan Race calls a "debilitating relativism" (Race 1983: 90). That is, in the absence of a metaframework for religious pluralism, we could still insist, dogmatically, that all religions are equally true and effective paths, but we would not be able to provide a coherent explanation of *how* all these religions—with their vastly different doctrines, practices, and soteriological goals—can possibly have salvific efficacy and doctrinal truth.[35] And as McKim has shown, *any* second-order pluralist framework will inevitably have a doctrinally inclusivist dimension, however minimal.

7. The Contemporary Relevance of Vivekananda's Vedāntic Universal Religion

There is, of course, much more that could be said about Vivekananda's Vedāntic harmonization of the world's religions, but I will conclude this chapter by making a brief case for its continued relevance. Since the British philosopher John Hick first presented his groundbreaking quasi-Kantian theory of religious pluralism several decades ago, numerous theologians and philosophers of religion have debated its merits and proposed numerous alternative theories of pluralism.

[35] Long (2017: 259–60) defends the inclusivist dimension of Vivekananda's religious pluralism along similar lines.

The fact remains, however, that the vast majority of recent pluralist theories continue to be rooted in Western, and especially Christian, theological paradigms. What is urgently needed now is a broader cross-cultural approach to religious pluralism that takes seriously the pluralist views developed in both Western and non-Western religious traditions. To this end, I will briefly explore some of the ways that Vivekananda can be brought into fruitful conversation with two of the leading Christian religious pluralists, John Hick (1922–2012) and Perry Schmidt-Leukel (1954–).

Hick is justly famous for his groundbreaking theory of religious pluralism, which holds that all the major world religions are equally capable of effecting the "transformation of human existence from self-centeredness to Reality-centredness" (Hick 1989: 14).[36] To address the thorny problem of conflicting religious truth-claims, Hick appeals to a quasi-Kantian ontology: he posits an unknowable "Real *an sich*" and distinguishes it from the "Real as humanly-thought-and-experienced" (1989: 239–40). According to Hick, then, the various personal and non-personal ultimates taught by the various world religions are different culturally conditioned ways of conceiving one and the same noumenal Real (1989: 246).

Vivekananda's Vedāntic theory of religious pluralism, I would argue, has at least two major advantages over Hick's quasi-Kantian theory. First, as numerous scholars have contended (and as I have argued in detail elsewhere), one of the most serious weaknesses of Hick's theory is that it downgrades the ultimates of various religions to non-noumenal status, thereby failing to honor the self-understanding of most religious practitioners, who take their respective ultimates to have full-blown ontological reality.[37] As George Mavrodes puts it, "Hick's view suggests that almost all of the world's religious believers are wildly mistaken about the objects of their worship and adoration" (Hick 2001: 69n6). Vivekananda, in contrast to Hick, follows Ramakrishna in holding that the personal and non-personal ultimates of various religions correspond to different *ontologically real* aspects of one and the same Infinite Divine Reality. Hence, while Hick maintains that the Real *an sich* is *neither* personal *nor* impersonal (Hick 1989: 350), Vivekananda holds that the Infinite Reality is *both* personal *and* impersonal. Arguably, then, his Vedāntic pluralist theory is better equipped than Hick's to honor the self-understanding of practitioners of various religions.

[36] Actually, as I argue in Maharaj (2018: 117–52), Hick initially endorsed a different Aurobindonian theory of religious pluralism between 1970 and 1974 that comes much closer to Vivekananda's Vedāntic theory. However, by 1976, Hick abandoned this Aurobindonian theory in favor of the well-known quasi-Kantian theory that I discuss here.

[37] See Maharaj (2018: 139–40), Mavrodes's objections to Hick's theory in Hick (2001: 62–69), McKim (2012: 111–12), Netland (1986: 255–66), and Heim (1995: 34).

Second, from a Vivekanandan perspective, Hick's quasi-Kantian ontology fails to provide a sufficiently strong basis for religious cosmopolitanism. While Hick upholds the equal salvific efficacy of all the major world religions, he does not furnish a plausible philosophical rationale for *learning* from religions other than one's own. For Hick, the world religions are not complementary in any meaningful sense, since none of the various religious ultimates correspond to ontologically real aspects of the Real *an sich*. Hence, by exposing ourselves to other religious traditions, we can learn, at best, about the background cultural assumptions informing different religious conceptions of the ultimate reality, but we cannot learn anything about the ultimate reality itself.[38]

Vivekananda's Vedāntic universal religion, I would suggest, furnishes a much stronger philosophical basis for religious cosmopolitanism than does Hick's quasi-Kantian theory. For Vivekananda, the various theistic and nontheistic ultimates of different religions genuinely complement one another, since they correspond to different ontologically real aspects and forms of one and the same Infinite Divine Reality. Accordingly, religious practitioners can gain deeper insight into the inexhaustible nature of the Infinite Reality by learning from other religions. With respect to spiritual practice, since each of the four Yogas cultivates a different part of the human personality, and each religion corresponds to at least one of the four Yogas, we can enrich our spiritual lives and develop a more harmonious and balanced personality by incorporating some of the religious disciplines taught in other religions into our own spiritual practice. Moreover, the more religions we learn about, the closer we can come to discovering the religion in our own "soul," which is uniquely suited to our individual nature and temperament.

Finally, I would like to indicate briefly how Vivekananda's Vedāntic universal religion anticipated key aspects of the intriguing new "fractal" theory of religious diversity proposed by the contemporary theologian Perry Schmidt-Leukel in his Gifford Lectures (Schmidt-Leukel 2017). According to Schmidt-Leukel's fractal paradigm, the "cultural diversity at the global level is reflected in the diversity within each culture and this again is, to some extent, reflected, on a still smaller scale, in the individual" (2017: 227). Hence, he argues that many of the differences *between* the various world religions can be found *within* each particular religion, as well as *within* each individual religious practitioner. To his credit, Schmidt-Leukel does discuss Vivekananda's Vedāntic universal religion, but he makes the typical mistake of taking it to be based on an inclusivist hierarchy of Dvaita, Viśiṣṭādvaita, and Advaita (2017: 54–58). Against Schmidt-Leukel, I hope to have shown in this chapter that Vivekananda only endorsed

[38] For similar criticisms of Hick, see Long (2010: 151–61), Heim (1995: 7), and Maharaj (2018: 146–47).

this hierarchical universal religion for a brief period from mid-1894 to mid-1895 and that his final account of the Vedāntic universal religion, from late 1895 up to his death, was grounded not in the three stages of Dvaita, Viśiṣṭādvaita, and Advaita but in the robustly pluralist paradigm of the four Yogas.

In fact, Vivekananda's nuanced account of religious diversity in terms of the four Yogas exhibits a fractal pattern remarkably similar to the one identified by Schmidt-Leukel over a century later. At the intercultural level, Vivekananda—as we have already seen—maintains that each of the world religions "represents one" of the four Yogas (*CW* 8:152). Strikingly, though, he also anticipated Schmidt-Leukel in claiming that intercultural differences are reflected at both the intracultural and intrasubjective levels. In a passage from his lecture on "The Ideal of Karma-Yoga" already quoted in section 4 of this chapter, Vivekananda notes that the "divisions" between the four Yogas—namely, "work, love, psychology, and knowledge"—are "not very marked and quite exclusive of each other" and, hence, that each Yoga "blends into the other" (*CW* 1:108). Accordingly, at the *intracultural* level, Vivekananda claims that each religion, while predominantly emphasizing one Yoga more than the other three, nonetheless contains elements of the other Yogas to varying degrees. At the *intrasubjective* level, this same pattern reappears: "It is not that you can find men who have no other faculty than that of work, nor that you can find men who are no more than devoted worshippers only, nor that there are men who have no more than mere knowledge" (*CW* 1:108). Although most individuals possess one faculty to a greater degree than the other three faculties, they nonetheless also have these other faculties to a lesser degree. It is also highly significant that Vivekananda explicitly linked his sophisticated fractal paradigm to a full-blown religious pluralist position, the view that "[a]ll religions and all methods of work and worship lead us to one and the same goal" (*CW* 1:108). Here again, Vivekananda anticipated Schmidt-Leukel, who similarly argues that "a fractal interpretation of religious diversity . . . ultimately tends toward religious pluralism" (Schmidt-Leukel 2017: 237).

Vivekananda, then, can be seen as a valuable ally in Schmidt-Leukel's efforts to develop a fractal-based interreligious theology. More generally, in our contemporary climate of religious strife and violence, Vivekananda's Vedāntic religious cosmopolitanism is not merely of academic interest, as it can play a vital role in fostering mutual respect—and mutual learning—among the world's religious practitioners.

PART II

THE EXPERIENTIAL BASIS OF RELIGION

4

"The Science of Religion"

Vivekananda's Critique of Scientism and His Defense of the Scientific Credentials of Religion

A central aspect of Vivekananda's thought is his emphasis on spiritual experience, which he refers to variously as "superconscious perception" (*CW* 1:165), "realisation" (*CW* 1:165), "direct perception" (*CW* 4:122), "direct experience" (*CW* 1:126), "Anubhūti" (*CW* 3:377), and "*aparokṣānubhūti*" (*BCW* 9:33 / *CW* 7:142). As he puts it, "The end and aim of all religions is to realise God" (*CW* 6:82). Accordingly, he consistently subordinates doctrinal religious belief to the direct realization of spiritual truths like God and the soul:

> Religion is realising, and I shall call you a worshipper of God when you have become able to realise the Idea. Before that it is the spelling of words and no more. It is this power of realisation that makes religion; no amount of doctrines or philosophies, or ethical books, that you may have stuffed into your brain, will matter much—only what you *are* and what you have *realised*. (*CW* 5:265)

As has been well documented, Vivekananda's emphasis on the primacy of spiritual experience has been massively influential in shaping modern and contemporary articulations of Vedānta and Hinduism both within and outside of India.[1]

However, numerous recent scholars have criticized Vivekananda's appeal to spiritual experience on various grounds. For instance, Anantanand Rambachan (1994a: 94–112) and C. Mackenzie Brown (2012: 151–53) have argued, in opposition to Vivekananda, that spiritual experience is epistemically bankrupt, since it is inherently subjective and not amenable to empirical verification.[2] Scholars have also claimed that Vivekananda's privileging of spiritual experience over scripture marks a radical departure from the traditional Advaita Vedānta of Śaṅkara, who held that the Upaniṣads are the primary, if not the sole, means of knowing Brahman (Rambachan 1994a: 41–63, 113–25; Halbfass 1988: 378–402).

Vivekananda's critics, I will argue, have not sufficiently appreciated his multifaceted cosmopolitan rationale for emphasizing spiritual experience and his

[1] See, for instance, Bharati (1970: esp. 278), Rambachan (1994a: 6–7), and R. King (1999: 7–34).
[2] I address Rambachan's criticisms of Vivekananda in detail in section 5 of chapter 6.

Swami Vivekananda's Vedāntic Cosmopolitanism. Swami Medhananda, Oxford University Press. © Oxford University Press 2022. DOI: 10.1093/oso/9780197624463.003.0005

sophisticated arguments in support of its epistemic value. As a philosophically minded denizen of late nineteenth-century British-ruled India, Vivekananda was influenced not only by Indian thought-currents but also by scientific, philosophical, and theological developments in the West. He was, in short, a philosophical cosmopolitan, whose views on spiritual experience cannot be understood apart from the global intellectual context within which he articulated and defended them. Chapters 4 through 6 aim to shed new light on Vivekananda's views on spiritual experience by paying careful attention to his cosmopolitan philosophical method of drawing upon, and critically engaging, both Indian and Western ideas.

This chapter focuses on his multivalent doctrine of the "science of religion," which embodies his attempt to defend the scientific credentials of religion while also criticizing the scientism that was becoming prevalent during his time. Section 1 briefly elaborates the global cosmopolitan context within which he appealed to this "science of religion." For Vivekananda, the combined forces of scientific advancement, critical thinking, and globalization had precipitated nothing less than a global crisis of religious belief. His sustained effort to reground religion in spiritual experience, I contend, is best understood as a response to this global crisis. Section 2 examines the negative, polemical dimension of Vivekananda's "science of religion"—namely, his prescient critique of various forms of scientism. As we will see, his critique of scientism resonates with contemporary discussions of scientism in the philosophy of science. Section 3 shows how his critique of scientism clears the way for the positive, constructive dimension of his science of religion: namely, his defense of what I call a "wide empiricism." He claims that experience is the primary source of knowledge, but he widens the category of experience to encompass both sensory experience and supersensuous experience. While sensory experience is the basis of the natural sciences, supersensuous experience is the basis of the science of religion.

Chapter 5 discusses Vivekananda's philosophical argument for the epistemic value of supersensuous experience, which is central to his defense of a wide empiricism. Chapter 6 then demonstrates the relevance of his argument to contemporary philosophical debates and addresses some of the most important criticisms of his views on spiritual experience.

1. *Vivekananda's Appeal to Spiritual Experience as a Response to the Global Crisis of Religious Belief*

Vivekananda's emphasis on the primacy of spiritual experience has to be understood within his late nineteenth-century historical context. As the contemporary historian Frank Turner notes, "Between 1750 and 1870—from the publication of the *Encyclopédie* [of Diderot] to the early work of Nietzsche and of Darwin's *Descent of man*—the relationship of science and religion in the western world passed from fruitful co-operation and modest tensions to harsh public conflict . . . " (2010: 87). Darwin's revolutionary book *On the Origin of Species* (1859) sent shockwaves throughout the Western world, and Christian theologians scrambled either to attack Darwin's theory of evolution through natural selection or to accommodate at least parts of it within Christian doctrine (Brooke 1991: 374–437). In the popular imagination, there was a growing sense of a fundamental conflict between science and religion (Russell 2000: 12–17). Influential books attesting to this conflict began to proliferate, including John William Draper's *History of the Conflict between Religion and Science* (1874) and Andrew Dickson White's *A History of the Warfare of Science with Theology* (1896). The philosopher John Stuart Mill, in his book *Three Essays on Religion* (1874), attacked many of the traditional arguments for God's existence in the light of modern science. In 1860, the prominent British scientist Thomas Henry Huxley memorably remarked that "extinguished theologians lie about the cradle of every science as the strangled snakes beside that of Hercules" (quoted in Brooke 1991: 420).

Vivekananda, as an avid philosophy student at Scottish Church College in the 1880s, devoured the work of Western thinkers like T. H. Huxley, J. S. Mill, Charles Darwin, Auguste Comte, Herbert Spencer, Immanuel Kant, and Arthur Schopenhauer. Indeed, he became convinced that modern Western science and philosophy had undermined the very foundations of many traditional religious beliefs. In an 1895 lecture delivered in America, he gave voice to this growing crisis of religious belief in dramatic terms:

> At the beginning of this century it was almost feared that religion was at an end. Under the tremendous sledge-hammer blows of scientific research, old superstitions were crumbling away like masses of porcelain. Those to whom religion meant only a bundle of creeds and meaningless ceremonials were in despair; they were at their wit's end. Everything was slipping between their fingers. For a time it seemed inevitable that the surging tide of agnosticism and materialism would sweep all before it. There were those who did not dare utter what they thought. Many thought the case hopeless and the cause of religion lost once and for ever. But the tide has turned and to the rescue has come—what? The study of comparative religions. By the study of different religions we find that in essence they are one. When I was a boy, this scepticism reached me, and it seemed for a time as if I must give up all hope of religion. But fortunately for me I studied the Christian religion, the Mohammedan, the Buddhistic, and

> others, and what was my surprise to find that the same foundation principles taught by my religion were also taught by all religions. (*CW* 1:317)[3]

Vivekananda voiced here the widespread sentiment that religion—understood solely or primarily as a "bundle of creeds," a set of dogmatic religious beliefs—had been severely undermined, if not destroyed, by the "tremendous sledge-hammer blows" of modern science and skepticism.[4] Tellingly, he then waxed autobiographical, noting that as a boy, he had himself become skeptical about religion until he studied, and compared, many different religions and found that "in essence they are one." What he elliptically alludes to here was his own personal spiritual crisis as a student, when he had almost lost faith in religion and began to approach prominent Hindu and Christian religious figures like Debendranath Tagore, asking them, "Have you seen God?" (*CW* 3:345–46).

As we saw in chapter 1, the young Vivekananda's turning point came in 1882, when he met his future guru Ramakrishna. His own account of this fateful encounter is highly significant:

> He [Ramakrishna] used the most simple language, and I thought "Can this man be a great teacher?"—crept near to him and asked him the question which I had been asking others all my life: "Do you believe in God, Sir?" "Yes," he replied. "Can you prove it, Sir?" "Yes." "How?" "Because I see Him just as I see you here, only in a much intenser sense." That impressed me at once. For the first time I found a man who dared to say that he saw God, that religion was a reality to be felt, to be sensed in an infinitely more intense way than we can sense the world. (*CW* 4:179)

In Ramakrishna, the young Vivekananda found someone who believed in God not because some scripture or religious authority told him to but because he had directly perceived God. The analogy Ramakrishna drew between sensory experience and spiritual experience is also important, since—as we will see in chapter 5—it became a key aspect of Vivekananda's later philosophical defense of the epistemic value of spiritual experience. Just as we believe that ordinary sense-objects like tables and chairs exist because we perceive them through our five senses, Ramakrishna told Vivekananda that he believed in God's existence because he directly perceived God.

Vivekananda was also deeply impressed by the fact that Ramakrishna practiced a variety of *sādhanas* in different religious traditions—including Advaita Vedānta, Tantra, Vaiṣṇavism, Christianity, and Islam—and declared, on

[3] For a similar passage, see *CW* 1:366–67.
[4] For detailed discussion of Vivekananda's treatment of this issue, see Green (2016).

the basis of his own spiritual experiences, that all religious paths lead to the common goal of realizing God in one or more of His innumerable forms and aspects. As Vivekananda put it, he learned from Ramakrishna "the central secret that the truth may be one and yet many at the same time, that we may have different visions of the same truth from different standpoints . . . " (*CW* 4:181). Vivekananda clearly had this idea in mind when he remarked, in the passage from the 1895 lecture quoted earlier, that it was the "study of comparative religions" that had rescued him from the abyss of skepticism. He made this point explicit later in the same 1895 lecture:

> The next idea that I want to bring to you is that religion does not consist in doctrines or dogmas. It is not what you read, nor what dogmas you believe that is of importance, but what you realise. . . . The end of all religions is the realising of God in the soul. That is the one universal religion. If there is one universal truth in all religions, I place it here—in realising God. (*CW* 1:324)

By regrounding religion in spiritual experience rather than in mere creedal belief, Vivekananda sought to address at a stroke three of the most serious problems facing religion in the late nineteenth century: the problem of conflicting religious truth-claims, the problem of religious fanaticism and violence, and the problem of reconciling religion with modern science and philosophy.

In an era of increasing globalization, Vivekananda insisted that it was no longer possible for us to ignore the fact that there were a variety of religions other than our own. However, as soon as we recognize religious diversity, we are faced with the formidable problem of deciding which of the many world religions to accept, since different religions appear to conflict with one another on various points of doctrine and spiritual practice. As he puts it, "the Christian claims that his religion is the only true one, because it was revealed to so-and-so. The Mohammedan makes the same claim for his religion; his is the only true one, because it was revealed to so-and-so" (*CW* 1:368). After rehearsing an imagined debate between a Christian and a Muslim regarding ethics as taught in their respective scriptures, Vivekananda asks: "How is this to be decided? Certainly not by the books, because the books, fighting between themselves, cannot be the judges. Decidedly then we have to admit that there is something more universal than these books . . . " (*CW* 1:368). As I discussed at length in the previous chapter, Vivekananda follows Ramakrishna in claiming that the universal basis of all religions is the direct experience of God. Even if the various religions *do* conflict on certain points of doctrine, religious doctrines are secondary, since they are only different means to the primary goal of realizing the Divine Reality in any of His innumerable forms or aspects. From Vivekananda's standpoint, then, the extraordinary diversity of religious views turns out not to be a problem but a boon: since *all* religions ultimately lead to salvific spiritual experience, and different religions appeal to people of differing temperaments and belief-systems, each person can follow the religion that best suits him or her.

Vivekananda also argues that religious fanaticism and conflict stem primarily from dogmatic adherence to certain beliefs and customs as the be-all and end-all of religion:

> Why is there so much disturbance, so much fighting and quarrelling in the name of God? There has been more bloodshed in the name of God than for any other cause, because people never went to the fountain-head; they were content only to give a mental assent to the customs of their forefathers, and wanted others to do the same. What right has a man to say he has a soul if he does not feel it, or that there is a God if he does not see Him? (*CW* 1:127)

For Vivekananda, religious conflicts arise because people fail to go to the "fountain-head" of all religions: direct spiritual experience. While beliefs and customs vary considerably from one religion to another, all religions are based on the common foundation of spiritual experience. Hence, according to Vivekananda, one of the best ways to reduce religious strife and violence throughout the world is to recognize the primacy of spiritual experience over religious doctrine.

2. *Vivekananda's Critique of Scientism*

By regrounding religion in spiritual experience, Vivekananda also attempted to establish a rigorous "science of religion," which could withstand scientific and philosophical scrutiny. He referred to the "science of religion" no fewer than thirteen times in the *Complete Works*.[5] As De Michelis (2004: 64) has noted, "the idea of a 'science of religion' had become common currency in Brahmo circles by the second half of the nineteenth century." The Brāhmo leaders Akshay Kumar Dutt, Rajnarayan Bose, and Keshab Chandra Sen had all attempted to prove that religion was not a set of dogmatic beliefs but a "science" grounded in empirical verification (De Michelis 2004: 62–64; Baier 2019: 246–51). Keshab, for instance, argued in an 1880 lecture that "[b]etween God-vision and the spirit of science in the nineteenth century there is no discord, but rather concord" (K. C. Sen 1901: 405). According to Keshab, since the first principle of all sciences is "Prove all things and hold fast that which is true," religion is also a science, since

[5] See *CW* 6:81, *CW* 6:308, *CW* 7:38, *CW* 7:431, *CW* 3:5, *CW* 9:286, *CW* 1:165, *CW* 1:199, *CW* 4:215, *CW* 6:136, *CW* 4:285, *CW* 1:14, *CW* 1:367.

religion is grounded not in "trust" and "dreamy speculations" but in "the direct apprehension of God and Heaven in consciousness" (K. C. Sen 1901: 396–97). Vivekananda was almost certainly influenced by these earlier Brāhmo efforts to develop a "science of religion." However, I will make the case in chapters 4 through 6 that his specific theorization of religion as a "science" grounded in empirical verification has a number of distinctive features that are absent from the work of Brāhmos like Keshab.

In Vivekananda's hands, the "science of religion" had both negative and positive dimensions: it served as a critique of the prevailing climate of scientism in the late nineteenth century and as a defense of the scientific credentials of religion. He never used the term "scientism," nor was the term current during his time.[6] Nonetheless, he frequently criticized various forms of what would now be called "scientism," and—as I will argue—his critique of scientism formed an integral part of his case for the primacy of spiritual experience. In the past few decades, scientism has become a hotly discussed topic in scholarly circles.[7] To appreciate the subtlety and prescience of Vivekananda's late nineteenth-century critique of scientism, it will help to consider briefly contemporary discussions of three of the primary forms of scientism as well as three of the major philosophical arguments *against* scientism.

As the philosopher of science Samir Okasha notes, "scientism," in popular usage, is a pejorative term for "science-worship—the over-reverential attitude towards science found in many intellectual circles" (2002: 121). Susan Haack similarly defines scientism, in its popular, pejorative sense, as "an exaggerated kind of deference towards science, an excessive readiness to accept as authoritative any claim made by the sciences, and to dismiss every kind of criticism of science or its practitioners as anti-scientific prejudice" (2007: 17–18). Let us call this understanding of scientism "CS," short for the "Common Understanding of Scientism." Rik Peels has also distinguished two neutral (i.e., non-pejorative), narrower, and more philosophically precise senses of the term "scientism." He defines "epistemological scientism"—let us call this "ES"—as the view that only the natural sciences deliver genuine knowledge (Peels 2018: 33). By contrast, "ontological scientism"—let us call this "OS"—is the view that the only entities that *exist* are those that are discoverable through the natural sciences (Peels 2018: 35).

This is not the place to discuss all the various arguments for and against these different forms of scientism. I will only outline here three of the most important arguments against scientism, which are especially relevant to an understanding of Vivekananda's views. The first argument targets an underlying assumption

[6] For one of the earliest uses of the term "scientism" in the contemporary sense, see Hayek (1942: 267–91).

[7] See, for instance, Boudry and Pigliucci (2017), De Ridder, Peels, and van Woudenberg (2018), Williams and Robinson (2015), Sorell (1991).

of all forms of scientism (CS, ES, and OS)—namely, scientific realism. Michael Liston defines scientific realism as "the view that well-confirmed scientific theories are approximately true; the entities they postulate do exist; and we have good reason to believe their main tenets" (2019). Though not all scientific realists subscribe to scientism, all proponents of scientism clearly subscribe to scientific realism.[8] After all, the scientistic belief in the epistemic value and great explanatory power of science obviously presupposes the scientific realist thesis that scientific theories are more or less truth-tracking.

One of the most influential arguments *against* scientific realism is the "pessimistic induction" argument first rigorously formulated by Larry Laudan (Laudan 1981a). According to Laudan, there are innumerable examples of past scientific theories that were highly successful at the time they were first proposed but which later proved to be false, including the "phlogiston theory of chemistry," the "caloric theory of heat," and "the electromagnetic aether" (1981a: 33). He concludes, therefore, that we have no good reason to believe that our *current* scientific theories are even approximately true.

Another common argument that directly targets both the epistemological and ontological forms of scientism is the "argument from nonscientific assumptions and principles in science," which Jeroen De Ridder, Rik Peels, and René van Woudenberg summarize as follows:

> There are certain principles that are indispensable for doing science, but that are not themselves the result of the science. These principles are held to be indispensable for science in the sense that if they cannot be rationally believed or known, then science cannot deliver rational belief or knowledge. . . . Among the basic assumptions and principles that scientists would seem to have to embrace in order to do science are epistemic theses—for example, that our cognitive faculties, such as perception or logical reasoning, are broadly reliable . . . —metaphysical theses—for example, that the world behaves in a regular way, has done so for times immemorial, and will continue to do so—and semantic principles—for example, that if a name refers to a thing and another name refers to a thing, and the things referred to have all the same properties, then the names refer to numerically the same thing. (2018: 19)

According to this argument, then, ES and OS must be false, because they presuppose a host of epistemic, metaphysical, and semantic beliefs and principles that are themselves not justified by science.[9]

[8] For an explanation of the difference between scientific realism and scientism as well as their interrelation, see Sankey (2008: 20–21).

[9] For formulations of this argument, see van Woudenberg (2011: 176–77) and Midgley (1992: 108).

Very recently, Alvin Plantinga has presented an argument against epistemological scientism that targets what he takes to be its empiricist underpinnings:

> Now what sorts of belief underlie scientism? Where does it come from? For the most part it would seem to originate in versions of empiricism. Empiricism comes in several forms, but fundamentally it is the idea that experience is our only source of knowledge. Empiricism thus precludes the idea that we can attain knowledge by way of reason as well as by way of experience. (Plantinga 2018: 223–24)

Plantinga then critically examines the forms of sensory empiricism advocated by John Locke, David Hume, and in the twentieth century by the logical positivist A. J. Ayer and his followers. He argues that all forms of empiricism have fatal problems, such as the "self-referential problem"—namely, that empiricism presupposes theses that are themselves not empirically grounded (Plantinga 2018: 224–25). He concludes, therefore, that "if scientism is grounded in these sorts of empiricism, it is poorly grounded indeed" (Plantinga 2018: 225).

I would argue that Vivekananda, in the 1890s, both identified and critically interrogated all three major forms of scientism that are currently being discussed (CS, ES, and OS). He repeatedly singled out for attack what he called "scientific popery" and "scientific superstition"—an excessive reverence for everything scientific and the tendency to accept uncritically the findings of modern science (in other words, CS):

> In olden times the churches had prestige, but today science has got it. And just as in olden times people never inquired for themselves—never studied the Bible, and so the priests had a very good opportunity to teach whatever they liked—so even now the majority of people do not study for themselves and, at the same time, have a tremendous awe and fear before anything called scientific. You ought to remember that there is a worse popery coming than ever existed in the church—the so-called scientific popery, which has become so successful that it dictates to us with more authority than religious popery.
>
> These popes of modern science are great popes indeed, but sometimes they ask us to believe more wonderful things than any priest or any religion ever did. (*CW* 9:212)[10]

In a shrewd reversal of the commonly held view that modern science had debunked the claims of dogmatic religion, Vivekananda remarked, with biting sarcasm, that science had become a new dogmatic religion in its own right. He

[10] For a similar passage, see *CW* 2:74.

may have had in mind late nineteenth-century thinkers like T. H. Huxley and Ernst Haeckel, who—as the historian John Hedley Brooke notes—inflated "Darwin's science" into "a naturalistic world-view, and thence into a rival religion" (Brooke 1991: 417). Haack, as we have just seen, echoes Vivekananda when she diagnoses in our contemporary culture "an exaggerated kind of deference towards science, an excessive readiness to accept as authoritative any claim made by the sciences" (2007: 17–18).

In an 1899 lecture delivered in Los Angeles, Vivekananda attacked the rampant scientism of his day—including CS, ES, and OS—by appealing to an argument that resonates with the contemporary pessimistic induction argument:

> For practical purposes, let us talk in the language of modern science. But I must ask you to bear in mind that, as there is religious superstition, so also there is a superstition in the matter of science. There are priests who take up religious work as their speciality; so also there are priests of physical law, scientists. As soon as a great scientist's name, like Darwin or Huxley, is cited, we follow blindly. It is the fashion of the day. Ninety-nine per cent of what we call scientific knowledge is mere theories. And many of them are no better than the old superstitions of ghosts with many heads and hands, but with this difference that the latter differentiated man a little from stocks and stones. True science asks us to be cautious. Just as we should be careful with the priests, so we should be with the scientists. Begin with disbelief. Analyse, test, prove everything, and then take it. Some of the most current beliefs of modern science have not been proved. Even in such a science as mathematics, the vast majority of its theories are only working hypotheses. With the advent of greater knowledge they will be thrown away. (*CW* 2:28)

Vivekananda criticized what he perceived to be the scientistic tendency during his time to accept blindly the findings of science as indisputable facts. He argues that the vast majority of scientific findings are nothing more than "mere theories" or "working hypotheses" that have not yet been proved to be true. Indeed, he claims that the majority of current scientific theories—even in mathematics—will eventually be discarded. As we have just seen, many contemporary philosophers like Laudan have defended precisely such an "anti-realist" stance toward science by appealing to the pessimistic induction argument: since innumerable scientific theories in the past that were once highly successful and widely held to be true were later proved to be wrong, we have good reason to believe that our *current* scientific theories will also be proved wrong eventually. Like Laudan, Vivekananda rejects an uncritical scientific realism in favor of a critical openness to the possibility that even the most deeply entrenched scientific dogmas of our day might later be falsified.

On numerous occasions, Vivekananda specifically targeted both ontological and epistemological forms of scientism (OS and ES). For instance, in the preface to *Rāja-Yoga*, he claims that "Rāja-Yoga does not, after the unpardonable manner of some modern scientists, deny the existence of facts which are difficult to explain" (*CW* 1:121). The "facts" he has in mind here include "various extraordinary phenomena" like "miracles," "answers to prayers," and—much more importantly—spiritual experiences of supersensuous realities like God and the soul (*CW* 1:121). Some scientists, he claims, deny the existence of such phenomena on the grounds that they cannot be explained by the methods of modern natural science. Vivekananda argues that these proponents of ontological scientism presuppose without justification the highly controversial philosophical thesis that everything that exists is discoverable through the natural sciences. In fact, as we will see in the next section, he specifically argues against this ontological thesis by defending the view that we can gain knowledge of *metaphysical* realities like God and the soul through supersensuous perception.

In an unfinished article on "The Fundamentals of Religion," Vivekananda also criticized epistemological scientism by anticipating two of the contemporary arguments against scientism discussed earlier—namely, Plantinga's critique of the empiricist basis of scientism as well as the argument from nonscientific assumptions and principles in science. The relevant passage from his article is long but philosophically rich, so it deserves to be quoted in full:

> There is a great outcry going over the world against metaphysical knowledge as opposed to what is styled physical knowledge. This crusade against the metaphysical and the beyond-this-life, to establish the present life and the present world on a firmer basis, is fast becoming a fashion to which even the preachers of religion one after the other are fast succumbing. . . .
>
> Now, no one denies that our senses, as long as they are normal, are the most trustworthy guides we have, and the facts they gather in for us form the very foundation of the structure of human knowledge. But if they [those who deny metaphysical knowledge] mean that all human knowledge is only sense-perception and nothing but that, we deny it. If by physical sciences are meant systems of knowledge which are entirely based and built upon sense-perception, and nothing but that, we contend that such a science never existed nor will ever exist. Nor will any system of knowledge, built upon sense-perception alone, ever be a science.
>
> Senses no doubt cull the materials of knowledge and find similarities and dissimilarities; but there they have to stop. In the first place the physical gatherings of facts are conditioned by certain metaphysical conceptions, such as space and time. Secondly, grouping facts, or generalisation, is impossible without some abstract notion as the background. The higher the generalization,

> the more metaphysical is the abstract background upon which the detached facts are arranged. Now, such ideas as matter, force, mind, law, causation, time, and space are the results of very high abstractions, and nobody has ever sensed any one of them; in other words, they are entirely metaphysical. Yet without these metaphysical conceptions, no physical fact is possible to be understood. Thus a certain motion becomes understood when it is referred to a force; certain sensations, to matter; certain changes outside, to law; certain changes in thought, to mind; certain order singly, to causation—and joined to time, to law. Yet nobody has seen or even imagined matter or force, law or causation, time or space. (*CW* 4:377–78)

Vivekananda begins by noting the prevalence of an empiricist outlook that rejects "metaphysical knowledge" in favor of "physical knowledge." He almost certainly has in mind empiricist thinkers like David Hume, Auguste Comte, and John Stuart Mill, who held that sensory experience is the ultimate source of all knowledge. Vivekananda's stance toward empiricism is dialectical: while he admits that the "facts" learned through our senses "form the very foundation of the structure of human knowledge," he rejects the empiricist thesis that "all human knowledge is only sense-perception and nothing but that." As we will see in the next section, his main argument against a narrowly sensory empiricism is that it unjustifiably rules out the possibility of knowledge gained through supersensuous perception.

In the remainder of the quoted passage, Vivekananda anticipates Plantinga in criticizing forms of epistemological scientism that are based on sensory empiricism: "If by physical sciences are meant systems of knowledge which are entirely based and built upon sense-perception, and nothing but that, we contend that such a science never existed nor will ever exist." He seems to have in mind here the positivist philosophy of Comte, which was quite fashionable during his time. Vivekananda had read Comte's work as an undergraduate,[11] and he refers to "August[e] Comte" in *Bhakti-Yoga* (*CW* 3:61) and to "the modern positivists" and "modern Comtists" in one of his 1896 lectures on "Practical Vedānta" (*CW* 2:342). Comte rejected both the "theological" and "metaphysical" attitudes of mind in favor of the "positivist" or scientific attitude, which he defined as the pursuit of knowledge solely on the basis of empirical observation and verification (Harré 2003: 11–26, esp. 13; Laudan 1981b: esp. 146). As Laudan notes, "Comte used the requirement of verifiability as a stick with which to beat the metaphysicians" (1981b: 145). Comte's positivism, as Vivekananda recognized,

[11] For detailed information on Vivekananda's studies at Scottish Church College, see Dhar (1975: 51–61).

was tantamount to epistemological scientism: only the empirical sciences can deliver knowledge, since the sciences alone are based on sensory observation.

Vivekananda's subtle argument against epistemological scientism can be seen as an early articulation of the "argument from nonscientific assumptions and principles in science" that is now being discussed in debates about scientism. He argues that scientific inquiry presupposes a whole host of metaphysical concepts—such as time, space, matter, force, law, and causation—that science itself cannot justify. According to Vivekananda, the senses only furnish the "materials of knowledge" for science, but metaphysical concepts are needed in order to arrive at scientific theories on the basis of these sensory materials. The scientist, he argues, cannot even gather together various pieces of physical evidence without presupposing the metaphysical concepts of space and time. Further, we cannot make any generalizations on the basis of sensory data unless we employ a host of metaphysical categories like causation, law, and force. For Vivekananda, then, any form of epistemological scientism proves to be self-defeating, since scientific inquiry itself presupposes metaphysical concepts that cannot be justified through science.

3. *Vivekananda's Defense of a Wide Empiricism*

While Vivekananda wholeheartedly endorses the empiricist insistence on the need for verification through direct experience, he rejects a narrowly sensory empiricism, the view that all knowledge derives only from the five senses. Instead, he endorses a *wide* empiricism that encompasses both sensory perception as well as supersensuous perception. Indeed, he begins his lecture on "Religion and Science" by grounding the "science of religion" in such a wide empiricism:

> Experience is the only source of knowledge. In the world, religion is the only source where there is no surety, because it is not taught as a science of experience. This should not be. There is always, however, a small group of men who teach religion from experience. They are called mystics, and these mystics in every religion speak the same tongue and teach the same truth. This is the real science of religion. (*CW* 6:81)

The first sentence signals his endorsement of a certain form of empiricism: "Experience is the only source of knowledge." However, in stark contrast to the major Western empiricists, Vivekananda accords scientific status to religion by widening the concept of experience to include religious experience. For Vivekananda, natural sciences like physics and chemistry are based on sensory experience, while the science of religion is based on *supersensuous* experience.

He provides a more nuanced account of wide empiricism in his lecture on "Cosmology," dated December 18, 1895:

> There are two worlds, the microcosm, and the macrocosm, the internal and the external. We get truth from both of these by means of experience. The truth gathered from internal experience is psychology, metaphysics, and religion; from external experience, the physical sciences. (*CW* 2:432)

Truth, according to Vivekananda, derives from either "external experience" or "internal experience." By "external experience" he means sensory experience,[12] on which all the "physical sciences" are based. It is worth noting that contemporary philosophers like Haack and van Woudenberg defend something akin to Vivekananda's view of the physical sciences. Haack, for instance, argues that natural science is the "long arm of common sense"—that is, an extension and refinement of "the resources on which we all rely in the most ordinary of everyday empirical inquiry" (2007: 93–122). [13] Internal experience, Vivekananda claims, is the source of the truths not only of "religion" but also of "psychology" and "metaphysics." If religion is based on supersensuous experience, psychology and metaphysics are typically based on other forms of "internal experience" like, presumably, introspection and self-inquiry.

In his Bengali essay "*Hindudharma o Śrīrāmakṛṣṇa*" (1901; "Hinduism and Sri Ramakrishna"), Vivekananda provides a slightly different account of wide empiricism:

> Truth is of two kinds: (1) that which is cognizable by the five ordinary senses of man, and by inferential reasoning based thereon; (2) that which is cognizable by the subtle, supersensuous power born of Yoga (*jāhā atīndriya sūkṣma yogaja śaktir grāhya*).
>
> Knowledge acquired by the first means is called "science" (*vijñāna*); and knowledge acquired by the second is called "Veda."
>
> The whole body of supersensuous truths (*jñānarāśi*), having no beginning or end, and called by the name of "Veda," is ever-existent, and the Creator Himself is creating, preserving, and destroying the universe with the help of these truths.
>
> The person in whom this supersensuous power (*atīndriya śakti*) is manifested is called a "Rishi," and the supersensuous truths (*alaukik satya*) which he realises by this power are called "Veda."

[12] It should be noted that he clearly accepts that sensory experience should be aided, whenever necessary, by instruments like microscopes and telescopes, since he refers to such instruments in numerous places (for instance, at *CW* 1:414 and *CW* 1:158).

[13] For a similar view, see van Woudenberg (2018: 167–89, esp. 169–71).

The attainment of this Rishihood and this supersensuous perception of Veda is the true experiential verification of religion (*ei ṛṣitva o vedadraṣṭṛtva lābh karāi yathārta dharmānubhūti*). And so long as this does not develop in the life of an initiate, so long is religion a mere empty word to him, and it is to be understood that he has not yet taken the first step in religion.

The authority of Veda extends to all ages, climes, and persons; that is to say, its application is not confined to any particular place, time, or person. (*BCW* 6:3 / *CW* 6:181; translation modified)

In this passage, Vivekananda claims that truth derives from sensory and supersensuous experience. Sensory experience—together with inferential reasoning based on sensory experience—yields the truths discovered by the natural sciences (*vijñāna*) like physics, chemistry, and biology.[14] Sensory experience clearly corresponds to what he called "external experience" in his earlier "Cosmology" lecture.

However, in his "Cosmology" lecture, he claimed that "internal experience" was the source of the truths not only of "religion" but also of "psychology" and "metaphysics" (*CW* 2:432). By contrast, his formulation of a wide empiricism in this later passage does not explicitly accommodate metaphysical and psychological knowledge. Supersensuous experience, he claims here, yields the "body of supersensuous truths" which he refers to as "Veda." The Sanskrit-derived Bengali word *veda*, which derives from the verbal root *vid* ("to know"), literally means "Knowledge." In a striking move, Vivekananda defines "Veda" etymologically as the body of supersensuous truths—concerning God, the soul, and so on—known through Yogic perception. Hence, it is clear from the context that by "Veda" he does *not* mean the well-known Indian scriptures like the Ṛg Veda, Yajur Veda, and so on. For Vivekananda, the "authority of Veda extends to all ages, climes, and persons"; hence, spiritual experience alone can furnish a universal basis for religion. None of us can be truly religious, Vivekananda claims, until we gain direct experiential knowledge of the supersensuous realities propounded in our religious scriptures.

The problem with this formulation of a wide empiricism is that it does not seem to be compatible with the fact that, in various other places in his work, he clearly accepts the possibility of metaphysical knowledge. We need only recall from the previous section his own argument that the physical sciences presuppose various metaphysical concepts such as matter, force, causation, and law that cannot themselves be justified by these sciences (*CW* 4:377–78). It is, of course, possible that Vivekananda's understanding of wide empiricism evolved

[14] In this context, he uses the term "*vijñāna*" ("science") in the narrow sense of the natural sciences, so he is not denying the scientific status of religion.

from his 1895 "Cosmology" lecture to his 1901 "*Hindudharma o Śrīrāmakṛṣṇa*" essay. However, there is no evidence from his post-1895 work that he ever repudiated the possibility of gaining knowledge of metaphysical and psychological truths. Hence, I think it would be more plausible to take his formulation of wide empiricism in the "Cosmology" lecture to represent his true position, which he held until the end of his life. Accordingly, his narrower formulation of wide empiricism in "*Hindudharma o Śrīrāmakṛṣṇa*"—which problematically excludes metaphysical and psychological knowledge—needs to be supplemented and corrected by his earlier formulation of wide empiricism in terms of internal and external experience.[15]

Vivekananda's introduction to *Rāja-Yoga* contains his most detailed and systematic defense of the scientific status of religion on the basis of a wide empiricism. In the opening paragraph, he delineates some of the key features of the "exact sciences":

> All our knowledge is based upon experience. What we call inferential knowledge, in which we go from the less to the more general, or from the general to the particular, has experience as its basis. In what are called the exact sciences, people easily find the truth, because it appeals to the particular experiences of every human being. The scientist does not tell you to believe in anything, but he has certain results which come from his own experiences, and reasoning on them when he asks us to believe in his conclusions, he appeals to some universal experience of humanity. In every exact science there is a basis which is common to all humanity, so that we can at once see the truth or the fallacy of the conclusions drawn therefrom. Now, the question is: Has religion any such basis or not? (*CW* 1:125)

According to Vivekananda, sciences like physics, chemistry, and astronomy exhibit three basic features. First, all sciences are based on "universal experience," in that they appeal to sense-data that is, in principle, accessible to everyone. Second, the sciences present hypotheses or theories that invite empirical verification. If we follow the steps laid out by the scientist, each of us can verify for ourselves the "truth or the fallacy" of the scientist's conclusions. Hence, third, the

[15] One might ask whether and how Vivekananda's wide empiricism accommodates mathematical truths, which are arguably known through a priori reasoning. As far as I am aware, he never explicitly addressed this issue. It is clear, however, that he considered mathematics to be a genuine science. He notes, for instance, that "algebra, geometry, astronomy, and the triumph of modern science—mixed mathematics—were all invented in India" (*CW* 2:511). Since Vivekananda had read Mill, he may have endorsed a form of mathematical empiricism akin to the one elaborated by Mill in chapters 5 and 6 of Book II of *A System of Logic* (1843). As a wide empiricist, Vivekananda would likely have maintained that mathematical knowledge derives from inferential reasoning based on sensory experience. Some recent philosophers of mathematics have continued to defend versions of mathematical empiricism (Gillies 2000: 41–57).

sciences do not require us to "believe in anything" or to take anything on faith; instead, we need not accept what any scientist tells us until we have confirmed a given scientific theory ourselves.

On the basis of his wide empiricism, Vivekananda proceeds to argue that genuine religion is, indeed, scientific, since it exhibits all three of these key features of science. Even though most people mistakenly think that religion is nothing but a set of doctrines that one must uncritically swallow or accept on faith, he claims that the *founders* of all religions taught these doctrines on the basis of their own direct experience. As he puts it, "Thus it is clear that all the religions of the world have been built upon that one universal and adamantine foundation of all our knowledge—direct experience. The teachers all saw God; they all saw their own souls . . . " (*CW* 1:126). Here, it is clear that his case for the scientific status of religion hinges on his wide empiricism. If we equate "experience" with *sensory* experience, then religion clearly would not count as a science. For Vivekananda, however, experience can be either sensory or supersensuous. The physical sciences are based on the former, while religious science is based on the latter.

He also argues that the science of religion, like all sciences, invites empirical verification:

> Our business is to verify, not to swallow. Religion, like other sciences, requires you to gather facts, to see for yourself, and this is possible when you go beyond the knowledge which lies in the region of the five senses. Religious truths need verification by everyone. (*CW* 6:133)[16]

The science of religion, like any other science, prescribes a systematic procedure for verifying its claims. In the course of his book *Rāja-Yoga*, Vivekananda details the "eight-limbed" (*aṣṭāṅga*) procedure taught in Patañjali's *Yogasūtra*, a graded series of ethical and spiritual practices like chastity, truthfulness, sense-restraint, and meditation, culminating in the "superconscious" state of *samādhi*, which gives us "[m]etaphysical and transcendental knowledge" of supersensuous realities like God and the soul (*CW* 1:183). Since the science of religion is based on empirical verification, it does not require us to believe any of its claims until we have verified them for ourselves. He puts this in the form of a motto: "Believe nothing until you find it out for yourself" (*CW* 1:131).

Vivekananda was well aware that many people would be skeptical of his claims about the empirical verifiability of religion, so he took great pains to anticipate some of their objections. One such objection is that religion is not really a science, since the procedures for verifying religious claims are radically different from the verificatory methods typically found in sciences like chemistry and

[16] For similar passages, see *CW* 1:9, *CW* 7:9, and *CW* 1:128.

astronomy. Anticipating this objection, Vivekananda argues that each science has its own unique procedures of verification:

> The science of Rāja-Yoga proposes to put before humanity a practical and scientifically worked out method of reaching this truth. In the first place, every science must have its own method of investigation. If you want to become an astronomer and sit down and cry "Astronomy! Astronomy!" it will never come to you. The same with chemistry. A certain method must be followed. You must go to a laboratory, take different substances, mix them up, compound them, experiment with them, and out of that will come a knowledge of chemistry. If you want to be an astronomer, you must go to an observatory, take a telescope, study the stars and planets, and then you will become an astronomer. Each science must have its own methods. I could preach you thousands of sermons, but they would not make you religious, until you practiced the method. These are the truths of the sages of all countries, of all ages, of men pure and unselfish, who had no motive but to do good to the world. They all declare that they have found some truth higher than what the senses can bring to us, and they invite verification. They ask us to take up the method and practice honestly, and then, if we do not find this higher truth, we will have the right to say there is no truth in the claim, but before we have done that, we are not rational in denying the truth of their assertions. So we must work faithfully using the prescribed methods, and light will come. (*CW* 1:128–29)

Vivekananda's key point is that "[e]ach science must have its own methods." Astronomy, for instance, often involves observing distant objects through a telescope, while chemistry involves mixing together substances and experimenting with them. The majority of contemporary philosophers of science agree with Vivekananda that there is no single "scientific method" that is common to all the sciences.[17] As Thomas Nickles puts it, "There is no such thing as 'the' scientific method, let alone agreement on what exactly it is" (2013: 115). Alex Rosenberg also echoes Vivekananda in his claim that "different sciences perforce employ methods suited to their own domains and not those of others" (2017: 203).

Vivekananda goes on to argue that since each science has its own unique methods, it would be a mistake to expect that the particular methods employed in the science of religion must be identical, or even similar, to methods employed in other sciences. The science of religion, he claims, prescribes certain ethical and spiritual practices that, when carried out properly, will put us in a position

[17] See, for instance, Andersen and Hepburn (2015: section 6.1), Nickles (2013: 101–20), Dupré (1993: 233), and Laudan (1983).

to verify religious truth-claims by enabling us to experience for ourselves the supersensuous truths of religion, such as God or the soul.

He further argues that the *difficulty* of these ethical and spiritual practices does not in any way impugn the empirical verifiability of religion:

> It is comparatively easy to observe facts in the external world, for many instruments have been invented for the purpose, but in the internal world we have no instrument to help us. . . . The science of Rāja-Yoga, in the first place, proposes to give us such a means of observing the internal states. The instrument is the mind itself. The power of attention, when properly guided, and directed towards the internal world, will analyse the mind, and illumine facts for us. (*CW* 1:129)

If, say, an astronomer claims that there is a star in a certain nebula, we can easily verify her claim by looking through a sufficiently powerful telescope and seeing whether there really is a star in that nebula. Since sciences like astronomy and chemistry make claims about physical objects that are perceivable through the five senses, their instruments of investigation are correspondingly physical. However, since religions make claims about supersensuous realities, the primary instrument for investigating these inner spiritual realities is the cultivated mind itself.[18] It should hardly be a surprise that the arduous mental investigation of the "internal world" requires a great deal more practice and effort than most external investigations. After all, the internal methods of religion, unlike the external procedures of the physical sciences, require a high degree of ethical and spiritual development, which most of us lack, at least initially.

In this context, we can address a potential objection to Vivekananda's bold thesis that religion can be verified in a "scientific" manner. Aren't there disaffected practitioners of mystical traditions like Advaita Vedānta and Zen Buddhism who have given up after practicing for years without ever having the kind of experience the traditions promise? If there is even one such person, then—supposing that person is sincere and trustworthy—wouldn't that be grounds for doubting Vivekananda's thesis that the truths of religion can be verified in a "scientific" manner?

I believe Vivekananda would respond that these disaffected practitioners failed to attain the spiritual goal of their respective traditions not because these traditions make false promises but because either the practitioners themselves were not sufficiently sincere and wholehearted in practicing the ethical and

[18] There is a complexity here, since Vivekananda, as we will see in chapter 9, accepts the Sāṃkhyan view that the mind itself is a subtle form of matter. A more nuanced way of stating Vivekananda's position, then, is that the mind is the primary instrument of Rāja-Yoga until the attainment of *samādhi*, at which point the mind is transcended.

spiritual methods taught in their traditions, or they *were* sufficiently sincere and wholehearted but had not yet attained the requisite level of purity and spiritual development. To use an analogy, verifying religious truth-claims is less like learning to use a very powerful and complicated telescope in order to view distant galaxies—a feat that many people could presumably pull off if they put in the requisite time and effort—and more like verifying Fermat's Last Theorem, which states that no three positive integers a, b, and c satisfy the equation $a^n + b^n = c^n$ for any integer value of n greater than 2. Around 1637, Pierre de Fermat introduced this theorem and noted that he had a proof, but he never ended up publishing that proof. For centuries, some of the best mathematical minds tried and failed to verify Fermat's Last Theorem, which was consequently downgraded to the status of a "conjecture." Finally, in 1994, Andrew Wiles came up with a proof of Fermat's Last Theorem. Would those disaffected mathematicians prior to Wiles—who spent years trying unsuccessfully to prove Fermat's Last Theorem—have been justified in concluding that the theorem was either false or unprovable? I think not. Now that Fermat's Last Theorem has been proved by Wiles and subsequently verified by many others, we can say for sure that the theorem was verifiable all along but that it was incredibly difficult to verify. I believe Vivekananda would hold a similar view with respect to the verifiability of religious truth-claims: while religion can, and has been, verified by many great saints in the past and present, verifying religion is nonetheless extremely difficult, since it requires wholehearted effort and a very high degree of ethical and spiritual development that usually takes many lifetimes to achieve.[19]

One might also raise the objection that there appears to be a contradiction between Vivekananda's claim that we can verify religious truth-claims by engaging in ethical and spiritual practices and a core doctrine of his salvific pluralism discussed in the previous chapter—namely, that a religion's salvific efficacy is largely independent of its doctrinal truth. Vivekananda, we should recall, privileges spiritual practice over religious doctrines, which he refers to as mere "secondary details" (*CW* 1:257). Accordingly, he holds that even if a religion teaches mostly false doctrines, it can still lead to salvation so long as it inculcates ethical and spiritual practices aimed at diminishing egoism. Is he not contradicting himself by claiming that salvific efficacy—which is connected with ethical and spiritual practices—is independent from truth, while also holding that truth can be verified by means of ethical and spiritual practices?

[19] The analogy is not perfect, since it is comparatively easy for well-trained contemporary mathematicians to understand and verify Andrew Wiles's proof of Fermat's Last Theorem, but in the case of religion, every person who wants to verify its truth-claims must become more like Wiles himself! Of course, the recorded biographies and teachings of the great religious saints of the past have helped others to make progress on the religious path, but the fact remains that there seems to be no "shortcut" to verifying religious truth-claims.

To address this objection, we should remind ourselves of Vivekananda's definition of religion, discussed in section 5 of the previous chapter. According to Vivekananda, all religions have two features in common. First, every religion posits some kind of ideal state, reality, or condition beyond the senses—what he calls an "Ideal Unit Abstraction" (*CW* 2:62). Second, every religion prescribes ethical practices that lead to the realization of this ideal. With this definition of religion in the background, we can defuse the objection raised in the previous paragraph. For Vivekananda, a religion's salvific efficacy is largely, *but not completely*, independent of its doctrinal truth. Even if a religion teaches mostly false doctrines, it nonetheless holds at least one *true* doctrine—namely, that one can attain an ideal state of existence through the performance of certain ethical practices. Hence, by engaging in the ethical practices taught by a particular religion, we can verify the truth of at least one doctrine of that religion by seeing whether we are able to attain an ideal state of existence through those practices.

To conclude this chapter, Vivekananda's entire case for the scientific credentials of religion rests on his controversial doctrine of wide empiricism: while the five senses afford knowledge of the natural world, supersensuous perception affords knowledge of transcendental realities like God and the soul. But why should we believe that supersensuous perception is a source of knowledge in the first place? Wouldn't it be far more reasonable to restrict our knowledge-claims to sensory experience, with which we are all familiar? As we will see in the next chapter, Vivekananda directly tackles these questions by presenting a subtle philosophical argument in support of the epistemic value of supersensuous perception.

5

Perceiving God

A Vivekanandan Argument for the Epistemic Value of Supersensuous Perception

How comes, then, the knowledge which the Vedas declare? It comes through being a Rishi. This knowledge is not in the senses; but are the senses the be-all and the end-all of the human being? Who dare say that the senses are the all-in-all of man?

—Swami Vivekananda (1897; *CW* 3:252–53)

The previous chapter discussed Vivekananda's "science of religion," at the heart of which lies his wide empiricism, the view that sensory experience and supersensuous experience are the twin sources of all our knowledge. Scholars criticizing Vivekananda's views on spiritual experience have tended to assume that he dogmatically assumes the truth of wide empiricism and fails to provide any cogent arguments in support of the highly controversial thesis that supersensuous perception is a means of knowledge. C. Mackenzie Brown, for instance, argues that Vivekananda overlooks the fact that mystical experiences are merely subjective and, hence, cannot possibly provide knowledge of objective realities. As Brown puts it, "For Vivekananda, personal experiences of sages like Kapila are accepted as infallible without critical assessment of such experiences—without awareness that experiences are largely inseparable from personal and cultural interpretation" (2012: 153).

In this and the next chapter, I argue that such criticisms of Vivekananda are unjust, because he does, in fact, present a sophisticated and novel philosophical argument for the epistemic value of supersensuous perception in *Rāja-Yoga*. To my knowledge, no scholar has even acknowledged, let alone grappled with, this argument in Vivekananda's work. Moreover, this argument is crucial to his wide empiricism and to his broader defense of the scientific status of religion.

Section 1 sets the stage for understanding Vivekananda's argument by discussing traditional Indian views on perception and testimony. Section 2 then reconstructs Vivekananda's argument for the epistemic value of supersensuous perception (AEV). I devote the remaining four sections of the chapter to refining

Swami Vivekananda's Vedāntic Cosmopolitanism. Swami Medhananda, Oxford University Press. © Oxford University Press 2022. DOI: 10.1093/oso/9780197624463.003.0006

and developing Vivekananda's AEV into a more systematic seven-premise argument (AEV_S) by drawing upon his own ideas as well as contemporary analytic philosophy. Premises 1 and 2 of AEV_S are discussed in section 3, premise 3 in section 4, premise 4 in section 5, and premise 5 in section 6. The next chapter will address some of the most serious objections to the seven-premise AEV_S and to Vivekananda's specific views on spiritual experience.

1. *Perception and Testimony in Traditional Indian* Pramāṇa *Epistemology*

This section briefly summarizes those aspects of traditional Indian *pramāṇa* epistemology that are important for understanding Vivekananda's argument for the epistemic value of supersensuous perception.[1] All of the traditional Indian philosophical schools were concerned with the epistemological question of how knowledge is obtained. Hence, they developed an epistemology based on one or more *pramāṇas* ("means of knowing"), such as perception, inference, and testimony. As B. K. Matilal notes, a *pramāṇa* is "the 'most effective' causal factor that gives rise to a particular cognitive episode" (1986: 35). Another important point to note is that the majority of traditional philosophers in all six of the Vedic schools—Mīmāṃsā, Vedānta, Nyāya, Vaiśeṣika, Sāṃkhya, and Yoga—hold that a *pramāṇa* is infallible and, therefore, necessarily generates only veridical cognition (i.e., *pramā*) (Phillips 2019: sec. 1.1).[2] The infallible nature of the *pramāṇas* follows analytically from the very definition of a *pramāṇa* as "*pramā-karaṇam*"—that is, as the instrumental cause of a veridical cognition (*pramā*).[3] How, then, do we account for cases of perceptual illusion, such as mistaking a rope for a snake? The standard account of such cases would be that any non-veridical cognition, such as the illusory perception of a snake, is generated not by a genuine *pramāṇa*—in this case, *pratyakṣa-pramāṇa* (the perceptual means of knowledge)—but by a *pseudo-pramāṇa* (in this case, *pratyakṣa-ābhāsa*, the mere "appearance of perception") (Phillips 2019: sec. 1.1; Dasti 2012: 2–3). As Stephen Phillips puts it, "You don't really *see* an illusory snake; you only think you see one" (2019: sec. 1.1). Typically, then, traditional Indian philosophers in the Vedic

[1] I found the following discussions of Indian *pramāṇa* epistemology to be especially helpful: Perrett (2016: 49–77), Phillips (2019), Mohanty (2000: 11–38), Arnold (2001), and Matilal (1986).

[2] I say "majority," rather than "all," since Jonardon Ganeri (2010) has made a plausible case that at least some Naiyāyikas, including Mādhavadeva and perhaps Gaṅgeśa, did not take *pramāṇas* to be unerring. For a rebuttal to Ganeri's view, see Dasti and Phillips (2010).

[3] This definition of *pramāṇa* is ubiquitous in classical Indian epistemology. See, for instance, 1.8 of the Advaita Vedānta epistemological treatise *Vedāntaparibhāṣā*. The Naiyāyika Jayanta also uses the same definition of *pramāṇa*, as noted by Dasti and Phillips (2010: 537).

schools have held that a *pramāṇa* always generates veridical cognition, while a pseudo-*pramāṇa* (*pramāṇa-ābhāsa*) always generates non-veridical cognition.

Different schools of Indian philosophy accept a varying number of *pramāṇas* and often differ in how they define them. The materialist Cārvāka school, for instance, accepts only perception (*pratyakṣa*) as a means of knowledge, while Sāṃkhya and Yoga accept perception, inference (*anumāna*), and testimony (*śabda*). Nyāya accepts the latter three *pramāṇas*, along with *upamāna* (comparison). Bhāṭṭa Mīmāṃsā and post-Śaṅkara Advaita Vedānta, meanwhile, accept all four of these *pramāṇas*, along with two others, non-perception (*anupalabdhi*) and postulation (*arthāpatti*).

Various Indian schools also differ on the question of how the validity of a cognition is apprehended. Nyāya upholds *parataḥ-prāmāṇyavāda*, the doctrine that the validity of a cognition can only be apprehended through a second cognition. According to Nyāya, for instance, the validity of a cognition depends on whether it corresponds to reality (Perrett 2016: 51). By contrast, Mīmāṃsā, Advaita Vedānta, and Sāṃkhya all uphold *svataḥ-prāmāṇyavāda*, the doctrine that the validity of a cognition is apprehended through that very cognition itself.[4] The Bhāṭṭa Mīmāṃsaka Pārthasārathimiśra conceived the doctrine of *svataḥ-prāmāṇya* as the epistemic principle that one is *prima facie* justified in taking one's cognitions to be veridical, unless one has good reasons to doubt their veridicality (Taber 1992; Arnold 2001). As Eliot Deutsch has noted, Advaita Vedāntins beginning with Śaṅkara also accepted this epistemic understanding of *svataḥ-prāmāṇyavāda*:

> An idea is held to be true or valid, then, the moment it is entertained . . . and it retains its validity until it is contradicted in experience or is shown to be based on defective apprehension. For example, according to the theory, if under the conditions of normal light and good eyesight I see an object and judge it to be a table, I immediately and rightfully trust my judgment that the object is a table and that I may safely place a book or a glass upon it. Whenever a cognition arises or a judgment takes place, it generates assurance about its truth. The judgment may be mistaken, but this is learned only later (e.g., the book falls through the "table"). *Svataḥprāmaṇyavāda* is thus a kind of perverse pragmatism. Instead of "truth" happening to an idea, it is "falsity" that happens. A cognition, in other words, is like the accused in court who is considered innocent

[4] I have deliberately defined *svataḥ-prāmāṇyavāda* in a general way, since different thinkers interpreted the doctrine in a number of ways. For instance, Arnold (2001), building on the argument of Taber (1992), has suggested that the Bhāṭṭa Mīmāṃsā commentators Bhaṭṭa Uṃveka and Pārthasārathimiśra respectively defended "causal" and "doxastic" interpretations of *svataḥ-prāmāṇyavāda*. McCrea (2018) discusses Sucaritamiśra's subtly different interpretation of *svataḥ-prāmāṇyavāda*.

until proven guilty; it is considered true until it is shown in experience to be false. (1988: 86–87)

As we will see in the next section, Vivekananda's argument for the epistemic value of supersensuous perception has as one of its key premises this epistemic conception of *svataḥ-prāmāṇyavāda* endorsed by the Bhāṭṭa Mīmāṃsaka Pārthasārathimiśra and Advaita Vedāntins.

For the purposes of this chapter, I will focus on the *pramāṇas* of perception and testimony, especially as discussed in the tradition of Advaita Vedānta, which is most relevant to an understanding of Vivekananda's views. Different schools define *pratyakṣa* (perception) in a number of ways, though they all agree that sensory perception is the most basic and common form of perception. Most schools also take as a form of *pratyakṣa* the inner perception of mental states such as fear and happiness (Chadha 2015). Moreover, many schools—including Nyāya-Vaiśeṣika, Sāṃkhya-Yoga, and Buddhism—take *pratyakṣa* to include yogic perception (often called *yogaja-pratyakṣa* or *yogi-pratyakṣa*), though they differ in their understanding of the objects of yogic perception.[5] For the Naiyāyikas, yogic perception includes the supernormal perception of sensory objects that are extremely distant or extremely small, as well as the perception of *non*-sensory objects like the Ātman and *dharma* (duty or moral law) (Sinha 1934: 337–47; Dasti 2010: 115–52). Vijñānabhikṣu, in his commentary on Patañjali's *Yogasūtra* 1.7, holds that *pratyakṣa* encompasses not only sensory perception but also the supersensuous perception of the Ātman/Puruṣa as well as *īśvara*'s own non-sensory mode of perception (Rukmani 2007: 61). The question of whether Advaita Vedānta accepts yogic perception—and, if so, what its objects are—is a complicated one, since various figures within the Advaitic tradition seem to hold differing views on the issue. I will discuss Advaitic views on yogic perception and spiritual experience a bit later in this section.

All the Vedic philosophical schools accept *śabda* (verbal testimony) as a valid means of knowledge. Verbal testimony is understood in a broad sense to include testimony about things in the external world—which can be perceived by the senses—as well as scriptural testimony (*śruti*) about supersensuous realities like *dharma*, God (*īśvara*), and Ātman/Brahman. However, schools have debated various questions regarding *śruti*, including its status, the nature of the knowledge it conveys, and whether it has an author. Mīmāṃsakas argue that the Vedas are eternal, uncreated, authorless (*apauruṣeya*), and therefore, infallible. Naiyāyikas, by contrast, maintain that *īsvara* is the author of the Vedas.

[5] For detailed discussion of yogic perception, see Sinha (1934: 335–67). For an account of the Pūrva Mīmāṃsā rejection of yogic perception, see McCrea (2009).

Let us now examine in some detail the views on *pratyakṣa-pramāṇa* and *śabda-pramāṇa* in the tradition of Advaita Vedānta beginning with Śaṅkara. Śaṅkara accepted perception, inference, and verbal testimony as valid means of knowledge.[6] Regarding the Vedas in particular, Śaṅkara followed the Mīmāṃsakas in holding that the Vedas are authorless, eternal, uncreated, and (therefore) infallible (Rambachan 1991: 33–34). However, as Anantanand Rambachan (1991: 38) has shown, Śaṅkara's particular understanding of the authorlessness of the Vedas actually represents a kind of middle way between Nyāya and Mīmāṃsā. In Śaṅkara's view, *īśvara* reveals the Vedas "in the same linguistic form at the beginning of each creation to qualified seers." Hence, for Śaṅkara, the authorlessness of the Vedas is compatible with the view that the Vedas were recorded—but not authored—by seers. Śaṅkara also followed the Mīmāṃsakas in holding that the world itself originated from Vedic words. Rambachan explains Śaṅkara's position on this issue: "Vedic words occur in the mind of *Prajāpati* when He is intent on creation, and, corresponding to them, He creates the universe" (1991: 36). As we will see in the next section, Vivekananda developed his own understanding of the Vedas in explicit opposition to the traditional view of Śaṅkara and the Mīmāṃsakas.

Śaṅkara's views on the status of the Vedas in relation to the other *pramāṇa*s are also very important. According to Śaṅkara, "one *pramāṇa* does not contradict another, since every *pramāṇa* makes known only what is *not* an object of another *pramāṇa*" (*BṛUpBh* 2.1.20, pp. 472–73).[7] In general, Śaṅkara construes *pratyakṣa* narrowly as sensory perception and, therefore, claims that the Vedas alone provide knowledge of supersensuous realities like *dharma* and the nondual Ātman. He makes his position clear in his commentary on verse 18.66 of the *Bhagavad-Gītā*:

> The validity of the Vedas holds good only with regard to matters . . . which are not known through other *pramāṇa*s such as perception (*pratyakṣa*), but not with regard to objects of perception and so on, because the validity of the Vedas lies in revealing what cannot be perceived (*adṛṣṭa-darśana-arthatvāt*). . . . Surely, even a hundred Vedic texts cannot become valid if they assert that fire is cold or non-luminous! (*BhGBh* 18.66, pp. 757–58)

According to Śaṅkara, *pratyakṣa* is the means of knowing sensory objects, while *śruti* is the means of knowing supersensuous realities like the Ātman, which cannot be perceived by the senses. Indeed, he frequently makes the stronger

[6] For a thorough discussion of Śaṅkara's epistemology, see Rambachan (1991).

[7] *na ca pramāṇaṃ pramāṇāntareṇa viruddhyate, pramāṇāntara-aviṣayam eva hi pramāṇāntaraṃ jñāpayati.*

claim that the Upaniṣads are the *only* means of knowing the nondual Ātman. For instance, in his commentary on *Brahmasūtra* 2.1.6, he explicitly rejects the view that Brahman may be known through *pramāṇa*s other than scripture, arguing that Brahman cannot be known through perception, since it is not a sense object, and it cannot be known through inference, since it is "devoid of all grounds of inference" (*liṅgādi abhāvāt*) (*BSBh* 2.1.6, 188). He concludes, therefore, that Brahman "is to be known through scripture alone (*āgamamātra*)" (*BSBh* 2.1.6, 188).

However, Śaṅkara significantly complicates his position on this issue in his commentary on *Brahmasūtra* 1.1.2, where he claims that "*śruti* etc., as well as *anubhava* etc., are valid means of knowing Brahman as far as possible; for the knowledge of Brahman culminates in *anubhava*, and it relates to an existing entity" (*BSBh* 1.1.2, p. 8).[8] There has been intense scholarly controversy regarding the meaning of this textual crux. Many scholars have interpreted Śaṅkara as claiming here that *both* scripture *and* spiritual experience (*anubhava*) are valid means of knowing Brahman and that scriptural knowledge of Brahman culminates in the direct experience of Brahman.[9] Rambachan, by contrast, argues that what Śaṅkara means is that *anubhava*, as well as other *pramāṇa*s like inference, are only valuable *supplements* to scripture, which is the one and only *pramāṇa* for gaining knowledge of Brahman (1991: 113–16; 1994b: 721–24). Meanwhile, other scholars have suggested a variety of other interpretations of this passage (B. Gupta 2009: 267–79; Preti 2014).

It is beyond the scope of this chapter to enter into this interpretive controversy. For present purposes, I wish only to make the relatively uncontroversial point that Śaṅkara's views on scripture and its relation to the other *pramāṇa*s are ambiguous and have accordingly invited a variety of conflicting interpretations. Is scripture the sole means of knowing Brahman? Or is spiritual experience an additional means of knowing Brahman alongside scripture? If spiritual experience is an additional *pramāṇa* for knowing Brahman, is it a special form of *pratyakṣa* or is it a fourth *pramāṇa* different from perception, inference, and testimony? What is the precise relationship between scripture and spiritual experience? Since Śaṅkara's own answers to these questions were not clear-cut, later Advaitins defended a variety of conflicting views on these questions.

Vivekananda's understanding of Advaita Vedānta, as I already pointed out at the end of chapter 1, was mediated not only by his reading of Śaṅkara and his training under Ramakrishna but also by his acquaintance with a variety of post-Śaṅkara Advaitic texts like *Vivekacūḍāmaṇi*, *Avadhūta-Gītā*, *Aparokṣānubhūti*,

[8] *śrutyādayaḥ anubhavādayaḥ ca yathāsaṃbhavam iha pramāṇam anubhavāvasānatvāt bhūtavastuviṣayatvāt ca brahmajñānasya.*

[9] A. Sharma (1992), Phillips (2001), Devaraja (1962: 36–71), and Murty (1959: 112).

Aṣṭāvakra-Saṃhitā, *Pañcadaśī*, and *Vicāra-Sāgar*.[10] Hence, in order to understand Vivekananda's views on spiritual experience and scripture, we need some understanding of post-Śaṅkaran views in the Advaitic tradition.

One of the key points of contention between the two major post-Śaṅkaran schools of Advaita Vedānta—namely, the Vivaraṇa school inaugurated by Padmapāda and the Bhāmatī school inaugurated by Vācaspati Miśra—concerned the question of the respective roles of scripture and spiritual experience vis-à-vis the knowledge of Brahman. While both schools agreed that hearing Upaniṣadic scripture is *necessary* for the knowledge of Brahman, they diverged on the question of whether hearing scripture is also *sufficient* for the knowledge of Brahman. The textual crux in relation to this dispute is Bṛhadāraṇyaka Upaniṣad 2.4.5: "My dear Maitreyī, the Self . . . should be realized—should be heard of, reflected on, and meditated upon" (*ātmā vā are draṣṭavyaḥ śrotavyo mantavyo nididhyāsitavyo maitreyi*). According to the Bhāmatī school, the three practices of *śravaṇa*, *manana*, and *nididhyāsana* are chronologically sequential: after hearing the Upaniṣadic *mahāvākya* (like "*tat tvam asi*" ["Thou art That"]), we must reflect on the scriptural teaching and then meditate on it in order to attain the knowledge of Brahman. Hence, for the Bhāmatī school, while *śravaṇa* is a necessary first step in the attainment of liberative knowledge, *nididhyāsana* is the immediate cause of liberative knowledge. According to the Vivaraṇa school, by contrast, *śravaṇa* is the immediate cause of the knowledge of Brahman, while *manana* and *nididhyāsana* are merely supplementary aids in preparing the mind to be fully receptive to the scriptural teachings.[11] In this context, Alan Preti makes the important point that in spite of this key difference between the Bhāmatī and Vivaraṇa schools on the question of the immediate cause of liberative knowledge, both schools nonetheless agree that "*brahmajñāna* cannot be attained independently of *śruti*" (2014: 729).

A large number of popular post-Śaṅkaran Advaitic texts strongly emphasized the need for the spiritual experience of Brahman in *nirvikalpa samādhi*.[12] One such text is *Vivekacūḍāmaṇi*, which Vivekananda knew very well and frequently quoted.[13] Verse 364 of this text runs as follows:

[10] For a good discussion of some of these post-Śaṅkaran textual influences on Vivekananda, see Madaio (2017).

[11] For a detailed account of the debate between the Bhāmatī and Vivaraṇa schools on this issue, see Ram-Prasad (2001: 197–209).

[12] See, for instance, verses 364–65 of *Vivekacūḍāmaṇi* (Madhavananda 1921: 161), verse 124 of *Aparokṣānubhūti* (Vimuktananda 1938: 67), verses 181–215 of *Vedāntasāra* (Sadānanda 1931: 109–22), verses 1.53–64 of *Pañcadaśī* (Vidyāraṇya 1967: 25–31), and *Jīvanmuktiviveka* (Vidyāraṇya 1996).

[13] See, for instance, his references to *Vivekacūḍāmaṇi* at *CW* 2:306–7 and *CW* 3:421–22.

Reflection on Brahman is a hundred times greater than hearing, and meditation is a hundred thousand times greater than reflection. But *nirvikalpa samādhi* is infinite in its results.

[*śruteḥ śataguṇaṃ vidyān mananaṃ mananād api*
nididhyāsaṃ lakṣaguṇam anantaṃ nirvikalpakam] (Madhavananda 1921: 161)

Here, the poet conceives *śravaṇa*, *manana*, and *nididhyāsana* as progressively superior stages, culminating in *nirvikalpa samādhi*, which is infinitely superior to the practices leading up to it. In the very next verse, he makes clear that *nirvikalpa samādhi* alone results in the liberative knowledge of Brahman: "It is only through *nirvikalpa samādhi*, and not otherwise, that the truth of Brahman is clearly and definitely known" (*nirvikalpakasamādhinā sphutaṃ brahmatattvam avagamyate dhruvam* | *nānyathā* . . .) (Madhavananda 1921: 161). In verse 474 of *Vivekacūḍāmaṇi*, the poet states that for the knowledge of Brahman, "scripture, reasoning, and the words of the guru are all *pramāṇa*s, and one's own self-authenticating spiritual experience is also a *pramāṇa*" (*śāstraṃ yuktir deśikoktiḥ pramāṇaṃ cāntaḥsiddhā svānubhūtiḥ pramāṇam*) (Madhavananda 1921: 205; my translation). This should remind us of Śaṅkara's statement in his commentary on *Brahmasūtra* 1.1.2, which has been interpreted by some scholars as upholding the view that both *śruti* and *anubhava* are *pramāṇa*s for knowing Brahman.

One other Advaitic text is worth mentioning to round out the historico-philosophical background necessary for fully appreciating Vivekananda's views on spiritual experience. The Advaita Vedāntin Dharmarāja Adhvarīndra, in his influential epistemological treatise *Vedāntaparibhāṣā*, follows the Vivaraṇa school in holding that the immediate cause of liberative knowledge is *śravaṇa* (Adhvarīndra 1942: 207–19). Interestingly, he defines the veridical knowledge generated by *pratyakṣa-pramāṇa* as "Pure Consciousness alone" (*pratyakṣapramā tu atra caitanyam eva*) (Adhvarīndra 1942: 8). Moreover, he makes a key distinction between determinate perception (*savikalpaka-pratyakṣa*) and indeterminate perception (*nirvikalpaka-pratyakṣa*). Determinate perceptions encompass ordinary perceptions like the perception of a jar, which involve the apprehension of a relation between the perceiving subject and the object of knowledge. Indeterminate perceptions, by contrast, do not involve the apprehension of any kind of relation between subject and object. According to Dharmarāja, one important form of *nirvikalpaka-pratyakṣa* is the supersensuous perception of nondual Brahman that arises from hearing the Upaniṣadic teaching "*tat tvam asi*" (Adhvarīndra 1942: 32–37).[14] Hence, for Dharmarāja, the liberative knowledge of Brahman arises from a scripturally generated spiritual

[14] For discussion, see B. Gupta (1995: 226–37).

experience, which he explicitly characterizes as a special indeterminate form of perception (*pratyakṣa*). It should be clear, then, that even a Vivaraṇa-leaning text like *Vedāntaparibhāṣā* accords prominence to spiritual experience.

With this background in place, I will argue that Vivekananda defends the epistemic value of supersensuous perception through a subtle and original critical engagement with traditional Indian *pramāṇa* epistemology—especially the doctrine of *svataḥ-prāmāṇyatā* and the wide range of Advaitic views on the role of, and relation between, scripture and spiritual experience in generating the knowledge of Brahman.

2. *Reconstructing and Refining Vivekananda's Argument*

As I will discuss in detail in chapter 7, one of the most pressing problems in post-Kantian Western philosophy was the following: even if God exists, is it possible for us to *know* God? Vivekananda was well aware that philosophers like Immanuel Kant and Herbert Spencer had answered this question in the negative. According to Kant and Spencer, while it is necessary and valuable for us to have faith in God, we can never have knowledge of God. In contrast to these philosophers, Vivekananda defends an affirmative answer to the question. In numerous places in his work, he ingeniously argues for the epistemic value of supersensuous perception on the basis of the traditional epistemic doctrine of *svataḥ-prāmāṇyatā*.

He provides an especially clear and detailed formulation of this argument in his commentary on Patañjali's *Yogasūtra* 1.7 in his book *Rāja-Yoga*. He translates the *sūtra*, which enumerates the three means of knowledge (*pramāṇas*) accepted in Yoga philosophy, as follows: "Direct perception, inference, and competent evidence are proofs" (*pratyakṣānumānāgamāḥ pramāṇāni*) (*CW* 1:204). His commentary on this *sūtra* deserves to be quoted at length:

> There are also three kinds of proof. *Pratyakṣa*, direct perception; whatever we see and feel, is proof, if there has been nothing to delude the senses. I see the world; that is sufficient proof that it exists. Secondly, *anumāna*, inference; you see a sign, and from the sign you come to the thing signified. Thirdly, *āptavākya*, the direct evidence of the Yogis, of those who have seen the truth. We are all of us struggling towards knowledge. But you and I have to struggle hard, and come to knowledge through a long tedious process of reasoning, but the Yogi, the pure one, has gone beyond all this. Before his mind, the past, the present, and the future are alike, one book for him to read; he does not require to go through the tedious processes for knowledge we have to; his words are proof, because

> he sees knowledge in himself. These, for instance, are the authors of the sacred scriptures; therefore the scriptures are proof. If any such persons are living now their words will be proof. Other philosophers go into long discussions about *āptavākya* and they say, "What is the proof of their words?" The proof is their direct perception. Because whatever I see is proof, and whatever you see is proof, if it does not contradict any past knowledge. There is knowledge beyond the senses, and whenever it does not contradict reason and past human experience, that knowledge is proof. Any madman may come into this room and say he sees angels around him; that would not be proof. In the first place, it must be true knowledge, and secondly, it must not contradict past knowledge, and thirdly, it must depend upon the character of the man who gives it out. I hear it said that the character of the man is not of so much importance as what he may say; we must first hear what he says. This may be true in other things. A man may be wicked, and yet make an astronomical discovery, but in religion it is different, because no impure man will ever have the power to reach the truths of religion. Therefore we have first of all to see that the man who declares himself to be an *āpta* is a perfectly unselfish and holy person; secondly, that he has reached beyond the senses; and thirdly, that what he says does not contradict the past knowledge of humanity. Any new discovery of truth does not contradict the past truth, but fits into it. And fourthly, that truth must have a possibility of verification. If a man says, "I have seen a vision," and tells me that I have no right to see it, I believe him not. Everyone must have the power to see it for himself. No one who sells his knowledge is an *āpta*. All these conditions must be fulfilled; you must first see that the man is pure, and that he has no selfish motive; that he has no thirst for gain or fame. Secondly, he must show that he is superconscious. He must give us something that we cannot get from our senses, and which is for the benefit of the world. Thirdly, we must see that it does not contradict other truths; if it contradicts other scientific truths reject it at once. Fourthly, the man should never be singular; he should only represent what all men can attain. (*CW* 1:204–6)

Since I will be referring to this long passage throughout the chapter, I will refer to it as "passage A." Vivekananda's core argument for the epistemic value of supersensuous perception—which I will abbreviate as "AEV"—is as follows. We ordinarily take our sensory perceptions to be proof that what we perceive actually exists. As he puts it, "I see the world; that is sufficient proof that it exists." This everyday behavior is justified, he claims, on the basis of the following general epistemic principle: "whatever we see and feel, is proof, if there has been nothing to delude the senses." Let us call this Vivekananda's *Principle of Perceptual Proof* (hereafter "PP"). By conceiving "direct perception" (*pratyakṣa*) as "proof," he is implicitly drawing upon the epistemic principle of the intrinsic validity (*svataḥ-prāmāṇyatā*) of cognitions espoused by traditional Advaita Vedāntins and Bhāṭṭa Mīmāṃsakas like Pārthasārathimiśra. Vivekananda also holds that direct perception (*pratyakṣa*) encompasses both sensory perception and supersensuous perception—a view, as we saw in the previous section, also held by Naiyāyikas, Sāṃkhya-Yoga thinkers, and post-Śaṅkara Advaita Vedāntins like Dharmarāja. This is clear from the fact that Vivekananda refers to the "direct perception" of Yogis who claim to have attained "knowledge beyond the senses."

He then goes on to defend another epistemic principle: the testimony of an "*āpta*"—a credible person—about her perception of some entity constitutes "proof" for others that that entity exists. Let us call this Vivekananda's *Principle of Testimonial Proof* (hereafter "TP"). Crucially, he includes credible Yogis under the category of an *āpta*. Hence, if we accept PP and TP, then the "words" of a Yogi who claims to have perceived a supersensuous reality constitute "proof" for others that that supersensuous reality exists. On the basis of TP, Vivekananda further claims that "the scriptures are proof," since *āpta*s include "the authors of the sacred scriptures." Here again, he is implicitly applying *svataḥ-prāmāṇyatā* to cognitions generated by *śabda-pramāṇa* (i.e., verbal testimony). Accordingly, he translates the word "*āgama*" in *Yogasūtra* 1.7—another term for verbal testimony—as "competent evidence," which he takes to be one of three "proofs," alongside direct perception and inference. On the basis of PP and TP, Vivekananda concludes: "There is knowledge beyond the senses, and whenever it does not contradict reason and past human experience, that knowledge is proof." In other words, he claims that some people have, indeed, attained knowledge of supersensuous realities like God and the soul.

I believe Vivekananda's core argument for the epistemic value of supersensuous perception (AEV) is a sophisticated and promising one. Indeed, as we will see, numerous contemporary analytic philosophers have made very similar arguments on the basis of epistemic principles akin to those defended by Vivekananda.

Nonetheless, I think Vivekananda's AEV requires further refinement and amplification in order to be fully plausible. In the remainder of this chapter, I will present and defend a more refined and systematized version of Vivekananda's AEV by drawing upon the conceptual resources of contemporary analytic philosophy as well as Vivekananda's own lectures and writings. I will call this seven-premise argument "AEV$_s$" (with the subscript "s" standing for "systematized"), in order to distinguish it from Vivekananda's own AEV. While AEV$_s$ is not an argument that Vivekananda actually made, I refer to it as a "Vivekanandan argument," since it takes its bearings from his own ideas and arguments. The seven-premise AEV$_s$ runs as follows:

Let "mystics" stand for subjects who have had experiences as of an ultimate reality.

A Vivekanandan Argument for the Epistemic Value of Supersensuous Perception (AEV$_S$)

1. Mystics exist.
2. Experiences as of an ultimate reality are perceptual in nature, since they are sufficiently similar to sense-perceptual experiences.
3. *Perception as Epistemic Justification* (PEJ): When a subject *S* has a perceptual experience as of *F*, *S* is thereby rationally justified in believing that she has a veridical perceptual experience of *F*, unless she has good reasons to doubt the veridicality of her perceptual experience as of *F*.
4. At least some mystics have no good reasons to doubt the veridicality of all or most of their experiences as of an ultimate reality.

Therefore,

5. At least some mystics are rationally justified in believing that at least some of their experiences as of an ultimate reality are veridical. (*from* 1–4)
6. *Perceptual Testimony as Epistemic Justification* (PTEJ): People other than *S* are rationally justified in believing that *S*'s perceptual experience as of *F* is as *S* reports it to be, unless they have good reasons to doubt *S*'s sincerity or trustworthiness.
7. People other than mystics have no good reasons to doubt the sincerity or trustworthiness of all or most mystics who claim to have had veridical experiences of an ultimate reality.

Therefore,

8. People other than mystics are rationally justified[15] in believing that at least some mystics have had at least some veridical experiences of an ultimate reality. (*from* 5–7)

While AEV$_S$ takes its bearings from Vivekananda's AEV, the two arguments differ in a number of subtle ways. First, while Vivekananda repeatedly uses the somewhat vague term "proof," I use the more precise language of rational justification. Second, Vivekananda claims that direct perception encompasses both sensory

[15] Throughout AEV$_S$, I say "rationally justified" instead of "justified," in order to rule out non-rational forms of justification like pragmatic justification.

and supersensuous perception, but it is not clear from passage A what reasons he has for conceiving supersensuous experience as a form of perception. Hence, premise 2 of AEV$_S$ includes a clause about the sufficient similarity between sensory experiences and supersensuous experiences. Third, in premises 3 and 6 of AEV$_S$, I have tried to provide more precise formulations of Vivekananda's PP and TP respectively, the two *svataḥ-prāmāṇya*-based epistemic principles at the core of his AEV. Fourth, I have added premises 4 and 7 in order to complete the argument, and I will show later in the chapter that while Vivekananda does not explicitly state premises 4 and 7 in passage A, he does so elsewhere. Fifth and finally, the conclusion to Vivekananda's AEV—namely, that "there is knowledge beyond the senses"—seems too strong to me, so I have reformulated it in terms of rational justification in conclusion 8 of AEV$_S$. In the remainder of this chapter, I will explain each of the seven premises of AEV$_S$ and refer to Vivekananda's work as well as contemporary analytic philosophy to clarify and support these premises.

3. *Premises 1 and 2: Perceiving Ultimate Reality*

Premise 1 of AEV$_S$ is uncontroversial, because it only states that some people have experiences *as of* an ultimate reality—that is, experiences that *seem* to their subjects to have ultimate reality as their phenomenal content. Hence, premise 1 does not presuppose the veridicality of such experiences. According to Vivekananda, people who have had experiences as of an ultimate reality include "the authors of the sacred scriptures"—like the Vedas, the Bible, and the Koran—all of whom claimed to have directly perceived the supersensuous realities described in these books. Another such person was Vivekananda's guru Ramakrishna, who "dared to say that he saw God" (*CW* 4:179). Moreover, as we saw in chapter 1, Vivekananda himself reported having had numerous mystical experiences. He was also well aware that many people have experiences as of an ultimate reality that are *not* veridical. As he puts it in passage A, "Any madman may come into this room and say he sees angels around him. . . . " A bit later in passage A, he delineates four criteria for determining whether "the man who declares himself to be an *āpta*" really *is* an *āpta*, that is, "one who has seen the truth." I will discuss these four criteria later under premise 6, but for now, I only wish to emphasize Vivekananda's carefully qualified language: a person who "declares" that she has experienced ultimate reality may not, in fact, have had such an experience.

The other significant point to note about premise 1 is its characterization of the object of putative mystical experiences as "ultimate reality." In passage A, Vivekananda characterizes the object of supersensuous perception in very broad terms as "the truth." "Yogis," as he puts it, are those who "have seen the truth." I believe he quite deliberately employs the broad term "truth," because—as he notes in numerous other places—different mystics throughout the world have experienced this supersensuous truth in various ways. For instance, in his 1900 lecture "Is Vedānta the Future Religion?," he claims that Vedānta "denies emphatically that any one book can contain all the truths about God, soul, the ultimate reality" (*CW* 8:124). Taking a clue from this statement, I have chosen in premise 1 to characterize the object of putative mystical experiences as "ultimate reality," since Vivekananda himself uses this term in a broad sense to encompass "God" as well as the "soul."

Hence, contrary to what some scholars have claimed, Vivekananda did not subscribe to the "common core" or "perennialist" thesis that all mystical experiences are phenomenologically identical.[16] Indeed, he frequently distinguishes three fundamental types of mystical experience: the realization of one's own individual soul, the theistic experience of a personal God, and the non-theistic realization of the impersonal nondual Brahman/Ātman. For instance, in his "Paper on Hinduism" (1893), he explicitly distinguishes the mystical experience of the individual "soul" (with a lowercase "s") from the mystical experience of "God," which he characterizes as the "all-merciful universal Soul" (with an uppercase "S"):

> If there is a soul in him which is not matter, if there is an all-merciful universal Soul, he [the Hindu] will go to Him direct. He must see Him, and that alone can destroy all doubts. So the best proof a Hindu sage gives about the soul, about God, is: "I have seen the soul; I have seen God." (*CW* 1:13)

It is important to recall from chapter 1 that Vivekananda's understanding of the term "God" is very broad, since it encompasses both the personal God of theism and the impersonal nondual Brahman. In his lecture "The Sages of India," for instance, he declares that "our religion preaches an Impersonal Personal God" (*CW* 3:249).

Indeed, in a Bengali conversation with his disciple Saratcandra Cakravarti in 1897, Vivekananda distinguished the theistic realization of the personal God from the Advaitic realization of nondual Brahman:

> Suppose someone is cultivating that type of devotion (*bhakti*) to God (*īśvara*) which Hanumān represents. The more intense the attitude (*bhāva*) becomes, the more will the pose and demeanor of that aspirant, nay even his physical configuration, be cast in that mold. . . . Taking up any such attitude (*bhāva*), the worshipper becomes gradually shaped into the very form of his Ideal. The ultimate stage of any such attitude is called *bhāva-samādhi*. By contrast, the aspirant in the path of *jñāna*, pursuing the process of *neti, neti* ["not this,

[16] Rambachan (1994a: 111) mistakenly attributes this "common core" view to Vivekananda. I argue against Rambachan's interpretation of Vivekananda in section 5 of the next chapter.

> not this"], such as "I am not the body, nor the mind, nor the intellect," and so on, attains *nirvikalpa-samādhi* when he is established in Pure Consciousness (*cinmātrasattāi avasthita hole*). It requires striving through many births to reach perfection or the ultimate stage with regard to a single one of the devotional attitudes. But Sri Ramakrishna, the king of the realm of devotional attitudes (*bhāvarājyer rājā*), perfected himself in no fewer than eighteen different forms of *bhāva*! (*BCW* 9:11 / *CW* 6:463–64; translation modified)

Here and elsewhere, Vivekananda distinguishes two fundamentally different experiences of the ultimate reality: the *bhakta*'s realization of the loving personal God (*īśvara*) in *bhāva-samādhi* and the Advaitic *jñānī*'s realization of "Pure Consciousness" (*cinmātrasattā*) in *nirvikalpa-samādhi*. Significantly, he also emphasizes that theistic *bhāva-samādhi* itself takes numerous forms, depending on the particular *bhāva* that gives rise to it. These devotional *bhāvas* include, for instance, *dāsya-bhāva* ("attitude of a servant"), *vātsalya-bhāva* ("attitude of a parent"), *mādhurya-bhāva* ("attitude of a lover"), *sakhī-bhāva* ("attitude of a friend"), and *santāna-bhāva* ("attitude of a child"). He further claims that Ramakrishna practiced to perfection no fewer than eighteen *bhāvas*, each of which culminated in a different type of theistic spiritual experience.

It should now be clear why I have decided to characterize the object of supersensuous perception broadly as "ultimate reality" in premise 1 and in the rest of Vivekananda's argument. He clearly intended AEV to apply to a wide variety of theistic and non-theistic mystical experiences. Hence, in AEV_s, I follow Vivekananda in taking the term "ultimate reality" to encompass the personal God, the impersonal nondual Brahman, as well as the individual soul.

Numerous passages from Vivekananda's work lend support to premise 2 of AEV_s. In passage A, he translates *pratyakṣa* as "direct perception," claiming that *pratyakṣa-pramāṇa* encompasses not only sensory experiences—"whatever we see and feel" through our "senses"—but also the supersensuous experiences of Yogis. He makes this clear when he asserts that the "proof" of the "words" of Yogis, or *āptavākya*s, is "their direct perception" of supersensuous truths. There are many other places in his lectures and writings where he explicitly claims that the *pramāṇa* of direct perception or *pratyakṣa* includes both sensory perception and supersensuous perception (which he refers to as "*alaukikapratyakṣam*" in his "Reply to the Madras Address" [*CW* 4:340]). For instance, in his lecture "The Sages of India," he remarks: "The proof, therefore, of the Vedas is just the same as the proof of this table before me, *pratyakṣa*, direct perception. This I see with the senses, and the truths of spirituality we also see in a superconscious state of the human soul" (*CW* 3:253).[17]

[17] See also *CW* 1:415.

In passage A, Vivekananda specifies two fundamental commonalities between sensory perception and supersensuous perception. First, his very translation of *pratyakṣa* as "direct perception" indicates that both the ordinary perception of a sense-object like a table and the yogic perception of a supersensuous reality like God have in common a phenomenological directness or immediacy. The philosopher of religion William Alston echoes Vivekananda in explaining the directness of the mystical perception of God as follows: "The experience is *direct*. One seems to be *immediately* aware of God rather than through being aware of something else. It is like seeing another human being in front of you, rather than like seeing that person on television" (2004: 137). Second, Vivekananda holds that subjects tend to make truth-claims on the basis of their perceptions, whether these perceptions are sensory or supersensuous. That is, just as ordinary people generally tend to think that a given sense-object exists *because* they perceive it, mystics tend to think that supersensuous realities like God and the soul exist *because* they perceive them. As he puts it, "I see the world; that is sufficient proof that it exists." Similarly, when mystics make claims about the reality of supersensuous entities like God, their "proof" for their claims "is their direct perception." William James, in *The Varieties of Mystical Experience* (1900), described this characteristic of mystical experiences as their "noetic quality": "mystical states seem to those who experience them to be also states of knowledge" (James [1900] 2002: 295). Like James, Vivekananda holds that the supersensuous perceptions of Yogis lead them to think that they have attained "knowledge beyond the senses."

In fact, Vivekananda often emphasizes that supersensuous perceptions have a much stronger noetic quality than sensory perceptions. For instance, in his commentary on *Yogasūtra* 1.49, he remarks:

> The central idea of the Yogis is that just as we come in direct contact with objects of the senses, so religion even can be directly perceived in a far more intense sense. The truths of religion, as God and Soul, cannot be perceived by the external senses. (*CW* 1:232)

According to Vivekananda, supersensuous perceptions are "far more intense" than ordinary sensory perceptions. This should remind us of his recollection of his early encounter with Ramakrishna, quoted in the previous chapter: "For the first time I found a man who dared to say that he saw God, that religion was a reality to be felt, to be sensed *in an infinitely more intense way* than we can sense the world" (*CW* 4:179; emphasis added). In such passages, I take him to be making the phenomenological point that supersensuous perceptions have a much stronger noetic quality than sensory perceptions. For the purposes of premise 2, it is sufficient to note that for Vivekananda, supersensuous perceptions generally carry a much stronger conviction about their veridicality than do ordinary sense perceptions. The question of whether and how this phenomenological conviction bears on the issue of epistemic justification will be addressed in the next section's discussion of premise 3 of AEV$_S$.

Premise 2 is, of course, highly controversial, and in section 1 of the next chapter, I will discuss one of the most serious objections to this premise—namely, the objection that supersensuous experiences are not sufficiently similar to sensory experiences, since only the latter, but not the former, can be adequately crosschecked. I will argue there that Vivekananda provided a cogent response to this crosscheckability objection, which can be further strengthened by drawing on some aspects of the recent work of William Alston.

4. Premise 3: Perception as Epistemic Justification

In passage A, as we have seen, Vivekananda upholds the *Principle of Perceptual Proof* (PP), which he formulates as follows: "[W]hatever we see and feel, is proof, if there has been nothing to delude the senses." Affirming the *svataḥ-prāmāṇyatā* of perceptual experiences, he claims that we are justified in taking our perceptions to be veridical *unless* we have good reasons to doubt their veridicality.

Elsewhere, he clarifies the defeasibility condition for PP:

> With regard to fallacies, it must be remembered that direct perception itself can only be a proof, provided the instrument, the method, and the persistence of the perception are all maintained pure. Disease or emotion will have the effect of disturbing the observation. *Therefore direct perception itself is but a mode of inference.* Therefore all human knowledge is uncertain and may be erroneous. (*CW* 8:270; emphasis in original)

If I see a snake slithering in front of me, I would *not* be justified in taking my visual experience of the snake to be veridical if, for instance, my visual faculty is physically damaged or if I recently ingested a hallucinogenic drug that makes me prone to seeing things that are not really there. I think Vivekananda is best understood as implying a distinction between what contemporary epistemologists call *prima facie* justification and *ultima facie* (or "all-things-considered") justification.[18] Let us take Vivekananda's own example of seeing the world. If I see the world, I am *prima facie* justified in believing that the world exists. If I reflect further on my perception of the world and conclude that I have no good reasons to believe that my perception is not veridical, then I have *ultima facie* justification

[18] For this distinction, see Pryor (2000: 534) and Senor (1996).

for believing that the world exists. This *ultima facie* justification, I would suggest, is what Vivekananda calls "sufficient proof": "I see the world; that is sufficient proof that it exists." Regarding his cryptic claim that "direct perception itself is but a mode of inference," I think the context makes clear that he is not directly equating perception with inference but noting that the move from *prima facie* to *ultima facie* justification for believing that a given perception is veridical typically requires a process of inferential reasoning through which one determines whether there are any good reasons for doubting the perception's veridicality. For Vivekananda, however, even this "sufficient proof" is defeasible; as he puts it, "all human knowledge . . . may be erroneous." After all, since he had read Descartes and Hume, he was well aware of external-world skepticism. In fact, just a few pages before passage A, he acknowledges that we can never rule out the possibility that the world does not exist even though we perceive it: "what reason is there to believe in the testimony of the senses?" (*CW* 1:199).

At this point, however, we should recall from our discussion of premise 2 of AEV$_S$ that Vivekananda takes *pratyakṣa-pramāṇa* to encompass both sensory perception as well as supersensuous perception. Hence, his initial characterization of "*pratyakṣa*" in terms of specifically *sensory* perception is misleading, since he does not mean to restrict *pratyakṣa* to sensory perception alone. He makes this clear a bit later in passage A when he addresses the question of why we should believe the mystical testimony of *āpta*s, trustworthy sages who claim to have perceived supersensuous realities like God. Vivekananda answers this question as follows: "The proof is their direct perception. Because whatever I see is proof, and whatever you see is proof, if it does not contradict any past knowledge." Here, he conceives *pratyakṣa-pramāṇa* in a broad manner, taking it to include both ordinary sense-perceptual experience as well as the supersensuous experience of Yogis.

In numerous places in his corpus, Vivekananda formulates PP even more directly than he does in passage A. He provides perhaps his clearest formulation of PP in his lecture "Steps to Realisation" (1895) delivered in New York:

> What is the proof of God? Direct perception, *pratyakṣa*. The proof of this wall is that I perceive it. God has been perceived that way by thousands before, and will be perceived by all who want to perceive Him. But this perception is no sense-perception at all; it is supersensuous, superconscious. . . . (*CW* 1:415)

According to Vivekananda, direct perception serves equally as the "proof of God" and as the "proof of this wall." That is, if I am justified in believing that there is a wall in front of me because I perceive it, I am also justified in believing that God exists because I perceive Him. In his lecture "The Sages of India" (1897), he makes exactly the same argument: "The proof, therefore, of the Vedas is just the same as the proof of this table before me, *pratyakṣa*, direct perception. This I see with the senses, and the truths of spirituality we also see in a superconscious state of the human soul" (*CW* 3:253).[19]

Vivekananda was prescient in defending the epistemic value of supersensuous perception on the basis of PP, since numerous recent analytic philosophers of religion and epistemologists have defended principles very similar to PP, which go by various names such as the "principle of credulity" (Swinburne 2004: 303–22), "perceptual dogmatism" (Pryor 2000), "critical trust" (Kwan 2009; Hick 2006: 129), and "phenomenal conservatism" (Huemer 2001: 98–118). I have found the work of Richard Swinburne especially helpful in sharpening Vivekananda's PP and TP into premises 3 (PEJ) and 6 (PTEJ) of AEV$_S$ respectively. Swinburne argues that if we accept two uncontroversial "principles of rationality"—namely, the "Principle of Credulity" and the "Principle of Testimony"—then we are rationally justified in believing that putative mystical experiences of God are probably veridical and, therefore, that God probably exists.[20] I will discuss Swinburne's Principle of Credulity here and his Principle of Testimony in the next section. Swinburne formulates the Principle of Credulity as follows:

> (in the absence of special considerations), if it seems (epistemically) to a subject that *x* is present (and has some characteristic), then probably *x* is present (and has that characteristic); what one seems to perceive is probably so. (2004: 303)

For Swinburne, "special considerations" include the unreliability of the subject or of the conditions in which the perceptual experience occurred as well as the strong likelihood that *x* does not exist (2004: 310–15).

My formulation of PEJ (premise 3 of AEV$_S$) is similar to Swinburne's Principle of Credulity, the only minor difference being that while Swinburne's principle is probabilistic ("probably *x* is present"), PEJ is framed in terms of rational justification: "When a subject *S* has a perceptual experience as of *F*, *S* is thereby rationally justified in believing that she has a veridical perceptual experience of *F*, unless she has good reasons to doubt the veridicality of her perceptual experience as of *F*."

Vivekananda's justification of PP also resonates strongly with recent justifications of similar epistemic principles by analytic philosophers. Vivekananda takes PP to be an indispensable principle that all rational people accept implicitly in their day-to-day lives. Accordingly, he frequently refers to ordinary perceptual experiences, like seeing a table or a wall. He takes it to be a sign of

[19] For very similar passages, see *CW* 4:34 and *CW* 4:122. As he puts it in "Addresses on Bhakti-Yoga," "We have to go beyond the intellect; the proof of religion is in direct perception. The proof of the existence of this wall is that we see it . . . " (*CW* 4:34).

[20] It should be noted that in his book, Swinburne (2004) combines the argument from religious experience with numerous other arguments to make a cumulative case for the overall likelihood that God exists.

rational behavior to accept that what *seems* to us to be the case actually *is* the case. As he puts it, "The proof of this wall is that I perceive it." From Vivekananda's perspective, he need not present additional philosophical arguments in favor of PP, since it is an indispensable principle of rationality that we all take for granted at a pre-philosophical level. Swinburne echoes Vivekananda in taking the Principle of Credulity to be a necessary "principle of rationality" that we presuppose in our everyday lives (2004: 303). In fact, Swinburne even uses the same ordinary example of a table as Vivekananda did: "Quite obviously having the experience of it seeming . . . to you that there is a table there . . . is good evidence for supposing that there is a table there" (2004: 303).

More recently, John Hick has justified the "principle of critical trust"[21] along very similar lines. Hick's formulation of this principle closely echoes Vivekananda's PP and Swinburne's Principle of Credulity: "we accept what appears to be there as being there, except when we have reason to doubt it" (2006: 129). Hick also follows Vivekananda and Swinburne in arguing for the indispensability of this principle in our daily lives:

> The implicit principle by which we all live, then, is critical trust. We could not live on any other basis. If I did not trust my perception of the solid wall in front of me I would walk into it and injure myself. If I did not trust my perception of cars moving along the road I would be run over. If I did not trust my perception of the telephone I would not use it. If I did not trust my perception of the visitors who have come to lunch I would not prepare any food for them. We live all the time by a trust which is the most basic kind of faith. And we do not feel any need to justify it—which, as we have seen, is in any case not possible. Critical trust, then, is part of our working definition of sanity. We would count as insane someone who lacks it. (2006: 130)

Hick's argument supports Vivekananda's justification of PP as an indispensable principle of rationality. Indeed, Hick's example of trusting the "perception of the solid wall in front of me" echoes Vivekananda's statement that "[t]he proof of this wall is that I perceive it" (*CW* 1:415). Also like Vivekananda, Hick adds that the principle is not "a blind but a critical trust," because it is "always in principle open to revision" (2006: 130). It might turn out, for instance, that what I think is a wall in front of me is, in fact, a holographic projection, in which case I would conclude that my perception of a wall was not veridical. Hick's point, however, is that perceptions are innocent until proven guilty: we are justified in taking them to be veridical unless we have reason to believe that they are not. As he puts it, "it is rational to trust our experience *except* when we have a reason not to" (Hick

21 Hick borrows this term from Kwan (2009).

2006: 131; emphasis in original). Vivekananda, in the course of elaborating PP, similarly claims that "whatever we see and feel is proof, if there has been nothing to delude the senses" (*CW* 1:204).

Vivekananda, in a passage just a few pages before passage A, provides another philosophical argument in support of PP:

> The sensible world will be the limit to our knowledge if we cannot go farther, if we must not ask for anything more. This is what is called agnosticism. But what reason is there to believe in the testimony of the senses? I would call that man a true agnostic who would stand still in the street and die. If reason is all in all, it leaves us no place to stand on this side of nihilism. (*CW* 1:199)

Here, Vivekananda suggests that accepting PP—believing in "the testimony of the senses"—is the only way to avoid sheer "nihilism," by which he means a debilitating global skepticism about the existence of the external world. He also anticipates the possible response of a hard-core philosophical skeptic who argues for the greater rationality of accepting radical external-world skepticism over PP. Vivekananda's response to such a hypothetical PP-skeptic is that the skeptic commits a self-contradiction by endorsing external-world skepticism at an intellectual level while also implicitly *accepting* PP and the reality of the external world in his everyday life. A true skeptic, Vivekananda claims, "would stand still in the street and die." That is, the PP-skeptic would lose the ability to function in the world, since engaging in any action whatsoever presupposes that what *seems* to be the case *is* the case. For Vivekananda, then, the only alternative to accepting PP is a thoroughgoing external-world skepticism, which he takes to be a view that is very difficult, if not impossible, coherently to hold. Since he was familiar with Mīmāṃsā philosophy, it is possible that he was influenced by Kumārila Bhaṭṭa's very similar justification of *svataḥ-prāmāṇyavāda*: "He who out of delusion is concerned about a contradiction [of his cognition], even though one has not arisen, will be filled with doubt and meet with failure in all his actions."[22]

Swinburne echoes Vivekananda in claiming that failure to accept the Principle of Credulity would land us in a "sceptical bog" (2004: 304n10). While Swinburne does not develop this argument at all, Vivekananda helps clarify the precise nature of this skeptical bog. For Vivekananda, failure to accept PP would land us in the skeptical bog of practical paralysis: we would not be able to act in the world, since virtually all our everyday activities presuppose that what we perceive through our senses actually exists.

[22] *utprekṣeta hi yo mohād ajātam api bādhakam | sa sarvavyavahāreṣu saṃśayātmā kṣayaṃ vrajet ||* (Kumārila's *Bṛhaṭṭīkā* as preserved at Śāntarakṣita's *Tattvasaṃgraha* 2871; cited and translated in Taber 1992: 216).

Thus far, I have been arguing, in the context of premise 3 of AEV$_S$, that Vivekananda generally takes perception to be *defeasible* epistemic justification. My perception of a chair under normal circumstances makes me rationally justified in believing that there is a chair in front of me, but it is still always possible that I am mistaken. Vivekananda clearly believes that all sense-perceptual experiences furnish defeasible epistemic justification. However, his stance on supersensuous perceptions is more complicated. In numerous places, he distinguishes "lower" and "higher" spiritual experiences. He considers divine visions to be a genuine but lower form of spiritual experience. In a conversation with his disciple Saratcandra Cakravarti, Vivekananda recalled a vision he had as a young boy in which he saw a figure whom he later thought was "the Lord Buddha" (*CW* 7:123). He then went on to distinguish such divine visions from the highest realization of the Ātman in *nirvikalpa samādhi*:

> When the mind is purified, when one is free from the attachment for lust and gold, one sees lots of visions, most wonderful ones! But one should not pay heed to them. The aspirant cannot advance further if he sets his mind constantly on them. Haven't you heard that Sri Ramakrishna used to say, "Countless jewels lie uncared for in the outer courts of my beloved Lord's sanctum." We must come face to face with the Ātman; what is the use of setting one's mind on vagaries like those? (*BCW* 9:45 / *CW* 7:123)

He clearly accepts the genuineness of divine visions, but he considers them to be lower spiritual experiences than the salvific realization of the Ātman, in part because he does not think that divine visions are sufficient for liberation. Similarly, in *Rāja-Yoga*, he distinguishes "lower states of *Samādhi*," which "give us visions" of divine "beings," from the "highest grade of *Samādhi*," when "we see the real thing, when we see the material out of which the whole of these grades of beings are composed . . . " (*CW* 1:159).

For Vivekananda, another key difference between divine visions and the highest realization of God is that the former, but not the latter, can be doubted by the subject of experience:

> The stage beyond consciousness is inspiration (*Samādhi*); but never mistake hysterical trances for the real thing. . . . There is no external test for inspiration, we know it ourselves; our guardian against mistake is negative—the voice of reason. (*CW* 7:60)

He seems to have in mind here the "lower states of *Samādhi*" mentioned in *Rāja-Yoga*—states in which we have "visions" of divine beings. Vivekananda points out that in the case of all such divine visions, there is always the possibility of mistakenly taking a hysterical "trance" for a veridical spiritual experience. Hence, if we have such a divine vision, we should exercise our reason to determine whether our experience is, in fact, veridical. For Vivekananda, then, neither divine visions nor ordinary sensory experiences can be self-authenticating, since the experience itself does not guarantee its veridicality.[23]

By contrast, he maintains that the highest state of *samādhi*—the highest supersensuous perception of God or the Ātman—*is* self-authenticating, in that the experience itself guarantees its veridicality to its epistemic subject. Take, for instance, this passage from his "Paper on Hinduism" (1893):

> He [God] reveals Himself to the pure heart; the pure and the stainless see God, yea, even in this life; then and then only all the crookedness of the heart is made straight. Then all doubt ceases. . . . The Hindu does not want to live upon words and theories. . . . If there is a soul in him which is not matter, if there is an all-merciful universal Soul, he will go to Him direct. He must see Him, and that alone can destroy all doubts. So the best proof a Hindu sage gives about the soul, about God, is: "I have seen the soul; I have seen God." (*CW* 1:13)

Here and in numerous other passages, Vivekananda claims that the highest realization of God destroys "all doubts" in the person who has that experience.[24] There is a weak and a strong sense in which we can have a perceptual experience that removes all our doubts about its veridicality. In the weak sense, this removal of all doubts would amount to a merely subjective certitude of the veridicality of our experience. I might have an experience that is so vivid and overwhelming that I cannot doubt its reality, but it is still possible that my experience is not veridical. However, in the strong sense, the absence of doubt would not be a merely subjective certitude but an *infallible* certitude. In that case, my experience of God precludes all doubts in the sense that it is self-authenticating: it guarantees, all by itself, its own veridicality.

Vivekananda, I would suggest, holds that the highest supersensuous perception of God is self-authenticating in the strong sense: the experience itself has built into it an infallible certitude of its own veridicality. Accordingly, he was fond of quoting Muṇḍaka Upaniṣad 2.2.9, which declares that the highest realization of Brahman is self-authenticating: "When the Supreme is seen, the knot of the heart-strings is rent, all doubts are cut asunder (*chidyante sarvasaṃśayāḥ*), and one's *karma* is entirely exhausted."[25] In his lecture "The Great Teachers of the World" (1900), he claims that the great "Prophets" like Jesus Christ and the

[23] Rambachan (1994a: 107) mistakenly claims that Vivekananda takes all experiences of God to be "self-validating."

[24] See also, for instance, *CW* 2:474 and *CW* 4:128.

[25] This is a modified version of Sri Aurobindo's translation (Aurobindo 2001: 141).

Buddha had the "direct perception" of God, a state that he proceeds to describe by paraphrasing the same verse from Muṇḍaka Upaniṣad: "All doubts vanish for ever, and all the crookedness of the heart is made straight, and all bondages vanish, and the results of action and *karma* fly when He is seen . . . " (*CW* 4:128). For Vivekananda, then, the highest realization of God carries with it an infallible certitude that dispels all doubts about its veridicality for its epistemic subject.[26]

In his lecture "Steps to Realisation," he similarly claims that the highest supersensuous perception of the "Truth" furnishes infallible conviction of its veridicality:

> Truth has such a face that any one who sees that face becomes convinced. The sun does not require any torch to show it; the sun is self-effulgent. If truth requires evidence, what will evidence that evidence? If something is necessary as witness for truth, where is the witness for that witness? We must approach religion with reverence and with love, and our heart will stand up and say, this is truth, and this is untruth. (*CW* 1:415)

Vivekananda may have had in mind here the traditional debate between Advaita Vedāntins and Naiyāyikas on the question of whether the validity of a cognition is apprehended intrinsically (*svataḥ*) or extrinsically (*parataḥ*). Naiyāyikas, as I discussed in section 1, uphold *parataḥ-prāmāṇyavāda*, the doctrine that the validity of a cognition can only be apprehended through a second cognition. Advaita Vedāntins, by contrast, uphold *svataḥ-prāmāṇyavāda*, the doctrine that a cognition and its validity are apprehended together. One of the Advaitin's main arguments in support of *svataḥ-prāmāṇyavāda* is that the alternative doctrine of *parataḥ-prāmāṇya* leads to an infinite regress, since one would need a third cognition to verify the validity of the second cognition, and so forth. Vivekananda employs a similar infinite regress argument to support the self-authenticating nature of the highest realization of God: "If truth requires evidence, what will evidence that evidence?" Hence, he upholds the view that just as the sun is "self-effulgent," the highest realization of God furnishes an infallible conviction of its own veridicality to its epistemic subject.

We are now in a better position to understand the rational justification in play in premise 3 of AEV$_S$. In the case of all sense-perceptual experiences as well as all supersensuous perceptions *other than* the highest realization of God, *S* has *defeasible* rational justification for believing that her experience is veridical. By contrast, in the case of the highest supersensuous perception of God, *S* has

[26] Likewise, Vivekananda's statement elsewhere that the "superconscious state makes no mistakes" (*CW* 8:45) can be taken to mean that the highest spiritual experience is self-authenticating.

non-defeasible rational justification for believing that her experience is veridical, since the experience itself guarantees to *S* its own veridicality.

In his lecture on "Reason and Religion," Vivekananda claims that "physics or chemistry has no internal mandate to vouch for its truth, which religion has" (*CW* 1:367). I take him to mean that religion has an "internal mandate" in the sense that it is grounded in the self-authenticating perception of God, which infallibly guarantees its truth at the phenomenological level. The physical sciences, by contrast, have no such internal mandate, since they are based on sensory experiences, which can never be self-authenticating. Let us recall Vivekananda's statement, already quoted, that religion is "a reality to be felt, to be sensed in an infinitely more intense way than we can sense the world" (*CW* 4:179). For Vivekananda, while all perceptual experiences have a noetic quality, different types of perceptual experience exhibit varying degrees of noetic strength. The highest supersensuous perception of God has a maximally strong noetic quality, since it is a self-authenticating experience that carries with it an infallible conviction of its veridicality. Lower types of supersensuous perception—such as the vision of some form of God—have a much stronger noetic quality than sensory experiences, but they nonetheless fall short of being self-authenticating. Finally, sense-perceptual experiences have a comparatively weaker noetic quality than *any* supersensuous perceptions, of either the lower or the higher type.

Many contemporary philosophers of religion who have defended the epistemic value of mystical experience nonetheless deny the logical possibility of a *self-authenticating* mystical experience.[27] Robert Oakes (1981; 2005), by contrast, defends the logical possibility of a self-authenticating mystical experience. The key question is whether we should accept what Oakes calls the "Phenomenological Indiscernibility Postulate" (PIP), according to which a veridical mystical experience is necessarily indistinguishable from a delusory mystical experience at the phenomenological level (2005: 415–16). Oakes argues that while PIP applies to the vast majority of perceptual experiences, it is logically possible for an omnipotent God to perform the "epistemic miracle" of bringing about self-authenticating experiences of Himself by suspending the applicability of PIP to these experiences (1981: 106–7). In *Infinite Paths to Infinite Reality* (Maharaj 2018: 201–11), I provide a detailed defense of Oakes's line of reasoning by drawing upon Ramakrishna's mystical testimony and teachings. Vivekananda follows Ramakrishna in accepting the logical possibility of self-authenticating mystical experiences. Moreover, Vivekananda's claim that the highest spiritual experiences have an "internal mandate" to vouch for their truth indicates that he does not take PIP to apply to such spiritual experiences.

[27] See, for instance, Yandell (1993: 163–75), Alston (1991: 80–81), and Gellman (1997: 47).

5. *Premise 6: Perceptual Testimony as Epistemic Justification*

As we have seen in section 2, Vivekananda defends the *Principle of Testimonial Proof* (TP) in passage A. He translates *āgama* in *Yogasūtra* 1.7 as "competent evidence"—the verbal or written testimony of a trustworthy person (an "*āpta*").[28] He claims that an *āpta*'s "words are proof," thereby asserting the *svataḥ-prāmāṇyatā* of cognitions arising from testimony. He then goes on to explain why:

> Other philosophers go into long discussions about *āptavākya* and they say, "What is the proof of their words?" The proof is their direct perception. Because whatever I see is proof, and whatever you see is proof, if it does not contradict any past knowledge. (*CW* 1:205)

Here, it is clear that he is focusing on verbal testimony based on perception (*pratyakṣa*) rather than on inference (*anumāna*). In this passage, he justifies TP on the basis of PP: since an *āpta*'s direct perception of *F* is sufficient "proof" for him that *F* exists, the *āpta*'s testimony about his perception of *F* constitutes "proof" of the existence of *F for others*. On this point, Vivekananda largely follows Vyāsa's commentary on *Yogasūtra* 1.7. Vyāsa explains *āgama* as follows: "Something which has been seen or inferred by a trustworthy person (*āptena*) is mentioned by word (*śabdena*) in order that his knowledge [thereof] may pass over to some other person (*svabodhasaṃkrāntaye*)" (Woods 1914: 20–21; translation slightly modified). While Vyāsa conceives *āgama* as testimony based on both perception and inference, Vivekananda conceives *āgama* as perceptual testimony alone. Premise 6 of AEVs (PTEJ) represents a refinement of Vivekananda's TP: "People other than *S* are rationally justified in believing that *S*'s perceptual experience as of *F* is as *S* reports it to be, unless they have good reasons to doubt *S*'s sincerity or trustworthiness."

Vivekananda clarifies his justification of PP and TP in his commentary on *Yogasūtra* 1.49: "The idea is that we have to get our knowledge of ordinary objects by direct perception, and by inference therefrom, and from testimony of people who are competent" (*CW* 1:232). He argues that in ordinary life, we are only able to get on in the world by assuming that our cognitions derived from perception, inference, and testimony are "innocent until proven guilty" (to use Deutsch's phrase, already quoted in section 1); that is, we assume that our everyday cognitions are veridical unless we have some reason to doubt them. As

[28] In conversation with Saratcandra Cakravarti, Vivekananda similarly remarked: "*Śabdas* are again divided into two classes, the Vedic *Śabda* and *śabdas* in common human use (*vaidika o laukika bhede śabda ābār dvidhā vibhakta*). I found this position in [the Nyāya book called] *Śabdaśaktiprakāśikā*" (*BCW* 9:22 / *CW* 6:499).

we already discussed in the previous section, Vivekananda believes that this assumption is an eminently reasonable one, since *not* accepting this assumption would land us in a debilitating "nihilism."

In passage A, Vivekananda focuses especially on *mystical* testimony—that is, *āptavākya* understood as "the direct evidence of the Yogis" who have attained supersensuous knowledge. He claims that the Yogi's "words are proof, because he sees knowledge in himself." He goes on to note, however, that "[a]ny madman may come into this room and say he sees angels around him; that would not be proof." It is at this point that he delineates four criteria for determining whether the person claiming to have supersensuous knowledge is competent (i.e., is truly an *āpta*). First, the person must be "unselfish and holy," since purity is a precondition for supersensuous perception. More generally, he insists on the importance of assessing the person's "character." This first criterion debars from being an *āpta*, for instance, anyone who has a "selfish motive" for deceiving us, who is prone to being deceived or deluded, or who is not mentally stable. Second, the person must claim to have knowledge of a supramundane reality that lies "beyond the senses." Third, what the person says must "not contradict the past knowledge of humanity." Vivekananda's third criterion entails that verbal testimony must not contradict perception or inference—a view that was widely held by traditional Indian philosophical schools. For instance, as we saw in the previous section, Śaṅkara insists that in cases where verbal testimony contradicts sense-perception, we should reject testimony in favor of perception. Fourth, what the person says "must have a possibility of verification." That is, any one of us should, in principle, be able to verify the person's perceptual testimony by having the same kind of perceptual experience ourselves.

Swinburne has defended a "Principle of Testimony" that is strikingly similar to PTEJ and Vivekananda's TP. After introducing the Principle of Credulity, Swinburne appeals to the Principle of Testimony in order to establish that the existence of *x* is probable not only for the subject undergoing the experience but also for others:

> (in the absence of special considerations) the experiences of others are (probably) as they report them. (2004: 322)

The "special considerations" Swinburne mentions include evidence that the person reporting her experiences generally "misremembers or exaggerates or lies" (2004: 322). Swinburne argues that these special considerations do not generally obtain in the case of mystical testimony, and some of the reasons he gives echo Vivekananda's criteria for qualifying as an *āpta*. Vivekananda, we should recall, insists that an *āpta* must be a "perfectly unselfish and holy person" (*CW* 1:205). Similarly, Swinburne argues that a good test to verify a mystic's claims is to check whether her "lifestyle has undergone a change," since it is reasonable to expect that someone who believes that God exists will be naturally inclined to engage in "prayer, worship, and self-sacrifice" (2004: 323). Swinburne also follows Vivekananda in defending the Principle of Testimony as a fundamental "principle of rationality" that is indispensable in everyday life. Finally, just as Vivekananda argued that there was "knowledge beyond the senses" on the basis of PP and TP, Swinburne argues for the "considerable evidential force of religious experience" on the basis of the Principles of Credulity and Testimony (2004: 326).

In passage A and in numerous other places, Vivekananda boldly claims that the world's religious scriptures are paradigmatic instances of *āptavākya*. *Āpta*s include "the authors of the sacred scriptures; therefore the scriptures are proof." He elaborates this claim in his commentary on *Yogasūtra* 1.49:

> By "people who are competent," the Yogis always mean the Rishis, or the Seers of the thoughts recorded in the scriptures—the Vedas. According to them, the only proof of the scriptures is that they were the testimony of competent persons, yet they say the scriptures cannot take us to realisation. We can read all the Vedas, and yet will not realise anything, but when we practise their teachings, then we attain to that state which realises what the scriptures say, which penetrates where neither reason nor perception nor inference can go, and where the testimony of others cannot avail. (*CW* 1:232)

In spite of his allegiance to Vedānta, Vivekananda breaks dramatically with traditional Vedānta in his understanding of scripture and its relation to spiritual experience. Most fundamentally, he rejects the traditional Mīmāṃsā/Vedānta view of the eternality and authorlessness (*apauruṣeyatva*) of the Vedas. In his "Notes Taken Down in Madras" (1892–93), he affirms the eternality not of the *words* of the Vedas but of the "spiritual laws" taught in them:

> The Vedas are *anādi*, eternal. The meaning of the statement is not, as is erroneously supposed by some, that the words of the Vedas are *anādi*, but that the spiritual laws inculcated by the Vedas are such. These laws which are immutable and eternal have been discovered at various times by great men or Rishis, though some of them are forgotten now, while others are preserved. (*CW* 6:103)

In stark contrast to Mīmāṃsā and traditional Vedānta, Vivekananda claims that the Vedas were authored by mystics who described, in these texts, their own supersensuous experiences of eternal spiritual laws and ultimate truths. As he puts it elsewhere, "In their books the writers, who are called Rishis, or sages, declare they experienced certain truths, and these they preach" (*CW* 1:126).[29]

Since Vivekananda conceives the scriptures as records of the supersensuous experiences of mystics, he argues that the scriptures can only be verified or proved through supersensuous perception. As he puts it, "The proof, therefore, of the Vedas is just the same as the proof of this table before me, *pratyakṣa*, direct perception" (*CW* 3:253). For Vivekananda, then, while we can gain mediate or intellectual knowledge of ultimate reality through the Vedas, we can attain full-blown *spiritual* knowledge of ultimate reality only through direct supersensuous perception.[30] As we have seen in section 1, Śaṅkara's own views on this issue are complicated since, in his commentary on *Brahmasūtra* 1.1.2, he claims that the knowledge of Brahman "culminates in *anubhava*," which seems to leave the door open for Vivekananda's view that scriptural knowledge finds its ultimate validation in the spiritual experience of Brahman.

One of Vivekananda's main reasons for holding this view is that the Vedāntic scriptures themselves self-reflexively subordinate scriptural knowledge to spiritual experience. In his lecture "The Vedānta in All its Phases," he puts this point as follows:

> This unique idea that religion is to be realised is in India alone. *Nāyam ātmā balahīnena labhyo na medhayā na bahunā śrutena*—"This Ātman is not to be reached by too much talking, nor is it to be reached by the power of intellect, nor by much study of the scriptures" [Muṇḍaka Upaniṣad 3.2.4]. Nay, ours is the only scripture in the world that declares, not even by the study of the scriptures can the Ātman be realised—not talks, not lecturing, none of that, but It is to be realised. (*CW* 3:345)[31]

Citing a verse from Muṇḍaka Upaniṣad as evidence, Vivekananda claims that the Vedāntic scriptures themselves declare that scriptural knowledge must culminate in spiritual realization. An even more important scriptural source-text for Vivekananda is Bṛhadāraṇyaka Upaniṣad 2.4.5: "My dear Maitreyī, the Self . . . should be realized—should be heard of, reflected on, and meditated upon" (*ātmā vā are draṣṭavyaḥ śrotavyo mantavyo nididhyāsitavyo maitreyi*). He quotes this scriptural passage repeatedly in his lectures.[32] Crucially, he interprets *śravaṇa*,

[29] Similarly, in *Rāja-Yoga*, he defines the "scriptures" as the "testimony of competent persons" (*CW* 1:232).

[30] For a good discussion of Vivekananda's view on this issue, see Rambachan (1994a: 41–50).

[31] Elsewhere, he similarly remarks: "One peculiarity of the Vedas is that they are the only scriptures that again and again declare that you must go beyond them" (*CW* 5:311).

[32] See, for instance, *CW* 2:152, *CW* 3:25, *CW* 4:245, and *CW* 2:419–20.

manana, and *nididhyāsana* as chronologically sequential stages culminating in spiritual realization:

> The Vedas teach three things: this Self is first to be heard, then to be reasoned, and then to be meditated upon. When a man first hears it, he must reason on it, so that he does not believe it ignorantly, but knowingly; and after reasoning what it is, he must meditate upon it, and then realise it. (*CW* 5:302–3)

For Vivekananda, after gaining intellectual knowledge of the Ātman through scripture, we must proceed to reflect, and then to meditate, on the Ātman in order to attain the liberative spiritual experience of the Ātman. As discussed in section 1 of this chapter, Vivekananda's interpretation of this scriptural passage is in line with the Bhāmatī school of Advaita as well as medieval Advaitic texts like *Vivekacūḍāmaṇi*.

However, Vivekananda's understanding of scripture and its relation to spiritual experience is even more radical than that of any earlier Advaitins in at least one crucial respect. Whenever followers of the Bhāmatī school and medieval Advaitic texts referred to "*śruti*," they meant the Vedas—especially the Upaniṣads. Vivekananda, by contrast, accepts *all* the world's religious scriptures as equally valid. It is highly significant that in passage A, he refers to "the authors of the sacred scriptures" in general as *āptas*. In fact, in numerous places, he emphatically rejects the traditional view that the Vedas are the only source of religious truths. As he puts it, "All scriptures, all truths are Vedas in all times, in all countries; because these truths are to be *seen*, and any one may discover them" (*CW* 7:9).[33] All the world's religious scriptures are equally valid, since they are all records of universal spiritual truths that were directly realized by sages of various countries.

From this universalist standpoint, Vivekananda severely criticizes the "bigotry" of Vedic orthodoxy:

> Such bigotry is characteristic of the orthodox element of all religions. For instance, the orthodox followers of the Vedas claim that the Vedas are the only authentic word of God in the world; that God has spoken to the world only through the Vedas; not only that, but that the world itself exists by virtue of the Vedas. Before the world was, the Vedas were. Everything in the world exists because it is in the Vedas. A cow exists because the name ["]cow["] is in the Vedas; that is, because the animal we know as a cow is mentioned in the Vedas. The

[33] Similarly, he states: "It is a marvelous book—these spiritual revelations of the world. The Bible, the Vedas, the Koran, and all other sacred books are but so many pages, and an infinite number of pages remain yet to be unfolded. I would leave it open for all of them" (*CW* 2:374).

language of the Vedas is the original language of God, all other languages are mere dialects and not of God. (*CW* 6:47)

Here, he attacks two traditional Mīmāṃsā and Vedāntic views on scriptures that were discussed in section 1: that the Vedas are the only valid scripture and that "the world itself exists by virtue of the Vedas." His tone of mockery suggests that he considers the latter view to be patently implausible, and he traces both orthodox views to a bigoted and ethnocentric outlook that refuses to accept the universality of spiritual truths.

It is also significant that Vivekananda, in a passage from *Rāja-Yoga* already quoted, claims that the "Yogis" hold that "the only proof of the scriptures is that they were the testimony of competent persons, yet they say the scriptures cannot take us to realisation." In the context of this passage, I think it is plausible to assume that by "Yogis" he means followers of the Yoga school of philosophy. In other words, he traces his own preferred view of scripture as records of the spiritual experiences of seers to the Yoga school. Some recent scholars of Yoga philosophy have supported Vivekananda's view in this regard (Grinshpon 1997: 129–38; Bryant 2009: 36–38). Yohanan Grinshpon, for instance, argues that the *Yogasūtra*, as well as Vyāsa's commentary thereon, both suggest a "radical mystico-yogic orientation" (1997: 134). *Yogasūtra* 1.6, for instance, includes "*pramāṇa*" as one of the mental *vṛtti*s that needs to be restrained. Since the very next *sūtra* mentions *āgama* as one of the three *pramāṇa*s, Patañjali may be implying that scriptural knowledge must ultimately give way to the spiritual experience of *samādhi*. Similarly, Vyāsa, in his commentary on *Yogasūtra* 1.43, claims that *nirvitarka-samādhi*—which Vivekananda translates as the "*Samādhi* called 'without question'" (*CW* 1:229)—is the "supreme perception, the seed of both scriptural testimony and inference, and that from which both scriptural testimony and inference arise" (*tat paraṃ pratyakṣam. tac ca śrutānumānayor bījam. tataḥ śrutānumāne prabhavataḥ*) (Rukmani 2007: 212). As Grinshpon notes, this statement suggests that "Vyāsa sees the Veda as derivative, secondary to the non-verbal meditative state of yogic consciousness from which Vedic teachings seem to 'spring'" (1997: 136). Arguably, then, there is some plausibility in Vivekananda's attempt to trace his own views on scripture and spiritual experience to the Yoga school of philosophy.

Hence, two of the primary traditional sources for key aspects of Vivekananda's views on scripture and its relation to spiritual experience are Yoga philosophy as well as texts like *Vivekacūḍāmaṇi* in the tradition of Advaita Vedānta. However, as Rambachan (1994a: 19–35) has shown, Vivekananda's views on this issue were also strongly shaped by Ramakrishna and Brāhmo thinkers like Debendranath Tagore and Keshab Chandra Sen. As I already noted in chapter 1, Debendranath and Keshab had emphatically subordinated religious scriptures to the direct spiritual realization of God. Ramakrishna would often express a similar view—as, for instance, in this remark to a pundit on June 30, 1884:

> But seeing is far better than hearing. Then all doubts disappear. It is true that many things are recorded in the scriptures; but all these are useless without the direct realization of God, without devotion to His Lotus Feet, without purity of heart. (*K* 478 / *G* 476)

Hence, Vivekananda followed not only Ramakrishna but also Brāhmos like Debendranath and Keshab in privileging spiritual experience over scriptural knowledge. Vivekananda's broad understanding of scripture as encompassing not just the Vedas but *all* the world's religious scriptures can also be traced to the teachings of Ramakrishna and Keshab, both of whom held that all the world religions are different paths to the same goal of God-realization.

6. *Premises 4 and 7: Absence of Rebutting and Undercutting Defeaters*

According to PEJ, when a person *S* has a perceptual experience as of *F*, *S* is thereby rationally justified in believing that she has a veridical perceptual experience of *F only if* she has no good reasons for doubting the veridicality of her perceptual experience as of *F*. Hence, in order to establish that at least some mystics are justified in believing that at least some of their experiences as of an ultimate reality are veridical (premise 5), premise 4 is necessary: at least some mystics have no good reasons to doubt the veridicality of all or most of their experiences as of an ultimate reality.

Likewise, according to premise 6 of AEVs, people other than *S* are rationally justified in believing that *S*'s perceptual experience as of *F* is as *S* reports it to be, *unless* they have good reasons to doubt *S*'s sincerity or trustworthiness. Hence, in order to establish that people other than mystics are justified in believing that at least some mystics have had at least some veridical experiences of an ultimate reality (conclusion 8), premise 7 is necessary: people other than *S* have no good reasons to doubt the sincerity or trustworthiness of all or most mystics who claim to have had veridical experiences of an ultimate reality.

Premises 4 and 7 are, of course, closely related, since the "good reasons" mystics might have for doubting the veridicality of their experiences as of an ultimate reality are the same "good reasons" people *other* than these mystics might have for doubting the veridicality of these mystics' experiences as of an ultimate reality. These "good reasons" amount to various defeaters for premises 3 and 6. Following John Pollock and Joseph Cruz (1986: 196), we can divide these defeaters into two categories: rebutting defeaters and undercutting defeaters. A rebutting defeater for some belief that *p* is a reason for holding the negation of *p* or for holding some proposition, *q*, incompatible with *p*. An undercutting defeater for some belief that *p* is a reason for supposing that one's ground for believing *p* is not sufficiently indicative of the truth of the belief.[34]

With respect to AEVs, rebutting defeaters for PEJ and PTEJ would be good reasons for believing that an ultimate reality such as God or the nondual Ātman does not exist. Having read Hume, Mill, and other Western thinkers, Vivekananda was well aware of some of the major arguments against God's existence—especially the argument from evil, to which he frequently referred.[35] In *Rāja-Yoga*, he clarifies his stance on all such arguments against God's existence:

> The field of reason, or of the conscious workings of the mind, is narrow and limited. There is a little circle within which human reason must move. It cannot go beyond. Every attempt to go beyond is impossible, yet it is beyond this circle of reason that there lies all that humanity holds most dear. All these questions, whether there is an immortal soul, whether there is a God, whether there is any supreme intelligence guiding this universe or not, are beyond the field of reason. Reason can never answer these questions. What does reason say? It says, "I am agnostic; I do not know either yea or nay." (*CW* 1:181)

Vivekananda argues that reason has inherent limits and, therefore, can neither prove nor disprove the existence of an ultimate reality such as God or the Ātman. In chapter 7, I will discuss in detail his subtle stance on the limits of reason and his reasons for thinking that no argument against God's existence can ever succeed. As we will see in that chapter, he defends his rational agnosticism by drawing upon traditional Vedāntic arguments as well as the modern Western arguments of Kant and William Hamilton, among others. Moreover, he also specifically refutes what he takes to be the single most serious argument against God's existence—namely, the argument from evil—by defending a Vedāntic *karma*-based theodicy. On the side of ultimate reality, then, he lends support to PEJ and PTEJ by arguing that it is not possible to prove that God or the nondual Ātman does not exist.

Undercutting defeaters for PEJ and PTEJ would be good reasons for believing that the ground of all or most mystics for believing that their perceptual experiences as of an ultimate reality are veridical is not sufficiently indicative of the truth of the belief. Vivekananda was well aware of one such

[34] These formulations of rebutting and undercutting defeaters are taken from Brogaard (2013: 270).

[35] See, for instance, *CW* 6:52–53.

undercutting defeater: namely, that those claiming to have perceived God likely suffer from some sort of psychological abnormality—such as mental illness or hyperemotionalism—which makes them prone to hallucination or self-deception. In fact, on one occasion, he told his disciple Surendranāth Dāsgupta about one of his own earlier experiences of *nirvikalpa samādhi*, and his disciple asked him, "Might not this state as well be brought about by a derangement of the brain?" Vivekananda responded as follows:

> A derangement of the brain! How can you call it so, when it comes neither as the result of delirium from any disease, nor of intoxication from drinking, nor as an illusion produced by various sorts of queer breathing exercises—but when it comes to a normal man in full possession of his health and wits? (*CW* 5:392)

This statement contains Vivekananda's basic support of PEJ and PTEJ against undercutting defeaters. He claims that we would only have good reason to believe that mystics are deluded if we could establish either that they suffer from some sort of mental or physical disease that makes them prone to "delirium," or that they are under the influence of an intoxicant, or that they have engaged in practices that make them prone to hallucinations. In fact, however, he claims that many of those who claim to have perceived ultimate reality are physically and psychologically normal and "in full possession" of their "health and wits." In sum, then, he lends support to PEJ and PTEJ by arguing that we have no good reason to believe that God does not exist or that all mystics are liars or suffer from some sort of psychological abnormality which makes them prone to hallucinations.

Recent analytic philosophers of religion have defended premises 4 and 7 of AEV_S on very similar grounds. Like Vivekananda, Swinburne claims that there is "no good proof of the non-existence of God" and that "[m]ost religious experiences are had by people who normally make reliable perceptual claims, and have not recently taken drugs" (2004: 315). In line with both Vivekananda and Swinburne, Caroline Franks Davis has examined in detail the evidence in support of the claim that all or most mystics suffer from a pathology such as hypersuggestibility, deprivation and maladjustment, mental illness, or abnormal physiological states (1989: 193–223). Davis concludes that "the evidence overwhelmingly supports the view that most subjects of religious experiences . . . have no underlying pathology" and that "relatively few religious experiences are induced by hallucinogenic drugs" (1989: 221).[36]

Premises 1 through 4 of AEV_S, if true, make plausible the conclusion that at least some mystics are rationally justified in believing that at least some of their

[36] Gellman (1999: 55–74) has defended a similar position.

experiences as of an ultimate reality are veridical. Premises 5 through 7, if true, make plausible the further conclusion that non-mystics are also rationally justified in believing that at least some mystics have had at least some veridical experiences of an ultimate reality. The next chapter will address some of the main philosophical challenges to different premises of AEVs and to Vivekananda's specific views on spiritual experience.

6

Addressing Philosophical Challenges to Supersensuous Perception

The previous chapter reconstructed Vivekananda's argument for the epistemic value of supersensuous perception (AEV) and then further refined and developed it into a seven-premise argument (AEV$_s$) by drawing upon his own ideas as well as contemporary analytic philosophy. This chapter will address some of the most serious objections that have been leveled against different premises of AEV$_s$ and against Vivekananda's views on spiritual experience. Since I will be referring to various premises of AEV$_s$ throughout this chapter, I reproduce the full argument here:

Let "mystics" stand for subjects who have had experiences as of an ultimate reality.

A Vivekanandan Argument for the Epistemic Value of Supersensuous Perception (AEV$_s$)

1. Mystics exist.
2. Experiences as of an ultimate reality are perceptual in nature, since they are sufficiently similar to sense-perceptual experiences.
3. *Perception as Epistemic Justification* (PEJ): When a subject *S* has a perceptual experience as of *F*, *S* is thereby rationally justified in believing that she has a veridical perceptual experience of *F*, unless she has good reasons to doubt the veridicality of her perceptual experience as of *F*.
4. At least some mystics have no good reasons to doubt the veridicality of all or most of their experiences as of an ultimate reality.

Therefore,

5. At least some mystics are rationally justified in believing that at least some of their experiences as of an ultimate reality are veridical. (*from* 1–4)
6. *Perceptual Testimony as Epistemic Justification* (PTEJ): People other than *S* are rationally justified in believing that *S*'s perceptual experience as of *F* is as *S* reports it to be, unless they have good reasons to doubt *S*'s sincerity or trustworthiness.

Swami Vivekananda's Vedāntic Cosmopolitanism. Swami Medhananda, Oxford University Press. © Oxford University Press 2022. DOI: 10.1093/oso/9780197624463.003.0007

7. People other than mystics have no good reasons to doubt the sincerity or trustworthiness of all or most mystics who claim to have had veridical experiences of an ultimate reality.

Therefore,

8. People other than mystics are rationally justified in believing that at least some mystics have had at least some veridical experiences of an ultimate reality. (*from* 5–7)

Section 1 discusses one of the most important objections to premise 2 of AEVs—namely, that supersensuous experiences are not sufficiently similar to sensory experiences, since only the latter, but not the former, can be adequately crosschecked. The philosopher of religion William Alston, I argue, provides a plausible response to this crosscheckability objection that resonates strongly with Vivekananda's views.

Section 2 addresses the "speckled hen" objection, which contemporary epistemologists have leveled against principles of perceptual dogmatism akin to premise 3 (PEJ). According to this objection, some perceptual experiences have the content that *p* without justifying the belief that *p*. For instance, if we take a quick glance at a hen with 48 speckles, we have a perceptual experience that represents the hen as having 48 speckles, yet we would not be justified in *believing* that the hen has 48 speckles, since it is not possible for normal humans to count that many speckles so quickly. I discuss several contemporary responses to the speckled hen objection and argue that Jessie Munton's new line of response is especially promising. According to Munton, the objection fails because a normal human's momentary perceptual experience of a 48-speckled hen represents the hen not as having 48 speckles but as having an *indeterminate* number of speckles.

Section 3 addresses the gullibility objection to principles of default trust in testimony akin to premise 6 (PTEJ). According to some contemporary epistemologists, principles such as PTEJ open the floodgates to gullibility, since such principles do not require *positive* reasons for believing that the testifier is sincere and trustworthy. Building on the recent work of philosophers like Tyler Burge and Robert Audi, I argue that PTEJ is an indispensable principle of rationality and that the defeater clause built into PTEJ is sufficient to block the gullibility objection.

Section 4 discusses some objections to premises 4 and 7 of AEVs. According to the conflicting claims objection, mystics have characterized ultimate reality in numerous conflicting ways on the basis of their experiences—a fact that calls into question their epistemic value. Vivekananda, I argue, follows Ramakrishna in claiming that the apparently conflicting mystical reports about ultimate reality are actually complementary, since they describe different forms and aspects of one and the same impersonal-personal Divine Reality. I then discuss some of the Mīmāṃsaka Kumārila's main criticisms of yogic perception and testimony, and I explore how Vivekananda might have responded to these criticisms.

Finally, section 5 addresses Anantanand Rambachan's specific criticisms of Vivekananda's views on spiritual experience and the "science of religion." Drawing on chapters 4 through 6, I argue that Rambachan misunderstands or oversimplifies Vivekananda's views in numerous respects. Most seriously, Rambachan overlooks Vivekananda's argument for the epistemic value of spiritual experience, which plays a pivotal role in his overall defense of the experiential basis and scientific credentials of religion.

1. *The Crosscheckability Objection to Premise 2*

Some contemporary philosophers of religion have challenged premise 2 of AEV_S by arguing that putative mystical experiences are, in fact, quite different from sensory experiences in important respects. If it can be shown that mystical experiences are not sufficiently similar to sensory experiences, then mystical experiences would not be perceptual in nature, and PEJ—even if valid—would apply to sense-perceptual experiences but *not* to mystical experiences. Hence, if premise 2 can be shown to be implausible, then any attempt to establish the epistemic value of mystical experience on the basis of PEJ would fail.

Critics of premise 2 argue that one of the major differences between mystical experiences and sensory experiences is that claims based on the latter, but not the former, can be directly crosschecked.[1] If I claim to see an oak tree a short distance away from me, someone standing next to me can crosscheck my claim by seeing whether there really is an oak tree in front of me. Let us call this the "other observers" test.[2] That same person can crosscheck my claim in a different way by walking toward the exact spot where I claim to see the oak tree and seeing whether she runs into it. Let us call this the "predictive efficacy" test.[3] The "other observers" test and the "predictive efficacy" test are two of the most common procedures for crosschecking claims based on sensory experiences, but there are, of course, many other tests for sensory experiences as well, which I will not discuss here.[4]

Philosophers such as Evan Fales and Anthony O'Hear argue that one reason why sense-perceptual experiences have epistemic value, while mystical

[1] See Fales (1996a), Gale (1991: 302–43), O'Hear (1984: 25–55), and Clark (1984). I have discussed the crosscheckability objection in more detail in Maharaj (2018: 219–31).

[2] I borrow the term "other observers test" from Alston (2004: 144). For other formulations of the other observers test, see Fales (1996a), Gale (1991: 302), and O'Hear (1984: 45–46).

[3] For appeals to the predictive efficacy test, see Fales (1996a: 27) and O'Hear (1984: 45–46).

[4] See, for instance, the list of eleven crosschecking procedures for sensory experiences in Gale (1991: 302).

experiences do not, is that the former, but not the latter, can be crosschecked by means of direct procedures like the "other observers" test and the "predictive efficacy" test.[5] As Fales puts it, "When St. Teresa is receiving an inner locution, we can't call on St. John of the Cross to contemplate and independently confirm the message Teresa says God is sending. St. John of the Cross-Check he's not" (1996a: 34). One obvious rejoinder to Fales is that there *are* crosschecking procedures for verifying the veridicality of mystical experiences, though these procedures are quite different from the kind of crosschecks used to verify sensory experiences. Some common mystical checking procedures include, for instance, seeing whether the putative mystic has been morally and spiritually transformed by her spiritual experience and determining whether the mystic's experientially based claims accord with the teachings of the religious scriptures accepted in her tradition. While Fales acknowledges these kinds of mystical crosschecking procedures, he argues that all such mystical crosschecks lack "epistemic bite," since they are markedly inferior to the more "direct and independent" checking procedures for sensory experiences (1996a: 34).

William Alston has defended the epistemic force of mystical crosschecking procedures against critics like Fales by arguing that their line of reasoning exhibits two vices: "epistemic imperialism" and the "double standard" (1991: 209–50). Fales is guilty of epistemic imperialism, since he makes the unwarranted assumption that claims based on experiences of God must be subject to the *same kind* of crosschecks used for sensory experiences (Alston 1991: 216). As Alston puts it, "there is no reason to suppose it *appropriate* to require the same checks and tests for them [reports of perception of God] as for sense-perceptual reports, and every (or at least sufficient) reason to suppose it inappropriate" (1991: 216). Most fundamentally, since God cannot be perceived by the physical senses, it is unreasonable to suppose that reports of experiences of God should be subject to checking procedures appropriate to sensory experiences.[6] Second, although Fales claims that the "other observers" test is "more direct and independent" than the kind of crosschecking procedures frequently employed by mystics, even the "other observers" test is epistemically circular, since another observer can only verify a sense-perceptual report—such as my claim that I see an oak tree in front of me—on the basis of her *own* sensory experience, which would itself require crosschecking, ad infinitum. Alston contends, therefore, that those who fault mystics for employing crosschecks that are indirect or epistemically unreliable are guilty of a "double standard," because they overlook the fact that the crosschecks for verifying sensory experiences are just as epistemically circular as mystical crosschecks (1991: 249–50).[7]

5 Fales (1996a), O'Hear (1984: 25–55), and Gale (1991: 302–43).
6 For a good discussion of this point, see Gellman (1997: 26–27).
7 For similar arguments, see Wainwright (1981: 105) and Kwan (2009: 547).

How might Vivekananda make a contribution to these contemporary debates about whether mystical claims can be adequately crosschecked? First of all, it is interesting to note that Vivekananda himself is as insistent as critics like Fales about the need to verify mystical claims. Indeed, as we have seen in chapter 4, Vivekananda defends religion as a bona fide "science" by arguing that religion, like any other science, invites empirical verification. "Religious truths," as he puts it, "need verification by everyone" (*CW* 6:133). According to Vivekananda, religious claims are based on spiritual experiences, which we can all directly verify by engaging in the relevant spiritual practices and seeing whether we have the same spiritual experiences ourselves.

In numerous places, he also accepts another valid, but less direct, method of verifying a mystic's claims: namely, by checking whether the mystic's character has been positively transformed as a result of her spiritual experience. As he puts it, "we have first of all to see that the man who declares himself to be an *āpta* [one who has realized God] is a perfectly unselfish and holy person" (*CW* 1:205). Vivekananda gives two reasons for thinking that people who have realized God should be highly moral and saintly. First, he notes—in accordance with all Indian spiritual traditions—that ethical behavior is an essential prerequisite for attaining spiritual experience in the first place. As he puts it, "A man may be wicked, and yet make an astronomical discovery, but in religion it is different, because no impure man will ever have the power to reach the truths of religion" (*CW* 1:205). Second, he claims that we can judge whether someone has really attained the highest *samādhi* by evaluating the "effects" of that spiritual experience in that person's life. According to Vivekananda, one who has attained *samādhi* "comes out enlightened, a sage, a prophet, a saint, his whole character changed, his life changed, illumined" (*CW* 1:181).[8] A number of contemporary philosophers have defended Vivekananda's line of reasoning (Gutting 1983: 152; Gellman 1997: 32–33, 75). Gary Gutting, for instance, argues that if God "is indeed an extraordinarily good, wise, and powerful being, there is reason to think that intimate contact with it [God] will be of great help in our efforts to lead good lives" (1983: 152). In other words, God's own moral perfection should rub off on those who have experienced Him.

Vivekananda also anticipated Alston's powerful critique of Fales by arguing that it is unreasonable to expect that the methods for verifying mystical claims should be the same as the methods for verifying claims in sciences like physics or chemistry. Vivekananda makes this argument in the following passage from *Rāja-Yoga*, already quoted in chapter 4:

[8] Both of these mystical checking procedures were strongly emphasized by Ramakrishna, who was one of the major influences on Vivekananda. See my discussion in Maharaj (2018: 219–31).

> The science of Rāja-Yoga proposes to put before humanity a practical and scientifically worked out method of reaching this truth. In the first place, every science must have its own method of investigation. If you want to become an astronomer and sit down and cry "Astronomy! Astronomy!" it will never come to you. The same with chemistry. A certain method must be followed. You must go to a laboratory, take different substances, mix them up, compound them, experiment with them, and out of that will come a knowledge of chemistry. If you want to be an astronomer, you must go to an observatory, take a telescope, study the stars and planets, and then you will become an astronomer. Each science must have its own methods. (*CW* 1:128)[9]

His main argument is succinctly captured in the final sentence: "Each science must have its own methods." If the methods for verifying claims in each of the physical sciences like chemistry and astronomy differ substantially, it is only reasonable to expect that the methods for verifying claims in the science of religion will also be unique. Nonetheless, two of the mystical crosschecking procedures he most frequently emphasizes are at least *analogous* to those used to verify sense-perceptual claims. Verifying a mystic's claims by engaging in spiritual practices in order to have the same experience for ourselves is akin to the "other observers" test for sense-perceptual claims. Moreover, the indirect method of examining the moral character of a person who claims to have realized God is analogous to the "predictive efficacy" test for sense-perceptual claims. On this basis, Vivekananda argues that mystical crosschecking procedures have epistemic bite, even though they are not identical to sensory crosschecking procedures.

Vivekananda's defense of the epistemic value of the unique methods for verifying religious claims is very similar to that of Alston, who argues as follows:

> It can easily be seen that not all our standard belief-forming practices work like sense perception. Consider introspection. If I report feeling excited, there are no conditions under which my report is correct *if and only if* someone who satisfies those conditions also feels excited. Introspective reports can be publicly checked to a certain extent, but not in that way. Again, the fact that we can't use perceptual checks on mathematical reports has no tendency to show that rational intuition cannot yield objective truths. Different belief-forming practices work differently. (2004: 144)

Alston begins with the premise that the "other observers" test used to verify sense-perceptual claims obviously cannot be used to verify introspective or

[9] For a similar passage, see *CW* 7:64–5, where Vivekananda explains why "[e]ach science requires its own particular method and instruments."

mathematical claims. Nonetheless, this fact does not typically deter us from granting epistemic weight to introspective and mathematical claims. Similarly, he argues that the fact that mystical crosschecking procedures differ substantially from sensory crosschecking procedures does not constitute a good reason for believing that the former have less epistemic force than the latter. Echoing Vivekananda's claim that "[e]ach science must have its own methods," Alston notes that "[d]ifferent belief-forming practices work differently."

Having defended the epistemic force of the procedures for verifying the claims of mystics, Vivekananda argues that the science of religion is on an equal footing with any other science with respect to the possibility of direct verification:

> They [sages] all declare that they have found some truth higher than what the senses can bring to us, and they invite verification. They ask us to take up the method and practice honestly, and then, if we do not find this higher truth, we will have the right to say there is no truth in the claim, but before we have done that, we are not rational in denying the truth of their assertions. (*CW* 1:128–29)

It is not rational, Vivekananda argues, to dismiss the claims of mystics without first verifying these claims by employing the methods they prescribe and seeing whether we have the same mystical experiences ourselves. Yet, as we have seen in chapter 4, he detected precisely such an *irrational* tendency to dismiss mystical claims a priori among many of his contemporaries. He traced this tendency to the prevailing climate of scientism—or "scientific popery," as he liked to put it (*CW* 9:212). From Vivekananda's perspective, the natural sciences have gained so much prestige that many people tend to dismiss claims about any realities, such as God or the soul, that cannot be perceived through the senses. Here, Vivekananda went one step further than Alston by suggesting that what Alston calls "epistemic imperialism"—that is, taking the sense-perceptual belief-forming practice as the epistemic standard by which to judge all other belief-forming practices—is symptomatic of an increasingly hegemonic scientism. Accordingly, Vivekananda's critique of scientism plays an important role in his defense of the epistemic value of mystical experience.

2. *The Speckled Hen Objection to Premise 3*

Numerous contemporary epistemologists have presented various objections to versions of PEJ (premise 3 of AEV_S).[10] I will focus here on the speckled hen objection, which Nicholas Silins summarizes as follows:

[10] Two major objections to PEJ that I will not discuss here are cognitive penetration and Bayesian objections, discussed at length in Tucker (2013).

> [S]uppose you get a look at a speckled hen in good light, but without enough time to carefully count the number of speckles on it. The objection . . . can be put as follows. First, your experience does have a content about how many spots face you—say to the effect that *H* has 48 spots. Second, your experience does not justify you in believing that *H* has 48 spots. After all, forming a belief that *H* has 48 spots without carefully counting might seem no more likely to be right than a guess. So, the critic concludes, some experiences have the content that *p* without giving you justification to believe that *p*. (2015: sec. 1.3.2)[11]

If this speckled hen objection succeeds, then it would show that principles of perceptual justification like PEJ and James Pryor's perceptual dogmatism (Pryor 2000) are too permissive, since accepting such a principle would allow that certain perceptions that clearly do *not* furnish epistemic justification—like the perception of a hen with 48 spots—actually do.

Perceptual dogmatists have adopted a variety of strategies for rebutting the speckled hen objection.[12] One of the most popular strategies is to distinguish seemings from sensations or perceptual experiences.[13] For instance, Berit Brogaard (2013; 2018) claims that perceptual experiences usually give rise to phenomenal "seemings"—that is, the way something appears or looks to us—and it is these seemings, when appropriately related to perceptual experiences, that have epistemic force. Our visual experience of a hen with three speckles would ordinarily make it seem to us that the hen has three speckles. Hence, we would have *prima facie* justification for believing that the hen has three speckles on the basis of that phenomenal seeming. By contrast, in the case of a hen with 48 speckles, Brogaard (2013: 282) argues that while our visual experience represents the hen as having 48 speckles,[14] we would not be justified in believing that the hen has 48 speckles, since our visual experience does not make it *seem* to us that the hen has 48 speckles. After all, for human beings "whose psychology is in the normal range" (Brogaard 2018: 61), it is simply not possible to "translate" the momentary visual "image" of a 48-speckled hen into the "number" 48 (Brogaard 2013: 283).

Brogaard's line of response to the speckled hen objection to perceptual dogmatism has been challenged on several fronts. Some philosophers have questioned the distinction made by Brogaard and others between perceptual experience and phenomenal seeming, arguing that it is more intuitively plausible to equate the

[11] In Silins's rendering of the example, the hen actually has "17 spots," but my hen has "48 spots" to match the 48 spots in Tucker's example, which I discuss subsequently.

[12] See, for instance, Nanay (2009), Tucker (2010), Pace (2017), Brogaard (2013; 2018), and Munton (2020).

[13] See Tucker (2010), Bergmann (2013), and Brogaard (2013; 2018).

[14] One caveat here is that Brogaard (2018: 61), in a more recent article, notes that "one could question whether the envisaged experience represents the hen as 48-speckled."

two.[15] As Elijah Chudnoff and David Didemonico (2015: 535) put it, "for it to visually seem to you that there is a red light ahead is for you to have a visual experience part of whose content is that there is a red light ahead." Chudnoff and Didemonico (2015: 539–40) have also questioned the assumption—shared by Brogaard and others—that a normal person's visual experience of a 48-speckled hen represents to that person that there is a hen with 48 speckles. They suggest that our visual experience of this hen may have as part of its content all 48 speckles, yet *without* having as part of its content "that there is a hen with 48 speckles" (Chudnoff and Didemonico 2015: 540).

Very recently, Jessie Munton (2020) has defended a promising new strategy for responding to the speckled hen problem that avoids the potential drawbacks of Brogaard's line of response. Instead of distinguishing perceptual experiences from phenomenal seemings, Munton challenges the "pictorialist" assumption at the basis of the speckled hen objection—the assumption "that we visually perceive general, determinable properties only in virtue of determinate properties or more specific, local features of our visual experience" (2020: 1). According to Munton, the very premise of the speckled hen problem—namely, that our visual experience represents the hen as having 48 speckles—presupposes a conception of visual experience as akin to an "image" or "picture," just as "a clear photograph of a hen represents it as speckled in virtue of representing it as having some determinate number of speckles" (2020: 7).

Munton rejects this pictorialist conception of visual experience in favor of the view that "visual perception frequently starts from a position of uncertainty, and is routinely able to acquire information about general properties in the absence of more specific information" (2020: 1). She defends this alternative view on the basis of recent empirical work on the perception of numerosity:

> [W]e are capable of perceiving number *directly*, in the sense that numerosity is a primary visual property. We can visually experience the numerosity of a set independently of its other features. In particular, the visual system does not need to represent or count the individual members of the set to arrive at an impression of its numerosity. (Munton 2020: 10–11)

Equipped with this understanding of visual experience, Munton claims not so much to solve as to *dissolve* the speckled hen problem, since she denies its foundational premise that our visual experience represents the hen as having 48 speckles. As she puts it, "A quick glance at a speckled hen justifies a belief that it is speckled to some rough degree, but fails to justify a belief that it has any particular number of speckles, because that is the content of the experience"

[15] Huemer (2001: 59–71), Chudnoff and Didemonico (2015), and Tolhurst (1998).

(2020: 18).[16] Our indeterminate visual experience of the 48-speckled hen only represents it as having a large number of speckles. Hence, according to PEJ, we would not be justified in believing that the hen has exactly 48 speckles on the basis of our visual experience.

3. The Gullibility Objection to Premise 6

Contemporary philosophers working on the epistemology of testimony have been actively debating whether, and under what conditions, one is justified in believing that *p* on the basis of someone else's testimony that *p* (Lackey and Sosa 2006). Numerous epistemologists have defended principles of default trust in testimony akin to Vivekananda's *Principle of Testimonial Proof* (TP) and premise 6 of AEVs (PTEJ).[17] Tyler Burge (1993: 467), for instance, defends the "Acceptance Principle," according to which "a person is entitled to accept as true something that is presented as true and that is intelligible to him, unless there are stronger reasons not to do so." Other philosophers, by contrast, have argued that such principles are too permissive and that default trust in a speaker's testimony is "an epistemic charter for the gullible and undiscriminating" (Fricker 1994: 126). According to Elizabeth Fricker, we should have *positive reasons* for believing a speaker's testimony. As she puts it, "rational prudence dictates that one should bestow trust only where it is due; where one has good grounds to believe one's informant competent and sincere" (Fricker 2006: 243). Fricker then goes on to argue that it is often feasible to determine a speaker's competence and sincerity before accepting her testimony.

Like Fricker, Jennifer Lackey (2006; 2008) contends that a rational agent must have "positive reasons" for believing a speaker's testimony. She presents the following thought-experiment in order to lend intuitive plausibility to her view that positive reasons are needed for justified belief in testimony:

> Sam, an average human being, is taking a walk through the forest one sunny morning and, in the distance, he sees someone drop a book. Although the individual's physical appearance enables Sam to identify her as an alien from another planet, he does not know anything about either this kind of alien or the planet from which she comes. Now, Sam eventually loses sight of the alien, but he is able to recover the book that she dropped. Upon opening it, he immediately notices that it appears to be written in English and looks like what

[16] Munton is thinking of a hen with a large number of speckles, such as 48 or 72. If the hen only had, say, three speckles, then even a quick glance at it *would* justify our belief that it has three speckles.

[17] See, for instance, Swinburne (2004: 322–24), Burge (1993), Coady (1992), Strawson (1994), and Green (2006).

> we on Earth would call a diary. Moreover, after reading the first sentence of the book, Sam forms the corresponding belief that tigers have eaten some of the inhabitants of the author's planet during their exploration of Earth. It turns out that the book is a diary, the alien does communicate in English, and it is both true and reliably written in the diary that tigers have eaten some of the inhabitants of the planet in question. (Lackey 2008: 168–69)

This scenario, Lackey stipulates, rules out the possibility that Sam has any positive reasons for believing that the alien is sincere and trustworthy. In this scenario, Lackey claims that it is "plainly irrational" for Sam to believe that tigers have eaten some of the inhabitants of the alien's planet on the basis of her diary (2008: 169). She gives various reasons why the alien's testimony should not be trusted. For instance, "it may very well be accepted practice in alien society to be insincere and deceptive when testifying to others," or "normal alien psychology may be what we Earthlings would consider psychosis" (Lackey 2008: 169). Since Sam cannot rule out such possibilities, it is rational for Sam to withhold belief. However, it follows from an epistemic principle such as PTEJ or Burge's Acceptance Principle that Sam *is* justified in holding the belief, since such principles only require that Sam does not possess "any relevant undefeated defeaters" for accepting the alien's report (Lackey 2008: 170). She concludes, therefore, that rationally justified belief in a speaker's testimony requires positive reasons for believing that the speaker is sincere and trustworthy.

How might we defend PTEJ against the arguments of Fricker and Lackey? We should recall from the previous chapter that Vivekananda's primary justification of TP is that it is an indispensable principle of rationality through which we "get our knowledge of ordinary objects" (*CW* 1:232). Contemporary epistemologists have defended PTEJ along similar lines. First, they claim that critics of PTEJ like Fricker severely underestimate the sheer pervasiveness of our everyday reliance on testimony as a source of justified beliefs. As Swinburne (2004: 322) puts it, "Clearly most of our beliefs about the world are based on what others claim to have perceived—beliefs about geography and history and science and everything else beyond immediate experience are thus based. We do not normally check that an informant is a reliable witness before accepting his reports." Contrary to Fricker, it is simply not the case that in quotidian contexts—such as in asking for directions or the time of day or the location of the nearest supermarket—we first try to determine a speaker's sincerity and trustworthiness before believing her testimony (Burge 1993: 468–69). Hence, accepting Fricker's strictures would have the unwanted consequence of denying rational status to the vast majority of our testimonially generated beliefs.

Second, Fricker also underestimates the extent to which our very efforts to determine a speaker's trustworthiness often rely, either directly or indirectly, on testimonial evidence, thereby landing us either in a circularity or regress. As Robert Audi (1997: 417) notes, "It is doubtful that we can always avoid relying on testimony, at least indirectly, in appraising testimony. One's sense of an attester's track record, for instance, typically depends on what one believes from testimony, as where one news source serves as a check on another."[18] Likewise, P. F. Strawson points out that even when we determine a speaker's trustworthiness on the basis of perception, our perceptions themselves are often shaped by what we have previously learned on the basis of testimony:

> [M]uch, perhaps most, of what we see we could not see *as* what we do see it *as*, without the benefit of such instruction. It is precisely from such instruction that the majority of the concepts which figure in any veridical account of our perceptions derive their origin. I see that the petrol gauge on my car reads zero. *Could* I see *this* if I had not been *told* that what I am looking at is an *instrument* with a certain specific *function?* I hear the clock strike twelve. Could I hear *this* without grasp of the concept of a clock and of the number system? (1994: 26; emphasis in original)

Finally, in light of the fact that testimonially generated beliefs are woven into the very fabric of our lives, many philosophers have argued that default trust in testimony is a fundamental mark of rational behavior.[19] Like Strawson, Audi (1997: 418) contends that default trust in testimony plays an "essential role in concept acquisition and language learning." Ironically, then, even the kind of skepticism about PTEJ voiced by philosophers like Fricker and Lackey may not be possible without a prior acceptance of PTEJ. As Audi (1997: 418) puts it, the "initial success [of default trust in testimony] in producing knowledge early in our lives may indeed be a condition for our intelligibly questioning that very success when we have learned to be skeptical."

As for Lackey's thought-experiment of Sam and the alien, Timothy Perrine (2014: 3231) makes a persuasive case that even though Sam has no positive reasons for believing that the alien is insincere or untrustworthy, Sam does have good reasons to *doubt* the alien's sincerity and trustworthiness, precisely because he is faced with a "radically new source of testimony" and "he knows many of the ways in which testimony can go awry." Hence, even if we accept Burge's Acceptance Principle, Sam has a defeater that disqualifies his belief from being rationally held.[20]

[18] Coady (1992: 97) makes a similar point.

[19] See Coady (1992), Burge (1993), Strawson (1994), and Audi (1997).

[20] As Perrine (2014: 3232) notes, Lackey herself defines normative defeaters as "doubts or beliefs that S *should have* (whether or not S does have them) given the presence of certain available evidence" (Lackey 2008: 45).

I would argue that Perrine's rebuttal of Lackey's thought-experiment equally supports PTEJ, which has a similar defeater clause: "People other than *S* are rationally justified in believing that *S*'s perceptual experience as of *F* is as *S* reports it to be, unless they have *good reasons to doubt S*'s sincerity or trustworthiness." Sam, I would suggest, *does* have good reasons to doubt the alien's sincerity and trustworthiness. Since he knows nothing about such aliens, it is very well possible that the alien in question is insincere, deceptive, psychotic, or otherwise untrustworthy. Hence, according to PTEJ, Sam is not rationally justified in believing the alien's testimony.

4. *Objections to Premises 4 and 7: The Conflicting Claims Objection and Kumārila's Criticisms of Yogic Perception and Testimony*

Numerous philosophers of religion have challenged premises 4 and 7 of AEV_S on the grounds that mystics in various religious traditions have made conflicting claims about the nature of ultimate reality on the basis of their mystical experiences.[21] Advaitic mystics claim to have realized the impersonal nondual Brahman, while some Buddhist mystics claim to have attained the state of *nibbāna* or *śūnyatā*. Theistic mystics in different traditions have also reported incredibly diverse experiences of God—with some experiencing God as Christ, others as Allah, and still others as Rāma, Kṛṣṇa, Kālī, Śiva, or Viṣṇu. Since such claims about ultimate reality are mutually exclusive, the mystical experiences on which these claims are based are unreliable at best and delusive at worst.

Before explaining how Vivekananda would respond to the conflicting claims objection, I would first point out that this objection, even if successful, would not completely undermine premises 4 and 7. Even if mystical claims about ultimate reality do conflict, it would be unreasonable to conclude that all experiences as of ultimate reality are delusive. Take the following example. At exactly the same time, three people claim to see a flying object at the same location in the sky, but one of them claims that it is a bird, another claims that it is a plane, and the third person claims that it is a kite.[22] The fact that the reports of these three people conflict with each other does not support the conclusion that all of their experiences are delusive or that there *is* no flying object at all.[23] Rather, it would be far more plausible to conclude that there very likely *is* a flying object that all three people report having seen but that their respective claims about the object's *precise*

[21] See Flew ([1966] 2005: 126–27), Martin (1986: 87–88), and Fales (1996b: 143).

[22] My example is very similar to the examples found in Kwan (2006: 655) and Swinburne (2004: 317).

[23] This point is well made by Gellman (1997: 111–112) and Kwan (2006: 654–655).

nature are unreliable. Similarly, if the conflicting claims objection is successful, it would not establish that these mystics likely failed to experience any ultimate reality at all. Rather, the objection would establish that even if many mystics have had a veridical experience of an ultimate reality, at least some of these mystics are mistaken in their precise characterizations of ultimate reality.

In *Infinite Paths to Infinite Reality*, I have discussed in detail Ramakrishna's response to the conflicting claims objection (Maharaj 2018: 231–37). For Ramakrishna, mystics' apparently conflicting claims about ultimate reality are actually complementary, since different mystics experience different aspects and forms of one and the same impersonal-personal Infinite Divine Reality. Vivekananda, I suggest, would adopt his guru's line of response to the conflicting claims objection. Crucially, as we saw in chapter 2, Vivekananda fully accepted Ramakrishna's expansive ontology of God as the impersonal-personal Infinite Reality. In an 1896 lecture on Ramakrishna, Vivekananda explains that Ramakrishna had realized different forms and aspects of one and the same God by practicing a variety of *sādhanas* in both Hindu and non-Hindu religious traditions (*CW* 4:163–74). He then proceeds to draw the following lesson from Ramakrishna's life: "To learn this central secret that the truth may be one and yet many at the same time, that we may have different visions of the same truth from different standpoints, is exactly what must be done" (*CW* 4:181). Since God is the impersonal-personal Infinite Reality, different mystics "may have different visions" of the same God "from different standpoints."

In his second lecture on "Practical Vedānta" (1896), Vivekananda elaborates this view:

> The Impersonal God is a living God, a principle. The difference between personal and impersonal is this, that the personal is only a man, and the impersonal idea is that He is the angel, the man, the animal, and yet something more which we cannot see, because impersonality includes all personalities, is the sum total of everything in the universe, and infinitely more besides. "As the one fire coming into the world is manifesting itself in so many forms, and yet is infinitely more besides," so is the Impersonal. (*CW* 2:319–20)

In his rendering of Kaṭha Upaniṣad 2.2.9 at the end of this passage, Vivekananda uses the language of divine manifestation: the "Impersonal God" is "manifesting itself" in various personal forms and aspects. Hence, the reports of mystics often appear to conflict, since they experience different aspects and forms of one and the same impersonal-personal Infinite Reality.

One might argue that Vivekananda's line of response to the conflicting claims objection stands in tension with many of the premises of AEVs, which refer to "experiences as of an ultimate reality," not to "experiences as of a *manifestation* of ultimate reality." However, since both Ramakrishna and Vivekananda hold that there is an ontological continuity between ultimate reality and its various manifestations, they would maintain that an experience of a manifestation of ultimate reality *just is* an experience of ultimate reality itself. As I discussed in chapter 2, Vivekananda follows Ramakrishna in employing the water-wave analogy to convey the ontological parity of ultimate reality and its manifestations:

> Divine Mother can have form (*rūpa*) and name (*nāma*) or name without form; and as we worship Her in these various aspects we can rise to pure Being, having neither form nor name. . . . The sea calm is the Absolute; the same sea in waves is Divine Mother. (*CW* 7:26–27)

When we see a wave in an ocean, it would not make sense for us to say that we see a wave and *not* the ocean. Rather, we perceive the ocean itself in a particular form. Likewise, when mystics experience different aspects and manifestations of the Infinite Divine Reality, they all experience the Divine Reality itself.

As we saw in chapter 5, Vivekananda implicitly drew upon the Mīmāṃsaka Kumārila Bhaṭṭa's doctrine of *svataḥ-prāmāṇyatā* in order to defend some of the core premises of his argument for the epistemic value of supersensuous perception (AEV)—namely, the *Principle of Perceptual Proof* (PP) and the *Principle of Testimonial Proof* (TP). Interestingly, however, even if Kumārila would have accepted some version of PP and TP—at least on one understanding of Pārthasārathimiśra's interpretation of Kumārila (Taber 1992; Arnold 2001)—he would have rejected Vivekananda's AEV as well as AEV_S. In particular, while Kumārila might have accepted premises 3 (PEJ) and 6 (PTEJ) of AEV_S, he provided numerous reasons for denying premises 2, 4, and 7 of AEV_S. As a Mīmāṃsaka, Kumārila held that the Vedas, which are eternal and authorless, are the only source of knowledge about *dharma* and supersensuous matters in general. From this Mīmāṃsā standpoint, he rejected the doctrine of yogic perception (*yogajapratyakṣa*) defended by Buddhist, Jaina, and Nyāya thinkers, since yogic perception would constitute a rival means of knowing *dharma* (McCrea 2009: 56).

In opposition to premises 2 and 4 of AEV_S, Kumārila presents numerous arguments for denying the possibility of yogic perception, two of which I will focus on here. First, he claims that yogic perception does not meet the two necessary criteria for counting as perception:

> For there is no perception of yogins over and above common perception. Since it, too, is perception, it must be the apprehension of something that is present, and it must arise from an existing connection, like our perception.

(*Ślokavārttika*, "Pratyakṣapariccheda," 28cd–29; trans. in Taber 2005: 55, slightly modified here)[24]

According to Kumārila, ordinary sense perception has two essential features: it apprehends something present like a pot or a person, and it arises from the existing connection between a sense organ and a sense object. Since *dharma* is neither a sense object nor something that exists at present—since it will only come to be in the future (*bhāvya*)—yogic perception cannot possibly apprehend *dharma*.

Second, Kumārila rejects yogic perception on the basis of what Larry McCrea (2009: 59) aptly calls "an inference from the ordinary." As Kumārila puts it, "People can apprehend objects of a certain sort by certain means of knowledge now. It was the same even in other times" (*Ślokavārttika*, "Codanāsūtra," 113–115; trans. in McCrea 2009: 59).[25] According to Kumārila, since no one at present is endowed with yogic perception, it is not reasonable to suppose that people in the past—such as the alleged enlightened seers who authored scriptures—were capable of yogic perception either.

How would Vivekananda have responded to Kumārila's arguments against the possibility of yogic perception? With respect to Kumārila's first argument, Vivekananda could argue that Kumārila is guilty of epistemic imperialism, since he assumes that yogic perception must be "like our perception"—that is, ordinary sense perception (*asmatpratyakṣavat*). While it is certainly true that sense perception does apprehend existing objects like pots and always arises from a connection between a sense organ and a sense object, Kumārila gives no good reason for believing that *all* perception must exhibit these same features. In fact, as we saw in section 3 of the previous chapter, Vivekananda argues—in line with William Alston—that the two necessary features of perception are immediacy and noetic quality. Supersensuous perception is genuinely perceptual in nature, since it shares both of these features with ordinary sense perception.

With respect to Kumārila's second argument against the possibility of yogic perception, Vivekananda would challenge Kumārila's sweeping empirical generalization that *no one* at the present time has yogic perception (Kumārila's present time being roughly 700 CE). While it is certainly true that *most people*—whether living in Kumārila's or Vivekananda's time—do not have yogic perception, how could Kumārila possibly prove that not a single person has had yogic perception? In this context, the Naiyāyika Jayanta Bhaṭṭa argued that Kumārila illegitimately generalized from his *own* inability to have yogic perception: "The

[24] *na lokavyatiriktaṃ hi pratyakṣaṃ yoginām api || pratyakṣatvena tasyāpi vidyamānopalambhanam | satsamprayogatvaṃ vāpy asmatpratyakṣavad bhavet ||*

[25] *yajjātīyaiḥ pramāṇais tu yajjātīyārthadarśanam | bhaved idānīṃ lokasya tathā kālāntare 'py abhūt ||*

Naiyāyika reviews Kumārila's arguments and points out that the latter cannot say from his experience that a sage, though endowed with super-eyes, cannot perceive Dharma because Dharma and the excellent power of the eyes of a sage are imperceptible to him" (Bhaṭṭa 1978: 217). Vivekananda, on the basis of his own spiritual experiences and the reported experiences of Ramakrishna and many others, would follow Jayanta Bhaṭṭa in rejecting the premise of Kumārila's inductive inference: the fact that most people at present do not have yogic perception cannot justify us in concluding that *no one* has yogic perception. Indeed, since Vivekananda claimed to have had spiritual experiences himself, he could have turned Kumārila's inductive inference *against* him: since at least *one* person at present has yogic perception, some people in the past must also have had yogic perception.

Kumārila presents another objection to premise 7 of AEVs: even if yogic perception *is* possible, it would be epistemically useless, since there are always good reasons for doubting the authority of human testimony about supersensuous matters (McCrea 2009). Kumārila has in mind here Buddhists and Jainas in particular, who claimed that their scriptures were authoritative because they contained the teachings of enlightened beings—namely, the Buddha and the Jinas, respectively—who were endowed with supernormal perception. Let us examine three of Kumārila's main arguments for doubting the authority of human testimony about supersensuous matters.

First, he claims that humans often lie in general and, hence, their testimony should not be trusted:

> At all times, people are, for the most part, liars. Just as there can be no confidence in them now, in the same way there is no confidence in statements of things past. (*Ślokavārttika*, "Codanāsūtra," 144; trans. in McCrea 2009: 59)[26]

According to Kumārila, since most people are—and have always been—liars, we are not justified in believing their testimony. Since the Buddhist and Jaina scriptures are nothing but the testimony of supposedly enlightened beings, we are not justified in accepting their scriptures as trustworthy. For Kumārila, the Vedas alone are trustworthy and authoritative, precisely because they have no author.

Second, Kumārila argues that a mystic's testimony is epistemically useless to a non-mystic, since the non-mystic—who, by definition, does not have the mystic's yogic perception—is in no position to determine whether the mystic is really capable of yogic perception (McCrea 2009: 65–66). He makes this argument in the

[26] *sarvadā cāpi puruṣāḥ prāyeṇānṛtavādinaḥ | yathādyatve na visrambhas tathātītārthakīrtane ||*

specific context of Yogis who claim to be omniscient, but the argument is meant to apply more generally to testimony based on any kind of yogic perception:

> And you would need to postulate many omniscient persons—anyone who is not himself omniscient cannot know an omniscient person. And, if a person does not know him to be omniscient, then his statements would have no authority for that person, since he would not know their source, just as with the statements of any other person. (*Ślokavārttika*, "Codanāsūtra," 135–136; trans. in McCrea 2009: 65)[27]

As McCrea (2009: 65) nicely puts it, Kumārila's argument boils down to the logic of "it takes one to know one." In the case of testimony based on sense perception, we can always, in principle, crosscheck the testimony by employing our own faculty of sense perception. By contrast, in the case of mystical testimony, our only means of crosschecking it would be to have the same mystical experience as the testifier—which Kumārila rules out as a possibility. But for the sake of argument, even if person *T were* to have the same mystical experience as the one reported by the mystical testifier, then the mystical testimony would be epistemically redundant for *T*, since *T* would already have acquired that mystical knowledge through yogic perception herself.

Third, Kumārila makes the same conflicting claims objection—discussed earlier in this section—that is now being debated by philosophers of religion:

> Furthermore, when [human statements] concern objects beyond the range of the senses, they are false, because they are human statements. [In this inference] each of the extra-Vedic schools will serve as an example for the others. (*Ślokavārttika*, "Codanāsūtra," 126; trans. in McCrea 2009: 62–63)[28]

Since mystics in "extra-Vedic schools" like Buddhism and Jainism have made numerous conflicting claims about supersensuous matters, we have good reason to infer that all of these claims are false.[29]

How would Vivekananda have responded to Kumārila's three arguments against the epistemic value of mystical testimony? Earlier in this section, I have already discussed how Vivekananda would have responded to Kumārila's third argument, the conflicting claims objection. With respect to Kumārila's first

[27] *kalpanīyāś ca sarvajñā bhaveyur bahavas tava | ya eva syād asarvajñaḥ sa sarvajñaṃ na budhyate || sarvajño 'navabuddhaś ca yenaiva syān na taṃ prati | tadvākyānāṃ pramāṇatvaṃ mūlājñāne 'nyavākyavat ||*

[28] *api cālaukikārthatve sati puṃvākyahetukam | mithyātvaṃ vedabāhyānāṃ syād anyonyaṃ sapakṣatā ||*

[29] For a good discussion of Kumārila's conflicting claims objection, see McCrea (2009: 62–4).

argument that human testimony should not be trusted because humans are usually liars, Vivekananda could argue, first of all, that Kumārila's premise that humans usually lie is empirically false. It is significant that Kumārila's premise applies to human testimony in general and not just to mystical testimony. Is it really plausible to believe that people usually lie when we ask them what time it is, or how to get to a certain place, or whether it's raining outside? Would it not be more plausible to believe that human testimony about many matters is usually trustworthy?

Vivekananda could also contend that Kumārila's argument against the trustworthiness of human testimony undercuts PTEJ (premise 6 of AEV_s), which Kumārila should arguably accept, since he accepts the intrinsic validity (*svataḥ-prāmāṇyatā*) of cognitions based on testimony (*śabda*) in general, whether human or Vedic. If Kumārila is right that human testimony in general should not be trusted because humans usually lie, then we would always need to determine a speaker's trustworthiness before accepting her testimony even about the most mundane matters—a position that comes close to the position advocated by Fricker and Lackey, discussed in the previous section. Vivekananda, however, would side with Burge (1993), Perrine (2014), and other contemporary epistemologists in arguing that such a position is too stringent, as it would render unjustified a huge swath of our beliefs about the world that derive from human testimony, the trustworthiness of which we take for granted. If we really had to verify a speaker's trustworthiness before accepting her testimony about, say, what time it is or what the weather is like or how to get from point A to point B, then it is hard to see how we could go about our daily business. Ironically, as we saw in the previous chapter, this is precisely the kind of argument Kumārila himself made in defense of the intrinsic validity of all cognitions: "He who out of delusion is concerned about a contradiction [of his cognition], even though one has not arisen, will be filled with doubt and meet with failure in all his actions."[30]

Finally, as I already noted in chapter 5, Vivekananda explicitly rejected Kumārila's Mīmāṃsā doctrine that the Vedas are authoritative because they have no author. According to Vivekananda, it is much more plausible to believe that the Vedic scriptures are authoritative because they were authored by sages who directly perceived the eternal truths taught in those scriptures. As Vivekananda puts it, "the only proof of the scriptures is that they were the testimony of competent persons" (*CW* 1:232). Arguably, Vivekananda's position has greater *prima facie* plausibility than Kumārila's doctrine of the authorlessness of the Vedas, and if we accept Vivekananda's position, then Kumārila's denial of

[30] *utprekṣeta hi yo mohād ajātam api bādhakam* | *sa sarvavyavahāreṣu saṃśayātmā kṣayaṃ vrajet* || (Kumārila's *Bṛhaṭṭīkā* as preserved at Śāntarakṣita's *Tattvasaṃgraha* 2871; quoted and translated in Taber 1992: 216)

mystical knowledge and testimony would undermine the authority of the Vedas themselves.

With regard to Kumārila's second "it takes one to know one" argument, Vivekananda could respond that while it is true that most of us are not in an immediate position to share the mystic's experience, we *can* nonetheless see whether the mystic is "perfectly unselfish and holy" (*CW* 1:205), assuming the mystic is still living. And if the mystic is no longer living, we could rely on reliable accounts of the mystic's life to determine her character. If the mystic does prove to be unselfish and pure, then we would have no good reason to doubt the mystic's testimony, since moral perfection and purity are preconditions for genuine spiritual experience.

Kumārila might retort that a person's inner qualities like unselfishness and purity cannot always—if ever—be reliably judged on the basis of that person's outer behavior. After all, it is always possible that one is only *pretending* to be unselfish and saintly in order to gain the admiration of others or to achieve some other selfish end. Obversely, it is also possible for a highly moral and saintly person to give the impression that he is selfish and worldly in order to avoid praise and recognition.

We could defend Vivekananda's position by arguing that it is quite common for people to make judgments about a person's moral character on the basis of that person's observable behavior, and such judgments often (but not always) turn out to be correct. Of course, such a judgment may turn out to be mistaken, but this would be true not only for mystical testimony but also for testimony based on sense perception. For instance, if person *D* tells me that there is a blue jay on the branch of a tree outside my house, I might decide to trust *D*'s testimony on the basis of my judgment that *D* seems generally honest and does not seem to have any reason to lie to me. It is always possible, however, that *D is* lying to me about the blue jay for some reason unknown to me. Hence, as we discussed in section 1, Vivekananda could charge Kumārila with a double standard, since he grants epistemic value to testimony based on sense perception, but not to mystical testimony, even though we can never rule out the possibility that *either* kind of testimony is untrustworthy.

At this point, Kumārila could point out an important disanalogy between mystical testimony and sense-perceptual testimony. In the case of the blue jay example, I can always verify *D*'s trustworthiness by going outside and seeing whether there really is a blue jay on the tree branch. I think Vivekananda has available two lines of response to Kumārila. He could argue that even this sense-perceptual verificatory procedure is not perfect, since it is possible that *D* did lie to me about the blue jay but that it just so happened, by sheer coincidence, that there was a blue jay on the branch of a tree outside my house at the very moment I stepped outside.

However, as I already noted in section 1, Vivekananda also explicitly argues that there *is* an analogous verificatory procedure in the case of mystical testimony: we can engage in the ethical and spiritual practices recommended by the mystic in order to see whether we have the same mystical experience ourselves. If Kumārila were to respond that this is a much less direct and immediate verificatory procedure than, say, seeing whether there is a blue jay on a tree, then Vivekananda could charge Kumārila with epistemic imperialism, since there is no good reason to believe that mystical experiences could, or should, be verified *in the same way* as sense-perceptual experiences.

5. *Anantanand Rambachan's Criticisms of Vivekananda's Views on Spiritual Experience*

In his important and influential book *The Limits of Scripture: Vivekananda's Reinterpretation of the Vedas*, Anantanand Rambachan argues that there are a number of serious weaknesses in Vivekananda's defense of religion as a science grounded in spiritual experience (1994a: 106–12). To Rambachan's credit, he is one of the few scholars who has taken Vivekananda seriously as an original thinker and has carefully analyzed his philosophical arguments. However, I will argue in this section that Rambachan's criticisms of Vivekananda's views on spiritual experience stem largely from an oversimplification or misinterpretation of Vivekananda's positions.

As we saw in chapter 4, one of Vivekananda's main arguments in support of the scientific credentials of religion is that religious claims can be directly verified through spiritual experience. Of course, this argument presupposes that spiritual experience affords knowledge of supersensuous realities. To justify this controversial presupposition, Vivekananda—as we saw in section 2 of chapter 5—presented an argument in support of the epistemic value of supersensuous perception (AEV) based on epistemic principles of perception (PP) and testimony (TP). In chapter 5 and in the previous sections of this chapter, I have shown that more sophisticated versions of Vivekananda's AEV and of its key premises continue to be defended by contemporary epistemologists and philosophers of religion. Rambachan, I will contend, overlooks the crucial role of AEV in Vivekananda's overall defense of religion as an experientially grounded science.

According to Rambachan, Vivekananda's attempt to establish parallels between religion and natural science is philosophically weak:

> I have referred from time to time in this discussion to Vivekananda's attempts to equate the gain and verification of knowledge through *rājayoga* with the

> methods employed in science. The grounds, however, on which he draws his parallels leave many questions unanswered. Vivekananda's analogy with science is basically an analogy between religious experience and sense perception. The assumption is that both are verifiable in the same way. Almost all his examples, as well as his terminology, are drawn from the world of sense perception. There appear, however, to be very important differences between sensory experience and religious experience. (1994a: 107)

According to Rambachan, Vivekananda argues for the scientific status of religion by establishing parallels between religious experience and sense perception. This argument, Rambachan claims, is based on the "assumption" that both types of experience "are verifiable in the same way." Hence, Rambachan proceeds to point out some of the "very important differences" between sensory experience and religious experience, since he thinks that establishing these differences is sufficient to undermine Vivekananda's case for the scientific credentials of religion.

Before I address Rambachan's specific claims about what he sees as the major differences between sensory experience and spiritual experience, I wish to point out two mistakes in his broader interpretation of Vivekananda's views on spiritual experience. First of all, Rambachan claims that Vivekananda assumes that sensory experience and spiritual experience are both "verifiable in the same way." However, Rambachan presents no textual evidence in support of this claim. In fact, as we saw in chapter 4, Vivekananda explicitly *denies* this assumption, insisting rather that "[e]ach science must have its own methods" of verification (*CW* 1:128). For Vivekananda, the physical sciences and the science of religion share a common basis in experiential verification, but he argues that just as the methods for verifying claims in astronomy and chemistry differ, methods for verifying religious claims also differ quite naturally from verificatory methods in the other sciences.

Secondly, Rambachan assumes that Vivekananda's entire case for the scientific status of religion rests on establishing "parallels" between sensory experience and religious experience. In fact, however, Vivekananda presents such parallels only in support of his broader argument for the epistemic value of spiritual experience (AEV), which Rambachan overlooks entirely. Vivekananda tries to demonstrate that mystical experiences are *sufficiently similar* to sensory experiences in order to establish that both kinds of experience are perceptual in nature. If he is able to establish the plausibility of this premise, then the epistemic principles PP and TP would apply equally to sensory perception and supersensuous perception, and he would then be in a position to defend the epistemic value of supersensuous perception on the basis of these principles. Vivekananda's AEV, then, is the linchpin for establishing religion as a science based on direct experiential verification. Since Rambachan overlooks Vivekananda's AEV, many of his criticisms of Vivekananda actually target a straw man rather than Vivekananda's actual position.

Keeping in mind these general problems with Rambachan's approach, we can now consider some of his specific criticisms of Vivekananda. Rambachan enumerates a number of "very important differences between sensory experience and religious experience," which he believes Vivekananda overlooks. He claims, first, that Vivekananda takes mystical experience to be "self-validating," while "sense perception . . . is certainly not always self-validating," since "[t]he possibilities of sense illusion and deception are very well accepted" (1994a: 107). It should be noted, first, that Vivekananda was well aware that sensory perceptions are not self-validating. He makes this clear, for instance, when he claims that "whatever we see and feel, is proof, if there has been nothing to delude the senses" (*CW* 1:204). Here and elsewhere, Vivekananda acknowledges the possibility that sensory perceptions can be delusive. Moreover, I already noted in chapter 5 that Vivekananda's position—contrary to Rambachan's claim—is that *some*, but not all, spiritual experiences are self-validating. It is also not clear why the fact that some spiritual experiences differ from sensory experiences in being self-validating would be damaging in any way to Vivekananda's argument. As we saw in chapter 5, Vivekananda argues that sensory experiences and supersensuous experiences share two fundamental characteristics: immediacy and noetic quality. These common characteristics, Vivekananda argues, are sufficient to establish that both kinds of experience are perceptual in nature and, therefore, that PP and TP apply equally to both of them.

Rambachan argues that another fundamental difference between sensory experiences and mystical experiences is that the former, but not the latter, can be adequately verified:

> Even though these may not be readily apparent, there are definite criteria that are employed in validating sense experience. It might be argued that definite criteria are also available for verifying religious experience. But the problem here is reaching agreement on those criteria. In the case of sense perception, the criteria are widely accepted, but the criteria for evaluating religious experience in any particular community of shared beliefs may not be considered reliable in a community with different traditions. . . . In the case of his [Vivekananda's] common example of the wall, sight could be reinforced by touch and sound. The absence of anything to compare with this in religious experience must be taken into account whenever a parallel is drawn with sense perception. Agreement within a religious community on the criteria to be used in evaluating spiritual experience may be valid and genuine. There is always, however, the possibility that such agreement may be the result of a lack of awareness of alternatives, the

> sharing of erroneous beliefs, or the use of the same techniques to produce similar results. (1994a: 107)

Rambachan's argument essentially amounts to the crosscheckability objection discussed in section 1 of this chapter. According to Rambachan, there are reliable and "widely accepted" methods for verifying whether a sensory experience is veridical. If I see a wall, I can crosscheck my visual experience with my other senses—for instance, by walking to the wall and touching it. "The absence of anything to compare with this in religious experience," Rambachan argues, impugns the epistemic credentials of religious experience.[31]

However, as we have seen, this crosscheckability objection has been a major topic of debate among contemporary philosophers of religion for the past several decades. William Alston's response to the crosscheckability objection is especially relevant in this context. From Alston's perspective, Rambachan betrays an epistemic imperialism in assuming that mystical crosschecking procedures can only have epistemic force if they are the same as, or very similar to, sensory crosschecking procedures. Indeed, as I argued in section 1, Vivekananda himself anticipated such an Alstonian rebuttal to Rambachan's objection. Vivekananda argues that "[e]ach science must have its own methods" of verification (*CW* 1:128), so it is unreasonable to expect that mystical experiences must be verified in the same way as sensory experiences are.

Toward the end of the passage quoted earlier, Rambachan claims that crosschecking procedures for religious experiences are epistemically unreliable for a variety of reasons. A bit later in his book, Rambachan singles out for criticism one of Vivekananda's preferred methods for verifying spiritual experiences—namely, seeing whether the person has been morally and spiritually transformed as a result of her spiritual experience. With respect to this method, Rambachan writes: "Out of *samādhi*, says Vivekananda, one emerges with wisdom. This, however, does not help us very much unless there is some prior agreement on what constitutes wisdom. It is these very truth claims that need to be evaluated" (1994a: 108). However, Rambachan does not take into account the context of Vivekananda's statement, which I already quoted in the previous section. According to Vivekananda, one who has attained *samādhi* "comes out enlightened, a sage, a prophet, a saint, his whole character changed, his life changed, illumined" (*CW* 1:181). Clearly, what Vivekananda has in mind is that the person who has truly attained *samādhi* should have an exemplary moral character and exhibit saintliness and spiritual wisdom. Rambachan also ignores Vivekananda's argument in support of this verificatory method, which was discussed in the previous section. Since a very high level of ethical behavior

[31] C. Brown (2012: 152–53) makes a similar criticism of Vivekananda.

and purity are prerequisites for having any spiritual experience, it is only to be expected that someone who has had a genuine spiritual experience would exhibit moral goodness and saintliness. I also argued in section 1 that contemporary philosophers like Gary Gutting support Vivekananda's line of reasoning by providing plausible reasons for expecting that experiential contact with a loving and morally perfect God would result in moral and spiritual transformation.

Even more fundamentally, Rambachan seems to assume that the fact that the verificatory procedures for sensory experiences are "widely accepted" is sufficient to establish their epistemic reliability. However, as Alston has shown, even crosschecking procedures for sensory experiences are epistemically circular, since they invariably rely on sense perception. Let us take Rambachan's own example: we can verify our visual experience of a wall by determining whether we can perceive it through one of our other senses such as "touch and sound" (1994a: 107). This crosschecking procedure is blatantly epistemically circular, since it is itself based on other sensory experiences, which would need to be crosschecked in turn, ad infinitum. From Alston's perspective, since crosschecking procedures for *both* sensory experiences and mystical experiences are equally epistemically circular, people like Rambachan are guilty of a double standard when they take the former, but not the latter, to be epistemically reliable. Hence, Rambachan's crosscheckability objection is considerably weakened by the fact that he overlooks key aspects of Vivekananda's argumentation and fails to take into account Alston's cogent response to the crosscheckability objection.

Rambachan further criticizes Vivekananda's defense of religion as a science in the following passage:

> In seeking to present *rājayoga* as conforming to the methods of science, Vivekananda is constrained to modify considerably, if not misrepresent, the scientific process of gaining knowledge. He uses the word *experience* in the most general sense possible, when he speaks of all knowledge as being derived from experience. He does not specify the uniqueness and complexity of the "experience" through which knowledge is gained and corroborated in the physical sciences. (1994a: 108)

According to Rambachan, Vivekananda distorts the "scientific process of gaining knowledge" in order to portray religion as a science. However, I believe there are a number of reasons why Rambachan's criticism is unconvincing. First of all, Rambachan's final sentence is mistaken, because Vivekananda *does* "specify the uniqueness and complexity of the 'experience' through which knowledge is gained and corroborated in the physical sciences." Vivekananda's claim that "[e]ach science must have its own methods," which I already mentioned, indicates that he was well aware of the "uniqueness and complexity" of the methods employed in the various physical sciences such as astronomy and chemistry. Moreover, in a passage from an essay already quoted in chapter 4, Vivekananda claims that the knowledge acquired through the physical sciences derives from "the five ordinary senses of man," while knowledge about transcendental realities derives from "the subtle, supersensuous power born of Yoga" (*BCW* 6:3 / *CW* 6:181). On this basis, Vivekananda defends a wide empiricism, the view that all knowledge is grounded in either sensory experience or supersensuous experience. Rambachan is correct that Vivekananda conceives "experience" in a broad sense, but he does not explain why such a broad construal is problematic. Perhaps Rambachan's tacit assumption is that it is more plausible to restrict experience to sensory experience. However, as we have seen in chapter 4, Vivekananda anticipated precisely this move, arguing that the tendency among his late nineteenth-century contemporaries to restrict experience to sensory experience betrays a dogmatic scientism, an unjustified—and unscientific—refusal to accept the possibility of experience beyond the senses. Accordingly, Vivekananda consciously rejected the narrow empiricism of Comte and his followers in favor of a wide empiricism, which he took to be more philosophically justifiable. Arguably, then, Rambachan's unjustified dismissal of Vivekananda's wide construal of experience is itself a symptom of the very scientism that Vivekananda had singled out for criticism.

Moreover, Rambachan objects that Vivekananda distorts the "scientific process of gaining knowledge," but Rambachan himself fails to specify what he takes this scientific method of gaining knowledge to be. How can we know whether Vivekananda distorts the scientific process unless Rambachan tells us what it is? The burden is on Rambachan to define the scientific method and show how Vivekananda deviates from it.

Rambachan also does not take into account the debates in philosophy of science that have been raging since the early twentieth century regarding the so-called "scientific method" and whether it is even possible to demarcate science from putatively non-scientific endeavors. In fact, as I already noted in chapter 4, there *is* no uncontroversial definition of the "scientific method." The failure of all past attempts to provide a satisfactory account of the scientific method has led many contemporary philosophers of science to conclude, with Thomas Nickles, that "[t]here is no such thing as 'the' scientific method, let alone agreement on what exactly it is" (Nickles 2013: 115).[32] Moreover, Rambachan seems to think that there is an obvious and simple way to differentiate the method of the physical sciences from what he takes to be the *non*-scientific method of religion. However, he does not explain how to draw this line of demarcation. Indeed,

[32] For other references, see note 18 of chapter 4.

the prominent philosopher of science Larry Laudan, in his now classic essay "The Demise of the Demarcation Problem" (1983), surveys the history of failed attempts to distinguish the "scientific" from the "non-scientific" and concludes that the "evident epistemic heterogeneity of the activities and beliefs customarily regarded as scientific should alert us to the probable futility of seeking an epistemic version of a demarcation criterion" (1983: 124). More recently, both Maarten Boudry (2013: 84–86) and Evan Fales (2013: 247–55) have argued that there is no philosophically plausible and non-question-begging way to define science so as to exclude religious claims. These contemporary positions in the philosophy of science call into question Rambachan's assumption that science can be clearly demarcated from religion and, hence, leave the door open for Vivekananda's efforts to defend religion as a science grounded in direct experiential verification.

Rambachan also questions the cogency of Vivekananda's view that the nondual Ātman is directly perceived in *nirvikalpa samādhi*:

> We have seen that he [Vivekananda] speaks repeatedly about the necessity for a direct perception of the *ātman* if its very existence is to be certified beyond any doubt. Perception, however, whether ordinary or supersensuous, involves knowledge gained through objectification. It also implies a duality between the knower and the known. In Advaita, the definition of the *ātman* as the ultimate and only knower, incapable of being objectified by any faculty, is a fundamental tenet. . . . Thus, a suggestion about acquiring knowledge of the *ātman* through any kind of perception appears to deny its very nature. (1994a: 109)

According to Rambachan, since all perception involves subject-object duality, Vivekananda's claim that the nondual Ātman can be perceived in *nirvikalpa samādhi* is self-contradictory. Rambachan adduces as evidence the following passage in which Vivekananda himself claims that all knowledge is "objectification":

> You cannot by any possibility say you know Him; it would be degrading Him. You cannot get out of yourself, so you cannot know Him. Knowledge is objectification. . . . He is the Eternal Subject of everything. I am the subject of this chair; I see the chair; so God is the Eternal Subject of my soul. How can you objectify Him, the Essence of your souls, the Reality of everything? Thus, I would repeat to you once more, God is neither knowable nor unknowable, but something infinitely higher than either. He is one with us, and that which is one with us is neither knowable nor unknowable, as our own self. You cannot know your own self; you cannot move it out and make it an object to look at, because you are that and cannot separate yourself from it. Neither is it unknowable, for what is better known than yourself? It is really the centre of our knowledge. In exactly

> the same sense, God is neither unknowable nor known, but infinitely higher than both; for He is our real Self. (*CW* 2:133; quoted in Rambachan 1994a: 109)

On Rambachan's interpretation of this passage, Vivekananda claims that the Ātman cannot be known, since all knowledge involves objectification, and the eternal nondual Self can never be an object. Hence, Vivekananda contradicts himself by claiming, in other places, that the nondual Ātman is directly perceived in the state of *nirvikalpa samādhi*.

However, Rambachan overlooks some crucial nuances in this passage. Vivekananda expresses his overall position in the following key sentence: "God is neither knowable nor unknowable, but something infinitely higher than either." Since God is "our real Self," He cannot be known, because knowledge is "objectification," and our Self can never be an object. At the same time, the self is "better known" to us than anything else in the world. Echoing Śaṅkara and Descartes, Vivekananda claims that nothing is more certain to me than the fact that I exist. I *know* that I exist, yet this knowledge is clearly not knowledge of an object, since the self "is really the centre of our knowledge." I think Vivekananda is best understood here as distinguishing two kinds of knowledge: knowledge by objectification and knowledge by identity. Our ordinary knowledge of our own existence is a paradigmatic instance of knowledge by identity. He then proceeds to argue that we can know the nondual Ātman in the same way, by realizing our identity with the Ātman in *nirvikalpa samādhi*. Robert Forman (1993) has echoed Vivekananda in arguing that the nondual experience of Pure Consciousness is a form of "knowledge by identity."

Equipped with this key distinction between knowledge by objectification and knowledge by identity, we can make sense of Vivekananda's repeated claims that we can directly perceive and know the nondual Brahman in *nirvikalpa samādhi*. Indeed, in an 1898 conversation with his disciple Saratcandra Cakravarti, Vivekananda explicitly addressed the paradox highlighted by Rambachan:

> the Ātman alone is self-effulgent and known only through itself (*svayaṃjyotiḥ—svasaṃvedya*). How can that which is known only through itself (*svasaṃvedya*) be known with the help of something else? It is therefore that the *śruti* [Bṛhadāraṇyaka Upaniṣad 4.5.15] says, "*vijñātāram are kena vijānīyāt*" ["through what are you to know the Eternal Knower?"]. Whatever you know, you know by means of the instrument of the mind. But the mind is insentient; the mind is only able to function because of the pure Ātman behind it. Therefore, how can you know the Ātman with the mind? Know for certain that neither the mind (*mon*) nor the intelligence (*buddhi*) can reach the pure Ātman. The duality of knowledge and knower persists only so long as the mind and intelligence function (*jānājāniṭā ei paryanta*). When the mind becomes

> devoid all modifications (*vṛttihīn*), the mind itself gets suspended and it is then that the Ātman is directly perceived (*takhani ātmā pratyakṣa han*). It is this state which the *ācārya* Śaṅkara describes as "*aparokṣānubhūti*" [direct realization]. (*BCW* 9:33 / *CW* 7:142; translation modified)[33]

Citing a verse from the Bṛhadāraṇyaka Upaniṣad, Vivekananda observes that the Ātman cannot be known by means of anything else, since it is the "Eternal Knower" and, therefore, can never become an object of knowledge. In the Advaitic state of *nirvikalpa samādhi*, the mind is "suspended" and, hence, there is no longer any "duality of knowledge and knower." At the same time, he claims that in this state of *samādhi*, the "Ātman is directly perceived"—not as an object but as one's own Self.

Rambachan imputes to Vivekananda the view that "[p]erception . . . whether ordinary or supersensuous, involves knowledge gained through objectification" (1994a: 109). In fact, however, Vivekananda holds that the supersensuous perception of the nondual Ātman involves knowledge by *identity* rather than knowledge by objectification. In the state of *nirvikalpa samādhi*, we directly perceive the Ātman by *being* the Ātman. Vivekananda has in mind this knowledge by identity when he goes on to describe *nirvikalpa samādhi* as "direct realization," referring to the title of the Advaitic text *Aparokṣānubhūti*, which he attributes to Śaṅkara, though the text was almost certainly composed after Śaṅkara's time. On other occasions, Vivekananda similarly refers to *nirvikalpa samādhi* as "direct perception" (*pratyakṣa anubhava*) (*BCW* 9:22 / *CW* 6:498), and he claims that in *nirvikalpa samādhi*, one attains the "direct realization of Brahman" (*brahmer sākṣāt upalabdhi*) by *being* Brahman (*BCW* 9:22 / *CW* 6:499). The contradiction Rambachan finds in Vivekananda's account of *nirvikalpa samādhi* vanishes once we take into account his crucial distinction between knowledge by objectification and knowledge by identity.

Rambachan also fails to acknowledge that Vivekananda's understanding of *nirvikalpa samādhi* as the direct perception of Brahman is, in fact, in line with that of a host of earlier Advaita Vedāntins. Indeed, in the passage quoted earlier, Vivekananda explicitly refers to the text *Aparokṣānubhūti*, thereby signaling his alignment with the earlier Advaitic tradition. As we saw in the previous chapter, Śaṅkara himself seems to suggest, in his commentary on *Brahmasūtra* 1.1.2, that *anubhava* is an additional means of knowing Brahman alongside scripture. Moreover, numerous post-Śaṅkara Advaitins conceived *nirvikalpa samādhi* as the direct perception of Ātman/Brahman. The author of *Vedāntaparibhāṣā*, for instance, characterizes the nondual knowledge of Brahman as a form of

[33] For a similar passage, see *BCW* 9:62 / *CW* 7:139–40.

"*nirvikalpaka-pratyakṣa*" (indeterminate perception) (Adhvarīndra 1942: 32–37). In *Pañcadaśī* 1.64, Vidyāraṇya claims that *nirvikalpa samādhi* leads to the "immediate knowledge of the Ātman" (*aparokṣātmavijñānam*) (Vidyāraṇya 1967: 31). Similarly, the author of *Vivekacūḍāmaṇi*—a text Vivekananda knew well—declares in verse 365: "It is only through *nirvikalpa samādhi*, and not otherwise, that the truth of Brahman is clearly and definitely known" (Madhavananda 1921: 161). Vivekananda follows all of these earlier Advaitins in understanding the "perception" (*pratyakṣa*) or "knowledge" (*jñāna* or *vijñāna*) of Brahman in *nirvikalpa samādhi* as knowledge by identity.

Rambachan also claims that Vivekananda creates "a sharp dichotomy between experience and doctrine, accepting, in doing so, the possibility of a pure, uninterpreted experience" (1994a: 110). Rambachan then proceeds to argue that this dichotomy is untenable:

> Recent studies of mysticism and religious experience have brought into sharp focus the flaws of this assumption [of a pure, uninterpreted experience] and highlighted the complexity of the interplay between experience and doctrinal interpretation. In Vivekananda's view, a clear experience is followed later by the recording, in words, of its implications and significance. . . . In reality, however, no such dichotomy can be easily demonstrated, for language and experience are inseparable. Language does not merely provide labels for describing but, in fact, makes experience possible. . . . In fact, it would seem that an "uninterpreted experience" is a contradiction in terms. An experience always belongs to someone who is never free from a belief system of some kind. (1994a: 110)

Anyone familiar with the recent philosophical literature on mysticism will recognize that the position Rambachan endorses here is constructivism, the view that a mystic's pre-experiential beliefs and concepts play a key role in shaping or constructing mystical experience itself.[34] Indeed, in a footnote to this passage, Rambachan approvingly cites Steven Katz's influential edited volume, *Mysticism and Philosophical Analysis* (Katz 1978a), in which Katz, in his own contribution to the volume, provides a detailed defense of constructivism (Katz 1978b). We will be in a better position to understand and assess Rambachan's criticism of Vivekananda if we first briefly acquaint ourselves with Katz's argument.

Katz's primary polemical target is perennialism, the view that mystics in various religions have essentially the same kind of mystical experience but retroactively interpret their experiences in different ways.[35] One of the main problems

[34] For more detailed discussions of constructivist views, see Maharaj (2018: 162–69) and Gellman (2018: sec. 6).

[35] See Gellman (2018: sec. 4) and Maharaj (2018: 156–62) for discussions of perennialism.

with perennialism, Katz argues, is that it overlooks the obvious fact that mystical experiences across traditions differ quite dramatically at the phenomenological level. As Katz observes, "what the Buddhist experiences as *nirvāṇa* is different from what the Jew experiences as *devekuth*" (1978b: 38). Against perennialism, he endorses the following "epistemological assumption": "*There are NO pure* (i.e., *unmediated*) *experiences*. Neither mystical experience nor more ordinary forms of experience give any indication, or any grounds for believing, that they are unmediated" (1978b: 26). On the basis of this assumption, Katz defends the constructivist view that "there is a clear causal connection between the religious and social structure one brings to experience and the nature of one's actual religious experience" (1978b: 40). From Katz's perspective, an Advaitin mystic has an experience of the impersonal nondual Brahman while a Christian mystic has an experience of a loving personal God, because their respective theological beliefs play a major role in shaping their mystical experiences.

Rambachan clearly follows Katz in rejecting perennialism in favor of the constructivist position that "an 'uninterpreted experience' is a contradiction in terms." Rambachan also assumes that Vivekananda was a perennialist. "Vivekananda," Rambachan writes, "clearly seems to think that the experiences of mystics in all religious traditions are the same" (1994a: 111). In support of his claim, he quotes the following passage from Vivekananda's lecture "Religion and Science":

> There is always, however, a small group of men who teach religion from experience. They are called mystics, and these mystics in every religion speak the same tongue and teach the same truth. . . . As mathematics in every part of the world does not differ, so the mystics do not differ. They are all similarly constituted and similarly situated. Their experience is the same; and this becomes law. (*CW* 6:81)

Rambachan's criticism of Vivekananda should now be clear: he takes Vivekananda to be a perennialist and claims that constructivism is a more plausible position than perennialism.

However, I would dispute Rambachan's assumption that Vivekananda was a perennialist. In fact, as I already argued in section 3 of chapter 5, Vivekananda does *not* hold that all mystical experiences are phenomenologically identical. For instance, in several places, Vivekananda points out major phenomenological differences between theistic and non-theistic mystical experiences.[36] In light of his acceptance of the phenomenological diversity of mystical experiences, I believe that in the admittedly perennialist-sounding passage quoted in the previous

[36] See, for instance, *BCW* 9:11 / *CW* 6:463–64.

paragraph, where Vivekananda claims that the experience of all mystics "is the same," what he actually means is that while various experiences of the ultimate reality often differ at the phenomenological level, they are all the "same" in the sense of being experiences of *one and the same* ultimate reality. We should always keep in mind his expansive Ramakrishnan conception of ultimate reality as the impersonal-personal Infinite Reality which is perceived by mystics in different forms and aspects.[37]

Rambachan also overlooks the intricate debates between perennialists and constructivists that ensued in the years following the publication of Katz's 1978 volume. The fact is that both perennialism and constructivism remain highly controversial philosophical positions. Instead of considering the arguments on both sides of these debates, Rambachan assumes, without sufficient justification, the correctness of constructivism.

In the fifth chapter of my book *Infinite Paths to Infinite Reality* (Maharaj 2018), I discussed the perennialism-constructivism debate in detail and argued that Ramakrishna champions an alternative "manifestationist" approach to mystical experience that shares the primary advantages of both perennialism and constructivism while avoiding their respective weaknesses. For present purposes, I will briefly summarize the relevant parts of that chapter, but interested readers should consult that chapter for more detail and justification. As Katz and many others have pointed out, the primary weakness of perennialism is that it fails to acknowledge that mystical experiences both within and across religious traditions often differ at the phenomenological level. Constructivism has the major advantage that it *does* acknowledge the diversity of mystical experiences.

However, numerous philosophers have also pointed out three serious weaknesses in the constructivist position—none of which Rambachan considers.[38] First, since constructivism holds that mystical experiences are always conditioned by the mystic's prior belief-system, constructivists are not able to account for surprising or novel mystical experiences.[39] For instance, as I mentioned in chapter 1 of this book, Vivekananda described an occasion in early 1882 when Ramakrishna touched him "over the heart," and he reportedly had the Advaitic experience of *nirvikalpa samādhi*, in which the entire world—along with his "consciousness of the ego"—entirely vanished (*CW* 5:392). This first experience of *nirvikalpa samādhi* was entirely unexpected for Vivekananda, not only because he was not seeking such an experience but also because he was, at the time, a member of the theistic Brāhmo Samāj, which emphatically rejected the Advaitic doctrine of the impersonal nondual Brahman. Hence, the young

[37] I discussed this doctrine in detail in section 2 of chapter 2 of this book.
[38] I provide a more detailed critical discussion of constructivist theories in Maharaj (2018: 162–69).
[39] See, for instance, Forman (1990: 20–21), King (1988: 267), and Stoeber (1994: 8–13).

Vivekananda's theistic worldview could not possibly have shaped his Advaitic experience of *nirvikalpa samādhi*. Such instances of mystical novelty and surprise, which can easily be multiplied, provide strong counterevidence against the constructivist position.

Second, constructivists deny a key element in the self-understanding of most mystics, including Ramakrishna and Vivekananda: the conviction that their mystical experiences are epistemically sui generis in character.[40] As Anthony Perovich (1990) has convincingly documented, numerous mystics have described their mystical experience as a nondiscursive form of immediate knowledge that differs radically from ordinary, conceptually mediated cognition. Constructivists are unable to take such mystical testimony at face value, since they maintain that there is no difference between ordinary experience and mystical experience at the epistemic level. As Katz puts it, "the synthetic operations of the mind are in fact the fundamental conditions under which, and under which alone, mystical experience, as all experience, takes place" (1978: 62–63).

Third, the subjectivist element in all constructivist positions results in an ontologically deflationary account of the divine object of mystical experience.[41] Mystics typically believe that what they experience has fully objective reality. Constructivists, however, do not grant full ontological reality to the divine objects of mystical experience, since they maintain that the mystic's belief-system at least partly shapes what the mystic experiences. For instance, when analyzing a hypothetical mystic's statement "I experience *x*," Katz claims that "the mind is active in constructing *x* as experienced" (1978: 64). Therefore, constructivists have to deny the self-understanding of most mystics, who claim that what they experience has fully objective reality.

Ramakrishna, I argued in *Infinite Paths*, adopts what I call a "manifestationist" approach to mystical experience that can be seen as a dialectical alternative to both perennialism and constructivism (Maharaj 2018: 169–95). On the basis of his own richly varied mystical experiences, Ramakrishna affirmed that God is both personal and impersonal, both with and without form, both immanent in the universe and beyond it. He derives his manifestationist paradigm from this expansive ontology of God:

> [O]ne who constantly thinks of God can know God's real nature; he alone knows that God manifests Himself to seekers in various forms and aspects (*tini nānārūpe dekhā den, nānābhāve dekhā den*). God is personal (*saguṇa*) as well as impersonal (*nirguṇa*). . . . God manifests Himself to the devotee in the form

[40] For persuasive criticisms of this aspect of the constructivist position, see Perovich (1990), Almond (1988: 216), Wainwright (1981: 20), King (1988: 263), Jones (2016: 67), and Parsons (1999: 120–22).

[41] I develop this objection in more detail in Maharaj (2018: 168–69).

> the devotee loves most; God's love for the devotee knows no bounds. (*K* 101 / *G* 149–50)

According to Ramakrishna, the impersonal-personal Infinite Divine Reality *manifests* to different mystics in various forms and aspects. Hence, in contrast to perennialism, Ramakrishna's manifestationist paradigm is able to account for a wide range of mystical experiences. At the same time, Ramakrishna's manifestationism has two major advantages over constructivism. First, unlike constructivism, Ramakrishna's manifestationism readily accounts for surprising or novel mystical experiences. For Ramakrishna, the cause of a mystical experience is not the mystic's belief-system but God Himself, who can always choose to manifest Himself to a mystic in a form or aspect that the mystic was not expecting. Second, Ramakrishna is in a better position than constructivists to honor the self-understanding of most mystics in two respects, since he holds not only that mystical experiences are epistemically sui generis but also that mystics experience *fully real* manifestations of one and the same Infinite Divine Reality.

With this argumentation in the background, I would suggest that Vivekananda was *neither* a perennialist *nor* a constructivist. Rather, he followed his guru Ramakrishna in championing a manifestationist approach to mystical experience. I have already provided textual evidence for Vivekananda's manifestationism in my discussion of his response to the conflicting claims objection in the previous section. Like Ramakrishna, Vivekananda consistently holds that one and the same impersonal-personal Divine Reality "manifests" itself to different mystics in various forms and aspects (*CW* 2:319–20).

Hence, I believe that Rambachan makes three mistakes in criticizing Vivekananda's alleged perennialism from Rambachan's own preferred constructivist standpoint. First, Rambachan wrongly takes Vivekananda to be a perennialist. Second, Rambachan's failure to consider recent debates between perennialists and constructivists leads him to accept the constructivist position uncritically, without addressing the many serious objections that philosophers have raised against it. Third, Rambachan seems to assume that perennialism and constructivism are the only available options. I have argued, however, that Ramakrishna and Vivekananda actually championed an alternative manifestationist paradigm that has a number of advantages over both perennialism and constructivism (Maharaj 2018: 153–95).

In a recent book, Thomas J. Green rightly views Vivekananda as a participant in a "cosmopolitan religious culture" (2016: 2) and contends that Vivekananda's aim in emphasizing spiritual experience was to strip back "religion to those essential elements that could withstand the critique of secular reason" (2016: 78). In line with Green's approach, I argued in chapter 4 that Vivekananda's defense of religion as an experientially grounded science was a cosmopolitan response to the global crisis of religious belief in the late nineteenth century. As a creative and agential cosmopolitan thinker, Vivekananda drew selectively upon Western sources, championing the modern scientific method of empirical verification while also strongly criticizing the tendency toward scientism he detected in Comte, Huxley, and other Western figures. He was equally creative and dialectical in his engagement with Indian philosophical traditions. While he rejected the Mīmāṃsaka/Vedāntic doctrine of the authorlessness of the Vedas, he employed the traditional doctrines of *yogajapratyakṣa* and *svataḥ-prāmāṇyatā* as the basis for a highly original argument for the epistemic value of supersensuous perception that remains as timely as ever.

PART III
FAITH AND REASON

7

From Agnosticism to "Metagnosticism"

Vivekananda's Kantian-Vedāntic Critique of Theological Reason

This and the next chapter provide an in-depth examination of Vivekananda's views on faith and reason, which have not yet received sustained scholarly attention. I aim to demonstrate that he developed his positions through a subtle critico-constructive engagement with both Indian and Western thinkers. This chapter focuses on his views on the powers and limits of theological reason, while the next chapter discusses his three-stage account of religious faith. I will argue that Vivekananda's distinctive conception of the rationality and dynamics of religious faith makes an important contribution to contemporary discussions in the philosophy of religion.

The first two sections of this chapter provide the philosophical background necessary for understanding Vivekananda's cosmopolitan views on reason, which will be discussed in sections 3 through 5. Section 1 outlines the rational theology of the Nyāya school of Indian philosophy and contrasts it with the Vedāntic views of the classical Advaitin Śaṅkara and the modern mystic Ramakrishna. While Naiyāyikas attempt to prove God's existence through rational arguments, Śaṅkara and Ramakrishna uphold the Vedāntic view that reason is valuable in certain respects, but it can neither conclusively prove nor disprove the existence of supersensuous realities. As we will see, however, Śaṅkara and Ramakrishna part ways on the question of whether scripture or spiritual experience is paramount.

Section 2 sketches the views on reason of Immanuel Kant, William Hamilton, Herbert Spencer, and John Stuart Mill, all of whom Vivekananda had read as a young philosophy student. Kant set the agenda for subsequent philosophers and theologians in the West by denying both rational and supersensuous knowledge of God while also attempting to justify faith in God's existence on moral grounds. Hamilton and Spencer embraced Kant's doctrine of the unknowability of the Absolute but explored alternative strategies for justifying religious faith. Mill not only penned an influential book-length critique of Hamilton's views on faith and reason, but he also forcefully raised the problem of evil and refuted various traditional arguments for God's existence, conceding only that the argument from design has some, albeit minimal, rational force.

Swami Vivekananda's Vedāntic Cosmopolitanism. Swami Medhananda, Oxford University Press. © Oxford University Press 2022. DOI: 10.1093/oso/9780197624463.003.0008

Sections 3 through 5 show how Vivekananda developed his views on faith and reason through a cosmopolitan engagement with Kant, Hamilton, Spencer, and Mill on the one hand and with Śaṅkara and Ramakrishna on the other. I will contend in section 3 that Vivekananda sided with Ramakrishna against Śaṅkara in holding that spiritual experience, rather than scripture, is the only authoritative means of knowing Brahman. Moreover, while Vivekananda followed Vedānta and the Kantian tradition in arguing that reason can neither prove nor disprove God's existence, he also criticized Kantian thinkers from a Vedāntic standpoint, arguing that they were not justified in ruling out the possibility of supersensuous knowledge of God.

Section 4 discusses Vivekananda's stance toward rational arguments for God's existence. In spite of his rational agnosticism, he defended the (limited) rational force of the argument from religious experience, which infers God's existence from the testimony of mystics who claim to have realized God. Vivekananda claimed that the argument from religious experience provides an adequate rational basis for faith in God, which, in turn, has to be strengthened and deepened through spiritual practice, with the aim of attaining the direct spiritual experience of God. He also followed Mill and Ramakrishna in granting some degree of rational force to the argument from design for God's existence, though he maintained that this argument is much weaker than the argument from religious experience.

Section 5 shows how Vivekananda drew upon the Vedāntic ideas of Śaṅkara and Ramakrishna to refute the well-known argument from evil against God's existence, raised by Mill and many others. Vivekananda's theodicy, I argue, has two main dimensions. He argued that God created this world as a moral "gymnasium" in which we evolve spiritually through the experience of good and evil in the course of many lives. As we will see, the doctrines of *karma*, rebirth, and universal salvation all play a crucial role in his Vedāntic theodicy of spiritual evolution. However, he also appealed ultimately to a panentheistic metaphysics, according to which God has become everything in the universe, including both evildoers and the victims of evil and suffering. From the lofty heights of panentheistic spiritual experience, the problem of evil—which presupposes a difference between God and His suffering creatures—no longer arises.

1. The Indian Background: Nyāya, Śaṅkara, and Ramakrishna

In classical Indian thought, two of the most important theological traditions are the rational theology of Nyāya and the scripturally oriented theology of Vedānta. In this section, I will briefly outline the Nyāya view and contrast it with the

Vedāntic approaches of the classical Advaita Vedāntin Śaṅkara and the modern Vedāntin Ramakrishna.

The Naiyāyikas are well known for championing rational theology, the project of proving the existence of God (*īśvara*) through inferential reasoning independent of scripture.[1] Beginning with Uddyotakara, they were especially keen to defend versions of the design and cosmological arguments for God's existence. Udayana succinctly formulates the design argument[2] as follows:

> The existence of a creator of the universe is established by inference (*anumāna*): the universe, whose status as having a maker is disputed, does have a maker, since it is an effect (*kāryatvāt*).[3]

According to Udayana, since the universe is an "effect," and the property of being an effect is invariably concomitant with having an intelligent cause, the universe must have had an intelligent creator.[4] He then goes on to make the additional argument that the intelligent creator of the universe must have been the omniscient God, since God alone has the requisite knowledge of all the material causes of the universe (Dasti 2011: 4). Of course, as Udayana and his fellow Naiyāyikas were well aware, this argument is highly controversial, and they accordingly elaborated and refined the argument in various ways, defending it against various objections.[5]

Both Buddhists and Mīmāṃsakas attempted to refute Nyāya design arguments for God's existence primarily by targeting the *vyāpti* (invariable concomitance) at their core. Matthew Dasti helpfully summarizes their basic refutation of the Nyāya *vyāpti* as follows: "being grounded in the experience of ordinary, common artifacts and ordinary, common makers, no supposed *vyāpti* between products and makers may be cited to support inference of a wholly unique, Godlike creator of the manifest world" (2011: 9). That is, it is illegitimate to make an inductive inference from our ordinary experience that artifacts have makers—for instance, that a clay pot was made by a human potter—to the claim that this entire universe must have been created by an omniscient God, since there are no

[1] See Dasti (2011), Vattanky (1978), and Chemparathy (1972).

[2] There is some controversy about whether this argument is properly a design argument (Dasti 2011: 5–6; C. Brown 2008), a cosmological argument (Chakrabarti 1989), or some combination of the two (Patil 2009: 33). I follow Dasti and Brown in interpreting the Nyāya argument primarily as a design argument, though I do not have the space here to enter into this scholarly controversy.

[3] *viśvasya kartuḥ anumāna—siddhatvāt. vivāda—adhyāsita sakartukaṃ kartṛkaṃ kāryatvāt iti* (Udayanācārya 1995: 380). I follow Dasti's (2011: 2) translation, except that I prefer to translate "*kārya*" as "effect," not "product."

[4] I agree with Dasti (2011: 9), who notes that this "would be a much better argument if Nyāya developed a principled way to distinguish between accidental developments of structure (e.g., a lump of clay) and manifestly purposeful structure (e.g., pots)."

[5] See Dasti (2011), Patil (2009: 31–99), C. Brown (2008), and Chakrabarti (1989).

examples from our experience to support this claim.[6] The Naiyāyikas, in turn, defended the design argument against such refutations, primarily by arguing for the epistemic legitimacy of inferring new information that is not found in our experience.[7]

Śaṅkara explicitly rejects Nyāya rational theology in favor of the Vedāntic position that the Upaniṣads are the primary source of the knowledge of *īśvara*. *Brahmasūtra* 1.1.2 defines Brahman as "that from which [are derived] the birth etc. of this [universe]" (*janmādyasya yataḥ*). In his commentary on 1.1.2, Śaṅkara has the *pūrvapakṣin* (*prima facie* objector) ask whether this *sūtra* presents a Nyāya-like "inference" (*anumāna*) to the existence of *īśvara* from perceived features of the universe. Śaṅkara refutes this *pūrvapakṣa* position by arguing that all the *sūtras* of the *Brahmasūtra* have the purpose of "stringing together the flowers of the sentences of the Upaniṣads" (*BSBh* 1.1.2, p. 7).[8] *Brahmasūtra* 1.1.2, he notes, refers to Taittirīya Upaniṣad 3.1 (*yato vā imāni bhūtāni jāyante*, "That from which these beings take birth"). The realization of Brahman, he claims, arises only from "deliberation on the meaning of Upaniṣadic statements" and not from *anumāna* or any other *pramāṇas*. According to Śaṅkara, then, we learn from the Upaniṣads alone that Brahman is the material and efficient cause of the universe. It should be noted, however, that as an Advaita Vedāntin, Śaṅkara holds that Brahman is the cause of the universe only from the empirical (*vyāvahārika*) standpoint. From the ultimate (*pāramārthika*) standpoint, he upholds *vivartavāda*, the view that the sole reality is *nirguṇa* Brahman and that the universe does not exist and, hence, has no relation to Brahman (C. Brown 2008: 109–112).

Crucially, however, Śaṅkara does not dismiss reasoning altogether. Rather, he argues that inferential reasoning that does not contradict the Upaniṣads can enhance our understanding of Brahman insofar as it "aims to strengthen our understanding of the meaning" of these scriptural texts (*tadarthagrahaṇadārḍhyāya*) (*BSBh* 1.1.2, pp. 7–8). Later in his commentary on 1.1.2, Śaṅkara specifically refutes the Nyāya design argument by claiming that since Brahman is not an object of the senses, we cannot infer from the fact that the universe is a "mere effect" (*kāryamātram*) to the conclusion that Brahman must be its cause. As he puts it, "even when the mere effect [i.e., the universe] is cognized, one cannot ascertain whether it is related to Brahman [as its cause] or to something else"

[6] For details on Buddhist refutations of Nyāya design arguments, see Dasti (2011), Patil (2009: 100–193), and Vattanky (1978: 402).

[7] See Dasti's discussion of *pakṣa-dharmatā-bala* (2011: 11–14) and Vattanky (1978: 402–3).

[8] Throughout this chapter, the translated passages from Śaṅkara's commentary on the *Brahmasūtra* are based primarily on Gambhirananda's translation (Gambhirananda 2006), though I have sometimes modified his translation, and I have also consulted Thibaut's translation (Thibaut 1890). For discussions of Śaṅkara's views on reason, see Taber (1981), C. Brown (2008: 105–12), B. Gupta (2009: 89–119), and Murty (1959).

(*BSBh* 1.1.2, p. 8). Śaṅkara's criticism of the Nyāya design argument should remind us of the Buddhist objection that the *vyāpti* at the core of the design argument is invalid since *īśvara*, the alleged cause of the universe, is not an object of our ordinary experience.

In his commentary on *Brahmasūtra* 2.1.6, Śaṅkara clarifies his position on the role of reason in understanding Brahman. What he rejects is not reasoning per se but reasoning *independent* of the scriptures. Accordingly, he rejects "independent reasoning" (*śuṣkatarka*) and points out the "inconclusiveness of mere reasoning" (*kevalasya tarkasya vipralambhakatvam*) (*BSBh* 2.1.6, pp. 188–89). At the same time, he *endorses* "reasoning that accords with the scriptures" (*śrutyanugṛhītatarka*) (*BSBh* 2.1.6, p. 188). In his commentary on 2.1.11, he explains why independent reasoning is inconclusive:

> Reasoning that is independent of scripture and that springs from mere human conjecture is inconclusive. (*nirāgamāḥ puruṣotprekṣamātranibandhanāḥ tarkā apratiṣṭhitā bhavanti.*) For people's conjectures are endless (*utprekṣāyā niraṅkuśatvāt*). We see that an argument thought up with great effort by clever people is refuted by still more clever people; and the argument thought up by the latter are refuted, in turn, by still others. Hence, nobody can rely on any argument as conclusive, on account of the diversity of people's views (*puruṣamativairūpyāt*). (*BSBh* 2.1.11, p. 113)

Śaṅkara provides two reasons for the inconclusiveness of rational argumentation. First, he claims, in a Kantian vein, that any argument can always be met with an equally strong, if not stronger, counterargument. Second, since people's viewpoints and preferences differ considerably, an argument that appears to be conclusive to one person may appear *in*conclusive, or just plain wrong, to another person. Hence, for Śaṅkara, while we can never conclusively establish that Brahman is the material and efficient cause of the universe by means of independent reasoning, we *can* do so "by means of scripture and reasoning in accordance with scripture" (*āgamavaśena āgamānusāritarkavaśena*) (*BSBh* 2.1.11, p. 115).

In his commentary on the second *adhikaraṇa* of the *Brahmasūtra*, Śaṅkara appeals to various rational arguments in his efforts to refute the rival views of Sāṃkhya, Buddhism, Jainism, and others. For instance, in his commentary on *Brahmasūtra* 2.2.1, Śaṅkara appeals to a form of the design argument in order to refute the Sāṃkhyan view that insentient *pradhāna* is the cause of the universe:

> it is not seen in this world that any independent insentient thing that is not guided by some sentient being can produce modifications to serve some special purpose of a man; for what is noticed in the world is that houses, palaces, beds,

> seats, recreation grounds, etc., are made by intelligent engineers and others at the proper time and in a way suitable for ensuring or avoiding comfort or discomfort. So how can the insentient *pradhāna* create this universe, which cannot even be mentally conceived of by the intelligent and most far-famed architects, which is seen in the external context to consist of the earth etc. that are fit places for experiencing the results of various works, and in the context of the individual person, of the body and other things have different castes etc., in which the limbs are arranged according to a regular design, and which are seen as the seats for experiencing various fruits of actions? Even in the cases of earth etc. it is noticed that special creations take place under the control of potters and others. On that analogy, the possibility arises of *pradhāna* also being under the control of some conscious entity. . . . Accordingly, by reason of the impossibility of design (*racanā*) as well, the insentient *pradhāna* should not be inferred to be the cause of the universe. (*BSBh* 2.2.1, p. 221)

Śaṅkara argues, against the Sāṃkhyans, that an insentient entity cannot be the cause of the universe, since the universe exhibits various signs of design (*racanā*), which imply a conscious designer. Anticipating William Paley's famous design argument for God's existence, Śaṅkara makes the following analogical argument. It is commonly observed that things in this world that serve some special purpose—like houses and beds (Paley later used the example of a watch)—are made by conscious and intelligent people. This universe also seems to serve a special purpose—namely, the purpose of allowing people to work out the good and bad *karma* that they have accumulated in past lives. According to Śaṅkara, even the greatest human architects could not begin to fathom how to arrange the universe so as to serve as a suitable *karma-bhūmi*, a place for working out our individual *karma*. Therefore, we can infer from the various signs of design in the universe that its creator must be conscious and intelligent rather than insentient.

How are we to reconcile Śaṅkara's appeal to the design argument in his commentary on *Brahmasūtra* 2.2.1 with his *critique* of the Nyāya design argument in his earlier commentary on 1.1.2? What Śaṅkara rejects is the rational theology of Naiyāyikas, the view that inferential arguments like the design argument are the primary source of our knowledge of *īśvara*. As a Vedāntin, Śaṅkara defends the view that the primary source of our knowledge of Brahman is scripture, which alone tells us that Brahman is both the material and efficient cause of the universe. At the same time, Śaṅkara endorses—and himself engages in—reasoning that accords with scripture (*śrutyanugṛhītatarka*). Accordingly, in his commentary on 2.2.1, he refutes the Sāṃkhyan position by arguing that an insentient entity could not have produced this universe, which exhibits various signs of conscious design (*racanā*). From Śaṅkara's standpoint, the design argument does plausibly establish that this universe has a conscious creator, but the Upaniṣads alone can give us the *specific* knowledge that this conscious creator is none other than Brahman, which is both the material and efficient cause of the universe. For Śaṅkara, then, reasoning is beneficial insofar as it (1) strengthens our conviction of the truth of the Upaniṣads, (2) helps us resolve apparent contradictions in the scriptures, and (3) helps us refute non-Vedāntic views.

Like Śaṅkara, Ramakrishna strongly emphasized the limitations of the rational intellect. At several places in the *Kathāmṛta*, he highlighted our inability to "comprehend the nature of God" (*K* 341 / *G* 351) or to "understand God's ways" by means of the rhetorical question, "Can a one-seer pot hold ten seers of milk?" (*K* 229 / *G* 257). By likening the finite human mind to a "one-seer pot," Ramakrishna points to the fundamental limitations of the rational intellect and its inherent incapacity to grasp spiritual realities.

However, instead of dismissing reasoning altogether, Ramakrishna taught that four forms of reasoning are spiritually beneficial insofar as they help us to attain the ultimate goal of God-realization. First, he strongly encouraged people to practice discrimination or what he called *sad-asad-vicāra*—that is, reasoning "about the true and the false, about what is permanent and what is transitory" (*K* 501 / *G* 496). Second, he taught that reasoning about the scriptures is valuable only insofar as it serves as a means to the end of God-realization:

> There are many scriptures like the Vedas. But one cannot realize God without austerity and spiritual discipline. "God cannot be found in the six systems, the Vedas, or the Tantra."... It is true that many things are recorded in the scriptures; but all these are useless without the direct realization of God, without devotion to His Lotus Feet, without purity of heart. The almanac forecasts the rainfall of the year. But not a drop of water will you get by squeezing the almanac. No, not even one drop.
>
> How long should one reason about the texts of the scriptures? So long as one does not have direct realization of God. (*K* 478 / *G* 475–76)

While Śaṅkara tended to emphasize the self-sufficiency of scripture in providing knowledge of Brahman, Ramakrishna emphatically subordinated scriptural knowledge to direct spiritual experience. He comes close here to the Bhāmatī school of Advaita Vedānta, which—as we saw in chapter 5—holds that the hearing (*śravaṇa*) of scripture must be followed by reasoning about it (*manana*) and then meditation on the Ātman (*nididhyāsana*), which should culminate in the direct realization of the nondual Ātman.

Third, while Ramakrishna was skeptical of the pretensions of natural theology, he nonetheless believed that rational arguments for God's existence could strengthen one's religious faith. Take, for instance, the following dialogue between Ramakrishna and the devotee Śrīś:

ŚRĪŚ: "Sir, I feel that there is an All-knowing Person. We get an indication of His Knowledge by looking at His creation. Let me give an illustration. God has made devices to keep fish and other aquatic animals alive in cold regions. As water grows colder, it gradually shrinks. But the amazing thing is that, just before turning into ice, the water becomes light and expands. In the freezing cold, fish can easily live in the water of a lake: the surface of the lake may be frozen, but the water below is all liquid. If a very cool breeze blows, it is obstructed by the ice. The water below remains warm."

SRI RAMAKRISHNA: "That God exists may be known by looking at the universe. But it is one thing to hear of God, another thing to see God, and still another thing to talk to God. Some have heard of milk, some have seen it, and some, again, have tasted it. You feel happy when you see milk; you are nourished and strengthened when you drink it. You will get peace of mind only when you have seen God. You will enjoy bliss and gain strength only when you have talked to Him." (*K* 362 / *G* 368)

Śrīś sketches a form of the argument from design for God's existence: certain features of the natural world—such as the existence of natural mechanisms to keep fish alive in cold areas—suggest that the world was created by an omniscient and omnipotent God. In response to Śrīś's argument, Ramakrishna acknowledges that one may indeed see God's handiwork "by looking at the universe." However, he also points out that no such rational arguments are ever conclusive, so the only way to attain unshakable certainty of God's existence is to experience God directly.

Fourth, he encouraged the use of reason to refute arguments *against* God's existence. As I discussed at length in chapter 7 of *Infinite Paths*, Ramakrishna explicitly refuted the argument from evil against God's existence by defending a sophisticated theodicy on the basis of numerous rational arguments. His overall view, then, is that reasoning is valuable so long as it strengthens our faith in God and aids us in our efforts to realize God through spiritual practice.

2. *Can We Have Faith in an Unknowable God? Kant, Hamilton, Spencer, and Mill*

On the Western side, Vivekananda was especially influenced by the Kantian approach to reason and faith. In this section, I will briefly outline the views of Immanuel Kant, William Hamilton, Herbert Spencer, and John Stuart Mill—all of whom Vivekananda had read and to whom he explicitly referred at various points in his lectures and writings.

In his early philosophical thinking, Kant (1724–1804) was sympathetic to the rational theological approach of his predecessors G. W. Leibniz and Christian Wolff, and he even presented, in his book *The Only Possible Argument in Support of a Demonstration of the Existence of God* (*OPA*; 1763), an a priori "demonstration" of God's existence based on the possibility of an absolutely necessary being. However, in his epoch-making book *Critique of Pure Reason* (*CPR*; 1781, 1787), Kant did an about-face and argued against the very possibility of rational theology. He argued that since human reason is inherently limited, we can never gain knowledge of "supersensible" entities like God and the soul. In "The Ideal of Pure Reason" section, he specifically refutes, in turn, the ontological, cosmological, and "physico-theological" arguments—which he takes to exhaust all possible proofs of God's existence. Kant's stance toward the "physico-theological" argument, which is none other than the argument from design, is somewhat ambivalent (Wood 1978: 130–46). On the one hand, he echoes Buddhist critics of the Nyāya design argument in arguing that the inference from perceivable features of the universe to "obscure and unprovable grounds of explanation"—that is, an unperceivable divine designer—is unjustified (*CPR*, A626/B654). He also claims that the design argument is a disguised form of the ontological argument, which he already refuted in an earlier section (*CPR*, A629–630/B657–658). On the other hand, Kant remarks that the design argument "always deserves to be named with respect" (*CPR*, A623/B651) and acknowledges its "rationality and utility," denying only that it furnishes "apodictic certainty" of God's existence (*CPR*, A624/B652). Indeed, he even admits that the design argument "could at most establish a highest architect of the world, who would always be limited by the suitability of the material on which he works, but not a creator of the world, to whose idea everything is subject" (*CPR*, A627/B655).

For Kant, the inherent limitations of reason make it impossible either to prove or to disprove God's existence:

> the same grounds for considering human reason incapable of asserting the existence of such a being, when laid before our eyes, also suffice to prove the unsuitability of all counter-assertions. For where, by pure speculation of reason, will anyone acquire the insight that there is no highest being as the original ground of everything? (*CPR*, A640–641/B668–669)

Accordingly, Kant agrees with Vedāntins like Śaṅkara that reason has an "important negative use" (*CPR*, A640/B668), in that it can be used to refute attempts to disprove God's existence. As he puts it, the "objective reality" of the "highest being" "cannot of course be proved . . . but also cannot be refuted" (*CPR*, A641/B669). In "The Antinomies of Reason" section, he defends this rational agnosticism by showing that we have equally strong rational grounds for accepting a variety of theses and antitheses about supersensible entities like God.

However, in stark contrast to Vedāntins, Kant holds that human cognition is restricted to what we can know through sensible intuition and, hence, we can only cognize appearances (phenomena) and not things in themselves (noumena) (*CPR*, A249–253). Accordingly, he emphatically rejects the possibility of supersensible knowledge or experience of noumenal entities like God or the soul. At various points in the *Critique of Pure Reason*, Kant asserts that a hypothetical being endowed with "intellectual intuition," rather than sensible intuition, would be able to cognize things in themselves (*CPR*, A249). However, he insists that human beings do not possess such a faculty of intellectual intuition: "sensible intuition . . . is the only one possible for us" (*CPR*, A252). Accordingly, he explicitly contrasts his own critical philosophy, which humbly restricts human knowledge to the deliverances of sensible intuition, with "mysticism," which he defines as "the presupposition of an intuitive intellect . . . or intellectual intuition" (*LM* 425; Ak. 29:953). Such statements have led most Kant scholars to assume that Kant was an arch enemy of mysticism.[9]

Nonetheless, I have argued in a recent article that Kant was actually more sympathetic to certain forms of mysticism than he lets on (Maharaj 2017b).[10] In his pre-critical phase, he was so fascinated by the alleged visions of the Swedish mystic Emanuel Swedenborg (1688–1772) that he wrote the book *Dreams of a Spirit Seer* (1786), in which he defends the possibility of *indirect* mystical experience (hereafter IME), which I define as the indirect experience of a supersensible entity through the perception of something sensible (such as an image or a feeling) that is caused by that supersensible entity. Moreover, even in his critical period, Kant continued to defend the epistemic possibility of IME, since he accepted noumenal causality, which is all that is necessary for an IME. What Kant clearly and consistently denied in both his pre-critical and critical periods was the possibility of *direct* mystical experience—that is, the direct experience of a supersensible entity by means of a faculty of supersensible intuition.[11]

Interestingly, however, Kant's rational agnosticism did not lead him to embrace *religious* agnosticism. Rather, as he famously put it in the preface to the second edition of *CPR*, "I had to deny *knowledge* in order to make room for *faith*" (*CPR*, Bxxx). For Kant, the denial of both rational and supersensible knowledge of God and the immortal soul actually clears a space for a religious faith grounded securely in our *moral* consciousness. The details of Kant's account of the moral basis of religious faith are extremely complicated and at times obscure,

[9] See, for instance, Wood (1992: 394–416), Baelz (1968: 41), and Ward (1972: 168).

[10] For a recent book-length defense of a Kantian mysticism, see Palmquist (2019).

[11] For detailed discussion and justification of the claims in this paragraph, see Maharaj (2017b).

and some contemporary scholars have argued that his views on faith evolved in the course of his thinking.[12] Since my aim here is not to contribute to Kant exegesis, I will only provide a brief sketch of Kant's basic strategy for attempting to justify religious faith on moral grounds.

In the *Critique of Practical Reason* (1788), Kant argues that "it is morally necessary to assume the existence of God" (*CPrR*, 241; Ak. 5:125). He presents numerous subtly different versions of this moral justification of belief in God's existence in the works of his critical period. For present purposes, I will focus on the argument he presents in *Religion within the Boundaries of Mere Reason* (1793), which represents his most mature view on the matter. In this work, Kant argues as follows. In order to maintain our commitment to leading a moral life, we must believe that our moral behavior will be rewarded in an afterlife in the form of attaining the "Highest Good," an ideal state in which our happiness is exactly proportionate to our moral goodness. (In other words, we must believe that the better we are in this life, the happier we will be in the afterlife.) However, only a morally perfect, omnipotent, and omniscient God is capable of bringing about the Highest Good. Therefore, we must believe that God exists in order to be able to lead moral lives (*RB*, 58–60; Ak. 6:4–6). By means of this argument, Kant claims that he has established not the "*logical* certainty," but the "*moral* certainty," of God's existence (*CPR*, 689; A829/B857).

The Scottish philosopher William Hamilton (1788–1856) was strongly influenced by Kant as well as the common-sense philosopher Thomas Reid. In *Lectures on Metaphysics and Logic* (1859), Hamilton argues, in a Kantian vein, that philosophy has two main tasks: first, to admit "the weakness of our discursive intellect," and second, to demonstrate "that the limits of thought are not to be assumed as the limits of possibility" (1859: 25). Echoing Kant's claim that he had to "deny *knowledge* in order to make room for *faith*," Hamilton remarks: "A learned ignorance is thus the end of philosophy, as it is the beginning of theology" (1859: 25). According to Hamilton, philosophical reasoning should terminate in a rational acknowledgment of the inherent limitations of reason, which then opens up a space for religious faith.

While Hamilton follows Kant in emphasizing the space-clearing function of reason with respect to faith, he rejects Kant's moral justification of religious faith. In *On the Philosophy of the Unconditioned* (1829; Hamilton 1853: 9–44), Hamilton argues that Kant contradicts himself by denying theoretical knowledge of God and the immortal soul while affirming *practical* knowledge of these same noumenal entities. As he puts it, "If our intellectual nature be perfidious in one revelation, it must be presumed deceitful in all; nor is it possible for Kant to establish the existence of God, Freewill, and Immortality, on the presumed veracity

[12] For discussion of some of these complexities, see Pasternack and Fugate (2020).

of reason, in a practical relation, after having himself demonstrated its mendacity in a speculative" (1853: 25). Hamilton's criticism is not entirely clear, but he seems to be arguing that Kant overreaches in his efforts to establish the "moral certainty" of God's existence, since such moral certainty or knowledge flies in the face of the epistemic strictures of the first *Critique*. Having studied post-Kantian philosophy in Germany, Hamilton argues that Kant's doctrine of the practical knowledge of God paved the way for the metaphysical extravagances of the absolute idealists Schelling and Hegel. According to Hamilton, "Kant had annihilated the older metaphysic, but the germ of a more visionary doctrine of the absolute, than any of those refuted, was contained in the bosom of his own philosophy" (1853: 25).

In stark contrast to Kant, Hamilton attempts to ground religious faith in a novel argument based on "The Law of the Conditioned," which he elaborates as follows:

> The conditioned is the mean between two extremes—two inconditionates, exclusive of each other, neither of which *can be conceived as possible*, but of which, on the principles of contradiction and excluded middle, one *must be admitted as necessary*. On this opinion, therefore, reason is shown to be weak, but not deceitful. The mind is not represented as conceiving two propositions subversive of each other, as equally possible; but only, as unable to understand as possible, either of two extremes; one of which, however, on the ground of their mutual repugnance, it is compelled to recognize as true. (1853: 22)

Hamilton's basic argument, though opaque and notoriously problematic, seems to be as follows.[13] Through reason, we can only gain knowledge of conditioned entities—that is, phenomenal entities conditioned by space, time, causality, and so on. Our knowledge of these conditioned entities leads us to the thought of *unconditioned* (i.e., noumenal) entities like God and the immortal soul. According to Hamilton, these unconditioned entities must be either "absolute" (which, in his technical sense, means limited) or "infinite" (by which he means unlimited) (1853: 20). However, due to the limitations of reason, we cannot even conceive the possibility of the existence *either* of an absolute unconditioned entity *or* of an infinite unconditioned entity. At the same time, the law of non-contradiction entails that both these unconditioned entities cannot be false, and the law of the excluded middle entails that one of them must be true (Madden 1985: 842). Hence, we must, of necessity, believe that one of these unconditioned entities exists. On the basis of this bold but rather obscure argument, Hamilton explains how our "learned ignorance" paves the way for faith in God: "And by a wonderful

[13] For a detailed discussion of Hamilton's argument, see Madden (1985), 839–66.

revelation, we are thus, in the very consciousness of our inability to conceive aught above the relative and finite, inspired with a belief in the existence of something unconditioned beyond the sphere of all comprehensible reality" (1853: 22).

It was not long before philosophers began to criticize Hamilton's attempt to ground religious faith in his "Law of the Conditioned." In his *First Principles* (1862)—a book Vivekananda had read during his student days—Herbert Spencer (1820–1903) devoted a full chapter to "The Relativity of All Knowledge," in which he approvingly referred to Hamilton's *Philosophy of the Unconditioned* in support of the thesis that "the reality existing behind all appearances is, and must ever be, unknown" (1862: 55). However, Spencer, in effect, turned Hamilton's criticism of Kant against Hamilton himself by arguing that there is an "inconsistency" in Hamilton's position (1862: 76). On the one hand, Hamilton's claim that the Absolute is not even conceivable as possible entails a radical "scepticism," since it means that "we cannot rationally affirm the positive existence of anything beyond phenomena" (1862: 71). On the other hand, Hamilton claims that through a "wonderful revelation," our very inability to conceive of a reality beyond appearances compels us nonetheless to *believe* in its existence (Spencer 1862: 71). For Spencer, however, Hamilton's attempt to ground religious faith in a "wonderful revelation" was not only hazy and dogmatic but also contradicted his earlier skeptical assertion that the Absolute is not even conceivable.

While Spencer agreed with Hamilton that the Absolute is unknowable, he argued that Hamilton makes a "grave error" in holding that the Absolute is *inconceivable* (1862: 71). According to Spencer, while we can never have "definite consciousness" of the Absolute, we *do* have an "indefinite" consciousness of it (1862: 71). Spencer's basic argument is that our very knowledge of relative and limited entities presupposes the existence of an unlimited Absolute at their basis. As he puts it, "It is impossible to conceive that our knowledge is a knowledge of Appearances only, without at the same time assuming a Reality of which they are appearances; for appearance without reality is unthinkable" (1862: 72). Hence, in contrast to Hamilton, Spencer argues that "we are obliged to form a positive though vague consciousness of this which transcends distinct consciousness" (1862: 72). Our consciousness of the Absolute is "vague," since we cannot know its nature or attributes, but we *can* nonetheless be sure that the Absolute exists. Spencer puts this point as follows: "In the very denial of our power to learn *what* the Absolute is, there lies hidden the assumption *that* it is . . . " (1862: 72).

Just three years later, in 1865, John Stuart Mill (1806–1873) published an influential book-length refutation of Hamilton's philosophy (Mill 1889). Like Spencer, Mill argued that Hamilton committed a flagrant self-contradiction by denying knowledge of unconditioned entities like God while claiming that we are nonetheless certain—via "belief" or "faith"—that these unknowable entities exist. Hamilton, Mill argues, is not "warranted in giving back under the name of Belief, the assurance or conviction respecting these objects which he refuses under the name of knowledge. My position is, that the Infinite and Absolute which Sir William Hamilton has been proving to be unknowable, being made up of contradictions, are as incapable of being believed as of being known . . . " (1889: 79). Mill proceeds to argue—on various grounds that I do not have the space to discuss here—that Hamilton's Law of the Conditioned "rests on no rational foundation" (1889: 110). One of Mill's primary objections is that Hamilton fails to prove that our knowledge of conditioned entities necessarily leads us to the thought of two inconceivable entities, one of which must be true. According to Mill, since Hamilton's Law of the Conditioned is not a convincing argument, Hamilton is not justified in moving from a plausible rational agnosticism about the existence of unconditioned entities like God to the much stronger, and flagrantly *implausible*, position that we "must" necessarily *believe* that these very inconceivable entities actually exist. As Mill puts it, "Not content with maintaining that things which from the natural and fundamental law of the human mind, are for ever inconceivable to us, may, for aught we know, be true, he [Hamilton] goes farther, and says, we know that many such things are true" (1889: 98). However, whereas Spencer attempted to furnish a stronger rational foundation for faith in an unknowable Absolute than he believed Hamilton was able to provide, Mill departed from both Hamilton and Spencer in arguing that the most rational conclusion to draw from the unknowability of the Absolute is that we should not believe in an Absolute at all.

In his *Three Essays on Religion* (1874), Mill clarified his own views on the question of whether it is rational to believe that God exists. He critically assessed various traditional arguments for God's existence and argues that all of them fail *except* the argument from design, which "has some force," though "its force is very generally overrated" (1874: 168). According to Mill, Darwin's theory of evolution through the "survival of the fittest," if true, "would greatly attenuate the evidence for" a Divine Creator, since it would account for the adjustment of part to part in the natural world in wholly naturalistic terms (1874: 174). However, Mill believed that no one had yet been able to prove that natural selection could explain *all* instances of apparent design in the natural world. Therefore, he concluded that "in the present state of our knowledge, the adaptations in Nature afford a large balance of probability in favour of creation by intelligence" (1874: 174).

Mill believed, then, that the argument from design makes it more probable than not that this world was created by a divine being. However, he also forcefully raised the problem of evil at several points in *Three Essays on Religion*. He argued that the tremendous amount of natural evil we find in the world—along with the fact that a given person's happiness and suffering are generally not proportionate to "that person's good or evil deeds" (1874: 38)—indicates that this world is "clumsily made and capriciously governed" (1874: 112). Hence, if this world was indeed created by God, God could not be both omnipotent and perfectly good (1874: 38). Rather, he argued that the undeniable imperfections of this world suggest that God, if good, must be "extremely limited" in power (1874: 40). Indeed, the very fact that God, assuming He did create the world, had to resort to various "means" in order to achieve His purposes in the world suggests that He has only "limited power," since an omnipotent God would have achieved His ends by sheer divine fiat (1874: 177).

To sum up this section, we can say that Kant's arguments for the unknowability of noumenal entities like God, along with his trenchant refutations of traditional arguments for God's existence, helped precipitate a crisis of religious belief in the nineteenth century. Since many of Kant's successors, like Hamilton and Spencer, were unconvinced by Kant's own moral justification of religious faith, they attempted to justify religious faith in other ways. However, Mill was not alone in thinking that none of these post-Kantian strategies for justifying belief in God were successful and that modern scientific theories like Darwin's theory of evolution directly undermined key elements of traditional religious doctrine.

3. *Vivekananda's Cosmopolitan Views on the Powers and Limits of Reason*

In the remainder of this chapter, I will argue that Vivekananda articulated and defended his views on the scope of reason and the rational basis of religious faith through a dialectical engagement with many of the Western and Indian thinkers discussed in the previous two sections. The following passage from *Rāja-Yoga* contains a very clear statement of his views on the scope of theological reason:

> The field of reason, or of the conscious workings of the mind, is narrow and limited. There is a little circle within which human reason must move. It cannot go beyond. Every attempt to go beyond is impossible, yet it is beyond this circle of reason that there lies all that humanity holds most dear. All these questions, whether there is an immortal soul, whether there is a God, whether there is any supreme intelligence guiding this universe or not, are beyond the field of reason. Reason can never answer these questions. What does reason say? It says, "I am agnostic; I do not know either yea or nay." (*CW* 1:181)

Vivekananda adopted a position of rational agnosticism with respect to the existence of supersensible entities like God and the soul. Reason, he argued, can neither prove nor disprove the existence of supersensible entities. With respect to the scope of theological reason, he sided with Vedānta and the Kantian tradition against the rational theology championed by Naiyāyikas and Western theologians like William Paley. At the same time, he developed original positions on the positive uses of reason and the rational basis of faith through a dialectical engagement with Śaṅkara, Kant, Hamilton, Spencer, and Mill.

On August 19, 1883, the twenty-year-old Vivekananda, who was studying philosophy at Scottish Church College, had an interesting conversation with Ramakrishna and Mahendranāth Gupta, the author of the *Kathāmṛta*:

> Narendra said to M. [Gupta] that he had been reading a book by Hamilton, who wrote: "A learned ignorance is the end of philosophy and the beginning of religion."
>
> MASTER [Ramakrishna] (to M.): "What does that mean?"
>
> Narendra explained the sentence in Bengali. The Master beamed with joy and said in English, "Thank you! Thank you!" (*K* 255 / *G* 278)

The young Vivekananda paraphrased Hamilton's statement in *Lectures on Metaphysics and Logic* (1859), which I quoted in the previous section. Vivekananda's approving reference to Hamilton makes clear that from his college days, he was drawn toward a broadly Kantian-Hamiltonian position on the limits of theological reason. It is not surprising that Ramakrishna endorsed Hamilton's statement, since it agrees with his own view that the finite human intellect can never comprehend God, just as a "one-seer pot" cannot hold ten seers of milk. Hamilton's striking phrase "learned ignorance" also signals one of the positive uses of reason that Vivekananda and Ramakrishna both supported: reason can be a great help in spiritual life if it humbly reflects on its own limitations and opens itself to possibilities *beyond* reason.

Vivekananda was, of course, well aware that Kant's *Critique of Pure Reason* is one of the most systematic and rigorous exercises in "learned ignorance" to be found in the Western philosophical tradition. In *Rāja-Yoga*, Vivekananda singles out for praise Kant's rational demonstration of the limits of reason while also noting where he parts ways with Kant:

> Kant has proved beyond all doubt that we cannot penetrate beyond the tremendous dead wall called reason. But that is the very first idea upon which all Indian thought takes its stand, and dares to seek, and succeeds in finding something higher than reason, where alone the explanation of the present state is to be found. (*CW* 1:199)

Vivekananda's stance toward Kant is dialectical. On the one hand, Vivekananda finds strong support for his own Vedāntic position of rational agnosticism in Kant's *Critique of Pure Reason*, which argues that in light of our cognitive limitations, we can never know, by means of reasoning, whether supersensible entities like God and the soul exist. On the other hand, Vivekananda criticizes Kant from a Vedāntic standpoint, arguing that Kant was unjustified in ruling out the possibility of supersensible knowledge of noumenal entities. Against Kant, he argues that there is a form of knowing that is "higher than reason."

We should recall from the previous section that Kant aimed to "deny *knowledge*" of God and the soul in order to "make room for *faith*"—a faith that he conceived as a "moral certainty" of the existence of God and an immortal soul (A829/B857). In a striking passage toward the end of the first *Critique* (*CPR*), Kant clarifies his view of moral faith as follows:

> In this way enough is left to us, even after the frustration of all the ambitious aims of reason that wanders about beyond the boundaries of all experience, that we have cause to be satisfied with it from a practical point of view. Of course, no one will be able to boast that he *knows* that there is a God and a future life; for if he knows that, then he is precisely the man I have long sought. (*CPR*, A829/B857; emphasis in original)

There is an autobiographical poignancy in Kant's passing remark that he has "long sought" someone who "*knows* that there is a God and a future life." He seems to be alluding here to his own early quest to find someone who had either rational knowledge of God (as Leibniz and Wolff had claimed) or supersensible knowledge of God (as the mystic Swedenborg had claimed). As we have seen, Kant—in spite of his early flirtation with rational theology and his fascination with Swedenborg—ultimately rejected the possibility of both rational and supersensible knowledge of noumenal entities. However, he did concede that Swedenborg and other mystics may have had *indirect* knowledge of a noumenal entity through the perception of something sensory that was caused by that noumenal entity.

The parallel between Kant and Vivekananda is striking. Like Kant, Vivekananda, as a youthful agnostic, embarked on a quest to find someone who had realized God, asking various renowned spiritual personages in Calcutta, "Have you seen God?" (*CW* 3:345–46). Unlike Kant, however, Vivekananda believed that his quest was fulfilled when he encountered Ramakrishna, who "dared to say that he saw God" (*CW* 4:179). Just as Kant critically examined Swedenborg's mystical claims (Maharaj 2017b), Vivekananda was careful not to accept Ramakrishna's claims until he had verified them to his satisfaction. As Vivekananda put it to his disciple Sister Nivedita, "Let none regret that they were difficult to convince! I fought my Master for six years with the result that I know every inch of the way! Every inch of the way!" (*CW* 9:411). From Vivekananda's standpoint, Kant might have ruled out the possibility of supersensible knowledge of God in part because he was unable to find, in his European milieu at the time, someone like Ramakrishna who not only claimed to know God directly but also explained the spiritual methods by which anyone could realize God for themselves. Moreover, Vivekananda countered Kant's dismissal of the possibility of supersensible knowledge with a philosophical argument for the epistemic value of supersensible perception (AEV), which we discussed at length in chapters 5 and 6. On the basis of AEV, Vivekananda contended, against Kant, that we are rationally justified in believing that some people have experienced God through direct supersensuous perception. From Vivekananda's perspective, the burden is on the Kantian to disprove this argument.

In a section of "Lessons on Rāja-Yoga" (1896) intriguingly titled "Metagnosticism," Vivekananda clarifies his dialectical stance toward the Kantian tradition:

> "Repent, for the Kingdom of Heaven is at hand." The word "repent" is in Greek "metanoeite" ("meta" means behind, after, beyond) and means literally "go beyond knowledge"—the knowledge of the (five) senses—"and look within where you will find the kingdom of heaven."
>
> Sir William Hamilton says at the end of a philosophical work, "Here philosophy ends, here religion begins." Religion is not, and never can be, in the field of intellect. Intellectual reasoning is based on facts evident to the senses. Now religion has nothing to do with the senses. The agnostics say they cannot know God, and rightly, for they have exhausted the limits of their senses and yet get no further in knowledge of God. Therefore in order to prove religion—that is, the existence of God, immortality, etc.—we have to go beyond the knowledge of the senses. All great prophets and seers claim to have "seen God," that is to say, they have had direct experience. . . . Our business is to verify, not to swallow. (*CW* 6:132–33)

This passage begins with a highly original Vedāntic interpretation of Jesus's teaching in Matthew 3:2, "Repent, for the Kingdom of Heaven is at hand." Noting that the original Greek word for "repent" in this Biblical passage is "metanoeite," Vivekananda interprets Christ's teaching to mean: Go beyond sense-knowledge and realize God (the "Kingdom of Heaven") within your own soul. Interestingly, he then paraphrases Hamilton's statement about "learned ignorance," which he had quoted to Ramakrishna over a decade earlier: "Here philosophy ends, here religion begins." Vivekananda marshals Hamilton in support of the Vedāntic view that religion "is not, and never can be, in the field of the intellect." However, we should recall from the previous section that Hamilton's understanding of "religion" differed radically from Vivekananda's. Hamilton attempted to justify faith in God by arguing that even though God is unknowable and inconceivable, the "Law of the Conditioned" entails the necessary *belief* that God exists. Vivekananda seems to have Kant, Hamilton, and Spencer in mind when he remarks, "The agnostics say they cannot know God, and rightly, for they have exhausted the limits of their senses and yet get no further in knowledge of God." While Vivekananda agrees with Hamilton's rational agnosticism, he rejects his Kantian assumption that God is unknowable. From Vivekananda's Vedāntic perspective, Western thinkers like Kant, Hamilton, and Spencer are unjustified in dismissing the possibility of attaining supersensible knowledge of God through "direct experience." The final sentence in this passage—"Our business is to verify, not to swallow"—seems to be an implicit critique of the various (less than convincing) attempts made by Kant, Hamilton, and Spencer to justify faith in an unknowable God. For Vivekananda, faith that is not ultimately validated by one's own direct experiential knowledge remains empty and dogmatic. Hence, one must transcend sense-knowledge in order to move beyond the impasse of rational agnosticism. As I will discuss in detail in the next chapter, while he accepts the Kantian view that rational agnosticism clears a space for faith in God, he parts ways with Kantian agnostics in arguing that this faith must be verified ultimately through supersensible knowledge of God.

In an interesting passage from notes taken in Madras from 1892–1893, Vivekananda faults Herbert Spencer and other "Western philosophers" for failing to go beyond rational agnosticism:

> What is Spencer's unknowable? It is our Māyā. Western philosophers are afraid of the unknowable, but our philosophers have taken a big jump into the unknown, and they have conquered. (*CW* 6:104)

From Vivekananda's Vedāntic perspective, Western agnostics like Spencer confuse *māyā* with God. *Māyā*, the principle through which the One appears as many and the Divine appears to be undivine, *is* unknowable in the sense of being rationally inexplicable (*anirvacanīya*). By contrast, the ultimate reality—God or Brahman—is knowable through supersensuous perception. Vedānta, Vivekananda argues, *begins* with the rational agnosticism endorsed by Western philosophers like Kant, Hamilton, and Spencer but takes a decisive step beyond these thinkers by showing how to attain direct supersensuous knowledge of God. Interestingly, Spencer himself noted, in an 1899 postscript to his *First Principles* (1862), that his doctrine of the unknowability of ultimate reality had been criticized by several scholars:

> Several opponents have contended that it is illegitimate to assert of the Ultimate Reality lying behind Appearance, that it is unknown and *unknowable*. The statement that it is *unknowable* is said to assume knowledge greater than we

> can have: alike as putting an arbitrary limit to possible human faculty, and as asserting something concerning that of which we are said to know nothing: a contradiction. (1862: 103; emphasis in original)

Spencer's "opponents"—whom he unfortunately does not name—argue that he commits a self-contradiction by claiming to *know* that the ultimate reality is *un*knowable. Since Spencer himself insists that we can know nothing at all about ultimate reality, he should, by the logic of his own argument, remain strictly agnostic about whether or not the ultimate reality is knowable. Vivekananda can be seen as mounting a similar objection to Spencer from a Vedāntic standpoint: the fact that the ultimate reality cannot be known through reason does not justify Spencer, Kant, or Hamilton in ruling out the possibility of knowing the ultimate reality through *suprarational* spiritual experience.

Vivekananda further developed his views on faith and reason in critical dialogue with Śaṅkara. In an 1889 letter to the Advaita Vedānta pandit Pramadadās Mitra, Vivekananda asked a challenging question about Śaṅkara's understanding of the authority of the Vedas:

> Why does the *Vedāntasūtra* [i.e., *Brahmasūtra*] not provide any proof of the authority (*pramāṇa*) of the Vedas? At the very beginning [of the *Brahmasūtra*], it is said that the authoritative proof of the existence of God is the Vedas (*īśvarer pramāṇa veda*) and that the authority of the Vedas (*veda prāmāṇya*) is said to derive from the fact that the Vedas are "the breath of God" (*puruṣa-niḥśvasitam*). Is this not what in Western logic is called "argument in a circle"? (*BCW* 6:230 / *CW* 6:212; translation modified)[14]

Vivekananda's question concerns Śaṅkara's commentary on *Brahmasūtra* 1.1.3 ("*śāstrayonitvāt*"). According to Śaṅkara, this *sūtra* can be interpreted in two equally viable ways. On the one hand, the *sūtra* means that Brahman is the "*yoni*" of the Vedas in the sense of being their efficient and material cause (*BSBh* 1.1.3, p. 9). Śaṅkara goes on to quote a statement from Bṛhadāraṇyaka Upaniṣad 2.4.10 in support of this interpretation: "Those that are called the Ṛg-Veda, [Yajur-Veda, etc.] are but the exhalation of this Great Being" (*asya mahato bhūtasya niḥśvasitam etad ṛgvedaḥ*) (*BSBh* 1.1.3, p. 10). When Vivekananda refers to the Vedas as "the breath of God," he clearly has in mind Śaṅkara's appeal to this scriptural verse. On the other hand, Śaṅkara claims that 1.1.3 also means, conversely, that the Vedas are the "*yoni*" of Brahman in the sense of being the "authoritative

[14] *vedāntasūtre veder kono pramāṇ keno dewā hoy nāi? prathamei balā hoyyāche, īśvarer pramāṇ ved ebong ved prāmāṇya "puruṣa-niḥśvasitam" boliyā; ihā ki pāścāṭya nyāye jāhāke* argument in a circle *bale, sei doṣduṣṭa nahe?*

means of knowing the real nature of Brahman" (*BSBh* 1.1.3, p. 10).[15] Vivekananda has in mind this latter interpretation of *sūtra* 1.1.3 when he refers to the Vedas as the "authoritative proof of the existence of God."

Vivekananda's concern is that *Brahmasūtra* 1.1.3, on either interpretation, fails to provide a convincing "proof of the authority" (*pramāṇa*) of the Vedas. If the *sūtra* means that the Vedas derive their authority from their source in Brahman, then we would have to ask, in turn, for proof that Brahman exists. Śaṅkara, Vivekananda claims, ends up arguing in a circle by claiming that the Vedas are the authoritative means of knowing (*pramāṇa*) the true nature of Brahman while also claiming that the authority of the Vedas derives from the fact that they originated from Brahman. Accordingly, as I argued in chapter 5, Vivekananda sides with Ramakrishna *against* Śaṅkara in arguing that the Vedas are records of the spiritual experiences of enlightened sages and, hence, depend for their validity on supersensuous perception. As Vivekananda puts it, "The proof . . . of the Vedas is just the same as the proof of this table before me, Pratyakṣa, direct perception" (*CW* 3:253). Hence, unlike Śaṅkara, Vivekananda holds that the Vedas derive their authority from supersensuous perception.

Vivekananda's overall stance toward Śaṅkara, then, is complex. He concurs with Śaṅkara that since Brahman can never be known through reasoning, we should have faith in the Upaniṣads, which teach us the true nature of Brahman. However, Vivekananda departs from Śaṅkara in arguing that the authority of the Upaniṣads and other scriptures depends ultimately on spiritual experience. He follows Ramakrishna in holding that our initial faith in scripture should lead us to engage in spiritual practice with the aim of verifying the scriptures ourselves by directly perceiving God.

4. *Vivekananda on Arguments for God's Existence*

Vivekananda, as we have seen, unambiguously endorsed rational agnosticism, the view that reason can neither prove nor disprove the existence of God or the soul. In light of his rational agnosticism, we might be surprised that he frequently defended one particular argument for God's existence. He made this argument, for instance, in his 1895 lecture "Steps to Realization":

> What is the proof of God? Direct perception, *pratyakṣa*. The proof of this wall is that I perceive it. God has been perceived that way by thousands before, and

[15] *athavā yathoktam ṛgvedādiśāstraṃ yoniḥ kāraṇaṃ pramāṇam asya brahmaṇo yathāvat svarūpādhigame.*

> will be perceived by all who want to perceive Him. But this perception is no sense-perception at all; it is supersensuous, superconscious. . . . (*CW* 1:415)

In chapter 5, I reconstructed from such passages Vivekananda's argument for the epistemic value of supersensuous perception (AEV), which concludes that "there is knowledge beyond the senses" (*CW* 1:205). In the passage just quoted, he turns AEV into an argument for God's existence by adding a second conclusion that follows directly from the previous one: a veridical supersensuous perception of God constitutes direct "proof" of God's existence. Contemporary philosophers of religion have defended a very similar "argument from religious experience" (hereafter ARE), which establishes God's existence on the basis of mystical testimony.[16] Since a veridical experience of *F* entails the existence of *F*, if we are justified in believing that certain mystics have had veridical experiences of an ultimate reality, then we are also justified in believing that an ultimate reality exists. For Vivekananda, ARE is the best possible rational argument for God's existence.

At the same time, he maintains, as a rational agnostic, that even ARE is not conclusive, though it does have significant rational force. In the following passage from his lecture "My Master" (1896), he clarifies his stance on the rational force of arguments for God's existence in general:

> There is but one solution of life, says the Hindu, and that solution is what they call God and religion. . . . That is our idea, but no amount of reasoning can demonstrate it; it can only make it probable, and there it rests. The highest demonstration of reasoning that we have in any branch of knowledge can only make a fact probable, and nothing further. . . . Facts have to be perceived, and we have to perceive religion to demonstrate it to ourselves. We have to sense God to be convinced that there is a God. We must sense the facts of religion to know that they are facts. Nothing else, and no amount of reasoning, but our own perception can make these things real to us, can make my belief firm as a rock. (*CW* 4:167)

He makes a key distinction here between probabilification and demonstration. Rational arguments, at best, can make "probable" God's existence, but they can never conclusively "demonstrate" God's existence. He employs the term "demonstration" in the sense of conclusive, incontrovertible knowledge. As a Kantian-Vedāntic rational agnostic, he denies the possibility of rationally demonstrating God's existence in this strong sense. Rather, he insists that conclusive, unshakeable knowledge of God can come only from "our own perception," by which he means the supersensuous perception of God. Nonetheless, he argues that ARE

[16] See, for instance, Swinburne (2004: 293–326), Gellman (1997), and Kwan (2006).

provides a sufficient rational basis for *faith* in God's existence, on the basis of which we should engage earnestly in spiritual practice with the aim of directly perceiving God for ourselves, thereby finally securing the conclusive proof of God's existence that no rational argument could ever provide.

While Vivekananda considers ARE to be the single strongest argument for God's existence, he also believes that the traditional argument from design has some, albeit very limited, rational force. He refers to the design argument in several of his lectures, and his stance toward it is somewhat ambivalent. In his lecture "The Cosmos: The Macrocosm" (1896), which I will discuss in more detail in chapter 10 in the context of his views on consciousness, Vivekananda remarks: "What is the most evolved notion that man has of this universe? It is intelligence, the adjustment of part to part, the display of intelligence, of which the ancient design theory was an attempt at expression" (*CW* 2:209). He does not present the design argument in all its details, since he assumed that his Western audience was familiar with it. Vivekananda's language of "adjustment of part to part" suggests that he likely had in mind William Paley's famous 1802 argument from design. Paley's argument runs as follows. When we inspect a watch, we find that "its several parts are framed and put together for a purpose, e.g. that they are so formed and adjusted as to produce motion, and that motion so regulated as to point out the hour of the day" (Paley 1802: 2). This adjustment of part to part in the watch makes it reasonable to infer that "the watch must have had a maker" (Paley 1802: 3). The natural world as a whole resembles the watch in its adjustment of part to part, though on a much vaster scale and with much greater complexity. Therefore, it is reasonable to infer that the natural world was designed by a great and powerful divine intelligence.

Vivekananda's apparently uncritical acceptance of the design argument here is somewhat misleading, since in other lectures, his stance toward the design argument is much more ambivalent and critical. The following passage from his lecture on "Vedic Religious Ideals" (1896) provides the clearest and most detailed account of his subtle stance toward the design argument:

> In short, out of the external world we can only get the idea of an architect, that which is called the Design Theory. It is not a very logical argument, as we all know; there is something childish about it, yet it is the only little bit of anything we can know about God from the external world, that this world required a builder. But this is no explanation of the universe. The materials of this world were before Him, and this God wanted all these materials, and the worst objection is that He must be limited by the materials. The builder could not have made a house without the materials of which it is composed. Therefore he was limited by the materials; he could only do what the materials enabled him to. Therefore the God that the Design Theory gives is at best only an architect, and

> a limited architect of the universe; He is bound and restricted by the materials; He is not independent at all. (*CW* 1:353)

Vivekananda sides with Śaṅkara and Ramakrishna against Nyāya in holding that while the argument from design cannot, on its own, prove the existence of God, the argument nonetheless does have some value. This passage also suggests that Vivekananda's views on the design argument were partly shaped by Kant, Mill, and Darwin. As I mentioned in section 2, Kant refutes the design argument while also conceding that it deserves "respect" (*CPR*, A623/B651) and that it "could at most establish a highest architect of the world, who would always be limited by the suitability of the material on which he works . . . " (A627/B655). Vivekananda echoes Kant almost verbatim when he suggests that the design argument establishes "at best" only a "limited architect of the universe" who is "bound and restricted by the materials." Like Kant, Vivekananda believes that the design argument at best makes probable the existence of a cosmic architect but not of the omnipotent God of theism.

Vivekananda also seems to have been influenced by Mill's discussion of the design argument, which I summarized in section 2. According to Mill, the argument from design "has some force" (1874: 168), even though Darwin's evolutionary theory does "attenuate" its force to some extent (1874: 174). Bankimchandra Chatterjee, in his influential essay "Mill, Darwin and Hinduism" (1875), went even further than Mill in arguing that Darwinian theory had completely undermined the design argument. As he put it, "Darwin has shown that this skilful construction [of the world] happens of itself" (B. Chatterjee 1986: 60). That Vivekananda was aware of these discussions of the anti-theological implications of Darwinian theory is clear from this remark in his 1895 lecture "Introduction to Jñāna-Yoga":

> At the beginning of the nineteenth century man tried to find God through reason, and Deism was the result. What little was left of God by this process was destroyed by Darwinism and Millism. (*CW* 6:41)

Vivekananda provides here a brief, high-altitude narrative of the fate of rational theology in the nineteenth-century Western world. The first sentence may be an allusion to Paley's famous 1802 argument from design. As we have seen, Vivekananda followed Kant and Mill in taking the design argument to make probable, at best, the existence of a limited divine architect. This seems to be what he has in mind when he refers to "Deism," the doctrine that a powerful divine being created the world but otherwise has nothing to do with it. However, Vivekananda's second sentence indicates that even the existence of a deistic God was jeopardized by "Darwinism and Millism." This remark reflects his awareness of Mill's, and perhaps even Bankim's, discussion of the implications of Darwinian evolution for the design argument. However, if we place this statement alongside Vivekananda's other, more positive statements about the design argument, I think we can say that Vivekananda's overall stance toward the design argument comes closer to Mill than to Bankim: Darwinian evolutionary theory has significantly undermined, but not completely destroyed, the rational force of the design argument.

5. *Vivekananda's Rational Response to the Problem of Evil*

As I have already noted, Vivekananda follows both Śaṅkara and Ramakrishna in holding that one valuable use of reason is to refute attempts to *disprove* God's existence. One of the most popular and formidable arguments against God's existence is the argument from evil: the sheer amount of evil and suffering in this world is incompatible with the existence of an omnipotent and perfectly good God. Both Śaṅkara and Ramakrishna, in spite of their insistence on the inherent limitations of the rational intellect, explicitly addressed this problem of evil and made use of various rational arguments in order to reconcile the existence of so much evil in the world with the existence of an omnipotent and morally perfect God (Maharaj 2018: 241–79).

Ramakrishna's theodicy, as I discussed at length in chapter 7 of *Infinite Paths to Infinite Reality*, has two key dimensions: a "saint-making" teleological framework and a panentheistic metaphysics. Ramakrishna claims that God permits evil in the world "in order to create saints" (*K* 37 / *G* 97). It is through the experience of good and evil, both in the world and in ourselves, that we gradually learn to combat our own evil tendencies—such as "anger, lust, and greed"—and to cultivate ethical and spiritual virtues that are necessary to realize God (*K* 37 / *G* 97). Crucial to Ramakrishna's saint-making theodicy are the three interrelated doctrines of *karma*, rebirth, and universal salvation. Each of us experiences happiness and suffering in this life in accordance with our own *karma*, which is the cumulative result of our own past behavior, earlier in this life and in our past lives. Moreover, Ramakrishna maintains that everyone, without exception, will eventually attain salvation, either in this life or in a future life (*K* 38 / *G* 98). He thereby parts ways with many theistic traditions that hold that some souls are bound for eternal damnation.

However, Ramakrishna ultimately appeals to a panentheistic metaphysics in response to a natural question raised by his saint-making theodicy: why would a loving God design this world as an arena for attaining saintliness in the first place if She knew that it would entail untold suffering for Her creatures?[17] Ramakrishna responds to this doubt by affirming, on the basis of his own spiritual experience of *vijñāna*, that "God Herself has become everything—the universe and its living beings" (*K* 878 / *G*, 818). From Ramakrishna's panentheistic standpoint of *vijñāna*, since God Herself has become everyone, including both the victims of suffering and the inflicters of suffering, the problem of evil—which presupposes a *difference* between God and Her suffering creatures—no longer arises.

Vivekananda, I would suggest, adopts Ramakrishna's two-pronged strategy for responding to the problem of evil. It is beyond the scope of this chapter to provide a detailed and comprehensive reconstruction of Vivekananda's theodicy. For present purposes, I will very briefly outline the saint-making teleology and panentheistic metaphysics at the heart of his theodicy. Echoing Ramakrishna, Vivekananda claims, in several places, that God created this world as a "gymnasium" for saint-making:

> It [this world] is a great gymnasium in which you and I, and millions of souls must come and get exercises, and make ourselves strong and perfect. This is what it is for. Not that God could not make a perfect universe; not that He could not help the misery of the world. (*CW* 4:207)[18]

According to Vivekananda, even though the omnipotent God could have created a world without any suffering, He chose to make this world a moral "gymnasium" in which we grow spiritually through encountering both good and evil, until we eventually attain spiritual perfection.

Interestingly, in his lecture "Steps of Hindu Philosophic Thought," Vivekananda claims that the problem of evil arises only for "dualists" who believe that God is different from His creatures (*CW* 1:397). From this dualistic standpoint, he responds to the problem of evil by arguing, in accordance with traditional Vedāntins as well as Ramakrishna, that this cosmic "gymnasium" is governed by the law of *karma* and rebirth:

> Then the question comes: If God is the ruler of this universe, why did He create such a wicked universe, why must we suffer so much? They [the dualists] say, it is not God's fault. It is our fault that we suffer. Whatever we sow we reap. He did not do anything to punish us. Man is born poor, or blind, or some other way. What is the reason? He had done something before, he was born that way. (*CW* 1:397)

[17] For a detailed discussion of Ramakrishna's theodicy, see Maharaj (2018: 268–73).
[18] He makes a very similar statement in *Karma-Yoga*: "The world is a grand moral gymnasium wherein we have all to take exercise so as to become stronger and stronger spiritually" (*CW* 1:80).

For Vivekananda, so long as we feel that we are *different* from God, we will naturally ask why a loving God permits us to suffer as much as we do. His answer is that we suffer because of our own past deeds, both in this life and in our past lives. Hence, *we* are responsible for our suffering, not God.[19] Nonetheless, Vivekananda repeatedly emphasizes that it is precisely through our varied experiences of both happiness and misery that we grow spiritually and inch our way closer to salvation.

Vivekananda was almost certainly aware of Mill's discussion of the problem of evil in *Three Essays on Religion* (1874). As we saw in section 2, Mill argues that the sheer extent of natural evil in the world—combined with the fact that a person's happiness and suffering are generally not proportionate to "that person's good or evil deeds" (1874: 38)—suggests that this world is "clumsily made and capriciously governed" (1874: 112) and, hence, could not have been created by an omnipotent God. Vivekananda's theodical appeal to the Vedāntic doctrines of *karma* and rebirth can be seen as a direct response to Mill's challenge. From Vivekananda's perspective, Mill is led to assume that our happiness and suffering are not proportioned to our "good or evil deeds," because he fails to accept rebirth and, hence, only considers our past deeds in *this* life. However, according to the universal law of *karma*, a person's happiness and suffering in this life are a result of that person's past behavior, *both* in this life *and* in previous lives. Moreover, Vivekananda's overall theodicy seeks to show, against Mill, that an omnipotent God permits all the evil we see in the world in order to help us evolve spiritually and attain salvation.

Vivekananda also follows Ramakrishna in accepting the doctrine of universal salvation and emphasizing its theodical implications. As he puts it, "every soul must eventually come to salvation" (*CW* 2:242). He continues: "No one will be left out. Through various vicissitudes, through various sufferings and enjoyments, each one of them will come out in the end" (*CW* 2:242). In sum, then, Vivekananda initially responds to the problem of evil raised by "dualists" by meeting them on their own terms: presupposing a difference between God and His creatures, he argues that this suffering-filled world is a grand gymnasium—governed by the law of *karma*—in which we all evolve spiritually through the course of many lives until we finally attain salvation.[20]

However, Vivekananda argues that the problem of evil can be fully resolved—or *dissolved*—only by ascending from a dualist to a nondualist standpoint. As

[19] It may seem here as if Vivekananda's appeal to the doctrines of *karma* and rebirth is dogmatic, but he presents various rational arguments in support of these doctrines elsewhere, especially in his 1895 article "Reincarnation" (*CW* 4:257–71) and his 1896 lecture "The Cosmos: The Microcosm" (*CW* 2:216–25). I discuss Vivekananda's arguments for rebirth in detail in Medhananda (forthcoming-b).

[20] Long (2016) emphasizes this aspect of Vivekananda's theodicy.

he puts it, "the non-dualists say that it is God Himself who has become this universe" (*CW* 1:402). Notice how closely Vivekananda echoes Ramakrishna's teaching that *vijñānīs* "realize that Brahman has become all this—the *jīvas* [individual souls], the *jagat* [universe], and the twenty-four cosmic principles" (*K* 479 / *G* 477). Indeed, as I have argued at length in the first three chapters of this book, Vivekananda reconceptualizes Advaita Vedānta in accordance with Ramakrishna's expansive and world-affirming philosophy of Vijñāna Vedānta. Like Ramakrishna, Vivekananda makes the striking claim that from the nondualistic standpoint, the problem of evil does not even arise, since there is nothing, and no one, *apart* from God. From the standpoint of Vivekananda's Integral Advaita, "There is no good, and there is no evil. God is all there is" (*CW* 6:53). Since the problem of evil raises the question of why God permits Her creatures to suffer, Vivekananda, as an Integral Advaitin, ultimately rejects the very terms of the question, insisting that there *are* no creatures separate from God for whom the problem of evil can even arise. Rather, God alone is playing in the form of everything and everyone in the universe: "[But] who cares for good and evil? Play! God Almighty plays. That is all. . . . You are the almighty God playing" (*CW* 2:470).

While Vivekananda maintains that the truth of Integral Advaita can be conclusively verified only through direct spiritual experience, he also provides rational arguments in support of the reasonableness of a nondualist metaphysics. In chapter 10, I will discuss in detail his argument for panentheistic cosmopsychism, the view that everything is Divine Consciousness, an argument based on the Sāṃkhyan doctrine that the effect pre-exists in its material cause as well as two sub-arguments: the argument for the epistemic value of supersensuous perception (discussed in chapter 5) and the argument from design.

Of course, much more can be said about Vivekananda's response to the problem of evil, but I hope I have done enough in this section to show that in spite of his insistence on the limitations of reason, he made copious use of rational arguments in order to respond to the problem of evil raised by thinkers like John Stuart Mill in the West and by the Buddhists in India.

To sum up this chapter, Vivekananda defended a nuanced position on the powers and limits of theological reason by integrating Kantian rational agnosticism within a Vedāntic framework shaped primarily by Ramakrishna and, to a lesser extent, by Śaṅkara. While Vivekananda denied the possibility of conclusively proving either that God exists or does not exist, he nonetheless highlighted four positive uses of reason. First, as his approving reference to Hamilton's statement about "learned ignorance" makes clear, Vivekananda believed that a self-critical reason is valuable insofar as it humbly admits its own constitutive limitations. Second, he held that certain arguments for God's existence—especially the argument from religious experience, but also, secondarily, the argument from design—make probable the existence of God. In particular, the argument from religious experience makes it reasonable to believe that God exists on the basis of the testimony of credible mystics who claim to have perceived God. For Vivekananda, this argument furnishes a rational basis for religious faith, which we should strive to strengthen and deepen through intensive spiritual practice culminating in the direct self-authenticating experience of God. Third, Vivekananda himself frequently made use of rational argumentation in order to refute arguments *against* God's existence—especially the argument from evil defended by Mill and others. Fourth, he claimed that reason is a valuable tool for distinguishing genuine spiritual experience from its counterfeits. As he puts it, "There is knowledge beyond the senses, and whenever it does not contradict reason and past human experience, that knowledge is proof" (*CW* 1:205). Accordingly, Vivekananda maintained that religious truths and experiences are "*above* reason" but do not *contradict* reason (*CW* 7:60; emphasis added). Equipped with an understanding of his views on the scope of reason and the rational basis of religious faith, we can now proceed to examine, in the next chapter, his innovative account of the nature and dynamics of faith itself.

8

The Will to Realize

Vivekananda's Doxastic Involuntarism and His Three-Rung Ladder of Religious Faith

Most persons are unconscious atheists who self-complacently think that they are devout believers.

—Swami Vivekananda (1894; *CW* 8:203)

In the previous chapter, we found that while Vivekananda denies the possibility of conclusively proving either the existence or the non-existence of God through rational arguments, he contends that the argument from religious experience nonetheless provides a secure rational foundation for religious faith: it is reasonable to believe that God exists on the basis of the testimony of credible mystics who claim to have experienced God.

However, as we will see in this chapter, he does not simply conceive religious faith as the rationally justified belief that God exists. My aim in this chapter is to reconstruct Vivekananda's nuanced and original views on religious faith, situating them in their historical context and demonstrating their relevance to contemporary debates in philosophy of religion and epistemology. Section 1 summarizes some of the most prominent late nineteenth-century views on religious belief and faith, ranging from the evidentialist positions of W. K. Clifford and T. H. Huxley to the anti-evidentialist fideism of William James. With this historical background in place, section 2 discusses Vivekananda's unique intervention in these late nineteenth-century debates about faith and reason. Vivekananda, who was familiar with Huxley's work and had extended discussions with James at Harvard in the 1890s, steered a middle course between Huxley and James by defending what I call an "expanded evidentalism." Religious faith is justified on evidentialist grounds, Vivekananda argues, because mystical experience and mystical testimony are valid sources of evidence that support the rationality of religious belief.

In sections 3 through 5, I argue that Vivekananda's various remarks about religious faith hint at a dynamic understanding of religious faith as consisting of three main stages: (1) faith as sub-doxastic intellectual assent (section 3), (2) faith

Swami Vivekananda's Vedāntic Cosmopolitanism. Swami Medhananda, Oxford University Press. © Oxford University Press 2022. DOI: 10.1093/oso/9780197624463.003.0009

as belief (section 4), (3) faith as self-authenticating realization (section 5). For Vivekananda, sincere spiritual aspirants at the first stage of faith do not yet *believe* that God exists but "assent" intellectually to God's existence and earnestly strive to acquire full-blown belief by engaging in ethical and spiritual disciplines that gradually remove the mental impurities that have accumulated in the course of many lives. Once they have attained a sufficiently high level of purity, the belief that God exists spontaneously arises in their hearts. In the context of this second stage of doxastic faith, I discuss Vivekananda's doxastic involuntarism, the view that we cannot simply adopt a belief at will. However, according to Vivekananda, the journey of faith culminates not in belief but in realization, the direct supersensuous perception of God which removes all doubts. Finally, section 6 brings Vivekananda into critical dialogue with the recent philosopher of religion William Alston, who was one of the first Western philosophers to distinguish doxastic and non-doxastic forms of religious faith.

1. *Evidentialism versus the Will to Believe: Clifford, Huxley, and James*

In 1877, the Cambridge mathematician and philosopher William Kingdon Clifford (1845–1879) published his article "The Ethics of Belief" (Clifford 1879: 177–211), which sparked heated debate in the late nineteenth century about the rationality of religious belief. In this article, Clifford defended a very stringent form of evidentialism: "it is wrong always, everywhere, and for anyone, to believe anything upon insufficient evidence" (1879: 186). On the basis of this principle, he argues that mystics and saints are never justified in forming beliefs about God on the basis of their spiritual experiences. Taking Mohammed as an example, Clifford contends that he was wrong in believing that he had a mystical "vision" of the angel Gabriel:

> What means could he [Mohammed] have of knowing that the form which appeared to him to be the angel Gabriel was not a hallucination . . . ? . . . [H]ow could he know that this strong conviction was not a mistake? (1879: 191)

According to Clifford, mystics like Mohammed are not justified in forming beliefs on the basis of their spiritual experiences because they have no way of knowing whether their experiences are veridical. However, numerous philosophers have pointed out that Clifford's evidentialist principle is far too stringent to be plausible, since it would disallow many necessary everyday beliefs, including our belief in the reality of objects in the external world.[1] After all, what non-circular

[1] For this objection, see Amesbury (2008: 28), Van Inwagen (1996), and Madigan (2009: 85–164).

evidence could I possibly offer that would justify my belief that the table in front of me is not a "hallucination"? Nonetheless, philosophers sympathetic to Clifford's evidentialist approach to belief have continued to defend less stringent forms of his evidentialist principle (Feldman 2000; Aikin 2014).

The British biologist Thomas Henry Huxley (1825–1895), a close friend of Clifford's, was well aware of his friend's provocative essay and even defended it against his critics (Byun 2017: 135–55). Nonetheless, in his own work, Huxley tended to defend a somewhat less stringent form of evidentialism.[2] Huxley coined the term "agnosticism" in 1869 and wrote several essays in 1889 explaining how he understood the term. He himself noted that Hamilton's and Spencer's Kantian views on the limits of reason played a major role in shaping his own agnostic position, though he was quick to add that he emphatically rejected their positive efforts to justify "faith" in an unknowable Absolute (Huxley [1889] 1894a: 227). Regarding the positive side of Hamilton's and Spencer's projects, Huxley wrote in an 1863 letter, "I laugh at their beards as soon as they try to spin their own cobwebs" (quoted in Byun 2017: 124n324). He provided a clear formulation of his agnostic principle in his essay "Agnosticism" (1889):

> Positively the principle may be expressed: In matters of the intellect, follow your reason as far as it will take you, without regard to any other consideration. And negatively: In matters of the intellect do not pretend that conclusions are certain which are not demonstrated or demonstrable. That I take to be the agnostic faith. . . . (Huxley [1889] 1894a: 246)

Huxley's agnostic principle, as formulated here, is considerably weaker than Clifford's evidentialist principle, since Huxley is concerned not with the ethics of *belief* but with the ethics of claims to *certainty* or *knowledge* (Van Harvey 2013; Byun 2017). According to Huxley's evidentialist principle, we should not claim to be "certain" of anything that has not been "demonstrated" or that is not "demonstrable." In other places, however, Huxley muddies the waters by endorsing a more stringent form of evidentialism that comes much closer to Clifford's principle. For instance, in an 1884 essay, Huxley writes: "It [agnosticism] simply means that a man shall not say he knows or believes that which he has no scientific grounds for professing to know or believe" (quoted in Byun 2017: 126–27). This formulation of the agnostic principle encompasses *both* knowledge and belief. Notice also that he specifies here that we must justify our beliefs with "scientific" evidence.

[2] For detailed discussion of Huxley's evidentialist principle, see Van Harvey (2013) and Byun (2017).

In fact, Huxley devotes a great deal of energy to explaining what counts as "scientific" evidence (Byun 2017: 74–119). The most reliable evidence, he claims, is that based on direct sensory observation, though when such observational evidence is unavailable—as, for instance, in the case of past events—he also admits the validity of "testimonial evidence" and "circumstantial evidence" (Huxley [1876] 1896: 56). Significantly, his narrow understanding of "scientific" evidence leads him to follow Clifford in dismissing mystical experience as an invalid source of belief or knowledge. In "The Value of Witness to the Miraculous" (1889), Huxley specifically targets the mystical testimony of the British Quaker mystic George Fox (1624–1691):

> It needs no long study of Fox's writings, however, to arrive at the conviction that the distinction between subjective and objective verities had not the same place in his mind as it has in that of an ordinary mortal. When an ordinary person would say "I thought so and so," or "I made up my mind to do so and so," George Fox says, "It was opened to me," or "at the command of God I did so and so.". . . Fox hears voices and he sees visions. . . . But this modern reproduction of the ancient prophet, with his "Thus saith the Lord," "This is the work of the Lord," steeped in supernaturalism and glorying in blind faith, is the mental antipodes of the philosopher, founded in naturalism and a fanatic for evidence, to whom these affirmations inevitably suggest the previous question: "How do you know that the Lord saith it?" "How do you know that the Lord doeth it?" and who is compelled to demand that rational ground for belief, without which, to the man of science, assent is merely an immoral pretence. And it is this rational ground of belief which the writers of the Gospels, no less than Paul, and Eginhard, and Fox, so little dream of offering that they would regard the demand for it as a kind of blasphemy. ([1889] 1894b: 189–91)

Huxley accuses Fox and other religious believers and mystics of "blind faith" since they fail to provide a "rational ground" for their belief in the form of "evidence." Of course, Huxley was aware that Fox took his mystical experiences as evidence for his beliefs about God. However, Huxley argues that Fox's mystical experiences were merely "subjective" experiences that Fox unjustifiably *took* to be "objective" ones. Like Clifford, Huxley claims that mystics like Fox have no way of knowing that their spiritual experiences are veridical. Notice also that Huxley contrasts the "supernaturalism" and "blind faith" of Fox with the "naturalism" of the "philosopher" and the "man of science." It becomes clear here that Huxley's commitment to scientific naturalism is at the root of his dismissal of the possibility of supersensuous knowledge.

The Harvard philosopher and psychologist William James (1842–1910), in his now classic essay "The Will to Believe" (1896), defended the legitimacy of religious faith in explicit opposition to the evidentialist arguments of Huxley and "that delicious *enfant terrible* Clifford" (1897: 8).[3] As James puts it, his essay is a "justification of faith, a defence of our right to adopt a believing attitude in religious matters, in spite of the fact that our merely logical intellect may not have been coerced" (1897: 1–2). His broadly Pascalian argument is as follows. The religious option, he argues, is "a genuine option that cannot by its nature be decided on intellectual grounds" (1897: 11). For James, there are no conclusive rational arguments proving either the truth or the falsity of religion. Moreover, he specifies that an option is "genuine" if it is "forced," "momentous," and "living" (1897: 3)—which means, as G. L. Doore succinctly explains, that "it is an unavoidable decision that one finds to be of great personal significance, and where the doctrines in question are not impossible for one to come to believe" (1983: 354). According to James, since the religious option is a "genuine" one in this technical sense, we are justified in having religious faith based not on sufficient evidence but on the *hope* that religion is true, since the stakes are infinitely high, and if we do not believe, we lose the possibility of attaining the infinite good that religion promises. There are numerous complexities in, and interpretive controversies surrounding, James's justification of faith in "The Will to Believe,"[4] but this brief summary will suffice for the purpose of contextualizing Vivekananda's views.

Scholars discussing James's views on faith have focused almost exclusively on "The Will to Believe," even though he continued to write on faith in his later work. In fact, I will make the case that his justification of religious faith evolved in certain respects from "The Will to Believe" to his two later essays, "Reason and Faith" (written in 1906 and published in 1927) and "Faith and the Right to Believe" (written in 1909 or 1910 and published in 1911). I will also argue that Vivekananda likely played a role in the evolution of James's thinking about religious faith.

James first met Vivekananda in 1894 but had more extensive discussions with him in 1896, when Vivekananda delivered several lectures on Vedānta philosophy at Harvard University, which James and other Harvard philosophers had attended.[5] James admired Vivekananda in spite of his philosophical differences with him.[6] In a 1900 letter to Mrs. Ole Bull (a friend of Vivekananda's), James wrote that Vivekananda "is simply a wonder for oratical power" and that "the Swami is an honour to humanity" (quoted in Burke 1992–1999: vol. 4, 554).

[3] Hollinger (1997) claims that James misrepresented Clifford's evidentialist argument.

[4] See, for instance, Wernham (1987), Hick (1990: 59–60), H. Brown (1997: 488–519), and Christian (2005).

[5] Frederick (2012), Burke (1992–1999: vol. 2, 186–87), Burke (1992–1999: vol. 4, 548–57).

[6] On the philosophical differences between James and Vivekananda, see Frederick (2012) and Burke (1992–1999: vol. 4, 548–57).

James owned and—judging from his flyleaf annotations—read carefully Vivekananda's *Yoga Philosophy* (the original title of *Rāja-Yoga*) in which, as I discussed in chapters 4 and 5, Vivekananda argues that religion is a rigorous "science" based on supersensuous experiences that invite verification (Algaier 2020: 264; Frederick 2012: 41–43). James also owned a copy of the published transcript of Vivekananda's lecture on "The Vedānta Philosophy" (*CW* 1:357–65) and the subsequent question-and-answer session (*CW* 5:297–310), both of which were held at the Graduate Philosophical Society of Harvard University on March 25, 1896 (Algaier 2020: 217). In this question-and-answer session, Vivekananda claimed that through the practice of the "internal science" of Yoga, one can attain direct "knowledge" of "one's Self" (*CW* 5:299). Norris Frederick has made a plausible case that "Vivekananda's argument that religious experiences, like scientific truths, are based on 'experimentation, observation, and verification,' must have appealed greatly to James" (2012: 41).

Indeed, there is strong evidence that Vivekananda played a role in deepening James's interest in religious experience, culminating in his writing the classic treatise *The Varieties of Religious Experience* (1900), which explicitly refers to passages from Vivekananda's *Rāja-Yoga* and several of his published lectures ([1900] 2002: 310, 396). In *Varieties*, James, in stark contrast to Clifford and Huxley, did not dismiss religious experiences as merely subjective. Instead, James *defended* the epistemic value of religious experience, arguing that "[m]ystical states, when well developed, usually are, and have the right to be, absolutely authoritative over the individuals to whom they come" ([1900] 2002: 327). Significantly, while James made no mention at all of religious experience in "The Will to Believe," he explicitly argued in *Varieties* that the testimony of mystics in various religious traditions can furnish a rational basis for religious faith, even for *non*-mystics:

> They [mystical states] break down the authority of the non-mystical or rationalistic consciousness, based upon the understanding and the senses alone. They show it to be only one kind of consciousness. They open out the possibility of other orders of truth, in which, so far as anything in us vitally responds to them, we may freely continue to have faith. ([1900] 2002: 327)[7]

As we have seen in chapters 5 and 7, Vivekananda made precisely this argument, in a more detailed and rigorous way than James did here, in his lectures and writings in the 1890s—especially in *Rāja-Yoga*. According to Vivekananda's

[7] James makes a similar claim in *Pragmatism*: "we may well believe, on the proofs that religious experience affords, that higher powers exist and are at work to save the world on ideal lines similar to our own" ([1907] 1987: 619).

argument from religious experience, it follows from certain uncontroversial epistemic principles—namely, *The Principle of Perceptual Proof* and *The Principle of Testimonial Proof*—that the testimony of mystics who claim to have experienced God make it reasonable for us to believe that God exists and, on the basis of this belief, to engage in spiritual practices with the aim of experiencing God for ourselves.

In *Pragmatism* (1907), James explicitly credited Vivekananda with defending a "mystical method" for verifying religious truth-claims:

> The paragon of all monistic systems is the Vedânta philosophy of Hindostan, and the paragon of Vedântist missionaries was the late Swami Vivekananda who visited our shores some years ago. The method of Vedântism is the mystical method. You do not reason, but after going through a certain discipline you see, and having seen, you can report the truth. ([1907] 1987: 552–53)

While James had various philosophical reasons for rejecting Vivekananda's Vedāntic monism in favor of "pluralism," he was evidently impressed with Vivekananda's defense of the epistemic value of religious experience. Hence, I believe it is plausible to infer that James's own defense of religious experience as a source of knowledge in *Varieties* and later works was at least partly inspired by his extended discussions with Vivekananda and his careful study of Vivekananda's work.

Significantly, in his later essays "Reason and Faith" and "Faith and the Right to Believe," James introduced three new elements into his justification of religious faith that were entirely absent from "The Will to Believe." First, while "The Will to Believe" defended the right to believe in the face of "insufficient evidence" either for or against religion, his later essays came somewhat closer to the evidentialist position of Clifford and Huxley in arguing that faith is based on the *probability* that religion is true. As he put it in "Reason and Faith," "Reason claims certainty and finality for her conclusions. Faith is satisfied if hers seem probable and practically wise" (James 1927: 198). In "Faith and the Right to Believe," he similarly claimed, "We must go in for the more probable alternative as if the other one did not exist, and suffer the full penalty if the event belie our faith" ([1911] 1987: 1099). James's probabilistic grounding of religious faith in these later essays was not present in "The Will to Believe."[8]

Second, James argued in "Reason and Faith," in opposition to Clifford and Huxley, that religious experience constitutes a major source of evidence that tilts the probability in favor of religious faith:

[8] I disagree here with James Wernham, who claims that James's post-"Will to Believe" essays on faith do not hold that theism is more probable than atheism (1990: 105–14, esp. 114).

> But religious experience, strictly and narrowly so-called, gives Reason an additional set of facts to use. They show another possibility to Reason, and Faith then can jump in. . . . Reason, operating on our other experiences, even our psychological experiences, would never have inferred these specifically religious experiences. She could not suspect their existence for they are discontinuous with natural experience and invert its values. But as they come and are given, creation widens to our view. They suggest that our natural experience, so called, may only be a fragment of reality. They soften Nature's outlines and open out the strangest possibilities and perspectives. This is why it seems to me that Reason, working in abstraction from specifically religious experiences, will always omit something, and fail to reach completely adequate conclusions. This is why "religious experience," peculiarly so called, needs, in my opinion, to be carefully considered and interpreted by everyone who aspires to reason out a true religious philosophy. (1927: 200–201)

James argues here that the abundant evidence of religious experience—including one's own religious experience as well as the extensive testimony of mystics—provides a rational basis for religious faith by making it more probable than not that our ordinary experience is only a "fragment of reality." It is, as I have argued, hardly a coincidence that Vivekananda defended a very similar view in several lectures attended by James and in numerous works like *Rāja-Yoga*, which James had read. As far as I am aware, no scholar of James has acknowledged the likelihood that Vivekananda played a role in shaping James's later views on religious faith.

Third, in both later essays, James outlined a "faith-ladder," a sequence of seven steps in the development of faith, which was not explicitly formulated in "The Will to Believe":

1. There is nothing absurd in a certain view of the world being true, nothing self-contradictory;
2. It *might* have been true under certain conditions;
3. It *may* be true, even now;
4. It is *fit* to be true;
5. It *ought* to be true;
6. It *must* be true;
7. It *shall* be true, at any rate true for me. ([1911] 1987: 1096)[9]

[9] James orders his faith-ladder somewhat differently in "Reason and Faith" (1927: 198). As Wernham (1990) points out, James sketched at least *six* subtly different "faith-ladders" in different writings after "The Will to Believe." For the purposes of this chapter, I will focus on James's faith-ladders in "Reason and Faith" and "Faith and the Right to Believe."

Unfortunately, James does not explain these steps in much detail, so it is difficult to determine how they relate to the specific arguments in his later essays, especially his claims about probability. Nonetheless, it is fairly clear that step 1 affirms the bare *logical possibility* that religion is true. It is possible that steps 2 and 3 are meant to affirm the *probability* that religion is true, though the terms "*might*" and "*may*" in these steps seem too weak to support such a probability claim.[10] Steps 4 through 7 encompass the passional dimension of faith, consisting primarily in the *hope* that religion is true. In his 1905 essay, James clarified the final step 7—"It *shall* be true"—as follows: "I will treat it as if it *were* true so far as my advocacy and actions are concerned" (James 1927: 198). For James, faith culminates not in certainty or knowledge of the truth of religion but in a *will to believe* that religion is true by trying to live in accordance with its truth.[11]

2. *Vivekananda's Vedāntic Intervention in Late Nineteenth-Century Debates about Faith*

Where did Vivekananda stand in these contemporary debates about religious faith? Although Vivekananda had extended discussions with William James, there are no references to James's work in the *Complete Works*, and it is unclear whether Vivekananda had read James's essay "The Will to Believe" or any of his other work. Vivekananda also did not refer to Clifford anywhere, but he did refer repeatedly to Huxley and was familiar with Huxley's work, especially his principle of agnosticism.[12]

It is significant that Vivekananda referred to the terms "agnosticism" or "agnostic" no fewer than thirty-nine times in the *Complete Works*. As Bernard Lightman (2002) has shown, although Huxley coined the term "agnosticism" in 1869 and took pains to define it in a specific way, by the mid-1880s, the term had become so popular in intellectual circles that it took on a life of its own, and various thinkers—to Huxley's chagrin—defined the term quite differently than Huxley had. As we saw in section 3 of the previous chapter, Vivekananda himself endorsed rational agnosticism, the view that reason can neither conclusively prove nor disprove the existence of supersensuous entities like God and the soul. As he puts it, "What does reason say? It says, 'I am agnostic; I do not *know* either yea or nay'" (*CW* 1:181; emphasis added). Vivekananda's use of the word "know" here indicates that his rational agnosticism concerns the impossibility

[10] Pappas (1992: 783) interprets step 3 as a probability claim.

[11] James's language of a "will to believe" should not mislead us into thinking that he was a doxastic voluntarist. In fact, James explicitly rejects doxastic voluntarism in "The Will to Believe" (1897: 4–5).

[12] Vivekananda refers to Huxley at *CW* 2:74, *CW* 2:28, *CW* 2:218, and *CW* 9:25.

of attaining, through reason, *conclusive knowledge* either that God exists or does not exist.

However, in the following passage from *Rāja-Yoga* (1896), he actually criticizes a different kind of "agnosticism":

> The next question will be: What proof is there that the state beyond thought and reasoning is the highest state? In the first place, all the great men of the world, much greater than those that only talk, men who moved the world, men who never thought of any selfish ends whatever, have declared that this life is but a little stage on the way towards Infinity which is beyond. In the second place, they not only say so, but show the way to every one, explain their methods, that all can follow in their steps. In the third place, there is no other way left. There is no other explanation. Taking for granted that there is no higher state, why are we going through this circle all the time; what reason can explain the world? The sensible world will be the limit to our knowledge if we cannot go farther, if we must not ask for anything more. This is what is called agnosticism. But what reason is there to *believe* in the testimony of the senses? I would call that man a true agnostic who would stand still in the street and die. If reason is all in all, it leaves us no place to stand on this side of nihilism. If a man is agnostic of everything but money, fame, and name, he is only a fraud. Kant has proved beyond all doubt that we cannot penetrate beyond the tremendous dead wall called reason. But that is the very first idea upon which all Indian thought takes its stand, and dares to seek, and succeeds in finding something higher than reason, where alone the explanation of the present state is to be found. . . . That is the science of religion, nothing else. (*CW* 1:199; emphasis added)

Vivekananda's use of the word "believe" in this passage, I would suggest, signals that what he means by "agnosticism" here is not the rational agnosticism that he endorses elsewhere—the view that it is impossible to attain *knowledge* of supersensuous entities through reason—but the far more stringent *belief*-agnosticism championed by Clifford and, at times, by Huxley. Clifford, we should recall, holds that "it is wrong always, everywhere, and for anyone, to *believe* anything upon insufficient evidence" (1879: 186; emphasis added). Huxley, in an 1884 essay that Vivekananda might very well have read, defines the principle of agnosticism in a similar manner: "a man shall not say he *knows or believes* that which he has no scientific grounds for professing to know or believe" (quoted in Byun 2017: 126–27; emphasis added). As we saw in the previous section, Huxley took this principle of agnosticism to undermine the grounds of religious belief as well as claims to mystical knowledge.

However, Vivekananda argues that such a belief-agnosticism is far too stringent, since it precludes belief not only in the existence of supersensuous entities like God or the soul but also in the existence of ordinary sense-objects. As he puts it, "what reason is there to believe in the testimony of the senses?" A "true agnostic," Vivekananda contends, would have to embrace "nihilism" and "stand still in the street and die," since he would not even be justified in believing that sense-objects exist. Vivekananda clearly follows Descartes and Buddhists like Vasubandhu in assuming (plausibly) that there is no non-circular evidence for the existence of this world of sense-objects that we all perceive.

Accordingly, just a few pages later in *Rāja-Yoga*, Vivekananda—as we saw in chapter 5—justifies the epistemic value of *both* sense-perception and supersensuous perception by defending *The Principle of Perceptual Proof* (PP), the epistemic principle that our perception of an entity is sufficient proof that that entity exists, so long as we have no good reasons for thinking that our perceptual experience is delusive. According to Vivekananda, we all accept PP, implicitly or explicitly, whenever we act on the basis of our beliefs about the external world. As he puts it, "I see the world; that is sufficient proof that it exists" (*CW* 1:204). On the basis of PP, he defends another epistemic principle, *The Principle of Testimonial Proof* (TP), according to which the testimony of a credible person about her perception of some entity constitutes "proof" for others that that entity exists. However, he goes on to argue that PP and TP equally justify beliefs formed on the basis of supersensuous perception and testimony about supersensuous perception. As I discussed in chapters 5 and 7, PP and TP are the key premises in Vivekananda's argument for the epistemic value of supersensuous perception (AEV) and his argument from religious experience for God's existence (ARE).

I believe that in order to bring out the full philosophical force of Vivekananda's critique of Huxleyan agnosticism in the passage from *Rāja-Yoga* quoted earlier, we should read this passage in conjunction with his defense of PP and TP a few pages later. This passage begins, let us recall, with a demand for "proof" of the existence of a superconscious state "beyond thought and reasoning." For Vivekananda, this proof consists in the testimony of "all the great men of the world" who claim to have perceived supersensuous realities like God and the soul in such a superconscious state. This proof, then, presupposes PP, TP, and ARE, which he soon goes on to defend.

With PP and TP in the background, Vivekananda then proceeds to argue that Huxleyan agnostics end up in a double-bind. On the one hand, if they consistently follow their own agnostic principle, then they land in a state of existential paralysis ("nihilism"), since they would not even be justified in believing that the sense-objects they perceive actually exist. On the other hand, if Huxleyan agnostics accept PP as the basis of their beliefs about objects in the external world, then they would also have to accept the legitimacy of beliefs formed on the basis of *supersensuous* perception, since PP applies to *all* perceptual experiences, including both sense-perception and supersensuous perception. Hence, from

Vivekananda's standpoint, Huxley and Clifford are not justified in dismissing mystical experiences as merely "subjective" experiences devoid of epistemic value. On the basis of this critique of Huxley's agnostic principle, Vivekananda defends his own Vedāntic position that religious faith is grounded in the testimonial evidence of mystics who claim to have attained the direct supersensuous perception of God and the soul. So while Vivekananda agrees with Huxley and Clifford that religious faith requires evidentialist justification, he appeals to PP, TP, and ARE in order to refute their narrow form of evidentialism, defending instead an *expanded evidentialism* that encompasses the evidence of both sense-perception and supersensuous perception.

I already discussed Vivekananda's relation to William James in the previous section, so I will only add a few further points here. Whether or not Vivekananda was aware of James's "The Will to Believe," he would certainly have been sympathetic to James's efforts to defend the legitimacy of religious belief against the overly stringent evidentialist principles of Clifford and Huxley. However, I think Vivekananda's expanded evidentialism places him somewhere *between* the narrow evidentialism of Clifford and Huxley on the one hand and the James of "The Will to Believe" on the other. In "The Will to Believe," James maintains that the evidence for religious belief is strictly undecideable in either direction. Vivekananda, by contrast, holds that while religious beliefs cannot be *conclusively* proved or disproved through rational argumentation, the argument from religious experience (ARE)—based on the evidence of mystical testimony—nonetheless lends some degree of *probability* to religious beliefs about an ultimate reality. As I suggested in the previous section, it seems likely that Vivekananda played a significant role in leading James to rethink his views on faith and to emphasize both probabilism and mystical evidentialism in the later essays on faith he wrote in the first decade of the twentieth century.

However, Vivekananda and the later James differ in their respective conceptions of the dynamics and development of religious faith. James's seven-rung faith-ladder, we should recall, begins with the *possibility* that religion is true and ends with the *will to believe* that religion is true. Vivekananda made numerous remarks about religious faith in various lectures and writings, primarily from 1894 to 1896. I will argue in the next three sections that his various remarks hint at a three-rung ladder of faith that differs in significant ways from that of James.

I suggest that the three rungs in Vivekananda's faith-ladder are as follows:

1. I *assent intellectually* to the proposition that God exists.
2. I *believe* that God exists.
3. I *know*, with absolute certainty, that God exists, since I have directly realized God.

To be sure, Vivekananda himself never presented such a three-rung faith-ladder so clearly and explicitly in any one place. Nonetheless, he did frequently contrast "intellectual assent" (stage 1) with "realisation" (stage 3),[13] and he insisted that those who merely intellectually assent to religion are, in fact, "atheists," since they do not really believe that God exists (*CW* 2:163–64). He also remarked in numerous passages that there is a stage *prior* to the realization of God in which one truly *believes* that God exists and has a correspondingly intense longing to realize Him (stage 2).[14] By putting all of these passages together, I will present a three-rung ladder of religious faith that I believe accords with Vivekananda's own views and intentions, even if he himself never presented such a faith-ladder so systematically. Sections 3, 4, and 5 will discuss, respectively, the first, second, and third stages of this Vivekanandan ladder of religious faith. At relevant points in the discussion, I will also compare Vivekananda's views with those of James, Clifford, and Huxley.

3. *Stage 1: Faith as Sub-Doxastic Intellectual Assent*

Vivekananda emphatically rejects the common equation of religious faith with religious belief. In fact, in his 1896 lecture on "Realisation" delivered in London, he argues that religious faith typically begins not with belief but with what he calls "intellectual assent":

> This is one great idea to learn and to hold on to, this idea of realisation.... Only the man who has actually perceived God and soul has religion. There is no real difference between the highest ecclesiastical giant who can talk by the volume, and the lowest, most ignorant materialist. We are all atheists; let us confess it. Mere intellectual assent does not make us religious. . . . Not one in twenty millions is a real Christian.
>
> So, in India, there are said to be three hundred millions of Vedāntins. But if there were one in a thousand who had actually realised religion, this world would soon be greatly changed. We are all atheists, and yet we try to fight the man who admits it. We are all in the dark; religion is to us a mere intellectual assent, a mere talk, a mere nothing. (*CW* 2:163–64)

He contrasts mere "intellectual assent" to the proposition that God exists with the supersensuous "realisation" of God. According to Vivekananda, the vast majority of people who profess to be religious believers are, in fact, "atheists"; they

[13] See, for instance, *CW* 2:372, *CW* 4:34, *CW* 9:246, *CW* 2:410, and *CW* 2:163–64.

[14] See section 4 of this chapter for discussion of such passages.

do not *believe* that God exists so much as they merely *assent intellectually* to the proposition that God exists, and they behave in their day-to-day lives as if God does *not* exist.

Although Vivekananda does not clearly define "intellectual assent," I think we can gather from this passage that intellectual assent to God's existence has two elements: (i) intellectual acceptance and affirmation of God's existence and (ii) verbal affirmation of God's existence. Vivekananda's negatively tinged qualifier "mere" in the phrases "mere intellectual assent" and "mere talk" indicates that the intellectual-cum-verbal affirmation involved in intellectual assent is sub-doxastic, since the person who merely intellectually assents to the proposition that God exists does not yet *believe* or *feel* that God exists and does not *act* in accordance with God's existence.

What is Vivekananda's justification for distinguishing between intellectual assent and belief? As I will discuss in detail in the next section, he argues that one who believes that *F* exists feels strongly inclined to act and behave in accordance with the existence of *F*. By contrast, one who merely *assents intellectually* to the existence of *F*, but does not *believe* that *F* exists, tends to act and behave as if *F* does *not* exist. Accordingly, Vivekananda rather startlingly declares that most so-called religious "believers" throughout the world are, in fact, "religious atheists," in that they act and behave no differently than atheists do (*CW* 2:44). For Vivekananda, one can infer what a person believes from observing how that person lives. As he puts it, "As soon as a man begins to believe there is a God, he becomes mad with longing to get to Him" (*CW* 2:46).

Vivekananda clearly believes that the overwhelming majority of people who have religious faith are at the first stage of sub-doxastic intellectual assent. However, in his lecture "The Real and the Apparent Man" (1896) delivered in New York, he further divides these people at the first stage of faith into the two categories of sincere intellectual assenters and insincere intellectual assenters:

> Religion can be realised. Are you ready? Do you want it? You will get the realisation if you do, and then you will be truly religious. Until you have attained realisation there is no difference between you and atheists. The atheists are sincere, but the man who says that he believes in religion and never attempts to realise it is not sincere. (*CW* 2:285)

For Vivekananda, the degree of one's sincerity in religious life can be measured in terms of the earnestness and intensity of one's efforts to *realize* God through spiritual practice. In other words, a sincere religious person at the first stage of religious faith is a spiritual aspirant who is sufficiently self-aware and honest to acknowledge that she does not yet *believe* that God exists but is sincerely striving to bring herself into a position to believe in God and, ultimately, to realize God.

Unfortunately, according to Vivekananda, the majority of people at the first stage of religious faith are not sufficiently sincere and honest even to recognize or admit that they do not yet believe that God exists. Instead, they consciously or unconsciously delude themselves and others into thinking that they have already arrived at the second stage of religious belief proper. He makes this point forcefully in his 1894 lecture on "The Love of God—II" delivered in Detroit:

> Religion nowadays has become a mere hobby and fashion. People go to church like a flock of sheep. They do not embrace God because they need Him. Most persons are unconscious atheists who self-complacently think that they are devout believers. (*CW* 8:203)

With Kierkegaardian fervor, Vivekananda declares that most people of faith are insincere, because they profess to believe in God, yet do not strive to realize God or to live in accordance with the belief that God exists.

During Vivekananda's time, there were heated and well-publicized debates between atheists and religious figures about the existence of God and the truth of Christian doctrine.[15] In his lecture "Preparatory and Supreme Bhakti Yoga" (1896) delivered in New York,[16] Vivekananda polemically claims that modern self-professed atheists are more laudable and sincere than most self-professed religious "believers":

> The vast majority of men are atheists. I am glad that, in modern times, another class of atheists has come into existence in the Western world—I mean the materialists. They are sincere atheists. They are better than the religious atheists, who are insincere, who fight and talk about religion, and yet do not want it, never try to realise it, never try to understand it. Remember the words of Christ: "Ask, and it shall be given you; seek, and ye shall find; knock, and it shall be opened unto you." These words are literally true, not figures or fiction.... Who wants God? That is the question. Do you think that all this mass of people in the world want God, and cannot get Him? That cannot be. (*CW* 2:44)

Such pronouncements, which he made repeatedly in both America and England, must have come as a shock to his predominantly Christian audiences. He reminds

[15] One of the most famous was an 1860 debate about evolution and religion between T. H. Huxley and Bishop Samuel Wilberforce held at Oxford. For details on this debate, see Gilley and Loades (1981). In his fourth "Practical Vedānta" lecture delivered in London, Vivekananda refers to another fierce debate about religion between "Herbert Spencer and Frederick [*sic*] Harrison" in the 1880s (*CW* 2:342). Eisen (1968) discusses this debate.

[16] In the *Complete Works*, this lecture is undated and incorrectly titled "Bhakti or Devotion." I am indebted to Swami Atmarupananda, who has determined the original title of the lecture as well as the date and venue.

them of Christ's words in Matthew 7:7, which he interprets as a call to seek and realize God through sincere spiritual practice. Most "Christians," he claims, are only Christians in name, since they *profess* belief in Christian doctrine—either hypocritically or self-deceptively—yet without responding to Christ's call to seek God. This widespread lack of sincerity in religious life, he says, is true not only of Christians but of the "vast majority" of religious people throughout the world, including India (as is clear from his remark in a passage quoted earlier that only "one in a thousand" of self-professed "Vedāntins" are *true* Vedāntins). Vivekananda, of course, is not endorsing atheism when he claims that "sincere atheists" are better than "insincere" religious people. Rather, he is encouraging the latter to be sincere spiritual aspirants who honestly admit that they do not yet believe in God and who strive to deepen their religious faith through ethical and spiritual practice.

Before we move on to consider the second stage of faith-as-belief, we should address one final question. According to Vivekananda, how does one arrive at the first stage of intellectual assent to religion? At different places in his lectures and writings, he indicates two main paths to intellectual assent. First, as I discussed at length in the previous chapter, he holds that one may arrive at the first stage of religious faith through intellectual reasoning. After assessing arguments both for and against the existence of God, one should arrive—to use the phrase of William Hamilton of which Vivekananda was fond—at a "learned ignorance," the recognition that reason is powerless to prove or disprove God's existence. However, Vivekananda further contends, via the argument from religious experience (ARE), that the testimony of mystics who claim to have realized God makes it more probable than not that God exists. As I noted in chapter 4, Vivekananda himself arrived at religious faith in such an intellectual manner. After having read Mill and other Western thinkers, the young Vivekananda became an agnostic and only arrived at the stage of intellectual assent to religion after he had met Ramakrishna, who assured him that he had seen God (*CW* 1:317).

Apart from this somewhat rarefied intellectual path to the first stage of religious faith, there is a far more common path to faith that Vivekananda also frequently acknowledges. Take, for instance, this passage from his lecture "The Methods and Purpose of Religion" (1896) delivered in London:

> So, says Vedānta, religion is to be realised now. And for you to become religious means that you will start without any religion, work your way up and realise things, see things for yourself; and when you have done that, then, and then alone, you have religion. Before that you are no better than atheists, or worse, because the atheist is sincere—he stands up and says, "I do not know about these things"—while those others do not know but go about the world, saying, "We are very religious people." What religion they have no one knows, because

> they have swallowed some grandmother's story, and priests have asked them to believe these things. . . . (*CW* 6:13–14)

Vivekananda clearly recognizes that many people inherit their religious faith from their family or culture. Moreover, he thinks that this is a perfectly legitimate path to faith, so long as these people honestly acknowledge that they are mere neophytes in the long and arduous journey of religious faith. As he puts it, "you will start without any religion, work your way up and realise things. . . . " As usual, he criticizes those who complacently or self-deceptively think that they are "very religious" even though they do not yet believe in God and do not make any effort to deepen their religious faith through sincere spiritual practice. From Vivekananda's standpoint, whether we arrive at the first stage of religious faith through intellectual inquiry or through familial or cultural influence, we should honestly admit that our journey of faith has just begun and strive to ascend to the higher stages of religious belief and direct realization.

4. *Stage 2: Faith as Belief*

In the following passage from his lecture "Preparatory and Supreme Bhakti Yoga" (1896), Vivekananda explains the second stage of religious belief as well as the conditions necessary for ascending from the first to the second stage:

> A great sage used to say, "Suppose there is a thief in a room, and somehow he comes to know that there is a vast mass of gold in the next room, and that there is only a thin partition between the two rooms. What would be the condition of that thief? He would be sleepless, he would not be able to eat or do anything. His whole mind would be on getting that gold. Do you mean to say that, if all these people really *believed* that the Mine of Happiness, of Blessedness, of Glory were here, they would act as they do in the world, without trying to get God?" As soon as a man begins to *believe* there is a God, he becomes mad with longing to get to Him. Others may go their way, but as soon as a man is sure that there is a much higher life than that which he is leading here, as soon as he feels sure that the senses are not all, that this limited, material body is as nothing compared with the immortal, eternal, undying bliss of the Self, he becomes mad until he finds out this bliss for himself. And this madness, this thirst, this mania, is what is called the "awakening" to religion, and when that has come, a man is beginning to be religious. But it takes a long time. All these forms and ceremonies, these prayers and pilgrimages, these books, bells, candles, and priests, are the preparations; they take off the impurities from the soul. And when the soul has become pure, it naturally wants to get to the mine of all purity, God

> Himself. Just as a piece of iron, which had been covered with the dust of centuries, might be lying near a magnet all the time, and yet not be attracted by it, but as soon as the dust is cleared away, the iron is drawn by the magnet; so, when the human soul, covered with the dust of ages, impurities, wickednesses, and sins, after many births, becomes purified enough by these forms and ceremonies, by doing good to others, loving other beings, its natural spiritual attraction comes, it wakes up and struggles towards God. (*CW* 2:46; emphasis added)

The "great sage" mentioned here is Ramakrishna, who often appealed to the analogy of the thief and the pot of gold.[17] Indeed, I would argue that it was Ramakrishna who played the most significant role in shaping Vivekananda's views on religious faith in general. The lesson Vivekananda draws from Ramakrishna's analogy is that "[a]s soon as a man begins to believe there is a God, he becomes mad with longing to get to Him." According to Vivekananda, our beliefs tend to be reflected in our behavior. Hence, if we really *believed* that God exists, we would act and think in accordance with this belief and exert our utmost efforts to realize God for ourselves. Of course, he is aware that by this criterion, there are very few religious believers in the world, in spite of the fact that—as we already noted in the previous section—there are countless people who, for self-serving reasons, confuse intellectual assent with religious belief. Indeed, in another lecture, Vivekananda remarks that Ramakrishna used to say that "not one in twenty millions in this world believed in God" (*CW* 1:407). For Vivekananda, then, there are very few people in the world who have made the ascent from the first to the second stage of religious faith.

In the passage just quoted, Vivekananda also explains how belief in God eventually arises. Sincere spiritual aspirants who do not yet believe in God practice various spiritual disciplines—such as "forms and ceremonies," "prayers and pilgrimages"—which "take off the impurities from the soul." Once the aspirant's mind becomes sufficiently purified through such spiritual practices in the course of "many births," the belief in God arises spontaneously. Vivekananda's reasoning seems to be as follows: so long as our mind is impure, our thoughts and feelings will revolve around sense-pleasures rather than God, and this world of the senses will consequently seem far more real to us than God does. Accordingly, he remarked in an 1887 conversation with his brother disciple Prasanna (who would later become Svāmī Triguṇātītānda): "So long as one has desires and cravings, one does not believe that God exists" (*K* 1157 / *G* 999).[18] Here again, Vivekananda was directly influenced by Ramakrishna, who taught

[17] In his lecture "My Master" (1896), Vivekananda explicitly mentions that it was Sri Ramakrishna who taught him this story of the thief and the pot of gold (*CW* 4:170–71).

[18] *jatakṣan kāmanā, vāsanā, tatakṣan īśvarke aviśvās.*

that "[o]ne cannot even believe that God exists until one's heart becomes pure" (*K* 185 / *G* 220).[19] It is also worth noting that there is at least one major Western precedent for Ramakrishna's and Vivekananda's view on this matter. The French Catholic thinker Blaise Pascal (1623–1662) suggested that if one is not yet able to believe that God exists, one should endeavor to cultivate belief in God's existence "not by increase of proofs of God, but by the abatement of the passions" ([1670] 2003: 68).

Tellingly, Vivekananda draws upon another analogy of Ramakrishna's—that of a magnet and a dust-covered piece of iron[20]—to illustrate both how belief in God arises and the affective dynamics involved in such belief. Just as a piece of iron covered with thick layers of dust is automatically attracted to a nearby magnet as soon as the dust is removed, the human soul becomes naturally attracted to God as soon as its impurities are removed through spiritual practices. Vivekananda makes two important philosophical points through this analogy.

First, though we cannot simply adopt a belief in God at will, we can prepare the *conditions* for belief in God by engaging in spiritual practices that remove the impurities we have accrued in the course of many lifetimes. Hence, he rejects what contemporary epistemologists call "doxastic voluntarism," the view that we can adopt beliefs at will.[21] With respect to the first stage of religious faith, Vivekananda maintains that we can *choose* whether or not to assent intellectually to the proposition that God exists. Crucially, however, Vivekananda holds that *belief* in God's existence is *in*voluntary. Hence, we cannot voluntarily ascend from the first stage of sub-doxastic assent to the second stage of belief. Nonetheless, what we can do, at the first stage of faith, is to engage voluntarily in spiritual disciplines that will purify our minds, thereby preparing the necessary conditions for the spontaneous arising of the belief that God exists, which is not under our direct control.

Second, Vivekananda affirms—through both the magnet analogy and the analogy of the thief and the pot of gold—that belief in God is necessarily accompanied by an intense longing to realize God. Just as a dust-free piece of iron is naturally attracted to a powerful magnet, the pure soul is naturally attracted to God. In his lecture "Steps to Realisation" (1895), he characterizes this second stage of belief in God as *śraddhā*: "Strong faith in God and the consequent eagerness to reach Him constitute *śraddhā*" (*CW* 1:407). If we interpret this statement in the light of the long passage quoted earlier, then it is clear that the "strong faith" he describes here must be the second stage of faith-as-belief, since it is accompanied by an intense longing to "reach" God.

[19] *antar śuddha nā hole īśvar āchen bole viśvāsī hoy nā!*

[20] See, for instance, Sri Ramakrishna's appeal to this analogy at *K* 124 / *G* 173–74.

[21] Vitz (2019) provides a good overview of doxastic voluntarism.

To convey the nature of the longing for God of those who have reached the second stage of religious belief, Vivekananda appeals to yet another of Ramakrishna's favorite analogies:

> A disciple went to his master and said to him, "Sir, I want religion." The master looked at the young man, and did not speak, but only smiled. The young man came every day, and insisted that he wanted religion. But the old man knew better than the young man. One day, when it was very hot, he asked the young man to go to the river with him and take a plunge. The young man plunged in, and the old man followed him and held the young man down under the water by force. After the young man had struggled for a while, he let him go and asked him what he wanted most while he was under the water. "A breath of air," the disciple answered. "Do you want God in that way? If you do, you will get Him in a moment," said the master. Until you have that thirst, that desire, you cannot get religion, however you may struggle with your intellect, or your books, or your forms. Until that thirst is awakened in you, you are no better than any atheist; only the atheist is sincere, and you are not. (*CW* 2:45)[22]

The disciple in this passage thinks that he is already at the second stage of belief in God; he thinks that he really wants God. His master, however, proves to him that he is deluding himself, since he lacks the intense longing for God that is the sure sign of belief in God. According to Vivekananda, then, we can avoid self-deception in our journey of faith by applying this test: we can be sure that we do not believe in God so long as we do not have an intense, all-consuming longing to realize God—a longing that is ultimately fulfilled in the third and final stage of God-realization.

5. *Stage 3: Faith as Self-Authenticating Realization*

For Vivekananda, as soon as a person begins to believe in God, she is consumed with a longing to realize God. In this second stage of religious belief, the spiritual aspirant devotes all her energy to spiritual practice with the aim of realizing God. Such a spiritual aspirant's sincere longing for God, when it becomes sufficiently intense, results in the direct realization of God, the third and culminating stage of religious faith. He describes this culminating stage of faith in his lecture "Realisation" (1896) delivered in London:

[22] Sri Ramakrishna appeals to this analogy at *K* 502 / *G* 497 and elsewhere.

> If you have seen a certain country, and a man forces you to say that you have not seen it, still in your heart of hearts you know you have. So, when you see religion and God in a more intense sense than you see this external world, nothing will be able to shake your belief. Then you have real faith. That is what is meant by the words in your Gospel, "He who has faith even as a grain of mustard seed." Then you will know the Truth because you have become the Truth. This is the watchword of the Vedānta—realise religion, no talking will do. (*CW* 2:165)

For Vivekananda, "real faith" consists neither in intellectual assent nor even in belief but in direct realization. At the second stage of religious belief, an aspirant might still be assailed by doubts on occasion, since she is not yet *certain* that God exists. However, once this aspirant realizes God for herself, then nothing can "shake" her belief. We should recall from chapter 5 that the highest spiritual experience, for Vivekananda, is self-authenticating, since it has an "internal mandate to vouch for its truth" (*CW* 1:367). In other words, a self-authenticating experience of God *guarantees* its own veridicality to its epistemic subject. We can always doubt the veridicality of our ordinary sense-perceptions, since they are not self-authenticating. Accordingly, as we have already seen, Vivekananda points out in *Rāja-Yoga* that we can never rule out the skeptical possibility that our senses deceive us: "what reason is there to believe in the testimony of the senses?" (*CW* 1:199). By contrast, at the culminating point of our journey of faith, we attain a self-authenticating experience of God which *assures* us of its veridicality. This is, I believe, what Vivekananda means when he declares: "when you see religion and God in a more intense sense than you see this external world, nothing will be able to shake your belief." Similarly, in a passage from his *Inspired Talks* (1895), I believe he has in mind "real faith"—that is, the culminating stage of faith as self-authenticating realization—when he remarks: "Faith is not belief, it is the grasp on the Ultimate, an illumination" (*CW* 7:60).

Vivekananda quotes Matthew 17:20 from the Bible in support of his understanding of the culminating point of faith. Jesus tells his disciples: "if you have faith like a grain of mustard seed, you will say to this mountain, 'Move from here to there,' and it will move, and nothing will be impossible for you." We can clarify Jesus's comparison of faith to a mustard seed by juxtaposing this statement with Matthew 13:32, where Jesus observes that the mustard seed "is the smallest of all seeds, but when it has grown it is larger than all the garden plants and becomes a tree, so that the birds of the air come and make nests in its branches." Vivekananda interprets Jesus's teaching from a Vedāntic perspective: our faith in God, which may be as paltry as a mustard seed in the beginning, should eventually mature into the self-authenticating realization of God, which constitutes "real faith." For Vivekananda, although our faith may begin as mere intellectual assent, if we are sincere, our faith will eventually flower into belief and, ultimately, realization. To support his view that Jesus understood the culminating point of faith as God-realization, Vivekananda, in numerous other lectures, quotes Jesus's famous teaching in Matthew 5:8, which I will discuss in more detail in the next section of this chapter: "Blessed are the pure in heart, for they shall see God" (*CW* 4:148).

We are now in a position to compare the respective faith-ladders of Vivekananda and William James. James's faith-ladder, we should recall, culminates in the will to believe in God, the resolve to think and behave "as if" God exists (James 1927: 198). James also holds out the possibility that through this process, one may eventually acquire the *belief* that God exists. Although the later James, likely in part due to the influence of Vivekananda, emphasized the evidential value of religious experience as a basis for faith, he never accepted the possibility of a self-authenticating experience of God. As an empiricist, James consistently held that we should "give up the doctrine of objective certitude" (1897: 17). Accordingly, James claimed that religious faith is, at best, based on the probability, rather than the certainty, that God exists. As he put it in his 1906 essay on faith, "Reason claims certainty and finality for her conclusions. Faith is satisfied if hers seem probable and practically wise" (1927: 198).

There are, then, two major differences between the faith-ladders of James and Vivekananda. First, Vivekananda's final stage of faith as self-authenticating realization is entirely absent from James's faith-ladder. For Vivekananda, we *can* achieve "objective certitude" of God's existence—which James deems to be impossible—through a self-authenticating realization of God that guarantees its own veridicality. Second, while James does take religious experience seriously, he never conceives the journey of faith as one that should culminate in religious experience. Vivekananda, by contrast, insists that we should not rest content with even a strongly held belief in God but should strive to *verify* this belief through intense spiritual practice, culminating in the confirmatory realization of God.

In effect, then, Vivekananda mediated between James on the one hand and Clifford and Huxley on the other by championing a mystical evidentialism. Vivekananda, as we saw in chapters 4 and 5, was as ardent as Clifford and Huxley in insisting on the need for the empirical "verification" of religion, but he argued against their narrow empiricism by defending the evidential value of supersensuous experience. Hence, while Vivekananda agreed with James that religious belief is rationally justified, Vivekananda parted ways with James in holding that the journey of faith should culminate not in mere belief but in a direct verification of this belief through the self-authenticating experience of God.

6. *Vivekananda's Relevance to Contemporary Debates about Faith*

This final section begins to explore how Vivekananda's Vedāntic views on faith can contribute to contemporary debates about faith in analytic philosophy of religion. William Alston, in his groundbreaking paper "Belief, Acceptance, and Religious Faith" (Alston 1996), challenged the then-prevailing conception of religious faith as propositional belief, arguing instead that faith takes two forms: faith as belief and faith as non-doxastic "acceptance." A number of contemporary philosophers of religion have followed Alston in distinguishing doxastic and non-doxastic forms of faith, but they continue to debate the precise nature of this non-doxastic faith and its relation to doxastic faith. Is non-doxastic faith best understood as acceptance (as Alston contends) or as "mental assent" (Schellenberg 2005: 127–66), "fiducial faith" (Audi 2011: 51–89), "affective faith" (Kvanvig 2013), a practical "assumption" (Golding 1990 and Howard-Snyder 2016), or otherwise?

In his 1996 paper, Alston referred to his distinction between doxastic and non-doxastic faith as a "startling discovery," observing that it had "completely escaped notice in the mountain of literature on faith" (1996: 20). Of course, Alston had in mind the "mountain" of *Western* philosophical literature on faith and seems to have been unaware that Vivekananda had distinguished genuine religious belief from sub-doxastic "intellectual assent" a century earlier. I wish to make a case for the contemporary relevance of Vivekananda's views on faith by bringing him into critical dialogue with Alston. I will focus here on Alston's 1996 paper, though I will also refer occasionally to his follow-up paper, "Audi on Nondoxastic Faith" (2007), which reaffirms his 1996 position while also clarifying it in certain respects.

Alston's 1996 paper is detailed and rigorously argued, and I will only summarize those aspects of his argument that are most relevant to our present discussion. Alston begins by adapting for his own purposes L. Jonathan Cohen's epistemic distinction between belief and acceptance (Cohen 1992). Alston provides the following list of six tendencies that indicate that x believes that p ("xBp"):

A. If xBp, then if someone asks x whether p, x will have a tendency to respond in the affirmative.
B. If xBp, then if x considers whether it is the case that p, x will tend to feel it to be the case that p, with one or another degree of confidence.
C. If xBp, then x will tend to believe propositions that she takes to follow from p.

D. If xBp, then x will tend to use p as a premise in theoretical and practical reasoning where this is appropriate.
E. If xBp, then if x learns that not-p, x will tend to be surprised.
F. If xBp, then x will tend to act in ways that would be appropriate if it were the case that p, given x's goals, aversions, and other beliefs. (2007: 131)[23]

Alston argues that belief differs from acceptance in two crucial respects. First, while both belief and acceptance exhibit A, C, D, E, and F to a greater or lesser extent, acceptance lacks B, the "spontaneous feeling of certainty" that p, which tends to accompany belief (1996: 25). Second, belief is involuntary, while acceptance is voluntary. Rejecting doxastic voluntarism, Alston argues that any number of ordinary examples show that belief is "not under direct voluntary control."[24] As he puts it, "If I were to try to do something that will bring it about, right away, that I believe that Salem is the capital of Massachusetts, I wouldn't know what button to push" (1996: 7). He argues that acceptance, in contrast to belief, *is* a voluntary act. Hence, for Alston, while we *can* choose to accept that p, we *cannot* choose to believe that p.

Equipped with this distinction between belief and acceptance, Alston then applies it to the issue of religious faith, and to Christian faith in particular. People of Christian faith, he argues, fall into two categories: those who *believe* Christian doctrines and those who *accept* them. For Alston, the paradigmatic case of a Christian believer is a person born into a devout Christian household who, at a young age, in effect *inherits* the Christian beliefs of his family and continues to hold Christian beliefs through adulthood without ever doubting them. As he puts it, Christian doctrines, for such people, have been "part of their repertoire of constant belief for as long as they can remember, and nothing has come along to shake it" (1996: 16).

However, Alston suggests that a "significant proportion" of Christians, "in these secular, scientistic, intellectually unsettled times," are not believers but *accepters* of Christian doctrine (1996: 16). Those who accept, rather than believe, Christian doctrines include those who remained "troubled by doubts" and who "take it as a live possibility that all or most central Christian doctrines are false" (1996: 16). Interestingly, he goes on to argue that the Christian accepter "is not necessarily inferior to the *believer* in commitment to the Christian life, or in the seriousness, faithfulness, or intensity with which she pursues it" (1996: 17).

Accordingly, Alston makes the case that Christianity does not "require its devotees to *believe* the articles of faith," since one can be just as good and sincere a

[23] In his earlier article, Alston provides a very similar list (1996: 4), but I refer to his 2007 formulation of the list, because it is a bit clearer and more succinct than the earlier one.

[24] Alston (1988) provides a detailed defense of doxastic involuntarism.

Christian by *accepting* the articles of faith without belief (1996: 21). As part of his case, he analyzes the statement in the Epistle to the Hebrews 11:6: "For whoever would draw near to God must believe that he exists and that he rewards those who seek him" (1996: 22). He interprets this Biblical statement as follows:

> But the Greek verb translated "believe" in the Revised Standard version . . . and in many other translations, is *pisteuo*, the verbal form of the noun *pistis*, "faith." In English we lack a verb cognate of "faith," and this leads translators to settle on "believe" as the nearest English verb. But once we come to realize that it is not always belief that constitutes the cognitive aspect of faith, we can see that a better translation would be "have faith that he exists". . . . Propositional "*faith*" can involve either belief or acceptance. (1996: 22)

On the basis of this and other scriptural and doctrinal evidence, Alston argues that Christianity calls on us not to *believe* Christian doctrine but to have *faith*, which can take the form of either belief or acceptance. Hence, he maintains that Christian accepters, as opposed to believers, are not missing anything "essential to being a Christian in the fullest sense" (1996: 21).

Let us now bring Alston into conversation with Vivekananda. There are, of course, numerous ways of staging this conversation. One might, for instance, compare Vivekananda's Vedāntic approach to faith with Alston's Christian approach. However, I believe there is a much more interesting and fruitful way of bringing these two thinkers into dialogue. Since Vivekananda himself repeatedly appealed to Biblical passages in support of his views on faith, I will draw upon Vivekananda's arguments with the aim of critically engaging Alston's views on faith *on Alston's own Christian terms*. For the purposes of this more direct debate between Vivekananda and Alston, I will focus on a fundamental aspect of faith that is common to Vivekananda's Vedānta philosophy and Christianity: the faith that God exists. Of course, as I have noted in chapter 5, Vivekananda's conception of God is much broader than Alston's since it encompasses both the loving personal God of theistic religions like Christianity and Islam as well as the impersonal nondual Brahman of Advaita Vedānta. However, since we are trying to bring Vivekananda into direct debate with Alston, let us simply assume that Vivekananda accepts Alston's narrower theistic conception of God.

Vivekananda, I believe, would agree with Alston on three issues. First, Vivekananda, as we have seen, anticipated Alston in upholding doxastic involuntarism. In fact, in an important article defending doxastic involuntarism, Alston specifically argues that it is "not within our power" simply to *choose* to believe that God exists "in the face of the lack of any significant inclination to suppose it to be true" (1988: 266–67). He further claims that what might *seem* to be a case of forming a belief in p—in this case, the proposition that God exists—is often something quite different: "S may be seeking, for whatever reason, to bring himself into a position of believing p; and S or others may confuse this activity, which can be undertaken voluntarily, with believing or judging the proposition to be true" (1988: 268). Vivekananda agrees with Alston on this point but goes further than Alston in making the normative claim that many people of faith "self-complacently" deceive themselves and others by claiming to believe that God exists but behaving in a way that betrays their *lack* of belief.

Second, Vivekananda also anticipated Alston in distinguishing the involuntary *belief* that God exists from a voluntary, non-doxastic *acceptance* of, or assent to, the proposition that God exists. Of course, while Vivekananda calls this non-doxastic epistemic attitude "intellectual assent," Alston calls it "acceptance," and there are—as we will see—important differences in their respective conceptions of this non-doxastic form of religious faith. It is worth mentioning, however, that Alston himself acknowledges that " 'assent' is not infrequently itself used for the mental act I call 'acceptance,' " noting that both Thomas Aquinas and John Locke used the term "assent" in this sense (1996: 8).

Third, Vivekananda's account of the second stage of faith-as-belief suggests that he would more or less accept Alston's list of six tendencies that characterize belief that p. Moreover, he would certainly concur with Alston that belief, as opposed to acceptance/assent, necessarily involves a "spontaneous feeling of certainty" (1996: 25). Hence, in the case of the proposition that God exists, Alston and Vivekananda share the view that the belief that God exists typically involves the *strong feeling* that God exists. They would also concur that this belief that God exists tends to have a significant influence on a person's everyday thought and behavior. I think Vivekananda would only object to the qualifying phrase "with one or another degree of confidence" in Alston's B. Vivekananda's remarks about belief strongly suggest that he takes belief to be an "all or nothing" affair, which does not admit the possibility of degrees of belief. For Vivekananda, the belief that God exists necessarily involves a very strong conviction that God exists. Interestingly, although Alston accepts degrees of belief, he admits that he is more sympathetic to the "all or nothing" view endorsed by Vivekananda: "I must confess to some uneasiness about the whole notion of degrees of belief. I am inclined to think that unqualified, flat-out belief that *p* requires that it seem unquestionable to S that *p*. On this view, belief excludes any doubts or uncertainty" (1996: 6). However, as I noted in my discussion of stages 2 and 3 of Vivekananda's faith-ladder, Vivekananda himself thinks that even the very strong conviction involved in the belief that God exists still admits the possibility of occasional doubts, since one can be entirely free from doubts only after *realizing* God.

In spite of these important similarities in the views of Alston and Vivekananda, I will argue that they differ markedly in their understanding of the precise nature of sub-doxastic faith and its relation to doxastic faith. Moreover, these differences reflect even more fundamental divergences in how Vivekananda and Alston conceive the dynamics of religious faith, the role of spiritual practice in religious life, and the ultimate goal of religious endeavor. Alston, as we have seen, claims that the primary difference between acceptance and belief is that the former lacks B, the second of the six tendencies involved in belief. To accept religious doctrines, he sums up, involves a "voluntary act of committing oneself to them" as well as a *tendency* to "use them as a basis for one's thought, attitude, and behavior" (1996: 17). Alston illustrates non-doxastic acceptance through the example of a defensive football captain who thinks that the quarterback is most likely to call a "fullback plunge" on the next play (1996: 10). In such a scenario, Alston claims, the defensive captain *accepts*, but does not *believe*, the proposition that the quarterback will call a fullback plunge, and proceeds to align his defense accordingly.

However, from Vivekananda's perspective, Alston's example of the defensive captain not only fails to capture the primary difference between religious acceptance and religious belief but also points to a deeper problem in Alston's understanding of the dynamics of religious life. Notice that in Alston's example, it is equally easy, from a practical standpoint, for the defensive captain to align his defense in any number of ways. Hence, as soon as he accepts the proposition that the quarterback will call a fullback plunge on the next play, the defensive captain is immediately able to align his defense accordingly. For Vivekananda, it is precisely this feature of Alston's example that makes it inapplicable to the case of sub-doxastic religious acceptance/assent. Even if we intellectually assent to the proposition that God exists and *resolve* to think and act in accordance with the truth of this proposition, it is incredibly difficult to do so in practice. Thinking and acting on the assumption that God exists requires nothing less than a radical shift in our existential orientation; it requires us to place God, rather than the "rascal ego" (*CW* 8:31), at the center of our lives. From Vivekananda's Vedāntic perspective, centering our thoughts and actions around God is extremely difficult for the vast majority of us, because we have various worldly attachments and desires, acquired and nourished in this life and in numerous past lives, which make us far more inclined to lead selfish, rather than God-centered, lives. Hence, one can think and act in a God-centered way only after having engaged in earnest ethical and spiritual practice in the course of numerous lives. Unlike Alston, then, Vivekananda would hold that the arduous endeavor to center our thoughts and actions in God once we have intellectually assented to the proposition that God exists is *nothing at all* like a defensive captain's effortless alignment of his defense the very moment he accepts the proposition that the quarterback will call a fullback plunge.

Of course, Alston, as a Christian, would not accept the Vedāntic doctrines of *karma* and rebirth. Nonetheless, like most Christians, he does accept the doctrine of original sin, which lies at the basis of our inherent tendency to live sinfully and selfishly and to forget God. As Saint Paul puts it, "I know that nothing good lives in me, that is, in my sinful nature. For I have the desire to do what is good, but I cannot carry it out" (Romans 7:18). Hence, even from Alston's Christian perspective, the example of the defensive captain seems difficult to square with the fact that our innately sinful tendencies make it extraordinarily difficult for us to think and act in a God-centered manner.[25]

The difference between non-doxastic and doxastic religious faith, then, is much starker for Vivekananda than it is for Alston. According to Alston, non-doxastic acceptance lacks only B (the feeling that p) from his list of six tendencies characterizing belief. For Alston, then, the religious accepter shares with the religious believer the *tendency* to act and think in a God-centered manner (hence the language of "tend" in his C, D, and F). By contrast, Vivekananda holds that a strong natural tendency to think and live in a God-centered manner is absent from the first stage of intellectual assent and is present only in the second stage of religious belief. He reasons that we cannot have a strong inclination to live for God until we genuinely believe that God exists. Hence, for Vivekananda, intellectual assent to the proposition that God exists definitely exhibits Alston's A—the *verbal affirmation* of God's existence—but lacks not only Alston's B but also C, D, and F.[26] He holds that a sincere spiritual aspirant at the first stage of intellectual assent *strives* to think and live in a God-centered manner, even though she still lacks the spontaneous tendency to do so. Let *s* stand for "a sincere intellectual assenter," *g* stand for "the proposition that God exists," and "*sAg*" stand for "*s* intellectually assents to *g*." In the case of *s*, I think Vivekananda would replace Alston's verb "tend" in C, D, and F with the verb "strive":

C′. If *sAg*, then *s* will *strive* to believe propositions that she takes to follow from *g*.

D′. If *sAg*, then *s* will *strive* to use *g* as a premise in theoretical and practical reasoning where this is appropriate.

F′. If *sAg*, then *s* will *strive* to act in ways that would be appropriate if it were the case that *g*, given *s*'s goals, aversions, and other beliefs.

Unlike Alston, Vivekananda maintains that the sincere spiritual aspirant's persistent *striving* to live in a God-centered manner matures into a natural *tendency* to so live only after she has ascended from intellectual assent to belief. For Vivekananda, even sincere spiritual aspirants at the first stage of intellectual assent have at least some "desires and cravings" (*K* 1157 / *G* 999) that make them

[25] Alston (2007: 133) gives an example of an army general, which has basically the same structure as his earlier defensive captain example.

[26] I am not sure whether Vivekananda would accept Alston's E with respect to the intellectual assenter, so I leave that question open.

more inclined to lead a selfish rather than a God-centered life. It is only after they have sufficiently curbed their egoistic tendencies that they will be able to form the (involuntary) *belief* that God exists, which is necessarily accompanied by the spontaneous tendency to think and act in a God-centered manner. However, Vivekananda holds that the sincere religious assenter has a clear-sighted recognition of where she stands and makes earnest efforts to ascend from intellectual assent to belief, and eventually from belief to God-realization.

Vivekananda also differs markedly from Alston in his understanding of the nature and dynamics of religious faith. According to Alston, " 'Faith that' has at least a strong suggestion of a weak epistemic position vis-à-vis the proposition in question" (1996: 12). Since "faith does not count as *knowledge*," a person's faith that God exists necessarily falls short of knowledge or certainty of God's existence (Alston 1996: 15). Vivekananda, in contrast to Alston, adopts a broader, stadial view of religious faith as a journey, spanning several lives, from weaker to stronger epistemic states. For a sincere spiritual aspirant, the journey of faith begins with sub-doxastic *intellectual assent* to the proposition that God exists and an earnest endeavor to live in a God-centered manner by engaging in intensive spiritual practice. After several lives of such spiritual practice, the aspirant's faith eventually matures into the *belief* that God exists. For Vivekananda, however, the faith-journey does not end with belief. Rather, the spiritual aspirant should continue her spiritual practices with even greater intensity until she attains the *knowledge* of God through self-authenticating spiritual experience.

Alston notes that "it is possible for acceptance to turn into belief as one gets deeper and deeper into the religion one has accepted" (1996: 18). Nonetheless, unlike Vivekananda, Alston does not think that all religious accepters *should* strive to become religious believers, since—as we have seen—he holds that the religious accepter "is not necessarily inferior to the *believer* in commitment to the Christian life, or in the seriousness, faithfulness, or intensity with which she pursues it" (1996: 17). Accordingly, he rejects the view that "the elect" is "restricted to the firm believers" (1996: 24). At the same time, Alston admits that religious belief is "the most desirable state possible" and that "there are many respects in which a firm belief in the major doctrines of the Christian faith is a superior position to a nonbelieving acceptance of them" (2007: 136). For instance, he observes that "the accepter will receive less comfort from her faith than the unquestioning believer, and she will be more troubled by doubts and waverings" (2007: 136).

From Vivekananda's perspective, there is a palpable tension in Alston's position on the relation between non-doxastic and doxastic faith. If religious belief is "the most desirable state possible," then surely it is both epistemically and normatively superior to non-doxastic faith. After all, why would a sincere Christian *not* want to receive maximal spiritual "comfort" and be less tormented by "doubts and waverings"? Arguably, then, Alston, in order to be consistent, should accept Vivekananda's normative view that a religious assenter/accepter should strive to attain the more desirable state of religious belief through earnest spiritual practice.

Vivekananda, however, would also contest Alston's claim that religious belief is "the most desirable state possible." For Vivekananda, while religious belief is certainly much more desirable than mere intellectual assent, the *most* desirable state is not belief but direct realization, the self-authenticating experiential knowledge of God. Of course, it might be tempting to chalk up this difference to Vivekananda's Vedāntic approach. However, as we have seen in chapter 6, Alston himself was one of the foremost defenders of the epistemic value of mystical experience (Alston 1991). While Alston does not accept the possibility of self-authenticating mystical experience, he does spend a great deal of energy defending mystical experience as full-blown knowledge. Indeed, his book *Perceiving God* (1991) is strewn with passages from the testimony of great Christian mystics like Saint Teresa who claim to have attained mystical knowledge of God. From Vivekananda's perspective, if Alston accepts that direct experiential knowledge of God is possible, then he should also accept that the most desirable epistemic state is not religious belief but the mystical knowledge of God.

Vivekananda, in contrast to Alston, argues that the Bible itself advocates a model of faith as a journey culminating in direct realization. As we saw in the previous section, Vivekananda appeals to Matthew 17:20—"He who has faith even as a grain of mustard seed"—to support his claim that "you have real faith" only "when you see religion and God in a more intense sense than you see this external world" (*CW* 2:165). While Matthew 17:20 does seem to enjoin us to strengthen our faith in God as much as possible, what Biblical evidence does Vivekananda have for equating the highest form of faith with *seeing* God—rather than, say, merely believing that God exists? In his lectures and writings, he was fond of referring to Matthew 5:8, one of the beatitudes from Jesus's Sermon on the Mount:

> Are you pure? If you are pure, you will reach God. "Blessed are the pure in heart, for they shall see God." . . . The pure heart is the best mirror for the reflection of truth, so all these disciplines are for the purification of the heart. And as soon as it is pure, all truths flash upon it in a minute; all truth in the universe will manifest in your heart, if you are sufficiently pure. (*CW* 1:413–14)[27]

He effuses that "[t]his sentence alone" from Jesus's Sermon "would save mankind if all books and prophets were lost" (*CW* 1:103). Vivekananda follows numerous

[27] Vivekananda also refers to Matthew 5:8 at *CW* 4:148 and numerous other places.

Christian mystics, like the Desert Father Saint Hesychios,[28] in interpreting the goal of *seeing* God as the direct mystical perception of God. According to Vivekananda, Matthew 5:8 not only declares the goal of religious life to be God-realization but also specifies that the means to attain this goal is the purification of one's heart. Hence, the sincere spiritual aspirant progresses in her journey of faith—from intellectual assent, to belief, to realization—by purifying her heart through the intensive practice of spiritual disciplines. Indeed, Jesus devotes much of his Sermon on the Mount to specifying the spiritual disciplines necessary for self-purification, such as striving to eliminate lust from one's heart (Matthew 5:28), to curb one's anger (Matthew 5:20–21), to love one's enemies (Matthew 5:44), and to help those in need (Matthew 5:42). Jesus concludes his Sermon by inculcating his disciples to strive to attain moral and spiritual perfection through all these purificatory disciplines: "Be ye therefore perfect, even as your Father which is in heaven is perfect" (Matthew 5:48).

With the Sermon on the Mount in the background, we can revisit the Epistle to the Hebrews 11:6 discussed by Alston: "For whoever would draw near to God must believe that he exists and that he rewards those who seek him" (Alston 1996: 22). Alston, we should recall, argues that a more accurate translation of the verb *pisteuo* is "have faith," which can mean either acceptance or belief. Such Biblical statements, Alston argues, suggest that a Christian can rest content with acceptance and need not strive to *believe* Christian doctrine. I am not sure that Vivekananda would dispute Alston's interpretation of *pisteuo*, but I think he *would* draw Alston's attention to the fact that Saint Paul urges us to "draw near to God." From Vivekananda's perspective, this Biblical statement—as well as the entire Sermon on the Mount and many other Biblical passages—supports his own Vedāntic view that the faith-journey is one in which one strives to draw nearer and nearer to God, with the ultimate aim of *seeing* God. Tellingly, Alston does not discuss the Sermon on the Mount at all, which inculcates us to draw nearer to God—and, ultimately, to see God—through an arduous process of self-purification. According to Vivekananda, then, true Christians should not rest content either with Alstonian acceptance or even with strong belief but should continue on their journey of faith until their hearts become so pure that they *perceive* God directly and all their doubts are dispelled.

Vivekananda's Biblically grounded epistemic linkage of the strength of our faith with the purity of our heart leads him to deviate from Alston on another crucial issue. Alston's paradigmatic Christian believers, we should recall, are "those born into Christianity," for whom Christian doctrine has been "part of their repertoire of constant belief for as long as they can remember" (1996: 18).

[28] See St. Hesychios's interpretation of Matthew 5:8 in *The Philokalia* (Palmer, Sherrard, and Ware 1979: 171).

Accordingly, he claims that "acceptance as well as belief is common among committed Christians" (1996: 20). In stark contrast to Alston, Vivekananda claims that "[n]ot one in twenty millions is a real Christian" (*CW* 2:163–64), since a "real Christian" is one who has *seen* God. For Vivekananda, the vast majority of Christians—and, indeed, followers of all religions—remain at the stage of intellectual assent. Only a tiny minority of people in the world even *believe* that God exists, since such belief can only arise in a heart sufficiently purified through spiritual disciplines practiced across multiple lives. Vivekananda, then, would emphatically reject Alston's assumption that one can imbibe religious belief from one's family or culture. In fact, as I noted earlier, he was scathing toward those who think that they are "very religious people" simply because "they have swallowed some grandmother's story, and priests have asked them to believe these things" (*CW* 6:13–14). For Vivekananda, such people are actually "unconscious atheists who self-complacently think that they are devout believers" (*CW* 8:203). Self-deception is so rampant in religious life, he claims, because if we think that we are already "believers," we conveniently spare ourselves the hard work of having to purify ourselves through the arduous spiritual disciplines inculcated in Jesus's Sermon on the Mount.

As I have already noted, Alston himself claims that it is "not within our power" to believe that God exists "in the face of the lack of any significant inclination to suppose it to be true" (1988: 266–67). Vivekananda would agree with Alston's doxastic involuntarism but insist that this "significant inclination" comes not from familial and cultural indoctrination but from a long and difficult process of self-purification. Tellingly, in a lecture delivered to a Christian audience in Detroit, Michigan, in 1894, Vivekananda appealed to another teaching from the Sermon on the Mount to justify his position:

> Let me tell you, brethren, if you want to live, if you really want your nation to live, go back to Christ. You are not Christians. . . . Go back to Christ. Go back to him who had nowhere to lay his head. . . . You cannot serve God and Mammon at the same time. All this prosperity, all this from Christ! Christ would have denied all such heresies. All prosperity which comes with Mammon is transient, is only for a moment. Real permanence is in Him. (*CW* 8:213)

Vivekananda refers here to Matthew 6:24: "No man can serve two masters: for either he will hate the one, and love the other; or else he will hold to the one, and despise the other. Ye cannot serve God and mammon." Jesus tells us that so long as we value or love the things of this world, we cannot truly value or love God. Vivekananda can be seen as drawing out the epistemic implications of Jesus's teaching. Following Ramakrishna, he maintains that we cannot even *believe* that God exists until we have attained a very high level of purity, since God will not seem real and lovable to us so long as we remain attached to the ephemeral things of this world. Accordingly, Vivekananda claims, "So long as one has desires and cravings, one does not believe that God exists" (*K* 1157 / *G* 999). Unlike Alston, then, Vivekananda views religious belief as a hard-won achievement gained through a long battle with our selfish tendencies and impulses (often in the course of multiple lives).

To sum up, I think there are five primary reasons why Vivekananda is a valuable interlocutor in contemporary philosophical discussions of religious faith. First, he was one of the first philosophers to distinguish sub-doxastic and doxastic forms of faith—a crucial distinction that Western philosophers of religion have only begun to explore and defend in the past several decades. Second, Vivekananda's doxastic involuntarism with respect to religious belief is a timely position that resonates strongly with contemporary arguments in epistemology against the view that beliefs can be adopted at will. Third, his unique Vedāntic view of religious faith as a journey from weaker to stronger epistemic states challenges the more static views of faith typically favored by contemporary philosophers of religion. Fourth, Vivekananda invites contemporary Christian philosophers and theologians to reflect more deeply on Jesus's rather demanding teachings in the Sermon on the Mount and their implications for understanding the dynamics of religious faith. From Vivekananda's standpoint, Jesus is at one with Vedāntic sages in holding that the journey of faith involves a strenuous process of self-purification culminating in the direct supersensuous perception of God: "Blessed are the pure in heart, for they shall see God." Fifth, Vivekananda's provocative thesis that faith culminates not in belief but in the *realization* of God is, as far as I am aware, entirely absent from contemporary Western discussions of faith. This thesis, moreover, has far-reaching implications for the question of whether and how religious faith can be justified or verified. In Vivekananda's view, since mystical experience is a source of knowledge, the highest form of religious faith meets even the most stringent evidentialist standards: religious belief is ultimately verified through a self-authenticating experience of God, which removes all doubts.

PART IV
CONSCIOUSNESS

9

Panentheistic Cosmopsychism

Vivekananda's Sāṃkhya-Vedāntic Solution to the Hard Problem of Consciousness

We now see that all the various forms of cosmic energy, such as matter, thought, force, intelligence and so forth, are simply the manifestations of that cosmic intelligence, or, as we shall call it henceforth, the Supreme Lord. Everything that you see, feel, or hear, the whole universe, is His creation, or to be a little more accurate, is His projection; or to be still more accurate, is the Lord Himself. It is He who is shining as the sun and the stars, He is the mother earth. . . . He is the speech that is uttered, He is the man who is talking. He is the audience that is here. . . . It is all He.

—Swami Vivekananda, "The Cosmos: The Microcosm" (1896; *CW* 2:211)

Conscious experience is such a pervasive feature of our lives that we usually take it for granted. We experience, for instance, the delicious taste of tiramisu, the shimmering colors of a rainbow, the sharp pain of a sprained ankle. What all these experiences have in common is an irreducibly subjective or qualitative character. As Thomas Nagel (1974) puts it, there is something *it is like* to be in any such experiential state. Recent philosophers have used technical terms like "qualia" and "phenomenal consciousness" to capture this subjective dimension of the experiential lives of human beings and (presumably) many other animals.

In spite of its familiarity, consciousness is notoriously difficult to explain. Philosophers throughout the world have puzzled over this ubiquitous feature of our everyday lives. What exactly *is* consciousness? What makes us conscious creatures rather than mere non-conscious automata? Does consciousness arise from states of the brain, and if so, how and why? The contemporary philosopher David Chalmers (1995; 1996) has made an influential distinction between "easy" and "hard" problems of consciousness. According to Chalmers, neuroscientists may very well be able to solve in the next century or two one of the "easy" problems of consciousness, such as the problem of pinpointing

Swami Vivekananda's Vedāntic Cosmopolitanism. Swami Medhananda, Oxford University Press. © Oxford University Press 2022. DOI: 10.1093/oso/9780197624463.003.0010

the neural correlates of particular conscious states (1995: 200–1). However, Chalmers argues that such a hypothetically complete and accurate science of physical correlations would still leave unanswered the one really *hard* problem of consciousness: namely, the problem of explaining *why* certain states of the brain are accompanied by, or give rise to, conscious experience.[1] Similarly, Joseph Levine (1983) has argued that even if scientists are able to identify the physical correlates of conscious experiences, there still remains an "explanatory gap" between physical states and consciousness that needs to be bridged. If a scientist were to tell me that pain is nothing but C-fibers firing, then I would be justified in protesting that such a materialist explanation of pain is inadequate, since it fails to account for how pain *feels* to me. No merely third-person scientific description of the physical correlates of our conscious experiences can explain the first-person qualitative dimension of these experiences.

Philosophers have proposed a wide range of solutions to the hard problem of consciousness, including eliminativism, materialist reductionism, epiphenomenalist dualism, interactionist dualism, and mysterianism.[2] For various reasons, many philosophers have not been satisfied with any of these theories of consciousness. As a result, a number of recent analytic philosophers of mind have begun to take seriously panpsychism, the apparently counterintuitive view that everything in the world is in some sense conscious.[3] Panpsychism is hardly a new view. Many Western philosophers have advocated forms of panpsychism, including Thales of Miletus, Baruch Spinoza, G. W. Leibniz, Josiah Royce, and W. K. Clifford (Skrbina 2005; Goff 2017b: sec. 1). While most analytic philosophers have not considered non-Western forms of panpsychism, some scholars have very recently begun to explore how ideas and arguments from Indian philosophical traditions—such as Vedānta,[4] Yogācāra Buddhism (Duckworth 2017), and Śaiva Nondualism (Biernacki 2016a; 2016b)—might be able to enrich contemporary debates about panpsychism.

Within the context of cross-cultural work on panpsychism, both Luca Gasparri (2019) and Miri Albahari (2020; 2019a) have identified points of affinity and divergence between certain forms of panpsychism and classical Advaita Vedānta in particular. Anand Vaidya (2020) has helpfully widened the

[1] Some philosophers formulate the hard problem in a narrower manner that presupposes the truth of materialism. Eugene O. Mills (1997: 109), for instance, defines the hard problem of consciousness as "the problem of explaining why physical processes give rise to conscious phenomenal experience." It is question-begging to pose the hard problem in a way that presupposes materialism, since doing so dogmatically rules out the possibility of a non-materialistic explanation of consciousness. Hence, I understand the hard problem of consciousness in a broader way: why does conscious experience exist and how does it arise?

[2] For a brief summary of some of the main approaches to consciousness, see section 1.

[3] See, for instance, Nagel (1979), Brüntrup and Jaskolla (2017), Seager (2020), Goff (2017a).

[4] Gasparri (2019: 130–42), Albahari (2020), Vaidya and Bilimoria (2015), and Vaidya (2020).

Vedāntic field by bringing recent work on panpsychism into dialogue not only with Advaita Vedānta but also with Viśiṣṭādvaita Vedānta and Ramakrishna's Vijñāna Vedānta.[5] Taking Vaidya's lead, I will provide in this and the next chapter the first detailed examination of Vivekananda's unduly neglected views on consciousness. Vivekananda, I argue, defends a distinctive form of panpsychism that has great contemporary relevance.

Section 1 of this chapter briefly outlines some of the main theories of consciousness proposed by recent analytic philosophers. Section 2 provides important historical context by outlining the views on consciousness of five of Vivekananda's prominent late-nineteenth-century contemporaries—namely, John Tyndall, T. H. Huxley, William James, W. K. Clifford, and Alfred Russel Wallace, some of whom Vivekananda referred to in his lectures and writings. Section 3 summarizes Ramakrishna's mystically grounded panentheistic worldview, which played a major role in shaping the views of his disciple Vivekananda.

With this background in place, I go on to provide a detailed reconstruction of Vivekananda's theory of consciousness in sections 4 and 5 of this chapter and in the next chapter. Section 4 of this chapter discusses Vivekananda's approach to the hard problem of consciousness and his critique of modern materialist theories of consciousness. In opposition to materialism, Vivekananda defends the Sāṃkhyan position that the insentient mind appears conscious because of the conscious soul (Puruṣa) behind it. However, as I discuss in section 5, he also criticizes certain aspects of Sāṃkhyan dualist metaphysics and ultimately defends a Sāṃkhya-Vedāntic metaphysics of panentheistic cosmopsychism, according to which the sole reality is Divine Consciousness, which manifests as everything in the universe.

In the next chapter, I will discuss Vivekananda's sophisticated philosophical arguments in support of panentheistic cosmopsychism, many of which anticipated arguments in contemporary philosophy of mind and religion. I will also elaborate in greater detail his account of divine manifestation, which explains how the single Divine Consciousness individuates into the various conscious perspectives of human subjects. Taken together, chapters 9 and 10 make the case that Vivekananda's panentheistic cosmopsychism, in light of its distinctive features and its potential philosophical advantages over rival positions, deserves to be taken seriously by contemporary philosophers of consciousness.

[5] Vaidya's discussion of Ramakrishna's Vijñāna Vedānta is based on my reconstruction of Ramakrishna's philosophy in the first chapter of my book *Infinite Paths to Infinite Reality* (Maharaj 2018).

1. Contemporary Analytic Responses to the Hard Problem of Consciousness

In the past few decades, there has been a resurgence of interest in consciousness among analytic philosophers of mind. Since the literature on the topic is extensive, my aim in this section is only to summarize nine of the main responses to the hard problem of consciousness in the recent literature: eliminativism, reductionism, mysterianism, interactionist substance dualism, epiphenomenalist dualism, property dualism, panpsychism, panprotopsychism, and neutral monism. I will focus especially on panpsychism, since it is most relevant to the concerns of this chapter.

Eliminativism is the view that there *is* no hard problem of consciousness, since conscious experience itself does not exist, even if it *seems* to many of us to exist. While some philosophers continue to defend eliminativism about consciousness (Dennett 1988; Rey 1997; Frankish 2016, 2017), most philosophers agree that eliminativism is implausible in the extreme, since it denies the reality of conscious experiences like the taste of coffee or the fragrance of a rose. Reductionism holds, in contrast to eliminativism, that conscious experience does exist but that it can be fully explained in terms of neural states or functional properties. There are numerous reductionist theories of consciousness, including functionalism, first-order representationalism, higher-order representationalism, self-representationalism, and neuronal reductionism.[6] However, as Nagel, Chalmers, and many others have argued, all such reductionist theories fail to explain the qualitative, "what it is like" dimension of conscious experience, which is precisely what calls for explanation.

Mysterianism is the view that the hard problem of consciousness is either temporarily or permanently insoluble. Nagel, for instance, claims that our present scientific methods are not equipped to explain how and why conscious experience arises from physical states but that future science may be able to provide an "objective phenomenology" that adequately explains the subjective character of conscious states (1974: 449–50). Colin McGinn (1991) goes even further than Nagel by arguing that the hard problem of consciousness is *permanently* insoluble. While McGinn believes that consciousness arises from physical states, he claims that our inherent cognitive limitations prevent us from understanding how this is possible.

In light of the various difficulties facing physicalist theories of consciousness, many Western philosophers have embraced some form of mind-body dualism, the view that mind and matter are ontologically distinct. Interactionist substance dualism, a view famously defended by Descartes and versions of which continue

[6] See, for instance, Churchland (1986), Nöe (2005), and Block (2002).

to be advocated by philosophers, is the view that mind and matter are ontologically distinct substances that can causally influence each other.[7] Interactionist substance dualism has several advantages over competing positions, since it not only accounts for the qualitative dimension of conscious experience but also supports the commonsense view that our mental states have a causal impact on the physical world. (For many people, it is just obvious that my desire to walk across the street, for instance, *causes* me to walk across the street.) Many contemporary philosophers, however, argue that the advantages of interactionist substance dualism are outweighed by its costs. First, it seems difficult to justify the existence of a non-physical soul or mind, particularly in the light of modern science and the waning of belief in God or souls (especially among Western academics). Second, interactionist substance dualists like Descartes face notorious difficulties in trying to explain how the mind interacts with the brain. Third, interactionist substance dualism requires us to deny the causal closure of the physical, the widely held view that physical events have only physical causes.

Epiphenomenalist dualism, in contrast to interactionist dualism, is the view that while mind and matter are ontologically distinct, mind is a mere byproduct of physical processes in the brain and, therefore, has no causal influence on physical events (T. H. Huxley 1890a; Robinson 2004). The advantage of epiphenomenalism over interactionist dualism is that the former accepts the causal closure of the physical, since it denies that mental events can affect physical events. Arguably, however, this advantage comes at too steep a cost, since epiphenomenalism flies in the face of the commonsense view that mental events are causally efficacious. Moreover, epiphenomenalists are hard pressed to provide a cogent explanation of *how* the mind arises from the brain. Meanwhile, some philosophers like Chalmers (1996) reject substance dualism in favor of property dualism, the view that there is only one substance—namely, matter—which has distinct physical and mental properties.

In light of the various difficulties facing traditional approaches to consciousness, numerous contemporary philosophers have begun to champion panpsychism, the view that consciousness is present everywhere, even in amoebas and electrons. Both Nagel (1979) and Galen Strawson (2008) have argued that if we rule out substance dualism, then we can infer the truth of panpsychism from two plausible premises: nonreductionism about consciousness and the denial of radical emergence. According to the first premise, no reductionist explanation of conscious experience in terms of its neural correlates or its functional role can resolve the hard problem of accounting for the qualitative, "what it is like" dimension of consciousness. According to the second premise, if we accept the plausible principle of *ex nihilo nihil fit* ("nothing comes from nothing"), then it

[7] Swinburne (1986), Lowe (2008), and Baker and Goetz (2011).

is unintelligible how consciousness can emerge from non-conscious entities. As Strawson puts it, "For any feature *Y* of anything that is correctly considered to be emergent from *X*, there must be something about *X* and *X* alone in virtue of which *Y* emerges, and which is sufficient for *Y*" (2008: 65). According to panpsychists, the best way to explain conscious experience while avoiding both reductionism and radical emergence is to adopt the view that human and non-human animal consciousness is grounded in, or constituted by, a more fundamental form of consciousness present everywhere.

There are two basic forms of panpsychism, depending on how one characterizes this fundamental form of consciousness. Micropsychism is the form of panpsychism according to which macro-level human and non-human animal consciousness derives from the more fundamental consciousness of *micro-level* entities like quarks or electrons (Goff 2017b). The most formidable problem facing micropsychist views is the "subject combination problem"—the problem of explaining how micro-subjects can combine to form macro-level conscious subjects (Chalmers 2017a).

In light of the subject combination problem, some contemporary philosophers have rejected micropsychism in favor of cosmopsychism, the view that human and non-human animal consciousness derives from "cosmic consciousness," the more fundamental consciousness of the universe as a whole.[8] Clearly, cosmopsychism avoids the subject combination problem, since it explains human and animal consciousness in terms of cosmic consciousness rather than the consciousness of micro-level entities. However, cosmopsychist views arguably face the obverse problem—variously called the "individuation problem" (Mathews 2011: 145), the "decombination problem" (Albahari 2020), and the "derivation problem" (Nagasawa and Wager 2017)—of explaining how the consciousness of the cosmos as a whole *individuates* into the conscious experiences of individual humans and non-human animals.

It is also important to note that the vast majority of contemporary philosophers discussing panpsychism take consciousness to be synonymous with mind or mentality. Philip Goff (2017b), for instance, defines panpsychism as "the view that mentality is fundamental and ubiquitous in the natural world." Similarly, Nagel writes, "By panpsychism I mean the view that the basic physical constituents of the universe have mental properties . . . " (1979: 181). However, since most Indian philosophical traditions take mind to be a subtle form of insentient matter, I believe it would be more accurate and helpful to define panpsychism more broadly as the view that *consciousness* is fundamental and ubiquitous.[9]

[8] Shani (2015, 2018), Nagasawa and Wager (2017), Mathews (2011).
[9] Vaidya (2020: 415) makes a similar point.

All forms of panpsychism have to address what Goff (2017b) calls the "incredulous stare" objection, the objection that it is deeply counterintuitive and implausible to ascribe even rudimentary forms of consciousness to the fundamental constituents of the universe, which seem to be insentient. Some contemporary philosophers have defended two views that are very similar to panpsychism—namely, panprotopsychism and neutral monism—which they claim are not vulnerable to the incredulous stare objection. Panprotopsychism is the view that human and non-human animal consciousness derives from *proto-consciousness*, which is present in all micro-level entities (Chalmers 2017b). Neutral monism, by contrast, is the view that the intrinsic nature of ultimate reality is neither physical nor mental and that human and non-human animal consciousness derives from ultimately neutral entities (Stubenberg 2016). Proponents of panprotopsychism and neutral monism claim that these views are not vulnerable to the incredulous stare objection against panpsychism, since they do not ascribe conscious experience to micro-level entities.

This necessarily brief and oversimplified survey of some of the most important recent responses to the hard problem of consciousness will provide the conceptual background for the remainder of this chapter, as it will enable us not only to identify precisely the various approaches to consciousness adopted by Vivekananda and his contemporaries but also to demonstrate the continued relevance of Vivekananda's views.

2. *Late Nineteenth-Century Western Views on Consciousness*

Remarkably, many of the contemporary approaches to consciousness outlined in the previous section were anticipated by late nineteenth-century thinkers (Leach and Tartaglia 2017; Pinch 2014–2015). As early as 1868, the Irish physicist John Tyndall (1820–1893) raised the hard problem of consciousness in the following striking passage, which became so widely read and cited that William James could refer to it in 1890 as "that lucky paragraph which has been quoted so often that every one knows it by heart" ([1890] 1950: 147):

> [T]he passage from the physics of the brain to the corresponding facts of consciousness is unthinkable. Granted that a definite thought, and a definite molecular action in the brain occur simultaneously, we do not possess the intellectual organ, nor apparently any rudiment of the organ, which would enable us to pass by a process of reasoning from the one phenomenon to the other. They appear together, but we do not know why. Were our minds and senses so expanded, strengthened, and illuminated as to enable us to see and feel the very molecules of the brain; were we capable of following all their motions, all their groupings,

> all their electric discharges, if such there be, and were we intimately acquainted with the corresponding states of thought and feeling, we should be as far as ever from the solution of the problem, "How are these physical processes connected with the facts of consciousness?" The chasm between the two classes of phenomena would still remain intellectually impassable. (Tyndall 1870: 16–17)

Anticipating Chalmers, Tyndall argued that a mere science of correlations leaves unanswered the really hard problem of explaining the *connection* between "physical processes" in the brain with "the facts of consciousness." Likewise, Tyndall's claim about the unbridgeable "chasm" between neural processes and conscious states anticipated Joseph Levine's argument about an "explanatory gap." Tyndall's preferred view is a form of mysterianism, though he seemed to remain noncommittal about whether the mystery is a temporary or a permanent one. His claim that "we do not possess the intellectual organ" to understand how conscious states are related to brain processes comes close to Colin McGinn's permanent mysterianism, the view that human cognitive limitations make the hard problem of consciousness insoluble. However, while McGinn takes for granted that conscious experience arises from neural processes, Tyndall remained resolutely noncommittal about physicalism, noting that the limits of science open up a space for a "theological" explanation of consciousness (1870: 18). Moreover, in the paragraphs following the passage just quoted, Tyndall raised the intriguing possibility that the mystery of consciousness may be temporary after all, since we are not entitled to assume that "man's present faculties end the series" (1870: 18). For Tyndall, it is possible that the human mind will eventually evolve into a superhuman form of mentality that may be able to penetrate the mysteries of consciousness.

In a widely read 1874 article, the prominent British scientist T. H. Huxley (1825–1895) defended the epiphenomenalist view that humans and other animals are "conscious automata" (1890a: 244) and that consciousness is a causally inert byproduct of neural processes:

> The consciousness of brutes would appear to be related to the mechanism of their body simply as a collateral product of its working, and to be as completely without any power of modifying that working as the steam-whistle which accompanies the work of a locomotive engine is without influence upon its machinery. (1890a: 240)

According to Huxley, just as a train's engine causes the steam-whistle to produce a sound that has no causal influence on the workings of the engine itself, bodily processes produce consciousness as a "collateral product" that has no causal influence on physical events. However, Huxley himself recognized that epiphenomenalism was insufficient on its own to solve the hard problem of consciousness. As he put it in a physiology textbook, "But what consciousness is, we know not; and how it is that anything so remarkable as a state of consciousness comes about as the result of irritating nervous tissue, is just as unaccountable as the appearance of the Djin when Aladdin rubbed his lamp in the story, or as any other ultimate fact of nature" (Huxley 1866: 193).[10] As a committed epiphenomenalist, Huxley was convinced that consciousness arose as a causally inert byproduct of physical processes. Nonetheless, he remained baffled about *how* consciousness arises from physical processes, ultimately taking the emergence of consciousness from insentient matter to be a brute "fact of nature" that cannot be explained.

The British philosopher and mathematician W. K. Clifford (1845–1879) critically engaged Huxley's approach to consciousness in an 1874 lecture entitled "Body and Mind." On the one hand, Clifford wholeheartedly endorsed Huxley's epiphenomenalism:

> Again, if anybody says that the will influences matter, the statement is not untrue, but it is nonsense. The will is not a material thing, it is not a mode of material motion. . . . The only thing which influences matter is the position of surrounding matter or the motion of surrounding matter. (1879: 56)

On the other hand, Clifford rejected Huxley's reluctant acceptance of the brute emergence of consciousness from physical processes. Anticipating Nagel and Strawson, Clifford argued that the impossibility of the brute emergence of consciousness from insentient matter makes it reasonable to accept either panpsychism or panprotopsychism:

> yet we cannot suppose that so enormous a jump from one creature to another should have occurred at any point in the process of evolution as the introduction of a fact entirely different and absolutely separate from the physical fact. It is impossible for anybody to point out the particular place in the line of descent where that event can be supposed to have taken place. The only thing that we can come to, if we accept the doctrine of evolution at all, is that even in the very lowest organisms, even in the Amoeba which swims about in our own blood, there is something or other, inconceivably simple to us, which is of the same nature with our own consciousness, although not of the same complexity—that is to say (for we cannot stop at organic matter,

[10] Huxley leaves this passage largely unaltered in later editions of the textbook, which suggests that even after he explicitly adopted an epiphenomenalist position in 1874, he continued to accept the sheer mysteriousness of consciousness.

> knowing as we do that it must have arisen by continuous physical processes out of inorganic matter), we are obliged to assume, in order to save continuity in our belief, that along with every motion of matter, whether organic or inorganic, there is some fact which corresponds to the mental fact in ourselves. The mental fact in ourselves is an exceedingly complex thing; so also our brain is an exceedingly complex thing. We may assume that the quasi-mental fact which corresponds and which goes along with the motion of every particle of matter is of such inconceivable simplicity, as compared with our own mental fact, with our consciousness, as the motion of a molecule of matter is of inconceivable simplicity when compared with the motion in our brain. (1879: 60–61)

Clifford based his argument on Charles Darwin's theory of gradual evolution through natural selection, which sent shockwaves throughout the Western world when it was introduced in 1859. According to Clifford, the Darwinian doctrine of gradual evolution rules out the possibility that consciousness suddenly emerged at some particular point in the evolutionary process, since such an enormous "jump" from non-conscious matter to consciousness is incompatible with evolutionary gradualism. Unlike Huxley, Clifford argued that the most reasonable way to account for the emergence of human consciousness is to posit that consciousness in some form was already present even in the "very lowest organisms" and in all forms of matter. It remains somewhat unclear whether Clifford endorsed panpsychism or panprotopsychism. The fact that he referred to the "quasi-mental" properties of all matter suggests that he might have been a panprotopsychist. Earlier in the passage, however, he clarified that the quasi-mentality of matter "is of the same nature with our own consciousness, although not of the same complexity," which may suggest the panpsychist view of an ontological continuity between human consciousness and more primitive forms of consciousness.

William James (1842–1910) was deeply interested in consciousness and critically engaged the work of both Huxley and Clifford in his article "Are We Automata?" (1879) and in his later book *The Principles of Psychology* (1890). James attacked the epiphenomenalist dualism of Huxley and Clifford, which he claimed "banishes" the mind to "a limbo of causal inertness, from whence no intrusion or interruption on its part need ever be feared" (1879: 3). He presented two main objections to epiphenomenalism, one negative and one positive. His negative argument was that it is counterintuitive in the extreme to deny the commonsense view that mental states are causally efficacious—that, for instance, the "thoughts in Shakespeare's mind" led him to write *Hamlet* ([1890] 1950: 132–33). James's positive argument was based on Darwinian evolution through natural selection: he provided various reasons for believing that consciousness was an evolutionary advantage for biological organisms, and he argued that the adaptive value of consciousness presupposed its causal efficacy in the physical world.

Although James was highly critical of Clifford's epiphenomenalism, he was much more sympathetic to—and, indeed, may have been influenced by—Clifford's appeal to pan(proto?)psychism. Like Clifford, James argued that it is highly unlikely that consciousness could have emerged suddenly from insentient matter. As James puts it, "we ought . . . to try every possible mode of conceiving of consciousness so that it may not appear equivalent to the irruption into the universe of a new nature non-existent to then" ([1890] 1950: 148). Also like Clifford, James argued that the Darwinian doctrine of gradual evolution, combined with the denial of the brute emergence of consciousness, entailed panpsychism or a similar view:

> And Consciousness, however small, is an illegitimate birth in any philosophy that starts without it, and yet professes to explain all facts by continuous evolution. *If evolution is to work smoothly, consciousness in some shape must have been present at the very origin of things.* Accordingly we find that the more clear-sighted evolutionary philosophers are beginning to posit it there. Each atom of the nebula, they suppose, must have had an aboriginal atom of consciousness linked with it. ([1890] 1950: 149; emphasis in original)

Tellingly, in his Harvard lecture notes from 1902 to 1903, James explicitly declared his "doctrine" to be "pluralistic pansychism" (quoted in Perry 1935: 373). Moreover, in several articles written between 1904 and 1905, James characterized ultimate reality as "pure experience" and claimed that both mental and physical states derived from pure experience (James 1912). However, there is considerable scholarly controversy regarding the precise nature of "pure experience" in James's philosophy. Is James's pure experience best understood as mental (panpsychism), protomental (panprotopsychism), or *neither* mental nor physical (neutral monism)?[11] Assessing this complicated interpretive issue is, of course, beyond the scope of this chapter. For present purposes, what is important is that James defended either full-blown panpsychism or a kindred position on consciousness.

One of the most fascinating figures in late nineteenth-century Europe was Alfred Russel Wallace (1823–1913), a brilliant and eccentric British biologist who, independently of his friend Darwin, developed a theory of evolution based on natural selection in 1858. Until around 1864, Wallace agreed with Darwin that natural selection was the primary driver of the evolution of all species, including

[11] These three interpretations of James's philosophy are defended respectively by Ford (1982), Cooper (1990, 2002), and Ayer (1968).

human beings (Kottler 1974). However, in July 1865, Wallace began to attend seances, which convinced him of the existence of spiritual beings that interacted with the physical world (Kottler 1974: 164). From that point on, he was a committed "spiritualist," even writing a book-length defense of spiritualism (Wallace 1896). Wallace's spiritualist convictions led him to rethink entirely his views on natural selection in relation to human beings. In *Contributions to the Theory of Natural Selection* (1870) and his later book *Darwinism* (1889), Wallace accepted Darwin's thesis that humans evolved from lower animals and argued that natural selection perfectly accounts for the various traits we find in plants and nonhuman animals as well as most (but not all) of the *physical* traits of humans. However, Wallace also argued, in stark contrast to Darwin, that natural selection fails to account for three major phenomena: the origin of life from matter; the origin of consciousness from matter; and the origin of the higher intellectual, aesthetic, and moral faculties of human beings. According to Wallace, the best way to account for these phenomena is to accept the doctrine of occasional spiritual interventionism—the view that higher spiritual beings intervened during these three crucial phases in an evolutionary process otherwise governed by natural selection.

In "The Limits of Natural Selection as Applied to Man"—the final chapter of his *Contributions*—Wallace argued that natural selection is unable to account for the emergence of consciousness (1870: 352). With regard to the question of the origin of consciousness, Wallace referred to the recent work of Tyndall and Huxley. Wallace approvingly quoted Tyndall's famous formulation of the hard problem of consciousness in which he declares that the "passage from the physics of the brain to the corresponding facts of consciousness is unthinkable" (1870: 361). However, instead of adopting Tyndall's noncommittal mysterianism, Wallace argued that consciousness could not possibly emerge from physical processes. Explicitly rejecting Huxley's physicalist view that "thoughts are expressions of molecular changes" at the level of matter, Wallace claimed that Huxley failed to bridge over the "chasm" separating matter from mind and that all such attempts to derive mind from matter are "inconsistent with accurate conceptions of molecular physics" (1870: 362). Anticipating Clifford's and James's arguments against the brute emergence of consciousness, Wallace argued that consciousness could not possibly emerge from a combination—no matter how complex—of unconscious material elements, since "[y]ou cannot have, in the whole, what does not exist in any of the parts" (1870: 365). According to Wallace, once we rule out the possibility that consciousness emerged from insentient matter, we are faced with a stark alternative between panpsychism and spiritualist dualism: "There is no escape from this dilemma,—either all matter is conscious, or consciousness is something distinct from matter, and in the latter case, its presence in material forms is a proof of the existence of conscious beings, outside of, and independent of, what we term matter" (1870: 365). He dismissed without argument the panpsychist view that "all matter is conscious," presumably because he took it to be absurd. Accordingly, Wallace argued that the best way to explain consciousness is to accept the view that "higher intelligent beings" were responsible for the emergence of consciousness (1870: 371A).

Vivekananda was aware of the views of many of these Western thinkers and kept abreast of the latest debates about consciousness, evolution, and other current issues. In his lectures and private letters, he referred to T. H. Huxley four times[12] and to Tyndall twice.[13] As I discussed in section 1 of the previous chapter, he also personally met William James at Harvard University in 1894 and 1896 and had extended discussions with him. Vivekananda did not refer to Clifford or Wallace anywhere in his lectures or writings, but it is still possible that he was aware of them.

I have not found any evidence that Vivekananda read the specific articles and books of the thinkers discussed in this section, though he very well might have read one or more of them. In any case, as we will see in this and the next chapter, some of Vivekananda's key arguments about consciousness resonate with those of Tyndall, Clifford, James, and Wallace. Whether or not Vivekananda had read the work of these thinkers, I will argue that he adopted a broadly cosmopolitan method in articulating and justifying his own unique Sāṃkhya-Vedāntic position on consciousness. That is, he articulated and defended his views on consciousness by drawing upon, and critically engaging, ideas and arguments in both Western and Indian philosophical traditions. Vivekananda's philosophical cosmopolitanism, then, is reflected not only in his explicit engagement with Indian and Western thinkers but also, more broadly, in his sustained effort to explain his philosophical views in a manner that both his Indian and Western contemporaries would find relevant and convincing.

3. *Ramakrishna's Mystically Grounded Panentheistic Cosmopsychism*

The key Indian philosophical sources for Vivekananda's understanding of consciousness were Sāṃkhya, Advaita Vedānta, and the teachings of his guru Ramakrishna. In this section, I will outline briefly Ramakrishna's teachings on consciousness, and in sections 4 and 5, I will discuss Vivekananda's extensive engagement with the philosophies of Sāṃkhya and Advaita Vedānta.

[12] *CW* 9:25, *CW* 2:74, *CW* 2:28, and *CW* 2:218.
[13] *CW* 2:218 and *CW* 2:74.

Ramakrishna's views on consciousness were grounded in his philosophy of Vijñāna Vedānta, outlined in section 1 of chapter 1 and explained in much greater detail in the first chapter of my book *Infinite Paths to Infinite Reality* (Maharaj 2018). For present purposes, what is crucial is his distinction between two fundamental stages of spiritual realization, which he calls "*jñāna*" and "*vijñāna*." According to Ramakrishna, *jñāna* is the Advaitic realization of one's true essence as the impersonal nondual Brahman, which is "immovable, immutable, inactive, and of the nature of Pure Consciousness (*bodha-svarūpa*)" (*K* 430 / *G* 430). The *jñānī* feels that Brahman alone is real and that everything else is unreal. However, Ramakrishna maintained that some rare souls, even after attaining *brahmajñāna*, can go on to attain the even greater state of *vijñāna*, a more intimate and expansive realization of God as the impersonal-personal Infinite Reality that has become everything in the universe. According to Ramakrishna, "The *vijñānī* sees that the Reality which is impersonal (*nirguṇa*) is also personal (*saguṇa*)" (*K* 51 / *G* 104). Hence, while the Advaitic *jñānī* dismisses Śakti (the personal God) as unreal, the *vijñānī* realizes that "Brahman and Śakti are inseparable" (*K* 568 / *G* 550). Moreover, while the *jñānī* dismisses the world as unreal, the *vijñānī* looks upon the world as a real manifestation of God. As Ramakrishna put it, "God, as Consciousness, has become the entire universe of the living and non-living" (*tini caitanyarūpe carācar viśve vyāpta hoye royechen*) (*K* 283 / *G* 300).

Ramakrishna explicitly declared that he had himself attained this panentheistic realization of *vijñāna*:

> Why should the universe be unreal? That is a speculation of the philosophers. After realizing God, one sees that it is God Herself who has become the universe and all living beings. The Divine Mother revealed to me in the Kālī temple that it was She who had become everything. She showed me that everything was Divine Consciousness (*sab cinmaya*). The Image was Consciousness, the altar was Consciousness, the water vessels were Consciousness, the doorsill was Consciousness, the marble floor was Consciousness—all was Consciousness. I found everything inside the room soaked, as it were, in Bliss—the Bliss of Saccidānanda. I saw a wicked man in front of the Kālī temple; but in him also I saw the Śakti of the Divine Mother vibrating. That was why I fed a cat with the food that was to be offered to the Divine Mother. I clearly perceived that the Divine Mother Herself had become everything—even the cat. . . . After realizing God, one sees all this aright—that it is She who has become the universe, living beings, and the twenty-four cosmic principles (*tinī jīva, jagat, caturviṃśati tattva hoyechen*). (*K* 335–36 / *G* 345)

In contemporary philosophical terms, we can say that Ramakrishna's mystical experience of *vijñāna* led him to accept a panentheistic form of cosmopsychism, according to which everything in the universe is one and the same Divine Consciousness manifesting in various forms. He specifically emphasized that this Divine Consciousness is present not only in sentient creatures like cats and human beings but also in insentient things like water vessels and marble floors.

As I already discussed in chapter 1, Ramakrishna considered his panentheistic worldview to be a world-inclusive form of Advaita. As he put it, "The *bhakta* also has a realization of oneness (*ekākār jñāna*); he sees that there is nothing but God. Instead of saying that the world is unreal like a dream, he says that God has become everything" (*K* 740 / *G* 700). Crucially, Ramakrishna explicitly contrasted his world-inclusive Advaitic philosophy with the world-denying Advaitic philosophy of Śaṅkara and his followers.

Vivekananda, I will argue, addressed the hard problem of consciousness largely by developing and defending the *vijñāna*-based panentheistic cosmopsychism taught to him by Ramakrishna. As we will see, Vivekananda frequently appealed to Advaita Vedānta in his efforts to explain and justify his panentheistic cosmopsychism, but we should always keep in mind that he followed Ramakrishna in championing a *world-inclusive* Integral Advaitic philosophy, according to which the world is a real manifestation of the impersonal-personal God.

4. *Vivekananda's Provisional Sāṃkhyan Mind-Consciousness Dualism*

With all this background in place, we can now embark on a detailed reconstruction of Vivekananda's theory of consciousness. On my interpretation, his solution to the hard problem of consciousness proceeds in two stages—the first Sāṃkhyan and the second Vedāntic—which I will discuss respectively in sections 4 and 5. In this section, I will discuss his provisional defense of Sāṃkhyan mind-consciousness dualism[14] over against modern materialist theories of consciousness. In the next section, I will argue that he identifies certain deficiencies in the philosophy of Sāṃkhya that lead him ultimately to champion a panentheistic form of Advaita Vedānta, which corrects for the weaknesses and lacunae in the Sāṃkhyan system. As we will see, he does not so much reject the Sāṃkhyan system as he dialectically incorporates it into his broader Vedāntic framework of panentheistic cosmopsychism.

[14] I borrow the phrase "mind-consciousness dualism" from Schweizer (1993).

In his lecture "The Science of Yoga" (1900) delivered in California, Vivekananda, like his contemporary Tyndall, raises the hard problem of consciousness in an acute form and hints at how it might be resolved:

> The mind cannot be analysed by any external machine. Supposing you could look into my brain while I am thinking, you would only see certain molecules interchanged. You could not see thought, consciousness, ideas, images. You would simply see the mass of vibrations—chemical and physical changes. From this example we see that this sort of analysis would not do.
>
> Is there any other method by which the mind can be analysed as mind? If there is, then the real science of religion is possible. The science of Rāja-Yoga claims there is such a possibility. We can all attempt it and succeed to a certain degree. There is this great difficulty: In external sciences the object is [comparatively easy to observe]. The instruments of analysis are rigid; and both are external. But in the analysis of the mind the object and the instruments of analysis are the same thing.... The subject and the object become one....
>
> External analysis will go to the brain and find physical and chemical changes. It would never succeed [in answering the questions]: What is the consciousness? What is your imagination? Where does this vast mass of ideas you have come from, and where do they go? We cannot deny them. They are facts. I never saw my own brain. I have to take for granted I have one. But man can never deny his own conscious imagination. (*CW* 7:431–32)[15]

Here, Vivekananda rejects two strategies for explaining consciousness that are still actively being discussed by contemporary philosophers of mind—namely, reductionism and eliminativism. As I discussed in section 1, while reductionism seeks to explain consciousness in terms of physical states of the brain, eliminativism goes to the extreme of claiming that first-person consciousness does not even exist. Against eliminativism, Vivekananda argues that first-person conscious experiences are "facts" that cannot be denied. Against reductionism, Vivekananda claims that through the methods of physical science, we might be able to demonstrate, at best, that certain "physical and chemical changes" in the brain correspond to certain states of consciousness. However, Vivekananda argues that such a third-person scientific analysis of the neural correlates of consciousness would still leave unanswered the question of the nature and origin of *first-person* conscious states such as "thought," "ideas," and "images." He thereby anticipates Nagel's argument against reductionism in his influential article "What Is It Like to Be a Bat?" (1974). As Nagel puts it, "every subjective phenomenon is essentially connected with a single point of view, and it seems inevitable

[15] The words and phrases in square brackets were supplied by the editor of the *Complete Works*.

that an objective, physical theory will abandon that point of view" (1974: 437). Vivekananda can also be seen as anticipating Chalmers's distinction between "easy" and "hard" problems of consciousness, since Vivekananda distinguishes the easy problem of identifying the neural correlates of consciousness from the hard problem of explaining the *nature* of consciousness and *how* and *why* it is correlated with certain brain states.

However, unlike Chalmers and Nagel and unlike any of his own contemporaries, Vivekananda argues that Rāja-Yoga—a method of meditative introspection—provides a unique scientific means of investigating subjective phenomena *without* abandoning the subjective point of view: namely, through the mind's analysis of itself. In "The Science of Yoga" lecture, he explains how the method of Rāja-Yoga can help clarify the nature of consciousness:

> The great problem is ourselves. Am I the long chain I do not see—one piece following the other in rapid succession but quite unconnected? Am I such a state of consciousness [for ever in a flux]? Or am I something more than that—a substance, an entity, what we call the soul? In other words, has man a soul or not? Is he a bundle of states of consciousness without any connection, or is he a unified substance? That is the great controversy. If we are merely bundles of consciousness, . . . such a question as immortality would be merely delusion. . . . On the other hand, if there is something in me which is a unit, a substance, then of course I am immortal. The unit cannot be destroyed or broken into pieces. Only compounds can be broken up. . . .
>
> The question is: Are we the substance [the soul] or this subtle matter, the changing, billowing mind? . . . Our minds are constantly changing. Where is the substance within? We do not find it. I am now this and now that. I will believe in the substance if for a moment you can stop these changes. . . .
>
> Yoga is the science that teaches us to stop the Citta [the mind-stuff] from getting into these changes. Suppose you succeed in leading the mind to a perfect state of Yoga. That moment you have solved the problem. You have known what you are. You have mastered all the changes. After that you may let the mind run about, but it is not the same mind any more. It is perfectly under your control. No more like wild horses that dash you down. . . . You have seen God. This is no longer a matter of speculation. . . . You have been yourself: I am the substance beyond all these changes. I am not the changes; if I were, I could not stop them. I *can* stop the changes, and therefore I can never be the changes. This is the proposition of the science of Yoga. . . . (*CW* 7:432–33)[16]

[16] The words and phrases in square brackets were supplied by the editor of the *Complete Works*. For a similar passage, see *CW* 6:95–96.

What is consciousness, and where does it come from? According to Vivekananda, Rāja-Yoga—which is based primarily on Patañjali's *Yogasūtra*—holds the key to answering these all-important questions. Since Yoga philosophy is based upon the dualist metaphysics of Sāṃkhya, we need a basic understanding of the Sāṃkhyan system to appreciate what Vivekananda is up to here.

According to Sāṃkhya, the eternal Puruṣa (Spirit or Self) alone is sentient, and everything else—including the mind—is only a modification of insentient Prakṛti (Primordial Nature). As Vivekananda explains, the English word "mind" corresponds to what Sāṃkhya philosophers call the "*antaḥkaraṇa*" (internal organ), which comprises the following four aspects: "First—*manas*, the cogitating or thinking faculty. . . . Second—*buddhi*, the will (sometimes called the intellect). Third—*ahaṃkāra*, the self-conscious egotism (from *aham*). Fourth—*citta*, the substance in and through which all the faculties act, the floor of the mind as it were . . . " (*CW* 8:39–40). It should be noted that Vivekananda is not deviating here from the traditional Sāṃkhyan triple schema of the *antaḥkaraṇa* as *manas*, *buddhi*, and *ahaṃkāra*. For Vivekananda, *citta*—as the "floor of the mind"—is not so much a fourth aspect of the *antaḥkaraṇa* as the foundation of *manas* itself.

Vivekananda explains the Sāṃkhyan approach to consciousness as follows: "Mind, intelligence, will, and everything else is insentient. But they are all reflecting the sentiency, the 'Cit' [Consciousness] of some being who is beyond all this, whom the Sāṅkhya philosophers call 'Puruṣa'" (*CW* 2:450). Sāṃkhya-Yoga, in other words, upholds a metaphysical dualism between the conscious Spirit and insentient matter. Crucially, even the mind (*antaḥkaraṇa*) is actually a subtle form of insentient matter, but it *appears* to be conscious because of the "light" of the Puruṣa behind it. As Vivekananda puts it, "By itself the mind has no light; but we see it reasons. Therefore there must be some one behind it, whose light is percolating through Mahat [cosmic consciousness] and consciousness [*ahaṃkāra*],[17] and subsequent modifications, and this is what Kapila calls the Puruṣa, the Self of the Vedāntin . . . " (*CW* 2:455–56). Obviously, Vivekananda intends the "light" of the Puruṣa illuminating the mind to be understood in metaphorical terms.

It is important to note that in Sāṃkhya philosophy, the *antaḥkaraṇa* is an essential part of the *liṅgaśarīra* or *sūkṣmaśarīra* (the fine or subtle body), the reincarnating entity that inhabits different physical bodies (*sthūlaśarīras*) from one life to the next (Larson 1969: 244). Vivekananda explains the Sāṃkhyan doctrine of reincarnation as follows:

[17] It may be confusing to contemporary readers that Vivekananda translates the Sanskrit term "*ahaṃkāra*"—commonly rendered by contemporary scholars as "ego-sense"—as "consciousness" (CW2:455) or "self-consciousness" (CW2:456). It should be kept in mind that for Vivekananda, *ahaṃkāra* itself is insentient but derives its consciousness from the sentient Puruṣa behind it.

> Each one of the Puruṣas is omnipresent; each one of us is omnipresent, but we can act only through the *liṅgaśarīra*, the fine body. The mind [*manas* and *buddhi*], the self-consciousness [*ahaṃkāra*], the organs [*indriyas*], and the vital forces [*prāṇas*] compose the fine body or sheath,[18] what in Christian philosophy is called the spiritual body of man. It is this body that gets salvation, or punishment, or heaven, that incarnates and reincarnates, because we see from the very beginning that the going and the coming of the Puruṣa or soul are impossible. (*CW* 2:456)

Sāṃkhya, then, upholds a three-tiered ontology of the self: the insentient grossly physical body (*sthūlaśarīra*), the insentient subtly physical body that reincarnates (*liṅgaśarīra*), and the conscious non-physical Spirit (Puruṣa). Moreover, Sāṃkhya philosophers accept the existence of multiple Puruṣas, each corresponding to a different *liṅgaśarīra*.

We can now come back to the long passage quoted earlier in which Vivekananda emphasizes the value of Rāja-Yoga in understanding consciousness. Rāja-Yoga, he claims, is the scientific method through which we can directly verify the existence of the eternal conscious Self. Through a series of graded ethical and spiritual practices, Rāja-Yoga teaches us to control, and eventually eliminate, all the fluctuations (*vṛttis*) of the mind, thereby enabling us to realize our true nature as the eternal Puruṣa apart from the body-mind complex.[19] Vivekananda reasons that if we are able to stop these mental fluctuations, then we can be certain that we are something *apart* from these fluctuations—namely, the transcendent Puruṣa. As he puts it elsewhere, "Only when the sea is stilled to mirror-like calmness, can the reflection of the moon be seen, and only when the 'mind-stuff,' the Citta[,] is controlled to absolute calmness, is the Self to be recognised" (*CW* 8:40). He also notes in numerous places that through Yogic practice, we can gain knowledge of our own past lives, thereby directly verifying the truth of reincarnation: "Verification is the perfect proof of a theory, and here is the challenge thrown to the world by the Ṛṣis. We have discovered the secret by which the very depths of the ocean of memory can be stirred up—try it and you would get a complete reminiscence of your past life" (*CW* 1:9). For Vivekananda, then, while the "external sciences" are helpless in the face of the hard problem of consciousness, the *internal* science of Rāja-Yoga is uniquely equipped to penetrate the mysteries of consciousness by enabling us to verify for ourselves whether or not we have an eternal soul.

[18] Likewise, in his lecture on "Sāṃkhya Cosmology" (1895), Vivekananda states: "The organs, the *prāṇa* functions, the mind and the *buddhi* combined, are called the finer body of man—the *liṅga* or *sūkṣma śarīra*" (CW2:438).

[19] For details, see Vivekananda's *Rāja-Yoga* (*CW* 1:119–313).

Vivekananda was well aware that many of his Western contemporaries would be inclined to dismiss his claims about the "scientific" status of Rāja-Yoga. Accordingly, as I discussed at length in chapter 5, he defended the scientific credentials of Rāja-Yoga by presenting an argument for the epistemic value of supersensous perception (AEV). It is important to note that when Vivekananda appeals to the "science" of Rāja-Yoga in his discussions of the hard problem of consciousness, he is not dogmatically presupposing the epistemic value of mystical experience. Rather, as I will discuss in the next chapter, AEV plays an important role in his philosophical justification of panentheistic cosmopsychism.

It is worth recognizing the originality and boldness of Vivekananda's approach to consciousness in his late nineteenth-century context. Vivekananda was, of course, hardly alone in raising the hard problem of consciousness. However, while thinkers like Tyndall, James, Huxley, and Wallace no doubt recognized the hard problem of consciousness, none of Vivekananda's contemporaries explored the possibility of addressing the hard problem through meditative practice and insight. To be sure, James, in his *Principles of Psychology* (1890), emphasized the importance of introspection for investigating conscious states:

> *Introspective Observation is what we have to rely on first and foremost and always.* The word introspection need hardly be defined—it means, of course, the looking into our own minds and reporting what we there discover. *Every one agrees that we there discover states of consciousness.* ([1890] 1950: 185; emphasis in original)

Clearly, James had in mind ordinary introspection, not the spiritual practice of meditation. Moreover, as we saw in section 2, James admitted that the hard problem of consciousness can never be resolved through ordinary introspection, which grants us only first-person access to our own mental states and, therefore, cannot elucidate how these mental states relate to physical processes. Indeed, James arrived at his own preferred solution to the hard problem of consciousness—namely, some form of panpsychism or panprotopsychism—not through introspection but through a philosophical critique of the view that consciousness emerged from non-conscious matter.[20]

In fact, it is only in the past few decades that philosophers and neuroscientists have begun to take seriously the possibility that spiritual techniques like meditation can help illuminate the nature of consciousness.[21] Jonathan Shear,

[20] Of course, in his later book *The Varieties of Religious Experience* (1900), James does explicitly discuss meditative techniques for penetrating the mysteries of consciousness. However, as I noted in section 1 of chapter 8, James wrote this book *after* he had met Vivekananda in 1896 and had read some of his work.

[21] For instance, see Forman (1990), Varela and Shear (1991), Lancaster (2004), Phillips (2009), Thompson (2015), Albahari (2019b), and Goff (2019: 205–16).

for instance, has argued that the insights afforded by Eastern meditative techniques—*if* epistemically valid—can help address the hard problem of consciousness by disclosing "the ground, deep layers, and mechanics of the unfolding of consciousness" (1997: 372–73). However, Shear also notes that this is a big "if," and he has not attempted to defend the epistemic value of meditative insight. In this regard, contemporary philosophers stand to learn a great deal from Vivekananda, who was one of the first to argue for the relevance of meditative techniques and spiritual experience to the hard problem of consciousness. Moreover, as I discussed in chapters 5 and 6, Vivekananda went even further than contemporary philosophers of consciousness in presenting a full-blown argument for the epistemic value of spiritual experience on the basis of general epistemic principles of perception and testimony.

For Vivekananda, the strongest evidence in support of the Sāṃkhyan theory of a conscious Self apart from the body-mind complex is the direct supersensuous knowledge of the Self achieved through the practice of Rāja-Yoga. Nonetheless, he also provides two supplementary arguments for the existence of a conscious soul.[22] He argues that scientists will never be able to prove that conscious experience arises from physical processes in the brain: "If matter and its transformations answer for all that we have, there is no necessity for supposing the existence of a soul. But it cannot be proved that thought has been evolved out of matter . . . " (*CW* 1:8). Vivekananda was certainly right that scientists in the late nineteenth century were nowhere close to demonstrating the physical basis of consciousness. However, is he justified in making the much stronger claim that scientists will *never* be able to prove that consciousness arises from matter? On what grounds does Vivekananda rule out the kind of temporary mysterianism endorsed by Nagel and, arguably, by his contemporary Tyndall?

In a Vivekanandan vein, we can ask whether contemporary neuroscience, for all its advances since the late nineteenth century, has made any significant progress in explaining how conscious experience can arise from the brain. We might consider, for instance, the recent "neurobiological theory of consciousness" proposed by the scientists Francis Crick and Christof Koch (1990), who suggest that 35–75 hertz neural oscillations in the cerebral cortex may be the basis of consciousness. However, as Chalmers has pointed out, even if scientists are eventually able to prove definitively that "these oscillations are the neural correlates of experience," they will not be one step closer to answering the question, "Why do the oscillations give rise to experience?" (1995: 204). As we have seen, this was precisely Vivekananda's point, when he claimed that no science of neural correlates could possibly explain the nature of consciousness or where

[22] As I discuss in Medhananda (forthcoming-b), Vivekananda also provides numerous arguments in support of reincarnation, which lend indirect support to the existence of a conscious soul.

it comes from. It is also important to recognize that Vivekananda's justification for his strong claim about the impossibility of proving the physical basis of consciousness derives in part from his argument from mystical insight. The fact that many yogis claimed to have attained direct supersensuous knowledge of the eternal conscious Self, coupled with the fact that scientists had not made appreciable progress in explaining the physical basis of consciousness, led Vivekananda to claim that scientists would *never* be able to prove the physical basis of consciousness.

In his lecture "The Real Nature of Man" (1896), delivered in London, Vivekananda presents another argument in support of the existence of a conscious soul apart from the body-mind complex:

> There is a great discussion going on as to whether the aggregate of materials we call the body is the cause of manifestation of the force we call the soul, thought, etc., or whether it is the thought that manifests this body. The religions of the world of course hold that the force called thought manifests the body, and not the reverse. There are schools of modern thought which hold that what we call thought is simply the outcome of the adjustment of the parts of the machine which we call body. Taking the second position that the soul or the mass of thought, or however you may call it, is the outcome of this machine, the outcome of the chemical and physical combinations of matter making up the body and brain, leaves the question unanswered. What makes the body? What force combines the molecules into the body form? What force is there which takes up material from the mass of matter around and forms my body one way, another body another way, and so on? What makes these infinite distinctions? To say that the force called soul is the outcome of the combinations of the molecules of the body is putting the cart before the horse. How did the combinations come; where was the force to make them? If you say that some other force was the cause of these combinations, and soul was the outcome of that matter, and that soul—which combined a certain mass of matter—was itself the result of the combinations, it is no answer. That theory ought to be taken which explains most of the facts, if not all, and that without contradicting other existing theories. It is more logical to say that the force which takes up the matter and forms the body is the same which manifests through that body. To say, therefore, that the thought forces manifested by the body are the outcome of the arrangement of molecules and have no independent existence has no meaning; neither can force evolve out of matter. (*CW* 2:75–76)

This is an excellent example of Vivekananda's cosmopolitan method of bringing classical Indian theories of consciousness to bear on contemporary Western debates. He begins by referring to the "great discussion" going on in the West regarding whether or not consciousness arises from physical processes. Although he does not mention any specific thinkers here, the details of the passage suggest that he had in mind the conflicting views of John Tyndall and T. H. Huxley. I believe Vivekananda was thinking primarily of Huxley when he referred to "schools of modern thought which hold that what we call thought is simply the outcome of the adjustment of the parts of the machine which we call body." We should recall from section 2 that this is precisely Huxley's epiphenomenalist view that we are "conscious automata" (1890a) and that thoughts are nothing but "expressions of molecular changes" (1890b: 154).

Moreover, Vivekananda's complex argument against this Huxleyan materialist stance on consciousness bears a striking resemblance to an argument against materialism presented by Tyndall in the same famous 1868 address in which he introduced the hard problem of consciousness. Tyndall's argument deserves to be quoted at length, since it helps clarify Vivekananda's own argument:

> In affirming that the growth of the body is mechanical, and that thought, as exercised by us, has its correlative in the physics of the brain, I think the position of the "Materialist" is stated as far as that position is a tenable one. I think the materialist will be able finally to maintain this position against all attacks; but I do not think, as the human mind is at present constituted, that he can pass beyond it. I do not think he is entitled to say that his molecular groupings and his molecular motions explain everything. In reality they explain nothing. The utmost he can affirm is the association of two classes of phenomena of whose real bond of union he is in absolute ignorance. The problem of the connection of the body and soul is as insoluble in its modern form as it was in the pre-scientific ages. Phosphorus is known to enter into the composition of the human brain, and a courageous writer has exclaimed, in his trenchant German, "Ohne phosphor kein gedanke" ["Without phosphorus, no thought"]. That may or may not be the case; but even if we knew it to be the case, the knowledge would not lighten our darkness. On both sides of the zone here assigned to the materialist he is equally helpless. If you ask him whence is this "matter" of which we have been discoursing, who or what divided it into molecules, who or what impressed upon them this necessity of running into organic forms, he has no answer. Science also is mute in reply to these questions. (1870: 17–18)

Tyndall argues that the Huxleyan materialist who strives to establish the physical basis of consciousness faces insuperable problems on "both sides of the zone" he occupies. On one side of this zone, the materialist is faced with the hard problem of consciousness: even a hypothetically complete science of the neural correlates of consciousness would leave unanswered the question of *how* or *why* conscious experience arises from physical processes in the brain.

On the other side of the zone, the materialist faces a different problem. Tyndall argues that *even if* scientists were able to demonstrate the molecular basis of consciousness, they would still not be able to explain "who or what" caused certain molecules to combine in such a way as to generate conscious experience in the first place.

Vivekananda's argument against a materialist approach to consciousness in his 1896 lecture can be seen as a skillful development of Tyndall's earlier argument. Like Tyndall, Vivekananda argues that any attempt to identify a physical basis for conscious experience only pushes the problem back a level or two rather than solving it. Even if we grant that a certain combination of molecules generates conscious experience, we would still need to determine how and why these molecules combined together in precisely that way. As Vivekananda puts it, "How did the combinations come; where was the force to make them?" He then develops Tyndall's argument further by anticipating the likely response of a Huxleyan materialist: we can simply posit another force—which itself has a physical basis—as the cause of the precise combination of molecules that generates conscious thought. In diagrammatic form, the Huxleyan materialist's argument would look as follows:

molecular $\text{grouping}_2 \rightarrow \text{force}_1 \rightarrow$ molecular $\text{grouping}_1 \rightarrow$ conscious experience

Vivekananda argues, however, that this materialist's answer is "no answer" at all, since it leads to an infinite regress. We can still ask what force was responsible for molecular grouping_2, and so on. At each level, the materialist would need to prove the physical basis of the prior forces ultimately causing conscious experience. And this is an impossible task, because of an infinite regress:

. . . molecular $\text{grouping}_4 \rightarrow \text{force}_3 \rightarrow$ molecular $\text{grouping}_3 \rightarrow \text{force}_2 \rightarrow$ molecular $\text{grouping}_2 \rightarrow \text{force}_1 \rightarrow$ molecular $\text{grouping}_1 \rightarrow$ conscious experience

At this point, instead of adopting Tyndall's noncommittal mysterianism, Vivekananda rejects the materialist account of consciousness in favor of the nonmaterialist view that "the force which takes up the matter and forms the body is the same which manifests through that body." I take him to mean that the very soul that forms and inhabits a particular physical body also makes possible all the conscious experiences associated with that body. This doctrine of the soul, Vivekananda argues, should be accepted because it avoids the problem of infinite regress and, thus, has greater explanatory power than the materialist theory of consciousness. We should remember, however, that he also has independent grounds for accepting the existence of a conscious soul—especially the argument from meditative insight.

Although Vivekananda's dialectic ends here, we can speculate a bit further about how this debate between Vivekananda and Huxley might have continued. Huxley, a vociferous champion of Darwinian evolution, might have responded to Vivekananda's objection by arguing that evolutionary mechanisms like natural selection are precisely the non-spiritual forces responsible for the formation of molecules that eventually led to the emergence of consciousness. A Darwinian could argue that consciousness emerged in the course of evolution through natural selection because it had adaptive value in the struggle for survival. It is reasonable to think, for instance, that the conscious feeling of pain significantly increased an animal's chances of survival in a hostile natural environment.

How might we defend Vivekananda's position against such an evolutionary argument for the physical basis of consciousness? First, it is worth pointing out that Huxley's epiphenomenalism—which denies the causal efficacy of mental events—would make it impossible for him even to make this evolutionary argument, since any argument for the adaptive value of consciousness *presupposes* the causal efficacy of conscious experiences.[23] A conscious experience like the feeling of pain, for instance, can only have adaptive value if it causes the animal to flee from danger. Second, as I will explain in detail in section 1 of the next chapter, Vivekananda explicitly argues against the view that consciousness gradually evolved from insentient matter. According to Vivekananda, since "something cannot be produced out of nothing," consciousness could not possibly have emerged from insentient matter (*CW* 2:75). Arguing that "every evolution presupposes an involution," he adopts the panpsychist position that consciousness must have been "involved" even in primordial matter and eventually became *manifest* in the course of the evolutionary process (*CW* 2:75).

Before concluding this section, I would like to indicate briefly the contemporary relevance of Vivekananda's Sāṃkhyan understanding of the relation between mind and consciousness. First, the philosopher Paul Schweizer points out a major advantage of Sāṃkhya over both Cartesian interactionist dualism and epiphenomenalism: "By including the mind in the realm of matter, mental events are granted causal efficacy, and are therefore able to directly initiate bodily motions" (1993: 849). Sāṃkhya, as we have seen, draws a line not between mind and body but between the conscious Spirit on the one hand and the insentient mind *and* body on the other. Since mind and body are both physical, Sāṃkhya has no trouble explaining how mental events can cause bodily actions. Hence, Sāṃkhya philosophy has a significant advantage over Cartesian interactionist dualism, which is faced with the formidable problem of explaining how an immaterial mind can interact with a material body. Moreover, in contrast to

[23] This is precisely the argument made by William James (1879) against Huxley's epiphenomenalism.

epiphenomenalism, Sāṃkhya has common sense on its side, since it accepts the causal efficacy of the mental.

Second, the Sāṃkhyan view that mind is a subtle form of matter resonates strongly with contemporary naturalistic theories of mind in cognitive science and philosophy. Chalmers makes a key distinction between the "phenomenal" and "psychological" properties of the mind: while psychological features of the mind such as learning and remembering may very well be explained someday wholly in terms of physical processes in the brain, the phenomenal (i.e., conscious) dimension of the mind eludes any such reductionist analysis (1996: 24). As Biernacki (2016a) has argued, the Sāṃkhyan approach to mind dovetails nicely with Chalmers's distinction between the phenomenal and the psychological. Like Chalmers, Sāṃkhya philosophers carefully separate out the conscious dimension of mind from its various psychological functions, arguing that only the latter can be explained fully in terms of physical processes. According to Sāṃkhya, the three basic psychological aspects of the mind (*antaḥkaraṇa*)—intellect/will (*buddhi*),[24] thought (*manas*), and ego-sense (*ahaṃkāra*)—are all subtle forms of insentient matter and, hence, lend themselves to naturalistic explanation. Schweizer clarifies the contemporary value of this Sāṃkhyan approach to mind: "A far wider range of cognitive phenomena are made available to naturalistic explanation on the Sāṃkhya-Yoga account, simply because the mind is included in the physical world" (Schweizer 1993: 858).[25] Indeed, Vivekananda himself highlighted precisely this advantage of the Sāṃkhyan doctrine of the materiality of the mind: "It is startling to find that the philosophers and metaphysicians of India stated ages ago that mind is material. What are our present materialists trying to do, but to show that mind is as much a product of nature as the body?" (*CW* 2:433). However, Vivekananda sides with Sāṃkhyans against Chalmers and many other contemporary thinkers in explaining the *conscious* dimension of mind by appealing to an underlying immaterial Soul.

5. *Vivekananda's Sāṃkhya-Vedāntic Metaphysics of Panentheistic Cosmopsychism*

As we saw in the previous section, Vivekananda's first-line response to the hard problem of consciousness is to appeal to the Sāṃkhyan position that the insentient mind is illuminated by the conscious Puruṣa. However, it is important to note that he does not subscribe to Sāṃkhyan metaphysics wholesale. In fact, he

[24] Larson (1969: 183–84), like Vivekananda, argues that *buddhi* is best construed as both intellect and will.

[25] Larson (2013) makes a similar point.

singles out for criticism three fundamental aspects of Sāṃkhyan metaphysics: the doctrine of multiple Puruṣas, the doctrine that insentient Prakṛti is the source of all creation, and the metaphysical dualism of Puruṣa and Prakṛti.[26] According to Vivekananda, problems internal to Sāṃkhyan metaphysics necessitate a transition from soul-matter dualism to spiritual monism. In particular, he defends a Vedāntic metaphysics of panentheistic cosmopsychism that incorporates key aspects of Sāṃkhyan metaphysics while also correcting for the latter's deficiencies and lacunae.

Vivekananda presents the following internal critique of the Sāṃkhyan doctrine of multiple Puruṣas:

> Can there be more than one Puruṣa? The Puruṣa, we have seen, is omnipresent and infinite. The omnipresent, the infinite, cannot be two. If there are two infinites A and B, the infinite A would limit the infinite B, because the infinite B is not the infinite A, and the infinite A is not the infinite B. Difference in identity means exclusion, and exclusion means limitation. Therefore, A and B, limiting each other, cease to be infinites. Hence, there can be but one infinite, that is, one Puruṣa. (*CW* 2:460–61)

According to Vivekananda, Sāṃkhyans themselves conceive the Puruṣa as both omnipresent and infinite. However, the notion of multiple infinites is incoherent, since the infinites would limit one another, thereby becoming finite. Hence, if the Puruṣa is truly infinite, it can only be one rather than multiple. For Vivekananda, then, the Sāṃkhyan doctrine of the infinitude of Puruṣa, when pushed to its logical conclusion, entails that there is only one Puruṣa—namely, the impersonal (*nirguṇa*) nondual Brahman of Advaita Vedānta.

Vivekananda also criticizes Sāṃkhyan atheism by presenting two main arguments for positing God (*īśvara*) as the efficient and material cause of all creation:

> The first point we will contend with Kapila is his idea of God. Just as the series of modifications of Prakṛti, beginning with the individual intellect [*buddhi*] and ending with the individual body, require a Puruṣa behind, as the ruler and governor, so, in the Cosmos, the universal intellect [*mahat*], the universal egoism [*ahaṃkāra*], the universal mind [*manas*], all universal fine and gross materials, must have a ruler and governor. How will the cosmic series

[26] Unfortunately, I do not have the space here to assess Vivekananda's criticisms of Sāṃkhya philosophy. For present purposes, I will simply outline his main criticisms of Sāṃkhya and then focus on his own preferred Vedāntic framework of panentheistic cosmopsychism and its implications for understanding consciousness.

> become complete without the universal Puruṣa behind them all as the ruler and governor? If you deny a universal Puruṣa behind the cosmic series, we deny your Puruṣa behind the individual series. If it be true that behind the series of graded, evolved individual manifestations, there stands One that is beyond them all, the Puruṣa who is not composed of matter, the very same logic will apply to the case of universal manifestations. This Universal Self which is beyond the universal modifications of Prakṛti is what is called Īśvara, the Supreme Ruler, God. (*CW* 2:460)

Understanding Vivekananda's objection requires a more detailed picture of Sāṃkhyan cosmology. According to Sāṃkhya, insentient Prakṛti is the material cause of all creation, which first becomes *mahat/buddhi*, which itself becomes *ahaṃkāra*, which in turn evolves into *manas*, the five sense-capacities (*buddhīndriyas*), the five action-capacities (*karmendriyas*), and the five subtle elements (*tanmātras*), and these *tanmātras* themselves evolve into the five gross elements (*mahābhūtas*). Sāṃkhyans claim that all these twenty-four cosmic principles (*tattvas*) exist for the sake of the conscious Puruṣa, which is entirely separate from nature. For a snapshot of the Sāṃkhyan dualist system, see Figure 9.1.

Vivekananda's objection is based on the Sāṃkhyan view that the macrocosm is reflected in the microcosm, so that each of the cosmic principles has

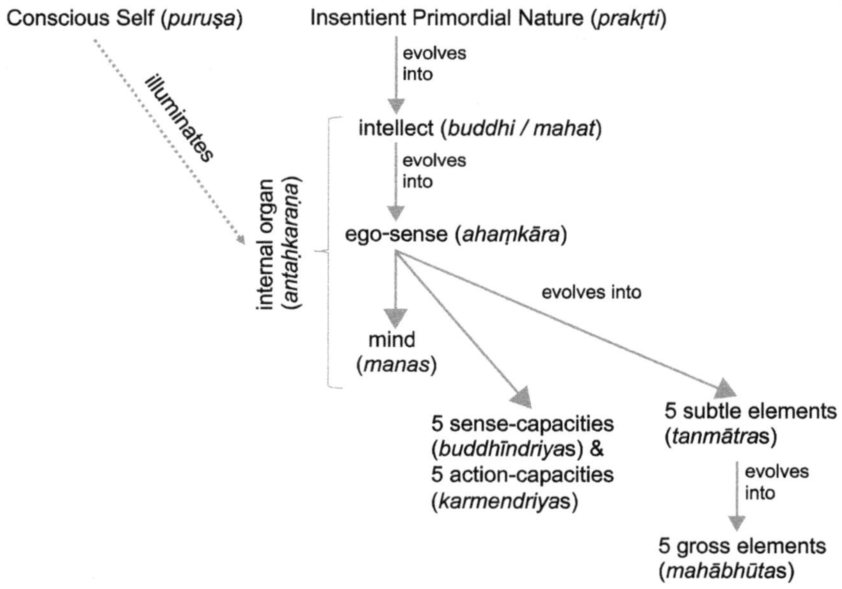

Figure 9.1 The Dualist System of Sāṃkhya

its individual counterpart.[27] For instance, according to Sāṃkhya, while *mahat* is the universal or cosmic intellect, *buddhi* is its counterpart at the individual level. Vivekananda now argues as follows: if Sāṃkhya holds that all the individual manifestations of Prakṛti exist for the sake of an individual Puruṣa, then it should also hold that all the *cosmic* manifestations of Prakṛti exist for the sake of a *universal* Puruṣa as their "ruler and governor." This universal Puruṣa, he claims, is none other than God (*īśvara*).

Vivekananda's second argument in favor of adding *īśvara* to the Sāṃkhyan system targets its doctrine of insentient Prakṛti (Nature):

> If their [the Sāṃkhyans'] Nature be absolute and the soul be also absolute, there will be two absolutes, and all the arguments that apply in the case of the soul to show that it is omnipresent will apply in the case of Nature, and Nature too will be beyond all time, space, and causation, and as the result there will be no change or manifestation. Then will come the difficulty of having two absolutes, which is impossible. What is the solution of the Vedāntist? His solution is that, just as the Sāṃkhya[n]s say, it requires some sentient Being as the motive power behind, which makes the mind think and Nature work, because Nature in all its modifications, from gross matter up to Mahat (Intelligence), is simply insentient. Now, says the Vedāntist, this sentient Being which is behind the whole universe is what we call *God*, and consequently this universe is not different from Him. It is He Himself who has become this universe. (*CW* 3:6–7)

According to Vivekananda, the Sāṃkhyan dualist system posits both Puruṣa and Prakṛti as absolutes, so if the absolute Puruṣa is omnipresent and beyond time, space, and causation, then the absolute Prakṛti must also be omnipresent and beyond time, space, and causation. In that case, however, there would be no "change or manifestation," since Prakṛti would be beyond nature altogether and unable to interact with it. He also makes an independent argument that it is impossible to have "two absolutes." He seems to have in mind his argument—mentioned earlier—that the notion of multiple infinite Puruṣas is incoherent, since they would limit each other. Similarly, two absolutes would limit each other and thereby lose their absolute status. To avoid this difficulty, we must posit a universal Puruṣa—God or *īśvara*—at the basis of Prakṛti. At the end of the passage, he also hints at the ultimate panentheistic worldview he favors: it is God "who has become this universe."

[27] Hence, as Larson (1969: 176–200) shows, Sāṃkhyan cosmology doubles as a psychology of the individual soul.

In a different lecture, Vivekananda argues in more detail that we should reject the spirit-matter dualism of Sāṃkhya in favor of a Vedāntic panentheism:

> Beyond this Prakṛti, and eternally separate from it, is the Puruṣa, the soul of the Sāṃkhya which is without attributes and omnipresent. The Puruṣa is not the doer but the witness. The illustration of the crystal is used to explain the Puruṣa. The latter is said to be like a crystal without any colour, before which different colours are placed, and then it seems to be coloured by the colours before it, but in reality it is not. The Vedāntists reject the Sāṃkhya ideas of the soul and nature. They claim that between them there is a huge gulf to be bridged over. On the one hand the Sāṃkhya system comes to nature, and then at once it has to jump over to the other side and come to the soul, which is entirely separate from nature. How can these different colours, as the Sāṃkhya calls them, be able to act on that soul which by its nature is colourless? So the Vedāntists, from the very first affirm that this soul and this nature are one. . . . The idea of the Advaitists is to generalise the whole universe into one—that something which is really the whole of this universe. And they claim that this whole universe is one, that it is one Being manifesting itself in all these various forms. They admit that what the Sāṃkhya calls nature exists, but say that nature is God. It is this Being, the Sat, which has become converted into all this—the universe, man, soul, and everything that exists. (*CW* 1:361–62)

He argues, rather swiftly, that the "huge gulf" Sāṃkhya posits between Puruṣa and Prakṛti makes it impossible for Prakṛti to interact in any way with Puruṣa. Hence, he claims that the Vedāntic view that Puruṣa and Prakṛti "are one" is more logically sound than Sāṃkhyan dualism. On this basis, he defends the panentheistic Advaitic view that God, the sole Reality, has become everything in the universe.

Crucially, Vivekananda's preferred nondual Vedāntic framework integrates within it all the elements of Sāṃkhya philosophy that he takes to be valid. In particular, he fully accepts the Sāṃkhyan doctrines that mind is a subtle form of matter and that conscious experience has a spiritual basis. He also accepts most of Sāṃkhyan cosmology, except that he equates *mahat* with *īśvara* (and perhaps tacitly assimilates Sāṃkhyan Prakṛti to *mahat*/*īśvara* as well). He makes this explicit in an 1896 letter to his disciple E. T. Sturdy in which he sketches a diagram illustrating his Vedāntic cosmology—one that was already discussed, in a different context, in chapter 2:

> I am working a good deal now upon the cosmology and eschatology of the Vedānta. . . . I intend to write a book later on in the form of questions and answers. The first chapter will be on cosmology, showing the harmony between Vedāntic theories and modern science.

Brahman	=	The Absolute
|		
Mahat or Īśvara	=	Primal Creative Energy (*CW* 5:102)

Unfortunately, he never found the time to write the book he had planned, so we will have to reconstruct his Vedāntic cosmology by drawing together various relevant passages in his work. As I noted in chapter 2, Brahman is the impersonal (*nirguṇa*) nondual Absolute, and the vertical line indicates that it is inseparable from *mahat*/*īśvara*, the "Primal Creative Energy" which he also frequently refers to as "Śakti" (*CW* 9:195). Echoing Ramakrishna's favorite teaching that "Brahman and Śakti are inseparable" (*K* 568 / *G* 550), Vivekananda holds that while the impersonal nondual Brahman is utterly transcendent, Śakti—that is, *mahat*/*īśvara*—is the same Absolute in its dynamic form as the personal God who creates, preserves, and destroys the universe.[28]

Vivekananda's equation of *īśvara* with *mahat* is highly significant, since it reflects how he integrates key aspects of the Sāṃkhyan system into his own broader Vedāntic cosmology. In Vivekananda's hands, the insentient *mahat* of Sāṃkhya morphs into the sentient "cosmic consciousness"[29] or "cosmic mind"[30] from which everything in the universe derives:

> What are you and I and all these souls? In our discussion of evolution and involution, we have seen that you and I must be part of the cosmic consciousness, cosmic life, cosmic mind, which got involved and we must complete the circle and go back to this cosmic intelligence which is God. This cosmic intelligence is what people call Lord, or God, or Christ, or Buddha, or Brahman, what the materialists perceive as force, and the agnostics as that infinite, inexpressible beyond; and we are all parts of that. (*CW* 2:231)

In Vivekananda's Vedāntic cosmology, *mahat*/*īśvara* manifests both as individual conscious souls (*jīvas*) and as insentient minds (*antaḥkaraṇas*). As he puts it, "According to the Sāṃkhya philosophy, the reactive state of the mind called Buddhi or intellect is the outcome, the change, or a certain manifestation of the Mahat or Cosmic Mind" (*CW* 1:361).[31] Vivekananda accepts unchanged the rest

[28] For details on Vivekananda's conception of the impersonal-personal God, see section 2 of chapter 2.

[29] Vivekananda equates "Mahat" with "cosmic consciousness" at least twice, at *CW* 8:363 and *CW* 2:231.

[30] Vivekananda explicitly equates "Mahat" with the "Cosmic Mind" in several places, including *CW* 1:360–61 and *CW* 2:267.

[31] I do not think Vivekananda means to imply that *buddhi* is a separate cosmic principle from *mahat*. Rather, he follows Sāṃkhya in taking *buddhi* to be the "individual Mahat" (*CW* 1:250–51), the microcosmic counterpart to the macrocosmic *mahat*.

of the Sāṃkhyan cosmology from *buddhi* down to the five *mahābhūta*s (gross elements).

In contemporary terms, I would suggest that this unique Vedāntic metaphysical worldview is best understood as a panentheistic form of cosmopsychism. As I discussed in detail in chapter 2 of this book, Vivekananda follows Ramakrishna in championing a world-affirming Integral Advaitic philosophy, according to which the sole reality is the impersonal-personal Infinite Divine Reality. We can now see that the personal aspect of the Infinite Reality is none other than Mahat/Īśvara/Śakti, the "cosmic consciousness" that not only *grounds*, but actually *is*, everything in the universe. Ultimately, then, Vivekananda solves the hard problem of consciousness by appealing to a Sāṃkhya-Vedāntic framework of panentheistic cosmopsychism. While he accepts the Sāṃkhyan view that the mind (*antaḥkaraṇa*) is insentient, he claims that all our conscious experiences are grounded not in the individual Puruṣa but in the all-pervasive Divine Consciousness. Figure 9.2 illustrates his panentheistic cosmopsychism in a nutshell.

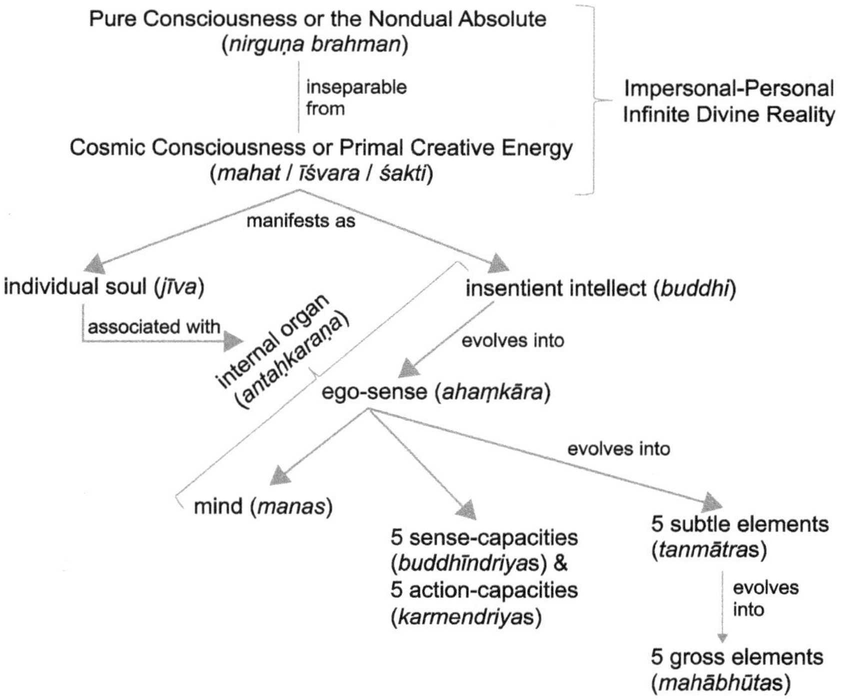

Figure 9.2 Vivekananda's Sāṃkhya-Vedāntic Framework of Panentheistic Cosmopsychism

It is important to note that Vivekananda's panentheistic cosmopsychism, in spite of its nondualism, preserves the Sāṃkhyan distinction between sentient and insentient entities. While he maintains that everything in the universe—including both sentient creatures and insentient entities—is a manifestation of the same Divine Consciousness, he does *not* hold that everything is conscious in the sense of being mental or sentient. Rather, he holds the Sāṃkhyan view that only entities with a mind (*antaḥkaraṇa*) are sentient. Surendranath Dasgupta succinctly explains why an *antaḥkaraṇa* is necessary for conscious experience:

> A question naturally arises, that if the knowledge forms [i.e., the *antaḥkaraṇa*] are made up of [the same][32] sort of stuff as the objective forms of matter are, why then should the puruṣa illuminate it [i.e., the *antaḥkaraṇa*] and not external material objects. The answer that Sāṃkhya gives is that the knowledge-complexes are certainly different from external objects in this, that they are far subtler and have a preponderance of a special quality of plasticity and translucence (*sattva*), which resembles the light of puruṣa, and is thus fit for reflecting and absorbing the light of the puruṣa. (1922: 241)

In other words, a physical structure must be sufficiently subtle and translucent to reflect the light of the Puruṣa. Gross physical entities like stones are insentient because they lack the subtlety and translucency (*sattva*) necessary to reflect the light of the Puruṣa. Human beings, dogs, and bats, by contrast, are sentient because their minds (*antaḥkaraṇas*) are sufficiently subtle and translucent to reflect the light of their respective Puruṣas. Vivekananda fully accepts this Sāṃkhyan view but replaces the individual Puruṣas of Sāṃkhya with the single Divine Cosmic Consciousness. According to Vivekananda, only entities endowed with a mind (*antaḥkaraṇa*) can be sentient because an *antaḥkaraṇa* is necessary to reflect the light of the all-pervasive Divine Consciousness. Since he does not ascribe mentality or sentience to everything in the universe, his panentheistic cosmopsychism is arguably in a better position than some other panpsychist theories to avoid the incredulous stare objection.

Now that we have a basic understanding of Vivekananda's overall metaphysical framework of panentheistic cosmopsychism, the next chapter will reconstruct his philosophical arguments in favor of panentheistic cosmopsychism and elaborate his account of how the Divine Cosmic Consciousness grounds the conscious perspectives of humans and non-human animals. I will argue that Vivekananda provides an account of grounding by self-limitation that offers a novel and promising resolution of the individuation problem.

[32] Dasgupta's original phrase is as follows: "... if the knowledge forms are made up of some sort of stuff as the objective forms of matter are...." Since this phrase is ungrammatical as it stands, I have supplied in brackets what I believe he meant.

10

Vivekananda's Justification of Panentheistic Cosmopsychism

Involution, Mystical Experience, and Grounding by Self-Limitation

In the previous chapter, we saw how Vivekananda arrived at a novel solution to the hard problem of consciousness through a cosmopolitan engagement with contemporary Western thinkers like T. H. Huxley and John Tyndall as well as the Indian philosophies of Sāṃkhya, Advaita Vedānta, and the Vijñāna Vedānta of his guru Ramakrishna. Vivekananda championed a metaphysics of panentheistic cosmopsychism, according to which the sole reality is Divine Consciousness, which manifests as everything and everyone in the universe. However, chapter 9 left unanswered a number of very important questions. Why should we believe that Vivekananda's panentheistic cosmopsychism is a plausible metaphysical worldview? What philosophical arguments does he provide in its favor? What exactly does he mean by "manifestation," and how does his cosmopsychist position handle the individuation problem? And how might Vivekananda's approach to consciousness enrich contemporary debates about consciousness and panpsychism? This chapter proposes to answer these questions.

Section 1 reconstructs Vivekananda's arguments for panpsychism and panentheistic cosmopsychism as presented in his lecture "The Cosmos: The Macrocosm" (1896). I show how he defends the key premises of his arguments by critically engaging both Indian and Western thought. I also argue that he anticipated key arguments in contemporary philosophy of mind and religion.

In section 2, I first note some problems and lacunae in Vivekananda's arguments as reconstructed in the previous section, and I then present more refined and complete versions of his arguments. These arguments are not ones that Vivekananda himself made but are nonetheless "Vivekanandan" in spirit, since they are based on his own ideas. Section 3 explains Vivekananda's account of grounding by self-limitation and shows how it addresses the individuation problem, which is generally considered to be the single most serious problem for cosmopsychist theories. I suggest that he follows Ramakrishna in explaining divine manifestation as a process by which God playfully limits or veils Himself through the individuating principle of *māyā*.

Swami Vivekananda's Vedāntic Cosmopolitanism. Swami Medhananda, Oxford University Press. © Oxford University Press 2022. DOI: 10.1093/oso/9780197624463.003.0011

Section 4 addresses some potential objections to Vivekananda's panentheistic cosmopsychism. Finally, section 5 brings Vivekananda into critico-constructive dialogue with Miri Albahari, who has recently criticized cosmopsychist theories and offered an alternative theory of universal consciousness based on classical Advaita Vedānta. I suggest that Vivekananda's model of grounding by self-limitation has unique conceptual resources for responding to Albahari's criticisms of cosmopsychism. Moreover, since Vivekananda's panentheistic cosmopsychism accepts the world as a real manifestation of Divine Consciousness, it arguably has significant philosophical advantages over Albahari's classical Advaitic approach to consciousness, which ultimately denies the reality of both the world and the grounding relation.

1. *Reconstructing Vivekananda's Argument for Panentheistic Cosmopsychism*

In numerous lectures, Vivekananda presents arguments in support of the plausibility of panentheistic cosmopsychism. Unfortunately, since he never wrote the definitive book on Vedāntic philosophy that he had planned, there is no single place in his corpus where he works out these arguments systematically and in detail. Perhaps his most detailed argument for panentheistic cosmopsychism occurs in the course of his lecture "The Cosmos: The Macrocosm," delivered in New York on January 19, 1896. The relevant passage from the lecture is long but needs to be quoted in full, since it is a continuous piece of reasoning:

> Next comes a very important question especially for modern times. We see that the finer forms develop slowly and slowly, and gradually become grosser and grosser. We have seen that the cause is the same as the effect, and the effect is only the cause in another form. Therefore this whole universe cannot be produced out of nothing. Nothing comes without a cause, and the cause is the effect in another form.
>
> Out of what has this universe been produced then? From a preceding fine universe. Out of what has man been produced? The preceding fine form. Out of what has the tree been produced? Out of the seed; the whole of the tree was there in the seed. It comes out and becomes manifest. So, the whole of this universe has been created out of this very universe existing in a minute form.... This coming out of the fine and becoming gross, simply changing the arrangements of its parts, as it were, is what in modern times [is] called evolution. This is very true, perfectly true; we see it in our lives. No rational man can possibly quarrel with these evolutionists. But we have to learn one thing more. We have to go one step further, and what is that? That every evolution

is preceded by an involution. . . . The whole of this universe was present in the cosmic fine universe. The little cell, which becomes afterwards the man, was simply the involved man and becomes evolved as a man. If this is clear, we have no quarrel with the evolutionists, for we see that if they admit this step, instead of their destroying religion, they will be the greatest supporters of it.

We see then, that nothing can be created out of nothing. . . . The whole series of evolution beginning with the lowest manifestation of life and reaching up to the highest, the most perfect man, must have been the involution of something else. The question is: The involution of what? What was involved? God. The evolutionist will tell you that your idea that it was God is wrong. Why? Because you see God is intelligent, but we find that intelligence develops much later on in the course of evolution. It is in man and the higher animals that we find intelligence, but millions of years have passed in this world before this intelligence came. This objection of the evolutionists does not hold water, as we shall see by applying our theory. The tree comes out of the seed, goes back to the seed; the beginning and the end are the same. The earth comes out of its cause and returns to it. We know that if we can find the beginning we can find the end. *E converso*, if we find the end we can find the beginning. If that is so, take this whole evolutionary series, from the protoplasm at one end to the perfect man at the other, and this whole series is one life. In the end we find the perfect man, so in the beginning it must have been the same. Therefore, the protoplasm was the involution of the highest intelligence. You may not see it but that involved intelligence is what is uncoiling itself until it becomes manifested in the most perfect man. That can be mathematically demonstrated. If the law of conservation of energy is true, you cannot get anything out of a machine unless you put it in there first. . . . There cannot be added in the economy of this universe one particle of matter or one foot-pound of force, nor can one particle of matter or one foot-pound of force be taken out. If that be the case, what is this intelligence? If it was not present in the protoplasm, it must have come all of a sudden, something coming out of nothing, which is absurd. It, therefore, follows absolutely that the perfect man, the free man, the God-man, who has gone beyond the laws of nature, and transcended everything, who has no more to go through this process of evolution, through birth and death, that man called the "Christ-man" by the Christians, and the "Buddha-man" by the Buddhists, and the "Free" by the Yogis—that perfect man who is at one end of the chain of evolution was involved in the cell of the protoplasm, which is at the other end of the same chain.

Applying the same reason to the whole of the universe, we see that intelligence must be the Lord of creation, the cause. What is the most evolved notion that man has of this universe? It is intelligence, the adjustment of part to part, the display of intelligence, of which the ancient design theory was an attempt at expression. The beginning was, therefore, intelligence. At the beginning that intelligence becomes involved, and in the end that intelligence gets evolved. The sum total of the intelligence displayed in the universe must, therefore, be the involved universal intelligence unfolding itself. This universal intelligence is what we call God. Call it by any other name, it is absolutely certain that in the beginning there is that Infinite cosmic intelligence. This cosmic intelligence gets involved, and it manifests, evolves itself, until it becomes the perfect man, the "Christ-man," the "Buddha-man." . . . This cosmic intelligence is what the theologians call God. . . .

We now see that all the various forms of cosmic energy, such as matter, thought, force, intelligence and so forth, are simply the manifestations of that cosmic intelligence, or, as we shall call it henceforth, the Supreme Lord. Everything that you see, feel, or hear, the whole universe, is His creation, or to be a little more accurate, is His projection; or to be still more accurate, is the Lord Himself. It is He who is shining as the sun and the stars, He is the mother earth. He is the ocean Himself. He comes as gentle showers, He is the gentle air that we breathe in, and He it is who is working as force in the body. He is the speech that is uttered, He is the man who is talking. He is the audience that is here. He is the platform on which I stand, He is the light that enables me to see your faces. It is all He. He Himself is both the material and the efficient cause of this universe, and He it is that gets involved in the minute cell, and evolves at the other end and becomes God again. He it is that comes down and becomes the lowest atom, and slowly unfolding His nature, rejoins Himself. This is the mystery of the universe. "Thou art the man, Thou art the woman, Thou art the strong man walking in the pride of youth, Thou art the old man tottering on crutches, Thou art in everything. Thou art everything, O Lord." This is the only solution of the Cosmos that satisfies the human intellect. (*CW* 2:207–11)[1]

This passage—hereafter referred to as "passage B"—contains Vivekananda's argument for panentheistic cosmopsychism (hereafter "APC"). In the first paragraph of passage B, he affirms the Sāṃkhyan doctrine of the pre-existent effect (*satkārya*): "the effect is only the cause in another form." According to Sāṃkhya, nothing new can ever be produced; rather, all effects are already present in another form in their respective material causes. The Sāṃkhya scholar Gerald James Larson summarizes two of the main arguments Sāṃkhyans provide in support of *satkāryavāda*: "First of all, non-being obviously can produce or do nothing. Second, the effect is made up of the same material as the cause, there being a difference only with respect to the appearance or modification

[1] Vivekananda makes a similar involution argument in numerous other places, including *CW* 2:74, *CW* 2:173, and *CW* 8:362–63.

of the material" (1969: 165).[2] Vivekananda presents both of these Sāṃkhyan arguments for *satkāryavāda*. He echoes the first Sāṃkhyan argument when he states that "nothing can be created out of nothing." Later in the same paragraph, he makes this same point in a slightly different way when he says that the notion of "something coming out of nothing" is "absurd." The intuition here is a powerful one: it just seems obvious that there must be a sufficient material cause for any existing entity. He provides three examples to make this intuition more plausible: this entire universe must have been produced from "a preceding fine universe"; human beings are produced from the "preceding fine form"; and a tree is produced from "the seed." Vivekananda also echoes the second Sāṃkhyan argument for *satkāryavāda*: it is a matter of empirical fact that "the cause is the effect in another form." If we examine the nature of any given effect, we will find that it is made of the same material as its material cause, only in a modified form.

In cosmopolitan fashion, Vivekananda then goes on to provide further support for the Sāṃkhyan doctrine of *satkārya* by appealing to two modern Western scientific theories: the doctrine of evolution and the law of the conservation of energy. As he puts it, "This coming out of the fine and becoming gross, simply changing the arrangements of its parts, as it were, is what in modern times [is] called evolution. This is very true, perfectly true. . . . "[3] Significantly, Vivekananda defines the doctrine of evolution in very general terms as a continuous process that molds pre-existing properties into other forms. He argues that a logical consequence of this modern doctrine of evolution is that "every evolution is preceded by an involution." That is, the modern scientific understanding of the evolutionary process implies *satkāryavāda*: since nothing truly novel can emerge through the evolutionary process, the evolved entity or property had to have been "involved"—that is, pre-existent in a latent form—in that from which it evolved. As Vivekananda puts it, "The little cell, which becomes afterwards the man, was simply the involved man and becomes evolved as a man."

Vivekananda was familiar with the views of Charles Darwin, T. H. Huxley, and Herbert Spencer—all of whom defended various forms of the doctrine of evolution—and he often referred to "Darwin" and "Darwinism" in his lectures and writings.[4] However, it is crucial to note that Vivekananda says nothing here about the *mechanism* of evolution. Indeed, in other places, he explicitly criticizes Darwin's preferred evolutionary mechanism of natural selection, arguing that

[2] Larson here summarizes the gist of *Sāṃkhyakārikā* IX, which gives reasons for accepting *satkāryavāda*.

[3] In fact, Vivekananda claims that the philosophies of Sāṃkhya and Yoga had a theory of evolution that anticipated modern evolutionary theory. See especially his evolutionary interpretation of *Yogasūtra* 4.2–3 at *CW* 1:291–93 and elsewhere. For helpful discussions of Vivekananda's views on evolution, see Killingley (1990) and C. Brown (2012: 131–54).

[4] See, for instance, *CW* 7:152–55 and *CW* 6:40.

while natural selection certainly operates in the "animal kingdom," it cannot account for the moral and spiritual qualities of human beings (*CW* 7:154). Hence, the modern doctrine of evolution that Vivekananda endorses as "perfectly true" is only the very general one that holds that presently existing entities did not emerge suddenly or out of nothing but evolved gradually from earlier entities in which the currently existing entities were already present in a latent form. For Vivekananda, then, modern scientific evidence for the truth of evolution lends further support to the ancient Sāṃkhyan doctrine of *satkārya*. Vivekananda also supports the Sāṃkhyan doctrine of the pre-existent effect by appealing to the law of the conservation of energy, which holds that the total amount of energy in the universe remains constant and that this energy only changes forms and manifests in a variety of ways. If this law is true, he argues, then nothing new can come into existence; rather, what exists now is only a "change" or "manifestation" of what existed previously.

After arguing for the view that the effect always pre-exists in its cause, Vivekananda goes on to refute emergentism, the view—held by many of his contemporaries—that consciousness emerged at a late stage in evolutionary history. He defines the emergentist position as follows: "It is in man and the higher animals that we find intelligence, but millions of years have passed in this world before this intelligence came." Vivekananda refutes emergentism by appealing to the doctrine of the pre-existent effect: "[W]hat is this intelligence? If it was not present in the protoplasm, it must have come all of a sudden, something coming out of nothing, which is absurd." According to Vivekananda, the emergentist view that conscious intelligence arose from non-conscious matter at a certain point in our evolutionary history is "absurd" because it is tantamount to holding that something can come from nothing, a position ruled out by the doctrine of the pre-existent effect. Since something cannot come from nothing, consciousness could not possibly have emerged from non-conscious matter.

Hence, he argues that the only way to avoid the "absurd" doctrine of emergentism is to assume that conscious intelligence was already "present in the protoplasm." In other words, he argues that the doctrine of the pre-existent effect, combined with the denial of emergentism, makes it reasonable to accept panpsychism, the view that consciousness is present in everything. Just as the entire tree was "involved"—that is, present in a latent form—in the seed from which it grew, consciousness was involved, in the distant past, even in the most primitive forms of matter and life. As he puts it, the "perfect man . . . was involved in the cell of the protoplasm. . . . "

Vivekananda was not alone among his contemporaries in defending panpsychism. In fact, as we saw in section 2 of the previous chapter, both W. K. Clifford and William James presented similar arguments for panpsychism. Like Vivekananda, James argued in his *Principles of Psychology* (1890), "*If evolution is to work smoothly, consciousness in some shape must have been present at the very origin of things*" ([1890] 1950: 149). Likewise, Clifford argued in an 1874 article that the "doctrine of evolution" rules out the possibility of emergentism—which would have amounted to an "enormous . . . jump from one creature to another"—and claimed, therefore, that there is consciousness or protoconsciousness "even in the Amoeba" (1879: 60–61). Vivekananda may even have been aware of the pan(proto?)psychist views of Clifford or James. However, Vivekananda was unique among his contemporaries in arguing for panpsychism on the basis of the doctrine of the pre-existent effect. For Vivekananda, since evolution presupposes material causation, it is an instantiation of the more general Sāṃkhyan doctrine that every effect pre-exists in its material cause.

It is also worth noting that contemporary philosophers of mind like Thomas Nagel and Philip Goff have advanced so-called "genetic" arguments for panpsychism that are very similar to Vivekananda's involution argument. Nagel argues for panpsychism on the grounds that "evolutionary biology . . . cannot account for the appearance of consciousness and of other phenomena that are not physically reducible" (2012: 14–15). Similarly, Goff (2013) defends a "sorites-style argument for panpsychism" based on the assumption of the truth of evolutionary theory. According to Goff, if we assume that emergentism is true and that consciousness does not admit of borderline cases, then "we will have to suppose that some utterly precise micro-level change—down to an exact arrangement of particles—marked the first appearance of consciousness . . . , and it is going to seem arbitrary that it was that utterly precise change that was responsible for this significant change in nature" (2017b).[5] Vivekananda's "involution" argument for panpsychism has great contemporary relevance in this respect, since his unique appeal to the doctrine of the pre-existent effect provides additional support for such genetic arguments.

We can also bring Vivekananda into dialogue with his contemporary Alfred Russel Wallace. As we saw in section 2 of the previous chapter, Wallace agreed with Vivekananda in rejecting an emergentist view of consciousness, but he would have rejected Vivekananda's panpsychism. According to Wallace, since the doctrine of evolution rules out the possibility of emergentism, we are left with a stark choice between the panpsychist view that "all matter is conscious" and the spiritualist view that "conscious beings" implanted consciousness in animals at a certain point in our evolutionary history (1870: 365). Since Wallace considered panpsychism to be a patently implausible position, he argued that the spiritualist position was the more reasonable one to adopt. Wallace, then, could have objected to Vivekananda's panpsychist conclusion by arguing that he overlooks the possibility of spiritualism. How might Vivekananda have responded to

[5] This is Goff's own summary of the argument of Goff (2013).

Wallace's objection? In his lecture "Reason and Religion," Vivekananda endorses the modern scientific principle of immanentism—the view that "the explanations of things are in their own nature, and that no external beings or existences are required to explain what is going on in the universe" (*CW* 1:371). Vivekananda, then, could have argued that Wallace violates the principle of immanentism by appealing to spiritual beings to explain the phenomenon of consciousness.

Now that Vivekananda takes himself to have established the plausibility of panpsychism in general, he goes on to inquire into the precise *nature* of the all-pervasive consciousness that is "involved" even in primitive matter: "The question is: The involution of what? What was involved? God." In passage B, he offers two reasons for conceiving the all-pervasive consciousness as God. First, he appeals to the "ancient design" argument: the universe displays "intelligence" in its "adjustment of part to part." Since I have already discussed his formulation of—and overall stance toward—the design argument in section 4 of chapter 7, I will not repeat my discussion here. As I argued there, Vivekananda followed Mill in holding that the design argument, though significantly weakened by Darwin's evolutionary theory, still gives us some reason to believe that this world was designed by a divine intelligence.

Second, he quotes Śvetāśvatara Upaniṣad 4.3 as scriptural support for panentheistic cosmopsychism, the view that the Divine Consciousness has become everything in the universe: "Thou art the man, Thou art the woman . . . Thou art everything, O Lord." Vivekananda's appeal to scriptural testimony here appears to be dogmatic. After all, he does not give us any reasons in passage B for accepting the truth of the Upaniṣads in the first place. However, as I discussed in chapter 5, there are numerous other places in Vivekananda's corpus where he does explain why scriptures like the Upaniṣads should be accepted as authoritative—namely, because these scriptures are records of the statements of enlightened "Rishis" who directly "realised" certain "supersensuous" facts (*CW* 2:60). For Vivekananda, it was the modern sage Ramakrishna who reaffirmed the panentheistic spiritual vision of these Upaniṣadic sages. In particular, as we saw in section 3 of chapter 9, Ramakrishna claimed to have attained the mystical state of *vijñāna*, which disclosed to him that the sole reality is an impersonal-personal "Divine Consciousness" (*K* 335–36 / *G* 345) that "has become the entire universe of the living and non-living" (*K* 283 / *G* 300).

Of course, even if people like Ramakrishna claim to have experienced the all-pervasive Divine Consciousness, what reason do we have to believe them? As I discussed in chapter 5, Vivekananda answers this question by presenting an argument for the epistemic value of supersensuous perception (AEV). Since I have already discussed his AEV in chapter 5, there is no need for me to go into the details here. Essentially, his argument for the rationality of believing the testimony of credible mystics is based on the general epistemic principles of *Perceptual Proof* and *Testimonial Proof*, both of which he takes to be uncontroversial and indispensable in everyday life. If we are rationally justified in believing the sense-perceptual testimony of ordinary people, then we are also rationally justified in believing the testimony of credible mystics like the Upaniṣadic Rishis and Ramakrishna who claim to have perceived that everything is Divine Consciousness. Vivekananda concludes, therefore, that the "words" of "Yogis" who "have seen the truth" count as "direct evidence" for the existence of the supersensuous realities they claim to have perceived (*CW* 1:204).

In passage B, then, Vivekananda moves from panpsychism in general to pantheistic cosmopsychism in particular by appealing to the argument from design and to scriptural testimony, which implicitly presupposes AEV. He concludes that "it is absolutely certain that in the beginning there is that Infinite cosmic intelligence" (*CW* 2:210) and that "[e]verything that you see, feel, or hear, the whole universe . . . is the Lord Himself" (*CW* 2:211).

2. *Refining and Developing Vivekananda's Argument*

I believe there is much of value in Vivekananda's APC, including his novel defense of panpsychism on the basis of the doctrine of the pre-existent effect and his defense of a distinctive cosmopsychist position. I have also shown how aspects of his argument resonate with contemporary philosophical arguments for panpsychism. At the same time, there are at least four problems with APC as presented in passage B. First, there are two missing premises in his argument for panpsychism. He argues for panpsychism on the basis of two premises: first, that the effect pre-exists in its cause, and second, that consciousness could not have emerged at a certain point in evolutionary history. However, this argument for panpsychism is incomplete without an additional premise: the denial of materialist reductionism. After all, if materialist reductionism holds, then consciousness would be identical to a brain state, and there would be no difficulty in explaining how consciousness—taken to be wholly physical—could have evolved from non-conscious matter at a certain point in the evolutionary process. Fortunately, as we saw in section 4 of the previous chapter, Vivekananda does explicitly refute materialist reductionism in his lecture "The Science of Yoga." In that lecture, he argues that even if we are one day able to identify the "physical and chemical changes" in the brain corresponding to different conscious experiences, we would still not be able to explain conscious experience itself (*CW* 7:432). As I noted earlier, his primary argument against reductionism anticipated Thomas Nagel's well-known 1974 argument. Vivekananda argues that "[t]he mind cannot be analysed by any external machine," because any such *objective* scientific analysis of the brain would require abandoning the *subjective* point of view with which conscious experiences are essentially connected (*CW* 7:431). Therefore, he concludes that consciousness cannot be identical to anything material, such as a particular state of the brain. Hence, Vivekananda's APC needs to be supplemented by his denial of materialist reductionism in his "Science of Yoga" lecture.

As we saw in the previous chapter, Vivekananda was also familiar with two dualistic theories of consciousness—namely, interactionist mind-brain dualism and Sāṃkhyan mind-consciousness dualism. Although he does not discuss these dualistic theories in passage B, he does explicitly criticize both forms of dualism in numerous other places in his work, as I will discuss later in this section. Vivekananda's APC would be stronger with an additional premise denying the plausibility of mind-brain dualism and mind-consciousness dualism.

Second, in passage B, he justifies the move from panpsychism to panentheistic cosmopsychism in particular by appealing to the argument from design and quoting a panentheistic statement from Śvetāśvatara Upaniṣad. However, as I have already discussed, his appeal to scripture is dogmatic unless it is supplemented by his argument for the epistemic value of supersensuous perception elaborated elsewhere, especially in *Rāja-Yoga*.

Third, I think the conclusions Vivekananda draws from his arguments in passage B are stated too strongly. For instance, he concludes that "intelligence *must* be the Lord of creation" and that "it is *absolutely certain* that in the beginning there is that Infinite cosmic intelligence" (*CW* 2:209–10; emphasis added). We should remember that he presented this argument in a lecture for a public audience, and it is typical of him to use strong language for the sake of rhetorical effect. In fact, however, as I discussed in chapter 7, Vivekananda subscribed to the traditional Vedāntic position that reason has certain fundamental limits when it comes to supersensuous matters. According to Vivekananda, rational arguments for God's existence—especially the argument from religious experience but also, secondarily, the argument from design—can, at best, make it *reasonable* to believe that God exists. However, such arguments can never definitively prove God's existence. Rather, for Vivekananda, we can only be absolutely certain of God's existence when we have realized Him directly for ourselves. As he puts it in the statement cited earlier, "What is the proof of God? Direct perception, *pratyakṣa*" (*CW* 1:415). Hence, in order for APC to be plausible and consistent with his own views on the inherent limits of reason expressed elsewhere, I think his very strong claims in passage B about absolute certainty and the rational necessity of accepting panentheistic cosmopsychism need to be weakened. From Vivekananda's perspective, in order to achieve absolute certainty of the truth of panentheistic cosmopsychism, we would have to follow in the footsteps of mystics like the Upaniṣadic sages and Ramakrishna, who attained the direct supersensuous perception of the all-pervading Divine Consciousness through intensive spiritual practice.

Fourth, I think Vivekananda's APC would be stronger and more perspicuous if it were split into two mutually supportive arguments—one in favor of panpsychism in general and the other in favor of panentheistic cosmopsychism in particular.

In order to address these problems and to facilitate cross-cultural philosophical dialogue, I have refined and developed Vivekananda's APC into the two arguments below: a Vivekanandan Argument for Panpsychism and a Vivekanandan Argument for Panentheistic Cosmopsychism. I call these "Vivekanandan" arguments, since Vivekananda himself did not make these arguments, but they nonetheless take their bearings from his views. I take both these arguments to be abductive ones (inferences to the best explanation).

Argument 1: A Vivekanandan Argument for Panpsychism

1. *Doctrine of the Pre-existent Effect*: If *c* is the material cause[6] of *e*, then *e* must already be present in some form in *c*.
2. *Denial of Materialist Reductionism*: Consciousness is not identical to anything material, such as a brain state.
3. *Denial of Emergentism*: Consciousness could not have emerged from nonconscious matter at a certain point in the evolutionary process. (*from* 1 and 2)
4. *Denial of Consciousness-Matter Dualisms*: Neither interactionist mind-brain dualism nor Sāṃkhyan consciousness-mind dualism is plausible.

Therefore,

5. *Plausibility of Panpsychism*: We are rationally justified in believing that consciousness is involved—that is, present in some form—even in primordial matter. (*from* 2–4)

Argument 2: A Vivekanandan Argument for Panentheistic Cosmopsychism

1. *Argument from Design*: The traditional argument that this universe presents evidence of design makes it reasonable to believe that there exists a divine intelligence.

[6] "Material cause" is the English equivalent of *upādāna-kāraṇa*, as opposed to the "instrumental cause" (*nimitta-kāraṇa*). It is important to note that in an Indian philosophical context, if *c* is the material cause of *e*, *c* can be either an insentient entity or a conscious being such as Brahman.

2. *Existence of Mystical Claims*: There are credible mystics, such as Ramakrishna, who claim to have directly perceived an impersonal-personal Divine Consciousness that manifests as everything in the universe.
3. *Argument for the Epistemic Value of Mystical Experience$_s$* (AEV$_s$)[7]: Given certain uncontroversial epistemic principles of perceptual justification and perceptual testimony as well as other premises, we are rationally justified in believing that the reported spiritual experiences of credible mystics are veridical.

Therefore,

4. *Plausibility of Panentheistic Cosmopsychism*: We are rationally justified in believing that there exists an impersonal-personal Divine Consciousness that manifests as everything in the universe. (*from* 1–3)

Some points should be noted regarding Argument 1. As I already noted, Vivekananda's own argument for panpsychism in passage B does not include premise 2, but I have included premise 2 in Argument 1, since it is necessary to complete his argument and he does defend premise 2 in his "Science of Yoga" lecture.

Premise 4 of Argument 1 is also not present in passage B, but Vivekananda defends the premise in numerous other places in his work. He criticized two forms of dualism in particular: interactionist mind-brain dualism and Sāṃkhyan consciousness-mind dualism. For instance, he discusses mind-brain dualism in this passage from his lecture "The Vedānta" (1897):

> In modern times, in Western countries, as physical science is making rapid progress, as physiology is step by step conquering stronghold after stronghold of old religions, the Western people do not know where to stand, because to their great despair, modern physiology at every step has identified the mind with the brain. But we in India have known that always. That is the first proposition the Hindu boy learns that the mind is matter, only finer. (*CW* 3:401)

He clearly has in mind contemporary religious people in the West who subscribed to the Cartesian view that the mind is a non-physical substance entirely different from, but in interaction with, the physical brain. He notes that recent scientific studies in physiology have demonstrated that the mind and brain are, in fact, identical in substance. Vivekananda's defense of the identity of mind and brain on the basis of empirical science anticipated similar efforts by philosophers

[7] To remind the reader, AEV$_s$ is the refined and systematized form of Vivekananda's argument for the epistemic value of supersensous perception (AEV), discussed in section 2 of chapter 5.

and scientists from the mid-twentieth century up to the present. As Paul Thagard (2018) notes, "The increasing integration of cognitive psychology with neuroscience provides evidence for the mind-brain identity theory according to which mental processes are neural, representational, and computational."

In his lecture "Prakṛti and Puruṣa" (1896), Vivekananda remarks:

> There is no difference between matter and mind, except in degree. The substance is the same in finer or grosser form; one changes into the other, and this exactly coincides with the conclusions of modern physiological research. By believing in the teaching that the mind is not separate from the brain, you will be saved from much fighting and struggling. (*CW* 2:444)

He notes here that physiological studies have shown how the mind and brain interact with, and change into, one another. One of Vivekananda's main criticisms of interactionist mind-brain dualism, then, is that it is unable to explain how a non-physical mind could interact with the physical brain. By contrast, he argues that the Indian philosophies of Sāṃkhya and Vedānta agree perfectly with modern scientific studies, which show that the mind is able to interact causally with the brain precisely because they are both material entities.

As I discussed in sections 4 and 5 of the previous chapter, while Vivekananda sides with Sāṃkhya in conceiving the mind as a subtle form of matter, he also criticizes its dualistic metaphysics. He argues that Sāṃkhyan mind-consciousness dualism sets up a "huge gulf to be bridged over" between the physical mind on the one hand and non-physical consciousness (Puruṣa) on the other (*CW* 1:361). Hence, Sāṃkhya is unable to explain how matter and consciousness interact with one another. As he puts it, "How can these different colours [of Nature or Prakṛti], as the Sāṃkhya calls them, be able to act on that soul which by its nature is colourless?" (*CW* 1:361). In sum, then, Vivekananda rejects both Western mind-brain dualism as well as Sāṃkhyan mind-consciousness dualism, primarily on the grounds that neither is able to explain the mutual interaction of two radically different entities.

It is also important to note that Argument 1 makes an abductive inference to panpsychism on the basis of a limited set of potential explanations of consciousness. In particular, I limit the abductive set to five potential explanations: materialist reductionism, emergentism, mind-brain dualism, mind-consciousness dualism, and panpsychism. In doing so, I obviously exclude any number of other potential explanations. My reasons for doing so are twofold. First, Vivekananda and many other (though certainly not all) late nineteenth-century intellectuals in India and the West considered these five explanations of consciousness to be the most serious live options. Second, the abductive set, in any case, could not possibly be exhaustive, since there are any number of logically possible theories of consciousness. Hence, I have adopted what Peter Lipton (2004: 59) considers to be the mainstream abductive approach—namely, to "start from a group of plausible candidates, and then consider which of these is the best, rather than selecting directly from the vast pool of possible explanations," which would include "all sorts of crazy explanations nobody would seriously consider." That said, if I had more space, I would certainly expand the abduction set to include at least a few more potential explanations, especially epiphenomenalism, property dualism, and illusionism (Frankish 2017).

Regarding Argument 2, premises 2 and 3 are missing from Vivekananda's own APC, but he defends very similar premises in *Rāja-Yoga*, as I have shown in chapter 5. In both Arguments 1 and 2, I have also replaced Vivekananda's language of "absolute certainty" and rational necessity with the weaker language of "rational justification."

Arguments 1 and 2 are also mutually supportive, since they provide independent grounds for believing that some form of panpsychism is true. Taken together, these two arguments, if successful, make it reasonable to believe not only that panpsychism is true but that the most plausible form of panpsychism is panentheistic cosmopsychism.

3. *Grounding by Self-Limitation and the Individuation Problem*

As I noted briefly in section 1 of the previous chapter, the most serious problem for cosmopsychists is the individuation problem: how is it possible for the single cosmic consciousness to individuate into the conscious experiences of multiple human and animal subjects, each of which has its own unique first-person perspective?[8] Before we examine Vivekananda's response to this question, we need a more precise formulation of the individuation problem itself. To this end, let us consider Itay Shani's helpful summary of Sam Coleman's articulation of the subject combination problem for *micropsychist* theories:

> He [Coleman] asks us to imagine two micro-subjects, Red and Blue, such that Red sees only red, while Blue sees only blue. Red and Blue combine, in turn, to form a macro-subject, call it Mac, which integrates their phenomenal worlds into a single perspective. The problem, says Coleman, is that Red's and Blue's

[8] I follow Mathews (2011) in referring to "the individuation problem" rather than to "the decombination problem," which is Miri Albahari's (2020) preferred term. I agree with Chalmers (2020: 365) that the term "decombination" is "misleading in suggesting that the universal mind must be a combination of the macro minds." "Individuation," the term I prefer, does not have the misleadingly mereological connotations of "decombination."

> perspectives do not survive *as points of view* within Mac's unified perspective. For example, Red's take on the world is that of seeing red, to the exclusion of all else, but Mac's perspective defies this condition: it may contain seeing blue, in addition to seeing red, or it may simply consist of seeing purple.... the original *perspectives* have disappeared from sight. (Shani 2015: 401)

Coleman's main point is that conscious perspectives are mutually exclusive as a matter of logical fact. Hence, micropsychist theories face the subject combination problem: it is difficult to conceive how, or in what sense, multiple micro-level consciousnesses can combine to form a single macro-level consciousness. Cosmopsychist theories, then, face the obverse individuation problem: how can the single cosmic consciousness, with its own cosmic perspective, individuate into multiple human and animal subjects, each with its own different conscious perspective?

In order to answer this question, most contemporary cosmopsychists have drawn upon Jonathan Schaffer's priority monism, the view that there exists only one basic entity, which grounds all other entities (Schaffer 2010). Combining cosmopsychism with priority monism yields priority cosmopsychism, the view that cosmic consciousness is the only basic entity, which grounds all individual conscious experiences. Proponents of priority cosmopsychism offer differing accounts of *how* cosmic consciousness grounds the conscious experiences of individual subjects.[9]

Philip Goff, for instance, defends a version of priority cosmopsychism based on "grounding by subsumption," which he defines as follows: "X grounds by subsumption Y iff [if and only if] Y is a partial aspect of X" (2020: 148).[10] According to Goff, then, the cosmic consciousness somehow *contains* within itself all the various human-level consciousnesses into which it individuates. However, Goff's cosmopsychist theory based on grounding by subsumption fails to provide a plausible and coherent response to the individuation problem. As several philosophers have shown, it is logically incoherent for a single unifying conscious perspective to contain within it multiple other conscious perspectives as "partial aspects," since these latter conscious perspectives would not survive *as points of view* within the broader unified perspective.[11]

Vivekananda's panentheistic cosmopsychism, I would argue, is a distinctive form of priority cosmopsychism that provides a novel account of the grounding relation. I would call his account of grounding "grounding by self-limitation," according to which X grounds by self-limitation Y if and only if X manifests as Y through a process of self-limitation. According to his panentheistic

[9] See, for instance, Goff (2017a: 220–55), Shani (2015, 2018), Nagasawa and Wager (2017).

[10] For a detailed discussion of grounding by subsumption, see Goff (2017a: 220–33).

[11] Coleman (2014), Shani (2015: 393–402), and Albahari (2020: 121–24).

cosmopsychism, then, the omnipotent Divine Cosmic Consciousness grounds the conscious experiences of individual subjects in the sense of *manifesting* as all of these individual subjects—with their own respective conscious perspectives—through a playful process of self-limitation. Vivekananda's account of grounding by self-limitation satisfies what Goff calls the "free lunch constraint"—the constraint that any adequate theory of grounding must account for the apparent paradox that if X grounds Y, then (a) Y is nothing over and above X, and yet (b) Y is not identical to X (2020: 146). For Vivekananda, the conscious perspectives of ordinary human subjects, as self-limited manifestations of the Divine Cosmic Consciousness, are nothing over and above the Divine Cosmic Consciousness while not being identical to it.

To gain a more precise understanding of Vivekananda's account of grounding by self-limitation, and whether and how it resolves the individuation problem, let us examine briefly the views of his guru Ramakrishna, which played an important role in shaping Vivekananda's own thinking on the matter. There are three key elements in Ramakrishna's account of how the single Divine Consciousness manifests as everything in the universe. The first two elements are contained in the following passage:

> This world is the *līlā* [sportive play] of God. . . . God alone has become all this (*īśvari sab hoye royechen*)—*māyā*, the universe, living beings (*jīva*), and the twenty-four cosmic principles. "As the snake I bite, and as the charmer I cure." It is God Herself who has become both Knowledge (*vidyā*) and ignorance (*avidyā*). She has become ignorant (*ajñāna*) through the *māyā* of ignorance (*avidyā-māyā*). Again, through the *māyā* of Knowledge (*vidyā-māyā*) and in the form of the guru, She dispels ignorance. . . . The *vijñānī* sees that it is God who has become all this. (*K* 437 / *G* 436)

First, Ramakrishna makes clear that he conceives divine manifestation in the maximally strong sense of becoming: God (*īsvara*) has literally "become" everything in the universe, including all sentient creatures and insentient entities. Second, he explains that God becomes both ignorant people and enlightened saints through *avidyā-māyā* and *vidyā-māyā* respectively. It is extremely important to note that Ramakrishna, unlike classical Advaita Vedāntins like Śaṅkara, does not conceive *māyā* as a principle of illusion. For Ramakrishna, *avidyā-māyā* and *vidyā-māyā* are twin principles of real divine manifestation. At the same time, he upholds the panentheistic view that God *in Her essence* remains perfectly pure and omnipotent even while manifesting as imperfect and limited creatures. Through *avidyā-māyā*, the immaterial, omniscient, omnipotent God takes the form of ignorance (*avidyā*)—that is, worldliness and selfish impulses like lust, anger, and greed—in those people who identify with their body-mind complexes and who, therefore, lack awareness of their divine nature. Through *vidyā-māyā*, God takes the form of knowledge (*vidyā*)—ethical and spiritual qualities like compassion, devotion, discrimination, and dispassion—in spiritual aspirants and enlightened saints who have realized their divine nature through intensive spiritual practice and God's grace. According to Ramakrishna, then, it is through these two forms of *māyā* that God manifests as all the various individual souls by limiting or veiling Herself in a spirit of sportive play.

Taken together, these two elements in Ramakrishna's account of divine manifestation raise the individuation problem in an acute form: if God has Her own divine perspective, then how is it logically possible for God to become different human beings, each with their own different conscious perspective? The third element in Ramakrishna's account of divine manifestation holds the key to understanding how he addresses the individuation problem. He presents a scheme of seven different levels of consciousness based on Tantric Kuṇḍalini-Yoga and his own spiritual experiences:

> Yoga is not possible if the mind dwells on "woman and gold." The mind of an ordinary person generally moves among the three lower centers: those at the sexual organ, at the organ of evacuation, and at the navel (*liṅga, guhya o nābhi*). After great effort and spiritual practice the Kula-Kuṇḍalinī is awakened. According to yogis, there are three nerves (*nāḍī*) in the spinal column: Iḍā, Piṅgalā, and Suṣumnā. Along the Suṣumnā are six lotuses, or centers (*padma*), the lowest being known as the Mūlādhāra. Then come successively Svādhiṣṭhāna, Maṇipura, Anāhata, Viśuddha, and Ājñā. These are the six centers. The Kuṇḍalinī, when awakened, passes through the lower centers and comes to the Anāhata, which is at the heart. It stays there. At that time the mind of the aspirant is withdrawn from the three lower centers. He feels the awakening of Divine Consciousness and sees Light. In mute wonder he sees that radiance and cries out: "What is this? What is this?"
>
> After passing through the six centers, the Kuṇḍalinī reaches the thousand-petaled lotus known as the Sahasrāra, and the aspirant goes into *samādhi*. . . . When the Kuṇḍalinī rises to the Sahasrāra and the mind goes into *samādhi*, the aspirant loses all consciousness of the outer world. He can no longer retain his physical body. . . . But the *īśvarakoṭi*s, such as the Incarnations of God, can come down from this state of *samādhi*. . . . Their minds move between the sixth and the seventh planes. They run a boat-race back and forth, as it were, between these two planes. (*K* 504–5 / *G* 499–500)

According to Ramakrishna, the minds of ignorant people usually remain concentrated at one of the three lower centers (Mūlādhāra, Svādhiṣṭhāna, Maṇipura), since they are preoccupied with egoistic and materialistic desires, especially lust and greed. Through spiritual practice, one can awaken the Kuṇḍalinī, which then ascends to the three higher centers (Anāhata, Viśuddha, Ājñā) in succession. As one's consciousness ascends through these higher centers, one realizes that one is not the body-mind complex but an eternal divine soul intimately related to God. At the sixth center (Ājñā), one "sees the form of the personal God" (*īśvarer rūp darśan hoy*) but there still remains a "slight barrier" (*āḍāl*) between the aspirant and God (*K* 504 / *G* 500). When the Kuṇḍalinī rises to the Sahasrāra, one goes into *nirvikalpa samādhi*, the Advaitic state in which one's individuality becomes entirely merged in the impersonal (*nirguṇa*) nondual Brahman. Ramakrishna adds, however, that the *īśvarakoṭi*—by which he means the *vijñānī*—can come down from the nondual state of *nirvikalpa samādhi* and shuttle back and forth between the sixth and seventh planes of consciousness. As a result, the *vijñānī* realizes that "the Reality which is impersonal and without attributes (*nirguṇa*) is also personal and with attributes (*saguṇa*)" (*K* 51 / *G* 104). When the *vijñānī* remains on the sixth plane of consciousness, he communes with the loving personal God, and when he ascends to the seventh plane, he realizes his identity with the impersonal nondual Brahman.

Ramakrishna addresses the individuation problem by combining his doctrine of God's playful self-limitation through *māyā* with his Tantric scheme of seven centers of consciousness. By means of Her own *avidyā-māyā*, the Divine Consciousness limits Herself by becoming ignorant people whose consciousness remains on the lower three planes and, hence, preoccupied with egoistic concerns and the desire for sense-gratification. God thereby limits Herself in such a way that She "loses" Her own divine perspective and enjoys instead the respective conscious perspectives of each of those ignorant people. I put "loses" in scare-quotes, because Ramakrishna is committed to the panentheistic view that God in Her essence (*svarūpa*) still remains perfectly pure, omnipotent, and divine. From Ramakrishna's perspective, the key to solving the individuation problem is to recognize that while the seven planes of consciousness exist simultaneously, no individual's consciousness can remain on more than one plane at any given time. So long as I am egoistic and worldly minded, my consciousness remains on one of the lower three planes, and I accordingly enjoy my own ignorant conscious perspective that is distinct from God's divine perspective. Through intensive spiritual practice over the course of many lives and by God's grace, I can gradually ascend to higher planes of consciousness, culminating in the Advaitic state of *nirvikalpa samādhi* on the seventh plane of consciousness. Once I reach this seventh plane, I lose my individual conscious perspective entirely, since my individuality is then completely merged in the Pure Consciousness of nondual Brahman. If I am a *vijñānī*, then even after the attainment of *nirvikalpa samādhi*, I can move between the sixth and seventh planes of consciousness, thereby sharing the divine conscious perspective of Śakti or the

Divine Cosmic Consciousness. Notice, however, that my own limited conscious perspective as an ignorant human being is not contained or subsumed within God's divine perspective. Hence, the threat of logical incoherence raised by the individuation problem is arguably averted.

We can now reconstruct Vivekananda's response to the individuation problem by taking as our clue the three key elements in Ramakrishna's account of divine manifestation: a very strong conception of divine manifestation as literal becoming, the doctrine of God's playful self-limitation through *māyā*, and the Tantric scheme of seven planes of consciousness. I will argue that Vivekananda, as an Integral Advaitin, accepts all three of these key elements, each of which I will now discuss in turn. First, there is strong evidence that he follows Ramakrishna in conceiving divine manifestation as literal becoming. Ramakrishna, as we have seen, uses forms of the Bengali verb "to become"—such as *hoyechen* and *hoye royechen*—when teaching that God manifests as everything in the universe. That Vivekananda follows his guru on this point is clear from his English translation of one of his favorite Upaniṣadic passages, Kaṭha Upaniṣad 2.2.9:

> As the one fire entering into the world manifests (*babhūva*) itself in various ways, even so that one Self, the Self of all, manifests Itself in every form. (*CW* 2:411)
>
> *agnir yathaiko bhuvanaṃ praviṣṭo rūpaṃ rūpaṃ pratirūpo babhūva* |
> *ekas tathā sarvabhūtāntarātmā rūpaṃ rūpaṃ pratirūpo bahiśca* ||

The Sanskrit verb *babhūva* derives from the verbal root *bhū*, which means "to become." Hence, the word *babhūva* literally means "became" or "becomes." Tellingly, Vivekananda translates *babhūva* as "manifests," which indicates that he understands divine manifestation in the sense of literal becoming. There are numerous similar passages throughout his work, such as the statement quoted in section 1: "He it is that comes down and *becomes* the lowest atom, and slowly unfolding His nature, rejoins Himself" (*CW* 2:211; emphasis added). Like Ramakrishna, then, Vivekananda holds that God has actually become everything and everyone in the universe, including both good and evil people.[12]

Second, Vivekananda also follows his guru in explaining the dynamics of divine manifestation by appealing to the doctrine of God's playful self-limitation through *māyā*. That this world is the sportive "play" or "fun" of God is a recurring theme in the *Complete Works*. For instance, in an 1897 conversation with a disciple, he remarked that "this creation of the universe is God's play" and then immediately quoted *Brahmasūtra* 2.1.33 (*lokavattu līlākaivalyam*), which states

[12] For details, see section 3 of chapter 2.

that Brahman creates this universe not out of necessity but in a spirit of sportive play (*BCW* 9:38 / *CW* 6:482). Likewise, in an 1896 class on the Muṇḍaka Upaniṣad, he explained that God playfully manifests as everything in the universe: "He is the man, the woman, the cow, the dog—in all animals, in the sin and in the sinner. He is the Sannyāsin, He is in the ruler, He is everywhere. . . . He is playing through all these things. Various forms—from the highest gods to the lowest worms—are all He" (*CW* 9:241).

For Vivekananda, *māyā* is the mechanism by which God playfully manifests as the universe. His clearest and most detailed account of divine manifestation is contained in his aptly titled lecture "The Absolute and Manifestation," delivered in London in 1896. His fundamental thesis is that "the Absolute is manifesting Itself as many, through the veil of time, space, and causation" (*CW* 2:135). Shortly thereafter, he explicitly defines "Māyā" as "the sum total of time, space, and causation" (*CW* 2:135). According to Vivekananda, then, the nondual Absolute manifests as everything in the universe through the individuating principle of *māyā*, the veil of time, space, and causation. Crucially, he then contrasts the classical Advaitic understanding of *māyā* as a principle of illusion with his own realist understanding of *māyā*.[13] He claims that time, space, and causation are perfectly real but "have no independent existence" apart from the Absolute (*CW* 2:136). As he puts it, "They [time, space, and causation] have no real existence; yet they are not non-existent, seeing that through them all things are manifesting as this universe" (*CW* 2:136). He clarifies the somewhat paradoxical ontological status of *māyā* by appealing to the metaphor of an ocean and its waves (not coincidentally, one of Ramakrishna's own favorite metaphors[14]):

> Thus we see, first, that the combination of time, space, and causation has neither existence nor non-existence. Secondly, it sometimes vanishes. To give an illustration, there is a wave on the ocean. The wave is the same as the ocean certainly, and yet we know it is a wave, and as such different from the ocean. What makes this difference? The name and the form, that is, the idea in the mind and the form. Now, can we think of a wave-form as something separate from the ocean? Certainly not. It is always associated with the ocean idea. If the wave subsides, the form vanishes in a moment, and yet the form was not a delusion. So long as the wave existed the form was there, and you were bound to see the form. This is Māyā.
>
> The whole of this universe, therefore, is, as it were, a peculiar form; the Absolute is that ocean while you and I, and suns and stars, and everything else

[13] For a more detailed discussion of Vivekananda's views on *māyā*, see section 3 of chapter 2.

[14] See, for instance, Ramakrishna's teaching at *K* 254 / *G* 277, already discussed in section 2 of chapter 2.

> are various waves of that ocean. And what makes the waves different? Only the form, and that form is time, space, and causation, all entirely dependent on the wave. As soon as the wave goes, they vanish. As soon as the individual gives up this Māyā, it vanishes for him and he becomes free. (*CW* 2:136)

According to Vivekananda, the nondual Absolute manifests as everything in the universe by limiting itself through the individuating principle of *māyā*. Just as the waves of an ocean are perfectly real but nonetheless evanescent and entirely dependent for their existence on the ocean itself, all the names and forms in this universe are real but impermanent manifestations of the eternal and omnipotent God, who always remains beyond all His limited manifestations.

Third, Vivekananda explicitly appeals to Ramakrishna's Tantric scheme of seven planes of consciousness in numerous places in his work.[15] For instance, he invokes the Tantric scheme in his lecture "Meditation" delivered in San Francisco in 1900:

> As this power of Kuṇḍalinī rises from one centre to the other in the spine, it changes the senses and you begin to see this world another [anew?]. It is heaven. You cannot talk. Then the Kuṇḍalinī goes down to the lower centres. You are again man until the Kuṇḍalinī reaches the brain, all the centres have been passed, and the whole vision vanishes and you [perceive] . . . nothing but the one existence. You are God. All heavens you make out of Him, all worlds out of Him. He is the one existence. Nothing else exists. (*CW* 4:237)

As a Ramakrishnan panentheistic cosmopsychist, Vivekananda maintains that nothing but God exists but that we cannot realize our true divine nature so long as our minds remain at the lower centers. In order to awaken the Kuṇḍalinī, we have to renounce sense-pleasures and engage in ethical and spiritual practices like meditation, unselfish service, and the worship of God. Through such spiritual practices, the Kuṇḍalinī gradually rises to higher centers, culminating in the realization that we ourselves "are God." So long as we identify with the ego, we will have our own conscious perspectives as limited and ignorant human beings, since our minds remain at the lower three centers. However, when we break our identification with the ego through spiritual practice, we can ascend to higher centers of consciousness, eventually realizing our identity with God. As he puts it, "Man only remains hypnotised with the false idea of an ego. When this ghost is off from us, all dreams vanish, and then it is found that the one Self only exists from the highest Being to a blade of grass" (*CW* 6:474–75).

[15] See, for instance, *CW* 1:169 and *CW* 7:253.

In his lecture "One Existence Appearing as Many," delivered in New York in 1896, he specifies that the different planes or centers of consciousness are mutually exclusive:

> We have seen how in the whole of this universe there is but One Existence; and that One Existence when seen through the senses is called the world, the world of matter. When It is seen through the mind, It is called the world of thoughts and ideas; and when It is seen as it is, then It is the One Infinite Being. . . . There is but one Being which the ignorant call the world. When a man goes higher in knowledge, he calls the very same Being the world of thought. Again, when knowledge itself comes, all illusions vanish, and man finds it is all nothing but Ātman. I am that One Existence. This is the last conclusion. There are neither three nor two in the universe; it is all One. That One, under the illusion of Māyā, is seen as many, just as a rope is seen as a snake. It is the very rope that is seen as a snake. There are not two things there, a rope separate and a snake separate. No man sees these two things there at the same time. . . . When we perceive the rope, we do not perceive the snake at all; and when we see the snake, we do not see the rope at all—it has vanished. (*CW* 3:20–21)

Vivekananda seems to come very close here to classical Advaita when he declares that "That One, under the illusion of Māyā, is seen as many, just as a rope is seen as a snake." He not only appeals to the classic Advaitic rope-snake analogy but also refers to *māyā* as an "illusion." However, as I already argued in detail in section 3 of chapter 2, what Vivekananda is actually doing here and elsewhere is subtly reinterpreting traditional Advaitic doctrines and analogies in a more realist manner that accords with his own Integral Advaitic position of panentheistic cosmopsychism. For Vivekananda, *māyā* is an "illusion" only in the sense that it is impermanent and has no independent existence apart from God. He then uses the rope-snake analogy not to illustrate the unreality of the world but to explain the *mutual exclusivity* of the different planes of consciousness: "When we perceive the rope, we do not perceive the snake at all; and when we see the snake, we do not see the rope at all. . . ."

We are now in a position to outline Vivekananda's distinctive solution to the individuation problem: how is it logically possible for God, with His own divine perspective, to manifest as various human beings, who enjoy their own different conscious perspectives? According to his Integral Advaitic metaphysics of panentheistic cosmopsychism, Divine Consciousness is the sole reality. By means of the individuating principle of *māyā*, this nondual Divine Consciousness—in its personal aspect as Śakti or the "Divine Mother" (*CW* 8:252–53)—manifests as everything in the universe through a process of playful self-limitation or self-veiling. As indicated in Figure 9.2 of the previous chapter, Śakti (or Mahat/

Īśvara) manifests as all the eternal individual souls (*jīvas*), each of which has its own unique conscious perspective. My conscious experiences, rooted in my own first-person perspective, result from the association of my *jīva* with my particular insentient *antaḥkaraṇa* in this life. Your conscious experiences, rooted in your different first-person perspective, result from the association of your conscious *jīva* with your insentient *antaḥkaraṇa* in this life.

In ignorant people, the Divine Consciousness manifests as *egoic* consciousness, concentrated at the three lower centers or planes of consciousness. As a result, ignorant people—who are nothing but different self-limited manifestations of God Himself—remain unaware of their own divine nature, and their conscious perspectives are grounded in their identification with the body-mind complex and their consequent preoccupation with worldly thoughts and desires. Those who engage in spiritual practice can ascend to higher planes of consciousness through the awakening of the Kuṇḍalinī. Vivekananda would often appeal to the analogy of "veils" to convey that our true nature is Divine Consciousness and that the aim of all spiritual practice is nothing but to remove the "veils" covering our divine nature. As he puts it in his lecture "The Real Nature of Man," "Every good thought that you think or act upon is simply tearing the veil, as it were; and the purity, the Infinity, the God behind, manifests Itself more and more" (*CW* 2:82). As we ascend to higher planes of consciousness, veil after veil covering the Divine Consciousness is removed, and our conscious perspective itself changes at each higher plane, until the Kuṇḍalinī finally rises to the Sahasrāra, and we realize our deepest nature as the Divine Consciousness. Hence, from Vivekananda's perspective, the conscious perspectives of various people are one and the same Divine Consciousness limited or "veiled" to varying degrees and in different ways, depending on their current plane of consciousness. In Vivekananda's rendering of the rope-snake analogy, as we have seen, the perception of the rope is mutually exclusive with the perception of the snake; we never see both the rope and the snake at the same time. Similarly, since the various planes of consciousness are mutually exclusive, our ignorant conscious perspectives and God's divine perspective are also mutually exclusive. So long as we enjoy our ignorant conscious perspectives, we do not, and cannot, share the perspective of Divine Consciousness. Conversely, when we realize our true nature as Divine Consciousness, we no longer have our ego-centered conscious perspectives.

Arguably, Goff's cosmopsychist theory based on grounding by subsumption is especially vulnerable to the individuation problem, since it seems to ascribe all our ordinary conscious experiences directly to the cosmic consciousness by conceiving the former as "partial aspects" of the latter (Goff 2017a). By contrast, Vivekananda's model of grounding by self-limitation does not entail that the Divine Cosmic Consciousness in any sense contains or subsumes the first-person conscious perspectives of different human and animal subjects. An example can help illustrate the dynamics of divine grounding by self-limitation. Let us assume that $human_1$ is afraid of dying, $human_2$ is not afraid of dying, $human_3$ is eager to make more money, and $human_4$ is perfectly content with the money she already has. According to Vivekananda's panentheistic cosmopsychism, God, through a playful process of self-limitation, has simultaneously manifested as all four of these human beings while still remaining perfect and divine in Her essential nature. God, in Her self-limited manifestation as $human_1$, is afraid of dying, while God, in Her self-limited manifestation as $human_2$, is not afraid of dying. God, in Her self-limited manifestation as $human_3$, is eager to make more money, while God, in Her self-limited manifestation as $human_4$, is not. So long as these human beings remain ignorant of their true nature as God, their minds will remain on the lower planes of consciousness; hence, they will think of themselves as individual body-mind complexes and have all their ordinary human mental states. However, once they attain God-realization, they will realize that they were simply different manifestations of God all along.

For Vivekananda, then, God, in Her essential nature, has *none* of the mental states enjoyed by the four human beings. At the same time, God, in Her self-limited manifestation as a particular human being, has all the mental states of that person alone. Since each person has a distinct individual soul, and God Herself has manifested all individual souls, each person enjoys her own unique mental states, while God in Her essence enjoys Her own divine perspective. Since Vivekananda's panentheistic cosmopsychism is based on grounding by self-limitation, it does not entail the combining or subsuming of perspectives at all. Hence, it arguably provides a more cogent solution to the individuation problem than many other cosmopsychist theories such as Goff's.

At this point, however, another question might be raised. Even if there is nothing logically incoherent in the idea of a perfect and omnipotent God manifesting as imperfect human beings, it is difficult to imagine *how* God can pull off such a feat without compromising Her own divine perfection. As is often the case, understanding how Ramakrishna addressed this question can help us gain insight into Vivekananda's own views on the matter. In a conversation with a visitor held on October 30, 1885, Ramakrishna appealed to God's omnipotence to explain how God can manifest as everything in the universe:

> But you must remember that everything is possible for God. She is formless, and again She assumes forms. She is the individual and She is the universe. She is Brahman and She is Śakti. There is no end to Her, no limit. Nothing is impossible for Her. (*K* 996 / *G* 920)[16]

[16] *kintu tẫte sab sambhabe! sei tinī nirākār sākār. tinī svarāṭ virāṭ! tinī brahma, tinī śakti! tẫr iti nāi,—śeṣ nāi; tẫte sab sambhabe.*

For Ramakrishna, due to our human cognitive limitations, we may very well find it difficult to fathom how Saccidānanda can become everything and everyone in the universe. Nonetheless, since God is omnipotent, She is capable of achieving things that we cannot even begin to comprehend. As Ramakrishna puts it, "everything is possible for God." Hence, in light of the unbridgeable gulf between the finite human mind and the omnipotent mind of God, we are never justified in inferring from *our* inability to understand how a perfect God can become this imperfect universe to the conclusion that God *cannot* become everything.

I think we can defend Vivekananda's panentheistic cosmopsychism along the same lines. Like Ramakrishna, Vivekananda frequently emphasizes God's omnipotence. For instance, in his 1893 lecture "The Hindu Religion," he affirms God's omnipotence from a panentheistic standpoint: "We [Hindus] believe in a God, the Father of the universe, infinite and omnipotent. But if our soul at last becomes perfect, it also must become infinite. But there is no room for two infinite unconditional beings, and hence we believe in a Personal God, and we ourselves are He" (*CW* 1:331). Hence, to explain how God can manifest as imperfect creatures while still remaining pure and perfect, Vivekananda could appeal to God's omnipotence. While even an omnipotent being arguably cannot do anything that is logically impossible—like making 2 + 2 equal to 5—He can, by definition, do anything that *is* logically possible. As Richard Swinburne puts it, "By God's being omnipotent I understand that he is able to do whatever it is logically possible (i.e. coherent to suppose) that he can do" (2004: 7). If my foregoing account of Vivekananda's grounding by self-limitation is convincing, then there is nothing logically incoherent in Vivekananda's view that the perfect and omnipotent God manifests as everything in the universe through a playful process of self-veiling. Vivekananda can then appeal to the doctrine of divine omnipotence to address the "how" question. It seems perfectly acceptable to appeal to God's omnipotence in answer to the question of *how* a perfect God manifests as this imperfect universe without compromising Her essential purity and perfection. After all, why should we limited human beings even expect to comprehend the capabilities of an omnipotent and omniscient being?

4. *Addressing Objections to Vivekananda's Panentheistic Cosmopsychism*

There are, of course, numerous possible objections to Vivekananda's panentheistic cosmospsychism and his arguments in favor of it. I will address some of these objections in this section. One could argue that there are obvious counterexamples to the doctrine of the pre-existent effect that plays such an important role in Vivekananda's argument. Premise 1 of Argument 1 formulates this doctrine as follows: "If *c* is the material cause of *e*, then *e* must already be present in some form in *c*." But in what sense, for instance, is liquid water already present in the non-liquid molecules of hydrogen and oxygen from which it emerges? The answer is that water, at an elemental level of description, is nothing but the combination of a certain ratio of hydrogen and oxygen molecules bonded together according to certain physical laws. Hence, the emergence of liquid water from non-liquid molecules actually *supports* the doctrine of the pre-existent effect, since the cause and effect are simply the non-liquid and liquid forms respectively of exactly the same substance (i.e., hydrogen and oxygen molecules).[17]

One might think that the way different colors combine to create a new color constitutes a potential counterexample to the doctrine of the pre-existent effect. In what sense, for instance, is the pigment purple already present in red and blue? However, purple is a secondary color, which is nothing but a mixture of the primary colors red and blue. Hence, the pigment purple—composed of a mixture of red and blue pigments—is already present in an *unmixed* form in the separate red and blue pigments themselves. In the case of both liquid water and the pigment purple, there is a more elemental level of description at which they are the same in substance as their respective causes.

One might also question Vivekananda's view that the single Divine Consciousness individuates into various human consciousnesses through a process of playful self-limitation. In the previous section, I argued that his account of grounding by self-limitation sidesteps the individuation problem, since the Divine Cosmic Consciousness does not contain or subsume the first-person conscious perspectives of different human and animal subjects. However, one might worry that God's omniscience is threatened if She, qua the cosmically perspectival *īśvara*, has no direct access to the perspectives of ordinary creatures. In that case, God presumably would not know what it is like to *be* such a creature from the inside.[18]

We can begin to defend Vivekananda's position against this objection by determining what exactly divine omniscience amounts to. Swinburne plausibly defines omniscience as knowledge of "whatever it is logically possible that he [God] know" (2004: 7). In light of the individuation problem discussed in the previous section, it is clear that it is, indeed, not logically possible for God, *in Her perfect divine essence*, to experience the world from the partial, and imperfect, conscious perspectives of ordinary creatures. Hence, God's omniscience is not threatened, since She is still capable of knowing everything that it is logically possible for Her to know.

[17] Along these lines, Strawson (2008: 60–70) explains in detail why the emergence of water from non-liquid molecules is "shiningly easy to grasp" (2008: 61), whereas the emergence of consciousness from insentient matter is incoherent.

[18] I owe this objection to Itay Shani.

However, one might still raise a related concern: can God resonate to the experiential lives of His creatures in the absence of unlimited first-person access to their conscious states? Linda Zagzebski (2008: 231–47) answers this question in the affirmative by arguing that omniscience is not only compatible with, but in fact *entails*, what she calls "omnisubjectivity," "the property of consciously grasping with perfect accuracy and completeness the first-person perspective of every conscious being" (2008: 231). Employing the model of human empathy, she suggests that "God's knowledge of our conscious lives is something like the perfection of empathy" (Zagzebski 2008: 237). For instance, when someone tries to empathize with her best friend who is grieving the recent death of her mother, she tries to *imaginatively simulate* her friend's grief as accurately as possible by putting herself in her friend's place, yet in this state of empathy, her simulated feeling of grief does not share the intentional object of her friend's actual grief (i.e., her recently deceased mother) (2008: 240). If human beings can usually only practice empathy imperfectly, an omniscient and omnipotent God must be omnisubjective in the sense of having "perfect total empathy" with all conscious beings, precisely because anything short of omnisubjectivity would mean that God would not know everything about the conscious lives of Her creatures, and hence would not be omniscient (2008: 242).

One might worry that if God empathized perfectly with all the conscious states of Her creatures, She would be tainted by unwholesome states like jealousy and hatred. Zagzebski responds to this worry by arguing that God empathizes with us by imaginatively simulating our emotions, yet without adopting the intentional objects of our emotions as Her own:

> [O]mnisubjectivity does not have the unwanted consequence that God fears, hates, or is angry at the things we fear, hate, or are angry at. . . . My suggestion, then, is that God does "get" what it's like to feel anger, lust, vengeance, and perverse pleasure, but God's copies of those states are not directed at anything and God is aware of the copies as copies. (2008: 243)

I think Zagzebski's model of omnisubjectivity can be fruitfully applied to Vivekananda's panentheistic cosmopsychism. Even though it is not logically possible for God to inhabit our first-person conscious states directly, God—by virtue of Her omniscience and omnisubjectivity—nonetheless knows exactly what it is like to be each one of Her creatures, with all their wholesome and unwholesome conscious states, through Her perfect total empathy. Although Vivekananda does not make this point himself, nothing he says rules out this possibility of divine omnisubjectivity.

One could also raise an objection to Vivekananda's doctrine that the universe is God's own playful self-limitation. Is this self-limitation real or only apparent? If it is real, then it would seem that God is not unlimited. If it is only apparent, then it would seem the universe is not real. We can respond to this objection by invoking Vivekananda's distinction between God's essence and Her manifestations, which was already discussed in the previous section. For Vivekananda, God's playful self-limitation is, indeed, real, but does not compromise Her omnipotence, since She remains perfectly pure and omnipotent in Her essence and self-limited only in Her various manifestations. Moreover, since the perfect Divine Consciousness is present in a latent form in all of Her self-limited manifestations, the self-limitation is ultimately only superficial and temporary, since it lasts only as long as we remain on the lower egoistic planes of consciousness.

In this context, it is worth noting, if only briefly, that Sri Aurobindo and Śaiva Nondualist philosophers have also defended metaphysical systems of panentheistic cosmopsychism similar to Vivekananda's and elaborated in great detail the dynamics of divine self-limitation. According to Śaiva Nondualists, the sole divine reality Śiva, by means of His *svātantrya-śakti* ("absolute freedom and power"), becomes various individual subjects by "subjecting Himself to *Māyā* and putting on the five *kañcukas* or cloaks which limit His universal knowledge and power" (Singh 1980: 13).[19]

Likewise, Aurobindo argues at length in *The Life Divine* (1940) that God's power of "self-limitation"—Her ability to limit Herself by manifesting as ignorant beings—is "not . . . a sign, proof or reality of weakness, but a sign, proof, reality—the greatest possible—of an absolute omnipotence" ([1939–40] 2005: 420). Aurobindo's views on divine self-limitation are especially relevant for our purposes, since his thought was directly influenced by Ramakrishna and Vivekananda (Maharaj 2020c; Medhananda forthcoming-c). Aurobindo can be seen as further developing and clarifying Ramakrishna's and Vivekananda's idea that God's self-limited manifestations are real but only superficial. In the course of explaining how God manifests as various ignorant creatures through self-limitation, Aurobindo characterizes the ontological status of divine self-limitation as follows:

> [A]ll ignorance is, when examined, a superficially exclusive self-forgetful concentration of Tapas, of the conscious energy of being in a particular line or section of its movement of which alone it is aware or which alone it seems to be on the surface. The ignorance is effective within the bounds of that movement and valid for its purposes, but phenomenal, partial, superficial, not essentially real, not integral. We have to use the word "real" necessarily in a quite limited and not in its absolute sense; for the ignorance is real enough, but it is not the whole truth of our being and by regarding it by itself even its truth is misrepresented to

[19] See also Dyczkowski (1989: 77–79).

> our outer awareness. In that true truth of itself it is an involved Consciousness and Knowledge evolving back to itself, but it is dynamically effective as an Inconscience and an Ignorance. ([1939–40] 2005: 611)

"Tapas," in Aurobindo's technical sense, is the "energy of being" of the Divine Consciousness that can be channeled or concentrated in various ways. Ignorance arises when this Tapas becomes so exclusively concentrated on a particular superficial level of consciousness that it "loses" its awareness of its own divine nature. I put "loses" in scare-quotes because Aurobindo insists that the perfect and all-knowing Divine Consciousness, *in Her essence*, can never really forget Herself. Nonetheless, through a process of exclusive concentration, Divine Consciousness manifests as various centers of consciousness that *are* ignorant of their divine nature. Aurobindo follows Vivekananda rather than Śaṅkara in holding that this ignorance is "perfectly real," but only "phenomenal" and "superficial," since it does not inhere in Divine Consciousness in Her essence but obtains only within the dynamics of Her world-manifestation. Like Vivekananda, Aurobindo also claims that the ignorant state of consciousness is nothing but an involved form of Divine Consciousness. Ignorance, as he puts it, is nothing but "the superficial and apparent self-forgetfulness of the One in its play of division and multiplicity" ([1939–40] 2005: 278). Since I have discussed Aurobindo's panentheistic cosmopsychism in detail elsewhere (Medhananda forthcoming-a), I will just note here that Vivekananda's account of grounding by self-limitation can be further developed and strengthened by drawing upon Aurobindo's philosophically sophisticated defense of divine self-limitation as a "sign" and "proof" of God's "absolute omnipotence" in *The Life Divine*.

Finally, one could raise objections to premise 2 of Argument 2: "There are credible mystics, such as Ramakrishna, who claim to have directly perceived an impersonal-personal Divine Consciousness that manifests as everything in the universe." One might argue that it is implausible to hold that perception alone could deliver the rich propositional knowledge that an impersonal-personal Divine Consciousness manifests as everything in the universe. Ramakrishna and Vivekananda, however, hold that a special spiritual experience—namely, what Ramakrishna calls "*vijñāna*"—does deliver precisely this propositional knowledge. According to Ramakrishna, after the attainment of *jñāna*—the knowledge of the impersonal nondual Brahman in *nirvikalpa samādhi*—certain divinely commissioned souls return to the world and attain the more expansive state of *vijñāna*:

> Those who realize Brahman in [*nirvikalpa*] *samādhi* come down also and see (*dekhen*) that it is Brahman that has become the universe and its living beings. . . . This is known as *vijñāna*. . . . The *vijñānī* further sees (*dekhe*) that

> the Reality which is Brahman is also the Bhagavān, the Personal God. (*K* 51 / *G* 104)[20]

On the basis of his own spiritual experiences, Ramakrishna declares that the *vijñānī* actually "sees" that the impersonal Brahman and the personal God are one and that this impersonal-personal Divine Reality has manifested as everything and everyone in the universe. Although spiritual experiences are ineffable by nature, he would sometimes use the analogy of wax to explain his unique state of *vijñāna*:

> Do you know what I see right now? I see that it is God Himself who has become all this. . . . I had a similar vision once before, when I saw houses, gardens, roads, men, cattle—all made of One Substance; it was as if they were all made of wax (*sab momer*). (*K* 1022 / *G* 941–42)

This analogy of wax helps clarify what the *vijñānī* perceives. For instance, when I look at figures of humans, animals, and trees made of wax, I see their various outer forms while also seeing that they are all nothing but the same wax in different shapes. Similarly, the *vijñānī* directly perceives that the universe and all living beings are nothing but different manifestations of one and the same impersonal-personal Divine Reality.

Even if one grants that certain mystics like Ramakrishna had a direct perception of God as everything, one might still raise the conflicting claims objection against premise 2 of Argument 2—an objection we have already discussed in section 4 of chapter 6. Haven't numerous other mystics had putative experiences of God that are quite different from *vijñāna*? For instance, Ramakrishna himself often noted that Advaitic mystics realize the impersonal nondual Brahman in *nirvikalpa samādhi* and, hence, dismiss both the personal God and the world as unreal. There might also be mystics in certain theistic traditions who perceive a personal God who is ontologically *distinct* from the world. Isn't premise 2 of Argument 2 undermined by the fact that various mystics have perceived the ultimate reality and its relation to the world in radically different ways? Assuming that all of these mystics are credible, then we would seem to be equally justified in accepting *all* of their conflicting mystical reports.

In section 4 of chapter 6, I argued that both Ramakrishna and Vivekananda responded to the conflicting claims objection by holding that these apparently conflicting mystical reports are actually complementary, since they refer to different aspects and forms of one and the same impersonal-personal Divine

[20] *jā̐rā samādhistha hoye brahmadarśan korechen, tā̐rāo neme ese dekhen je, jīvajagat tinī hoyechen. . . . eri nām vijñāna. . . . vijñānī dekhe jinī brahma tinī bhagavān. . . .*

Reality. In the specific context of Argument 2, it is important to recognize that Ramakrishna and Vivekananda accept a variety of spiritual experiences of God but hold that the panentheistic realization of God as everything is the culmination of spiritual experience. As I already noted in the previous paragraph, Ramakrishna fully accepted the Advaitic realization of the impersonal nondual Brahman but claimed that a select few divinely commissioned souls, after attaining Advaitic realization, go on to attain *vijñāna*, the even greater realization that the impersonal Brahman is one with Śakti, who manifests as the entire universe and all living beings. He would also often distinguish three classes of *bhakta*s:

> There are three kinds of devotees: inferior, mediocre, and superior (*adham bhakta, madhyam bhakta, uttam bhakta*). The inferior devotee says, "God is out there." According to him God is different from His creation. The mediocre devotee says: "God is the Antaryāmī, the Inner Controller. God dwells in everyone's heart." The mediocre devotee sees God in the heart. But the superior devotee sees that God alone has become everything; He alone has become the twenty-four cosmic principles. He finds that everything, above and below, is filled with God. (*K* 985 / *G* 909–10)

Ramakrishna hierarchizes three basic attitudes toward, and realizations of, God. He fully accepts the realization of God as "different from His creation" as well as the higher realization of God in our hearts, but he claims that the greatest devotee (*uttam bhakta*) is none other than the *vijñānī* who sees that God has become everything in the universe.

Likewise, Vivekananda often distinguished "three stages of spiritual growth in man" (*CW* 5:81) and claimed that they correspond to the Vedāntic philosophies of Dvaita, Viśiṣṭādvaita, and Advaita respectively:

> These are the salient points of the three steps which Indian religious thought has taken in regard to God. We have seen that it began with the personal, the extra-cosmic God. It went from the external to the internal cosmic body, God immanent in the universe, and ended in identifying the soul itself with that God and making one Soul, a unit of all these various manifestations in the universe. This is the last word of the Vedas. It begins with dualism, goes through a qualified monism, and ends in perfect monism. . . . (*CW* 2:253)

Like Ramakrishna, Vivekananda distinguishes three stages of spiritual realization: first, the realization of God as "extra-cosmic"; second, the realization of God as "immanent in the universe"; third, the Advaitic realization of God as everything in the universe. In the final Advaitic stage of realization, one realizes that God is not only *in* the universe but *is* the universe itself.[21]

We can now defend premise 2 of Argument 2 against the conflicting claims objection by appealing to Ramakrishna's and Vivekananda's hierarchical ordering of spiritual experiences of God. Although Vivekananda's own argument for the epistemic value of supersensuous experience (AEV) makes it reasonable to believe that numerous types of spiritual experience of God are veridical, premise 2 refers to the highest panentheistic realization of *vijñānīs* like Ramakrishna—a realization that supersedes other spiritual experiences, including Advaitic *nirvikalpa samādhi*, the realization of the extra-cosmic personal God, and the realization of God residing in our hearts.

5. *Which Advaita? Bringing Vivekananda into Dialogue with Miri Albahari*

Although micropsychism remains the most popular form of panpsychism in contemporary philosophy of mind, no proponent of micropsychism to date has been able to provide a fully convincing response to the formidable subject combination problem. As a result, some contemporary philosophers have begun to defend forms of cosmopsychism as an alternative to micropsychism.[22] Still others have rejected panpsychism altogether in favor of kindred theories like idealism (Kastrup 2018). In two provocative recent articles, Miri Albahari (2020; 2019a) has criticized some prominent contemporary theories of cosmopsychism, arguing that a metaphysical framework derived from classical Advaita Vedānta may provide a more satisfactory account of consciousness.[23] By way of concluding this chapter, I will bring Vivekananda's panentheistic cosmopsychism into critical dialogue with Albahari's classical Advaitic theory of consciousness.

According to Albahari, even if cosmopsychist theories avoid the subject combination problem, they still face the obverse, and equally formidable, "decombination problem"—the problem of explaining how the all-pervasive cosmic consciousness decombines or individuates into the conscious experiences of individual subjects.[24] In particular, she distinguishes two forms of the

[21] In section 7 of chapter 2 of this book, I argued that Vivekananda's doctrine of the three Vedāntic stages conflicts with his Integral Advaita philosophy, since he insists on the *necessity* of all three stages. However, if the necessity claim is dropped, the doctrine of three stages is perfectly consistent with the metaphysics of Integral Advaita. In the present context, I am appealing to Vivekananda's doctrine of the three stages *minus* the necessity claim.

[22] Shani (2015, 2018), Goff (2017a: 220–255), Nagasawa and Wager (2017), Mathews (2003, 2011).

[23] Since Albahari sees her two articles as complementary, I will focus on Albahari (2020) but also refer to Albahari (2019a) whenever I deem appropriate.

[24] Leidenhag (2019), like Albahari, criticizes cosmopsychist theories for failing to resolve the individuation problem.

decombination problem—which she calls the "perspective problem" and the "epistemic problem"—and argues that one or both of these problems is fatal to any cosmopsychist theory that conceives cosmic consciousness as a "*conscious subject of experience*" (2020: 121).[25]

What Albahari calls the "perspective problem" is essentially the individuation problem that we discussed in the previous section. Building on Sam Coleman's formulation of the subject combination problem, Albahari argues that cosmopsychist theories like Goff's, which hold that the singular perspective of cosmic consciousness somehow contains within it all our individual perspectives, are logically incoherent, since "perspectives cannot, as a matter of logical fact, survive being subsumed by a larger perspective" (2020: 122). Albahari further contends that cosmopsychist theories that conceive cosmic consciousness as an omniscient and perfect divine being face an additional "epistemic problem": how can mental states of imperfect and finite human beings—such as the "fear of mortality"—be "coherently ascribed to an absolute in the know" (2020: 122)?[26]

In light of what she perceives as the philosophical weaknesses of cosmopsychist theories, Albahari sketches an alternative metaphysical framework—which she calls, following Aldous Huxley, "Perennial Philosophy" or "Perennial Idealism"—based on the classical Advaita Vedānta of Śaṅkara and his followers. Following classical Advaitins, Albahari distinguishes between "relative" and "absolute" standpoints (which, I would add, correspond to the Sanskrit terms *vyāvahārika* and *pāramārthika* respectively). From the standpoint of absolute truth, the sole reality is the impersonal and nondual "universal consciousness"; hence, everything in this spatiotemporal universe—including all individual selves—is unreal. From the standpoint of relative truth, however, this nondual universal consciousness can be said to "ground" everything in this universe as well as "all individual conscious experience" (2020: 120). In contrast to cosmopsychists, Albahari claims that this nondual universal consciousness is "aperspectival" (2019a: 2), since it "does not belong to any subject or the cosmos" (2020: 124). Crucially, she adds that this universal consciousness is "experienceable" (2020: 124). According to her Advaitic framework, it is the illusory "sense of being a separate self" that prevents us from realizing that our conscious nature is "identical to universal consciousness" (2020: 120). Some mystics in various traditions claim to have eliminated the "illusion of self" by means of meditative techniques, thereby attaining the state of *nirvikalpa samādhi* in which they realized their identity with nondual universal consciousness. While she admits that

[25] She focuses on the cosmopsychist theories of Goff, Shani, and Mathews, but she takes her criticisms to apply to most forms of cosmopsychism.

[26] She provides some additional criticisms of very recent cosmopsychist theories in Albahari (2019a: 7–9).

determining the "psychological possibility" of *nirvikalpa samādhi* is beyond the scope of her article, she notes that "it is encouraging to encounter what might turn out to be 'empirical' evidence" (2020: 125–26).[27]

Since universal consciousness is nondual and *im*personal, Albahari argues that her Advaitic metaphysical framework has the major advantage of avoiding the decombination problem, which only arises for cosmopsychists who ascribe a "grand subjective perspective" to cosmic consciousness (2020: 124). She then devotes the brunt of her article to making intelligible the notion of nondual consciousness and explaining how it can ground our individual perspectives.[28]

I believe Albahari's article is an important intervention for three reasons. First, unlike most contemporary philosophers, she has made a sustained effort to demonstrate the relevance of Indian philosophical traditions to contemporary debates about consciousness. Hence, Albahari is a valuable ally for the small but growing number of philosophers—including myself—who are approaching consciousness from a cross-cultural perspective. Second, her emphasis on the experienceability of universal consciousness is also quite valuable, since the possibility of direct mystical verification of a theory of consciousness has not yet been taken seriously by the vast majority of contemporary philosophers of mind. Third, her criticisms of cosmopsychist theories are incisive and challenging, and will surely encourage cosmopsychists to refine and sharpen their views in the face of the decombination problem that she has so ably formulated.

That said, I believe there are two serious problems with Albahari's classical Advaitic metaphysics of universal consciousness. First and foremost, while her Advaitic metaphysical framework avoids at least certain forms of the decombination problem, it does so at the exceedingly high cost of denying the metaphysical reality of individual conscious experience as well as everything else in the universe.[29] As Albahari herself admits, her metaphysical framework can only be a viable one if it explains how "non-dual consciousness could coherently ground our individual conscious perspectives and their contents—as well as the objects that we take to be our mind-independent environment" (2020: 124). The problem, however, is that her classical Advaitic metaphysical commitments lead her to hold that nondual consciousness, precisely by virtue of its nonduality, *does not really ground anything at all*, since nothing exists other than nondual consciousness. According to classical Advaita Vedānta, if nondual consciousness really were to ground anything, then its nonduality would be compromised, since a ground entails something that is grounded. Hence, Albahari holds that nothing

[27] She elaborates this point in Albahari (2019b).

[28] Albahari is not the first to relate classical Advaitic ideas about consciousness to contemporary debates in philosophy of mind. See, for instance, Sarvapriyananda (2011).

[29] Anand Vaidya (2020) makes a similar criticism of the classical Advaitic approach to consciousness.

other than nondual consciousness—including individuals, their conscious perspectives, and all spatiotemporal entities—ultimately exists. Accordingly, she explicitly endorses Gauḍapāda's and Śaṅkara's Advaitic metaphysics of *ajāta* ("non-origination"), the doctrine that nondual Brahman alone exists and, hence, that there is no universe (2019a: 28–31). From the metaphysical standpoint of *ajāta*, Albahari admits that there *is* no true grounding relation between nondual consciousness and individual conscious subjects. Tellingly, she refers to the "pseudo-relation between aperspectival consciousness and subjects" (2019a: 32), and she claims that "accounts of grounding will only be expressible as relative rather than ultimate truths" (2020: 128).

The hard problem of consciousness arises from the need to explain the nature and origin of our individual conscious experiences. Ultimately, Albahari's classical Advaitic "solution" to the hard problem consists in denying the reality of human-level conscious experience altogether. Ironically, then, her position turns out to be a unique kind of eliminativism about human-level consciousness—a view widely considered to be implausible.[30]

Second, there is a philosophical and philological haziness in Albahari's exposition of her Advaitic metaphysical framework, which threatens to undermine her position from within. On the one hand, she claims that her metaphysical framework derives from the classical Advaita Vedāntins Gauḍapāda and Śaṅkara and modern exponents of Advaita like Ramana Maharshi and Nisargadatta Maharaj (Albahari 2019a: 10–11, 28–29; 2020: 119). On the other hand, she follows Aldous Huxley in calling her framework "Perennial Philosophy" or "Perennial Idealism," and she claims that her position is basically consistent with Huxley's own. In fact, however, Huxley's position in *The Perennial Philosophy* (1946) *differs* from classical Advaita Vedānta in at least three fundamental respects. First, although Huxley maintains that the "divine Ground of all existence" is a formless "spiritual Absolute," he adds the following crucial caveat: "The Absolute Ground of all existence has a personal aspect. The activity of Brahman is Isvara [the personal Lord]" (A. Huxley 1947: 29). While classical Advaitins like Śaṅkara conceive the ultimate reality as exclusively suprapersonal, Huxley holds that the Divine Ground is the suprapersonal nondual Absolute in its *transcendent* aspect and the personal Lord in its *dynamic* aspect. Second, it follows from Huxley's broad conception of the Divine Ground that the personal God—which is the real dynamic aspect of the "Divine Ground"—actually creates and sustains this universe. As he puts it, the "divine mind" imposes forms "upon a pre-existing chaos of formless matter" (A. Huxley 1947: 36). Classical Advaitins hold that nondual

[30] Both Vaidya (2020) and Gasparri (2019) make the point that classical Advaitic metaphysics amounts to a form of eliminativism. Vaidya further argues that Advaitic illusionism provides an unsatisfactory account of consciousness.

Brahman does not actually ground anything at all since the world is not ultimately real. Huxley, by contrast, maintains that the suprapersonal-cum-personal God is the real "Divine Ground" of this very real world. Third, Huxley explicitly criticizes one-sided spiritual philosophies that emphasize the reality of only one aspect of God at the expense of all other aspects:

> God may be worshipped and contemplated in any of his aspects. But to persist in worshipping only one aspect to the exclusion of all the rest is to run into grave spiritual peril. . . . [T]he complete transformation of consciousness, which is "enlightenment," "deliverance," "salvation," comes only when God is thought of as the Perennial Philosophy affirms Him to be—immanent as well as transcendent, supra-personal as well as personal—and when religious practices are adapted to this conception. (1947: 31)

For classical Advaitins, we achieve salvation by attaining the spiritual knowledge of our identity with the impersonal nondual Brahman. For Huxley, by contrast, the highest salvation consists in worshipping and experiencing God in all His "inexhaustible richness"—that is, as *both* personal and suprapersonal, *both* immanent and transcendent (1947: 30).

Ironically, Huxley's Perennial Philosophy comes much closer to the world-affirming Integral Advaitic philosophy of Ramakrishna and Vivekananda than to the world-negating philosophy of classical Advaita Vedānta. This is no coincidence, since Huxley's philosophical views were directly shaped by the teachings of Ramakrishna and Vivekananda. In 1939, Huxley began to visit Swami Prabhavananda, a monk of the Ramakrishna Order founded by Vivekananda, eventually becoming his initiated disciple. Huxley wrote a foreword to *The Gospel of Sri Ramakrishna* (1942), singling out for praise Ramakrishna's "most profound and subtle utterances about the nature of Ultimate Reality" (M. Gupta [1942] 1992: v). In the "List of Recommended Books" at the end of *The Perennial Philosophy*, he included *The Gospel of Sri Ramakrishna*. Thus, Huxley's broad conception of God as suprapersonal as well as personal and his doctrine of God's immanence in the world were almost certainly influenced by the world-affirming Advaitic philosophy of Ramakrishna and Vivekananda.

Albahari undermines her own position by trying to find support for her classical Advaitic metaphysical framework in Huxley's Perennial Philosophy, which explicitly criticizes the one-sidedness of the classical Advaitic position. Huxley, we should recall, sounds the warning: "But to persist in worshipping only one aspect [of God] to the exclusion of all the rest is to run into grave spiritual peril." This is precisely the mistake made by classical Advaitins like Albahari herself, who conceive the ultimate reality as suprapersonal nondual consciousness while denying the ultimate reality of both the personal God and the world. In short, then, Albahari's theorization of her classical Advaitic framework in terms of Huxley's Perennial Philosophy is either incoherent or self-undermining.

Indeed, I would argue that there is a full-blown aporia at the heart of Albahari's metaphysical framework of nondual consciousness. On the one hand, she explicitly subscribes to the *ajāta* metaphysics of classical Advaita, according to which the sole reality is the aperspectival, nondual consciousness, which does not ground anything at all. On the other hand, she sometimes comes closer to the world-affirming Advaitic philosophy of Ramakrishna, Vivekananda, and Huxley. Accordingly, she repeatedly *contrasts* her own position with "austere existence monism," according to which "the world as we appear to know it does not exist—only the ground does" (2019a: 4). She also sometimes claims that the nondual ground is an "inexhaustible yet unmanifest plenitude" (2019a: 26n52) and that "the world as it appears to us, with its tables, trees, atoms and people" is "a manifestation from the ground of aperspectival and unconditioned consciousness" (2019a: 3). But she simply cannot have it both ways. If she accepts the metaphysics of *ajāta*, then her position—all her protestations notwithstanding—*does* amount to an "austere existence monism," since she herself admits that nothing exists besides nondual consciousness and, hence, that there is really only a "pseudo-relation" between ground and grounded. In fact, it is not even accurate to refer to Albahari's nondual consciousness as a "ground" at all, since the concept of ground implies the existence of something grounded, but she explicitly denies the existence of the universe and individual souls. Conversely, if she really wants to distinguish her position from existence monism and hold that the world is a real "manifestation" of the nondual Reality, then she should repudiate the classical Advaitic metaphysics of *ajāta*, embracing instead a world-affirming Advaitic metaphysics that conceives the Divine Reality as both the aperspectival nondual Brahman *and* the dynamic personal Śakti. As it stands, however, Albahari vacillates between two fundamentally incompatible metaphysical frameworks: the world-denying metaphysics of classical Advaita and the world-affirming Advaitic metaphysics of Huxley, Ramakrishna, and Vivekananda. Hence, I believe the charge of logical incoherence that she levels against cosmopsychists like Goff can be leveled against her as well.

Does Vivekananda's panentheistic cosmopsychism fare any better than Albahari's classical Advaitic metaphysics of universal consciousness? His panentheistic cosmopsychism can be seen as a world-affirming Advaitic metaphysical framework that *subsumes* Albahari's narrower Advaitic metaphysics of universal consciousness. Vivekananda fully accepts the reality of the impersonal nondual Brahman. In fact, he claimed to have attained the Advaitic state of *nirvikalpa samādhi* on numerous occasions.[31] However, in contrast to classical Advaitins,

[31] See, for instance, *CW* 7:139.

Vivekananda also accepts the reality of Śakti or Īśvara, the personal and dynamic aspect of Brahman. Hence, while classical Advaitins dismiss the world as unreal, Vivekananda takes the world to be a real but impermanent manifestation of God. Moreover, he follows his guru Ramakrishna in holding that after attaining the nondual state of *nirvikalpa samādhi*, one can attain the even greater world-affirming Advaitic realization that the impersonal-personal Infinite Divine Reality has become everything in the universe. Hence, like Albahari, Vivekananda appeals to spiritual realization as an additional source of "empirical evidence" for his metaphysics of panentheistic cosmopsychism. However, as discussed in chapter 5, Vivekananda goes much further than Albahari in offering a full-blown defense of the epistemic value of mystical experience based on general epistemic principles of perception and testimony.[32] Moreover, while Albahari ultimately denies the reality of human-level consciousness, Vivekananda maintains that God as "Cosmic Consciousness" *actually grounds* individual conscious experience, which he takes to be a real manifestation of God. Arguably, Vivekananda's non-eliminativism about individual human consciousness makes it a more attractive option for contemporary philosophers than Albahari's eliminativist metaphysics of universal consciousness.

Of course, Albahari would likely object that Vivekananda's panentheistic cosmopsychism is not an attractive option, since it is vulnerable to the perspectival and epistemic forms of the decombination problem already outlined earlier in this section. However, as I have argued in the previous section, while cosmopsychist theories like Goff's—which are based on grounding by subsumption—do seem to be vulnerable to the perspectival (or individuation) problem, Vivekananda's panentheistic cosmopsychism is based on grounding by self-limitation, which is better equipped to handle the individuation problem. For Vivekananda, the Divine Cosmic Consciousness manifests as all individual consciousnesses through a playful process of self-limitation. Hence, unlike Goff, Vivekananda does not hold that cosmic consciousness somehow contains or subsumes the conscious perspectives of human and animal subjects within it.

What about the epistemic problem raised by Albahari? Applied to Vivekananda's framework, the epistemic problem is that it is logically incoherent for a perfect and omniscient God to "first-personally harbour" within Herself all the varied and often contradictory mental contents of ignorant people—such as, for instance, the fear of mortality (Albahari 2020: 122). However, Albahari's language of "harboring" indicates that she has in mind cosmopsychist theories based on grounding by subsumption. Vivekananda, I would argue, avoids the

[32] Albahari (2019b: 12) counters "four challenges that sceptics are likely to advance" against the thesis that mystical experiences have epistemic value. However, as far as I can tell, she does not supplement these *negative* arguments with any kind of positive argument for the epistemic value of mystical experience.

epistemic problem, since he does *not* ascribe any of our ignorant mental states to God. Rather, his account of grounding by self-limitation allows him to maintain that all these ignorant mental states belong not to God in Her essence—who remains perfect, omniscient, and omnipotent—but to God's *manifestations*. Through a playful process of self-veiling, God manifests as all the human beings in the world, each with his or her own unique conscious perspective and mental states. Since Vivekananda's panentheistic cosmopsychism does not entail that God in any sense contains all our ordinary mental states like the fear of mortality, it avoids the epistemic problem as framed by Albahari. Moreover, as we saw in section 3, Vivekananda can explain *how* a perfect Divine Being can manifest as imperfect creatures by appealing to God's omnipotence—which was the strategy adopted not only by Ramakrishna but also by Śaiva Nondualists and Sri Aurobindo.

Of course, much more would need to be said to clarify and defend fully Vivekananda's panentheistic cosmopsychism. However, I hope to have shown in chapters 9 and 10 that his cosmopsychist position is a sophisticated and original one that deserves to be taken seriously by contemporary philosophers of mind. To conclude, I will summarize six potential advantages of Vivekananda's distinctive cosmopsychist position over rival theories of consciousness. First, by conceiving mind as a subtle form of matter, Vivekananda not only accounts for the causal efficacy of mental states but also welcomes naturalistic explanations of a wide range of cognitive phenomena like learning, remembering, and information processing. Second, since he ascribes sentience to people and some non-human animals but *not* to entities like electrons and stones, he avoids one standard form of the incredulous stare objection. Third, his cosmopsychist position avoids the subject combination problem, which is the major pitfall for micropsychist theories. Fourth, since Vivekananda accepts the reality of human-level consciousness, his panentheistic cosmopsychism does not have the eliminativist implications of Albahari's classical Advaitic theory of universal consciousness, which ultimately denies the reality of both the grounding relation and human-level consciousness. Fifth, since his panentheistic cosmopsychism is based on grounding by self-limitation, it is arguably better equipped than many other cosmopsychist theories to address various forms of the individuation problem.[33] Sixth, he

[33] I believe Vivekananda's model of grounding by self-limitation may dovetail well with the model of "partial grounding" defended by Shani (2015). According to Shani, the Absolute's perspective partially grounds the conscious perspectives of relative subjects in that the latter perspectives *depend* on the former while also amounting to "something more" and are "not exhausted by this particular dependency relationship" (2015: 422). Vivekananda's grounding by self-limitation can be seen as a kind of partial grounding model, since he holds that God in Her divine essence does not share the conscious perspectives of Her self-limited manifestations as various creatures. For discussion of Shani's partial grounding model in relation to Aurobindo's cosmopsychism, see Medhananda (forthcoming-a).

makes the radical claim that his panentheistic cosmopsychism can be empirically verified through spiritual experience. While a small handful of contemporary philosophers have begun to consider the relevance of meditative techniques and spiritual experience to debates about consciousness, Vivekananda has gone much further than any of them in defending the epistemic credentials of spiritual experience on the basis of general epistemic principles. For too long, the philosophy of mind has been almost entirely isolated from the philosophy of religion. By bringing these two fields into fruitful dialogue, Vivekananda remains very much our contemporary.

Epilogue

From "Neo-Vedānta" to Cosmopolitan Vedānta

One of the dominant scholarly paradigms for studying modern Hinduism and Vedānta is the "Neo-Vedāntic" paradigm inaugurated by the German Indologist Paul Hacker (1913–1979). According to Hacker, modern Indian figures such as Swami Vivekananda, Sri Aurobindo, and Sarvepalli Radhakrishnan were "Neo-Hindus" who championed "pseudo-Vedāntic" philosophies shaped more by Western values than by indigenous Hindu traditions (1995: 296). Neo-Hindus, Hacker argues, disguised what were essentially Western ideas and values in superficially Indian garb in order to promote Indian nationalism (1995: 251). For instance, Hacker (1995: 239–41, 273–318) contends that Vivekananda's ethical doctrine of "Practical Vedānta" derived not from any indigenous Indian source but from Paul Deussen, who presumably acquainted Vivekananda—at some point in 1896—with Arthur Schopenhauer's derivation of an ethics of compassion from the Upaniṣadic teaching "*tat tvam asi*."

Against Hacker, I argued in section 5 of chapter 2 that Vivekananda's Vedāntic ethics was inspired not by Deussen but by Ramakrishna, who taught Vivekananda in 1884 the spiritually-grounded ethics of "*śivajñāne jīver sevā*"—the practice of serving others in a spirit of worship, "knowing that they are all manifestations of God" (*LP* 2.i.131 / *DP* 852). I am hardly alone in challenging Hacker's hermeneutic approach to modern Vedāntic figures. Scholars such as Beckerlegge (2006: 218–19), Green (2016: 130–31), and Killingley (1998: 145–59) have refuted Hacker's argument about Deussen's alleged influence on Vivekananda by identifying numerous passages in letters and lectures prior to his 1896 encounter with Deussen in which Vivekananda clearly articulated a Vedāntic ethics of social service. Other scholars have challenged Hacker's more general hermeneutic approach, arguing that it is reductive[1] and colored by his own Catholic theological commitments.[2]

Strikingly, countless contemporary scholars continue to refer to modern Vedāntins like Vivekananda and Aurobindo as "Neo-Vedāntins," even though many of these scholars reject—either in part or in full—Hacker's specific

[1] See Madaio (2017), Maharaj (2018: 45–50), and Nicholson (2020).

[2] See Halbfass ([1995] 2007) and Bagchee and Adluri (2013).

Swami Vivekananda's Vedāntic Cosmopolitanism. Swami Medhananda, Oxford University Press. © Oxford University Press 2022. DOI: 10.1093/oso/9780197624463.003.0012

arguments about the primarily Western provenance of modern Vedāntic ideas.[3] I will conclude this book by interrogating this seemingly benign practice and defending what I take to be a more nuanced and fruitful "cosmopolitan" hermeneutic approach to modern Indian thinkers.

First of all, the prefix "Neo" in the term "Neo-Vedānta" implies a dichotomy between so-called "traditional" Vedānta and newfangled forms of Vedānta, which is both misleading and question-begging. James Madaio (2017: 1) makes this point quite forcefully:

> [S]cholarly constructions of "Neo-Vedānta" consistently appeal to a high culture, staticized understanding of "traditional" Advaita Vedānta as the alterity for locating Vivekananda's "neo" or new teachings. In doing so, such studies ignore the diverse medieval and early modern developments in advaitic and Advaita Vedāntic traditions which were well-known to Vivekananda and other "Neo-Vedāntins."

As Madaio notes, Śaṅkara has usually been taken to be the paradigmatic figure of "traditional" Advaita Vedānta, so any deviations from Śaṅkara's philosophy are viewed as a break with tradition. Throughout this book, I have argued that Vivekananda does, indeed, deviate from Śaṅkara on a number of philosophical issues, including his emphasis on the importance of *nirvikalpa samādhi*, his acceptance of the ultimate reality of Śakti, his conception of the world as a real manifestation of Śakti, and his doctrine that all four Yogas are direct and independent paths to liberation. However, I have traced key elements in Vivekananda's views to the teachings of his guru Ramakrishna and to numerous pre-colonial Vedāntic texts, including the Upaniṣads, the *Bhagavad-Gītā*, the *Bhāgavata-Purāṇa*, *Vivekacūḍāmaṇi*, *Aparokṣānubhūti*, and *Aṣṭāvakra Saṃhitā*. Tellingly, Hacker himself admits that Ramakrishna was definitely *not* a "Neo-Hindu," since his religious "experiments involved not the slightest reinterpretation of traditional Hinduism" (1995: 234). However, Hacker thereby undermines his own case for Vivekananda as a "Neo-Hindu," since many of Vivekananda's major philosophical doctrines can be traced to Ramakrishna.

More fundamentally, it is perfectly natural for any philosophical or theological tradition to evolve over time. For instance, the twentieth-century Catholic theologian Karl Rahner (1974: 161–80) introduced a number of innovations within the Catholic tradition, such as the inclusivist doctrine that practitioners of non-Christian religions may be "anonymous Christians," who are unknowingly

[3] See, for instance, Halbfass (1988), Tapasyananda (1990: xxiii), Baumfield (1991), S. C. Chatterjee (1995), De Michelis (2004), Fort (2007), Hatcher (2008: 11–12), Panday (2012), and Baier (2019: 244–49).

saved through the grace of Christ. Likewise, the great Protestant philosopher of religion John Hick (1989) championed religious pluralism, denied the literal divinity of Jesus Christ, and rejected the traditional Christian doctrine of eternal damnation. Should we call Rahner a "neo-Catholic" and Hick a "neo-Protestant"? Or should we view Catholicism and Protestantism as continually evolving traditions rather than static ones? If we adopt the latter route, then we can view Rahner and Hick as innovative thinkers working *within* their respective theological traditions (Long 2019: 10). Similarly, instead of labeling modern Indian thinkers like Vivekananda and Aurobindo as "Neo-Vedāntins," I believe it would be more accurate and hermeneutically fruitful to view them as self-conscious innovators within the continually evolving tradition of Vedānta.[4]

Another reason to avoid the term "Neo-Vedānta" is its problematic historical provenance. As Brian Hatcher (2004) has pointed out, nineteenth-century Christian missionaries were the first to use the term "Neo-Vedānta." Threatened by modern Vedāntins like Rammohun Roy and Debendranath Tagore who championed a home-grown, ethically oriented Vedāntic monotheism, Christian missionaries in India strategically labeled them as "Neo-Vedāntins" in order to suggest that their views were "newfangled, contrived, and therefore dubious" (Hatcher 2004: 193). In the twentieth century, the Catholic scholar Hacker followed in the footsteps of these Christian missionaries by dismissing the thought of "Neo-Hindu" figures like Vivekananda as inauthentic and philosophically insignificant. Hence, even if we *intend* to use the term "Neo-Vedānta" in a non-normative sense, we cannot simply wish away the ideological baggage with which it has been saddled since the early nineteenth century.

This book has argued that Vivekananda is best seen not as a "Neo-Vedāntin" but as a cosmopolitan Vedāntin who, in the pursuit of truth, actively embraced the entire "universe" as his own "country" (*CW* 5:92). The first three chapters have shown how he creatively reconfigured many of the key tenets of Śaṅkara's Advaita Vedānta from the standpoint of his guru Ramakrishna's world-affirming and ethically oriented philosophy of Vijñāna Vedānta. Chapters 4 through 10 have gone on to argue that Vivekananda, through a critico-constructive engagement with a variety of Indian and Western thinkers, developed innovative positions on a wide range of philosophical issues, including the epistemic value of mystical experience, the scope of reason, the dynamics of religious faith, and the hard problem of consciousness. Along the way, I have also explored how his cosmopolitan philosophical views, when understood in all their subtlety, make valuable contributions to contemporary debates in the philosophy of religion, philosophy of mind, philosophy of science, theology, and epistemology.

[4] Mitra (2020: 2) makes a similar point.

Swami Vivekananda's Vedāntic Cosmopolitanism, then, should be seen as participating in a promising, but still nascent, movement away from the "Neo-Vedāntic" paradigm and toward a more fruitful cosmopolitan approach to colonial Indian thinkers.[5] Brian Hatcher, for instance, has persuasively argued that the "Neo-Hindu" hermeneutics—which interprets the ideas of colonial Indian thinkers as a nationalist response to Western colonialism—presupposes a reductive "billiard-ball theory of change," according to which modern Hindu thought is "the direct result of the 'impact' of Western thought" (2004: 201). This "impact-response" model, Hatcher claims, not only deprives Indian thinkers of agency and creativity but also overlooks the various ways that indigenous Indian sources and ideas contributed to the shaping of modern Hinduism and certain aspects of modern Western thought (2004: 201). In Hatcher's view, colonial Indian philosophers were neither "parrots" nor "patsies" but creative "poets" who "endeavored to work with the bits and pieces of a rapidly expanding and increasingly cosmopolitan intellectual world to create what might be for them and others meaningful expressions of Hindu belief" (2004: 202).

In a similar vein, Nalini Bhushan and Jay Garfield, in their groundbreaking book *Minds without Fear: Philosophy in the Indian Renaissance* (2017), have defended a cosmopolitan approach to a whole host of colonial Indian philosophers, including Vivekananda, Radhakrishnan, K. C. Bhattacharyya, A. C. Mukerji, Sri Aurobindo, and Muhammad Iqbal. Militating against the "Neo-Hindu" denigration of colonial Indian thinkers, Bhushan and Garfield emphasize the "productive dynamics" of their "cosmopolitan colonial context" (2017: 12). They clarify this rich cosmopolitan context as follows:

> These philosophers wrote in a context of cultural fusion generated by the British colonial rule of India. They were self-consciously writing both as Indian intellectuals for an Indian audience and as participants in a developing global community constructed in part by the British Empire. They pursued Indian philosophy in a language and format that rendered it both accessible and acceptable to the Anglophone world abroad. They were not abject subjects; they were intellectual agents. (Bhushan and Garfield 2017: 12)

For Bhushan and Garfield, the unique colonial context of these Indian philosophers did not reduce them to "abject subjects" but positively *enabled* them to cultivate a "cosmopolitan consciousness," the ability and willingness to engage critically and creatively with thought-currents both within and outside India (2017: 20–38).

[5] For references, see note 4 of the book's introduction.

Over half a century ago, Hans-Georg Gadamer emphasized that an interpreter's first task is to become aware of his or her own "pre-judgments" (*Vorurteile*) ([1960] 2006: 271–72). Scholars of colonial Indian philosophy would do well to turn their critical scrutiny on themselves by striving to identify the potentially distortive assumptions and *Vorurteile* informing their interpretations. If we adopt a reductive hermeneutic framework like that of "Neo-Vedānta" or "Neo-Hinduism," then it is hardly surprising that we will find little of enduring philosophical value in the work of Vivekananda and other thinkers living in British-ruled India. I propose, then, that we consign the terms "Neo-Hinduism" and "Neo-Vedānta" to the dustbin of history. Honoring the subtlety, creativity, and originality of colonial Indian philosophers demands a commensurately nuanced cosmopolitan hermeneutics—one that lets subalterns speak, in their own voice and on their own terms.

Bibliography

Abjajananda, Swami. 2003. *Monastic Disciples of Swami Vivekananda*, translated by Chhaya Ghosh. Mayavati: Advaita Ashrama.

Abjajānanda, Svāmī. 1983. *Svāmijīr Padaprānte*. Kolkata: Udbodhan.

Adhvarīndra, Dharmarāja. 1942. *Vedānta-Paribhāṣā*, translated by Swami Madhavananda. Kolkata: Advaita Ashrama.

Aikin, Scott. 2014. *Evidentialism and the Will to Believe*. London: Bloomsbury.

Albahari, Miri. 2002. "Against No-*Ātman* Theories of *Anattā*." *Asian Philosophy* 12.1: 5–20.

Albahari, Miri. 2019a. "Perennial Idealism: A Mystical Solution to the Mind-Body Problem." *Philosophers' Imprint* 19: 1–37.

Albahari, Miri. 2019b. "The Mystic and the Metaphysician: Clarifying the Role of Meditation in the Search for Ultimate Reality." *Journal of Consciousness Studies* 26.7–8: 12–36.

Albahari, Miri. 2020. "Beyond Cosmopsychism and the Great I Am: How the World Might Be Grounded in Advaitic 'Universal Consciousness.'" In *Routledge Handbook of Panpsychism*, edited by William Seager, 119–30. New York: Routledge.

Aleaz, K. P. 1993. *Harmony of Religions: The Relevance of Swami Vivekananda*. Calcutta: Punthi-Pustak.

Algaier, Ermine L. 2020. *Reconstructing the Personal Library of William James: Markings and Marginalia from the Harvard Library Collection*. Lanham, MD: Lexington Books.

Almond, Philip. 1988. "Mysticism and its Contexts." *Sophia* 27.1: 40–49.

Alston, William. 1988. "The Deontological Conception of Epistemic Justification." *Philosophical Perspectives* 2: 257–99.

Alston, William. 1991. *Perceiving God: The Epistemology of Religious Experience*. Ithaca, NY: Cornell University Press.

Alston, William. 1996. "Belief, Acceptance, and Religious Faith." In *Faith, Freedom, and Rationality*, edited by Jeff Jordan and Daniel Howard-Snyder, 3–27. Lanham, MD: Rowman & Littlefield.

Alston, William. 2004. "Religious Experience Justifies Religious Belief." In *Contemporary Debates in Philosophy of Religion*, edited by Michael Peterson and Raymond VanArragon, 135–44. Oxford: Blackwell.

Alston, William. 2007. "Audi on Nondoxastic Faith." In *Rationality and the Good: Critical Essays on the Ethics and Epistemology of Robert Audi*, edited by Mark Timmons, John Greco, and Alfred R. Mele, 123–39. New York: Oxford University Press.

Amarasiṃha. 1968. *Amarakoṣa*, edited by Haragovinda Śāstrī. Varanasi: Chowkhamba.

Amesbury, Richard. 2008. "The Virtues of Belief: Toward a Non-Evidentialist Ethics of Belief-Formation." *International Journal for Philosophy of Religion* 63.1: 25–37.

Andersen, Hanne and Brian Hepburn. 2015. "Scientific Method." *Stanford Encyclopedia of Philosophy*, http://plato.stanford.edu (accessed July 27, 2019).

Anonymous. 1989. *The Life of Swami Vivekananda by His Eastern and Western Disciples*, sixth edition. 2 vols. Kolkata: Advaita Ashrama.

Appiah, Kwame Anthony. 1997. "Cosmopolitan Patriots." *Critical Inquiry* 23.3: 617–39.

Arnold, Dan. 2001. "Intrinsic Validity Reconsidered: A Sympathetic Study of the Mīmāṃsaka Inversion of Buddhist Epistemology." *Journal of Indian Philosophy* 29: 589–675.

Audi, Robert. 1997. "The Place of Testimony in the Fabric of Justification and Knowledge." *American Philosophical Quarterly* 34: 405–22.

Audi, Robert. 2011. *Rationality and Religious Commitment*. New York: Oxford University Press.

Aurobindo, Sri. [1922–1928] 1997. *The Complete Works of Sri Aurobindo: Volume 19, Essays on the Gita*. Pondicherry: Sri Aurobindo Ashram.

Aurobindo, Sri. [1939–1940] 2005. *The Complete Works of Sri Aurobindo: Volumes 21–22, The Life Divine*. Pondicherry: Sri Aurobindo Ashram.

Aurobindo, Sri. 2001. *The Complete Works of Sri Aurobindo: Volume 18, The Upanishads—II: Kena and Other Upanishads*. Pondicherry: Sri Aurobindo Ashram.

Ayer, A. J. 1968. *The Origins of Pragmatism*. San Francisco: Freeman, Cooper.

Baelz, Peter R. 1968. *Christian Theology and Metaphysics*. London: Epworth Press.

Bagchee, Joydeep and Vishwa P. Adluri. 2013. "The Passion of Paul Hacker: Indology, Orientalism, and Evangelism." In *Transcultural Encounters between Germany and India*, edited by J. M. Cho, E. Kurlander, and D. T. McGetchin, 215–29. New York: Routledge.

Baier, Karl. 2019. "Swami Vivekananda: Reform Hinduism, Nationalism and Scientistic Yoga." *Interdisciplinary Journal for Religion and Transformation in Contemporary Society* 5: 230–57.

Baker, Mark C. and Stewart Goetz, eds. 2011. *The Soul Hypothesis*. London: Continuum.

Banerji, G. C. 1942. *Keshab Chandra and Ramakrishna*, second ed. Calcutta: Navavidhan Publication Committee.

Banhatti, G. S. 1989. *Life and Philosophy of Swami Vivekananda*. New Delhi: Atlantic Publishers.

Bareau, André. [1955] 2013. *The Buddhist Schools of the Small Vehicle*, translated by Sara Boin-Webb. Honolulu: University of Hawaii Press.

Barua, Ankur. 2014. "Hindu Responses to Religious Diversity and the Nature of Post-Mortem Progress." *Journal of Hindu-Christian Studies* 27: 77–94.

Barua, Ankur. 2020. "The Hindu Cosmopolitanism of Sister Nivedita (Margaret Elizabeth Noble): An Irish Self in Imperial Currents." *Harvard Theological Review* 113.1: 1–23.

Basu, Sankari Prasad, ed. 1982. *Letters of Sister Nivedita*, 2 vols. Calcutta: Nababharat Publishers.

Basu, Śaṅkarīprasād. 1977. *Vivekānanda o Samakālīn Bhāratavarṣa*, vol. 2. Kolkata: Maṇḍal Book House.

Batchelor, Stephen. 1997. *Buddhism without Beliefs*. New York: Riverhead Books.

Baumfield, Vivienne. 1991. "Swami Vivekananda's Practical Vedānta." Ph.D. dissertation, University of Newcastle upon Tyne.

Beckerlegge, Gwilym. 2000. *The Ramakrishna Mission: The Making of a Modern Hindu Movement*. New Delhi: Oxford University Press.

Beckerlegge, Gwilym. 2006. *Swami Vivekananda's Legacy of Service*. New Delhi: Oxford University Press.

Beckerlegge, Gwilym. 2013. "Swami Vivekananda (1863–1902) 150 Years On: Critical Studies of an Influential Hindu Guru." *Religion Compass* 7.10: 444–53.

Bergmann, Michael. 2013. "Externalist Justification and the Role of Seemings." *Philosophical Studies* 166: 163–84.

Bhajanananda, Swami. 1994. "Swami Vivekananda's Contribution to Moral Philosophy—Ontological Ethics." In *Swami Vivekananda: A Hundred Years Since Chicago*, edited by Swami Lokeswarananda, 559–81. Belur Math, Howrah: Ramakrishna Math and Ramakrishna Mission.

Bhajanananda, Swami. 2008. *Harmony of Religions from the Standpoint of Sri Ramakrishna and Swami Vivekananda*. Kolkata: Ramakrishna Mission Institute of Culture.

Bhajanananda, Swami. 2010. "Philosophy of Sri Ramakrishna." *University of Calcutta Journal of the Department of Philosophy* 9: 1–56.

Bharati, Agehananda. 1970. "The Hindu Renaissance and Its Apologetic Patterns." *Journal of Asian Studies* 29.2: 267–87.

Bhattacharya, Kamaleswar. 1973. *L'ātman-brahman dans le bouddhisme ancien*. Paris: École française d'Extrême-Orient.

Bhattacharyya, K. C. [1928] 2011. "Svaraj in Ideas." In *Indian Philosophy in English*, edited by Nalini Bhushan and Jay L. Garfield, 101–11. New York: Oxford University Press.

Bhaṭṭa, Jayanta. 1978. *Nyāya-Mañjarī*, translated by Janaki Vallabha Bhattacharya. Delhi: Motilal Banarsidass.

Bhaṭṭācārya Śāstrī, Dineścandra. 1990. *Vivekānander Vedāntacintā*. Kolkata: Ramakrishna Mission Institute of Culture.

Bhushan, Nalini and Jay L. Garfield, eds. 2011. *Indian Philosophy in English: From Renaissance to Independence*. New York: Oxford University Press.

Bhushan, Nalini and Jay L. Garfield. 2017. *Minds Without Fear: Philosophy in the Indian Renaissance*. New York: Oxford University Press.

Biernacki, Loriliai. 2016a. "A Cognitive Science View of Abhinavagupta's Understanding of Consciousness." *Sutra Journal*, http://www.sutrajournal.com.

Biernacki, Loriliai. 2016b. "Connecting Consciousness to Physical Causality: Abhinavagupta's Phenomenology of Subjectivity and Tononi's Integrated Information Theory." *Religions* 7: 1–11.

Block, Ned. 2002. "The Harder Problem of Consciousness." *Journal of Philosophy* 99.8: 391–425.

Boudry, Maarten. 2013. "Loki's Wager and Laudan's Error: On Genuine and Territorial Demarcation." In *Philosophy of Pseudoscience: Reconsidering the Demarcation Problem*, edited by Massimo Pigliucci and Maarten Boudry, 79–100. Chicago: University of Chicago Press.

Boudry, Maarten and Massimo Pigliucci, eds. 2017. *Science Unlimited? The Challenges of Scientism*. Chicago: University of Chicago Press.

Brogaard, Berit. 2013. "Phenomenal Seemings and Sensible Dogmatism." In *Seemings and Justification: New Essays on Dogmatism and Phenomenal Conservatism*, edited by Chris Tucker, 270–92. Oxford: Oxford University Press.

Brogaard, Berit. 2018. "Phenomenal Dogmatism, Seeming Evidentialism and Inferential Justification." In *Believing in Accordance with the Evidence*, edited by Kevin McCain, 53–67. Cham, Switzerland: Springer.

Brooke, John Hedley. 1991. *Science and Religion: Some Historical Perspectives*. Cambridge: Cambridge University Press.

Brown, C. Mackenzie. 2008. "The Design Argument in Classical Hindu Thought." *International Journal of Hindu Studies* 12.2: 112–27.

Brown, C. Mackenzie. 2010. "Vivekananda and the Scientific Legitimation of Advaita Vedānta." In *Handbook of Religion and the Authority of Science*, edited by James R. Lewis and Olav Hammer, 207–48. Leiden: Brill.

Brown, C. Mackenzie. 2012. *Hindu Perspectives on Evolution: Darwin, Dharma, and Design*. London: Routledge.

Brown, Hunter. 1997. "The Inadequacy of Wishful Thinking Charges Against William James's *The Will to Believe*." *Transactions of the Charles S. Peirce Society* 33.2: 488–519.

Brüntrup, Godehard and Ludwig Jaskolla, eds. 2017. *Panpsychism: Contemporary Perspectives*. Oxford: Oxford University Press.

Bryant, Edwin F. 2009. *The Yoga Sūtras of Patañjali*. New York: North Point Press.

Buchta, David. 2014. "Dependent Agency and Hierarchical Determinism in the Theology of Madhva." In *Free Will, Agency, and Selfhood in Indian Philosophy*, edited by Matthew R. Dasti and Edwin F. Bryant, 255–78. New York: Oxford University Press.

Burge, Tyler. 1993. "Content Preservation." *The Philosophical Review* 102: 457–88.

Burke, Marie Louise. 1992–1999. *Swami Vivekananda in the West: New Discoveries*, 6 vols. Kolkata: Advaita Ashrama.

Byun, Jiwon. 2017. "Thomas Henry Huxley's Agnostic Philosophy of Science." Ph.D. dissertation, University of British Columbia.

Cetanānanda, Svāmī. 1969. "*Nava Vṛndāvan o Śrīrāmakṛṣṇa*." *Udbodhan* 71: 144–52.

Chadha, Monima. 2015. "Perceptual Experience and Concepts in Classical Indian Philosophy." *Stanford Encyclopedia of Philosophy*, http://plato.stanford.edu (accessed July 28, 2019).

Chakrabarti, Arindam. 1989. "From the Fabric to the Weaver?" In *Indian Philosophy of Religion*, edited by Roy Perrett, 21–34. Dordrecht: Kluwer.

Chalmers, David. 1995. "Facing Up to the Problem of Consciousness." *Journal of Consciousness Studies* 2.3: 200–219.

Chalmers, David. 1996. *The Conscious Mind: In Search of a Fundamental Theory*. Oxford: Oxford University Press.

Chalmers, David J. 2017a. "The Combination Problem for Panpsychism." In *Panpsychism: Contemporary Perspectives*, edited by Godehard Brüntrup and Ludwig Jaskolla, 179–214. Oxford: Oxford University Press.

Chalmers, David J. 2017b. "Panpsychism and Panprotopsychism." In *Panpsychism: Contemporary Perspectives*, edited by Godehard Brüntrup and Ludwig Jaskolla, 19–47. Oxford: Oxford University Press.

Chalmers, David. 2020. "Idealism and the Mind-Body Problem." In *The Routledge Handbook of Panpsychism*, edited by William Seager, 353–73. New York: Routledge.

Chatterjee, Bankimchandra. 1986. "Mill, Darwin, and Hinduism." In *Bankimchandra Chatterjee: Sociological Essays: Utilitarianism and Positivism in Bengal*, edited and translated by S. N. Mukerjee and M. Maddern, 60–70. Calcutta: Ṛddhi.

Chatterjee, Satis Chandra. [1963] 1985. *Classical Indian Philosophies: Their Synthesis in the Philosophy of Sri Ramakrishna*, second ed. Calcutta: University of Calcutta.

Chatterjee, Satis Chandra. 1995. "Vivekananda's Neo-Vedantism and Its Practical Application." In *Vivekananda: The Great Spiritual Teacher*, edited by Swami Bodhasarananda, 255–80. Kolkata: Advaita Ashrama.

Chatterjee, Satischandra and Dhirendramohan Datta. 2008. *An Introduction to Indian Philosophy*. Calcutta: University of Calcutta.

Chaudhuri, Roma. 1995. "Vivekananda: His Place in Indian Philosophy." In *Vivekananda: The Great Spiritual Teacher*, edited by Swami Bodhasarananda, 281–95. Kolkata: Advaita Ashrama.

Chemparathy, George. 1972. *An Indian Rational Theology: Introduction to Udayana's* Nyāyakusumāñjali. Leiden: Brill.

Chetanananda, Swami. 1997. *God Lived with Them*. Kolkata: Advaita Ashrama.
Christian, Rose Ann. 2005. "Truth and Consequences in James's 'The Will to Believe.'" *International Journal for Philosophy of Religion* 58.1: 1–26.
Chudnoff, Elijah and David Didemonico. 2015. "The Epistemic Unity of Perception." *Pacific Philosophical Quarterly* 96: 535–49.
Churchland, Paul. 1986. *Neurophilosophy*. Cambridge, MA: MIT Press.
Clark, Ralph W. 1984. "The Evidential Value of Religious Experiences." *International Journal for Philosophy of Religion* 16.3: 189–202.
Clifford, William Kingdon. 1879. *Lectures and Essays*, vol. 2, edited by Leslie Stephen and Frederick Pollock. London: Macmillan & Co.
Coady, C. A. J. 1992. *Testimony: A Philosophical Study*. Oxford: Clarendon.
Cohen, Jonathan L. 1992. *An Essay on Belief and Acceptance*. Oxford: Clarendon.
Coleman, Sam. 2014. "The Real Combination Problem: Panpsychism, Micro-Subjects, and Emergence." *Erkenntnis* 79: 19–44.
Collins, Steven. 1982. *Selfless Persons*. Cambridge: Cambridge University Press.
Conze, Edward. 1962. *Buddhist Thought in India*. London: George Allen & Unwin.
Conze, Edward, trans. 1975. *The Perfection of Wisdom in Eight Thousand Lines & Its Verse Summary*. Bolinas, CA: Four Seasons Foundation.
Coomaraswamy, Ananda. 1964. *Buddha and the Gospel of Buddhism*. New York: Harper & Row.
Cooper, W. E. 1990. "William James's Theory of Mind." *Journal of the History of Philosophy* 28.4: 571–93.
Cooper, W. E. 2002. *The Unity of William James's Thought*. Nashville: Vanderbilt University Press.
Crick, Francis and Christof Koch. 1990. "Toward a Neurobiological Theory of Consciousness." *Seminars in the Neurosciences* 2: 263–75.
Crosby, Kate. 2014. *Theravada Buddhism: Continuity, Diversity, and Identity*. Oxford: Wiley Blackwell.
Dasgupta, Rabindra Kumar. 1999. *Swami Vivekananda's Neo-Vedānta*. Calcutta: The Asiatic Society.
Dasgupta, Surendranath. 1922. *A History of Indian Philosophy: Volume I*. Cambridge: Cambridge University Press.
Dasti, Matthew R. 2010. "Rational Belief in Classical India: Nyāya's Epistemology and Defense of Theism." Ph.D. dissertation, University of Texas at Austin.
Dasti, Matthew R. 2011. "Indian Rational Theology: Proof, Justification, and Epistemic Liberality in Nyāya's Argument for God." *Asian Philosophy* 21.1: 1–21.
Dasti, Matthew R. 2012. "Parasitism and Disjunctivism in Nyāya Epistemology." *Philosophy East and West* 62.1: 1–15.
Dasti, Matthew R. and Stephen Phillips. 2010. "*Pramāṇa* Are Factive—A Response to Jonardon Ganeri." *Philosophy East and West* 60.4: 535–40.
Datta, Bhupendranath. 1954. *Swami Vivekananda, Patriot-Prophet: A Study*. Calcutta: Nababharat Publishers.
Datta, Mahendranāth. 1912. *Śrīmat Vivekānanda Svāmījīr Jīvaner Ghaṭanāvalī: Akhaṇḍa Saṃskaran*. Kolkātā: D. Mahendra Publishing Committee.
Datta, Mahendranāth. 1943. *Śrīśrīrāmakṛṣṇer Anudhyān*. Kolkātā: D. Mahendra Publishing Committee.
Davies, Tony. *Humanism*. 1997. London: Routledge.

Davis, Caroline Franks. 1989. *The Evidential Force of Religious Experience*. Oxford: Clarendon Press.

Davis, Leesa. 2010. *Advaita Vedānta and Zen Buddhism*. London: Continuum.

De Michelis, Elizabeth. 2004. *A History of Modern Yoga*. London: Continuum.

Dennett, Daniel. 1988. "Quining Qualia." In *Consciousness and Contemporary Science*, edited by A. J. Marcel and E. Bisiach, 42–77. New York: Oxford University Press.

De Ridder, Jeroen, Rik Peels, and René van Woudenberg, eds. 2018. *Scientism: Prospects and Problems*. Oxford: Oxford University Press.

De Smet, Richard. 1972. "Is the Concept of 'Person' Congenial to Śaṅkara Vedānta?" *Indian Philosophical Annual* 8: 199–205.

De Smet, Richard. 1987. "Forward Steps in Saṅkara Research." *Darshana International* 26: 33–46.

Deutsch, Eliot. 1988. *Advaita Vedānta: A Philosophical Reconstruction*. Honolulu: University of Hawaii Press.

Devaraja, N. K. 1962. *An Introduction to Śaṅkara's Theory of Knowledge*. Delhi: Motilal Banarsidass.

Devdas, Nalini. 1968. *Svāmī Vivekānanda*. Bangalore: The Christian Institute for the Study of Religion and Society.

Dhar, Sailendra Nath. 1975. *A Comprehensive Biography of Swami Vivekananda*, 2 vols. Madras: Vivekananda Prakashan Kendra.

Dhīreśānanda, Svāmī. 1962. "*Svāmī Vivekānanda o Advaitavāda*." *Udbodhan* 65.2: 73–80 and 65.3: 80–81, 138–44.

Dhyānānanda, Svāmī. 1988. "*Vivekānanda-Vicār*." In *Cintānāyak Vivekananda*, edited by Svāmī Lokeśvarānanda, 84–96. Kolkata: Ramakrishna Mission Institute of Culture.

Doore, G. L. 1983. "William James and the Ethics of Belief." *Philosophy* 58: 353–64.

Draper, John William. 1874. *History of the Conflict between Religion and Science*. New York: D. Appleton.

Drew, Rose. 2011. *Buddhist and Christian? An Exploration of Dual Belonging*. London: Routledge.

Duckworth, Douglas. 2017. "The Other Side of Realism: Panpsychism and Yogācāra." In *Buddhist Philosophy: A Comparative Approach*, edited by Steven M. Emmanuel, 29–43. Hoboken, NJ: Wiley Blackwell.

Dupré, John. 1993. *The Disorder of Things: Metaphysical Foundations of the Disunity of Science*. Cambridge, MA: Harvard University Press.

Dutta, Tapash Sankar. 1982. *A Study of the Philosophy of Vivekananda*. Calcutta: Sribhumi Publishing.

Dyczkowski, Mark S. G. 1989. *The Doctrine of Vibration: An Analysis of the Doctrines and Practices of Kashmir Shaivism*. Delhi: Motilal Banarsidass.

Eisen, Sydney. 1968. "Frederic Harrison and Herbert Spencer: Embattled Unbelievers." *Victorian Studies* 12.1: 33–56.

Elkman, Stuart. 2007. "Religious Plurality and Swami Vivekananda." In *Beyond Orientalism*, edited by Eli Franco and Krain Preisendanz, 505–11. Delhi: Motilal Banarsidass.

Fales, Evan. 1996a. "Mystical Experience as Evidence." *International Journal for Philosophy of Religion* 40.1: 19–46.

Fales, Evan. 1996b. "Scientific Explanations of Mystical Experiences, Part I: The Case of St Teresa." *Religious Studies* 32.2: 143–63.

Fales, Evan. 2013. "Is a Science of the Supernatural Possible?" In *Philosophy of Pseudoscience: Reconsidering the Demarcation Problem*, edited by Massimo Pigliucci and Maarten Boudry, 247–62. Chicago: University of Chicago Press.

Feldman, Richard. 2000. "The Ethics of Belief." *Philosophy and Phenomenological Research* 60.3: 667–95.

Flew, Antony. [1966] 2005. *God and Philosophy*. New York: Prometheus Books.

Ford, Marcus Peter. 1982. *William James's Philosophy*. Amherst: University of Massachusetts Press.

Forman, Robert, ed. 1990. *The Problem of Pure Consciousness: Mysticism and Philosophy*. New York: Oxford University Press.

Forman, Robert. 1993. "Mystical Knowledge: Knowledge by Identity." *Journal of the American Academy of Religion* 61.4: 705–38.

Fort, Andrew. 2007. "*Jīvanmukti* and Social Service in Advaita and Neo-Vedānta." In *Beyond Orientalism*, edited by Eli Franco and Karin Preisendanz, 489–504. Delhi: Motilal Banarsidass.

Frankish, Keith. 2016. "Illusionism as a Theory of Consciousness." *Journal of Consciousness Studies* 23: 11–39.

Frankish, Keith, ed. 2017. *Illusionism as a Theory of Consciousness*. Exeter, UK: Imprint Academic.

Frauwallner, Erich. 1953. *Geschichte der indischen Philosophie, Band I*. Salzburg: Otto Müller.

Frederick, Norris. 2012. "William James and Swami Vivekananda: Religious Experience and Vedanta/Yoga in America." *William James Studies* 9: 37–55.

Fricker, Elizabeth. 1994. "Against Gullibility." In *Knowing From Words: Western and Indian Philosophical Analysis of Understanding and Testimony*, edited by Bimal Krishna Matilal and Arindam Chakrabarti, 125–61. Dordrecht: Springer.

Fricker, Elizabeth. 2006. "Testimony and Epistemic Autonomy." In *The Epistemology of Testimony*, edited by Jennifer Lackey and Ernest Sosa, 225–51. Oxford: Oxford University Press.

Gadamer, Hans-Georg. [1960] 2006. *Truth and Method*, second ed., translated by W. Glen-Doepel, Joel Weinsheimer, and Donald G. Marshall. London: Continuum.

Gale, Richard. 1991. *On the Nature and Existence of God*. Cambridge: Cambridge University Press.

Gambhirananda, Swami, trans. 1957–1958. *Eight Upaniṣads*, 2 vols. Kolkata: Advaita Ashrama.

Gambhirananda, Swami, trans. 1984. *Bhagavad Gītā with the Commentary of Śaṅkarācārya*. Kolkata: Advaita Ashrama.

Gambhirananda, Swami, trans. 2006. *Brahma-Sūtra-Bhāṣya of Śrī Śaṅkarācārya*. Kolkata: Advaita Ashrama.

Gambhīrānanda, Svāmī. 1984. *Yuganāyak Vivekānanda*, 3 vols. Kolkātā: Udbodhan.

Gambhīrānanda, Svāmī. 1988. "*Kārye Pariṇata Vedānta*." In *Cintānāyak Vivekānanda*, edited by Svāmī Lokeśvarānanda, 129–42. Kolkata: Ramakrishna Mission Institute of Culture.

Ganeri, Jonardon. 2001. *Indian Logic: A Reader*. Surrey, UK: Curzon Press.

Ganeri, Jonardon. 2010. "The Study of Indian Epistemology: Questions of Method—A Reply to Matthew Dasti and Stephen H. Phillips." *Philosophy East and West* 60.4: 541–50.

Ganeri, Jonardon. 2016. "A Manifesto for a Re:emergent Philosophy." *Confluence* 4: 134–41.

Ganeri, Jonardon. 2017. "Freedom in Thinking: The Immersive Cosmopolitanism of Krishnachandra Bhattacharyya." In *The Oxford Handbook of Indian Philosophy*, edited by Jonardon Ganeri, 718–36. New York: Oxford University Press.

Gasparri, Luca. 2019. "Priority Cosmopsychism and the Advaita Vedānta." *Philosophy East and West* 69.1: 130–42.

Gellman, Jerome. 1997. *Experience of God and the Rationality of Theistic Belief.* Ithaca, NY: Cornell University Press.

Gellman, Jerome. 1999. *Mystical Experience of God: A Philosophical Inquiry*. Burlington, VT: Ashgate.

Gellman, Jerome. 2018. "Mysticism." *Stanford Encyclopedia of Philosophy*, http://plato.stanford.edu (accessed July 29, 2019).

Ghoṣāl, Bipin Bihārī. [1881] 1987. *Mukti eboṅg tāhār Sādhan*. Kolkata: Udbodhan.

Gilley, Sheridan and Ann Loades. 1981. "Thomas Henry Huxley: The War between Science and Religion." *Journal of Religion* 61.3: 285–308.

Gillies, Donald. 2000. "An Empiricist Philosophy of Mathematics and its Implications for the History of Mathematics." In *The Growth of Mathematical Knowledge*, edited by Emily Grosholz and Herbert Breger, 41–57. Dordrecht: Springer.

Glassé, Cyril and Huston Smith, eds. 2001. *The New Encyclopedia of Islam*. Walnut Creek, CA: AltaMira Press.

Goff, Philip. 2013. "Orthodox Property Dualism + Linguistic Theory of Vagueness = Panpsychism." In *Consciousness Inside and Out: Phenomenology, Neuroscience, and the Nature of Experience*, edited by Richard Brown, 75–91. Dordrecht: Springer.

Goff, Philip. 2017a. *Consciousness and Fundamental Reality*. New York: Oxford University Press.

Goff, Philip. 2017b. "Panpsychism." *Stanford Encyclopedia of Philosophy*, http://plato.stanford.edu (accessed December 7, 2020).

Goff, Philip. 2019. *Galileo's Error*. New York: Pantheon Books.

Goff, Philip. 2020. "Cosmopsychism, Micropsychism and the Grounding Relation." In *The Routledge Handbook of Panpsychism*, edited by William Seager, 144–56. New York: Routledge.

Gold, Jonathan C. 2015. *Paving the Great Way: Vasubandhu's Unifying Buddhist Philosophy*. New York: Columbia University Press.

Golding, Alvin. 1990. "Toward a Pragmatic Conception of Religious Faith." *Faith and Philosophy* 7.4: 486–503.

Green, Christopher R. 2006. "The Epistemic Parity of Testimony, Memory, and Perception." Ph.D. dissertation, University of Notre Dame.

Green, Thomas J. 2016. *Religion for a Secular Age: Max Müller, Swami Vivekananda, and Vedānta*. Surrey, UK: Ashgate.

Gregg, Stephen E. 2019. *Swami Vivekananda and Non-Hindu Traditions*. London: Routledge.

Griffiths, Paul J. 2001. *Problems of Religious Diversity*. Malden, MA: Blackwell.

Grimm, Georg. 1958. *The Doctrine of the Buddha*. Berlin: Akademie-Verlag.

Grinshpon, Yohanan. 1997. "Yogic Revolution and Tokens of Conservatism in Vyāsa-Yoga." *Journal of Indian Philosophy* 25: 129–38.

Gupta, Bina. 1995. *Perceiving in Advaita Vedānta: Epistemological Analysis and Interpretation*. Delhi: Motilal Banarsidass.

Gupta, Bina. 2009. *Reason and Experience in Indian Philosophy*. Delhi: Indian Council of Philosophical Research.

Gupta, Mahendranath. [1942] 1992. *The Gospel of Sri Ramakrishna*, translated by Swami Nikhilananda. New York: Ramakrishna-Vivekananda Center.

Gupta, Mahendranāth. [1902–1932] 2010. *Śrīśrīrāmakṛṣṇakathāmṛta: Śrīma-kathita*. 1 vol. Kolkātā: Udbodhan.

Gutting, Gary. 1983. *Religious Belief and Religious Skepticism*. Notre Dame: University of Notre Dame Press.

Haack, Susan. 2007. *Defending Science within Reason: Between Scientism and Cynicism*. Amherst, NY: Prometheus Books.

Hacker, Paul. 1953. *Vivarta: Studien zur Geschichte der illusionistischen Kosmologie und Erkenntnistheorie der Inder*. Wiesbaden: Mainz Verlag.

Hacker, Paul. [1971] 1977. "Der religiöse Nationalismus Vivekanandas." In *Paul Hacker: Kleine Schriften*, edited by Lambert Schmithausen. Wiesbaden: Franz Steiner Verlag, 565–79.

Hacker, Paul. 1995. *Philology and Confrontation: Paul Hacker on Traditional and Modern Vedānta*, edited by Wilhelm Halbfass. Albany, NY: SUNY Press.

Halbfass, Wilhelm. 1988. *India and Europe: An Essay in Philosophical Understanding*. Albany: SUNY Press.

Halbfass, Wilhelm. 1991. *Tradition and Reflection: Explorations in Indian Thought*. Albany: SUNY Press.

Halbfass, Wilhelm. [1995] 2007. "Practical Vedānta." In *The Oxford India Hinduism Reader*, edited by Vasudha Dalmia and Heinrich von Stietencron, 169–82. New Delhi: Oxford University Press.

Hamilton, William. 1853. *Discussions on Philosophy and Literature*. New York: Harper & Brothers.

Hamilton, William. 1859. *Lectures on Metaphysics and Logic: Volume 1*. Boston: Gould & Lincoln.

Harré, Rom. 2003. "Positivist Thought in the Nineteenth Century." In *The Cambridge History of Philosophy*, edited by Thomas Baldwin, 11–26. Cambridge: Cambridge University Press.

Harvey, Peter. 2013. *An Introduction to Buddhism*, second ed. Cambridge: Cambridge University Press.

Harvey, Van. 2013. "Huxley's Agnosticism." *Philosophy Now* 99 (online; unpaginated).

Hatcher, Brian A. 2004. "Contemporary Hindu Thought." In *Contemporary Hinduism*, edited by Robin Rinehart, 179–211. Santa Barbara, CA: ABC Clio.

Hatcher, Brian A. 2008. *Bourgeois Hinduism, or the Faith of the Modern Vedāntists*. New York: Oxford University Press.

Hayek, Friedrich. 1942. "Scientism and the Study of Society: Part I." *Economica* 9.35: 267–91.

Hayes, R. P. 1994. "Nāgārjuna's Appeal." *Journal of Indian Philosophy* 22: 299–378.

Heim, S. Mark. 1995. *Salvations: Truth and Difference in Religion*. Maryknoll, NY: Orbis.

Hick, John. 1988. "A Concluding Comment." *Faith and Philosophy* 5: 449–55.

Hick, John. 1989. *An Interpretation of Religion*. London: Macmillan.

Hick, John. 1990. *Philosophy of Religion*, fourth ed. Englewood Cliffs, NJ: Prentice Hall.

Hick, John. 1991. "Reply (to Mesle)." In *Problems in the Philosophy of Religion*, edited by Harold Hewitt, 82–5. Houndmills, UK: Macmillan.

Hick, John. 1995. *A Christian Theology of Religions: The Rainbow of Faiths*. Louisville: Westminster John Knox Press.

Hick, John, ed. 2001. *Dialogues in the Philosophy of Religion*. London: Palgrave.

Hick, John. 2006. *The New Frontier of Religion and Science: Religious Experience, Neuroscience, and the Transcendent*. Basingstoke, UK: Palgrave Macmillan.

Hohner, Terrance and Carolyn Kenny. 2014. *Swami Vivekananda in the West: A Chronology*, third ed. Portland, OR: Vedanta Society of Portland. [http://vedanta.org/wp-content/uploads/2016/10/Swami-Vivekananda-in-the-West-A-Chronology.pdf.]

Hollinger, David A. 1997. "James, Clifford, and the Scientific Conscience." In *The Cambridge Companion to William James*, edited by Ruth Anna Putnam, 69–83. Cambridge: Cambridge University Press.

Howard-Snyder, Daniel. 2016. "Does Faith Entail Belief?" *Faith and Philosophy* 33.2: 142–62.

Huemer, Michael. 2001. *Skepticism and the Veil of Perception*. Lanham, MD: Rowman & Littlefield.

Huemer, Michael. 2013. "Phenomenal Conservatism Über Alles." In *Seemings and Justification: New Essays on Dogmatism and Phenomenal Conservatism*, edited by Chris Tucker, 329–49. Oxford: Oxford University Press.

Huxley, Aldous. 1947. *The Perennial Philosophy*. London: Chatto & Windus.

Huxley, T. H. 1866. *Lessons in Elementary Physiology*. London: Macmillan & Co.

Huxley, T. H. [1876] 1896. "Lectures on Evolution [New York]." In T. H. Huxley, *Science and Hebrew Tradition: Essays*, 46–138. New York: D. Appleton & Co.

Huxley, T. H. [1889] 1894a. "Agnosticism." In T. H. Huxley, *Collected Essays*, vol. 5, 209–62. Suffolk: Richard Clay & Sons.

Huxley, T. H. [1889] 1894b. "The Value of Witness to the Miraculous." In T. H. Huxley, *Collected Essays*, vol. 5, 160–91. Suffolk: Richard Clay & Sons.

Huxley, T. H. 1890a. "On the Hypothesis that Animals Are Automata, and Its History." In T. H. Huxley, *Methods and Results: Essays*, 199–250. New York: D. Appleton & Co.

Huxley, T. H. 1890b. "On the Physical Basis of Life." In T. H. Huxley, *Methods and Results: Essays*, 130–65. New York: D. Appleton & Co.

Isherwood, Christopher. 1965. *Ramakrishna and His Disciples*. Kolkata: Advaita Ashrama.

James, William. 1879. "Are We Automata?" *Mind* 4.13: 1–22.

James, William. [1890] 1950. *The Principles of Psychology: Volume 1*. New York: Henry Holt.

James, William. 1897. "The Will to Believe." In William James, *The Will to Believe and Other Essays in Popular Philosophy*, 1–31. New York: Longmans Green & Co.

James, William. [1900] 2002. *Varieties of Religious Experience*. London: Routledge.

James, William. [1907] 1987. *Pragmatism*. In William James, *Writings: 1902–1910*, 479–624. New York: Library of America.

James, William. [1911] 1987. "Faith and the Right to Believe." In William James, *Writings: 1902–1910*, 1095–101. New York: Library of America.

James, William. 1912. *Essays in Radical Empiricism*. New York: Longmans, Green & Co.

James, William. 1927. "Reason and Faith." *The Journal of Philosophy* 24.8: 197–201.

Jennings, J. G. 1948. *The Vedāntic Buddhism of the Buddha*. London: Oxford University Press.

Jones, Richard H. 2016. *Philosophy of Mysticism: Raids on the Ineffable*. Albany: SUNY Press.

Kant, Immanuel. 1992. *The Only Possible Argument in Support of a Demonstration of the Existence of God*. In Immanuel Kant, *Theoretical Philosophy: 1755–1770*, translated by David Walford, 107–202. Cambridge: Cambridge University Press.

Kant, Immanuel. 1996. *Critique of Practical Reason*. In Immanuel Kant, *Practical Philosophy*, translated by Mary J. Gregor, 133–271. Cambridge: Cambridge University Press.

Kant, Immanuel. 1996. *Religion within the Boundaries of Mere Reason*, translated by George di Giovanni, in Immanuel Kant, *Religion and Rational Theology*, 39–216. Cambridge: Cambridge University Press.

Kant, Immanuel. 1997. *Lectures on Metaphysics*, translated by Karl Ameriks and Steve Naragon. Cambridge: Cambridge University Press.

Kant, Immanuel. 1998. *Critique of Pure Reason*, translated by Paul Guyer and Allen Wood. Cambridge: Cambridge University Press.

Kastrup, Bernardo. 2018. "The Universe in Consciousness." *Journal of Consciousness Studies* 25.5–6: 125–55.

Katz, Steven, ed. 1978a. *Mysticism and Philosophical Analysis*. New York: Oxford University Press.

Katz, Steven. 1978b. "Language, Epistemology, and Mysticism." In *Mysticism and Philosophical Analysis*, edited by Steven Katz, 22–74. New York: Oxford University Press.

Keith, A. B. 1923. *Buddhist Philosophy in India and Ceylon*. London: Oxford University Press.

Killingley, Dermot. 1990. "*Yogasūtra* IV, 2–3 and Vivekānanda's Interpretation of Evolution." *Journal of Indian Philosophy* 18: 151–79.

Killingley, Dermot. 1998. "Vivekananda's Western Message from the East." In *Swami Vivekananda and the Modernization of Hinduism*, edited by William Radice, 145–59. Delhi: Oxford University Press.

King, Richard. 1989. "*Śūnyatā* and *Ajāti*: Absolutism and the Philosophies of Nāgārjuna and Gauḍapāda." *Journal of Indian Philosophy* 17: 385–405.

King, Richard. 1999. *Orientalism and Religion: Postcolonial Theory, India and "The Mystic East."* London: Routledge.

King, Sallie B. 1988. "Two Epistemological Models for the Interpretation of Mysticism." *Journal of the American Academy of Religion* 56.2: 257–79.

Kopf, David. 1979. *The Brahmo Samaj and the Making of the Modern Indian Mind*. Princeton, NJ: Princeton University Press.

Kottler, Malcolm Jay. 1974. "Alfred Russel Wallace, the Origin of Man, and Spiritualism." *Isis* 65.2: 144–92.

Kvanvig, Jonathan L. 2013. "Affective Theism and People of Faith." *Midwest Studies in Philosophy* 37: 109–28.

Kwan, Kai-Man. 2006. "Can Religious Experience Provide Justification for the Belief in God? The Debate in Contemporary Analytic Philosophy." *Philosophy Compass* 1.6: 640–61.

Kwan, Kai-Man. 2009. "The Argument from Religious Experience." In *The Blackwell Companion to Natural Theology*, edited by William Lane Craig and J. P. Moreland, 498–552. New York: Blackwell.

Lackey, Jennifer. 2006. "It Takes Two to Tango: Beyond Reductionism and Non-Reductionism in the Epistemology of Testimony." In *The Epistemology of Testimony*, edited by Jennifer Lackey and Ernest Sosa, 160–89. Oxford: Oxford University Press.

Lackey, Jennifer. 2008. *Learning from Words*. Oxford: Oxford University Press.

Lackey, Jennifer and Ernest Sosa, eds. 2006. *The Epistemology of Testimony*. Oxford: Oxford University Press.

Lamotte, Étienne. 1988. *History of Indian Buddhism*, translated by Sara Boin-Webb. Louvain-La-Neuve: Institut Orientaliste.

Lancaster, Brian L. 2004. *Approaches to Consciousness: The Marriage of Science and Mysticism*. London: Routledge.

Larson, Gerald James. 1969. *Classical Sāṃkhya*. Delhi: Motilal Banarsidass.

Larson, Gerald James. 2013. "Materialism, Dualism, and the Philosophy of Yoga." *International Journal of Hindu Studies* 17.2: 181–219.

Laudan, Larry. 1981a. "A Confutation of Convergent Realism." *Philosophy of Science* 48: 19–49.

Laudan, Larry. 1981b. "Towards a Reassessment of Comte's 'Méthode Positive.'" In *Science and Hypothesis*, edited by Larry Laudan, 141–62. Dordrecht: Springer.

Laudan, Larry. 1983. "The Demise of the Demarcation Problem." In *Physics, Philosophy and Psychoanalysis*, edited by R. S. Cohen and Larry Laudan, 111–27. Dordrecht: D. Reidel.

Leach, Stephen and James Tartaglia. 2017. *Consciousness and the Great Philosophers*. London: Routledge.

Leidenhag, Joanna. 2019. "Unity between God and Mind? A Study on the Relationship between Panpsychism and Pantheism." *Sophia* 58: 543–61.

Levine, Joseph. 1983. "Materialism and Qualia: The Explanatory Gap." *Pacific Philosophical Quarterly* 64: 354–61.

Lightman, Bernard. 2002. "Huxley and Scientific Agnosticism: The Strange History of a Failed Rhetorical Strategy." *The British Journal for the History of Science* 35.3: 271–89.

Lipton, Peter. 2004. *Inference to the Best Explanation*, second ed. London: Routledge.

Liston, Michael. 2019. "Scientific Realism and Antirealism." *Internet Encyclopedia of Philosophy*, http://www.iep.utm.edu/sci-real/.

Long, Jeffery D. 2008. "Advaita and Dvaita: Bridging the Gap—The Ramakrishna Tradition's both/and Approach to the Dvaita/Advaita Debate." *Journal of Vaishnava Studies* 16.2: 49–70.

Long, Jeffery D. 2010. "(Tentatively) Putting the Pieces Together: Comparative Theology in the Tradition of Sri Ramakrishna." In *The New Comparative Theology*, edited by Francis Clooney, 151–61. London: Continuum.

Long, Jeffery D. 2016. "Like a Dog's Curly Tail: A Hindu Theodicy in the Tradition of Sri Ramakrishna." In *Comparing Faithfully: Insights for Systematic Theological Reflection*, edited by Michelle Voss Roberts, 107–25. New York: Fordham University Press.

Long, Jeffery D. 2017. "The Eternal Veda and the 'Truth which Enlightens All': Correspondences and Disjunctures between *Nostra Aetate* and Swami Vivekananda's Vedantic Inclusivism." In *The Future of Interreligious Dialogue: A Multireligious Conversation on* Nostra Aetate, edited by Charles L. Cohen, Paul F. Knitter, and Ulrich Rosenhagen, 249–61. Maryknoll, NY: Orbis.

Long, Jeffery D. 2019. "Religious Experience, Hindu Pluralism, and Hope: *Anubhava* in the Tradition of Sri Ramakrishna." *Religions* 10: 1–17.

Long, Jeffery D. 2020. "A Complex Ultimate Reality: The Metaphysics of the Four Yogas." *Religions* 11: 1–19.

Lowe, E. J. 2008. *Personal Agency: The Metaphysics of Mind and Agency*. Oxford: Oxford University Press.

Loy, David. 1988. *Nonduality: A Study in Comparative Philosophy*. New Haven, CT: Yale University Press.
MacPhail, Jean C. 2013. "Learning in Depth: A Case Study in Twin 5X5 Matrices of Consciousness." Ph.D. dissertation, University of Viadrina.
Madaio, James. 2017. "Rethinking Neo-Vedānta: Swami Vivekananda and the Selective Historiography of Advaita Vedānta." *Religions* 8: 1–12.
Madden, Edward H. 1985. "Sir William Hamilton, Critical Philosophy, and the Commonsense Tradition." *The Review of Metaphysics* 38.4: 839–66.
Madhavananda, Swami, trans. 1921. *Vivekacūḍāmaṇi*. Mayavati: Advaita Ashrama.
Madhavananda, Swami, trans. 2009. *The Bṛhadāraṇyaka Upaniṣad with the Commentary of Śaṅkarācārya*. Kolkata: Advaita Ashrama.
Madigan, Timothy J. 2009. *W. K. Clifford and "The Ethics of Belief."* Newcastle, UK: Cambridge Scholars Publishing.
Mahadevan, T. M. P. 1965. *Swami Vivekananda and the Indian Renaissance*. Coimbatore: Sri Ramakrishna Mission Vidyalaya Teachers College.
Maharaj, Ayon. 2017a. "Swami Vivekananda's Vedāntic Critique of Schopenhauer's Doctrine of the Will." *Philosophy East and West* 67.4: 1191–221.
Maharaj, Ayon. 2017b. "Kant on the Epistemology of Indirect Mystical Experience." *Sophia* 56: 311–36.
Maharaj, Ayon. 2018. *Infinite Paths to Infinite Reality: Sri Ramakrishna and Cross-Cultural Philosophy of Religion*. New York: Oxford University Press.
Maharaj, Ayon. 2019. "'Infinite Paths, Infinite Doctrines': Some Reflections on Perry Schmidt-Leukel's Fractal Approach to Religious Diversity from the Standpoint of the Ramakrishna-Vivekananda Tradition." In *Incarnation, Prophecy, Enlightenment: Perry Schmidt-Leukel's Fractal Interpretation of Religious Diversity*, edited by Paul Knitter and Alan Race, 100–114. Maryknoll, NY: Orbis.
Maharaj, Ayon. 2020a. "*Asminnasya ca tadyogaṃ śāsti*: Swami Vivekananda's Interpretation of *Brahmasūtra* 1.1.19 as a Hermeneutic Basis for Samanvayī Vedānta." In *Swami Vivekananda: His Life, Legacy, and Liberative Ethics*, edited by Rita Sherma, 9–28. Lanham, MD: Rowman & Littlefield.
Maharaj, Ayon. 2020b. "*Śivajñāne jīver sevā*: Reexamining Swami Vivekananda's Practical Vedānta in the Light of Sri Ramakrishna." *Journal of Dharma Studies* 2: 175–87.
Maharaj, Ayon. 2020c. "Seeing Oneness Everywhere: Sri Aurobindo's Mystico-Immanent Interpretation of the Īśā Upaniṣad." In *The Bloomsbury Research Handbook of Vedānta*, edited by Ayon Maharaj, 309–40. London: Bloomsbury.
Majumdār, Rameścandra. 1988. "*Ācārya Vivekānanda*." In *Cintānāyak Vivekananda*, edited by Svāmī Lokeśvarānanda, 9–32. Kolkata: Ramakrishna Mission Institute of Culture.
Malkovsky, Bradley. 1997. "The Personhood of Śaṅkara's *Para Brahman*." *Journal of Religion* 77.4: 541–62.
Martin, Michael. 1986. "The Principle of Credulity and Religious Experience." *Religious Studies* 22.1: 79–93.
Matchett, Freda. 1981. "The Teaching of Rāmakrishna in Relation to the Hindu Tradition and as Interpreted by Vivekānanda." *Religion* 11: 171–84.
Mathews, Freya. 2003. *For Love of Matter: A Contemporary Panpsychism*. Albany, NY: SUNY Press.
Mathews, Freya. 2011. "Panpsychism as Paradigm." In *The Mental as Fundamental*, edited by Michael Blamauer, 141–56. Frankfurt: Ontos Verlag.

Matilal, B. K. 1986. *Perception: An Essay on Classical Indian Theories of Knowledge*. Oxford: Clarendon Press.

Matilal, B. K. 2002. "The Logical Illumination of Indian Mysticism." In *The Collected Essays of Bimal Krishna Matilal: Mind, Language and World*, edited by Jonardon Ganeri, 38–64. Delhi: Oxford University Press.

McCrea, Larry. 2009. "'Just Like Us, Just Like Now': The Tactical Implications of the Mīmāṃsā Rejection of Yogic Perception." In *Yogic Perception, Meditation and Altered States of Consciousness*, edited by Eli Franco, 55–70. Wien: Verlag der Österreichischen Akademie der Wissenschaften.

McCrea, Larry. 2018. "Justification, Credibility, and Truth: Sucaritamiśra on Kumārila's Intrinsic Validity." *Wiener Zeitschrift für die Kunde Südasiens* 57: 99–115.

McGinn, Colin. 1991. *The Problem of Consciousness*. Oxford: Blackwell.

McKim, Robert. 2012. *On Religious Diversity*. New York: Oxford University Press.

Medhananda, Swami. 2020. "Was Swami Vivekananda a Hindu Supremacist? Revisiting a Long-Standing Debate." *Religions* 11.7: 1–28.

Medhananda, Swami. Forthcoming-a. "The Playful Self-Involution of Divine Consciousness: Sri Aurobindo's Evolutionary Cosmopsychism and His Response to the Individuation Problem." *The Monist*.

Medhananda, Swami. Forthcoming-b. "From Good to God: Swami Vivekananda's Vedāntic Virtue Ethics." *International Journal of Hindu Studies*.

Medhananda, Swami. Forthcoming-c. "'A Great Adventure of the Soul': Sri Aurobindo's Vedāntic Theodicy of Spiritual Evolution." *International Journal of Hindu Studies*.

Medhācaitanya, Brahmacārī. 1988. "*Svāmī Vivekānander Navavedānta*." In *Cintānāyak Vivekānanda*, edited by Svāmī Lokeśvarānanda, 169–83. Kolkata: Ramakrishna Mission Institute of Culture.

Midgley, Mary. 1992. *Science as Salvation: A Modern Myth and Its Meaning*. London: Routledge.

Mill, John Stuart. 1874. *Three Essays on Religion*. New York: Henry Holt & Co.

Mill, John Stuart. 1889. *An Examination of Sir William Hamilton's Philosophy*, sixth ed. London: Longmans, Green, & Co.

Mills, Ethan. 2009. "From Comparative to Cross-Cultural Philosophy." In *Comparative Philosophy Today and Tomorrow*, edited by Sarah Mattice, Geoff Ashton, and Joshua Kimber, 120–28. New Castle upon Tyne, UK: Cambridge Scholars Publishing.

Mills, Eugene O. 1997. "Giving Up on the Hard Problem of Consciousness." In *Explaining Consciousness: The Hard Problem*, edited by Jonathan Shear, 109–16. Cambridge, MA: MIT Press.

Mitra, Arpita. 2018. "The Dawn of Religious Pluralism?—The Importance of the 1893 World's Parliament of Religions at Chicago." *Prabuddha Bharata* 123: 39–47.

Mitra, Arpita. 2020. "From *Līlā* to *Nitya* and Back: Śrī Rāmakṛṣṇa and Vedānta." *Religions* 11: 1–15.

Mohanty, J. N. 2000. *Classical Indian Philosophy*. Lanham, MD: Rowman & Littlefield.

Munton, Jessie. 2020. "Visual Indeterminacy and the Puzzle of the Speckled Hen." *Mind & Language* 35: 1–21.

Murti, T. R. V. 1955. *The Central Philosophy of Buddhism: A Study of the Mādhyamika System*. London: George Allen & Unwin.

Murty, K. Satchidananda. 1959. *Revelation and Reason in Advaita Vedānta*. Bombay: Asia Publishing House.

Nagasawa, Yujin and Khai Wager. 2017. "Panpsychism and Panprotopsychism." In *Panpsychism: Contemporary Perspectives*, edited by Godehard Brüntrup and Ludwig Jaskolla, 113–29. Oxford: Oxford University Press.
Nagel, Thomas. 1974. "What Is It Like to Be a Bat?" *Philosophical Review* 83.4: 435–50.
Nagel, Thomas. 1979. "Panpsychism." In Thomas Nagel, *Mortal Questions*, 181–95. Cambridge: Cambridge University Press.
Nagel, Thomas. 2012. *Mind and Cosmos: Why the Materialist Neo-Darwinian Conception of Nature is Almost Certainly False*. New York: Oxford University Press.
Nakamura, Hajime. 1980. *Indian Buddhism: A Survey with Bibliographical Notes*. Delhi: Motilal Banarsidass.
Ñāṇamoli, Bhikkhu and Bhikkhu Bodhi, trans. 1995. *The Middle Length Discourses of the Buddha*. Kandy: Buddhist Publication Society.
Nanay, Bence. 2009. "How Speckled Is the Hen?" *Analysis* 69.3: 1–4.
Neevel, Walter. 1976. "The Transformation of Śrī Rāmakrishna." In *Hinduism: New Essays in the History of Religions*, edited by B. L. Smith, 53–97. Leiden: Brill.
Netland, Harold. 1986. "Professor Hick on Religious Pluralism." *Religious Studies* 22: 255–66.
Neufeldt, R. W. 1987. "The Response of the Ramakrishna Mission." In *Modern Indian Responses to Religious Pluralism*, edited by Harold Coward, 65–84. Albany: SUNY Press.
Neufeldt, R. W. 1993. "Reflections on Swami Vivekananda's Speeches at the World Parliament of Religions, 1893." *Journal of Hindu-Christian Studies* 6: 1–3.
Nicholson, Andrew J. 2020. "Vivekananda's Non-Dual Ethics in the History of Vedānta." In *Swami Vivekananda: His Life, Legacy, and Liberative Ethics*, edited by Rita Sherma, 45–64. Lanham, MD: Rowman & Littlefield.
Nickles, Thomas. 2013. "The Problem of Demarcation: History and Future." In *Philosophy of Pseudoscience: Reconsidering the Demarcation Problem*, edited by Massimo Pigliucci and Maarten Boudry, 101–20. Chicago: University of Chicago Press.
Nikhilananda, Swami. 1953. *Vivekananda: A Biography*. Calcutta: Advaita Ashrama.
Nityaswarupananda, Swami, trans. 2008. *Aṣṭāvakra Saṃhitā*. Kolkata: Advaita Ashrama.
Nivedita, Sister. 1910. *The Master as I Saw Him*. London: Longmans, Green & Co.
Nöe, Alva. 2005. *Action in Perception*. Cambridge, MA: MIT Press.
Oakes, Robert. 1981. "Religious Experience and Epistemological Miracles: A Moderate Defense of Theistic Mysticism." *International Journal for Philosophy of Religion* 12: 97–110.
Oakes, Robert. 2005. "Transparent Veridicality and Phenomenological Imposters: The Telling Issue." *Faith and Philosophy* 22.4: 413–25.
O'Hear, Anthony. 1984. *Experience, Explanation and Faith: An Introduction to the Philosophy of Religion*. London: Routledge.
Okasha, Samir. 2002. *Philosophy of Science: A Very Short Introduction*. Oxford: Oxford University Press.
Olson, Carl. 2011. Review of *Interpreting Ramakrishna: Kali's Child Revisited* by Swami Tyagananda and Pravrajika Vrajaprana. *The Journal of Asian Studies* 70.4: 1210–11.
Oostveen, Daan F. 2018. "Multiple Religious Belonging: Hermeneutical Challenges for Theology of Religions." *Open Theology* 3: 38–47.
Pace, Michael. 2017. "Experiences, Seemings, and Perceptual Justification." *Australasian Journal of Philosophy* 95.2: 226–41.
Paley, William. 1802. *Natural Theology*. Philadelphia: H. Maxwell.

Palmer, G. E. H., Philip Sherrard, and Kallistos Ware, trans. and ed. 1979. *The Philokalia: Volume 1*. London: Faber and Faber.

Palmquist, Stephen R. 2019. *Kant and Mysticism*. Lanham, MD: Rowman & Littlefield.

Panday, Dulal Chandra. 2012. *Swami Vivekananda's Neo-Vedanta in Theory and Practice: A Critical Study*. Kolkata: Ramakrishna Mission Institute of Culture.

Pappas, Gregory Fernando. 1992. "William James and the Logic of Faith." *Transactions of the Charles C. S. Peirce Society* 28.4: 781–808.

Paranjape, Makarand R., ed. 2015. *Swami Vivekananda: A Contemporary Reader*. New Delhi: Routledge.

Paranjape, Makarand R. 2020. *Swami Vivekananda: Hinduism and India's Road to Modernity*. New Delhi: HarperCollins.

Parsons, William B. 1999. *The Enigma of the Oceanic Feeling: Revisioning the Psychoanalytic Theory of Mysticism*. New York: Oxford University Press.

Pascal, Blaise. [1670] 2003. *Pensées*, translated by W. F. Trotter. Mineola, NY: Dover Pascal.

Pasternack, Lawrence and Courtney Fugate. 2020. "Kant's Philosophy of Religion." *Stanford Encyclopedia of Philosophy*, http://plato.stanford.edu/ (accessed August 24, 2020).

Patil, Parimal G. 2009. *Against a Hindu God: Buddhist Philosophy of Religion in India*. New York: Columbia University Press.

Peels, Rik. 2018. "A Conceptual Map of Scientism." In *Scientism: Prospects and Problems*, edited by Jeroen De Ridder, Rik Peels, and René van Woudenberg, 29–56. Oxford: Oxford University Press.

Perovich, Anthony. 1990. "Does the Philosophy of Mysticism Rest on a Mistake?" In *The Problem of Pure Consciousness: Mysticism and Philosophy*, edited by Robert Forman, 244–50. New York: Oxford University Press.

Perreira, Todd LeRoy. 2012. "Whence Theravāda? The Modern Genealogy of an Ancient Term." In *How Theravāda Is Theravāda? Exploring Buddhist Identities*, edited by Peter Skilling, Jason A. Carbine, Claudio Cicuzza, and Santi Pakdeekham, 443–71. Chiang Mai: Silkworm Books.

Perrett, Roy W. 2016. *An Introduction to Indian Philosophy*. Cambridge: Cambridge University Press.

Perrine, Timothy. 2014. "In Defense of Non-Reductionism in the Epistemology of Testimony." *Synthese* 191: 3227–37.

Perry, Ralph Barton. 1935. *The Thought and Character of William James*. Boston: Little, Brown & Co.

Phillips, Stephen H. 2001. "Could There Be Mystical Evidence for a Nondual Brahman? A Causal Objection." *Philosophy East and West* 51.4: 492–506.

Phillips, Stephen H. 2009. "From Yogic Integration and Control to Metaphysical Holism." In *Understanding Consciousness: Recent Advances*, edited by Swami Sarvabhutananda, 148–63. Kolkata: Ramakrishna Mission Institute of Culture.

Phillips, Stephen H. 2019. "Epistemology in Classical Indian Philosophy." *Stanford Encyclopedia of Philosophy*, http://plato.stanford.edu (accessed July 28, 2019).

Pinch, Adela. 2014–2015. "The Appeal of Panpsychism in Victorian Britain." *Romanticism and Victorianism on the Net* 65: 1–24.

Plantinga, Alvin. 2018. "Scientism: Who Needs It?" In *Scientism: Prospects and Problems*, edited by Jeroen De Ridder, Rik Peels, and René van Woudenberg, 221–32. Oxford: Oxford University Press.

Pollock, John L. and Joseph Cruz. 1986. *Contemporary Theories of Knowledge*. Savage, MD: Rowman & Littlefield.

Preti, Alan A. 2014. "*Brahmānubhava* as *Überpramāṇa* in Advaita Vedānta: Revisiting an Old Debate." *Philosophy East and West* 64.3: 718–39.

Pryor, James. 2000. "The Skeptic and the Dogmatist." *Noûs* 34.4: 517–49.

Race, Alan. 1983. *Christians and Religious Pluralism: Patterns in the Christian Theology of Religions*. London: SCM Press.

Raghuramaraju, A. 2015. "Universal Self, Equality and Hierarchy in Swami Vivekananda." *The Indian Economic and Social History Review* 52.2: 185–205.

Rahner, Karl. 1974. *Theological Investigations: Volume XII, Confrontations 2*, translated by David Bourke. New York: Seabury Press.

Rambachan, Anantanand. 1990. "Swami Vivekananda's Use of Science as an Analogy for the Attainment of *Mokṣa*." *Philosophy East and West* 40.3: 331–42.

Rambachan, Anantanand. 1991. *Accomplishing the Accomplished: The* Vedas *as a Source of Valid Knowledge in Śaṅkara*. Honolulu: University of Hawaii Press.

Rambachan, Anantanand. 1994a. *The Limits of Scripture: Vivekananda's Reinterpretation of the Vedas*. Honolulu: University of Hawaii Press.

Rambachan, Anantanand. 1994b. "Response to Professor Arvind Sharma." *Philosophy East and West* 44.4: 721–24.

Ram-Prasad, Chakravarthi. 2001. *Knowledge and Liberation in Classical Indian Thought*. Basingstoke, UK: Palgrave.

Reigle, David. 2015. "The Ātman-Brahman in Ancient Buddhism." In Kamaleswar Bhattacharya, *The Ātman-Brahman in Ancient Buddhism*, ix–xviii. Cotopaxi, CO: Canon Publications.

Reigle, David and Nancy Reigle. 2015. "*Ātman/Anātman* in Buddhism and Its Implication for the Wisdom Tradition." In David and Nancy Reigle, *Studies in the Wisdom Tradition*, 1–28. Cotopaxi, CO: Eastern School Press.

Rey, Georges. 1997. "A Question about Consciousness." In *The Nature of Consciousness: Philosophical Debates*, edited by Ned Block, Owen Flanagan, and Güven Güzeldere, 461–82. Cambridge, MA: MIT Press.

Rigopoulos, Antonio. 2019. "Tolerance in Swami Vivekānanda's Neo-Hinduism." *Philosophy and Social Criticism* 45.4: 438–60.

Rhys Davids, C. A. F. 1934. *Outlines of Buddhism*. London: Methuen.

Robinson, W. S. 2004. *Understanding Phenomenal Consciousness*. New York: Cambridge University Press.

Rosenberg, Alex. 2017. "Strong Scientism and its Research Agenda." In *Science Unlimited? The Challenges of Scientism*, edited by Maarten Boudry and Massimo Pigliucci, 203–24. Chicago: University of Chicago Press.

Rowe, William. 1982. "Religious Experience and the Principle of Credulity." *International Journal for Philosophy of Religion* 13: 85–92.

Rukmani, T. S., ed. 2007. *Yogavārttika of Vijñānabhikṣu: Volume 1, Samādhipāda*. Delhi: Munshiram Manoharlal.

Russell, Colin A. 2000. "The Conflict of Science and Religion." In *The History of Science and Religion in the Western Tradition*, edited Gary B. Ferngren, 12–17. New York: Garland Publishing.

Sadananda, Swami. 1931. *Vedāntasāra*, translated by Swami Nikhilananda. Mayavati: Advaita Ashrama.

Sankey, Howard. 2008. *Scientific Realism and the Rationality of Science*. Aldershot, UK: Ashgate.

Saradananda, Swami. 2003. *Sri Ramakrishna and His Divine Play*, translated by Swami Chetanananda. St. Louis: Vedanta Society of St. Louis.

Sarvapriyananda, Swami. 2011. "Ancient Wisdom, Modern Questions—Vedantic Perspectives in Consciousness Studies." In *Spirituality and Science of Consciousness*, edited by Swami Sarvabhutananda, 285–303. Kolkata: Ramakrishna Mission Institute of Culture.

Sastri, Sivanath. 1911. *History of the Brahmo Samaj: Volume I*. Calcutta: R. Chatterji.

Satprakashananda, Swami. 1978. *Swami Vivekananda's Contribution to the Present Age*. St. Louis: Vedanta Society of St. Louis.

Sāradānanda, Svāmī. [1909–1919] 2009. *Śrīśrīrāmakṛṣṇalīlāprasaṅga*. 2 vols. Kolkātā: Udbodhan.

Schaffer, Jonathan. 2010. "Monism: The Priority of the Whole." *Philosophical Review* 119.1: 31–76.

Scheffler, Samuel. 1999. "Conceptions of Cosmopolitanism." *Utilitas* 11.3: 255–76.

Schellenberg, J. L. 2005. *Prolegomena to a Philosophy of Religion*. Ithaca, NY: Cornell University Press.

Schmidt-Leukel, Perry. 2005. "Exclusivism, Inclusivism, Pluralism: The Tripolar Typology—Clarified and Reaffirmed." In *The Myth of Religious Superiority*, edited by Paul Knitter, 13–27. Maryknoll, NY: Orbis Books.

Schmidt-Leukel, Perry. 2007. *Understanding Buddhism*. Delhi: Pentagon Press.

Schmidt-Leukel, Perry. 2017. *Religious Pluralism and Interreligious Theology*. Maryknoll, NY: Orbis.

Schweizer, Paul. 1993. "Mind/Consciousness Dualism in Sāṅkhya-Yoga Philosophy." *Philosophy and Phenomenological Research* 53.4: 845–59.

Seager, William, ed. 2020. *The Routledge Handbook of Panpsychism*. London: Routledge.

Sen, Amiya P. 2013. *Swami Vivekananda*, second ed. New Delhi: Oxford University Press.

Sen, Keshub Chunder. 1901. *Lectures in India*. London: Cassell and Company.

Senor, Thomas D. 1996. "The Prima/Ultima Facie Distinction in Epistemology." *Philosophy and Phenomenological Research* 56.3: 551–66.

Shani, Itay. 2015. "Cosmopsychism: A Holistic Approach to the Metaphysics of Experience." *Philosophical Papers* 44.3: 389–437.

Shani, Itay. 2018. "Beyond Combination: How Cosmic Consciousness Grounds Ordinary Experience." *Journal of the American Philosophical Association* 4.3: 390–410.

Sharma, Arvind. 1992. "Is *Anubhava* a *Pramāṇa* According to Śaṅkara?" *Philosophy East and West* 42.3: 517–26.

Sharma, Arvind. 1998. *The Concept of Universal Religion in Modern Thought*. London: Macmillan.

Sharma, B. N. K. 1962. *Philosophy of Śrī Madhvācārya*. Delhi: Motilal Banarsidass.

Sharma, Jyotirmaya. 2013. *A Restatement of Religion: Swami Vivekananda and the Making of Hindu Nationalism*. New Haven, CT: Yale University Press.

Shear, Jonathan. 1997. "The Hard Problem: Closing the Empirical Gap." In *Explaining Consciousness: The Hard Problem*, edited by Jonathan Shear, 359–78. Cambridge, MA: MIT Press.

Siderits, Mark. 2011. "Buddhas as Zombies: A Buddhist Reduction of Subjectivity." In *Self, No Self? Perspectives from Analytical, Phenomenological, and Indian Traditions*,

edited by Mark Siderits, Evan Thompson, and Dan Zahavi, 308–31. New York: Oxford University Press.
Siegel, Susanna. 2012. "Cognitive Penetrability and Perceptual Justification." *Noûs* 46.2: 201–22.
Sil, Narasingha P. 1997. *Swami Vivekananda: A Reassessment.* Selinsgrove, PA: Susquehanna University Press.
Silins, Nicholas. 2015. "Perceptual Experience and Perceptual Justification." *Stanford Encyclopedia of Philosophy*, http://plato.stanford.edu (accessed July 29, 2019).
Singh, Jaideva. 1980. *Pratyabhijñāhṛdayam: The Secret of Self-Recognition.* Delhi: Motilal Banarsidass.
Sinha, Jadunath. 1934. *Indian Psychology: Perception.* London: Kegan Paul, Trench, Trubner & Co.
Skrbina, David. 2005. *Panpsychism in the West.* Cambridge, MA: MIT Press.
Smart, Ninian. 2009. "Models for Understanding the Relations between Religions." In *Ninian Smart on World Religions: Volume 2*, edited by John J. Shepherd, 268–77. Surrey: Ashgate.
Sorell, Tom. 1991. *Scientism: Philosophy and the Infatuation with Science.* London: Routledge.
Spencer, Herbert. 1862. *First Principles*, sixth ed. London: Watts & Co.
Srivastava, R. S. 1965. *Contemporary Indian Philosophy.* Delhi: Munshiram Manoharlal.
Stevens, John A. 2018. *Keshab: Bengal's Forgotten Prophet.* New York: Oxford University Press.
Stoeber, Michael. 1994. *Theo-Monistic Mysticism: A Hindu-Christian Comparison.* London: Macmillan.
Strawson, Galen. 2008. "Realistic Monism: Why Physicalism Entails Panpsychism." In Galen Strawson, *Real Materialism and Other Essays*, 53–74. Oxford: Clarendon.
Strawson, P. F. 1994. "Knowing From Words." In *Knowing From Words: Western and Indian Philosophical Analysis of Understanding and Testimony*, edited by Bimal Krishna Matilal and Arindam Chakrabarti, 23–28. Dordrecht: Springer.
Stubenberg, Leopold. 2016. "Neutral Monism." *Stanford Encyclopedia of Philosophy*, http://plato.stanford.edu (accessed December 7, 2020).
Swinburne, Richard. 1986. *The Evolution of the Soul.* Oxford: Oxford University Press.
Swinburne, Richard. 2004. *The Existence of God*, second ed. Oxford: Clarendon Press.
Śaṅkarācārya. 2007. *Brahmasūtram: Śāṅkarabhāṣyopetam.* Delhi: Motilal Banarsidass.
Śaṅkarācārya. 2011. *Īśādi Nau Upaniṣad: Śāṅkarabhāṣyārtha.* Gorakhpur: Gita Press.
Śaṅkarācārya. 2012. *Śrīmadbhagavadgītā Śāṅkarabhāṣya Hindī-anuvādasahita.* Gorakhpur: Gita Press.
Śaṅkarācārya. 2013. *Bṛhadāraṇyaka Upaniṣad.* Gorakhpur: Gita Press.
Śraddhānanda, Svāmī. 1994. *Bandi Tomāi: Ramakrishna-Vivekananda Bhāvāñjali.* Kolkata: Udbodhan.
Taber, John. 1981. "Reason, Revelation and Idealism in Śaṅkara's Vedānta." *Journal of Indian Philosophy* 9: 283–307.
Taber, John. 1992. "What Did Kumārila Bhaṭṭa Mean by *Svataḥ Prāmāṇya*?" *Journal of the American Oriental Society* 111.2: 204–21.
Taber, John. 2005. *A Hindu Critique of Buddhist Epistemology: Kumārila on Perception.* London: RoutledgeCurzon.
Tagore, Devendranath. 1916. *The Autobiography of Maharshi Devendranath Tagore*, translated by Satyendranath Tagore and Indira Devi. London: Macmillan.

Tapasyananda, Swami. 1988. *Adhyātma Rāmāyaṇa: Original Sanskrit with English Translation*. Mylapore, Madras: Sri Ramakrishna Math.

Tapasyananda, Swami. 1990. *Bhakti Schools of Vedānta*. Madras: Sri Ramakrishna Math.

Tapasyananda, Swami. 1995. "Vivekananda's Contribution to Vedantic Thought." In *Vivekananda: The Great Spiritual Teacher*, edited by Swami Bodhasarananda, 223–31. Kolkata: Advaita Ashrama.

Thagard, Paul. 2018. "Cognitive Science." *Stanford Encyclopedia of Philosophy*, http://plato.stanford.edu (accessed December 7, 2020).

Thibaut, George. 1890. *The Vedānta-Sūtras with the Commentary by Śaṅkarācārya: Part I*. Oxford: Clarendon.

Thompson, Evan. 2015. *Waking, Dreaming, Being*. New York: Columbia University Press.

Tolhurst, William. 1998. "Seemings." *American Philosophical Quarterly* 35.3: 293–302.

Tucker, Chris. 2010. "Why Open-Minded People Should Endorse Dogmatism." *Philosophical Perspectives* 24: 529–45.

Tucker, Chris, ed. 2013. *Seemings and Justification: New Essays on Dogmatism and Phenomenal Conservatism*. Oxford: Oxford University Press.

Turner, Frank M. 2010. "The Late Victorian Conflict of Science and Religion as an Event in Nineteenth-Century Intellectual and Cultural History." In *Science and Religion: New Historical Perspectives*, edited by Thomas Dixon, Geoffrey Cantor, and Stephen Pumfrey, 87–110. Cambridge: Cambridge University Press.

Tyagananda, Swami and Pravrajika Vrajaprana. 2010. *Interpreting Ramakrishna: Kālī's Child Revisited*. New Delhi: Motilal Banarsidass.

Tyndall, John. 1870. "On the Methods and Tendencies of Physical Investigation." In John Tyndall, *Scientific Addresses*, 5–19. New Haven, CT: Charles C. Chatfield & Co.

Udayanācārya. 1995. *Ātmatattvaviveka*, translated by N. S. Dravid. Shimla: Indian Institute of Advanced Study.

Vaidya, Anand. 2020. "A New Debate on Consciousness: Bringing Classical and Modern Vedānta into Dialogue with Contemporary Analytic Panpsychism." In *The Bloomsbury Research Handbook of Vedānta*, edited by Ayon Maharaj, 393–422. London: Bloomsbury.

Vaidya, Anand and Purushottama Bilimoria. 2015. "Advaita Vedānta and the Mind Extension Hypothesis: Panpsychism and Perception." *Journal of Consciousness Studies* 22.7–8: 1–24.

Van Inwagen, Peter. 1996. "'It Is Wrong, Everywhere, Always, and for Anyone, to Believe Anything upon Insufficient Evidence.'" In *Faith, Freedom, and Rationality*, edited by Jeff Jordan and Daniel Howard-Snyder, 137–54. Lanham, MD: Rowman & Littlefield.

Van Woudenberg, René. 2011. "Truths that Science Cannot Touch." *Philosophia Reformata* 76.2: 169–86.

Van Woudenberg, René. 2018. "An Epistemological Critique of Scientism." In *Scientism: Prospects and Problems*, edited by Jeroen De Ridder, Rik Peels, and René van Woudenberg, 167–89. Oxford: Oxford University Press.

Varela, Francisco J. and Jonathan Shear, eds. 1991. *The View from Within: First-Person Approaches to the Study of Consciousness*. Thorverton: Imprint Academic.

Vattanky, John. 1978. "Aspects of Early Nyāya Theism." *Journal of Indian Philosophy* 6: 393–404.

Vidyāraṇya, Svāmī. 1967. *Pañcadaśī*, translated by Swami Swahananda. Madras: Sri Ramakrishna Math.

Vidyāraṇya, Svāmī. 1996. *Jīvan-Mukti-Viveka*, translated by Swami Mokshadananda. Kolkata: Advaita Ashrama.

Vimuktananda, Swami, trans. 1938. *Aparokshanubhuti*. Mayavati: Advaita Ashrama.

Vitz, Rick. "Doxastic Voluntarism." 2019. *The Internet Encyclopedia of Philosophy*, http://www.iep.utm.edu/.

Vivekananda, Swami. [1957–1997] 2006–2007. *The Complete Works of Swami Vivekananda: Mayavati Memorial Edition*. 9 vols. Calcutta: Advaita Ashrama.

Vivekānanda, Svāmī. [1964] 2009. *Svāmī Vivekānander Vāṇī o Racanā*, fourth edition. 10 vols. Kolkātā: Udbodhan.

Wainwright, William. 1981. *Mysticism: A Study of Its Nature, Cognitive Value and Moral Implications*. Brighton, UK: Harvester Press.

Wallace, Alfred Russel. 1870. *Contributions to the Theory of Natural Selection*. New York: Macmillan & Co.

Wallace, Alfred Russel. 1889. *Darwinism*. London: Macmillan & Co.

Wallace, Alfred Russel. 1896. *Miracles and Modern Spiritualism*. London: George Redway.

Walser, Joseph. 2018. *Genealogies of Mahāyāna Buddhism*. London: Routledge.

Ward, Keith. 1972. *The Development of Kant's View of Ethics*. Oxford: Blackwell.

Warder, A. K. 2004. *Indian Buddhism*. Delhi: Motilal Banarsidass.

Wernham, James C. S. 1987. *James's Will-to-Believe Doctrine: A Heretical View*. Kingston: McGill-Queen's University Press.

Wernham, James C. S. 1990. "James's Faith-Ladder." *Journal of the History of Philosophy* 28.1: 105–14.

White, Andrew Dickson. 1896. *A History of the Warfare of Science with Theology*. London: Macmillan.

Williams, Richard N. and Daniel N. Robinson. 2015. *Scientism: The New Orthodoxy*. London: Bloomsbury.

Wood, Allen. 1978. *Kant's Rational Theology*. Ithaca, NY: Cornell University Press.

Wood, Allen. 1992. "Rational Theology, Moral Faith, and Religion." In *Cambridge Companion to Kant*, edited by Paul Guyer, 394–416. Cambridge: Cambridge University Press.

Woods, James Haughton, trans. 1914. *The Yoga-System of Patañjali*. Cambridge, MA: Harvard University Press.

Yandell, Keith. 1993. *The Epistemology of Religious Experience*. Cambridge: Cambridge University Press.

Zagzebski, Linda. 2008. "Omnisubjectivity." In *Oxford Studies in Philosophy of Religion*, vol. 1, edited by Jonathan L. Kvanvig, 231–47. New York: Oxford University Press.

Index

For the benefit of digital users, indexed terms that span two pages (e.g., 52–53) may, on occasion, appear on only one of those pages.

Note: Figures are indicated by *f* following the page number and Vivekananda's lectures are indicated by "(lecture)" and his essays are indicated by "(essay)"

Abjajānanda, Svāmī, 72
"Absolute and Manifestation, The" (lecture), 71–72, 351
Acceptance Principle (Burge), 206, 207, 208
Adhvarīndra, Dharmarāja, 169–70
Adhyātma-Rāmāyaṇa, 38–39, 51
Advaita Vedānta (Śaṅkara). *See also* Śaṅkarācārya (Śaṅkara)
  acceptance of *svataḥ-prāmāṇyavāda*, 164–65, 187
  Albahari on metaphysical framework based on, 364–70
  Bhāmatī school, 168, 191, 241
  contemporary scholarship on, 300–1
  infallibility of *pramāṇas*, 163–64
  Narendra's acceptance of, 23–25
  Ramakrishna's harmonization with Rāmānuja, 31–33
  Tagore on, 19–20
  tenets of, 22, 72
  validity of cognition, 185
  Vivaraṇa school, 168, 169–70
  Vivekananda on universal religion and, 101–6
  Vivekananda's harmonization with Dvaita and Viśiṣṭādvaita, 85–90
  Vivekananda's reconceptualization of, 43–90
AEV (Vivekananda's argument for the epistemic value of supersensuous perception), 9–10, 170–72
AEV$_s$. *See* argument for the epistemic value of supersensuous perception (AEV$_s$)
agnosticism, 2, 117–18, 124, 125, 128, 143–44, 182, 194
  of Buddha, 129–30
  of Kant, 243–44
  of Vivekananda, 249–54
  of William Hamilton, 247–48
"Agnosticism" (T. H. Huxley), 266, 273
Albahari, Miri, 11–12, 300–1, 363–70
al-Ḥallāj, Manṣur, 104
Alston, William, 11, 178
  "Audi on Nondoxastic Faith," 286
  "Belief, Acceptance, and Religious Faith," 286–88
  comparative analysis with Vivekananda on faith, 288–96
  direct experience of mystical perception of God, 177
  double standard, 200, 216, 221
  epistemic imperialism, 200, 203, 212, 217, 220, 221
  Perceiving God, 293
  response to crosscheckability objection, 198
  verification of religious claims, 202–3
Amarakośa, 131
antaḥkaraṇa (insentient mind), 316–17, 324, 326*f*, 328–31
anti-evidentialist fideism. *See* James, William
Aparokṣānubhūti, 37, 167–68, 225–26
Appiah, Kwame Anthony, 7
Aquinas, Thomas, 289
"Are We Automata?" (James), 308–9
Argument for Panentheistic Cosmopsychism (APC), 333–40. *See also* panentheistic cosmopsychism, Vivekananda's justification of
  "Cosmos" excerpt, 333–35
  design argument, 339
  evolution as preceded by involution, 336
  pre-existent effect doctrine (*satkāryavāda*), 335–38
  refutation of emergentism, 337
  scriptural support, 339–40
argument for the epistemic value of supersensuous perception (AEV$_s$), 9–10, 162–96, 255–56, 318
  overview, 162–63
  absence of rebutting and undercutting defeaters (premises 4 and 7), 193–96

argument for the epistemic value of supersensuous perception (AEVs) (*cont.*)
analysis in AEVs framework, 172–74, 176, 179, 183, 185–86, 193, 194, 195–96
Perception as Epistemic Justification (PEJ), 173, 180, 193, 194–95
perception as epistemic justification (premise 3), 178–86
perception of ultimate reality (premises 1 and 2), 174–78
perceptual testimony as epistemic justification (premise 6), 187–93
Perceptual Testimony as Epistemic Justification (PTEJ), 173, 180, 187, 194–95
Principle of Perceptual Proof (PP), 171–72, 173–74, 178, 179, 180–82, 187–89, 269–70, 274–75, 339–40
Principle of Testimonial Proof (TP), 172, 173–74, 180, 187–89, 269–70, 274–75, 339–40
reconstruction and refinement of Vivekananda's AEV, 170–74
traditional Indian *pramāṇa* epistemology and, 163–70
argument from religious experience (ARE), 256–57, 264, 274–75
arguments for God's existence, Vivekananda on 255–59
Aṣṭāvakra-Saṃhitā, 23–24, 37, 167–68
Audi, Robert, 198, 207–8
"Audi on Nondoxastic Faith" (Alston), 286
Aurobindo, Sri, 3–4, 48, 359–60, 369–70, 372–74, 375
Avadhūta-Gītā, 38–39, 167–68
Ayer, A. J., 149
Ādi Brāhmo Samāj, 20
Āpta (credible person)
criteria for, 188–89, 201, 216, 220–21
Vivekananda's descriptions of, 172, 174, 187, 189
"Ātman, The" (lecture), 71–72, 86–90

babhūva (becomes/manifests), 350
Baier, Karl, 40–41, 42
Bhattacharyya, K. C., 375
Beckerlegge, Gwilym, 77–78, 92–93, 372
"Belief, Acceptance, and Religious Faith" (Alston), 286–88
belief in God (stage 2 of Vivekananda's faith-ladder), 276, 280–83, 289
Bhagavad-Gītā, 18, 35–36, 38–39, 48, 49, 50, 74, 78–79, 80–81, 98–99, 102, 120, 166
bhakta, 30–31, 33, 56. *See also vijñāna* (special spiritual experience)
Bhakti-Yoga, 36, 78–84, 109
"Bhakti-Yoga" (lecture), 82
Bhakti-Yoga (Vivekananda), 36–37, 55–57, 81–82, 152–53
Bhartṛprapañca, 54
Bhattacharyya, K. C., 3–5, 7
Bhaṭṭa, Jayanta, 212–13
Bhaṭṭa, Kumārila
arguments against epistemic value of mystical testimony, 211–14
comparison of Vivekananda's views to, 214–17
conflicting claims objection and, 211–17
justification of *svataḥ-prāmāṇyavāda* (intrinsic validity of cognitions), 182
Bhaṭṭācārya Śāstrī, Dineścandra 75–76
Bhāgavata-Purāṇa, 18, 35–36, 38–39, 56
Bhushan, Nalini, 3–4, 48, 375
Bible
Alston's references to, 287–88, 294
quotations of, 290–91
supersensuous perception in, 174
Vivekananda's references to, 284–85, 293–94, 295–96
Biernacki, Loriliai, 324
"Body and Mind" (Clifford), 307
Bose, Rajnarayan, 146–47
Boudry, Maarten, 222–23
Brahman (ultimate reality). *See also* Śakti (personal God)
attainment of *brahmajñāna*, 37, 58, 73, 82–83, 168, 312
inseparability of Śakti from, 30–31, 38, 50–58, 329
Śaṅkara on, 52, 53, 54–55, 56, 67
Viśiṣṭādvaita doctrine of, 31–32, 67
Vivekananda on impersonal-personal God, 50–58, 75, 210, 227–28, 325
Brahmasūtra
Śaṅkara's commentary on, 59–60, 166–67, 169, 190, 225–26, 238, 239–41, 254–55
Vivekananda's commentary on, 39–40, 56–57, 72, 255, 350–51
Vivekananda's study of, 38–39, 48, 49, 102, 120
Brāhmo Samāj, 8, 19–25
debates over influence on Vivekananda, 17–18
leaders of, 19–21
rational monotheism of, 20, 22
social reform initiatives in, 20, 22

British rule of India, seen as divinely ordained, 20
Brogaard, Berit, 204–5
Brooke, John Hedley, 149–50
Brown, C. Mackenzie, 141, 162
Buddha
teachings on God and the soul, 129–30
as true *avatāra*, 74
Buddhism
  at Advaita stage, 105–6
  doctrine of yogic perception and, 211, 213
  perception of ultimate reality, 165
  Ramakrishna on, 39
  refutes Nyāya design arguments, 237–39
  non-substantialist understandings of ultimate reality, 129–35
  Vivekananda on, 39, 93, 129–35
"Buddhistic India" (lecture), 129–30
Burge, Tyler, 198, 206, 207, 208, 215
Burke, Marie Louise, 3, 101

Caitanya, 39–40, 74
Candrakīrti, 131–32
casteism, Vivekananda's critique of, 39, 73, 74
Catholic tradition, 373–74
Cārvāka school, 164
Chalmers, David J., 11, 299–300, 303, 319–20, 324
Chatterjee, Bankimchandra, 258–59
Chatterjee, Satischandra, 45
Christianity. *See also* Bible
  Alston on belief vs. acceptance in faith, 287–88, 294–95
  Darwin's theory of evolution and, 142–43
  at Dvaita stage, 105–6
  monotheistic God in, 95–96
  original sin doctrine, 290–91
  purification of mind through social service, 117
  Ramakrishna's practice of, 109–10
  sinner vs. divinity of the soul, 68–69
  suppression of Advaitic spiritual experience, 104
  Vivekananda on New Testament, 104
Chudnoff, Elijah, 204–5
Clifford, W. K., 267, 270, 285, 301, 311
  as advocate of panpsychism, 300, 307–9
  belief-agnosticism of, 273
  "Body and Mind," 307
  "Ethics of Belief, The," 265–66
  evidentialism of, 11, 264
  on evolution, 337–38
Closed Inclusivism about Truth$_f$ (CIT$_f$), 96–97
Cohen, L. Jonathan, 286
Coleman, Sam, 345–46, 364
"Common Bases of Hinduism, The" (lecture), 70–71
compassion to all beings, 27
Complete Works of Swami Vivekananda
  critique of editorial treatment of, 3
  Nivedita's introduction, 88
  philosophical ideas and arguments, 2–3
  references to agnostic/agnosticism in, 272–73
  references to *līlā* (sportive play of God) in, 350–51
  references to science of religion in, 146–47
Comte, Auguste, 143, 152–53, 230–31
conflicting claims objection to AEV$_s$, 198–99, 209–17, 361–63
conscious automata (T. H. Huxley), 306–7, 320–21
consciousness. *See also* panentheistic cosmopsychism; panentheistic cosmopsychism, Vivekananda's justification of
  Chalmers on easy vs. hard problems of, 299–300
  late nineteenth-century Western views on, 305–11
  neurobiological theory of, 319–20
  philosophical theories of, 302–5
conservation of energy law, 336–37
constructivism (theory of mystical experience), 226–30
Contributions to the Theory of Natural Selection (Wallace), 309–11
cosmic consciousness, 304, 316, 329, 330. *See also* panentheistic cosmopsychism, Vivekananda's justification of
"Cosmology" (lecture), 154, 155–56
cosmopolitan consciousness, 3–5
cosmopolitan Vedānta, epilogue, 372–76
cosmopsychism (theory of consciousness), 304
"Cosmos: The Macrocosm, The" (lecture), 257, 299, 333–40. *See also* panentheistic cosmopsychism, Vivekananda's justification of
Crick, Francis, 319–20
critical trust (Hick), 181–82
Critique of Pure Reason (Kant), 243–46, 250–51
crosscheckability objection to AEV$_s$, 198, 199–203, 220–21
Cruz, Joseph, 193–94

Darwin, Charles, 142–43, 149–50, 248–49, 258–59, 308. *See also* evolution through natural selection
Darwinism (Wallace), 309–10

Dasgupta, R. K., 45
Dasgupta, Surendranath, 331
Dasti, Matthew, 237–38
Datta, Bhupendranath, 21–22
Datta, Mahendranāth, 21
Datta, Narendranāth (pre-monastic name).
  acts in *Nava Vṛndāvan* play, 21
  association with Sādhāran Brāhmo Samāj, 21–22, 23
  early education of, 1–2
  early phase (1878–1884): from Brāhmo theism to Advaita Vedānta, 18, 19–25
  later phase (1884–1886): from acosmic Advaita to Integral Advaita, 18, 25–35
  Ramakrishna's descriptions of, 22–23, 28–30, 34
  Ramakrishna's direct instructions to, 28, 30, 31, 33, 34–35, 45–46, 144
  Ramakrishna's influence on, 8, 17–42
  skepticism about religion as college student, 143–45, 251–52, 279
  spiritual experiences of, 22–23, 24–25, 28–29, 228–29
Datta, Viśvanāth (father of Vivekananda), 1–2, 28
Davis, Caroline Franks, 195
debilitating relativism (Race), 135
decombination problem for cosmopsychism, 363–64, 365–66, 369
deification of world, Vivekananda's 58–68
deism, 258–59
De Michelis, Elizabeth, 17, 21–22, 40–41, 42, 146–47
"Demise of the Demarcation Problem, The" (Laudan), 222–23
De Ridder, Jeroen, 148
Descartes, René, 178–79, 224, 273–74, 302–3
design argument, 235, 236–39, 240–41, 257–59, 339, 341–42
Deussen, Paul, 77–78, 372
Deutsch, Eliot, 164–65
Devī, Bhuvaneśvarī, 1–2
Didemonico, David, 204–5
"Discourses on Jñāna-Yoga" (lecture), 58
Divine Cosmic Consciousness, 328–31, 346–47, 349–50, 368–69. *See also* panentheistic cosmopsychism, Vivekananda's justification of
Divine Ground (A. Huxley), 366–67
Divine Mother. *See* Śakti (personal God)
"Divine Mother, The" (lecture), 53–54
divine omniscience, 356, 357–58, 359, 364, 369–70
Divine Oneness. *See* Integral Advaita (of Vivekananda)
Divine Reality. *See* Brahman (ultimate reality)
divine self-limitation (Aurobindo), 359–60
Doore, G. L., 267–68
double standard (Alston), 200, 216, 221
doxastic involuntarism, 264–96. *See also* faith
doxastic voluntarism, 11, 282, 287
Draper, John William, 142–43
Dreams of a Spirit Seer (Kant), 244
Dutt, Akshay Kumar, 146–47
Dvaita Vedānta (Madhva)
  Vivekananda on universal religion and, 101–6
  Vivekananda's harmonization of, 70–72, 85–90

eisegesis, 49
eliminativism (theory of consciousness), 302, 314–15, 366
emergentism (theory of consciousness), 337–39
epiphenomenalist dualism (theory of consciousness), 303, 306–8, 323–24. *See also* Clifford, W. K.; Huxley, Thomas Henry
epistemic imperialism (Alston), 200, 203, 212, 217, 220
ethical behavior, Vivekananda on, 201
ethical humanism, 124, 125
"Ethics of Belief, The" (Clifford), 265–66
ethics of Oneness. *See* Integral Advaita (of Vivekananda)
evidentialism. *See* Clifford, W. K.; Huxley, Thomas Henry
evil
  rational response to problem of, 259–63
  Vijñāna Vedānta on, 261–62
evolution through natural selection
  Darwin on, 308–9, 336–37
  emergentism vs., 337–39
  Huxley as proponent of, 323
  Wallace on, 309–11
exact sciences, 156–57
Exclusivism about Salvation (ES), 94
Exclusivism about Truth$_f$ (ET$_f$), 96
Exclusivism about Truth$_p$ (ET$_p$), 95–96
exclusivism/inclusivism/pluralism typology (Race), 91. *See also* religious cosmopolitanism, and Vivekananda's harmony of religions
expanded evidentialism, 11, 274–75
explanatory gap (Levine), 300, 306
extrinsic validity of cognitions. *See parataḥ-prāmāṇyavāda* (extrinsic validity of cognitions doctrine)

faith
faith-as-belief (stage 2 of Vivekananda's faith-ladder), 276, 280–83, 289
faith as self-authenticating realization (stage 3 of Vivekananda's faith-ladder), 283–85, 293, 296
faith as sub-doxastic intellectual assent (stage 1 of Vivekananda's faith-ladder), 276–80, 282, 289, 291–92
stages of faith, 11, 264–65
T.H. Huxley's views on, 266–67
Vivekananda's views on, 272–96
W. James's views on, 267–72
W.K. Clifford's views on, 265–66
"Faith and the Right to Believe" (James), 268, 270
faith-healing, 41–42
faith-ladder (James), 271–72, 285.
faith-ladder, of Vivekananda, 275–76, 285. *See also* faith
Fales, Evan, 199–200, 222–23
Fermat's Last Theorem, 159–60
fetishism, 125–26
First Principles (Spencer), 247
"Four Paths of Yoga" (essay), 82–83, 109
four Yogas as direct paths to liberation, Vivekananda's doctrine of, 78–84, 93, 106–23, 138
Fox, George, 267
Frederick, Norris, 268–69
free lunch constraint (Goff), 346–47
Fricker, Elizabeth, 206, 207–8, 215
frogs in a well analogy (*kūpa-maṇḍuka*), 6
"Fundamentals of Religion, The" (essay), 126, 151–53
"Future of India, The" (lecture), 120

Gadamer, Hans-Georg, 376
Gale, Richard, 199
Gambhīrānanda, Svāmī, 75–76
Ganeri, Jonardon, 4–5
Garfield, Jay L., 3–4, 48, 375
Gasparri, Luca, 300–1
Gauḍapāda, 365–67
Ghoṣāl, Bipin Bihārī, 37
"God in Everything" (lecture), 62–64, 66
Goff, Philip, 304–5, 338, 346–47, 354–55, 369
Gold, Jonathan C., 131–32
Gospel of Sri Ramakrishna, The (Gupta), 367
Gosvāmī, Vijayakṛṣṇa, 20
"Great Teachers of the World, The" (lecture), 184–85
Green, Thomas J., 44–45, 92–93, 230–31, 372
Gregg, Stephen, 91
Griffiths, Paul, 92, 94, 96
Grinshpon, Yohanan, 192–93
grounding by self-limitation, Vivekananda on, 11–12, 346–56
grounding by subsumption (Goff), 346, 354–55, 369–70
gullibility objection, 198, 206–9
Gupta, Mahendranāth, 21, 23, 32, 250
Gutting, Gary, 201, 220–21
gymnasium analogy, 236, 260, 261

Haack, Susan, 147, 154
Hacker, Paul, 77–78, 372, 374, 375
Haeckel, Ernst, 149–50
Halbfass, Wilhelm, 100
Hamilton, William, 194, 235–36
critique of, 247–48, 266
learned ignorance, 250, 252–53, 262–63, 279
Lectures on Metaphysics and Logic, 245, 250
On the Philosophy of the Unconditioned, 245–47
Hanumān, Ramakrishna on, 85–86
hard problem of consciousness (Chalmers), 11. *See also* panentheistic cosmopsychism
contemporary responses to, 302–5
harmony of religions, Vivekananda's doctrine of, 91–138. *See also* religious cosmopolitanism of Vivekananda
four Yogas at basis of universal religion (1895–1901), 93, 106–23, 138
nuances of final religious pluralist position, 93, 129–35
questions regarding final views, 93, 124–28
scholarly debates over, 91–93
three Vedāntic stages at basis of universal religion (1894–1895), 92–93, 101–6
"Harmony of Religions" (lecture), 100–1
Harvard University lectures, by Vivekananda, 106–7, 133, 268–69
Hastie, William, 2
Hatcher, Brian, 374, 375
Haṭha-Yoga, 125–26
hermeneutic method, of Vivekananda, 48–50
Hesychios, Saint, 293–94
Hick, John, 93, 126, 135–37, 181–82, 373–74
Hinduism
distinguished from Vedānta, 119–21
God-realization, 117
"Hinduism and Sri Ramakrishna" (essay), 120–21, 154–56
"Hindu Religion, The" (lecture), 356
"Hints on Practical Spirituality" (lecture), 65–66

History of the Conflict between Religion and Science (Draper), 142–43
History of the Warfare of Science with Theology, A (White), 142–43
Hohner, Terrance, 3
Hume, David, 149, 152, 178–79
Huxley, Aldous, 364–65, 366–68
Huxley, Thomas Henry, 149–50, 270, 285, 301
  "Agnosticism," 266, 273
  epiphenomenalism of, 306–7, 320–21
  evidentialism of, 11, 264, 266–67
  James's critique of, 308–9
  "Value of Witness to the Miraculous, The," 267
  Vivekananda on materialist views of, 322–23
  Vivekananda's critique of agnosticism of, 274–75
  Vivekananda's critique of scientism of, 230–31
  Vivekananda's study of, 142–43, 272, 311
  Wallace's critique of, 310–11
hypnotism, 41–42

"Ideal of a Universal Religion, The" (lecture), 79–80, 114–16, 119, 125–26
"Ideal of Karma-Yoga, The" (lecture), 108–9, 138
Ideal Unit Abstraction (IUA), 124–25, 161
Imitation of Christ, The (Thomas à Kempis), 38–39
immanentism, 338–39
immersive cosmopolitanism (Bhattacharyya), 4–5
impersonal-personal God, 50–58, 75, 210, 227–28, 229–30, 312–13, 361. *See also* Brahman (ultimate reality); Śakti (personal God)
Inclusivism about Salvation (IS), 94–95, 102–3, 113
Inclusivism about Truth$_f$ (IT$_f$), 96, 102–3, 104, 106, 121, 122, 128
Inclusivism about Truth$_p$ (IT$_p$), 95
incredulous stare objection to panpsychism (Goff), 305
Indian National Congress, 20
indirect mystical experience (Kant), 244
individuation problem, 304, 345–56
  Vivekananda's grounding by self-limitation and, 11–12, 345–56
inference from the ordinary (McCrea), 212
Infinite Paths to Infinite Reality (Maharaj), 25, 186, 210, 228, 229, 259, 312
innate divinity of the soul, 68–72
insentient mind (*antaḥkaraṇa*), 316–17, 324, 326*f*, 328–31
insentient Prakṛti as creator doctrine, of Sāṃkhya, 325–27
insider-outsider scholarship dichotomy, 12–13
Inspired Talks (Vivekananda), 284
Integral Advaita (of Vivekananda), 8, 43–90
  overview, 45–47
  four Yogas as direct paths to liberation, 78–84
  harmonization of Dvaita, Viśiṣṭādvaita, and Advaita, 50, 85–90
  impersonal-personal God, 50–58, 75, 210, 227–28, 229–30
  innate divinity of the soul, 68–72
  legacy of Ramakrishna passes to Swami Vivekananda, 18, 38–42
  Practical Vedānta and ethics of Oneness, 73–78
  Ramakrishna's scriptural support for, 18, 35–37
  scholarly debates over Vivekananda's Vedānta philosophy, 43–45
  two-pronged hermeneutic method, 48–50
  world as real manifestation of God, 58–68
intellectual assent (stage 1 of Vivekananda's faith-ladder), 276–80, 282, 289, 291–92
intellectual slavery, 4–5
interactionist substance dualism (theory of consciousness), 302–3, 323–24, 341, 343–44
intrinsic validity of cognitions. *See svataḥ-prāmāṇyavāda* (intrinsic validity of cognitions doctrine)
"Introduction to Jñāna-Yoga" (lecture), 258–59
involution. *See* Argument for Panentheistic Cosmopsychism (APC)
Iqbal, Muhammad, 375
Isherwood, Christopher, 21
Islam
  at Dvaita stage, 105–6
  monotheistic God in, 95–96
  Ramakrishna's practice of, 109–10
  suppression of Advaitic spiritual experience, 104
  universal brotherhood, 117
"Is Vedānta the Future Religion?" (lecture), 174–75
Īśā Upaniṣad, comparison of interpretations by Vivekananda and Śaṅkara, 62–64

Jainism, 124, 125, 127, 213, 214, 239
James, William, 11, 301
  anti-evidentialist fideism of, 264
  "Are We Automata?" 308–9
  comparison of Vivekananda's faith-ladder to, 275–76
  critique of epiphenomenalist dualism, 308–9

"Faith and Reason to Believe," 268, 270
faith-ladder, 271–72, 285
on genuine religion option, 267–72
pluralistic pansychism, 309
Pragmatism, 270
Principles of Psychology, The, 308–9, 318, 337–38
pure experience, 309
"Reason and Faith," 268, 270–71, 285
on Tyndall's quotation, 305
Varieties of Mystical Experience, The, 177, 269, 270
Vivekananda's influence on, 268–72, 275, 311
"The Will to Believe," 267–68, 269, 270, 275
Jīvanmuktiviveka, 37
jñāna, Ramakrishna contrasts with *vijñāna*, 25–27, 30–35, 58, 63–64, 312–13
Jñāna-Yoga, 36, 78–84, 109, 113, 133
Judaism, monotheistic God in, 95–96

Kant, Immanuel, 10.
Critique of Pure Reason, 243–46, 250–51
on design argument, 258
Dreams of a Spirit Seer, 244
Only Possible Argument in Support of a Demonstration of the Existence of God, The, 243
Religion within the Bounds of Reason Alone, 245
on unknowability of the Absolute, 235–36, 242–43
Vivekananda's dialectical stance toward, 250–53
Vivekananda's study of, 143, 170, 194
Kapila, 316, 325–26
karma and rebirth, 259, 260–61, 290–91, 316–17
Karma-Yoga, 78–84, 109, 134
"Karma-Yoga" (lecture), 78, 128
Karma-Yoga (Vivekananda), 83–84
Kathāmṛta (Gupta), 21, 23, 32, 241
Katz, Steven, 226–27, 228, 229
Kaṭha Upaniṣad, 38–39
Kālī. *See* Śakti (personal God)
Kenny, Carolyn, 3
Killingley, Dermot, 372
King, Richard, 131–32
knowledge by identity, 224–26
knowledge by objectification, 224–25
Koch, Christof, 319–20
Kopf, David, 21
Koran, 174
Kṛṣṇa, 85–86
Kumārila, 182, 209–17
Kuṇḍalinī, awakening of
Ramakrishna on, 348–50
Vivekananda on, 352–53, 354

Lackey, Jennifer, 206–7, 208–9, 215
Larson, Gerald James, 335–36
Laudan, Larry, 148, 150, 152–53, 222–23
learned ignorance (Hamilton), 250, 252–53, 262–63, 279
Lectures on Metaphysics and Logic (Hamilton), 245, 250
Leibniz, G. W., 243, 251, 300
"Lessons on Bhakti-Yoga" (lecture), 117–18
"Lessons on Rāja-Yoga" (essay), 252–53
Levine, Joseph, 299–300, 306
Liberation and Spiritual Practice (Ghoṣāl), 37
Life Divine, The (Aurobindo), 48, 359–60
Lightman, Bernard, 272–73
Limits of Scripture, The (Rambachan), 217
Lipton, Peter, 344–45
Liston, Michael, 147–48
līlā (sportive play of God), 34, 347–48, 350–51, 358–59
Locke, John, 149, 289

Madaio, James, 37, 373
Madhva, 56
magnet analogy, 280–82
Maharaj, Nisargadatta, 366–67
Maharaja of Cooch Behar, 20
Maharshi, Ramana, 366–67
Mahābhārata, 38–39
Mahāyāna Buddhism, 130–35
manifestationist paradigm (Ramakrishna), 228, 229–30
Manusmṛti, 38–39
materialist reductionism (theory of consciousness), 340–41
Matilal, B. K., 163–64
Mavrodes, George, 136
Mazoomdar, Pratap Chandra, 21–22
māyā
individuating principle of, 11–12, 32, 33, 34, 351
Ramakrishna on, 347–48, 349–50
Śaiva Nondualists on, 359
Śaṅkara on, 59–60, 65–66, 68
Vivekananda on, 59–61, 63, 64–67, 68, 351–52, 353–54
"Māyā and Freedom" (lecture), 66–67
"Māyā and Illusion" (lecture), 59–60
McCrea, Larry, 212, 214
McGinn, Colin, 302, 306

McKim, Robert, 92, 94, 95–96, 121–23, 134–35
"Meditation" (lecture), 352
mental illness, 194–95
metagnosticism, 252–53
metaphysical dualism of Puruṣa and Prakṛti, of Sāṃkhya, 327–28, 344
"Methods and Purpose of Religion, The" (lecture), 107–8, 119–20, 279–80
micropsychism (theory of consciousness), 304, 363
"Mill, Darwin and Hinduism" (Chatterjee), 258
Mill, John Stuart, 10
  critique of, 247–49
  design argument, 258–59, 339
  Three Essays on Religion, 142–43, 248–49, 261
  Vivekananda's rejection of empiricist thesis of, 152
  Vivekananda's study of, 142–43, 235–36, 242
mind-body dualism (theory of consciousness), 302–3, 341
mind-brain dualism (theory of consciousness). *See* interactionist substance dualism
mind-brain identity theory (theory of consciousness), 343–44
mind-consciousness dualism of Sāṃkhya, 313–24, 341, 343–44
  Vivekananda's provisional defense of, 313–24
Minds without Fear (Bhushan and Garfield), 375
Miśra, Vācaspati, 168
Mīmāṃsā. *See svataḥ-prāmāṇyavāda* (intrinsic validity of cognitions doctrine), Kumārila, Pārthasārathimiśra
Modern India (Vivekananda), 6
Mukerji, A. C., 375
multiple Puruṣas doctrine, of Sāṃkhya, 325
Munton, Jessie, 198, 205–6
Murti, T. R. V., 131–32
"My Master" (lecture), 256–57
mysterianism (theory of consciousness), 302, 306
mystical experience, three types of, 175
mystical testimony. *See* argument for the epistemic value of supersensuous perception (AEV_s)
Mysticism and Philosophical Analysis (Katz), 226–27, 228
mythology, in religion, 127

Nagel, Thomas, 299, 302, 303–4, 307, 314–15, 338, 340–41
"Naturalness of Bhakti-Yoga, The" (lecture), 80–81
Nava Vidhān (New Dispensation), Brāhmo Samāj sect, 20–21
Nava Vṛndāvan (play), 21
Nāgārjuna, 131–32
Nārada, 26–27
"Necessity of Religion, The" (lecture), 3, 124–25, 133–34
Neo-Hindus/Hinduism, use of term, 372, 376
Neo-Vedānta, use of term, 372–75, 376
neutral monism (theory of consciousness), 305
Nickles, Thomas, 158, 222–23
nirvāṇa, 39, 85–86, 134–35
nirvikalpa samādhi
  basis for Vivekananda's focus on meditation and, 37
  ontological reality of Divine Mother and, 54
  Ramakrishna on Kuṇḍalinī-Yoga as means to, 348–50
  Ramakrishna on *vijñāna* and, 26, 30–31, 34–35, 360–61
  Rambachan's critique of Vivekananda's views on, 223–26
  Vivekacūḍāmaṇi on, 168–69
  Vivekananda on divine visions vs., 183
  Vivekananda on service to *jīvas* and, 76–77
  Vivekananda's experience of, 22–23, 25, 194–95, 228–29, 368–69
Nivedita, Sister (M. Noble), 35, 47, 88–90
non-origination doctrine (*ajāta*), 365–66, 368
"Notes Taken Down in Madras" (essay), 189
numerosity, perception of (Munton), 205–6
Nyāya
  direct perception (*pratyakṣa*), 171–72
  rational theology and design argument, 235, 236–38, 240–41
  validity of cognition, 163–64, 185
Nyāyasūtra (Gautama), 38–39
Nyāya-Vaiśeṣika, 165–66

Oakes, Robert, 186
occasional spiritual interventionism doctrine (Wallace), 309–10
ocean-wave analogy, 53–54, 65–66, 210–11, 351–52
O'Hear, Anthony, 199–200
Okasha, Samir, 147
omnipotence. *See* divine omniscience
omnisubjectivity (Zagzebski), 358
"One Existence Appearing as Many" (lecture), 64, 353
oneness. *See* Integral Advaita (of Vivekananda)

Only Possible Argument in Support of a Demonstration of the Existence of God, The (Kant), 243
On the Origin of Species (Darwin), 142–43
On the Philosophy of the Unconditioned (Hamilton), 245–47
Open Inclusivism about Truth$_f$ (OIT$_f$), 97, 122–23
Open Pluralism about Truth$_f$ (OPT$_f$), 97, 101, 117
other observers test, 199–200, 202–3

Padmapāda, 168
Paley, William, 240–41, 249–50, 257
panentheistic cosmopsychism (theory of consciousness) 11, 261–62, 299–331
  overview, 299–301
  diagram of Vivekananda's framework for, 330*f*
  mystical grounding of, by Ramakrishna, 311–13
  Vivekananda on Sāṃkhya-Vedāntic metaphysics of, 324–31
  Vivekananda's diagram of Vedāntic cosmology, 328
panentheistic cosmopsychism, Vivekananda's justification of, 11–12, 332–71
  overview, 332–33
  addressing objections to, 356–63
  Albahari's views and, 363–70
  Argument for Panentheistic Cosmopsychism (APC), 333–40
  grounding by self-limitation and individuation problem, 345–56
  Ramakrishna on manifestations of Divine Consciousness, 347–52
  refinement and development of APC, 340–45
  six potential advantages, 370–71
panprotopsychism (theory of consciousness), 305, 307–8, 318
panpsychism (theory of consciousness)
  advocates of, 300, 303–4
  Clifford on, 307–8
  cross-cultural work on, 300–1
  definitions of, 304
  genetic arguments for, 338
  James on, 318
  two forms of, 304
  Wallace's refutation of, 338–39
Pañcadaśī (Vidyāraṇya), 37, 38–39, 167–68, 225–26
"Paper on Hinduism" (lecture), 68–69, 91, 97–100, 101, 102–3, 107, 175, 184
parataḥ-prāmāṇyavāda (extrinsic validity of cognitions doctrine), 164, 185
pariṇāmavāda doctrine, 67, 68
Parliament of the World's Religions, Chicago (1893)
  "Paper on Hinduism" lecture, 68–69, 91, 97–100, 101, 102–3, 107, 175, 184
Pascal, Blaise, 281–82
Patañjali, 70, 157, 165, 170, 192. *See also* *Yogasūtra* (Patañjali)
Paul, Saint, 290–91, 294
pāramārthika-vyāvahārika doctrine, 57
Pārthasārathimiśra, 9–10, 164, 165–66, 171–72, 192, 211, 237–38
Peels, Rik, 147, 148
Perceiving God (Alston), 293
Perception as Epistemic Justification (PEJ), 173, 180, 193, 194–95, 198, 199, 203, 205–6
perception of ultimate reality. *See* argument for the epistemic value of supersensuous perception (AEV$_s$)
perceptual dogmatism (Pryor), 204
Perceptual Testimony as Epistemic Justification (PTEJ), 173, 180, 187, 194–95, 206, 207–9, 215. *See also* argument for the epistemic value of supersensuous perception (AEV$_s$)
Perennial Idealism (Albahari), 11–12, 363–70
perennialism (theory of mystical experience), 226–30
Perennial Philosophy, The (A. Huxley), 366–68
permanent mysterianism (McGinn), 302, 306
Perovich, Anthony, 229
Perrine, Timothy, 208–9, 215
perspective problem (Albahari), 364
phenomenal seemings (Brogaard), 204–5
Phenomenological Indiscernibility Postulate (PIP) (Oakes), 186
Phillips, Stephen, 163–64
Plantinga, Alvin, 149, 152–53
Pluralism about Salvation (PS), 94–95, 99, 101, 103, 104–5, 112–13, 114, 115, 116, 121, 122, 123, 126, 133, 135
Pluralism about Truth$_f$ (PT$_f$), 96, 97, 98–99, 114, 115, 116, 121, 122, 123, 133
Pluralism about Truth$_p$ (PT$_p$), 95–96
pluralistic pansychism (James), 309
Pollock, John, 193–94
positive reasons, for belief in testimony (Lackey), 206–7
Practical Vedānta, 27–28, 73–78, 372
"Practical Vedānta" (lectures), 53, 57–58, 59, 60–61, 75–78, 88, 152–53, 210

Pragmatism (James), 270
Prajñāpāramitāsūtra, 38–39, 131
"Prakṛti and Puruṣa" (lecture), 344
pramāṇa epistemology, 163–70
pratyāhāra, 41–42
predictive efficacy test, 199–200, 202
pre-existent effect doctrine (*satkāryavāda*), 335–38
"Preparatory and Supreme Bhakti Yoga" (lecture), 280–82
Preti, Alan, 168
Principle of Credulity (Swinburne), 180–81, 182, 188–89
Principle of Perceptual Proof (PP), 171–72, 173–74, 178, 179, 180–82, 187–89, 211, 217, 218–19, 269–70, 274–75, 339–40
Principle of Testimonial Proof (TP), 172, 173–74, 180, 187–89, 206, 207, 211, 217, 218–19, 269–70, 274–75, 339–40
Principle of Testimony (Swinburne), 188–89
Principles of Psychology, The (James), 308–9, 318, 337–38
problem of evil, Vivekananda's rational response to, 259–63
property dualism (theory of consciousness), 303
proto-consciousness, 305
Pryor, James, 204
pure experience (James), 309

Race, Alan, 91, 135
Radhakrishnan, Sarvepalli, 372, 375
radical emergence, 303–4
Rahner, Karl, 373–74
"Ramakrishna" (lecture), 85
Ramakrishna, Sri. *See also* Vijñāna Vedānta (Ramakrishna)
  claims to see God, 144
  on conflicting claims objection, 210
  descriptions of Narendra, 22–23, 28–30, 34
  direct instruction of Narendra, 28, 30, 31, 33, 34–35, 45–46, 250
  on divine manifestation, 347–52
  on four beneficial forms of reasoning, 241–42
  imparting of spiritual experience to Narendra, 24–25
  influence on Vivekananda, 10, 11–12, 192–93, 280–82
  on Kālī, 30
  Keshab's relationship with, 20–22
  manifestationist approach to mystical experience, 228, 229–30
  mystical grounding of panentheistic cosmopsychism by, 311–13
  practice of multiple traditions, 109–10, 144–45, 210
  reason and supersensuous realities, 235, 236, 241–42
  on Śaṅkarācārya, 73
  on Tantric Kuṇḍalini-Yoga, 348–50
  teachings of, 69, 73, 74, 76–77, 80–82, 84, 85–86, 88–89, 110–11, 113–14, 117, 259–60, 261–62, 356, 369–70
  Vivekananda's descriptions of, 74, 118, 174, 175–76, 177–78
Ramakrishna and His Disciples (Isherwood), 21
Ramakrishna Mission, 40, 77
"Ramakrishna Paramahamsa" (lecture), 109–10, 111–13, 122
Rambachan, Anantanand, 82–83, 84, 141, 166, 167, 192–93, 217–31
rational agnosticism, defined, 255.
Ratnakūṭasūtra, 131–32
Rāja-Yoga, 78–84, 109, 125–26, 314–16, 317–18, 319
Rāja-Yoga (Vivekananda), 345
  on belief-agnosticism, 273–75
  on divinity of soul, 70
  on "eight- limbed" (*aṣṭāṅga*) procedure in *Yogasūtra*, 157–59
  on faith as self-authenticating realization, 284
  on faith-healers and hypnotism, 41–42
  on four Yogas as direct paths, 79, 126
  on Haṭha-Yoga, 125–26
  James's study of, 271
  on limits of reason, 194, 250–51
  on lower vs. higher visions, 183–84
  on scope of theological reason, 249–50
  on scripture as testimony, 192, 269–70
  on supersensuous perception, 151, 162, 341
  on three means of knowledge (*pramāṇas*), 170
  on verification of religious claims, 201–2, 268–69
  on wide empiricism, 156
Rāmānuja, 31–32, 56, 69–70, 74
"Real and the Apparent Man, The" (lecture), 65–66
real faith. *See* realization (stage 3 of Vivekananda's faith-ladder)
"Realisation" (lecture), 58–59, 283–84
realization (stage 3 of Vivekananda's faith-ladder), 276, 283–85
"Real Nature of Man, The" (lecture), 320–21, 354
reason, limitations of, 194, 249–55
"Reason and Faith" (James), 268, 270–71, 285

"Reason and Religion" (lecture), 186, 338–39
reductionism, 302, 303–4, 314–15
Reid, Thomas, 245
Reigle, David, 131–32
religion, criteria of, 125, 161
"Religion and Science" (lecture), 119, 153, 227
"Religions of India, The" (lecture), 103, 105–6
Religion within the Bounds of Reason Alone (Kant), 245
religious atheists, 277, 278–79, 294–95
religious cosmopolitanism of Vivekananda, 8–9, 91–138. *See also* harmony of religions, Vivekananda's doctrine of
  contemporary relevance, 93, 135–38
  four main facets of, 117–23
religious doctrine, as subordinate to spiritual experience, 142–46
religious faith. *See* faith
religious fanaticism and conflict, 146
religious pluralism. *See also* religious cosmopolitanism of Vivekananda
  Hick's quasi-Kantian theory of, 135–37
  Ramakrishna on, 32–33
  Schmidt-Leukel's fractal theory of, 137–38
  in Vivekananda's harmony of religions doctrine, 93, 129–35, 136–38
"Reply to the Address at Ramnad" (lecture), 6–7
"Reply to the Madras Address" (essay), 101–3, 105–6, 176
rooted cosmopolitanism, 7
rope-snake analogy, 64, 178–79, 353, 354
Rosenberg, Alex, 158
Roy, Rammohun, 374
Royce, Josiah, 300

Sadānanda, 67
Saddharmasmṛtyupasthānasūtra, 132–33
"Sages of India, The" (lecture), 52, 107, 175, 176, 179–80
salvific efficacy of religions, 94–97
Sanyāl, Trailokyanāth, 21
Satprakashananda, Swami, 43–44
Sādhāran Brāhmo Samāj
  Narendra's association with, 21–22, 23
  rational monotheism of, 20
Sāṃkhya, 311
  comparison of Śaṅkara's views on design argument to, 239–40
  dualist system of, 326*f*
  infallible nature of the pramāṇas, 163–64
  pre-existent effect doctrine (*satkārya*), 11–12, 335–37
  Vivekananda's critique of insentient Prakṛti as creator doctrine, 325–27
  Vivekananda's critique of metaphysical dualism of Puruṣa and Prakṛti, 327–28, 344
  Vivekananda's critique of multiple Puruṣas doctrine, 325
  Vivekananda's provisional defense of mind-consciousness dualism of, 313–24
Sāṃkhya-Yoga, 165, 171–72
Sāradānanda, Svāmī, 20–21
Schaffer, Jonathan, 346
Schmidt-Leukel, Perry, 93, 126, 135–36, 137–38
Schopenhauer, Arthur, 77, 143, 372
Schweizer, Paul, 323–24
science of religion doctrine, of Vivekananda, 9, 141–61
  overview, 141–42
  critique of scientism, 146–53
  defense of wide empiricism, 9, 153–61, 221–22
  subordination of religious doctrine to spiritual experience, 142–46
  verification of religious claims, 201–2, 203, 268–69
"Science of Yoga, The" (lecture), 314–15, 317, 340–41, 343
scientific method, use of term, 158, 222–23
scientism
  definitions of, 147
  scholarly debates over, 146–49
  Vivekananda's critique of, 149–53, 203, 230–31
Scottish Church College, 2, 22
self-authenticating spiritual experience, 169, 183–86, 219, 283–85, 293, 296
self-limitation
  Aurobindo on divine, 359–60
  grounding by and individuation problem, 11–12, 345–56
  manifestation as playful, 353–54
Sen, Amiya P., 44–45
Sen, Keshab Chandra, 17, 20–22, 40, 146–47, 192–93
service, ethics of. *See also* Practical Vedānta
  Ramakrishna on, 27, 35, 74–75
  Vivekananda on, 61–62, 75–78
Shani, Itay, 345–46
Shear, Jonathan, 318–19
sin, in Christianity, 68–69
Smart, Ninian, 93, 129–30, 133, 134–35

social reform initiatives, in organizations of Brāhmo Samāj, 20, 22
"Soul, God and Religion" (lecture), 2, 103–6
speckled hen objection to AEV/AEV$_S$, 198, 203–6
Spencer, Herbert, 143, 170, 235–36, 242, 247, 252–54, 266
Spinoza, Baruch, 300
sportive play of God, 34, 347–48, 350–51, 358–59
stages of faith, Vivekananda on. *See* faith
stages of realization, Vivekananda on, 362–63. *See also* faith
"Steps of Hindu Philosophic Thought" (lecture), 260–61
"Steps to Realisation" (lecture), 179, 185, 255–56, 282
Strawson, Galen, 303–4, 307
Strawson, P. F., 207–8
sub-doxastic intellectual assent. *See* intellectual assent (stage 1 of Vivekananda's faith-ladder)
subject combination problem for micropsychism, 304, 345–46
subsumption. *See* grounding by subsumption (Goff)
supersensuous experience. *See* science of religion doctrine, of Vivekananda
supersensuous perception, addressing challenges to AEV/AEV$_S$, 10, 197–231
  overview, 197–99
  conflicting claims objection to premises 4 and 7, 209–17
  crosscheckability objection to premise 2, 198, 199–203, 220–21
  gullibility objection to premise 6, 206–9
  Kumārila's arguments against epistemic value of mystical testimony, 211–14
  Perception as Epistemic Justification (PEJ), 198, 199, 203, 205–6
  Perceptual Testimony as Epistemic Justification (PTEJ), 206, 207–9, 215
  Principle of Perceptual Proof (PP), 211, 217, 218–19
  Principle of Testimonial Proof (TP), 206, 207, 211, 217, 218–19
  Rambachan's criticism of science of religion, 217–31
  speckled hen objection to premise 3, 203–6
"Svaraj in Ideas" (Bhattacharyya lecture), 4
svataḥ-prāmāṇyavāda (intrinsic validity of cognitions doctrine), 9–10, 164–65, 187
Svāmijīr Padaprānte (Abjajānanda), 72
Swami Vivekananda in the West (Burke), 3
Swedenborg, Emanuel, 244, 251–52
Swinburne, Richard, 180–81, 182, 188–89, 195, 207, 356
Śaiva Nondualism, 300, 359, 369–70
Śakti (personal God)
  inseparability of Brahman from, 30–31, 38, 50–58, 329
  manifestation as playful self-limitation, 353–54
  Narendra's ecstatic love for, 22, 28–30, 35
  in Vijñāna Vedānta, 312–13
  Vivekananda's lecture on, 53–54
Śaṅkaradigvijaya, 73
Śaṅkarācārya (Śaṅkara), 224. *See also* Advaita Vedānta (Śaṅkara)
  on *māyā*, 59–60, 65–66
  on path to *mokṣa*, 78–79, 80–81, 83–84, 190
  on perception vs. testimony, 188
  on personal God, 51–52, 53, 54–55, 56
  reason and supersensuous realities, 235, 236, 238–41
  on scriptural knowledge of Brahman, 166–67
  on the individual soul, 69–71
  on Upaniṣads, 61–64, 144, 166–67, 238–39, 240–41, 254–55
  Vivekananda's criticism of, 73
  Vivekananda on narrowness of heart of, 73–74
Śāstrī, Śivanāth, 20, 22
Śivamahimnastotram, 113
Śuddhānanda, Svāmī, 72
Śūnyatā, 39

Tagore, Debendranath, 19–20, 22, 24, 192–93, 374
Tantra, 44, 125
Tapasyananda, Swami, 45
Tathāgatagarbhasūtra, 131–32
text-torturing, use of term, 8, 40, 49–50
Thagard, Paul, 343–44
Thales, 300
theological reason
Vivekananda's Kantian-Vedāntic critique of, 235–63
Theosophy, 42
Theravāda Buddhism, 130–35
thief and pot of gold analogy, 280–82
Three Essays on Religion (Mill), 142–43, 248–49, 261
threefold typology, regarding truth and salvific efficacy, 94–97

three stages of Vedānta, Vivekananda's doctrine of, 85–90, 101–6
Tipiṭaka, 131–33
Totāpurī (guru of Ramakrishna), 37
truth and salvific efficacy, 94–97
Turner, Frank, 142–43
Tyndall, John, 301, 305–6, 310–11, 320–22

Udayana, 237
Uddyotakara, 237
universal religion, 8–9, 49, 108. *See also* religious cosmopolitanism of Vivekananda
universal salvation, 259, 261
unrooted cosmopolitanism (Bhattacharyya), 4–5
Upaniṣads
  comparison of interpretations by Vivekananda and Śaṅkara on Īśā, 61–64
  Śaṅkara's commentary on, 61, 141, 166–67, 238–39, 240–41, 254–55
  Tagore's commentary on, 19
  Vivaraṇa school vs. Bhāmatī school on, 168
  Vivekananda's commentary on, 73, 74, 102–3, 120–21, 184–85, 190–91, 210, 224–25, 255, 339, 350
  Vivekananda's Integral Advaitic philosophy and, 48, 49, 50, 59–60

Vaidya, Anand, 300–1
Vaiśeṣika, 163–64
"Value of Witness to the Miraculous, The" (T. H. Huxley), 267
Varieties of Mystical Experience, The (James), 177, 269, 270
Vasubandhu, 131–32, 273–74
Vāṇī o Racanā, 3
Veda, use of term, 154–55
Vedas. *See also* Upaniṣads
  infallible nature of the *pramāṇas*, 163–64
  Kumārila's commentary on, 211, 213
  Ramakrishna's commentary on, 241
  Śaṅkara's commentary on, 166–67, 254–55
  verbal testimony, 165–66
  Vivekananda's commentary on, 174, 189–91, 215–16, 254–55
  Vivekananda's study of, 38–39
"Vedānta and Privilege" (lecture), 67–68
"Vedānta in All its Phases, The" (lecture), 51, 106–7, 190–91, 343–44
Vedāntaparibhāṣā (Adhvarīndra), 169–70, 225–26
"Vedānta Philosophy, The" (lecture), 106–7, 268–69
Vedāntasāra (Sadānanda), 67
Vedic orthodoxy, bigotry of, 191–92
"Vedic Religious Ideals" (lecture), 257–58
verbal testimony, 165
Vicāra-Sāgar, 167–68
Vidyāraṇya, 225–26
vijñāna (special spiritual experience of Ramakrishna). *See also* Vijñāna Vedānta (Ramakrishna)
  Ramakrishna contrasts with *jñāna*, 25–27, 30–35, 58, 63–64, 312–13
  Ramakrishna's panentheistic standpoint of, 259–60, 339, 348–50, 360–62, 363
  Vivekananda on, 58–59, 67
Vijñānabhikṣu, 165
Vijñāna Vedānta (Ramakrishna). *See also* Ramakrishna, Sri
  contemporary scholarship on, 300–1
  ethics of service, 27–28, 74–75
  harmonization of Śaṅkara and Rāmānuja, 31–33
  on problem of evil, 261–62
Viśiṣṭādvaita Vedānta (Rāmānuja), 31–32, 67, 69–71, 72, 76–77, 85–90, 101–6, 300–1
Viṣṇu-Purāṇa, 80–81
vital assimilation, 5, 7
vivartavāda doctrine (world as illusory), 67–68
Vivekacūḍāmaṇi, 37, 38–39, 167–69, 191, 192–93, 225–26
Vivekananda, Swami, as cosmopolitan philosopher, 1–13
  early education of, 1–2
  immersive cosmopolitanism and, 5–7
  organization of book, 7–13
  travels and lectures, 2, 3, 4, 5–7
  views on Western occult and Spiritualist thought, 41–42
Vivekananda, Swami. *See also* Datta, Narendranāth (pre-monastic name)
  assumption of monastic name, 38
  meets and influences W. James, 268–72, 275
  Ramakrishna's influence on, 17–42
Vivekanandan Argument for Panentheistic Cosmopsychism, 342–43, 345
Vivekanandan Argument for Panpsychism, 342, 343–45
Vyāsa, 187, 192

Wallace, Alfred Russel, 301, 309–11, 338–39
Walser, Joseph, 132–33
watch analogy (Paley), 257
"Way to the Realisation of a Universal Religion, The" (lecture), 116, 117, 118, 126–27

Western occult ideas, 41–42
"What Is It Like to Be a Bat?" (Nagel), 314–15
White, Andrew Dickson, 142–43
wide empiricism, 9, 153–61, 221–22
Wiles, Andrew, 159–60
"Will to Believe, The" (James), 267–68, 269, 270, 275
Wolff, Christian, 243, 251
"Women of India, The" (lecture), 50–51
"Work Before Us, The" (lecture), 5–6, 69
world
  as illusory (*vivartavāda* doctrine), 67–68
  as moral gymnasium, 236, 260, 261
"Worshipper and Worshipped" (lecture), 53
Woudenberg, René van, 148, 154

Yoga, 163–64
Yoga Philosophy. *See* *Rāja-Yoga* (Vivekananda)
Yoga school of philosophy, 192
Yogasūtra (Patañjali), 70, 157, 165, 170, 172, 177, 187, 189, 192, 316
Yogavāsiṣṭha, 37
Yogācāra Buddhism, 300

Zagzebski, Linda, 358

www.ingramcontent.com/pod-product-compliance
Lightning Source LLC
Chambersburg PA
CBHW072052290825
31867CB00004B/347
9780197624463